Correspondence of
THOMAS GRAY

Edited by the late
PAGET TOYNBEE
and
LEONARD WHIBLEY
Fellow of Pembroke College
Cambridge

IN THREE VOLUMES

Volume I. 1734–1755

OXFORD
AT THE CLARENDON PRESS
1935

OXFORD
UNIVERSITY PRESS
AMEN HOUSE, E.C. 4
London Edinburgh Glasgow
New York Toronto Melbourne
Capetown Bombay Calcutta
Madras Shanghai
HUMPHREY MILFORD
PUBLISHER TO THE
UNIVERSITY

PRINTED IN GREAT BRITAIN

36-5664

Correspondence of
THOMAS GRAY

Thomas Gray

from the painting by J. G. Eckhardt
in the National Portrait Gallery

PREFACE

IT is desirable at the outset to explain the collaboration between the late Dr. Toynbee and myself. In September 1925 a letter from Dr. Toynbee to *The Times Literary Supplement*, followed a fortnight later by one from me, brought us into correspondence and acquaintance. Dr. Toynbee had already undertaken to edit Gray's Correspondence for the Delegates of the Oxford Press, and I had for some time been collecting material connected with Gray's life at Cambridge.

It was at once arranged that I should assist in the work: our collaboration was carried on almost entirely by correspondence, and from the first exhange of letters in October 1925 until the day before Dr. Toynbee died in May 1932, over a thousand letters passed between us. Apart from information which I volunteered, different problems were discussed and the results of our investigations were combined. This procedure was followed until November 1930, when, after Dr. Toynbee had nearly completed his work of annotation, a serious illness obliged him to retire to a nursing-home, and it was not until August 1931 that he resumed his work, which he brought to a conclusion at the end of the year. The manuscript went to press in January 1932, and the first proofs were being revised by Dr. Toynbee when he died on 13 May 1932.

On the invitation of the Delegates I undertook the revision and completion of the work. I had not seen the notes before they were sent to press, and I made myself responsible for them in their final form. There were problems which required further investigation for their solution, there were letters which on examination had to be transposed in date, there were additions to be made in the light of fuller knowledge; and, in order that the notes might not run to excess, some excisions seemed desirable. The result on balance has been a reduction in the amount of annotation.

While Dr. Toynbee had been engaged in the preparation of the notes, there had been, in general, a division of labour between us. As is explained more fully in the Introduction, Dr. Toynbee was responsible for the verification of the text of the letters of which the originals are extant, while I made it my task to determine, as far as possible, the dates of letters for which there was not positive evidence. In the substance of the notes it may

v

be said that, for the most part, the notes on public characters and events, on quotations traced to their source, on plays and actors, on music and musicians were written by Dr. Toynbee. The notes on Cambridge and on persons and events in the University or the Colleges were generally contributed by myself or based on material which I had supplied. For most of the notes on the composition and publication of Gray's poems as well as of the poems written by West and Mason I was responsible.

At an early stage of the work it was realized that there were some subjects to which allusions were made in more than one letter, for which it was advisable to have a continuous treatment in the form of appendixes. By this means the notes were lightened and a separate discussion was possible of problems for which the evidence was derived from different letters. Other appendixes give the authentic text of documents relating to Gray. The appendixes have the initials of Dr. Toynbee or myself: those with both initials were originally written by Dr. Toynbee and revised or amplified by me. Dr. Toynbee also drew up Genealogical Tables of Gray and of some of his friends.

I have written a brief introduction, drawn up a list of the letters, and given a table of the chief events in Gray's life. In the Introduction some account is given of the previous editions of Gray's letters (based in part on materials left by Dr. Toynbee), of the sources, manuscript or printed, of the letters, and of the chief sources of information from which the notes are compiled.

In the choice of illustrations I have been fortunate to light on the portraits of some of Gray's friends painted at the time when he knew them, which have not been reproduced before. There does not seem to be any portrait of Thomas Wharton in existence, and the portrait of Norton Nicholls, which was included in Dawson Turner's sale in 1859, cannot be traced. To the owners of pictures and facsimiles grateful acknowledgement is made in the Lists of Illustrations printed in the different volumes.

While the book was passing through the press, the proof-sheets were read by Dr. R. W. Chapman and Dr. L. F. Powell, who made many suggestions for the improvement of the notes and were unwearied in their researches on obscure points, as well as by Mr. W. S. Lewis, of Farmington, Connecticut, who has applied his special knowledge of Horace Walpole to the elucidation of many problems, and by Mr. F. G. Stokes, who had given valuable help to Dr. Toynbee and to whom I am indebted for many criticisms and suggestions.

vi

Preface

Acknowledgement of help from many sources is made below. For information on special subjects, I must thank the Earl and Countess of Sandwich for notes concerning Miss Speed; Sir Frank Mackinnon for notes on the franking of letters; Mr. D. A. Winstanley, Vice-Master of Trinity College, Cambridge, for notes on the contest for the High Stewardship at Cambridge (see Appendix P); Mr. A. Watkin-Jones of Exeter College, Oxford, for notes on the relations between Gray and Thomas Percy (see Appendix N) as well as for tracing the originals of six letters of Gray in the United States. With Professor Roger Martin, Maître de Conférences at Montpellier University, who has recently published his *Essai sur Thomas Gray*, I have been in correspondence for some years, and I owe to him many valuable suggestions.

Miss E. G. Withycombe, of the Clarendon Press, undertook the exacting task of collating the text of the letters with the photographs or rotographs of the originals, and thus provided an additional check on the accuracy of the transcription. To her also I am indebted for compiling the Indexes and for much help in verifying references, &c. Mr. F. Page, of the Oxford University Press in London, was of great assistance in searching the newspapers and magazines for information on various points, and for collating the text of some letters. To the readers of the Press I am obliged for the care with which they read the proofs.

LEONARD WHIBLEY.

THE DIAL HOUSE
FRENSHAM, SURREY.

September, 1935.

vii

ACKNOWLEDGEMENTS

ACKNOWLEDGEMENT has been made in the Introduction to the owners of original letters, and in the Lists of Illustrations to the owners of pictures and letters for permission to reproduce them.

DR. TOYNBEE'S ACKNOWLEDGEMENTS

To my friend Mr. F. G. Stokes, editor of the *Journals of William Coles*, whose assistance is gratefully acknowledged in the preface to my *Correspondence of Gray, Walpole, West, and Ashton*, I am indebted once again for his never-failing readiness to undertake the tasks of transcribing and collating letters, copying extracts, verifying references, and consulting at the British Museum authorities not available to me.

For further assistance of various kinds, some of which is specifically mentioned in the body of the work, my acknowledgements are due to Mr. P. J. Anderson, formerly Librarian of Aberdeen University; the late Mr. A. L. Attwater, of Pembroke College, Cambridge; Mr. R. A. Austen Leigh; Mr. H. I. Bell, Keeper of MSS. at the British Museum; Mr. B. Benham, formerly Assistant Registrary of Cambridge University; Professor Edward Bensly; Mr. W. L. M. Benson and Mr. E. G. Benson; Mr. John Beresford; Mr. Reginald Blunt; Mr. Henry Broadbent, Librarian of Eton College; Dr. Arnold Chaplin, Harveian Librarian of the Royal College of Physicians; Professor A. C. Clark, of Oxford; Mr. C. H. Crouch, of Wanstead; Mr. Ivor Crouch, Secretary of the London Assurance; Mr. P. J. Dobell; M. F. Dominicé, of Geneva; Rev. J. Kestell Floyer, of Esher; Professor Cesare Foligno, of Magdalen College, Oxford; Dr. René Galland, of Bordeaux University; the late Mr. J. Herbert H. Gossett; Mr. H. C. Green, of Messrs. J. C. and J. Field; Mr. H. M. Hake, Director of the National Portrait Gallery; the Dowager Viscountess Harcourt; Viscount Harcourt; Mr. E. Harrison, Registrary of Cambridge University; the late Rev. M. J. B. Hayter, Master of the Charterhouse; Mr. Edward Hepburn; Dr. M. R. James, O.M., Provost of Eton; Miss Kathleen A. Jones, of St. Albans; Professor W. Powell Jones, of the Western Reserve University, Cleveland; Mr. Charles Ker, LL.D., of Glasgow; Dr. Keynes, formerly Registrary of Cambridge University; Mr. H. S. Kingsford, of the Society of Antiquaries; Mr. W. S. Lewis, of Farmington, Connecticut; the late Mr. Falconer Madan, F.S.A., former Bodley's Librarian; the late Dr. A. H. Mann, Organist of King's College, Cambridge; Mr. W. Westley Manning; Mr. W. A. Marsden, Keeper of Printed Books at the British Museum; Dr. Roger Martin, of Montpellier University; the late Mr. Percival Merritt, of Boston, Mass.; Professor Ellis H. Minns, of Pembroke College, Cambridge; the late Sir John Murray; Lt.-Col. Sir John Murray, of Albemarle Street; Mr. A. E.

Acknowledgements

Newton, of Philadelphia; Mr. T. C. Nicholas, Senior Bursar of Trinity College, Cambridge; Mr. F. Page, of Amen House; Mrs. Paston-Bedingfeld; the late Sir Henry Paston-Bedingfeld, Bart.; Capt. F. W. Pleadwell, of Washington, D.C.; Dr. L. F. Powell, Librarian of the Taylor Institution; Mr. C. W. Previté-Orton, Librarian of St. John's College, Cambridge; Mr. Gavin Ralston, Factor to the Earl of Strathmore at Glamis Castle; the Earl and Countess of Sandwich; Mr. A. F. Scholfield, Librarian of Cambridge University; the late Sir R. F. Scott, Master of St. John's College, Cambridge; the late Rev. Dr. H. P. Stokes; the Earl of Strathmore; Professor Harold Temperley, of Peterhouse, Cambridge; Professor C. B. Tinker, of Yale University; Mr. J. W. C. Turner, Bursar of Trinity Hall, Cambridge; the late Dr. T. A. Walker, of Peterhouse, Cambridge; Mr. Ross D. Waller, of Manchester University; Sir Wathen Waller, Bart.; Mr. D. A. Winstanley, Vice-Master of Trinity College, Cambridge.

I must also gratefully acknowledge my indebtedness to the *Dictionary of National Biography*; G. E. C.'s *Complete Peerage* and *Complete Baronetage*; the *Graduati Cantabrigienses*; Dr. J. and Dr. J. A. Venn's *Alumni Cantabrigienses*; and Mr. Austen Leigh's *Eton College Register*.

MR. WHIBLEY'S ACKNOWLEDGEMENTS

Much information concerned Gray's life at Cambridge. I am obliged to the Master and Fellows of Peterhouse and the Master and Fellows of Pembroke College for giving me access to College records and other documents. At Peterhouse my acknowledgements are due individually to the late Dr. T. A. Walker, Mr. Butterfield, Sir Hubert Sams, and Professor Temperley; at Pembroke above all to the late Mr. A. L. Attwater; to the late Mr. H. G. Comber, Professor Minns, and Mr. S. C. Roberts. I am also obliged to the late Sir Robert Scott, Master of St. John's College; to Dr. J. A. Venn, President of Queens' College; the late Dr. Giles, Master of Emmanuel College; Dr. Seward, Master of Downing College; Mr. E. Harrison, Registrary of the University; Mr. A. F. Scholfield, University Librarian; the late Rev. Dr. H. P. Stokes; Mr. S. G. Campbell, of Christ's College; Mr. H. M. Adams, Librarian of Trinity College; Mr. E. Abbott, of Jesus College; Mr. Pink, Assistant in the University Library; and Miss Bloxham, who is assisting Dr. Venn in the preparation of the next series of *Alumni Cantabrigienses*.

For other help my acknowledgements are due to Professor C. D. Abbott, Librarian of the University of Buffalo; Mr. R. A. Austen Leigh; Mr. E. A. Barber, Fellow of Exeter College, Oxford; Professor Edward Bensly; Rev. R. A. Bentley, Rector of Oddington; Rev. Dr. Blakiston, President of Trinity College, Oxford; Professor Richmond P. Bond, of the University of North Carolina; Mr. Julian P. Boyd, Assistant Librarian to the Historical Society of Pennsylvania; Mr. A. T.

Acknowledgements

Bolton, Curator of Sir John Soane's Museum; Mr. H. Broadbent, Librarian of Eton College; Rev. W. H. Brooke, Rector of Aston, Yorks.; Dr. I.Graham Callander, of the National Museum of Scotland; the Very Rev. Dr. Cranage, Dean of Norwich; Mr. C. H. Crouch, of Wanstead; Messrs. Colbeck and Radford; Mrs. Darwin, of Elston Hall, Newark (for information about the Wharton family); Messrs. Dobell; Mr. G. A. Falk; Professor Foligno, of Oxford; Mr. W. Marshall Freeman; Mr. S. Gibson, Keeper of the Archives at Oxford; Mr. Edward B. Hall, of Harvard University; Rev. Canon Harrison, Librarian of York Minster; Mr. Hiscock, Sub-Librarian of Christ Church; Dr. M. R. James, Provost of Eton; Mr. Hilary Jenkinson, of the Record Office; Professor Powell Jones, of the Western Reserve University, Cleveland; Mr. Geoffrey Keynes; Mr. A. T. Loyd, of Lockinge; Dr. David M. Little, of Harvard University; Mr. James Maclehose; Dr. H. W. Meikle, Librarian of the National Library of Scotland; Mr. Robert F. Metzdorf, of Rochester University, New York; Rev. Canon Mozley; the late Sir John Murray; Lt.-Col. Sir John Murray; Mr. R. A. B. Mynors, of Balliol College; Professor Namier; the Record Committee of the General Post Office; Sir Robert Rait, Principal of the University of Glasgow; the late Mr. J. F. P. Rawlinson, K.C.; Sir Humphry Rolleston; Rev. E. V. Simpkinson, Vicar of Kirk Merrington, Durham; Dr. W. Douglas Simpson, Librarian of Aberdeen University; Professor D. Nichol Smith, of Oxford; Mr. Ronald Syme, of Trinity College, Oxford; Professor Tolkien, of Oxford; Mr. A. C. Townsend, Librarian of the British Museum of Natural History; Mr. Iolo A. Williams; Rev. Canon Rowland Wilson, of Witley Rectory, Worcester.

CONTENTS OF VOLUME I

CONTENTS OF VOLUME II

CONTENTS OF VOLUME III

Contents

INTRODUCTION

PREVIOUS EDITIONS OF GRAY'S LIFE AND CORRESPONDENCE

MASON

WHEN Gray died he left to William Mason, who had been one of his closest friends, 'all his books, manuscripts, . . . & papers of all kinds to preserve or destroy at his own discretion'. Within a few months of Gray's death Mason had decided to publish an edition of Gray's poems and to write his life. The inception and progress of his book can be traced in letters written by Mason to three of his friends, Edward Beding-field, Horace Walpole, and Richard Hurd.[1] In January 1772 he wrote to Bedingfield: 'I beleive also on the last page of the pamphlet [the first part of *The English Garden*] I shall pledge myself to the publick as preparing for the press the Life of Mr Gray in wch his fragments &c will be inserted.'

The plan of his work was to select such letters, or parts of letters, of Gray as, with the assistance of a few notes, would 'give a regular and clear delineation of his character', and so 'Mr Gray will become his own biographer'. Mason had ample materials. Among Gray's papers he found Gray's letters to his father and mother, letters to West and from West: he had Gray's letters to himself, and Gray had kept many which Mason had written to him. Walpole and Wharton gave him a free choice of the letters that Gray had written to them, and if one

[1] See *The Correspondence of Horace Walpole and the Rev. William Mason*, edited by the Rev. J. Mitford, London, 1851, and *The Correspondence of Richard Hurd and William Mason*, edited by Leonard Whibley, Cambridge, 1932. The originals of Mason's letters to Bedingfield are in the Henry E. Huntington Library at San Marino, California. Edward Bedingfield (see Letter 210, n. 1), an intimate friend of Mason, and a great admirer of Gray, lived in York, and, as we learn from Mason's letters to him, Bedingfield had seen through the press the editions of Mason's *Poems* which were published in 1771 and 1773. As soon as he was ready to print the *Memoirs* Mason sought Bedingfield's help. 'Prepare yourself for fresh Labour', he wrote in March 1773, 'I will not call it trouble, because I know you cannot think it such, when I tell you it is to revise My Memoires of Mr Gray, wch I mean to put to the press when I come to York in May.' Later letters show that throughout the work Mason relied on Bedingfield's assistance. He welcomed notes which Bedingfield inserted, and in Gray's fragmentary poem on *The Alliance of Education and Government* he altered the original text by substituting in the last line but one for Gray's 'distant' Bedingfield's suggestion of 'neighbring'. 'Your epithet is for the better', Mason wrote.

xiii

or two of Gray's friends were unwilling for letters written to them by Gray to be published, Mason could draw on many others, Stonhewer, Palgrave, Beattie, Nicholls, and How.

Mason's plan was a good one and his material was abundant; but he spoilt his plan and wasted his material by falsifying the text of Gray's letters. He printed in all 130 'letters', 113 from Gray, 16 from West to Gray, and 1 from Algarotti.[1] Of about half of these (among them 53 out of the first 58), including Gray's letters to his father and mother, nearly all the letters that passed between Gray and West, and letters to Stonhewer and Palgrave, we have only the text that Mason printed. Of the rest the originals are in existence and we can trace Mason's treatment of them. Few are faithful to the original text: Mason omitted passages, and inserted phrases of his own to fill the gaps that he had made, or to cover the lack of connexion. At the outset of his work he stated: 'I will promise my reader that he shall, in the following pages, seldom behold Mr. Gray in any light than that of a Scholar and Poet.' This consideration moved him to represent Gray as maintaining a blameless decorum. Gray wrote in a colloquial style, with a sprinkling of slang. Mason altered all this: 'do not' for 'don't', 'written' for 'wrote', 'boast' for 'brag', 'simpleton' for 'oaf' are instances of his futility. Less trivial changes of Gray's phraseology may be traced by comparing Mason's text with that of the letters, from which the passages were taken (see Letter 218, nn. 2, 4).

A more serious corruption which impairs the value of Mason's text as a record of what Gray did or said at any particular date was due to his combining passages from different letters in a patchwork of his own and representing the combinations as actual letters. There are 30 'letters' printed by Mason, which we know were compounded of parts taken from 70 genuine letters, fragments from 2, 3, 4, or 5 letters being patched together. As the parts which Mason combined were taken from letters of different dates, the date which he arbitrarily gave to the combination could not be right for all of them, and sometimes by his negligence or ineptitude was not right for any of them. The fragments that were joined together might have intervals of years between them, and, so far as they

---

[1] These numbers do not include a note of Lady Schaub to Gray (Letter 154*) which was printed in Mason's narrative (*Memoirs*, p. 211), nor fragments of letters from and to Gray, which were printed in notes to the *Memoirs* or the *Poems*.

recorded facts, the facts were distorted in date; parts of letters
to different correspondents were sometimes combined. If necessary the text was altered to conceal the falsification.[1] As we
have positive evidence of Mason's treatment of letters of which
the originals survive, we can have no assurance that the other
letters were printed as Gray wrote them.[2]

Mason did not wish that the liberties which he had taken
should be detected; he was therefore anxious that the original
letters which had been lent to him should be destroyed. He
seems to have urged Walpole to burn Gray's juvenile letters, but
compromised on 'the infantine beginnings and conclusions of
some of them' being erased (see Letter 1, n. 2, and *Walpole–
Mason Correspondence*, vol. i, pp. 115, 117). Wharton let Mason
have the letters which Gray had written to him: Mason before
he returned them erased or cut out names (see Letter 120, n. 2),
and when Wharton died expressed his indignation that the
letters had not been burnt.[3] His principles were baldly stated
in a letter to Norton Nicholls (dated 31 Jan. 1775):[4]

'Mr Mason returns many thanks to Mr Niccols for the use he has
permitted him to make of these Letters. He will find that much
liberty has been taken in transposing parts of them &c for the press,
and will see the reason for it, it were however to be wished that the
originals might be so disposed of as not to impeach the Editors
fidelity, but this he leaves to Mr Niccols discretion, for People of
common sense will think the Liberty he has used very Venial.'

[1] A signal instance of Mason's method is afforded by the last letter in his
collection (*Memoirs*, pp. 394–5). It purports to be the last letter written by
Gray to Thomas Wharton. Mason dated it May 24, 1771, which was the
date of Gray's authentic last letter to Wharton (553). His fabrication begins
with the second paragraph of a letter of 24 Aug. 1770 (530). This is followed
by the last sentence from Gray's letter to Wharton of 2 Feb. 1771 (542) and
two sentences from the letter of 24 May 1771, after which a sentence from a
letter to Norton Nicholls of 20 March 1770 (513) is intruded, and the letter concludes with a sentence from the letter to Wharton of 24 May 1771. In all of
the extracts Mason has introduced purposeless changes in Gray's phraseology.
   A comparison of Mason's 'letter' of Gray to himself, dated Dec. 19, 1757
(*Memoirs*, pp. 25–9), with the five actual letters (257, 265, 266*, 269, 275)
from which he selected his extracts gives further illustration of his patchwork
and his garblings. Another composite letter to Wharton, dated June 22,
1760 (*Memoirs*, pp. 276–8), is made up of parts of letters written in July 1759,
January, April, and June 1768 (296, 308, 311, 313).
[2] Internal evidence points to other instances of letters being combined
(see preliminary notes to Letters 62, 110, 133).
[3] See Dr. Toynbee's letter to *The Times Literary Supplement* of 7 Feb. 1929.
[4] Printed from the original letter in the possession of Captain F. L.
Pleadwell of Washington, D.C.

Introduction

As Mason was convinced of 'the impropriety of keeping letters' we cannot doubt that he exercised the discretion allowed to him by Gray's will to destroy many letters which were in his control. It may be assumed that letters which Gray wrote to his mother from Eton and Cambridge,[1] as well as those which he wrote from abroad, and the letters which passed between Gray and West came into Mason's possession and were burnt by him. With the exception of two letters to West, both of which contained verse translations by Gray (22 and 105), the only letters which Mason kept were those which Gray wrote to Mason and some of his own to Gray.

Mason's work was published in March 1775:

The Poems of Mr. Gray. To which are prefixed Memoirs of his Life and Writings by W. Mason, M.A. 4to. York: *Printed by A. Ward; and sold by J. Dodsley, Pall-Mall, London, and J. Todd, Stonegate,* York, MDCCLXXV.

A second edition was printed in London and published in June 1775. One correction was made in the notes to meet Hurd's protest (see Letter 247, n. 5), and there were a few minor corrections and additions in the notes.

In 1778 Mason published an edition in 4 vols., 8vo. He stated in the Advertisment: 'There is little alteration in this pocket edition from the two in quarto which preceded it, except that the Poems of Mr. Gray are here placed before the Memoirs of his Life.'

THE WORKS OF LORD ORFORD

The Works of Horatio Walpole, Earl of Orford, 5 vols., 4to, London, MDCCXCVIII.

This publication was edited nominally by Robert Berry, but in reality by his daughter, Mary Berry. In vol. iv there are two letters from Walpole and Gray to West (83, 92), and in vol. v nineteen Letters of Gray to Walpole (in whole or in part) and six letters of Walpole to Gray. The originals of some of these letters are extant, and these show that Miss Berry was generally accurate in her transcription.

[1] Mason printed no letters of Gray to his parents except those written from abroad. Gray's life at Eton was dismissed in four lines (*Memoirs,* p. 3); his life at Cambridge was illustrated by letters to West and Walpole. The disproportion in Mason's treatment of the different periods of Gray's life is shown by the fact that to the eight years covering Gray's first residence at Cambridge, his foreign tour, and the year after his return he devoted two-fifths of the space occupied by the whole biography.

xvi

Introduction

MATHIAS

The Works of Thomas Gray with Memoirs of his Life and Writings by William Mason to which are subjoined Extracts Philological, Poetical and Critical from the Author's original Manuscripts selected and arranged by Thomas James Mathias. 2 vols. 4to. London, 1814.

The first volume contained a reprint of Mason's *Poems and Memoirs*, with seventeen of Gray's letters to Walpole, which had appeared in the *Works of Lord Orford*, and the *Letter occasioned by the death of the Rev. Norton Nicholls*, which Mathias had written in 1809. The second volume contained extracts from Gray's Commonplace-book and from Gray's notes on the *Systema Naturæ* of Linnæus written in his interleaved copy of that work.

MITFORD

In 1814 the Rev. John Mitford began the publication of his works relating to Gray,[1] the last of which was published in 1853. They were as follows:

1. *The Poems of Thomas Gray, with critical notes, a Life of the Author and an Essay on his Poetry.* 8vo. London, 1814.

The Life of Gray with Appendixes of biographical or literary interest was reprinted, with some changes and with variations in the Appendixes, in Mitford's later editions of Gray's works.[2] It added much to the meagre biography of Mason.

2. *The Works of Thomas Gray, in 2 vols.* 4to. London, 1816.

The first volume contained the poems and the life, &c., the second volume contained the letters 'with important additions and corrections from his own Manuscripts Selected and edited by the Rev. John Mitford'.

[1] In the Harvard College Library are two volumes of manuscript letters addressed to Mitford (formerly owned by Sir William Alexander Fraser), lettered 'Correspondence Papers &c. Relating to Gray, vol. i, 1812–15, vol. ii. 1816–43'. The letters throw light on the preparation of Mitford's editions of Gray's Works, 1816, 1835–6. There are also letters of Mitford to Dyce in the Dyce Collection at South Kensington referring to the edition of 1835–6.

[2] To a second edition of *Gray's Poems*, edited by the Rev. James Moultrie, and published at Eton in 1747, Mitford contributed 'An original Life of Gray (written expressly for this edition)'. He added a good deal of fresh matter to the *Life* that had appeared in his earlier editions. The text has many careless misprints.

Mitford thus described the contents of the second volume:

'The second volume contains all the letters of Gray which were published by Mr. Mason; together with those subsequently printed in the works of Lord Orford, and in the Gentleman's Magazine. In addition to these, the editor has been enabled, by the kindness of Richard Wharton, Esq., to enrich his work with many original letters from Gray to his most intimate and respected friend, Dr. Wharton.'

Herein lay the importance of the publication. Mitford printed ninety letters from Gray to Wharton, and claimed that the volume 'enables the public *for the first time* to read the genuine and uncorrupted correspondence of Gray, exactly in his own language and printed from his own manuscripts'. He denounced Mason's corruption of the letters that he had printed: 'in almost all, he has altered the style, and changed, in a greater or less degree, the truth and character of the original composition.'

3. From 1828 Mitford was engaged in preparing a new edition of the poems and letters. It was ultimately arranged that the book should be published in Pickering's Aldine series.

The Works of Thomas Gray. 4 vols. Sm. 8vo. London, 1835–6.[1]

In this edition Mitford added six letters to Wharton, six to Chute, and single letters to five other correspondents; he printed also in the fourth volume letters written by James Brown and others after Gray's death.

In the Advertisement Mitford stated that he had been 'permitted to peruse the very valuable correspondence' between Gray and Nicholls, which was in the possession of Dawson Turner, a relative of Nicholls, and he expressed the hope that this might be published.

4. This correspondence 'at the kind suggestion of Mr. Rogers' Mitford was allowed to publish in 1843.

The Correspondence of Thomas Gray and the Rev. Norton Nicholls. Sm. 8vo. London, 1843. [This was printed also as vol. v of the Aldine edition.]

This contains thirty-two letters from Gray to Nicholls and twelve from Nicholls to Gray, as well as letters to and from

---

[1] The different volumes were dated as follows: vol. i. 1836 (but as the Advertisement is dated April 1837, it could not have been published until some time in 1837), vols. ii and iii, 1835, vol. iv. 1836.

Nicholls after Gray's death and *Reminiscences of Gray* by Nicholls. There were also two letters of Gray to Walpole.

5. In 1850 Mitford, who had already been entrusted with the letters of Mason to Walpole for publication, was informed that the corresponding letters of Walpole to Mason were in possession of the Rev. William Alderson, son of Christopher Alderson, whom he had succeeded in the rectory of Aston (see Letter 453, n. 7). These letters were also put at his disposal, and he was thus enabled to publish:

The Correspondence of Horace Walpole and the Rev. William Mason. 2 vols. 8vo. London, 1851.

The correspondence is of value as it throws light on the composition of the *Memoirs*, on the choice of letters to be inserted, and on letters which Mason did not print and presumably destroyed. Walpole's account of the quarrel with Gray at Reggio is given at length.

6. Mr. Granville Penn, of Stoke Park, had collected manuscripts of Gray after they were first sold by auction in 1845. He gave Mitford access to letters from and to Gray,[1] which Mitford printed in his last book:

The Correspondence of Thomas Gray and William Mason, with Letters to the Rev. James Brown, D.D., Master of Pembroke College. 8vo. London, 1853.

In 1855 the book was reissued with sixty pages of 'Additional Notes', in which Mitford corrected many errors in the text and notes of the first issue. The book made an important addition to Gray's correspondence. It contained seventy-one letters from Gray to Mason, twenty-four from Mason to Gray, and thirty-six from Gray to Brown with some other letters. In the Preface Mitford wrote that he still had 'some materials, partly relating to Gray and partly to those connected with him, that may serve to illustrate what is already published'. These

---

[1] In a 'Catalogue Briefly Descriptive of Various Books and Original Manuscripts of the Poet Gray', issued as a preliminary to an intended sale of Mr. Penn's collection in 1851, there is a note: 'The fact of so little justice being done to Gray's memory by his Correspondence, as printed in the work of Mason, has induced the Proprietor of this Collection to afford every facility to the Rev. John Mitford to gather from the whole, whatever might be considered useful for further illustration of the Poet's Character and Writings; and with this view the Correspondence has recently been announced by the Rev. Editor for publication.'

materials remained in his note-books until they were published by Tovey in *Gray and his Friends* (see below).

Mitford's lifelong labours on Gray's correspondence were of signal value. He published in all about 350 letters of Gray and about 50 letters from West, Mason, and Nicholls to Gray. He was the first to bring to light and to print from the originals the letters to Wharton, Nicholls, Mason, and Brown. For many of the letters to Brown, for the letters from Nicholls to Gray, and for some letters which he left unpublished in his note-books we still depend upon Mitford's printed or manuscript text. In addition, Mitford was an industrious collector of information relating to Gray: he had read widely in the memoirs and letters of Gray's time, he had sought the help of those who still preserved traditions of Gray which they had received from his contemporaries. This information he used in his Life of Gray and in the notes with which he illustrated the letters.

While we recognize the great contribution which Mitford made to our knowledge, there are defects which detract from the value of his work. The text of the letters, as printed, has many inaccuracies: many mistakes were made in his transcription or his proof-reading: he left obvious errors uncorrected, and many reappeared in editions which were stereotyped. Important words were occasionally omitted to the detriment of the sense. Mitford's text is so often proved wrong by a comparison with the originals, that in letters for which we have no other authority it has sometimes seemed necessary to suggest corrections. He did not take trouble to determine the dates of the letters, and left many out of order and some very much out of the reckoning.

GOSSE

Edmund (afterwards Sir Edmund) Gosse contributed to the English Men of Letters Series a *Life of Gray* which was published in 1882. It had been rapidly written between December 1881 and March 1882. The biography has many errors of fact and unwarranted assumptions. Unhappily, it has been accepted as reliable.

Two years later there appeared:

The Works of Thomas Gray in Prose and Verse, edited by Edmund Gosse. 4 vols. 8vo. London, 1884.

The second and third volumes contained the letters written by Gray. Gosse expressed his disappointment that he had not collected 'a sheaf of lost letters', and he was able to add only three letters which had not been published before. He entered on the inheritance of Mitford's labours, and had the advantage of being able to arrange in one sequence the letters which Mitford had gradually brought to light and published in three different collections. He had in the Preface to the *Life* found fault with Mitford for failing to date the letters correctly; but it cannot be said that Gosse made any systematic effort to correct the dates, or to arrange the letters in order.

In printing the letters Gosse 'followed Mitford's latest collations, except as regards the very numerous letters addressed to Wharton'. These, he stated, 'I have scrupulously printed, as though they had never been published before, direct from the originals, which exist, in a thick volume, among the Egerton MSS., in the Manuscript department of the British Museum. The Wharton letters are so numerous and so important, and have hitherto been so carelessly transcribed, that I regard this portion of my labours, mechanical as it is, with great satisfaction.' The statement seems to indicate, without any loophole of ambiguity, that whereas the Wharton letters had been carelessly transcribed before (i.e. by Mitford, for no one else had transcribed them) Gosse was scrupulously printing them 'direct from the originals', and had himself undertaken the mechanical labour of transcription. Gosse's statement was put to the proof by Tovey, who, in an Appendix to the first volume of his edition of *Gray's Letters* (published in 1900), pointed out, with a polite irony, the many coincidences of error in the texts of Mitford and Gosse. These could not be explained on any assumption except that Gosse was reproducing (with occasional corrections) Mitford's text and not that of the original letters. Gosse ignored the exposure, and when two years later he issued a 'Revised edition' of his book, although he made other changes in the Preface, he left the statement that the letters had been printed 'direct from the originals' as he had written it eighteen years before.

The question remained open until in 1931 the Honourable Sir Evan Charteris, in *The Life and Letters of Sir Edmund Gosse* (p. 190), offered the following explanation:

'Unfortunately Gosse had employed some one else to copy the letters in the Egerton MSS., and the copyist, wearying of the script, and finding that the letters had been published by Mitford, soon began to copy from the printed word in preference to the MSS. Mitford's edition of the letters differed from the originals, and those differences faithfully reappeared in the work of the copyist. Gosse's amanuensis had let him down.'

Thus Gosse's reiterated assertion that the Wharton letters had been 'scrupulously printed direct from the originals' and by his own labours of transcription is proved devoid of truth. In the words of his biographer he had 'been deluded into putting forward a claim that turned out not to be justified'.

TOVEY

In 1885 seventeen volumes of *Common Place Books and Recollections of the Rev. John Mitford*, 1847–56, were acquired by the British Museum (*Add. MSS.* 32559–32575). The third and fourth volumes contained transcripts of letters and other manuscripts written by Gray, and other notes referring to Gray and his friends. It was chiefly from these notes of Mitford that the Rev. Duncan C. Tovey began his long labours on Gray in his book:

> *Gray and his Friends. Letters and Relics in great part hitherto unpublished.* 8vo. Cambridge, 1890.

This was followed ten years later by the first volume of his edition of Gray's letters, the other two volumes being published later:

> *The Letters of Thomas Gray, including the Correspondence of Gray and Mason.* 3 vols. 8vo (vol. i, 1900, vol. ii, 1904, vol. iii, 1912).

With the letters published in *Gray and his Friends*, he added about 20 letters, and printed in all about 370 letters of Gray as well as 24 letters from Mason and 1 from Nicholls to Gray.

He claimed to 'have given a truer text of this collection of letters'. His claim was justified, and in the letters to Wharton he avoided the grosser errors of Mitford and Gosse. He corrected some of the dates that had hitherto been wrongly ascribed, and added many notes of value.

In all his work on Gray, including his edition of Gray's *English Poems* (1898) and his chapter on Gray in the *Cambridge History of English Literature* (1913), Tovey showed admirable sense and judgement. On many questions for the determination of which the evidence was not available to him he suggested solutions which were certainly right.

TOYNBEE

In the course of inquiries for Walpole letters Dr. Paget Toynbee discovered in the possession of the late Sir Francis E. Waller, Bart., a collection of letters of Gray, Walpole, West, and Ashton, which was put at his disposal. These letters with letters of the same correspondents from other sources were published in 1915:

> *The Correspondence of Gray, Walpole, West and Ashton (1754–1771) Chronologically arranged and edited with Introduction, Notes and Index.* 2 vols. 8vo. Oxford, 1915.

In the collection there were 89 hitherto unpublished letters from Gray to Walpole (32 written while Gray was an undergraduate at Cambridge), 4 from Walpole to Gray, as well as other letters, which had before this been printed in an incomplete form.

THE PRESENT EDITION

The present edition was projected by Dr. Toynbee. He traced twenty-three letters that had not been published before, three more have come to light since his death. With the new letters first published in *The Correspondence of Gray, Walpole, West and Ashton*, and with other letters from printed sources, the edition contains 500 letters or parts of letters from Gray, and 86 letters to Gray from West, Walpole, Mason, Nicholls, and other correspondents.

Text. The text of the letters, for which Dr. Toynbee was responsible, is that of the original manuscripts so far as they have been available. Nearly three-fourths of the letters have been printed from the originals, either from photographic reproductions or from transcripts made by Dr. Toynbee and others for the purpose of this edition, or transcripts made at an earlier date for *The Correspondence of Gray, Walpole, West and Ashton*, edited by Dr. Toynbee (1915), or for *The Correspondence of Richard Hurd and William Mason*, edited by Leonard Whibley (1932). The text is printed as Gray or his correspondents wrote it, with the spelling, punctuation, use of capitals, and abbreviations of the originals. The text printed from the transcripts of the manuscripts has been carefully checked, while the book was in proof, and every endeavour has been made to insure its fidelity. It must be remembered that in all handwriting there are possible ambiguities, which may be differently interpreted. Of the letters of which the originals have not been traced the text now printed is that of the first printed versions or of transcripts made by Mitford and others. The most important printed sources are Mason's *Memoirs*, the *Works of Lord Orford*, and Mitford's different collections, of which some account has been given above. With the knowledge that we possess of the neglect of Mason and Mitford to transcribe correctly, we have no reason to accept as Gray's text obvious mistakes, which they printed. Errors in Greek, Latin, or French have generally been corrected. If the correction is serious it is mentioned in the notes, but misspellings and false accents have been corrected *sub silentio*. It has seemed possible to detect more serious mistakes in Mitford, and attention has been called to such as seemed capable of correction. In particular he appears to have been at fault in deciphering obliterated passages in Gray's letters to Brown.

Some letters are reprinted from the *Gentleman's Magazine* (380, 399*), others from books not directly concerned with Gray: part of a letter to Christopher Anstey (343) from John Anstey's *Life of his father*, letters to Bonstetten (515, 520, 523) from Friedrich Matthisson's *Auserlesene Gedichte*, one letter to Beattie (444) and one from him, from Sir William Forbes's *Life and Writings of James Beattie*; other letters are derived from the Catalogues of Auction Sales or of Booksellers. It is always possible that other letters of Gray may come to light.[1]

List of Letters. It was necessary at an early stage of the work to make a provisional list of letters, with numbers in sequence. The discovery of new letters, the transposition of letters owing to the correction of the dates previously attached, the decision taken, when the work had been some time in progress, to insert in the text notes on non-extant letters, made it necessary to use

---

[1] Dr. Clerke and the Rev. William Robinson were intimate friends of Gray. Mason printed one letter to Clerke, but there were many others (see preliminary note to Letter 318). Robinson declined to help Mason, when he was writing the *Memoirs* (see preliminary note to Letter 380); one letter to him was printed in the *Gentleman's Magazine*. Dr. Toynbee was informed by Mr. A. K. Carlyon of Roselyon, Harrow on the Hill, that he had heard that a packet of letters from Gray to Thomas Carlyon (see Letter 136, n. 3) had been preserved at Tregehan, the family seat, and that in one of them, 'Gray described with much vigour of language the practical joke played upon him at Peterhouse, which led to his removal to Pembroke Hall'. In spite of a careful search at Tregehan no trace of them has been found. There are also said to have been letters from Gray to Algarotti in existence.

starred numbers to mark changes after the original list had been drawn up.[1]

Non-extant letters. Notes are inserted, in the text, describing letters known to have been written by Gray at an approximately certain date of which mention is made in extant letters or in the letters of his correspondents. The notes are given numbers in chronological sequence. It has not seemed advisable generally to insert notes of letters written to Gray, with the following exceptions:

1. Letters from West to which reference is made in Gray's letters to him are noted to show, as far as possible, the complete correspondence.

2. In cases in which it is known that on some particular occasion many letters passed of which only some have survived the missing letters are noted, in order to make it easier to understand the letters which are extant. This is the case with letters concerning the publication of Bentley's Designs (169** ff.), and with letters concerning the offer of the Laureateship to Gray (258* ff.).

3. Letters are noted of which the contents are known, as the Duke of Grafton's letter to Gray (478) and Cole's letter to Gray of 22 Dec. 1770 (538), to which Gray's letter of the same date (539) is a reply.

Dating of Letters. A consistent effort has been made to fix the correct dates of the letters, or, where this is not possible, to determine the approximate dates. Gray himself was erratic in dating his letters: sometimes he gives a precise date, but he might omit the year, or the day of the month, sometimes he combines the day of the week with the year, sometimes, as is only to be expected, he made mistakes.[2] Mason, apart from his combination of parts of letters of different dates, sometimes inserted dates many of which are demonstrably inaccurate.[3] Wharton endorsed many letters, apparently a long time after they were written, with the dates of the years (in some cases with an alternative), but his memory was often at fault, and correction is necessary.[4]

[1] Three numbers in the list, 205 A, 261A, 511A, are attached to copies of poems and to part of Gray's Journal in the Lakes and Yorkshire, which were not letters. The reasons why they are printed are stated in the notes.

[2] Mistakes in the year will be found in Letters 353, 354, in the month in Letters 193, 266*, in the day in Letters 6, 10.

[3] Instances of Mason's errors occur in Letters 26, 43, 379.

[4] Wharton's endorsements are wrong in Letters 115, 116, 123, 137, 163, 169*.

For the purpose of this edition the dates of Gray's residence at Cambridge have been traced, and thus a most important clue for dating many letters has been supplied. College records, which determine, within narrow limits, the date of Gray's return to Cambridge on different occasions, the duration of his residence, and the date of his departure, are still in existence. At Peterhouse the book of accounts for 'Hall Commons' (i.e. for dinners and suppers in Hall) shows the charges made to those resident for each week or half-week, and makes it possible to determine within a margin of two or three days whether Gray was in Cambridge at any particular time. In the same way, after Gray had migrated to Pembroke, the Butler's book of 'Sizings for Bread and Ale' contains against the names of all members on the Boards marks for each week, showing within a day or two the details of their residence. From these records, combined with references in Gray's letters or his pocket-books, and in other documents, a chart of his life has been drawn up, which shows, as far as our information goes, where he was from day to day for the greater part of his life. This chart has been used in drawing up the Chronological Table printed below.

Postmarks, where they are found on the outside of extant letters, afford positive evidence of date. It is to be noted that generally, when Gray was writing from Cambridge or elsewhere out of town, the postmark is a day later than the day of writing. This is not invariably the case, and letters from London often bear the postmark of the day when the letter was written.

Internal evidence, such as reference to events of which the date is known, the connexion of allusions in one letter with those in another, is of great importance: it is unnecessary to illustrate this in detail, but mention may be made of the dates of publication of books mentioned in the letters, which is sometimes decisive.

The application of these methods of external and internal evidence has enabled a more correct and more precise dating of the letters than has hitherto been possible. Letters have been transferred in date, very many dates of letters hitherto accepted have been corrected, and many letters dated vaguely by the year or month have had the dates more nearly determined. The dates of some sixty letters in all have been altered or more closely defined. It has not, of course, been possible to settle the dates of all letters: some can only be conjecturally dated, the dates of some few remain uncertain.

Gray's Handwriting. It seems doubtful whether, except for the letters written during Gray's first residence, any certain inference of date can be drawn from the handwriting. Gray seems to have fixed his handwriting during his foreign tour, and it would probably be difficult to trace any distinct variation thereafter. He wrote with a small crow-quill (as Cole informs us), and this enabled him to maintain the regularity of his small, neat script. If the pen that he used were broader or softer, this would affect his writing: it is noteworthy that the addresses on the outside of his letters are written in a larger and bolder hand, and for these he may have used an ordinary goose-quill. In some letters, written in the last year or two of his life, there are differences traceable, which may have been due to illness. The specimens of his handwriting, reproduced in facsimile in this work, have been chosen to enable the opinion that has been advanced to be tested.

Notes. The notes are intended to comment on the men or things that interested Gray, to give an account of his friends and acquaintances, to explain his allusions to events, whether in public affairs or in college life, to illustrate his journeys, to trace the composition and publication of his poems, and to discuss his references to books, plays, and operas. The sources from which information has been particularly derived are given below. Gray's own manuscripts have been constantly used. College records are important to explain college events: contemporary correspondence, whether published or unpublished, is of great value in illustration or explanation. It is only right to record that any one who studies Gray's letters is under great obligation to the researches of Mitford and Tovey.

THE MANUSCRIPTS OF THE LETTERS

The letters to Wharton, except one (268) printed by Mason, of which the original is missing, are in the British Museum (Egerton 2400) with manuscripts of Gray's poems in Gray's or Wharton's handwriting. Of the letters to or from Walpole the originals still in existence, except two (119, 167), are in the possession of Sir Wathen Arthur Waller, Bart, at Woodcote, Warwick. The letters to or from Mason are in the collection of Mr. A. T. Loyd of Lockinge (with two letters to West and four to Brown). The letters to John Chute are in the possession of Mr. Charles L. Chute of the Vyne, Hampshire. The letters to Nicholls, except one (477), are

in the Eton College Library. The letters to or from Beattie, of which
the originals are extant, are in the Aberdeen University Library.
The letters to Edward Bedingfield, now printed for the first time,
are in the Henry E. Huntington Library at San Marino, California.
The letters from Hurd to Gray are in the library of the Bishop of
Worcester at Hartlebury Castle. The letters to or from How are in
the British Museum (*Add. MS.* 26889, see Appendix O).[1]

The letters to Brown have been widely dispersed. A brief note
may be given of their history. Mason printed only one letter to
Brown (367): this was a formal letter intended to be sent to How,
which How kept and put at Mason's disposal. It seems prob-
able that Brown was not willing to let Mason publish any other of
Gray's letters to him. We can trace in all forty-two letters to Brown.
At some time, possibly after Brown's death, the letters came into
Mason's hands, and passed from him to Stonhewer, and from Ston-
hewer to Mr. Bright. Thirty-nine of them were included in Mr.
Bright's sale in 1845; three of these were presented by Captain
Montagu Montagu, R.N., to the Bodleian. Thirty-six were acquired
by Mr. Penn, and were sold in single lots in 1854.

Of the forty-two letters it has been possible to trace the originals
of twenty-four, divided among the following owners: the British
Museum, the Bodleian, the Library of Pembroke College, Cambridge, the Eton College Library, the Fitzwilliam Museum, the
Pierpont Morgan Library, the Pennsylvania Historical Society, the
Harvard College Library, Messrs. Quaritch, Messrs. Maggs, and
the Rosenbach Company of Philadelphia and New York.

Eight letters to Mary Antrobus and one to her mother were sold
at Messrs. Sotheby's on 8 July 1915. Photographs of six of the letters
to Mary Antrobus were kindly supplied by Mr. A. E. Newton, the
Pennsylvania Historical Society, and the Rosenbach Company. The
letter to Mrs. Antrobus is in the Charles A. Brown Collection of
Autographs and Manuscripts at the University of Rochester, New
York. Of this Mr. Robert F. Metzdorf has sent a photograph.

Other letters, chiefly single letters to different correspondents, are,
or were formerly, owned as follows: letters to Thomas Percy and James
Dodsley, by the British Museum; letters to Walpole, one by Haver-
ford College Library, and one by Messrs. Knight, Frank and Rutley;
letters to Birkett and Ashby, by Pembroke College, Cambridge;
letters to Cole and Stonhewer, by Mr. R. B. Adam; a letter to
Robert Dodsley, by Eton College; a letter to Palgrave, by Lady
Charnwood; a letter to Alderson, by Canon Rowland A. Wilson;
one letter to Ashton, by Messrs. Quaritch, and one by the Henry E.

[1] Photographs or rotographs were obtained of the letters to Wharton,
Mason, Bedingfield, Nicholls, of the correspondence with Beattie, of most
of the letters to Brown of which the originals have been found, and of other
single letters.

Introduction

Huntington Library, San Marino, California; one letter to Mrs. Jennings, by the Society of Antiquaries, and another by Mr. G. H. Last; a letter from Miss Speed, by the Pierpont Morgan Library; and a letter from Thomas Warton, by Trinity College, Oxford.

To the owners, whether institutions or individuals, grateful acknowledgement is due for photographic reproductions or transcripts of letters, and for permission to publish them. Thanks are especially due to Sir Wathen Arthur Waller, Bart., and Mr. A. T. Loyd of Lockinge, for allowing their great collections of original letters to be used and also for settling doubtful points in the manuscripts.

Sources of information illustrating the letters

MANUSCRIPTS.

1. *Gray's own manuscripts.*

(*a*) Commonplace-book in three volumes. This was left by Mason to Stonhewer, and by Stonhewer to Pembroke College. It contains notes of Gray's reading and copies of most of his own poems, many of them dated, and of poems by Walpole and West. The entries may, with fair probability, be dated approximately as made between 1737 and 1761.

(*b*) Note-books and detached notes made on his travels. There is a note-book of his travels in France, owned by Sir John Murray (printed in Gosse, *Works*, vol. i, pp. 237 ff.), and detached notes of his travels in France and Italy, in the Morris Collection at Eton (printed by Tovey in *Gray and his Friends*, pp. 203 ff.). Of his journeys in England and Scotland there are note-books, owned by Sir John Murray, described by Gray as follows: (1) Suffolk 1761, Southampton 1764, Old Park, Hartlepool 1765. (2) Scotland, Glamis 1765, Bishoprick, Old Park &c., Cumberland 1769. (3) Kent, Denton, and Ramsgate, London and Kent 1766, 1768. (4) Cumberland and Westmorland, and Lancashire and Yorkshire 1769.

The note-books generally contain notes on antiquities and natural history. Two of them (2 and 4) have the complete Journal of his Tour in the Lakes and Yorkshire (see Letter 505, n. 1).

(*c*) Various note-books on his reading are in the British Museum, the Pierpont Morgan Library, and elsewhere.

(*d*) Pocket-diaries. It was Gray's custom for many years to keep a pocket-diary. In these diaries he made notes of the budding and flowering of plants, &c. (the source in some instances of the botanical Calendars sent to Wharton). In some years he wrote notes of the symptoms of his ill health in Latin. At intervals he made entries of his receipts and expenses, and these sometimes give us definite dates of his journeys, &c.

After Gray's death Mason found pocket-diaries for twelve years, between 1754 and 1770, and wrote brief notes of the contents in blank pages of Gray's Commonplace-book. The diaries seem to have remained at Aston after Mason's death, and Mitford, who visited William Alderson at Aston, quotes from six of them. Two of these, the diaries for 1755 and 1760, are in the Pembroke College Library.

2. *College documents.*

(*a*) Cook's or Butler's accounts which give records of residence (discussed above).

(*b*) College Registers or Order Books referring to the transaction of College business, the election of Fellows, &c.

(*c*) College Admission Books giving the dates of admission of students with details of their age, parentage, &c.

(*d*) College books of account, in which, for example, Gray's expenses at Peterhouse and Pembroke are entered, and from which information is derived as to the rooms he occupied in College.

(*e*) The Library Register, still preserved at Pembroke, shows the books borrowed by Gray (many of them while he was still at Peterhouse).

3. *Other manuscripts.*

(*a*) Cole's voluminous manuscripts in the British Museum contain many references to Gray and his contemporaries. A copy of Mason's *Memoirs* with notes by Cole was lent by Samuel Rogers to Mitford, who printed the notes in Appendix D to the first volume of his edition of *Gray's Works* (1836). Two volumes of Cole's diaries, edited by Mr. F. G. Stokes, have been published.

(*b*) Mason's Commonplace-book is in the York Minster Library. His letters to Wharton are with Gray's letters to Wharton in the British Museum (Egerton 2400). Mason's letters to Christopher Alderson, his curate at Aston (138 in number), have been lent by their present owner, the Rev. Canon Rowland Wilson.

(*c*) Unpublished notes of Walpole, letters of Mann to Walpole, and a letter of Nicholls to Temple owned by Mr. W. S. Lewis, have been used.

PRINTED SOURCES.

Of contemporary writings the letters of Walpole, Mason, Hurd, and others are of obvious importance. The *Gentleman's Magazine* and John Nichols's *Literary Anecdotes* and *Illustrations* present a great deal of information. The London newspapers (most of which were published twice a week) are important for allusions to contemporary events. Cradock's *Memoirs*, Granger's *Letters*, Polwheles's *Traditions and Recollections*, and Egerton Brydges's *Autobiography* contain references to Gray.

Introduction

Cantabrigia Depicta, A Concise and Accurate Description of the University and Town of Cambridge (the earliest edition of which, that has been traced, was published in 1763) contains *An Exact List of the Posts, Coaches, Stage Waggons and other Carriers to or from Cambridge*. This is of service in giving the posts and the means of communication between Cambridge and London and elsewhere.

Mention should also be made of Mr. Ralph Straus's *Robert Dodsley*, which contains *A Chronological List of all the Books published by Robert Dodsley* (1735–64), with the precise date of publication. This has proved of the greatest use in connexion with many books mentioned by Gray.

BOOKS QUOTED BY SHORT TITLES

Mason, *The Poems of Mr. Gray to which are prefixed Memoirs of his Life and Writings*. First Edition, 1775.
— Mason, *Poems*.
Mason, *Memoirs*.

Mitford, *The Works of Thomas Gray, in 2 volumes*, 1816.
— Mitford (1816).

Mitford, *The Works of Thomas Gray*, 4 vols., 1835–6: the fifth volume containing the correspondence of Gray and Nicholls was added in 1843.
— Mitford (1835–43).

Mitford, *The Correspondence of Thomas Gray and William Mason with Letters to the Rev. James Brown*, 1853 (second edition, corrected, 1855).
— Gray–Mason, 1853.

Mitford, *The Correspondence of Horace Walpole and the Rev. William Mason*. 2 vols., 1851.
— Walpole–Mason Correspondence.

Gosse, *Gray*, in English Men of Letters Series, 1882.
— Gosse, *Life*.

Gosse, *The Works of Thomas Gray*. 4 vols., 1884.
— Gosse, *Works*.

Tovey, *The Letters of Thomas Gray*. 3 vols. (1900, 1904, 1912).
— Tovey.

Toynbee, *The Correspondence of Gray, Walpole, West and Ashton*. 2 vols., 1915.
— Toynbee (1915) or Gray–Walpole Correspondence.

The Correspondence of Richard Hurd and William Mason and Letters of Richard Hurd to Thomas Gray. 1932.
— Hurd–Mason Correspondence.

LIST OF LETTERS

THE list of letters indicates the dates when, the places at which the letters were written, and the names of Gray's correspondents to whom, or by whom, each letter was written. Letters to Gray from his correspondents are shown as '*From* Walpole', &c.; non-extant letters of which note has been taken in the text have the names of the correspondent in italics.

A further purpose served by the list is to give the source from which the text of each of the letters has been derived. Nearly three-fourths of the letters have been printed from the original manuscripts, (see Introduction). Other letters come from printed sources or from manuscript transcripts of letters of which the originals cannot now be traced.

In the Introduction an account has been given of the chief manu-scripts, and acknowledgement has been made to the owners who have allowed their manuscripts to be photographed or copied. A reference to the account will explain the abbreviated form under which the names of institutions or individual owners are indicated in the list.

Of the printed sources the most important are William Mason's *Memoirs of the Life and Writings of Mr. Gray* (1775), *The Works of Lord Orford* (1798), and the editions in which, at different times, Mitford published Gray's correspondence. Other printed sources include books not directly connected with Gray, Magazines, and Sale Cata-logues. Precise indications of the particular editions of Mitford and of other printed sources are given in the preliminary notes to the letters. The transcripts (indicated by T in the sixth column of the list) include two made by Gray himself (58**, 261 A), others made by Cole, Fess, copyists whose names are not known, and seven by Mitford (in one of his note-books now in the British Museum).

[Two numbers survive in the list (387, 396) with no letters attached to them. The letters were transposed in date after the general order had been settled.]

No. of Letter	Date	Place	Correspondent	Original Source	Printed Source or Transcript
	1734				
1	16 Apr.		Walpole	Waller	
2	31 Oct.	Cambridge	,,	,,	
3	17 Nov.	,,	,,	,,	
4	8 Dec.	,,	,,	,,	
5	Dec.	,,	,,	,,	
6	23 Dec.	,,	,,	,,	
	1735				
7	6 Jan.	,,	,,	,,	
8	12 Jan.	,,	,,	,,	
9	14 Jan.	,,	,,	,,	
10	19 Jan.	,,	,,	,,	
11	21 Jan.	,,	,,	,,	
12	27 Jan.	,,	,,	,,	
13	4 Feb.	,,	,,	,,	
14	25 Feb.	,,	,,	,,	
15	5 Mar.	,,	,,	,,	
15*	c. 1 July	,,	*From West*		
16	3 July	,,	Walpole	Waller	
17	c. 15 Oct.	,,	*From* Walpole		Mrs. Toynbee
18	14 Nov.	Oxford	*From West*		Mason
19	c. 20 Dec.	Cambridge	West		,,
	1736				
20	3 Jan.	London	Walpole	Waller	
21	11 Mar.	Cambridge	,,	,,	
22	8 May		West	Loyd	
22*	9 May	Oxford	*From West*		
22**	May	Cambridge	West		Mason
23	24 May	Oxford	*From* West		,,
24	11 June	London	Walpole	Waller	
25	15 July	,,	,,	,,	
26	Aug.	Burnham	,,	,,	
27	26 Sept.	,,	,,	,,	
28	3 Oct.	London	,,	,,	
29	8 Oct.	,,	Birkett	Pemb. Coll.	
30	Oct.	Cambridge	*From* Birkett	,,	
31	12 Oct.	London	Walpole	Waller	
32	27 Oct.	Cambridge	,,	,,	
33	Dec.	,,	West		Mason
34	22 Dec.	Oxford	*From* West		,,
35	29 Dec.	Cambridge	Walpole	Waller	
	1737				
36	16 Jan.	,,	,,	,,	
37	March		West		Mason
38	4 July	Oxford	*From West*		,,
39	July	Cambridge	Walpole	Waller	
40	22 Aug.	London	West		Mason
41	c. 22 Aug.	,,	Walpole	Waller	

No. of Letter	Date	Place	Correspondent	Original Source	Printed Source or Transcript
	1737				
41*	Oct. or Nov.	London	*From West*		
42	c. 12 Nov.	London	Walpole	Waller	
43	2 Dec.	Oxford	*From* West		Mason
44	29 Dec.	Cambridge	Walpole	Waller	
	1738				
45	10 Jan.	,,	,,	,,	
46	15 Jan.	,,	,,	,,	
47	22 Jan.	,,	West		Mason
48	21 Feb.	London	*From* West		,,
49	23 Feb.	Cambridge	Walpole	Waller	
50	7 Mar.	,,	,,	,,	
51	20 Mar.	,,	,,	,,	
52	28 Mar.	,,	,,	,,	
53	June	,,	West		Mason
54	30 June	,,	Ashton		Mitford (T)
55	29 Aug.	London	*From* West		Mason
55*	c. 7 Sept.	Cambridge	*Ashton*		
56	Sept.	,,	West		Mason
57	17 Sept.	London	*From* West		,,
58	19 Sept.	,,	Walpole	Waller	
58*	Dec.	,,	West		Mitford (T)
	1739				
58**	Jan.	Epsom	*From West*		Gray (T)
59	1 Apr.	Amiens	Mrs. Gray		Mason
60	12 Apr.	Paris	West		,,
61	21 Apr.		Ashton		Mitford (T)
61*	Apr. or May		*West*		
62	c. 15 and 22 May		West		Mason
63	29 May		Ashton	Huntington	
63*	June	London	*From West*		
63**	June	Rheims	*West*		
64	21 June	,,	Mrs. Gray		Mason
65	July	,,	Gray and Walpole to Ashton		Mitford (T)
66	25 Aug.	,,	Ashton		,,
67	11 Sept.	Dijon	Philip Gray		Mason
68	18 Sept.	Lyons	West		,,
69	24 Sept.	London	*From* West to Gray and Walpole	Waller	
70	28 Sept.	,,	*From* West		Mason
71	13 Oct.	Lyons	Mrs. Gray		,,
72	25 Oct.	,,	Philip Gray		,,
73	7 Nov.	Turin	Mrs. Gray		,,
74	16 Nov.	,,	West		,,
75	21 Nov.	Genoa	,,		,,
76	9 Dec.	Bologna	Mrs. Gray		,,
77	19 Dec.	Florence	,,		,,

Note. The dates of letters written by Gray from France and Italy were New Style.

No. of Letter	Date	Place	Correspondent	Original Source	Printed Source or Transcript
	1740				
78	15 Jan.	Florence	West		Mason
78*	Feb. or Mar.	London	*From West*		
78**	Mar. or Apr.	Florence	*West*		
79	12 Mar.	,,	Wharton	Egerton	
80	19 Mar.	,,	Mrs. Gray		Mason
81	2 Apr.	Rome	,,		,,
82	15 Apr.	,,	,,		,,
83	16 Apr.	,,	Walpole and Gray to West		Orford
84	Apr.	London	*From* West		Mason
85	14 May	Rome	Walpole and Gray to Ashton	Quaritch	
86	20 and 21 May	Tivoli	West		Mason
87	May	Rome	,,		,,
88	14 June	Naples	Mrs. Gray		,,
89	5 June (o.s.)	London	*From* West		,,
90	10 July	Florence	Philip Gray		,,
91	16 July	,,	West		,,
92	31 July	,,	Walpole and Gray to West		Orford
93	21 Aug.	,,	Mrs. Gray		Mason
93*	Aug.	London?	*From West*		
94	25 Sept.	Florence	West		Mason
95	9 Oct.	,,	Philip Gray		,,
	1741				
96	12 Jan.	,,	,,		,,
96*	c. Apr.	,,	*West*		
96**	Apr.	London?	*From West*		
97	21 Apr.	Florence	West		Mason
98	c. 1 Sept.	Dover	*Chute*		
99	7 Sept.	London	Chute	Chute	
99*	Sept.		*From Conway*		
	1742				
100	28 Mar.	Popes	*From West*		Mason
101	c. 1 Apr.	London	West		,,
102	4 Apr.	Popes	*From West*		,,
103	8 Apr.	London	West		,,
104	c. 12 Apr.	Popes	*From West*		,,
105	23 Apr.	London	West	Loyd	
106	5 May	Popes	*From West*		Mason and Prideaux
107	8 May	London	West		Mason
108	11 May	Popes	*From West*		,,
108*	c. 20 May	London	*Chute*		
109	24 May	,,	Chute	Chute	
110	27 May	,,	West		Mason
110*	c. 3 June	Stoke	*West*		
111	17 June	,,	Ashton		Mitford (T)
112	July	London	Chute and Mann	Chute	

No. of Letter	Date	Place	Correspondent	Original Source	Printed Source or Transcript
	1743				
113	25 Oct. (1743 or 1744)	Cambridge	Chute	Chute	
114	27 Dec.	,,	Wharton	Egerton	
	1744	,,			
115	26 Apr.	Cambridge	,,	Egerton	
	1745				
116	14 Nov.	Stoke	,,	,,	
	1746				
117	3 Feb.	Cambridge	Walpole	Waller	
118	28 Mar.	,,	,,	,,	
119	7 July	,,	,,	Haverford	
120	10 Aug.	Stoke	Wharton	Egerton	
121	11 Sept.	,,	,,	,,	
122	c. 6 Oct.	London	Chute	Chute	
123	8 Oct.	,,	Wharton	Egerton	
124	12 Oct.	Cambridge	Chute	Chute	
125	20 Oct.	,,	Walpole	Waller	
126	23 Nov.	,,	Chute	Chute	
127	11 Dec.	,,	Wharton	Egerton	
128	22 Dec.	,,	Walpole		Orford
129	27 Dec.	,,	Wharton	Egerton	
	1747				
130	Jan.	,,	Walpole		Orford
131	8 Feb.	,,	,,	Waller	
132	c. 15 Feb.	,,	,,	,,	
133	c. 22 Feb.	,,	,,		Mason
134	1 Mar.	,,	,,		,,
135	17 Mar.	,,	Wharton	Egerton	
136	26 Mar.	,,	,,	,,	
137	c. 10 Apr.	,,	,,	,,	
138	13 May	Stoke	Walpole	Waller	
139	c. 15 June	Cambridge	,,		Mitford
140	Aug.	Stoke	,,	Waller	
141	9 Sept.	,,	,,	,,	
142	Nov.	Cambridge	,,		Orford
143	30 Nov.	,,	Wharton	Egerton	
143*	c. Dec.	,,	*Whalley*		
	1748				
144	Jan. or Feb.	,,	Walpole	Waller (part)	Orford (part)
145	5 June	London	Wharton	Egerton	
146	19 Aug.	Stoke	,,	,,	
147	c. 1748	Cambridge	Cole	R. B. Adam	
147*	c. 1748?	,,	Chute	Chute	
	1749				
148	9 Mar.	,,	Wharton	Egerton	
149	25 Apr.	,,	,,	,,	
150	8 Aug.	,,	,,	,,	
151	7 Nov.	,,	Mrs. Gray		Mason
152	12 Nov.	,,	Walpole	Waller	

No. of Letter	Date	Place	Correspondent	Original Source	Printed Source or Transcript
	1750				
153	12 June	Stoke	Walpole		Orford
154	9 Aug.	,,	Wharton	Egerton	
154*	Sept.	,,	*From* Lady Schaub		Mason
155	Oct.	,,	*From* Miss Speed		Mitford (T)
156	18 Dec.	Cambridge	Wharton	Egerton	
	1751				
157	11 Feb.	,,	Walpole	Waller	
158	20 Feb.	,,	,,		Orford
159	3 Mar.	,,	,,		,,
160	16 Apr.	,,	,,	Waller	
161	8 Sept.	,,	,,	,,	
162	29 Sept.	,,	,,	,,	
163	10 Oct.	,,	Wharton	Egerton	
164	26 Nov.	,,	Walpole	Waller	
165	31 Dec.	,,	,,	,,	
165*	c. Dec.	,,	Mason		Mitford
	1752				
166	9 Apr.	London	Wharton	Egerton	
167	28 May	Cambridge	Walpole		*The Times*
168	8 July	Stoke	,,	Waller	
169	July	,,	,,		Orford
169*	29 Sept.	,,	Wharton	Egerton	
169**	Nov.	London	*From Robert Dodsley*		
169*₊*	Nov.	Cambridge	*Dodsley*		
169***	c. 15 Dec.	London	*From Dodsley*		
170	17 Dec.	Cambridge	Walpole	Waller	
171	19 Dec.	,,	Wharton	Egerton	
	1753				
171*	c. 11 Feb.	London	*From Walpole*		
172	12 Feb.	Cambridge	Dodsley	Eton	
173	13 Feb.	,,	Walpole	Waller	
173*	c. 15 Feb.	London	*From Walpole*		
173**	c. 17 Feb.	Cambridge	*Walpole*		
174	20 Feb.	London	*From* Walpole	Waller	
175	27 Feb.	Stoke	Walpole	,,	
176	15 Mar.	,,	Wharton	Egerton	
177	28 June	Cambridge	,,	,,	
178	14 July	,,	,,	,,	
179	24 July	Durham	Brown	Morgan	
180	21 Sept.	,,	Mason	Loyd	
181	23 Sept.	Hull	*From* Mason	,,	
182	26 Sept.	Durham	Mason	,,	
183	18 Oct.	Stoke	Wharton	Egerton	
184	5 Nov.	,,	Mason	Loyd	
184*	c. 1754	Cambridge	Brockett	Brit. Mus.	

No. of Letter	Date	Place	Correspondent	Original Source	Printed Source or Transcript
	1754				
185	15 Feb.	Cambridge	Walpole	Waller	
186	3 Mar.	,,	,,	,,	
187	17 Mar.	,,	,,	,,	
188	11 Apr.	,,	,,	,,	
189	23 May	,,	,,	,,	
189*	23 May	,,	*Chute*		
190	20 July	Stoke	*Wharton*		
191	13 Aug.	,,	Wharton	Egerton	
192	18 Sept.	,,	,,	,,	
193	10 Nov.	Cambridge	,,	,,	
194	26 Dec.	,,	,,	,,	
	1755				
195	1 Mar.	London	*From* Mason	Loyd	
196	9 Mar.	Cambridge	Wharton	Egerton	
197	27 June	Hanover	*From* Mason	Loyd	
198	22 July	The Vyne	Walpole	Waller	
199	6 Aug.	Stoke	Wharton	Egerton	
200	8 Aug.	,,	Walpole	Waller	
201	10 Aug.	,,	,,	,,	
202	14 Aug.	,,	,,	,,	
203	14 Aug.	,,	Chute	Chute	
204	21 Aug.	,,	Stonhewer		Mason
205	21 Aug.	,,	Wharton	Egerton	
205A			Text of the Bard	,,	
206	10 Sept.	Tonbridge	*From* Mason	Loyd	
207	14 Oct.	Stoke	Walpole	Waller	
2c8	18 Oct.	,,	Wharton	Egerton	
209	26 Nov.	Wadworth	*From* Mason	Loyd	
210	25 Dec.	Cambridge	Bedingfield	Huntington	
211	25 Dec.	London	*From* Walpole	Waller	
212	25 Dec.	Chiswick	*From* Mason	Loyd	

VOLUME II

No. of Letter	Date	Place	Correspondent	Original Source	Printed Source or Transcript
	1756				
213	9 Jan.	Cambridge	Wharton	Egerton	
214	25 Jan.	,,	,,	,,	
215	29 Apr.	,,	Bedingfield	Huntington	
216	8 June	,,	Mason	Loyd	
217	14 June	,,	*Wharton*		
218	23 July	Stoke	Mason	Loyd	
219	30 July	,,	Walpole	Waller	
220	30 July	,,	Mason	Loyd	
221	4 Aug.	,,	Walpole	Waller	
222	27 Aug.	,,	Bedingfield	Huntington	
223	29 Aug.	,,	Walpole	Waller	
224	8 Sept.	The Vyne	,,	,,	
225	12 Sept.	,,	,,	,,	
226	19 Sept.	,,	,,	,,	
227	21 Sept.	,,	,,	,,	
228	15 Oct.	Stoke	Wharton	Egerton	
229	12 Nov.	,,	,,	,,	
230	19 Dec.	Cambridge	Mason	Loyd	
231	29 Dec.	,,	Bedingfield	Huntington	
	1757				
231*	7 Jan.	,,	*From* Hurd	Hartlebury	
232	12 Feb.	,,	Bedingfield	Huntington	
233	17 Feb.	,,	Wharton	Egerton	
234	3 Mar.	,,	,,	,,	
235	11 Mar.	London	Walpole	Waller	
236	17 Apr.	Cambridge	Wharton	Egerton	
237	23 Apr.	,,	Mason	Loyd	
237*	c. Apr.	,,	*From* Hurd	Hartlebury	
238	24 or 31 May	,,	Mason	Loyd	
239	11 June	,,	,,	,,	
240	11 July	Stoke	Walpole		Orford
241	25 July	,,	Brown	Loyd	
242	1 Aug.	,,	Mason	,,	
243	10 Aug.	,,	Walpole	Waller	
244	10 Aug.	,,	Bedingfield	Huntington	
245	14 Aug.	,,	Brown	Morgan	
245*	16 Aug.	Cambridge	*From* Hurd	Hartlebury	
246	17 Aug.	Stoke	Wharton	Egerton	
247	25 Aug.	,,	Hurd		Mitford
247*	28 Aug.	Cambridge	*From* Hurd	Hartlebury	
248	7 Sept.	Stoke	Mason	Loyd	
249	7 Sept.	,,	Wharton	Egerton	
250	28 Sept.	,,	Mason	Loyd	
251	7 Oct.	,,	Wharton	Egerton	
252	13 Oct.	,,	Walpole	Waller	
253	13 Oct.	,,	Mason	Loyd	
254	21 Oct.	,,	Walpole	Waller	
255	31 Oct.	,,	Wharton	Egerton	
256	31 Oct.	,,	Bedingfield	Huntington	

xl

No. of Letter	Date	Place	Correspondent	Original Source	Printed Source or Transcript
	1757				
256*	c. 2 Dec.	Andover	*From* Butler		Mason
257	8 Dec.	Cambridge	Wharton	Egerton	
258	12 Dec.	,,	,,	,,	
258*	c. 13 Dec.	London	*From Mason*		
258**	c. 15 Dec.	Cambridge	*Mason*		
258*ₓ*	c. 17 Dec.	London	*From Mason*		
259	19 Dec.	Cambridge	Mason	Loyd	
260	c. 27 Dec.	,,	*Mason*		
	1758				
261	5 Jan.	Syon Hill	*From* Mason	Loyd	
261A			Gray's Copy of Mason's Ode		Gray (T)
262	13 Jan.	Cambridge	Mason	Loyd	
263	16 Jan.	Syon Hill	*From* Mason	,,	
263*	c. 16 Jan.	Cambridge	*Butler*		
264	17 Jan.	,,	Walpole	Waller	
265	22 Jan.	,,	Mason	Loyd	
265*	c. 23 Jan.	Andover	*From* Butler		Mason
266	31 Jan.	Cambridge	Bedingfield	Huntington	
266*	3 Feb.	,,	Mason	Loyd	
267	21 Feb.	,,	Wharton	Egerton	
268	8 Mar.	,,	,,		Mason
269	24 Mar.	,,	Mason	Loyd	
270	9 Apr.	,,	Wharton	Egerton	
271	18 June	,,	,,	,,	
272	20 June	,,	Mason	Loyd	
273	22 July	Stoke	Walpole	Waller	
273*	Aug.	,,	Palgrave	Lady Charnwood	
274	9 Aug.	,,	Wharton	Egerton	
275	11 Aug.	,,	Mason	Loyd	
276	18 Aug.	,,	Stonhewer		Mason
277	31 Aug.	,,	Wharton	Egerton	
278	6 Sept.	,,	Palgrave		Mason
279	7 Sept.	,,	Brown	Harvard	
280	16 Sept.	,,	Wharton	Egerton	
281	28 Oct.	,,	Brown		Mitford
282	9 Nov.	,,	Wharton	Egerton	
283	9 Nov.	,,	Mason	Loyd	
283*	Nov.?	,,	Mary Antrobus		Maggs
284	Nov.	Aston	*From* Mason	Loyd	
284*	c. 28 Nov.	Stoke	Mason	,,	
285	2 Dec.	,,	Wharton	Egerton	
	1759				
286	18 Jan.	London	Mason	Loyd	
287	22 Jan.	Aston	*From* Mason	,,	
288	25 Jan.	,,	,, ,,	,,	
289	14 Feb.	London	Walpole	Waller	

No. of Letter	Date	Place	Correspondent	Original Source	Printed Source or Transcript
	1759				
290	15 Feb.	London	*From* Walpole	Waller	
291	1 Mar.	Cambridge	Mason	Loyd	
292	10 Apr.	London	,,	,,	
293	3 May	,,	Mary Antrobus	A. E. Newton	
294	28 May	,,	Brown	Fitzwilliam Museum	
295	c. May?	,,	*Mary Antrobus*		
296	21 July	,,	Wharton	Egerton	
297	23 July	,,	Mason	Loyd	
298	24 July	,,	Palgrave		Mason
299	8 Aug.	,,	Brown	Loyd	
299*	11 Aug.	,,	,,	,,	
299**	c. 20 Aug.	,,	*Miss Speed*		
300	25 Aug.	Stoke	*From* Miss Speed	Morgan	
301	c. 15 Sept.	London	Mary Antrobus	Rosenbach	
302	8 Sept.	,,	Mrs. Antrobus	Rochester	
303	18 Sept.	,,	Wharton	Egerton	
304	6 Oct.	Stoke	Mason	Loyd	
304*	27 Oct.	London	Mrs. Jennings	Antiquaries	
305	24 Nov.	,,	Mary Antrobus	Rosenbach	
306	28 Nov.	,,	Wharton	Egerton	
307	1 Dec.	,,	Mason	Loyd	
	1760				
308	23 Jan.	,,	Wharton	Egerton	
309	c. 28 Mar.	,,	Brown	Pennsylvania	
310	c. Apr.	,,	Walpole		Orford
311	22 Apr.	,,	Wharton	Egerton	
311*	May	,,	*Macpherson*		
312	7 June	,,	Mason	Loyd	
313	c. 20 June	,,	Wharton	Egerton	
314	27 June	,,	Mason	Loyd	
315	29 June	[London]	Stonhewer		Mason
316	26 July	London	Brown		Mitford
317	7 Aug.	Cambridge	Mason	Loyd	
318	12 Aug.	,,	Clerke		Mason
319	Aug.	Strawberry Hill	*From* Walpole	Waller	
319*	c. 31 Aug.	Cambridge	Mason	Loyd	
320	2 Sept.	,,	Walpole	Waller	
321	21 Oct.	London	Wharton	Egerton	
322	23 Oct.	,,	Brown	Pennsylvania	
323	25 Oct.	,,	,,	Quaritch	
324	c. 28 Oct.	,,	Walpole	Waller	
324*	c. Oct.	,,	Mrs. Jennings	Last	
325	8 Nov.	,,	Brown	Eton	
326	28 Nov.	Aston	*From* Mason	Loyd	

Note. For Letters 301, 302 see Addendum in Vol. II.

No. of Letter	Date	Place	Correspondent	Original Source	Printed Source or Transcript
	1760				
327	10 Dec.	London	Mason	Loyd	
328	Dec.	,,	Walpole		Orford
	1761				
329	8 Jan.	Aston	*From* Mason	Loyd	
330	22 Jan.	London	Mason	,,	
331	31 Jan.	,,	Wharton	Egerton	
332	9 Feb.	,,	Brown	Eton	
333	9 May	,,	Wharton	Egerton	
333*	May?	,,	Walpole	Waller	
334	26 May	,,	Brown	Pemb. Coll.	
335	13 June	,,	,,		Mitford
336	23 June	Cambridge	Wharton	Egerton	
337	19 July	,,	,,	,,	
338	20 July	Aston	*From* Mason	Loyd	
339	Aug.	Cambridge	Mason	,,	
340	2 Sept.	,,	Percy	Brit. Mus.	
341	Sept.?		Anstey		Anstey
342	8 Sept.	London	Wharton	Egerton	
343	10 Sept.	,,	Walpole	Waller	
344	19 Sept.	,,	Brown		Morrison Catalogue
345	24 Sept.	,,	,,		K. Fess (T)
346	c. 20 Oct.	,,	Mason	Loyd	
347	22 Oct.	,,	Brown		Transcript at Pemb. Coll.
348	22 Oct.	,,	Wharton	Egerton	
349	7 Nov.	,,	Brown	Loyd	
350	13 Nov.	,,	Wharton	Egerton	
351	8 Dec.	Cambridge	Mason	Loyd	
351*	Dec.	,,	Stonhewer		Mason
351**	Dec.	,,	Walpole	Waller	
	1762				
352	11 Jan.	Cambridge	Mason	Loyd	
353	11 Jan.	,,	Wharton	Egerton	
354	5 Feb.	,,	Mason	Loyd	
355	11 Feb.	,,	Walpole	Waller	
356	28 Feb.	,,	,,		Orford
357	17 Mar.	,,	Mason	Loyd	
358	4 June	,,	Wharton	Egerton	
359	21 June	,,	Mason	Loyd	
360	10 July	York	Wharton	Egerton	
361	19 July	Old Park	Brown		Mitford
362	1 Sept.?	,,	Mason	Loyd	
363	4 Dec.	Cambridge	Wharton	Egerton	
364	21 Dec.	,,	Mason	Loyd	
	1763				
365	15 Jan.	Aston	*From* Mason	,,	
366	8 Feb.	Cambridge	Mason	,,	
367	Feb.	,,	Brown	Brit. Mus.	
368	6 Mar.	,,	Mason	Loyd	

List of Letters

No. of Letter	Date	Place	Correspondent	Original Source	Printed Source or Transcript
	1763				
369	24 Apr.	Pisa	*From* Algarotti	Loyd	
370	25 Apr.	,,	*From* How	Brit. Mus.	
371	28 June	York	*From* Mason	Loyd	
372	July	Cambridge	Mason	,,	
373	5 Aug.	,,	Wharton	Egerton	
374	9 Sept.	,,	Algarotti		Transcript in Brit. Mus.
375	10 Sept.	,,	How	Brit. Mus.	
376	12 Sept.	,,	Walpole	Waller	
377	19 Sept.	,,	,,	,,	
378	29 Sept.	Spa	*From* How	Brit. Mus.	
379	8 Oct.	Cambridge	Mason	Loyd	
380	10 Oct.	,,	Robinson		Gent. Mag.
381	8 Nov.	Brussels	*From* How	Brit. Mus.	
382	Nov.	London	How	,,	
	1764				
383	27 Jan.	Cambridge	Walpole	Waller	
384	31 Jan.	,,	,,	,,	
385	21 Feb.	,,	Wharton	Egerton	
386	18 Mar.	,,	Walpole	Waller	
387	No letter corresponding to this number				
388	25 Apr.	Cambridge	Walpole	Waller	
389	10 July	,,	,,	,,	
390	10 July	,,	Wharton	Egerton	
391	17 Aug.	,,	Walpole	Waller	
391*	Sept. or Oct.	London	Mary Antrobus	Pennsylvania	
392	1 or 8 Oct.	Southampton	Brown	Brit. Mus.	
393	13 Oct.	,,	,,	Pennsylvania	
394	25 Oct.	London	,,		Mitford
395	29 Oct.	,,	,,		,,
396	No letter corresponding to this number				
397	19 Nov.	London	Nicholls	Eton	
398	30 Dec.	Cambridge	Walpole	Waller	
	1765				
399	17 Jan.	,,	Mason	Loyd	
399*	March	,,	Bentham		Gent. Mag.
400	March	,,	Palgrave		Mason
400*	14 Apr.	,,	Walpole	Waller	
401	29 Apr.	,,	Wharton	Egerton	
402	May?	London	Brown	Pemb. Coll.	
403	20 May	,,	,,	Bodleian	
404	23 May	,,	Mason	Loyd	
405	4 June	York	Bedingfield	Huntington	
406	6 June	,,	Wharton	Egerton	
407	8 July	Old Park	Mason	Loyd	
408	22 July	Aston	*From* Mason	,,	
409	15 Aug.	Old Park	Brown		Tovey
410	30 Aug.	Aberdeen	*From* Beattie		Forbes
411	8 Sept.	Glamis	Beattie	Aberdeen	

List of Letters

No. of Letter	Date	Place	Correspondent	Original Source	Printed Source or Transcript
	1765				
412	30 Sept.	Glamis	Wharton	Egerton	
413	2 Oct.	,,	Beattie	Aberdeen	
414	2 Nov.	London	Brown	Bodleian	
415	8 Nov.	,,	Mason	Loyd	
416	10 Nov.	,,	Walpole	Waller	
417	19 Nov.	Paris	*From* Walpole	,,	
418	13 Dec.	Cambridge	Walpole		Orford
418*	Dec.	,,	Mary Antrobus	Rosenbach	

xlv

VOLUME III

No. of Letter	Date	Place	Correspondent	Original Source	Printed Source or Transcript
	1766				
419	25 Jan.	Paris	*From* Walpole		Orford
420	5 Mar.	Cambridge	Wharton	Egerton	
421	15 May	London	Brown		Mitford
422	26 Aug.	Cambridge	Nicholls	Eton	
423	26 Aug.	,,	Wharton	Egerton	
424	c. 26 Aug.	,,	Mason	Loyd	
425	23 Sept.	,,	Nicholls	Eton	
426	24 Sept.	,,	Walpole	Waller	
426	c. 23 Sept.	,,	*Stonhewer*		
427*	5 Oct.	,,	Mason	Loyd	
428	9 Oct.	London	,,	,,	
429	13 Oct.	,,	Nicholls	Eton	
430	23 Oct.	,,	Brown		Mitford
431	18 Nov.	,,	,,	Rosenbach	
	1767				
432	19 Jan.	Cambridge	Nicholls	Eton	
433	27 Jan.	,,	Mason	Loyd	
434	2 Feb.	London	*From* Mason	,,	
435	15 Feb.	Cambridge	Mason	,,	
436	28 Mar.	,,	,,	,,	
437	30 Mar.	Aberdeen	*From* Beattie		Mason
438	1 Apr.	Bath	*From* Mason	Loyd	
439	May	London	Mary Antrobus	Rosenbach	
440	23 May	,,	Mason	Loyd	
441	c. 28 May	,,	Brown		Mitford
442	2 June	,,	,,		,,
443	6 June	,,	,,		,,
444	6 June	,,	Mason	Loyd	
445	21 June	Aston	Wharton	Egerton	
446	10 July	Old Park	Mason	Loyd	
447	15 July	York	*From* Mason	,,	
448	19 July	Old Park	Mason	,,	
449	26 July	,,	,,	,,	
450	27 July	York	*From* Mason	,,	
451	9 Aug.	Old Park	Mason	,,	
452	12 Aug.	,,	Beattie	Aberdeen	
453	11 Sept.	,,	Mason	Loyd	
454	31 Oct.	York	Brown	Maggs	
455	5 Nov.	London	Nicholls	Eton	
456	17 Dec.	Cambridge	,,	,,	
457	24 Dec.	,,	Beattie	Aberdeen	
458	24 Dec.	,,	Walpole	Waller	
459	28 Dec.	,,	Wharton	Egerton	
460	31 Dec.	,,	Nicholls	Eton	
	1768				
461	8 Jan.	,,	Mason	Loyd	
462	12 Jan.	,,	How	Brit. Mus.	

No. of Letter	Date	Place	Correspondent	Original Source	Printed Source or Transcript
	1768				
463	17 Jan.	Cambridge	Wharton	Egerton	
464	28 Jan.	,,	Nicholls	Eton	
465	c. 1 Feb.	,,	James Dodsley	Brit. Mus.	
466	1 Feb.	,,	Beattie	Aberdeen and A. H. H. Murray	
467	3 Feb.	,,	Nicholls	Eton	
468	14 Feb.	,,	Walpole		Orford
469	16 Feb.	Aberdeen	*From* Beattie	Aberdeen	
470	18 Feb.	London	*From* Walpole		Orford
471	25 Feb.	Cambridge	Walpole		,,
472	26 Feb.	London	*From* Walpole		,,
473	6 Mar.	Cambridge	Walpole		,,
474	8 Mar.	London	*From* Walpole	Waller	
475	15 Mar.	Cambridge	Wharton	Egerton	
476	27 Apr.	London	Brown		Gosse
477	29 May	,,	Nicholls		Mitford
477*	27 July	,,	*From Duke of Grafton*		
478	27 or 28 July	,,	Duke of Grafton		Mason
479	29 July	,,	Mary Antrobus		Mitford
480	1 Aug.	,,	Wharton	Egerton	
481	1 Aug.	,,	Mason	Loyd	
482	3 Aug.	,,	Nicholls	Eton	
483	6 Aug.	Blundeston	*From* Nicholls		Mitford
484	8 Aug.	Hornby Castle	*From* Mason	Loyd	
485	27 Aug.	London	Nicholls	Eton	
486	7 Sept.	Cambridge	Mason	Loyd	
487	31 Oct.		Beattie	Aberdeen	
488	8 Nov.		Nicholls	Eton	
488*	Dec.		*Palgrave*		
489	29 Dec.		Mason	Loyd	
	1769				
490	2 Jan.		Nicholls	Eton	
491	26 Jan.		,,	,,	
491*	end Jan.		Percy [?]	Brit. Mus.	
492	Apr.	London	Walpole	Waller	
493	20 Apr.		Wharton	Egerton	
494	c. 20 Apr.		Brown		Mitford
495	26 May	Cambridge	Walpole	Waller	
496	7 June		Nicholls	Eton	
497	12 June		Stonhewer		Mason
498	14 June	Blundeston	*From* Nicholls		Mitford
499	24 June	Cambridge	Nicholls	Eton	
500	3 July	Blundeston	*From* Nicholls		Mitford
501	16 July	Cambridge	Beattie	Aberdeen	
502	17 July		Wharton	Egerton	
503	26 Aug.	Old Park	Mason	Loyd	
504	10 Oct.	Lancaster	Brown		Mitford

No. of Letter	Date	Place	Correspondent	Original Source	Printed Source or Transcript
	1769				
505	18 Oct.	Aston	Wharton	Egerton	
506	29 Oct.	Cambridge	,,	,,	
507	2 Nov.		Stonhewer	R. B. Adam	
507*	Nov.	Aberdeen	*From* Beattie	Aberdeen	
508	27 Nov.	Bath	*From* Nicholls		Mitford
508*	Nov.	Cambridge	Wharton	Egerton	
509	2 Dec.		Mason	Loyd	
509*	4 Dec.	London	*From* Hurd	Hartlebury	
510	14 Dec.	,,	Mason	Loyd	
	1770				
511	3 Jan.	Cambridge	Wharton	Egerton	
511A			Continuation of Journal	Murray	
512	6 Jan.	Cambridge	Bonstetten and Gray to Nicholls	Eton	
512*	Feb. or Mar.	,,	Lort		Sotheby
512**	Feb. or Mar.	London	*From Bonstetten*		
513	20 Mar.	Cambridge	Nicholls	Eton	
513*	Mar. 1770 to Apr. 1771		*From Bonstetten*		
514	4 Apr.	Cambridge	Nicholls	Eton	
514*	Apr. and May		*To and from Mason*		
515	12 Apr.	Cambridge	Bonstetten		Matthisson
516	12 Apr.		Farmer		Sale Catalogue
517	14 Apr.		Nicholls	Eton	
518	15 Apr.		Warton		Transcript in Brit. Mus.
519	18 Apr.		Wharton	Egerton	
520	19 Apr.		Bonstetten		Matthisson
521	20 Apr.	Winchester	*From* Warton	Trin. Coll. Oxon.	
522	1 May	Aberdeen	*From* Beattie	Aberdeen	
523	9 May	Cambridge	Bonstetten		Matthisson
524	22 May	London	Nicholls	Eton	
525	22 May		Brown	Pennsylvania	
525*	c. 24 May		*Mason*		
526	26 May	Blundeston	*From* Nicholls		Mitford
527	c. 2 June	Cambridge	Nicholls	Eton	
527*	23 June		Alderson	R. A. Wilson	
528	24 June		Nicholls	Eton	
529	2 July		Beattie		Mason
530	24 Aug.		Wharton	Egerton	
531	7 Sept.		Mason	Loyd	
532	12 Sept.		Walpole	Waller	
533	14 Sept.		Nicholls	Eton	
534	18 Sept.		Walpole	Waller	
535	24 Oct.	Cambridge	Mason	Loyd	
536	25 Nov.		Nicholls	Eton	
537	28 Nov.	Blundeston	*From* Nicholls		Mitford

No. of Letter	Date	Place	Correspondent	Original Source	Printed Source or Transcript
	1770				
538	22 Dec.	Milton	*From Cole*		
539	22 Dec.	Cambridge	Cole		Cole (T)
	1771				
540	26 Jan.		Nicholls	Eton	
541	31 Jan.	Blundeston	*From Nicholls*		Mitford
541*	Jan. or Feb.	Cambridge	Ashby	Pemb. Coll.	
542	2 Feb.		Wharton	Egerton	
543	24 Feb.		Nicholls	Eton	
544	8 Mar.		Beattie		Forbes
545	16 Mar.	Blundeston	*From Nicholls*		Mitford
545*	17 Mar.	Cambridge	Walpole		Mason
545**	c. 23 Mar.		*Walpole*		
546	25 Mar.	London	*From Walpole*	Waller	
547	27 Mar.	,,	*From Mason*	Loyd	
547*	c. 13 Apr.	Cambridge	*Stonhewer*		
548	15 Apr.	London	*From Mason*	Loyd	
549	29 Apr.	Blundeston	*From Nicholls*		Mitford
550	3 May	Cambridge	Nicholls	Eton	
551	14 May	Blundeston	*From Nicholls*		Mitford
552	20 May	London	Nicholls	Eton	
553	24 May		Wharton	Egerton	
554	27 May	Blundeston	*From Nicholls*		Mitford
555	22 June	London	Brown	Bodleian	
556	28 June		Nicholls	Eton	
557	29 June	Paris	*From Nicholls*		Mitford

CHRONOLOGICAL TABLE

THE following table serves a double purpose. The first column shows where Gray was at different dates: it records his places of residence, his journeys, and where he stayed. By a reference to this column the place from which any particular letter was written can be traced.

The second column gives the more important events in Gray's uneventful life and records the dates of the composition and publication of his works. The numbers of the letters are given for some of the entries. It should be noted that some of the dates are approximate, and that the time spent on Gray's journeys from place to place is not always stated.

1716 26 Dec. to c. 1725 } Living in Cornhill.	26 Dec. Born at his father's house in Cornhill.
c. 1725 to 1734 Sept. } At School at Eton.	4 July. Entered at Peterhouse.
1735 9 Oct. to 31 July } Cambridge.	9 Oct. Admitted at Peterhouse.
31 July to } London and else- 18 Oct. } where.	
18 Oct. to 24 Dec. Cambridge	22 Nov. Admitted at Inner Temple.
24 Dec. to } London. 1736 23 Jan. }	
23 Jan. } to } Cambridge. 12 Feb. }	9 Feb. Dr. Audley's Opinion (App. A). 12 Feb. His Aunt Sarah Gray died and left him her property.
12 Feb. to 5 Mar. London.	
5 Mar. } to } Cambridge. 6 June }	May. *Hymeneal* on the Marriage of the Prince of Wales in the Cambridge *Gratulatio* (23).
6 June to } London and Burnham. 22 Oct. }	
1737 23 Oct. to } Cambridge. 28 July }	Mar. *Luna est habitabilis* (Tripos Verses, 35).
28 July to } London and else- 15 Nov. } where.	
1738 15 Nov. to } Cambridge. 27 Apr. }	
27 Apr. to 26 May. London(?).	
26 May to 14 Sept. Cambridge.	
14 Sept. to } London. 1739 18 Mar. (O.S.) }	
29 Mar. (N.S.)[1] to } Journey to 4 Apr. } Paris.	29 Mar. Began his tour to France and Italy with Walpole (59).

[1] The dates during Gray's journey are in New Style.

1

1739 4 Apr. to 2 June. Paris.
2 June to 7 Sept. Rheims.
7–15 Sept. Journey to Lyons.
13 Sept. to ⎫ Lyons with excur-
31 Oct.　　⎭ sion to Geneva.
31 Oct. ⎫ Journey from Lyons
　　to　⎬ by Turin, Genoa,
16 Dec. ⎭ Bologna to Florence.

16 Dec. to ⎫ Florence.
1740 21 Mar.　⎭

21–25 Mar. Journey to Rome.
25 Mar. ⎫ Rome with excursions
　　to　⎬ to Tivoli and Naples.
4 July　⎭

4–7 July. Journey to Florence.

7 July ⎫ Florence with excur-　　*De Principiis Cogitandi* begun (sometime
　　to　⎬ sion to Bologna in　　in 1740).
1741 24 Apr. ⎭ Aug. 1740.

24 Apr. to 3 May. To Bologna　　*c.* 3 May. Quarrel with Walpole at
and Reggio, and at Reggio.　　Reggio.

3 May to 15 July. Venice.
15 July ⎫ Journey by Padua,　　21 Aug. *Ode* written in the album at the
　　to　⎬ Verona, Milan, Lyons,　　*Grande Chartreuse.*
12 Sept. ⎭ and Paris to London.

1 Sept. (O.S.) ⎫ London　with　　6 Nov. Philip Gray died.
　　to　　　⎬ visits　(prob-　　Winter (1741–2). *Agrippina* begun (101).
1742 28 May　　⎭ ably to Stoke).　　Mar.(?). *Hymn to Ignorance* written.
28 May to ⎫ Stoke.　　　　　　1 June. West died (110*).
19 June　⎭　　　　　　　　1 June. *Ode on the Spring* sent to West.

19 June to *c.* 15 July. London.
c. 15 July to ⎫ Stoke and Lon-　　Aug. *Eton Ode, Sonnet on the death of West,*
15 Oct.　　⎭ don.　　　　　and *Hymn to Adversity* composed.

15 Oct. ⎫　　　　　　　　　15 Oct. Returned to Peterhouse as a
　　　　⎮　　　　　　　　　　Fellow-commoner.
　　to　⎬ Cambridge.　　　　21 Oct. Jonathan Rogers died.
　　　　⎮　　　　　　　　　Dec.(?). Mrs. Gray and Mary Antrobus
1743 23 June ⎭　　　　　　　　retired from Cornhill to Stoke.

23 June to ⎫ Stoke and London.
30 Sept.　⎭

30 Sept. ⎫　　　　　　　　　Dec. Admitted to degree of Bachelor of
　　to　⎬ Cambridge.　　　　Laws (114).
1744 8 July　⎭

8 July to ⎫ Stoke and London.
5 Oct.　⎭

5 Oct. to ⎫ Cambridge.
1745 12 May　⎭

12 May to ⎫ Stoke and London.
13 Sept.　⎭

| 1745 | 13 Sept. to 7 Nov. Cambridge.
7–22 Nov. London and Stoke. | 8 Nov. Reconciliation with Walpole and Ashton (116). |

1746 22 Nov. to } Cambridge.
13 July
13 July to 10 Oct. London and Stoke (with an excursion to Hampton Court and other places (120)).
10–30 Oct. Cambridge.
30 Oct. to 15 Nov. London.

1747 15 Nov. to 8 May } Cambridge (with a few days' absence in February).

1 Mar. *Ode on the Cat* sent to Walpole (134).

8–22 May. Stoke and London.
22 May to 16 Aug. Cambridge.
16 Aug. to 23 Oct. London, Stoke, Strawberry Hill, &c.

30 May. *Eton Ode* published (139).

1748 23 Oct. to 8 Apr. } Cambridge.

15 Jan. Dodsley's *Collection of Poems* (containing three poems by Gray) published (144).
25 Mar. Fire in Cornhill. Gray's house burnt (145).

8 Apr. to 5 Nov. London and Stoke with visit to Strawberry Hill and perhaps visit to Cobham &c. (191, n. 22).

Aug.(?). *Alliance of Education and Government* begun (146).

1749 5 Nov. to 21 May } Cambridge.
21 May to 27 June } Stoke and London.
27 June to 14 Sept. Cambridge.
14–26 Sept. Stoke(?).
26 Sept. to 23 Nov. Cambridge.

5 Nov. Mary Antrobus died (151).

1750 23 Nov. to 5 Jan. } Stoke and London.
5 Jan. to 3 June } Cambridge.
3 June to 15 Nov. } Stoke.
15 Nov. to 7 Dec. London.

12 June. The *Elegy* finished and sent to Walpole (153).
Oct.(?). The *Long Story* sent to Lady Cobham (155).

1751 7 Dec. to 10 Mar. } Cambridge.
10–29 Mar. London.
29 Mar. to 6 June. Cambridge.

15 Feb. The *Elegy* published (157).

1751 6 June to ⎫ Stoke and London.
     2 Sept. ⎭

     2 Sept. ⎫ Cambridge (with brief
       to   ⎬ visit to Abbots Ripton
1752 2 Apr. ⎭ in Sept.
     2–15 Apr. London.
     15 Apr. to 21 June. Cambridge.
     21 June ⎫ Stoke (with visits to
       to   ⎬ Strawberry Hill and
     13 Oct. ⎭ London.

July or (before). *Progress of Poesy* begun (169).

     13 Oct. to ⎫ Cambridge.
1753 22 Feb. ⎭
     22 Feb. ⎫
       to   ⎬ Stoke.
     13 Apr. ⎭

11 Mar. Mrs. Gray died (176).
29 Mar. *Six Poems with Bentley's Designs* published (175).

     13 Apr. to 16 July. Cambridge.
     16 July to 3 Oct. Trip to the north and visit to Durham.
     3–4 Oct. Cambridge.
     4 Oct. to ⎫ Stoke and London.
     21 Dec. ⎭

     21 Dec. to ⎫ Cambridge.
1754 21 Jan. ⎭
     21 Jan. to 8 Feb. London(?).
     8 Feb. to 16 June. Cambridge.
     16 June ⎫ Stoke (with tour to
       to   ⎬ Northants, Warwick,
     27 Sept. ⎭ &c.) and London.
     27 Sept. to ⎫ Cambridge
     20 Dec. ⎭

Dec. (or before). *Progress of Poesy* finished (194).

     20–27 Dec. Away from Cambridge.

     27 Dec. to ⎫ Cambridge.
1755 24 Apr. ⎭

1754–5. The *Bard* and *Ode on Vicissitude* begun (196).
1755.[1] Offer of Secretaryship to Earl of Bristol at Lisbon declined.

     24 Apr. to 15 July. London, Stoke, the Vyne, &c.
     15–31 July. The Vyne with trip to Portsmouth, Southampton, Winchester, &c.
     1 Aug. ⎫ Stoke (with visit to
       to   ⎬ Strawberry Hill) and
     26 Nov. ⎭ London.

     26 Nov. to ⎫ Cambridge.
1756 3 Apr. ⎭

5 Mar. Migration from Peterhouse to Pembroke (214).

[1] Walpole in his brief *Memoir of Gray* (App. Y) says in the winter of 1755: the winter of 1754–5 seems to have been meant.

1756   3–8 Apr. London.
   8 Apr. to 16 June. Cambridge.
   16 June to 3 Dec. London and
    Stoke (with visit to Straw-
    berry Hill).

   3 Dec. to ⎫ Cambridge.
1757   5 Mar. ⎭

            Feb. Tuthill deprived of his Fellowship
            at Pembroke (App. G).

   5 Mar. to 2 Apr. London.
   2 Apr. to 17 June. Cambridge.
   17 June ⎫ London and Stoke
    to ⎬ with visit to Straw-   8 Aug. *Odes* published (240, n. 2).
   4 Dec. ⎭ berry Hill.

   4 Dec. ⎫ Cambridge (with a   15 Dec. Poet Laureateship offered to
     ⎪ brief visit to Abbots   Gray and declined (258*).
    to ⎬ Ripton at the end of
1758   16 Apr. ⎭ Jan).   Jan. (or before). *Epitaph on Mrs. Clerke*
            composed (266).

   16 Apr. to 15 May. London.
   15 May ⎫ Cambridge (with tour
    to ⎬ to Ely, Peterborough,
   29 June ⎭ &c.).
   29 June ⎫ London and Stoke,   July(?). *Epitaph on a Child* written for
    to ⎬ Hampton Court and   Wharton (271).
   31 July ⎭ Strawberry Hill, &c.
   31 July to ⎫ Stoke with brief visit   Sept. Mrs. Rogers died (281).
   12 Dec. ⎭ to London in Oct.

   12 Dec. to ⎫ London.
1759   15 Feb. ⎭
   15 Feb. to 4 Mar. Cambridge.
   4 Mar. to 29 June. London.
   29 June to 9 July. Cambridge.
   9 July ⎫ London with excur-   July. Gray took up his residence in
    to ⎬ sion to Strawberry   London (296).
   23 Sept. ⎭ Hill, &c.
   23 Sept. to ⎫ Stoke (at Lady   Sept. Alderman Nutting died (302).
   15 Oct. ⎭ Cobham's).

   15 Oct. ⎫ London with visit to
    to ⎬ Strawberry Hill in
1760   28 June ⎭ June, &c.   Mar. Lady Cobham died (311).
   28 June to ⎫ Shiplake.   June to July. Gray and Miss Speed
   21 July ⎭   stayed with Mrs. Jennings (318).
   21–29 July. London.
   29 July to 6 Oct. Cambridge.

   6 Oct. to ⎫ London.
1761   15 June ⎭   Apr. (or before). *The Fatal Sisters* and
            The Descent of Odin composed (471,
            n. 1a).

   15–29 June. Cambridge.

1761 29 June to⎫ Tour in Suffolk
    11 July   ⎭ and Norfolk.
    11 July to⎫ Cambridge.
    8 Sept. ⎭
    8 Sept. to⎫ London.
    19 Nov. ⎭

    19 Nov.⎫
    to   ⎬ Cambridge.
1762 22 Mar.⎭

    22 Mar. to 30 May. London.
    30 May to 1 July. Cambridge.
    1 July to⎫ York and Old Park.
    11 Nov. ⎭
    11–18 Nov. Journey to London.
    18–25 Nov. London.

    25 Nov. to⎫ Cambridge.
1763 6 May   ⎭
    6 May ⎫ London with 'a little
    to   ⎬ jaunt to Epsom and
    16 June⎭ Boxhill'.
    16 June to 19 Sept. Cambridge.
    19 Sept. to⎫ 'A ramble away
    4 Oct.   ⎭ from Cambridge.'
    4 Oct. to 4 Nov. Cambridge.
    4 Nov. to 8 Dec. London.

    8 Dec. to⎫ Cambridge.
1764 16 May ⎭

    16 May to 25 June. London.
    25 June to 4 Sept. Cambridge.
    4 to 25 Sept. London.
    25 Sept. to 22 Oct. Winchester,
    Southampton, Salisbury, Wilton, Stonehenge, &c.
    22 Oct. to 21 Nov. London.

    21 Nov. to⎫ Cambridge.
1765 30 Apr. ⎭
    30 Apr. to⎫ London with visit
    27 May ⎭ to Windsor.
    27 May⎫ York and Old Park
    to   ⎬ with visits to Hartlepool.
    18 Aug.⎭

Aug. *Epitaph on Sir W. Williams* composed (339).
Oct. Song (*Thyrsis*) written for Miss Speed.
12 Nov. Miss Speed married to Baron de la Perrière (353).
Nov. Gray gave up his lodgings in London (347).
Sometime in this year *The Triumph of Owen* and other imitations of Welsh poetry composed (App. M).

Nov. Gray's name suggested for the Regius Professorship of Modern History (363).

March(?). *The Candidate* composed (App. P).

1765 18 Aug. to 17 Oct. Journey to
Glamis, stay at Glamis, with
excursion to the Highlands.
7–14 Oct. Journey by Perth,
Stirling, and Edinburgh to
Old Park.
14–28 Oct. Old Park.
28 Oct. to 2 Dec. London.

1766 2 Dec. to ⎱ Cambridge.
16 Apr. ⎰
16 Apr. to 16 May. London.
16 May ⎱ Canterbury and Den-
to ⎱ ton with excursion to
4 July ⎰ Margate and Dover.
4–17 July. London.
17–24 July. Cambridge.
24 July to 3 Aug. Away from Cambridge.
3 Aug. to 11 Sept. Cambridge.
11–22 Sept. Suffolk and Norfolk.
22 Sept. to 6 Oct. Cambridge.
6 Oct. to 5 Dec. London.

1767 5 Dec. to ⎱ Cambridge.
20 Apr. ⎰
20 Apr. to 13 June. London
with excursion to Chiswick,
Strawberry Hill, &c., at the
end of May.
13–15 June. Cambridge.
15 June to 1 July. Aston (with a
visit to Dovedale and the
Peak) and York.
1 July to 24 Oct. Old Park with
visits to Rokeby and Richmond, Hartlepool, Carlisle,
Keswick, &c.
24 Oct. to 2 Nov. York.
2 Nov. to 14 Dec. London.

1768 14 Dec. to ⎱ Cambridge.
7 Apr. ⎰

7 Apr. ⎱ Ramsgate, Denton,
to ⎱ and other places in
15 July(?) ⎰ Kent.
15 July(?) to ⎱ London.
31 Aug. ⎰
1–15 Sept. Cambridge.
15 Sept. to 6 Oct. Lovingland,
Norwich, and Newmarket.
6 Oct. to ⎱ Cambridge.
10 Nov. ⎰

12 Mar. *Poems* published by Dodsley
(470).
4 May. Poems published by Foulis (487).
July. *Verses on Lord Holland's Villa* composed (App. T).
28 July. Appointed Regius Professor of
Modern History (477* ff.).

Oct.(?). New edition of *Poems* published
by Dodsley (487).

1768 10 Nov. to 23 Dec. London.

1769 23 Dec. to ⎱ Cambridge.
3 Apr. ⎰

3 Apr. to ⎱ London and else-   Apr. *Installation Ode* composed (493).
16 May ⎰ where.

16 May to ⎱ Cambridge.   1 July. Installation of Chancellor.
8 July ⎰

8–16 July. London.

18–23 July. York.

23 July to 29 Sept. Old Park with excursion to Hartlepool.

29 Sept. ⎱ Tour in the Lakes,
to ⎰ Lancashire and
15 Oct. ⎰ Yorkshire.

15–22 Oct. Journey to Cambridge by Leeds, Aston, &c.

22 Oct. to 4 Dec. Cambridge.

4–21 Dec. London.   Dec. Made acquaintance of Bonstetten and took him to Cambridge (508, 512).

1770 21 Dec. to ⎱ Cambridge.
21 Mar. ⎰

21 Mar. to 2 Apr. London.   Mar. Bonstetten left England (514).

2–23 Apr. Cambridge.

23 Apr. to ⎱ Thrapston and
7 May ⎰ Lovingland.

7–10. May. Cambridge.   2 July. Made his will (App. X).

10–31 May. London.

31 May to 3 June. Cambridge.

3–19 June. Aston.

19 June to 2 July. Cambridge.

2 July to 3 Aug. Tour in Worcestershire, Gloucestershire, Monmouthshire, Herefordshire, &c.

3–17 Aug. London.

1771 17 Aug. to ⎱ Cambridge.   Dec. James Brown elected Master of
1 Jan. ⎰   Pembroke (540).

1–17 Jan. London.

17 Jan. to 16 May. Cambridge.

16 May to 22 July. London.

22–30 July. Cambridge.   30 July. Died (App. W).

LIST OF ILLUSTRATIONS

VOLUME I

⁎ *Grateful acknowledgement is made to the owners of the original pictures, sketches, and letters, for permission to reproduce them.*

lix

ERRATA AND ADDENDA

VOLUME I

Page 51, n. 3, *for* nn. 3, 6 *read* nn. 2, 6

Page 59, n. 3, *for* Appendix A *read* Appendix B

Page 61, n. 1, *for* Appendix A *read* Appendix B

Page 142. n. 8, *for* between 1752 and 1758 *read* between 1754 and 1758.

Page 222, Letter 114, Preliminary Note, *for* notes 3 and 13 *read* notes 3 and 12

Page 231, Letter 119, *for* the Preliminary Note *read as follows*:
'Now first printed from the original. The manuscript is endorsed: "Original letter from Mr. Gray the Poet to Mr. Walpole, given me by Mr. W." The endorsement was, no doubt, made by J. Pinkerton, who printed a facsimile of the last three lines of the letter, as a specimen of Gray's handwriting in his *Walpoliana*.'

Page 267, n. 5 at end of note *add* 'She acted the part of Euanthe the heroine of the play.'

Page 287, n. 4, line 2, *for* in 1750 when he was sixty-four *read* on 5 June 1747

Page 313, n. 1, line 15 of note, *for* bought Strawberry Hill *read* moved to Strawberry Hill

Page 342, n. 4, *for* Bentley *read* Dodsley

Page 405, n. 14, *ad fin. for* Letters 302, 373 *read* Letters 303, 373

Page 420, n. 3, *for* Thomas Philips Jenkin *read* Jenkin Thomas Philips

VOLUME II

Pages 638–40, see Addendum, vol. ii, pp. xxxv–xxxvi.

VOLUME III

Page 487, n. 1, *for* 5 May *read* 4 May

Page 1149, last line of text 'a two months residence' *add to the notes* '7ª There is at Trinity College a book of Commons (headed *In Victualibus*). The indications of residence are not clear, but it seems probable that, from the time that Lord Richard entered the College in 1768 down to the date of this letter, he resided for a considerable part of each term. It seems possible that Gray wrote "two month's residence" by a slip for "two years residence".'

lx

1. GRAY TO WALPOLE[1]

[April 16, 1734][1a]

[   ][2]

I BELIEVE by your not making me happy in a longer letter than that I have just received, you had a design to prevent my tireing you with a tedious one; but in revenge for your neglect I'm resolved to send you one five times as long: S^r, do you think, that I'll be fob'd off[3] with eleven lines and a half? after waiting this week in continual expectation, & proposing to myself all the pleasure, that you, if you would, might give me; Gadsbud! I am provoked into a fermentation! when I see you next, I'll firk you, I'll rattle you with a Certiorari:[4] let me tell you; I am at

LETTER 1.—First printed by Toynbee (1915), No. 1. Mason (*Memoirs*, p. 16, n.) remarks : 'Mr. Walpole, on my informing him that it was my intention to publish the principal part of Mr. Gray's correspondence with Mr. West, very obligingly communicated to me the letters which he had also received from Mr. Gray at the same period. From this collection I have selected such as I thought would be most likely to please the generality of readers; omitting, though with regret, many of the more sprightly and humorous sort, because either from their personality, or some other local circumstance, they did not seem so well adapted to hit the public taste.' Of the thirty-eight extant letters from Gray to Walpole written between 1734 and 1739 Mason printed one and parts of five others.

[1] Horace Walpole (1717–97), third surviving son of Sir Robert Walpole, entered Eton in 1727, where he became an intimate friend of Gray, West, and Ashton. See Letter 2, n. 8.

[1a] The date of the month is supplied by the postmark (which in letters written from the country is usually a day later than the date of writing, see Letter 10, n. 1). The letter (in a round schoolboy hand) must have been written during Gray's holidays from Eton in 1734, in which year Passion Week (which is mentioned in the letter) ended on April 13.

[2] A piece containing the initial address (probably 'My Dearest Celadon', as in Letter 9) has been cut out, as in many of Gray's letters to Walpole; these excisions were no doubt made by Walpole, in accordance with the suggestion of Mason, who in a letter to Walpole, dated 4 Jan. 1774, while he was engaged upon his *Memoirs of the Life and Writings of Mr. Gray*, wrote: 'As to your preserving Mr. Gray's letters I have only to say that I wish when you look them over again, you would only erase some passages, for instance the infantine beginnings and conclusions of some of them, which are hardly fit for schoolboys, and yet will not be considered as written by a schoolboy; this was a liberty I once thought of taking myself, before I returned them.'

[3] 2 *Hen. IV*, ii. 1: '*Quickly*. I have been fubbed off, and fubbed off, and fubbed off, . . . that it is a shame to be thought on.'

[4] Congreve, *Double Dealer*, ii. 4: '*Sir Paul Plyant*. Gadsbud! I am provoked into a fermentation . . . I'll rattle him up, I warrant you, I'll firk him with a certiorari!'

present as full of wrath & choler, as—as—you are of wit & good-
nature; though I begin to doubt your title to the last of them,
since you have balked me in this manner: what an excuse do you
make with your Paſsion-week & fiddle-faddle, as if you could
ever be at a loſs what to say; why, I, that am in the country[5]
could give you a full & true account of half a dozen Intrigues,
nay I have an amour carried on almost under my window
between a boar & a sow, people of very good fashion, that come
to an aſsignation, and squeak like ten masquerades; I have
a great mind to make you hear the whole progreſs of the affair,
together with the humours of Miſs Pigsnies, the lady's Confidente; but you will think perhaps I invent it, & so I shall let it
alone: but I wonder you are not ashamed of yourself; in town,
and not able to furnish out an epistle as long as a Cows tail!
(excuse the rusticity of my simile) in short, I have tryed and
condemned you in my mind, all that you can alledge to save
yourself won't do; for I find by your excuses you are brought to
your derniere Chemise;[6] and as you stand guilty, I adjudge you
to be drawn to the place of execution, your chamber; where
taking pen in hand, you shall write a letter as long as this, to
him, who is nothing, when not

your sincere friend
& most devoted humble Serv[t]

[   ][7]   T: GRAY.

Addressed: To The Hon[rble] M[r] Horatio [Wal-]pole at the house of th[e
right] honourable Sr Robert [Walpole] in St James's Square[8] Lond[on]
Postmark: . . . N[9] 17 AP

[5] In what place is uncertain (see n. 9).
[6] This is no doubt an allusion to Cibber's comedy, *Love's Last Shift*, the
title of which had been rendered in French as *La Dernière Chemise de
l'Amour.*
[7] A postscript (apparently) has been cut out, carrying with it part of the
address on the other side (as indicated by the square brackets).
[8] Letters addressed by Gray to Horace Walpole in St. James's Square can
be assigned with certainty to a date anterior to 22 Sept. 1735, on which day,
as appears from the following announcement, his father transferred his
residence to Downing Street: 'Yesterday the Right Hon. Sir Robert Walpole,
with his Lady and Family removed from their House in St. James's Square,
to his new House adjoining to the Treasury in St. James's Park' (i.e. in
Downing Street). (*London Daily Post,* Tuesday, 23 Sept. 1735.)
[9] The postmark of the place is undecipherable, save for the impress of
a final N. It is possible that Gray at this time was staying with his uncle,
Rev. William Antrobus, Rector of Everdon, Northants (see Letter 283*,
n. 1). If so, the postmark may have been Northampton.

2. GRAY TO WALPOLE

[Cambridge, Oct. 31, 1734][1]

[   ][2]

FOR Gods sake send me your Quære's, & I'll do my best to
get information upon those Points, you don't understand:
I warrant, you imagine that People in one College, know the
Customs of others; but you mistake, they are quite little
Societies by themselves: yᵉ Dreſses, Language, Customs &c are
different in different Colledges: what paſses for Wit in one,
would not be understood if it were carried to another: thus the
Men of Peter-house, Pembroke & Clare-hall of course must be
Tories; those of Trinity, Rakes; of Kings, Scholars; of Sidney,
Wigs; of Sᵗ Johns, Worthy men & so on: now what to say about
this Terra Incognita, I don't know; First then it is a great old
Town, shapcd like a Spider, with a nasty lump in the middle of
it, & half a dozen scambling long legs: it has 14 Parishes,
12 Colledges, & 4 Halls, these Halls only entertain Students,
who after a term of years, are elected into the Colledges:[3] there
are 5 ranks in the University, subordinate to the Vice-
chancellour, who is chose annually: these are [Masters, Fellows,
Fellow-Commoners, Pensione][4]rs, & Sizers; The Masters of
Colledges are twelve grey-hair'd Gentlefolks, who are all mad
with Pride; the Fellows are sleepy, drunken, dull, illiterate
Things; the Fellow-Com: are imitatours of the Fellows, or else
Beaux, or else nothing: the Pension: grave, formal Sots, who
would be thought old; or else drink Ale, & sing Songs against
yᵉ Excise. The Sizers are Graziers Eldest Sons, who come to
get good Learning, that they may all be Archbishops of Canterbury: these 2 last Orders are qualified to take Scholarships;

LETTER 2.—First printed by Toynbee (1915), No. 2.
   [1] The date of the month is supplied by the postmark. The date 1735 has
been inserted in the original by Mason; but the actual date must be 1734,
when Gray was a freshman at Peterhouse.
   [2] A strip containing the initial address has been cut out (see Letter 1,
n. 2), carrying with it a line of the text on the other side.
   [3] Gray was mistaken—there was no difference between a 'Hall' and
a 'College' in Cambridge. The terms were used indifferently in the case of
Clare, Pembroke, and St. Catharine's. Gray himself dates from 'Pembroke
Hall' and 'Pembroke College' (see Letters 471, 473, 532, 534). The name
'Hall' survives only in the case of Trinity Hall.
   [4] Piece cut out (see n. 2); the missing words have been supplied in pencil
by Walpole.

one of which, your humble Servt has had given him:[5] first they
led me into the hall, & there I swore Allegiance to ye King;
then I went to a room, where I took 50000 Latin Oaths, such
as, to wear a Square Cap, to make 6 verses upon the Epistle or
Gospel every Sunday morning, to chant very loud in Chappel,
to wear a clean Surplice, &c: &c:[6] Now as to eating: the Fellow-
Com: dine at the Fellows Table, their Commons is worth 6^s-4^d
a-week, the Pensioners pay but 2^s-4^d; if any body don't like
their Commons, they send down into the Kitchen to know,
what's for Sizing:[7] the Cook sends up a Catalogue of what there
is; & they chuse, what they please: they are obliged to pay for
Commons, whither they eat it, or no: there is always Plenty
enough: the Sizers feast upon the leavings of the rest; as to drefs,
the Fell: Commoners usually wear a Prunella Gown with
Sleeves, a hat & no band; but their proper habit has its Sleeves
trimmed with Gold-lace, this they only wear at publick Ceremonies; neither do the Noblemen use their pr: Habit commonly,
but wear only a black Padesoy Gown: the Men of Kings are
a sort of University by themselves; & differ in Customs from all
the rest; every body hates 'em & when Almanzor[8] comes to
me, our Peoples stare at him, like a Lord-mayors Show, &
wonder to see a human Creature among them: if I tell you,

[5] Gray, who began residence at Peterhouse on 9 Oct. 1734, three weeks
before the date of this letter, had been appointed Cosin Scholar on 17 Oct.
(See *Peterhouse Admission Book*, ed. T. A. Walker, p. 267.)

[6] 'The provisions of the tenure of both Scholarships [the Cosin, and the
Hale, to which Gray was subsequently elected] were drafted on the same
model. They aimed at securing propriety of demeanour and the regular
pursuit of definite studies. With regulations as to the wearing of wide sleeved
gown and squared cap, the avoiding of extravagance in dress, and modest
deportment in Hall and elsewhere, were combined some particular require-
ments as to the student's mental fare. As Cosin Scholar Gray would be
forbidden to wear long locks or use hair powder. Whether as Cosin or Hale
Scholar, he would be required to study music under the College organist,
so as to take part in the chanting and singing of the Chapel choir; on each
Sunday and feast-day he would produce to the Master and to the President
or Senior Dean at dinner hour fair copies of Greek and Latin verses on a
subject taken from the Gospel for the day.' (T. A. Walker, 'Thomas Gray
at Peterhouse', in *Athenæum*, 20 Jan. 1906.)

[7] 'In his first year Gray's expenditure was very modest, the item "Sizings",
which represents specially ordered "extras" in dietary, amounting to a few
shillings only. In later years he became more luxurious. And in 1736–7
the charge for Sizings each quarter exceeded the charge for Commons.'
(T. A. Walker, *loc. cit.*)

[8] A character in Dryden's *Conquest of Granada*. The individual in question
was no doubt Thomas Ashton, now at King's, who with Gray ('Orosmades'),

I never stirr out, perhaps you won't believe me; especially when you know, there's a Club of Wits kept at the Mitre, all such as come from Eton; where Alm: would introduce me, if I so pleased:—yet you will not think it strange, that I don't go abroad, when I tell you, that I am got into a room;[9] such [a][10] hugeous one, that little i is quite lost in it; so [that][10] when I get up in the morning, I begin to travel [tow][10]ards the middle of it with might & main, & with much ado about noon bate at a great Table, which stands half-way it: so then, by that time, (after having pursued my journey full speed); that I arrive at the door, it is so dark & late, & I am so tired, that I am obliged to turn back again: so about Midnight I get to the bedside: then, thinks you, I suppose, he goes to sleep: hold you a bit; in this Country it is so far from that, that we go to bed to wake, & rise to sleep: in short, those that go along the street, do nothing but walk in their sleep: they run against every Post they meet: but I beg pardon, for talking so much of myself, since that's not, what you care for—(To be continued)

Addressed : To The Hon[rble] Horace Walpole Esq at the house of the right Hon[rble] S[r] Robert Walpole in S[t] James's Square London *Postmark:* CAMBRIDGE I NO

3. GRAY TO WALPOLE

With care   To mie Nufs att London   Present
Carridge pade   These

[Cambridge] 23[d] Sund[y] after Trin:

[Nov. 17, 1734][1]

Honner'd Nurse

THIS comes to let you know, that I am in good health; but that I should not have been so, if it had not been for your kind promise of coming to tend me yourself, & see the effect of

Walpole ('Celadon'), and Richard West ('Favonius' or 'Zephyrus'), had formed the 'Quadruple Alliance' at Eton. Ashton received the name of 'Almanzor' perhaps from having acted the part in a performance at Eton; just as John Dodd, another Eton contemporary, for a similar reason, as we know from Walpole, was called 'Tamerlane'.

[9] See Appendix K, on Gray's Rooms.
[10] MS. torn.
LETTER 3.—First printed by Toynbee (1915), No. 3.
[1] The date of the year is determined by the reference to Stevens (see n. 16).

your own Prescription: and I should desire of you, so please you, as how that, you would be so good as to be so kind, as to do me the favour of bringing down with you a quantity of it, prepared as your Grandmothers Aunt, poor Mrs Hawthorn (God[2] rest her soul, for she was as well a natured, a good Gentlewoman, as ever broke bread,[3] or trod upon Shoe-leather;[4] though I say it, that should not say it; for you know, she was related to me, & marry! not a jot the worse, I trow) used to make it: now I would not put you to this trouble, if I could provide myself of the Ingredients here; but truly, when I went to the Poticaries for a drachm of Spirit of Ridicule; the saucy Jackanapes of a Prentice-Boy fleered at me, I warrant ye, as who should say, you don't know your Errand: so by my troth, away ambles me I (like a fool as I came) home again, & when I came to look of your Receipt; to be sure, there was Sp^t of Ridicule in great Letters, as plain as the nose in one's face: & so, back hurries I in a making-Water-while, as one may say,[5] & when I came there, says I; you stripling, up-start, worsted-stocking, white-liver'd, lath-backed,[6] impudent Princox,[7] says I; abuse me! that am your betters every day in the week, says I; you ill-begotten, pocky, rascally, damned Son of a Bitch, says I—for you know, when he put me in such a perilous Pafsion, how could one help telling him his own—why, 'twould have provoked any Christian[8] in the world, tho' twere a Dog—to speak; & so if you'll be so kind, I'll take care you shall be satis-fied for your trouble: so, this is all at present from

> your ever-dutifull & most
> obedient & most affectionate,
> loving God-daughter
> Pru: Orosmades[9]

---

[2] This word was changed by Walpole into 'fudge', and then smudged.

[3] *Merry Wives of Windsor*, i. 4: 'an honest maid as ever broke bread.'

[4] *Julius Cæsar*, i. 1: 'As proper man as ever trod upon neat's leather.'

[5] Wycherley, *Plain Dealer*, iii. 1: '*Widow Blackacre.* O no; stay but a making-water while (as one may say) and I'll be with you again.'

[6] *Plain Dealer*, ii. 1: '*Widow Blackacre.* Thou pitiful, paltry, lath-backed fellow . . .'

[7] *Romeo and Juliet*, i. 5: *Capulet.* 'You are a princox, go!'

[8] For this word, which has been scored through, Walpole substituted 'man'.

[9] Orosmades was the name by which Gray was known among the members of the 'Quadruple Alliance' (see Letter 2, n. 8). 'Orosmades' is an alteration, which occurs in Lee's *Rival Queens*, ii. 1 (see *Mod. Lang. Rev.* xii.

A Discourse

Πάντα κόνις, κ̵̓ πάντα πιὸς,
    κ̵̓ πάντα τόβακκο[10]

If I should undertake to prove to you, that everything is Tobacco, it might be looked upon as an Absurdity after the rev[rd] & learn[d] D[n] Swift has made it so manifest, that every thing is a Pudding:[11] but I conceive it will not be so difficult to shew, that Tobacco is every thing (at least here) for there is not a soul in our Colledge (a body I should say) who does not smoke or chew: there's nothing but Whiffing from Fellow to Sizer; nay, even the very Chimnies, that they may'nt be thought partic'lar, must needs smoke, like the rest: whilst unfashionable I labour thro' clouds of it, with as much pains, as Milton's poor Devil took, when he travel'd through Chaos:[12]—but, as to the Guzzling affair, you mistook in thinking it was the Old fellows, that were with me; no 'twas a thousand times worse; they were all young ones—do but imagine me pent up in a room hired for the purpose, & none of the largest, from 7 a-clock at night, till 4 in the morning! 'midst hogsheads of Liquor & quantities of Tobacco, surrounded by 30 of these creatures, infinitely below the meanest People you could even form an Idea off; toasting bawdy healths & deafned with their unmeaning Roar; Jesus![13] but I must tell you of a fat Mortal, who stuck close to me, & was as drunk (as Mifs Edwards[14]—which story I'm afraid by the by, was too well-fancied, to be real) well! he was so maudlin & so loving & told me long Stories, interrupted by the sourest Interjections, with moral Discourses upon God knows what!

29–30), whence probably Gray took it, of Oromasdes, the name of the principal Zoroastrian divinity.

[10] This is a parody of the first line of an epigram by Glycon in the Greek Anthology: 'Πάντα γέλως, καὶ πάντα κόνις, καὶ πάντα τὸ μηδέν.' Gray's πιός is a pseudo-Greek word, to represent 'pie', as an equivalent of 'pudding' (see n. 11): 'All is dust, and all is pie, and all is tobacco.'

[11] Not Swift apparently, but Henry Carey, who in *A Learned Dissertation upon Dumpling* (1726) says: 'The universe itself is but a pudding of elements. Empires, kingdoms, states and republics are but puddings of people differently made up. The celestial and terrestrial orbs are decipher'd to us by a pair of globes or mathematical puddings.'

[12] *Paradise Lost*, Book ii, ll. 927 ff.

[13] This word has been scored through.

[14] This name has been heavily scored through, but is just decipherable; the person in question is perhaps the 'Mrs. Edwards, who died of drams', mentioned in Walpole's letter to Mann of 2 Dec. 1748.

that I was almost drunk too: oh—I must just beg lea[ve to men]¹⁵ tion one more, who, they tell me, has no fault, but that, he's a little too *foppish* & talks like a London-Rake; this fine Gentleman is quite master of the Spectator & retails it for ever; among the rest, he gave his humble Opinion of the present state of the Play-house; that Stevens¹⁶ had a very graceful Motion, spoke well, &c, but that he must needs give his Voice for Mʳ Quin;¹⁷ Mʳˢ Thurmond¹⁸ too was in great favour with him: as for the Opera's he could not understand them, but had heard Margaretta¹⁹ & Nicolini²⁰ highly commended by those, that were judges: by God, says another, those Opera's are the ruin of the nation; no honest people can go to 'em, & those, that do, are ashamed of themselves; else why should they go in Masques & Disguises thither—no body in the company found out his blunder, so no body laugh'd but I, which was taken for applause. you'll think it a strange compliment, when I tell you how often I thought of you, all the while: but will forgive me, when you recollect, that 'twas a great piece of Philosophy in me, to be able, in yᵉ midst of Noise & Disturbance, to call to mind the most agreeable thing in nature: when you could give me so much Pleasure, absent; what must you do, when with me? tho' perhaps its policy in you to stay away so long, that you may increase my Desire of seeing you: in your next send me word, how soon you design, to come to the relief

of your [   ]²¹

¹⁵ Piece cut out (see n. 21); the missing words have been supplied in pencil by Walpole.

¹⁶ Stevens (or Stephens) made his first appearance on the stage at Covent Garden on 19 Oct. of this year (1734), as Othello.

¹⁷ James Quin (1693–1766); he had played Othello at Drury Lane (his first appearance there for sixteen years) on 10 Sept. Articles comparing the acting of 'Mr. Stevens, the new actor', with that of Quin and Cibber appeared in the *Grub-street Journal* for 31 Oct., 7 Nov., and 14 Nov. (See *Gent. Mag.* 1734, p. 593.)

¹⁸ Mrs. Thurmond (*née* Lewis) played Desdemona to Quin's Othello at Drury Lane.

¹⁹ The Italian opera-singer, Francesca Margherita de l'Épine, known as Margherita, who sang for some years in London between 1692 and 1718, and died in England about 1750.

²⁰ Nicolino Grimaldi, known as Nicolini, performed in London between 1708 and 1717.

²¹ A piece containing the signature has been cut out.

4. GRAY TO WALPOLE

[Cambridge, Dec. 8, 1734][1]

[   ][2]

I (THO' I say it) had too much modesty to venture answering
your dear, diverting Letter, in the Poetical Strain myself: but,
when I was last at the DEVIL,[3] meeting by chance with the
deceased Mr Dennis[4] there, he offer'd his Service, &, being
tip'd with a Tester, wrought, what follows—[5]

From purling Streams & the Elysian Scene,
From Groves, that smile with never-fading Green
I reascend; in Atropos' despight
Restored to Celadon,[6] & upper light:
Ye gods, that sway the Regions under ground,
Reveal to mortal View your realms profound;
At his command admit the eye of Day;
When Celadon commands, what God can disobey?
Nor seeks he your Tartarean fires to know,
The house of Torture, & th' Abyfs of Woe;
But happy fields[7] & Mansions free from Pain,
Gay Meads, & springing flowers best please ye gentle Swain:
    That little, naked, melancholy thing
My Soul,[8] when first she tryed her flight to wing;

LETTER 4.—First printed by Toynbee (1915), No. 4.
    [1] The date of the month is supplied by the postmark; that of the year is
determined by the address (see Letter 1, n. 7).
    [2] See Letter 1, n. 2.
    [3] The Devil Tavern in Fleet Street (see *Dunciad*, i. 325, and note; and
Imitations of Horace, Epist. II. i. 41).
    [4] John Dennis, author and critic, the object of the ridicule of Swift
and Pope; he died on 6 Jan. of this year (1734). The name has been
scored through, but is still legible, and Walpole has written it in again
above.
    [5] These are no doubt the verses referred to by Horace Walpole in his
memoir of Gray (see Appendix Y), in which he says: 'One of his first pieces
of poetry was an answer in English verse to an epistle from H. W.'
    [6] Celadon (the name of the amorous shepherd in D'Urfé's pastoral
romance of *Astrée*, and hence that of the luckless swain in Thomson's
Summer, and of numerous others) was the pseudonym under which Walpole figured in his youthful correspondence with Gray and West (see
Letter 2, n. 8).
    [7] *Par. Lost*, i. 249.
    [8] Perhaps a reminiscence of Hadrian's lines to his soul:
            'Animula vagula blandula.
            Pallidula rigida nudula.'

9

Began with speed new Regions to explore,
And blunder'd thro' a narrow Postern door;
First most devoutly having said its Prayers,
It tumbled down a thousand pair of [Stairs],[9]
Thro' Entries long, thro' Cellars vast & deep,
Where ghostly Rats their habitations keep,
Where Spiders spread their Webs, & owlish Goblins sleep.
After so many Chances had befell,
It came into a mead of Asphodel:
Betwixt the Confines of yᵉ light & dark
It lies, of 'Lyzium yᵉ Sᵗ James's park:
Here Spirit-Beaux flutter along the Mall,
And shadows in disguise scate o'er yᵉ Iced Canal:
Here groves embower'd, & more sequester'd Shades,
Frequented by yᵉ Ghosts of Ancient Maids,
Are seen to rise: the melancholy Scene
With gloomy haunts, & twilight walks between[10]
Conceals the wayward band: here spend their time
Greensicknefs Girls, that died in youthful prime,
Virgins forlorn, all drest in Willow-green-i
With Queen Elizabeth and Nicolini.[11]
    More to reveal, or many words to use
Would tire alike your patience & my muse.
Believe, that never was so faithful found
Queen Proserpine to Pluto under ground,
Or Cleopatra to her Marc-Antony
As Orozmades[12] to his Celadony.

P:S:
Lucrece for half a crown will shew you fun,
But Mʳˢ Oldfield[13] is become a Nun.
Nobles & Cits, Prince Pluto & his Spouse
Flock to the Ghost of Covent-Garden house:
Plays, which were hifs'd above, below revive;
When dead applauded, that were damn'd alive:
The People, as in life, still keep their Pafsions,
But differ something from the world in Fashions.

⁹ Piece cut out; the missing word has been supplied in pencil by Walpole.
¹⁰ *Par. Lost*, ix. 1107: 'echoing walks between.'
¹¹ The well-known opera-singer (see Letter 3, n. 20).
¹² See Letter 3, n. 9.
¹³ Mrs. Oldfield (1683–1730), the actress, and mistress of General Charles Churchill.

Queen Artemisia[14] breakfasts on Bohea.
And Alexander wears a Ramilie.[15]

Addressed: To The Honble Horatio Walpole Esq at the house of the right
hon^ble Sr Robert Walpole in St James's Square London *Postmark:*
CAMBRIDGE 9 DE

5. GRAY TO WALPOLE

Præscript: you don't send me word when you think you shall
come to Sarag:[1]

From St Peters Charnel-house [Dec. 1734][2]

Dear Dimidium animæ meæ[3]

As you take a great deal of pleasure in concluding that I am
dead, & resolve not to let me live any longer; methinks you
ought to be good to my Ashes, & give 'em leave to rest in peace:
but instead of that, whereas I ought to be divested of all human
Pafsions, & forget the Pleasures of your World; you must needs
be diverting me, so that I made every nail in my Coffin start
with laughing: it happen'd, that on the 26th Instant at twelve
of the clock at midnight, being a hard frost; I had wrapt myself
up in my Shroud very snugg & warm; when in comes your
Letter, which (as I told you before) made me stretch my
Skeleton-jaws in such a horse-laugh, that all the dead pop'd up
their heads & stared: but to see the frowzy Countenances of the
Creatures especially one old Lady-Carcase, that made most
hideous Grimaces, & would needs tell me, that I was a very
uncivil Person to disturb a Woman of her Quality, that did me
the honour to lie so near me: & truly she had not been in such
a Surprise, this threescore & ten Year, come next March:
besides her Commode was discomposed, & in her hurry she had
lost her Wedding Ring, which she was buried in; nay, she said,

[14] Wife and sister of Mausolus, king of Caria, to whose memory she erected
the Mausoleum.
[15] A wig having a long plait behind tied with a bow at top and bottom.
(*O.E.D.*)
  LETTER 5.—First printed by Toynbee (1915), No. 5.
  [1] This name (the origin of which has not been traced) has been crossed
through by Walpole, who has substituted 'Cambr:'
  [2] The date of the month is conjectural, the postmark having been cut off
(see n. 5), but the reference to 'a hard frost' shows that it was winter; the
date of the year is determined by the address (see Letter 1, n. 8), if the
conjectural restoration (see n. 6) be correct.
  [3] Horace, 1 *Odes*, iii. 8.

11

she believed she should fall in fits, & certainly, that would be
her Death: but I gave her a Rowland for her Oliver, 'i'gad:
I told her Ladyship the more she stirred, the more she'd stink
& that to my knowledge, tho' she put a good face upon the
matter; she was not sound: so she lay'd her down very quietly,
and crept under her Winding-Sheet for fear of Spirits. now your
Arrival only can deliver me from such a state of Separation;
for, as your Soul is large enough to serve for both of us, it will
be ill-natured of you, if you don't reanimate my Corps: at least
I hope for a place in your heart, as formerly: tho', by your last
letter, but one; it seems, you have either forgot yourself, or
entertain a lefs favourable Opinion of me, than that; with
which you once honoured
                        your friend, the Defunct . . .
As my letter ends so prettily in that p. . . .⁴

Addressed: [To] [The Honᵇˡᵉ Horatio] Wal-[pole Esq at the house of t]he
right [Honᵇˡᵉ Sʳ Robert Wal]pole in [Sᵗ James's Square] [Lond]on⁵

6. GRAY TO WALPOLE

Dec: 24 [23] [1734]¹—Peter-house

[   ]²

AFTER having been very piously at Sᵗ Mary's church yesterday; as I was coming home; somebody told me, that you
was come, & that your Servant had been to enquire for me:

⁴ Three parts of the second leaf of the letter have been torn and cut off,
carrying away a part of the signature and postscript, as well as nearly the
whole of the address on the other side.
⁵ The address is restored conjecturally (see n. 4), on the analogy of that
of the previous letter.
LETTER 6.—First printed by Toynbee (1915), No. 22.
¹ The date is conjectural; in *Gray-Walpole Correspondence* this letter was
dated 1735. But it appears from Gray's letter to Walpole of 3 Jan. 1736
(Letter 20) that he spent the Christmas vacation of 1735 at home in London;
and his absence from Cambridge is confirmed by the Peterhouse books.
Further, in this letter he is evidently expecting Walpole's arrival in Cambridge for the first time. But Walpole went up to King's on 11 March
1735. Again, Gray's mention of his having been at St. Mary's church
the day before is difficult to explain if the year were 1735. It was the duty
of undergraduates to attend service at the University Church on Sundays,
but in 1735 Dec. 23 was Tuesday, not Sunday. On the other hand, the
year 1734 fits the circumstances; for Gray, as the Peterhouse books show,

whereupon throwing off all the Pruderie & Reserve of a
Cambridge Student, in a great extasie, I run in a vast hurry to
set the Bells a-ringing, & kindle a thousand Bonfires—when
amidst these Convulsions of Joy, I was stopt by one of our
Colledge, who inform'd me, that a fine Gentleman in a laced
hat & scarlet Stockings wanted me: so, you may conclude, as
soon as I set eyes on him, I was ready to eat him for having
your Livery on; but he soon checked me by acquainting me
'twas not You, that was come; but—Your Service: now undoubtedly after being so terribly bauked; one could not have
lived, but by the help of Hartshorn, Hungary-Water,[2a] & your
Journal, which gives one a greater Flow of Spirits, than ei[ther
of them.][3] [but, dear Celadon],[4] nothing gave me half so much
pleasure, as to find; that after the toil of the day was over, you
could be so good as to throw away a moment in thinking of me,
& had Spirits enough left, to make all the hideosities you underwent agreable by describing them:—by all that's frightful, I was
in agonies for you, when I saw you planted at the upper end of
a Table so elegantly set out; like the King of Monsters in
the Fairy-tales: never was any one's curiosity half so much
raised by a blot, as mine is by that in your Diary: 'tis so
judicious a Scratch, so genteel a Blurr, that I shall never be
easy, till I know what it conceals; no more than I shall be, till
I receive the things that are to come by word of mouth, w[ch] (if
'twere pofsible) would make me wish to see you more than ever:
[5]sure West is as much improved as he says[6] Plato[7] is; since you

was in residence during the whole of December that year, while Walpole
had not yet gone up to King's. The difficulty as to Gray's attending church
on 23 Dec. still remains, for that date in 1734 was a Monday. The most
probable explanation is that Gray, who was occasionally careless in dating
(see Letter 10), by an oversight wrote 24 instead of 23, in which case
'yesterday' would be 22 Dec., the fourth Sunday in Advent.

   [2] See Letter 1, n. 2.
   [2a] See Letter 9, n. 4.
   [3] Piece cut out (see n. 2); the missing words have been supplied in pencil
by Walpole.
   [4] Piece cut out; the missing words are supplied conjecturally from the
fragments of writing which have escaped the scissors.
   [5-5] This sentence has been heavily scored through, but is still decipherable.
   [6] Gray originally wrote 'you say', which he altered to 'he says'.
   [7] There are some grounds for supposing that 'Plato' may have been
William Cole (1714–82), the antiquary, who, though somewhat older, had
been at Eton with Gray, Walpole, and West, and was a friend of all three. (See
the references to 'Plato', in Nos. 19 and 94 of *Gray-Walpole Correspondence*; and

could have the conscience to persuade him to come to Cambridge⁵. . . .⁸

7. GRAY TO WALPOLE

To the faithful Miradolin,
third Son of the Vizier-azem.
Continuance of Health & long life.¹

WHEN the Dew of the morning is upon me, thy Image is before mine eyes; nor, when the night overshadoweth me, dost thou depart from me. shall I ne'er behold thine eyes, until our eternal meeting in yᵉ immortal Chioses² of Paradise; and sure at that hour, thy Soul will have little need of Ablution in the sight of Israphiel,³ the Angel of examination: surely, it is pure as the Snow on Mount Ararat, & beautiful as the cheeks of the Houries: the Feast of Ramadan⁴ is now past away, &

to Cole, in Gray's letters to Walpole of Aug. and 27 Oct., 1736—Letters 26 and 32.) At this time Cole was at Clare, but he migrated to King's in 1735 (see Letter 26, n. 17).

⁸ The second leaf, containing the remainder of the letter, and the address, &c., has been torn off.

LETTER 7.—First printed by Toynbee (1915), No. 6.

¹ Gray had evidently been reading *The Turkish Spy*, in which most of the oriental names and imagery in this letter have been traced by Professor Edward Bensly. Several letters (e.g. *Lett.* 1, *Bk.* i, and *Lett.* 1, *Bk.* iii, of *Vol.* vii; and *Lett.* 3, *Bk.* i, of *Vol.* viii) are addressed 'To *Mirmadolin*, Holy *Santone* of the Vale of *Sidon*'. Others (e.g. *Lett.* 2, *Bk.* ii, of *Vol.* vi) are addressed, 'To the *Vizier Azem* at the *Porte*', who in the index at the beginning of Vol. i is defined as 'the First Minister of State'.

² These are several times mentioned in *The Turkish Spy*; e.g. 'Houses . . . which might vie with the most delightful *Chioses* of the *Mussulman* Grandees' (*Lett.* 35, *Bk.* i, of *Vol.* iii); 'a little *Chiose* or bower' (*Lett.* 9, *Bk.* i, of *Vol.* iv); 'the *Chioses* of *Eden*, on the Banks of immortal Streams' (*Lett.* 8, *Bk.* iii, of *Vol.* v).

³ Israfil is the archangel who will sound the trumpet at the day of resurrection. (Hughes, *Dict. of Islam.*) He is called Israphiel in *The Turkish Spy*: 'May *Gabriel*, the *Friend* of the *Prophet*, pray for him; then *Michael*, *Israphiel*, and the *Messenger* of *Death* . . .' (*Lett.* 8, *Bk.* iii, of *Vol.* v.)

⁴ Properly speaking, Ramadan is not a feast, but a thirty days' fast, during the hours of daylight, throughout the ninth month of the Mahometan year. Gray presumably means Christmas (see n. 12). *The Turkish Spy*: 'I die in Contemplation of the same *Fasts* and *Feasts*, the nocturnal joys of *Ramezan*, the Revels and cheerful Illuminations of *Beiram*' (*Lett.* 17, *Bk.* iv, of *Vol.* vi). 'The successive variations of the *Great Fast* causing it sometimes to fall at the very Times of the most solemn *Festivals* among the *Nazarenes*, such as

14

thou thinkest not of leaving Candahar;[5] what shall I say unto thee, thou unkind one? thou has lost me in oblivion, & I am become as one, whom thou never didst remember: before; we were as two Palm-trees in the Vale of Medina, I flourish'd in thy friendship, & bore my head aloft: but now I wander in Solitarineſs, as a traveller in the sandy desarts of Barca, & pine in vain to tast of the living fountain of thy conversation: I have beheld thee in my Slumbers, I have attempted to seize on thee, I sought for thee & behold! thou wert not there! thou wert departed, as the smoke, or as the Shadows, when the Sun entreth his bed-chamber: were I to behold thy countenance, tho' afar off; my heart should bound as the Antelope; yea! my soul should be as light, as the Roe-buck on the hills of Erzerom. I swear by Abubekir,[6] thou art sweet in my thoughts as the Pine-apple of Damascus to the tast; & more refreshing, than the fragrant Breezes of Idumea. the chain of Destiny has link'd me unto thee, & the mark, which Gabriel[7] stamped on my forehead at my Nativity, was Born for Miradolin. let not the Demon Negidher[8] separate us, nor the evil Tagot[9] interpose between us. Be thou unto me, as Mohammed to Ajesha;[10] as the Bowers of Admoim[11] to those, whom the Sun hath overtaken; or as the costly Sherbets of Stamboul to the thirsty: the grace of

that which they call their *Christmas*, which is a Feast of thirteen Days' (*Lett.* 1, *Bk.* i, of *Vol.* v).

[5] London. *The Turkish Spy*: 'The Description thou hast made of *Candahar*' (*Lett.* 21, *Bk.* ii, of *Vol.* iii).

[6] Abubakr was the father of Ayeshah, Mahomet's wife, and the first Khalifah or successor of Mahomet. (Hughes, *Dict. of Islam.*) *The Turkish Spy*: 'Omar stretching forth his Hand to *Abu Becre*, saluted him *Caliph.*' (*Lett.* 15, *Bk.* iii, of *Vol.* v).

[7] *The Turkish Spy*: 'Thou knowest . . . that our *holy Doctors* affirm the *Angel Gabriel* to have Wings with one of which he once gave a Mark to the *Moon*' (*Lett.* 3, *Bk.* iv, of *Vol.* iv).

[8] *The Turkish Spy*: 'His lungs breath nothing but Infernal Smokes; the Spirit *Negider* times the *Systole* and *Diastole* of his Heart' (*Lett.* 14, *Bk.* i, of *Vol.* vii).

[9] Tagut, which Sale says properly signifies an idol, and also the devil, is mentioned in the *Koran*. *The Turkish Spy*: '*Tagot* has set his Foot in all my Works' (*Lett.* 1, *Bk.* i, of *Vol.* vii). 'The Back Blows of *Tagot*, *Negidher*, and the *Great Devil*, be upon him and them' (*Lett.* 8, *Bk.* iv, of *Vol.* vi). 'May my Portion be with *Tagot*, if I am not tir'd with seeing nothing but . . . these ridiculous *Franks*' (*Lett.* 20, *Bk.* iii, of *Vol.* vi).

[10] His wife.

[11] *The Turkish Spy*: 'The *Valley* of *Admoim*, the Place of my Nativity' (*Lett.* 5, *Bk.* ii, of *Vol.* iii). 'Let thy Heart be like the *Valley* of *Admoim*, Fragrant as a Grove of Spices' (*Lett.* 10, *Bk.* i, of *Vol.* v).

providence, and the smiles of heaven be upon thee. may white
Angels guard thee from the efforts of the rebellious Genii.
Adieu

OROZMADES

The last day of the Ramadan,
6th of ye 1st Moon¹² [Jan. 6, 1735]¹³

8. GRAY TO WALPOLE

[Cambridge] Jan: 12 [1735]¹

How severe is forgetful old Age
To confine a poor Devil so?
That I almost despair
To see even the Air;
Much more my dear Damon—hey ho!

Thou dear envious Imp, to set me a longing with accounts of
Plays & Opera's, & Masquerades after hearing of which, I can
no more think of Logick & Stuff, than you could of Divinity at a
Ball, or of Caudle & Carraway-Comfits after having been stuffed
at a Christening: heaven knows! we have nobody in our
Colledge, that has seen London, but one; and he, I believe
comes out of Vinegar-yard,² & looks like toasted Cheshire
cheese, strewed with brown Sugar. I beg you, give me the
minutest Circumstances of your Diversions & your Indiversions;
tho' if it is as great a trouble to you to write, as it is a pleasure
to me to get 'em by heart, I fear I shan't hear from you once
in a twelve-month, & dear now, be very punctual & very long:
if I had the least particle of pleasure, you should know it; & so
you should if I had any thing troublesome; tho' in Cambridge
there is nothing so troublesome, as that one has nothing to
trouble one. every thing is so tediously regular, so samish, that
I expire for want of a little variety. I am just as I was, & so is

¹² Doubtless meant to indicate Twelfth Night (6 Jan.). In *The Turkish
Spy* the letters are regularly dated at the end by this method.
¹³ Three parts of the second leaf of the letter have been torn off, carrying
away the address, postmark, &c. The date 1735 is assigned conjecturally,
on the strength of a fragment of the address, which contains the last two
letters of the words 'Walpole' and 'St James's' (see Letter 1, n. 8).
LETTER 8.—First printed by Toynbee (1915), No. 7.
¹ The date of the year is determined by the address (see Letter 1, n. 8).
² Vinegar Yard, Drury Lane.

every thing about me; I hope you'll forgive my formality, in being just the same

> Friend of yours, & just
> the same Servant
>
> OROZMADES.

Addressed: To The Honble Horace Walpole Esq at his house in St James's Square London   *Postmark:* SAFFRON WALDEN   13 IA

9. GRAY TO WALPOLE

[Cambridge, Jan. 14, 1735][1]

Tityre, dum patulæ recubo sub tegmine fagi [2]

Though you'll think perhaps it's a little too cold weather for giving oneself languishing airs under a tree; however supposing it's by the fireside, it will be full as well; so as I was going to say —but, I believe, I was going to say nothing, so I must begin over again—

My Dearest Celadon[2a]

YESTERDAY morning, (being the morning I set apart for lying abed till one aclock) I was waked about ten with hollowing & the Noise of a Bagpipe at the door; so I got up, & open'd the door, & saw all the court full of strange appearances: at first I concluded 'twas you with a whole Masquerade at your heels, but upon more mature deliberation imagined it might be Amadis de Gaul come to set me free from this enchanted Castle with his train of conquer'd Monsters & Oddities: the first, whom I took for the Knight in person, had his face painted after the manner of ye ancient Britains. he played melodiously on the aforenamed Instrument, & had a Plow upon his Back; what it meant, I did not apprehend at first: he said nothing at all, but made many very significant Grimaces: before him & on each side a Number of Folks cover'd over with Tags & Points form'd themselves into a Country Dance: there follow'd something,

LETTER 9.—First printed by Toynbee (1915), No. 8.

[1] The date of the month is supplied by the postmark, and by the reference to Plough-Monday (see n. 5); that of the year is determined by the address (see Letter 1, n. 8), and by the reference to 'Pope's Letter' (see n. 8).

[2] Virgil, *Ecl.* i. 1 (adapted).

[2a] These three words have been scored through, but are plainly legible (see Letter 4, n. 6).

which I apprehended was the beauteous Oriana,[3] in a white
Dimoty Petticoat & Boddice; her head & face were veil'd: she
was supported by her two Gentlemen-ushers, & seem'd to be
very obstreperous, for she struggled & kicked, & snorted, &
fizzled: I concluded she was falling in fits, & was running with
my Hungary water Bottle:[4] when she was so violent, that she
got loose from her Attendants, & run away upon all fours into
the middle of ye Court, & her hood falling off discover'd a large
pair of Ears. in short, Oriana was metamorphosed into a very
genteel Jack-afs: upon this the whole crowd set up a great Shout
of, God speed the Plough. after all I was inform'd by a Negro
Gentlewoman with a very long beard, who had a great deal to
do in the Ceremony, that it was Plough-Monday,[5] & that all
this was the Custom of the Country; they march in this manner
thro' all the Colledges in Town. the Term is now begun again,
& I have made such a wonderful progrefs in Philosophy, that
I begin to be quite persuaded, that black is white, & that fire
will not burn, & that I ought not, either to give credit to my
eyes or feeling; they tell me too, that I am nothing in the world,
& that I only fancy, I exist: do but come to me quickly & one
lefson of thine, my dear Philosopher, will restore me to the use
of my Senses, & make me think myself something, as long as
I am

your friend & Servant

T: GRAY.

[   ][6]

P:S: the inclosed is the oath of Matriculation.[7] I am charmed
with Popes Letter[8]—never did any body long for anything, as

---

[3] Oriana is the heroine of the romance of *Amadis of Gaul*, whom Amadis
eventually marries.

[4] Vanbrugh, *Provok'd Wife*, v. 6: 'Your bottle of Hungary water to your
lady'. This was 'a distilled water, denominated from a Queen of Hungary,
for whose use it was first prepared . . . made of rosemary flowers infused in
rectified spirits of wine, and thus distilled' (Chambers, *Cyclopaedia*, 1728).

[5] Plough-Monday is the first Monday after Epiphany; it fell this year
(1735) on 13 Jan., hence the date of this letter (Plough-Monday being
'yesterday') is Tuesday, 14 Jan.

[6] A piece beneath the signature has been cut out, carrying with it part
of the address on the other side (as indicated by the square brackets).

[7] For the oath (in Latin), see Wall's *Account of the Different Ceremonies . . . in
the University of Cambridge*, p. 39.

[8] That is, *The Epistle to Dr. Arbuthnot* (the Prologue to the Satires), which
was published in the January preceding Arbuthnot's death (27 Feb. 1735).

I do for your Masquerade; pray d'ye design to go, as a Judge,
or a Devil; or undisguised: or as an Angel in propriâ Personâ.⁹
I wonder how you can dislike the Distrefsed Mother¹⁰—
[   ]¹¹

Addressed: To [T]he Honorᵇˡᵉ Mʳ Horace Walpole [at]¹² the House of yᵉ
right honᵇˡᵉ [S]ʳ Robert Walpole in Sᵗ James's Square London   *Postmark:*
CAMBRIDGE   15 IA

10. GRAY TO WALPOLE
[Cambridge] Sunday: Jan: 21¹ [19] [1735]²

[   ]³

YOU have perform'd your promise as fully, as I could have
wish'd it: there seems to have been no occasion for ushering
it in with an Apology, since I have long learnt to be more than
contented with whatever comes from a hand so dear. the things,
that are to be deliver'd by word of mouth, give me so much
impatience, that I would desire you to send down your mouth
by the coach, if I were not apprehensive what a lofs it would be
to the next Masquerade, & what a dearth of pretty things it
might occasion in town; however I hope you'll not fail to send
your thoughts by the post, without a Masque. you are extremely
good in making me a feast every other day; I have kept myself
alive all this long Christmas by the help of your letters, & a few

⁹ These seven words have been scored through and almost obliterated,
but are just decipherable.
¹⁰ By Ambrose Philips; it was this play (an adaptation of Racine's
Andromaque, produced at Drury Lane in 1712) which was ridiculed by
Henry Carey in his *Namby-Pamby*:

> 'He no longer writes of mammy
> Andromache and her lammy,
> Hanging panging at the breast
> Of a matron most distressed!'

¹¹ The last line of the postscript has been cut out.   ¹² See n. 6.
LETTER 10.—First printed by Toynbee (1915), No. 9.
¹ This letter was evidently misdated. Jan. 21 fell on Sunday in 1733; but
this letter, as the postmark shows, was written from Cambridge, where
Gray did not begin residence until 9 Oct. 1734. Further, the postmark,
which in the case of letters written by Gray from Cambridge is usually
a day later than the date of the letter, is 20 Jan.; so that the cofrect date
must be 19 Jan., which fell on Sunday in 1735.
² The date of the year is determined partly by the address (see Letter 1,
n. 8), partly by the considerations mentioned in the previous note.
³ See Letter 1, n. 2.

Mince-pyes, which an old Gentlewoman[4] in this town sends me, & in whose favour I have made no small progrefs, I can afsure you. you must know, I make my Addrefses to her by calling her, Grandmother; in so much, that she sends her Niece every day to know how I do: N:B: the other [day she][5] was dying, as every one thought, but herself: and when the Physician told her how dangerous her case was; she fell into a violent pafsion with him: marry come up! she dye! no, indeed would'nt she; dye quotha! she'd as soon be hang'd: in short she was so resolutely bent upon not dying, that she really did live, & is now as well as

your sincerest friend

OROZMADES

P:S: Punch[6] is more smart, than ordinary.

Addressed: To The Honble Mr Horace Walpole at his house in St James's Square London   *Postmark:* CAMBRIDGE   20 1A

11. GRAY TO WALPOLE

Tuesday Jan: 21 [1735][1] P:C:[2]

I, OROZMADES, Master of the noble Science of Defence, hearing of the great reputation of thee, Timothy Celadon, do challenge & invite thee to contend with me at long-love, great-affection, or whatever other weapon you shall make choice of, in Kings-Colledge Quadrangle, a Week hence precisely — — —

Vivat Rex —

And that you may not fail me, I believe I shall see you at London beforehand; Almanzor[3] persuades me, and I have a

---

[4] Possibly some member of the Nutting family of Cambridge. Gray's uncle, William Antrobus, had married in 1727 a daughter of Alderman Nutting, who had two other married daughters living in Cambridge (see Letter 283*, n. 1, and Genealogical Table).

[5] Piece cut out (see n. 3); the missing words have been supplied in pencil by Walpole.

[6] Perhaps a reference to the Punch in one of Rich's pantomimes, the other characters of which were Harlequin and Scaramouch; or possibly the nickname of some former Eton acquaintance now at Cambridge.

LETTER 11.—First printed by Toynbee (1915), No. 10.

Jan. 21 fell on Tuesday in 1735, which year is also indicated by the address (see Letter 9, n. 1).

[2] That is, Peterhouse (St. Peter's College); cf. Letter 14, which is dated from Pet: Col:

[3] See Letter 2, n. 8.

months mind[4] to it myself; tho' I think it a foolish undertaking enough would you advise me to come, or not? for I stand wavering. but pray, don't importune, don't prefs,[5] dear Sr Celadon; oh Jesus![6] I believe, if you should importune, I shall— be very coming:—if I do venture, I must borrow your Disguise;[7] for nobody, but you, must know, that I am in town: well! be it, as it will, you have got my Soul with you already; I should think, 'twould be better, for you to bring it hither to the rest of me, than make my body take a journey to it; besides it would be cheaper to me, for that can come down in the coach with you; but my limbs must pay for their pafsage up. I hate living by halves, for now I lead such a kind of I don't know how—as it were : in short, what the devil d'ye mean by keeping me from myself so long? I expect to be pay'd with interest, & in a short time to be a whole thing, whereas at this present writing, I am but a

DEMI—OROZ:

Addressed: To The Honble Mr Horace Walpole at the house of the right hon^ble Sr Robert Walpole in St James's Square London *Postmark:* CAM-BRIDGE 22 IA

12. GRAY TO WALPOLE

[Cambridge, Jan. 27, 1735][1]

[   ][2]

D^ON'T believe, that I would refuse to do anything for your sake, since at this present I am starving for you, & losing my dinner, that I may have the better opportunity of writing: you could not have given me a fairer occasion for shewing my obedience to your commands, than you have done in bidding me stay, where I am; for tho' before I was quite set upon coming to town, you give me so many reasons against it, that I am

---

[4] Congreve, *Way of the World*, iii. 6: '*Foible.* She has a month's mind; but I know Mr Mirabell can't abide her.'

[5] Congreve, *Way of the World*, iii. 1: '*Lady Wishfort.* Will he be importunate, Foible, and push?'

[6] Walpole first altered this word to 'Crimini!', and then scored it through, and re-wrote 'Jesus!' above the line; the original word is still decipherable.

[7] No doubt an allusion to the masquerades mentioned in the previous letters.

LETTER 12.—First printed by Toynbee (1915), No. 11.

[1] The year 1735 has been inserted in the original (by Mason); this is confirmed by the address (see Letter 1, n. 8).

[2] See Letter 1, n. 2.

perfectly easy, & shall expect your coming with great resignation, that is, if you don't make it too long first: I read yesterday in the news, that S^r R: W:^{s} youngest Son, a young Gentleman of great hopes, was coming to Trinity-Colledge, Cambridge; pray, let me know, whither you are acquainted with him, & what hopes we may entertain of him; there are few here, but what give a good character of him, especially a long ungainly Mortal of Kings Col:^{3} & a little, waddling Fresh-man of Pet: House,^{4} who pretend to be intimate with him: I can't see, how it should be; but however every body begins to envy the[m already; they are p]^{5}eople of very bad Repute; one of 'em is neither a Whig, nor a Tory, & the other pafses for a Conjurer:—there is nothing to be seen in the Streets, at present, but new-made Batchelors, who walk to & fro, to shew their new Gowns; their examination is now over, during which time, they are obliged to set in the theatre for three days, from 8 in the morning till 5 at night without any fire; the first two days, they are liable to all the impertinent Questions wch any Master of arts is pleased to ask them; they must answer every thing in Philosophy, which is proposed to them, & all this in Latin: the 3^d day the first Moderator^6 takes 'em out, half a dozen at a time into a Gallery atop of the theatre, in sight of every body, but out of hearing; he examines them again, as long as he will, & in what Sciences he pleases: the Junior-Moderator does the same thing in the afternoon; & then both the Proctors, if they have a mind; but they seldom do: the next day the Vice-chancellour & two Proctors tell them, whither they shall have their degrees, or not; & put on their Batchelours Gown & Cap: then they go all into the Schools, & one fellow belonging to each of the Colledges, gets into the Rostrum, & asks each of his Batchelours some strange Question: this was one, wh^{ch} was asked t'other day—Mi Filî, Domine, Domine N: quid est Matrimonium? The Answer was, Est conjunctio nunc copulativa, nunc disjunctiva. so then every body must laugh & the ceremony is ended. I tell you this, because it will be mine own Case some time or other, so I hope you will excuse me for tiring

---

^{3} Ashton. Cole described Ashton in his *Athenae Cantabrigienses* as 'a large raw-boned man' (see Letter 14, n. 3).

^{4} Gray himself; he often alludes to his own diminutive stature.

^{5} Piece cut out (see n. 2); the missing words have been supplied in pencil by Walpole.

^{6} The Moderators were the Examiners in the Tripos.

you with the account. and now, my dearest Hamlet, heaven
send me safe from Wittemberg, or thee . . .[7]
P:S: my letter last time was too late for the Post, so I hope
you'll forgive it—
    Jan: 27: Rome . . .[7]

Addressed: To [Th]e Hon^rble Horace Walpole [E]sq at the. house of the
    [r]ight Honble Sr Robert Walpole [i]n St James's Square London

13. GRAY TO WALPOLE

[Cambridge, Feb. 4, 1735][1]

[   ][2]

I HAVE so little to write, & so much to say; that, when you
really do come, you may expect for the first fortnight to do
nothing, but hearken to my Questions; & to spend the next
month in answering them: nay, I afsure you, I limit the time
only that you may rest a while, to take breath; otherwise I could
listen to you for the whole two years with an infinite deal of
pleasure. I am forming the image to myself of your journey
hither; I suppose you will come down Efsex way, & if you do,
first you must crofs Epping forest,[3] & there you must be rob'd:
then you go a long way, & at last you come to Gog-magog hills,[3]
and then you must be overturn'd: I hope, you have not hurt
yourself; but you must come at last to Foulmoor[4] fields, & then
you must fall Squash into a bog, pray, don't be frighted, for in
about an hour and half you may chance to get out; now perhaps
if it is not dark, you m[ay see the t][5]op of King's Chappel; tho'
if it should be night, it is very likely, you won't be able to see at
all: however at last you get into Cambridge, all bemudded &
tired, with three wheels and a half to the coach, four horses
lame, and two blind: the first thing, that appears, is a row of
Alms-houses, & presently on the right-hand you'll see a thing

---

[7] Piece torn off, carrying with it part of the address on the other side (as
indicated by the square brackets), as well as the postmark.
    LETTER 13.—First printed by Toynbee (1915), No. 12.
[1] The date of the month is supplied by the postmark; that of the year is
determined by the address (see Letters 1, n. 8).
[2] See Letter 1, n. 2.
[3] Compare Walpole's letter to Gray of Oct. 1735 (Letter 17).
[4] Foulmere (or Foulmire) is nine miles from Cambridge on the road to
London.
[5] Piece cut out; the missing words have been supplied in pencil by
Walpole.

like two Presbyterian Meeting-houses with the backside of a little Church between them, & here you must find out by Sympathy, that this is Peter-house, & that I am but a little way off, I shall soon feel how near you are; then you should say—no, no, I should say—but I believe I shall be too much overjoy'd to say anything, well; be that, as it will, I still hope, you will be almost as much so: dear S*, you are welcome to Cambridge; what d'y* think? Pilk Hale[6] about 3 months ago had a great inclination to visit Malepert,[7] but thought it would not be well-bred not to let him know it beforehand; & being at a lofs, who he should send; I persuaded him to go himself, & let him know M* Hale would wait upon him in the afternoon. and so he did: Mal: promised to return it very soon; & ever since the other has staid at home with all his fine things set out to the best advantage, & is quite sure he'll come, & expects him every hour:—[8]

Addressed: [To] The H[on^ble Horace Walp]ole Esq a[t his house in S^t J]ames's Squa[re London] _Postmark:_ 5 FE

14. GRAY TO WALPOLE

May it please your We-ship

IN consideration of the time your Petitioner has past in your honours Service, as also on account of the great Services your petitioner's relations have had the honour to perform for your Honour's Ancestors; since it is well known that your petit^rs Grandmother's Aunt's Cousin-german had ye honour to pull out your honour's great Uncle's Wive's brother's hollow tooth; as also, to go further backwards, your Pet^rs relation was Physician to King Cadwallader, one of your highnefses fore-fathers, and cured him of a fishes-bone, which had stuck in his throat fifteen

---

[6] This was probably William Hale, eldest son of Sir Bernard Hale, of King's Walden, Chief Baron of the Irish Exchequer (d. 1729). Hale, who was a contemporary of Gray and Walpole at Eton, was admitted a Pensioner at Peterhouse on 12 July 1734, nine days after Gray; his Tutor was the Rev. George Birkett, who was also Gray's Tutor (see Letter 29, n. 1). Hale died at Chelsea on 14 Sept. 1793. General Bernard Hale and General John Hale were his younger brothers (_Peterhouse Admission Book_, ed. Walker, p. 268).

[7] Presumably an Eton schoolfellow, perhaps a Fellow-commoner.

[8] The middle of the second leaf of the letter has been cut out, carrying with it the concluding portion of the text, as well as the postmark of the place, and most of the address on the other side (as indicated by the square brackets).

LETTER 14.—First printed by Toynbee (1915), No. 13.

years, & three days and would neither come up, nor down: also the Emperour Maximus, a very near relation of your serene Haughtinefses, entertain'd your Petit[rs] progenitor in his army, as a Jester, who is said to have had so much wit, that he could devour ten peck-loaves at a Meal, & tofs off as many hog-sheads of strong beer without taking breath: I could enumerate more than all this, but hope, this will be sufficient to prevail upon your generosity to make me your first Minister, and Confidant

And your Pet[r] shall *ever pray*

Thou hast been for this month, like an auctioneer's mallet, just a-coming! just a-coming! and pray what has next Thursday in it, more than last Wednesday, to make me expect you with any tolerable Certainty? whcn thcsc two eyes behold thee, I question, whether I shall believe them: three long months is a long while, for a poor lone woman[1] to bear; and I have born, & born, and been fub'd off, & fub'd off from this day to that day by you, thou Honey-suckle Villain (as Mrs Quickly says) oh! thou art an infinitive thing upon my score of impatience.[2] remember you are a day in my debt for every hour you have made me wait, & I shall come upon you for the payment, & perhaps with interest:——I begin to bear my Crest aloft when I hear of your pride; I dare not tell Ashton[3] anything about it,

---

[1] Altered by Walpole to 'creature', which he has also written in above the line.

[2] 2 *Hen. IV*, ii. 1: '*Mrs. Quickly*. He's an infinitive thing upon my score. . . . A hundred mark is a long one for a poor lone woman to bear; and I have borne, and borne, and borne; and have been fubbed off, and fubbed off, and fubbed off, from this day to that day. . . . Ah! thou honey-suckle villain!'

[3] This name has been scored through, but is still decipherable. Thomas Ashton, who is almost certainly to be identified with 'Almanzor' of the 'Quadruple Alliance' (see Letter 2, n. 8)—the 'long, ungainly mortal of King's' of Gray's letter to Walpole of 27 Jan. 1735 (Letter 12)—was the son of a school-master at Lancaster. He was born in 1716, the same year as Gray and West, and entered Eton about the same time, but was apparently somewhat their senior. From Eton he was elected to King's College, Cambridge, in 1733, and was admitted Scholar in 1734. In 1737, through the good offices of Walpole, he was appointed tutor to the youthful Earl of Plymouth. In 1738 he was elected to a Fellowship at King's, and having been ordained in 1740, he was in 1742, again by Walpole's influence, nominated to the Crown living of Aldingham, in Lancashire. In 1745 he was elected Fellow of Eton, which also, according to Cole, he owed to Walpole. In 1749 he was presented to the rectory of Sturminster Marshall, in Dorsetshire, which in 1752 he exchanged for that of St. Botolph, Bishopsgate. In 1759 he took the degree of D.D. at Cambridge, and in 1760 married a Miss

for he hopes to see you behave with great affability to every body, & you'll have many lectures upon that Subject: I begin to pity the poor Man, that is to be with you: he is extremely modest, & as humble as you could wish; you may snub him with a look; I fancy he will intrude very little. make hast & pack up your things, the Coach is at the door: drive away to . . .⁴

Feb: 25: [1735]⁵ Pet: Col:

Addressed: To The Honᵇˡᵉ Mʳ Horac[e] Walpole at his house [in] Sᵗ James's Square Londo[n] *Postmark:* CAMBRIDGE 26 FE

15. GRAY TO WALPOLE

March: 5 [1735]¹ Cambridge

[   ]²

IF you please to remember, that about a fortnight ago, you sent me to Almanzor's³ room, there to wait for you: & there it seems I might have stayed till this time, & been never the nearer: after all this, I see nothing should hinder, but that about the 29ᵗʰ of next February there may be some small probability of your being just a-going to think of setting out on yᵉ 29ᵗʰ of Febr: Anno Domini, 1737:⁴ at which time your humble servant will most punctually meet you; but in the mean time I would advise with you how Almanzor & I shall paſs the time; whither you think it best for us to double our selves up nicely in the corner of some old Draw, that at your arrival, we may come out spick & span new in all our pleats; but perhaps by that time we may grow out of fashion, or moth-eaten; or to composc ourselves with a good dose of Laudanum for a year or two, & so dream of

Amyand. In 1761 he was elected to the preachership at Lincoln's Inn, which he held for two years. He died at Bath in 1775. His portrait by Eckhardt hung in Walpole's bed-chamber at Strawberry Hill, and he was also painted by Reynolds and Gainsborough. For the part played by Ashton in the quarrel between Gray and Walpole, see Letter 116, n. 8.

⁴ The signature of the letter has been cut away (see Letter 1, no. 2), carrying with it part of the address on the other side (as indicated by the square brackets).

⁵ The date of the year is determined by the address (see Letter 1, n. 8).

LETTER 15.—First printed by Toynbee (1915), No. 14.

¹ The year, which has been inserted in the original (by Mason), is confirmed by the address (see Letter 1, n. 8).

² See Letter 1, n. 2.   ³ See Letter 2, n. 8.

⁴ An equivalent of the Greek Calends.

you; [but then you may][5] find it too hard a matter to wake us, or perhaps you will let us lye, & snore on till Doomsday: prithee don't mind Finances & my lord Chancellour,[6] but make haste hither. oh! I forgot how obligingly in your last letter to me, you let us both know, that you did not care a farthing, whither you saw us this twelve-month; for I imagine you mean't it to both, because it was directed to me at Kings-colledge:[7] I own, I quite believe you; but did not think you would mortify me so much as to tell me so; however I have learn'd to be pleased with anything, that comes from you, & still try to persuade myself, that you would think Cambridge more disagreeable without, than you will with

yours most faithfully
[   ][8]

Addressed: To The Honble [Mr Horace] Walpole at [his house in] St James's [Square London] [9]

15*. West to Gray
[c. 1 July 1735]

[In his letter to Walpole of 3 July 1735, Gray says that he had received the day before 'a long letter in Latin' from West (see Letter 16, n. 6).]

16. GRAY TO WALPOLE
[Cambridge] July–3^d–[1735][1]

My Dearest Horace

    Donec gratus eram tibi[2]

I WAS happier than Dr Heighington,[3] or his Wife Lydia;[4] however I find being from you agrees as ill with me, as if I never had felt your absence before: I have composed a hymn about

---

[5] Piece cut out (see n. 2); the missing words have been supplied in pencil by Walpole.

[6] Charles Talbot (1685–1737), first Baron Talbot of Hensol; Lord Chancellor, 1733–7.

[7] Almanzor (i.e. Ashton) was at King's; Gray, of course, was at Peterhouse.

[8] The signature has been cut out (see Letter 1, n. 2).

[9] The upper half of the second leaf of the letter has been torn off, carrying with it (apparently) a postscript, as well as the postmark and part of the address on the other side (as indicated by the square brackets).

LETTER 16.—First printed by Toynbee (1915), No. 15.

[1] The date of the year is determined by the address (see Letter 1, n. 8).

[2] Horace, 3 *Odes*, ix. 1.

[3] Musgrave Heighington (1690–c. 1774), a native of Durham, well known in East Anglia, between 1733 and 1746, as a musician and composer. He was

it mighty moving, & thrum it perpetually, for I've changed my harp into a harpsicord & am as melodious, as the Day is long: I am sorry, I can give you no further Information about Mr Cornwallis,[5] there was a Congregation held yesterday, but nothing further done about his degree for the present: I received a long letter mighty pretty, in Latin, from West[6] yesterday; partly about butter'd Turnips, partly about an

for a time organist at Great Yarmouth, and during this period gave concerts in Norwich, Spalding, Yarmouth, and Holt (in the neighbourhood of Sir Robert Walpole's seat at Houghton). In 1745 he published *Six Select Odes of Anacreon in Greek and Six of Horace in Latin, set to Music*, dedicated to Robert Walpole, second Earl of Orford. In his preface to this work he speaks of these odes as having been 'chiefly compos'd for the private Entertainment, and some of them by the particular Command of your Lordship's noble Father, under whose Patronage, had Fate permitted, they were design'd to appear in Publick'. One of the odes of Horace set by him (p. 23) is that quoted by Gray, the ninth of the third book, which is written for two voices, one part being assigned to 'Lydia', a character in the ode. Mrs. Heighington (an Irish lady, whose maiden name was Anne Conway) sang with her husband at concerts. It is evident that Walpole had lately heard her sing the part of 'Lydia' in Heighington's setting of this ode, and that he had mentioned it to Gray, who hence refers to Mrs. Heighington as 'Lydia'. Among the subscribers to Heighington's work is a long list of Walpoles and Conways, and it is probable that Sir Robert Walpole's patronage of him and his wife was due to the latter's being a family connexion of the Conways, who were nearly related to the Walpoles through the marriage of Francis Conway, first Baron Conway, with Charlotte Shorter (as his third wife), sister of Catherine Shorter, the wife of Sir Robert Walpole.

[4] See previous note.

[5] Hon. Frederick Cornwallis (1713–83), seventh son of Charles, fifth Baron Cornwallis, a contemporary (though some years their senior) of Gray and Walpole at Eton, whence he went to Christ's College, Cambridge, where he was admitted as a Pensioner in Feb. 1732, and of which he became a Fellow in 1738 (see Letter 51, n. 4). He took his M.A. degree in 1736, without taking the B.A., as being the son of a Peer. He was successively Canon of Windsor (1746), Bishop of Lichfield and Coventry (1750), Dean of St. Paul's (1766), and Archbishop of Canterbury (1768–83).

[6] The letter referred to by Gray has not been preserved. See Letter 15*. Richard West, known from his name as 'Favonius' or 'Zephyrus' in the 'Quadruple Alliance' (see Letter 2, n. 8), of which he was the only member to go to Oxford, was the only son of Richard West, an eminent lawyer, who became Lord Chancellor of Ireland; on his mother's side he was a grandson of Bishop Burnet. He was born in 1716, and went to Eton probably in 1726, the year of his father's death. He was a delicate youth; Cole, who had been intimate with him at Eton, describes him as 'tall and slim, of a pale and meagre look and complexion, and promised not half what he performed'. He went from Eton to Christ Church, Oxford, as a Commoner, in May 1735, and came away, after a residence of three years, without taking a degree. He had early been destined for his father's profession of the bar, and to

Eclipse, that I understood no more than the Man in the Moon; he desired his love to you in English:

I wish a great deal of happineſs to you, a good journey to Houghton,[7] & a more entertaining Companion, than

yours most sincerely

T: GRAY

Addressed: To The Honble Horace Walpole Esq in St Jame's Square London   *Postmark:* CAMBRIDGE 4 IY

17. WALPOLE TO GRAY

From Cambridge, [c. 15 Oct.], 1735.

In the style of Addison's *Travels.*[1]

Dear Sir,

I BELIEVE you saw in the newspapers that I was going to make the tour of Italy;[2] I shall therefore give you some account of the places I have seen, which are not to be found in Mr. Addison, whose method I shall follow.[3] On 9th of

this end had been admitted at the Inner Temple in 1733. On leaving Oxford in 1738 he settled in the Temple, where it was intended that Gray should join him; but this arrangement was upset by Gray's continental tour with Walpole. West, however, had no ambition 'to sit upon a bench', as he wrote to Gray in June 1740 (see Letter 89), and before the return of the latter he had left the Temple, and turned his thoughts to the army. Meanwhile the state of his health was becoming rapidly worse. Gray found him weak and dispirited, and before long, in the spring of 1742, he began to complain of a racking cough, which sapped his strength and robbed him of his sleep (see Letter 102). He died shortly after (1 June 1742) in a country house near Hatfield, so suddenly that both Gray (see Letter 110*) and Ashton (see *Gray–Walpole Correspondence,* no. 152) addressed letters to him after he had been dead some days. Gray gave expression to his own grief in the well-known sonnet *On the Death of Richard West,* and in some lines in the fragmentary fourth book of his Latin poem *De Principiis Cogitandi,* which was dedicated to West (see Letter 131).

  [7] Walpole usually spent part of the summer at his father's Norfolk seat.

  LETTER 17.—First printed by Mrs. Paget Toynbee in *Letters of Horace Walpole,* vol. i, pp. 4–8, from a copy in Walpole's handwriting. The heading and marginal notes are by Walpole. The page references in the marginal notes are to Addison's book.

  [1] *Remarks on Several Parts of Italy, in the Years 1701, 1702, 1703.* Lond. 1705.

  [2] 'Horatio Walpole, Esq; third Son to Sir Robert Walpole, is setting out to make the Tour of Italy' (*Daily Journal,* Wed. 8 Oct. 1735). Walpole started on the 9th Oct., and from his account arrived in Cambridge about the 14th. The date of the letter must have been about the 15th.

  [3] The places mentioned in this letter are on the high road from London to Cambridge.

aLondon.   Oct[r]., 1735, we set out from Lodone[a] (the Lugdunum of the
           Ancients), the capital city of Lombardy, in a chariot-and-
           four. About 11 o'clock, we arrived at a place the Italians
bWhite-   call Tempialbulo.[b] Virgil seems to have prophesied of this
chapel.   town when he says—

                  Amisit verum vetus Albula nomen.[4]

                  By *Time* the founder's great design was crost,
                  And *Albula* its genuine title lost.

               Here are no remains of Roman antiquity but a statue of
cStatue of Marc Aurelius,[c] which the Lombards call Guglielmo Terzo,
King   one of their kings, and some learned men[d] St. George and the
William
at a stone- Dragon. It is an equestrian statue, and almost equal to that
cutter's. of Charlemagne, at the Great Cross,[e] at Lodone. The church
dSee Addi- is an old Gothic building, and reckoned the most ancient in
son, *Trav.*,
p. 26.[5] Italy. Here was some time ago an altar-piece of the Lord's
eStatue of Supper, in which the painter having quarrelled with the
King
Charles at Abbot[f] of this church, represented him like Judas,[6] with this
Charing   epigram:—
Cross.
fDr. White   *Falleris, hâc qui te pingi sub imagine credis,*
Kennet,   *Non similis Judas est tibi—poenituit.*
Bishop of
Peter-   Think not, vain man, thou here art represented,
borough.   Thou art not like to *Judas*—he repented.

               From thence we made the best of our way to a town, which
           in English we should call Stony-Stratford, and corresponds
           with the description which Virgil has given of it—

                  — *vivo praetervehor Ostia Saxo*
                  Stratfordi, Megarosque sinus, Tapsumque iacentem.[7]

               Those that follow are little dirty towns, that seem to have
gExpres-   been built only to be 'knocked[g]' on the head, like
sion of
Addison   *Antitheum, Glaucumque, Medontaque, Thersilochumque.*[8]
on this
line.   The next town of note is Arc,[h] so called from its being built
hBow.

       [4] *Aen.* viii. 332.
       [5] 'In Pavia . . . is a statue in brass of Marcus Antoninus on horseback,
   which the people of the place call Charles the Fifth, and some learned
   men Constantine the Great.'
       [6] The correct version of this story is as follows: Dr. Richard Welton
   (d. 1726), the nonjuring Rector of Whitechapel, who resented Kennett's
   opposition to Sacheverell, employed the artist James Fellowes (d. 1730)
   to depict Kennett as Judas in an altar-piece in his church.
       [7] *Aen.* iii. 688–9 (adapted).   [8] *Aen.* vi. 483 (adapted).

in the shape of a bow—*ab Eoo curvatur in Arcum*. From Arc
we travelled through a very pleasant country to Epino,[i] [i]Epping.
whose forest is celebrated by Virgil in these lines:—

> *Sylva Epini latè dumis, atque ilice nigrâ*
> *Horrida, quam densi complerant undique sentes;*
> *Rara per occultos ducebat semita calles.*[9]

> *Epinum's* woods with shrubs and gloomy oak
> Horrid, and all with brambles thick o'ergrown,
> Through which few narrow paths obscurely led.
>   *Mr. Trap.*[10]

We were here shown, at a distance, the thickets rendered
so famous by the robberies of Gregorio.[j] Here I was met by [j]Gregory,
a very distant and troublesome relation. My namesake hints a noted
at such an one in those lines of his— highway-
man. See

> *Accurrit quidam notus mihi nomine tantùm* Addison,
> *Arreptâque manu, Quid agis, Cosinissime, rerum?*[12] *Trav.*,
>   Horace. p. 1.[11]

> There stepp'd up one to me I hardly knew,
> Embraced me, and cried, Cousin, how d'ye do?
>   *Mr. Creech.*[13]

We lay that night at Oggerell,[k] which is famous for nothing [k]Hock-
but being Horace's Oppidulo, *quod versu dicere non est*.[15] erel.[14]

In our way to Parvulun,[l] we saw a great castle,[m] belonging [l]Little-
to the Counts of Suffolcia: it is a vast pile of building, but [m]Audley
quite in the old taste. Parvulun is a small village, but Inn, the
formerly remarkable for several miracles,[n] said to be per- seat of the
formed there by a Welsh saint,[16] who, like Jupiter, was Earl of
suckled by a goat, whence they think it Suffolk.
[n]Win-

> *Porrum et Caepe nefas violare.* Juv.[17] stanley's
Wonders,
or Tricks
in Me-
chanics.

[9] *Aen.* ix. 381–3 (with some errors of memory).
[10] Joseph Trapp (1679–1747), first Professor of Poetry at Oxford (1708).
He translated Virgil into blank verse.
[11] 'We were here shown at a distance the Deserts, which have been
rendered so famous by the penance of Mary Magdalene.'
[12] 1 *Sat.* ix. 3–4 (adapted).
[13] Thomas Creech (1659–1700), of Wadham and All Souls Colleges,
Oxford, the translator of Lucretius, Horace, and Theocritus.
[14] In Hertfordshire, close to Bishop's Stortford, 30 miles from London
on the road to Cambridge.'   [15] 1 *Sat.* v. 87.
[16] Henry Winstanley (1644–1703), draughtsman and engineer. The
'tricks in mechanics' mentioned by Walpole were shown, for the benefit
of his widow, at Winstanley's former house at Littlebury in Essex.
[17] Juvenal, *Sat.* xv. 9.

The wonders of Parvulun are in great repute all over Lombardy. We have very bad ways from hence to Pont Ossoria,° where are the ruins of a bridge that gives name to the town. The account they give of it is as follows:—St. Bona being desirous to pass over the river, met with a man who offered to carry her over; he took her up in his arms, and under pretence of doing her service, was going to ravish her; but she praying to the Virgin Mary for help, the wretch fell into the stream and was drowned, and immediately this bridge rose out of the water for her to go over. She was so touched with this signal deliverance, that she would not leave the place, but continued there till her death in exercises of devotion, and was buried in a little chapel at the foot of the bridge, with her story at length and this epitaph—*Hâc sita sunt fossâ Bonae Venerabilis ossa!*ᵖ

From Pont Ossoria we travelled by land to Nuovo Foroᑫ (the Novum Forum of Jockius), where are held the greatest races in all Italy. We were shown in the treasury of the Benedictines' Convent an ancient gold cup which cost an hundred guineas (a great sum in those days),[19] and given, as the friar told us that attended us, by a certain German Prince, he did not very well know who, but he believed his name was one King George.ʳ The inhabitants are wonderfully fond of horses, and to this day tell you most surprising stories of one Looby, a Boltognian. I saw a book dedicated to the head of that family, intituled *A Discourse on the Magnanimity of Bucephalus, and of the Duke of Boltogne's Horse Looby.*ˢ [22]

ᵒBone Bridge.[18]

ᵖEpitaph of Venerable Bede.
ᑫNewmarket.

ʳSee p. 78.[20]

ˢSee p. 30.[21]
Duke of Bolton.[23]

[18] Bournbridge, between Saffron Walden and Cambridge.
[19] A fling at George II's parsimony.
[20] 'I asked an abbot that was in the church, what was the name of this Gothic prince, who, after a little recollection, answered me, That he could not tell precisely, but that he thought it was one Julius Caesar.'
[21] 'When I was at Milan I saw a book newly published, that was dedicated to the present head of the Borromean family, and entitled *A discourse on the Humility of Jesus Christ, and of St. Charles Borromée.*'
[22] Looby, whose sire was Bay Bolton, won a royal plate at Newmarket. 'Last Monday was run the great Match at Newmarket, on which was depending upwards of 30,000 *l.* between the Duke of Bolton's Looby . . . against Mr. Panton's Conqueror, 4 miles for 300 Guineas a Side . . . which was won by Mr. Panton's Conqueror.' (*Daily Gazetteer*, Wed. 8 Oct. 1735—a few days before this letter was written.)
[23] Charles Paulet (1685–1754), third Duke of Bolton.

I staid here three days, and in my way to Pavia[t] stopped at the Palace of Delfini,[u] which is built on the top of a large barren mountain, and at a distance looks like the Ark resting on Mount Ararat. This mountain is called Gog, and opposite to one called Magog. They are very dangerous precipices, and occasioned the famous verse—

> *Incidit in Gogum qui vult vitare Magogon.*[v]

I need not repeat the history of Gog and Magog, it being known to every child, and to be found at large in most books of travels.

Pavia and its University are described by Mr. Addison, so I shall only mention a circumstance which I wonder escaped that learned gentleman. It is the name of the town, which is derived from the badneſs of the streets: *Pavia à non pavendo,* as *Lucus à non lucendo.*

Till next post, adieu!

Yours ever,
HORATIUS ITALICUS.

[t]Cambridge.
[u]Lord Godolphin's house on Gogmagog Hills.
[v]Incidit in Scyllam qui vult vitare Charibdim.

18. WEST TO GRAY

YOU use me very cruelly: You have sent me but one letter since I have been at Oxford, and that too agreeable not to make me sensible how great my loss is in not having more. Next to seeing you is the pleasure of seeing your handwriting; next to hearing you is the pleasure of hearing from you. Really and sincerely I wonder at you, that you thought it not worth while to answer my last letter. I hope this will have better success in behalf of your quondam school-fellow; in behalf of one who has walked hand in hand with you, like the two children in the wood,

> Through many a flowery path and shelly grot,
> Where learning lull'd us in her private maze.

The very thought, you see, tips my pen with poetry, and brings Eton to my view. Consider me very seriously here in a strange country, inhabited by things that call themselves Doctors and Masters of Arts; a country flowing with syllogisms and ale, where Horace and Virgil are equally unknown;

LETTER 18.—First printed in Mason's *Memoirs*, pp. 6–7.

consider me, I say, in this melancholy light, and then think if something be not due to

Yours.

Christ Church. Nov. 14. 1735.

P.S. I desire you will send me soon, and truly and positively, a history of your own time.¹

19. GRAY TO WEST

[c. 20 Dec. 1735]¹

²PERMIT me again to write to you, though I have so long neglected my duty, and forgive my brevity, when I tell you it is occasioned wholly by the hurry I am in to get to a place where I expect to meet with no other pleasure than the sight of you; for I am preparing for London in a few days at furthest. I do not wonder in the least at your frequent blaming my indolence, it ought rather to be called ingratitude, and I am obliged to your goodneſs for softening so harsh an appellation.² When you have seen one of my days, you have seen a whole year of my life; they go round and round like the blind horse in the mill, only he has the satisfaction of fancying he makes a progreſs, and gets some ground; my eyes are open enough to see the same dull prospect, and to know that having made four-and-twenty steps more, I shall be just where I was; I may, better than most people, say my life is but a span, were I not afraid lest you should not believe that a person so short-lived could write even so long a letter as this; in short, I believe I must not send you the history of my own time, till I can send you that also of the reformation.³ However, as the most undeserving people in the world must sure have the vanity to wish somebody

¹ An allusion to the *History of my own Time* (published in 1723–34) of West's maternal grandfather, Bishop Burnet.

LETTER 19.—First printed in Mason's *Memoirs*, pp. 7–8, in combination with part of another letter (Letter 22).

¹ Date conjectural; Gray speaks of 'preparing for London in a few days at farthest'. From the Peterhouse records it appears that he left Cambridge about 26 Dec. The letter was presumably written in the previous week.

²⁻² When this letter was reprinted in *Gray–Walpole Correspondence* (No. 21), the first eight lines were assumed to be a concoction of Mason's, and were omitted; but as the substance of the passage is probably Gray's it has now been restored.

³ Carrying on the allusion to the other history written by Mr. West's grandfather. *Mason.*—See postscript to Letter 18. Burnet's *History of the Reformation of the Church of England*, in 3 vols., was published 1679–1715.

had a regard for them, so I need not wonder at my own, in being pleased that you care about me. You need not doubt, therefore, of having a first row in the front box of my little heart, and I believe you are not in danger of being crouded there; it is asking you to an old play, indeed, but you will be candid enough to excuse the whole piece for the sake of a few tolerable lines.

20. GRAY TO WALPOLE

Jan: 3— [1736]¹ London

[   ]²

A THOUSAND thanks for the thousand happy New-years you sent me, & which, I suppose, a thousand good-natured people have made you a present of, in the overflowings of their zeal:

>—May each revolving year
>With blefsings crown'd, like this, returning smile
>On [   ],³ the happiest of his Kind—

I need not wish anything further, since (as I wish, what you do) to be sure you know my wishes already: Wise folks say the wise mans happinefs is in himself; pray, are you the wise man? they tell you too, that mortal happinefs is not of long continuance; heaven send, yours may last, till you wish for a little misery; nay! and longer still: I can't tell whither our situations are much changed, since this time twelvemonth; certain I am however, that there is a great alteration: I don't succeed to your diversions in town, I believe, & yet am absent from Cambridge without regret, nay with pleasure, tho' not infinitely happier here: —I have very little to tell you, as to the place, call'd London:— Adriano⁴ expired a few days ago, & his auncient Predecefsour Artaxerxes⁵ succeeds him for the present, wᶜʰ I think to visit to

LETTER 20.—First printed by Toynbee (1915), No. 23.
¹ The date of the year is determined by the references to the performances of *Adriano* and *Artaserse* (see nn. 4, 5), and of *Zara* (see n. 13).
² See Letter 1, n. 2.
³ The name (probably Celadon) has been cut out, carrying with it a word on the other side (see n. 15).
⁴ *Adriano* (adapted from Metastasio's *Adriano in Siria*, with music by Veracini) had been produced, as 'a new opera', at the King's Theatre in the Haymarket, on 29 Nov. 1735; it was performed several times in December, and was then withdrawn until the following February.
⁵ 'An opera call'd Artaxerses' (adapted from Metastasio's *Artaserse*, with music by R. Broschi and Hasse) was announced for performance at the

night: the [Town (in submiſsio]⁶n to your judgement) don't much admire Delane;⁷ Mʳˢ Porter⁸ acts in yᵉ Albion Queens,⁹ but I shall stay for another Play, before I see her; neither have I much inclination for old Cibber¹⁰ in Sʳ Courtly Nice,¹¹ nor for young Mʳˢ Cibber¹² in Voltaire's Zara,¹³ in wᶜʰ she performs the principal part for yᵉ first time of her appearance in that way: I went to King Arthur¹⁴ last night, which is exceeding fine; they have a new man to [suppl]¹⁵y Delane's place, one Johnson,¹⁶ with yᵉ finest person & face in the world to all appearance; but as awkward, as a Button-maker;¹⁷ in short, if he knew how to

King's Theatre in the Haymarket on the Saturday (10 Jan.) following the date of this letter.

⁶ Piece cut out; the missing words have been supplied in pencil by Walpole.

⁷ Dennis Delane (d. 1750), an Irish actor, who began his career in Dublin, and came to London in 1730.

⁸ Mary Porter (d. 1765) made her first appearance in 1699, and retired in 1743. After the retirement of Mrs. Oldfield (1730) she was the leading actress on the London stage. At this time (Jan. 1736) she was playing at Covent Garden.

⁹ By John Banks (fl. 1696); it was originally (1684) called *Island Queens*, but the name was changed to *Albion Queens* on its first production at Drury Lane in 1704. Mrs. Porter was playing the part of Queen Elizabeth.

¹⁰ Colley Cibber (1671–1757), actor, dramatist, and poet laureate (1730), the hero of the *Dunciad* on the deposition of Lewis Theobald (1688–1744), the original hero ('Tibbald'). He retired from the stage in 1733, but made several reappearances during the next twelve years. He played Sir Courtly Nice, one of his most famous parts, at Drury Lane on 29 Dec. 1735, and 2 Jan. 1736.

¹¹ *Sir Courtly Nice, or It cannot be*, comedy by John Crowne (d. c. 1703); it was first produced in 1685, and held the stage for upwards of a century.

¹² Susannah Maria Cibber (*née* Arne) (1714–66), singer and tragic actress; wife (1734) of Theophilus Cibber (son of Colley Cibber). She made her first appearance as an actress in the part of Zara at Drury Lane on 12 Jan. of this year, and was an immediate success.

¹³ Voltaire's *Zaïre*, the motive of which was borrowed from *Othello*, was produced in 1732; it was adapted for the English stage by Aaron Hill (see Letter 256, n. 6), and on its first appearance at Drury Lane had an uninterrupted run of fourteen nights.

¹⁴ *King Arthur, or the British Worthy*, by Dryden, music by Purcell, first produced in 1691. It had been revived by Giffard at Goodman's Fields on the previous 19 Dec., and ran for thirty-six nights.

¹⁵ Piece cut out; the missing word is supplied conjecturally from the fragments of writing which have escaped the scissors.

¹⁶ Originally an artist; he engaged himself to the managers of Drury Lane (Booth, Cibber, and Wilks), by whom, it was alleged, he was unfairly ousted from the best parts; he appears to have died c. 1742. He played the part of Arthur in *King Arthur* at Goodman's Fields.

¹⁷ This may be a glance at the actor Stevens (see Letter 3, n. 16).

manage his Beauties to advantage, I should not wonder, if all the Women run mad for him: the inchanted part of the play, is not Machinery, but actual magick: the second scene is a British temple enough to make one go back a thousand years, & really be in ancient Britain: the Songs are all Church-musick, & in every one of yᵉ Choruf's Mʳˢ Chambers[18] sung yᵉ chief part, accompanied with

Roarings, Squawlings & Squeakations dire[19]

Mʳˢ Giffard[20] is by way of Emmeline, & should be blind, but, heaven knows! I would not wish to see better than she does, & seems to do; for when Philidel[21] restores her to sight, her eyes are not at all better than before; she is led in at first, by a Creature, yᵗ was more like a Devil by half, than Grimbald[22] himself; she took herself for Madame la Confidente, but every body else took her to be in the Circumstances of Damnation: when Emmeline comes to her sight, she beholds this Mʳˢ Matilda[23] first, & cries out

Are Women all like thee? such glorious Creatures![24]

which set the people into such a laugh, as lasted the whole Act: the Frost Scene is excefsive fine; the first Scene of it is only a Cascade, that seems frozen; with the Genius of Winter asleep & wrapt in furs, who upon the approach of Cupid, after much quivering, & shaking sings the finest song in the Play: just after, the Scene opens, & shows a view of arched rocks coverd with Ice & Snow to yᵉ end of yᵉ Stage; between the arches are upon pedestals of Snow eight Images of old men & women, that seem frozen into Statues, with Icicles hanging about them & almost hid in frost, & from yᵉ end come Singers, viz: Mʳˢ Chambers, &c: & Dancers all rubbing their hands & chattering with cold with fur gowns & worsted gloves in abundance; there are several more beautiful Scenes; but rather than describe 'em, I ought to

[18] The same, no doubt, who subsequently made a hit as Polly Peachum in *The Beggar's Opera*, which she played to Lowe's Macheath.

[19] Milton, *Par. Lost*, ii. 628: 'Gorgons, and Hydras, and Chimæras dire.'

[20] Wife of the actor, who was manager of the theatre in Goodman's Fields. It was under his management that Garrick made his first appearance. Giffard played the part of Oswald, and his wife that of Emmeline, in *King Arthur*.

[21] An Airy Spirit.

[22] An Earthy Spirit—'the grossest, earthiest, ugliest fiend in hell'.

[23] Emmeline's attendant.

[24] Act iii, Sc. 2: '*Emmeline* (staring on *Matilda*). Are women such as thou? Such glorious creatures?'

beg pardon for interrupting your happine∫s so long, and conclude myself

your poor Servant ever

[   ]²⁵

21. GRAY TO WALPOLE

March: 11: [1736]¹—Cambridge:

My Dearest Horace

I WAS obliged by an unexpected accident to defer my journey
somewhat longer than Monday,² tho' it gave not at all the
more time for pleasure, if it had, I should have been at the
Masquerade with you: Ashton terrifies me with telling me, that
according to his latest Advices we are to remain in a State of
Separation from you the Lord knows how much longer; we are
inconsolable at the News, & weep our half Pint apiece every day
about it; if you don't make more haste, instead of us you may
chance to find a couple of Fountains by your fireside: if that
should be our fate I begg I may have the Honour of washing
your hands, & filling your Tea-kettle every morning, . . .³

Addressed: To The Honble Mr Horace Walpole near Whitehall⁴ Westminster
Postmark: SAFFRON WALDEN 12 MR

22. GRAY TO WEST

May: 8:—Cantabr: [1736]

My Dear West

MY letter enjoys itself, before its open'd, in imagining the
Confusion you'll be in, when you hear, that a Coach & six

²⁵ Signature cut off; the top of a 'd' is visible, so that Gray probably
signed himself Orozmades.

LETTER 21.—First printed by Toynbee (1915), No. 27.
¹ Gray had been away from Cambridge and had recently returned. The
Peterhouse records show that in 1735, 1737, and 1738 he was in residence
for the whole of March, but that in 1736 he was absent from c. 12 February
to c. 5 March. To this year the letter must be assigned.
² As Gray resumed residence in 1736 c. Friday, 5 March, this would be
1 March.   ³ The rest has been cut off.
⁴ That is, at the Treasury in Downing Street. Sir Robert Walpole had
removed from St. James's Square to the Treasury in Downing Street on
22 Sept. 1735. Among the publications announced in the *London Magazine*
for Oct. 1735 is 'Congratulatory verses to Sir *Robert Walpole* upon his
taking Possession as first Commissioner of the Treasury, of the new House
in St. *James*'s Park, in *September*, 1735'. (See Letter 1, n. 8.)
LETTER 22.—First printed in part (in a garbled text) in Mason, *Memoirs*,
pp. 7–10; first printed in full by Mitford in *Gray–Mason* (1853), pp. 1–4;
now reprinted from original.

is just stop'd at Christ-church Gates, & desires to speak with
you,[1] with a huddle of things in it, as different as ever met together in Noah's Ark; a fat one, and a lean one, and one, that
can say a little with his mouth, & a great deal with his pen;
& one that can neither speak, nor write; but you'll see 'em;
joy be with you; I hope too, I shall shortly see you; at least
in congratulatione Oxoniensi: my dear West, I more than ever
regret you;[2] it would be the greatest of pleasures to me, to
know wh[t] you do, wh[t] you read, how you spend your time,
&c: &c: & to tell you wh[t] I do not do, not read, & how I do not,
&c: &c: for almost all the employment of my hours may be best
explained by Negatives; take my word & experience upon it,
doing nothing is a most amusing businefs, & yet neither Something, nor nothing give me any pleasure; for this little while
last past, I have been playing with Statius; we yesterday had a
game at Quoits together, you'll easily forgive me for having
broke his head, as you have a little Pique to him

E LIB: 6to THEBAIDOS[3]

Then thus the King,[4] 'whoe'er the Quoit can wield,
And furthest send its weight athwart the field;
Let him stand forth his brawny arm to boast.'
Swift at the word, from out the gazing host
Young Pterelas with strength unequal drew
Labouring the Disc, & to small distance threw:
The Band around admire the mighty Mafs,
A slipp'ry weight, & form'd of polish'd Brafs;
The love of honour bad two Youths advance,
Achaians born, to try the glorious chance;

---

[1] An allusion to Walpole's approaching visit to Oxford, which took place
shortly after this date (see Walpole's letter to Geo. Montagu of 20 May 1736.
Walpole's companions may have been his tutor Whaley and his school-
fellow, Dodd. In his letter to Walpole after this visit West desires his 'Service
to Dod, and Mr Whaley'. (*Gray–Walpole Correspondence*, No. 32.)

[2] *Gratulatio Academiæ Oxoniensis, in Nuptias auspicatissimas illustrissimorum
Principum Frederici Principis Walliæ & Augustæ Principissæ de Saxo-Gotha.*
For West's contribution see Letter 23, n. 6.

[3] According to Mason (*Memoirs*, p. 8 n.), Gray's translation consisted
of 110 lines. Of these the translation of ll. 646–88 (making 59 lines in
English) was in this letter: the translation of the rest (ll. 704–24) making
27 lines must have been sent in another letter (see Letter 22**). The translation of ll. 689–703, making presumably 24 lines, is not extant.

[4] Adrastus (in margin in MS.).

A third arose, of Acarnania he,
Of Pisa one, & three from Ephyre;
Nor more for now Nesimachus's Son,[5]
By Acclamations roused, came towring on;
Another Orb upheaved his strong right hand,
Then thus, Ye Argive flower, ye warlike band,
Who trust your arms shall rase the Tyrian towers,
And batter Cadmus' Walls with stony Showers,
Receive a worthier load; yon puny Ball
Let Youngsters tofs:
He said, & scornful flung th' unheeded weight
Aloof; the champions trembling at the sight
Prevent disgrace, the palm despair'd resign;
All, but two youths, th' enormous Orb decline,
These conscious Shame withheld, & pride of noble line:
As bright & huge the spatious circle lay
With doubled light it beam'd against the Day;
So glittering shews the Thracian Godheads shield,
With such a gleam affrights Pangæa's field,
When blazing 'gainst the Sun it shines from far,
And clash'd rebellows with the Din of war:
   Phlegyas the long-expected play began,
Summon'd his strength, & call'd forth all the Man;
All eyes were bent on his experienced hand,
For oft in Pisa's sports his native land
Admired that arm, oft on Alpheus' Shore
The pond'rous brafs in exercise he bore;
Where flow'd the widest Stream he took his stand;
Sure flew the Disc from his unerring hand;
Nor stop'd till it had cut the further strand:
And now in Dust the polish'd Ball he roll'd,
Then grasp'd its weight, elusive of his hold;
Now fitting to his gripe, & nervous Arm
Suspends the crowd with expectation warm;
Nor tempts he yet the plain, but hurl'd upright
Emits the mafs, a prelude of his might;
Firmly he plants each knee, & o'er his head,
Collecting all his force, the circle sped;
It towers to cut the clouds; now thro' the Skies
Sings in its rapid way, & strengthens, as it flies;

[5] Hippomedon (in margin in MS.).

Anon with slack'ned rage comes quivering down,
Heavy & huge, & cleaves the solid ground.
  So from th'astonish'd Stars, her nightly train,
The Sun's pale sister, drawn by magic strain,
Deserts precipitant [her]⁶ darken'd Sphere;
In vain the Nations [wi]⁶th officious fear
Their cymbals tofs, & sounding brafs explore; ⎫
Th' Æmonian Hag enjoys her dreadful hour, ⎬
And smiles malignant on the labouring Power. ⎭

I wont plague you too much, & so break the affair in the middle, & give you leave to resume your Aristotle, instead of
Your friend & Servt
'I': Gray

Addressed: To Mr West of Christ Church Oxford   *Postmark:* CAMBRIDGE [date undecipherable]

22*.   West to Gray
[9 May 1736]

[Among the Walpole MSS. formerly in the Waller Collection was the cover of a letter addressed by West 'To Mr Thomas Gray at Peter-house College in Cambridge', bearing the postmark, 10 May, on the inside of which there was jotted down the following epigram of Martial (iii. 61), with the translation by West, which the latter sent to Ashton in July 1736 (see *Gray–Walpole Correspondence*, No. 38):

'Esse nihil dicis quicquid petis, Improbe Cinna,
  Si nil, Cinna petis, nil tibi, Cinna, nego.'

'Whenever Cinna asks a Favour,
  Oh! Tis but Nothing, S^r, he'll say;
Cinna, you are too Modest rather;
  Is't really Nothing? take it, Pray.'

It is possible that this cover belonged to a letter (no longer extant) in which West (who was then at Oxford) sent the epigram to Gray, and that the cover on which some one had copied the epigram was sent to Walpole.]

22**. GRAY TO WEST
[May,¹ 1736]

I SEND you my translation, which I did not engage in because I liked that part of the Poem, nor do I now send it to you

---

⁶ MS. torn.

LETTER 22**.—First printed in Mason's *Memoirs*, pp. 8–10, in a composite letter, dated by Mason 8 May 1736, containing also passages from Letters 19 and 22.   ¹ Before 24 May, the date of West's reply.

41

because I think it deserves it, but merely to show you how I mifspend my days.[2]

> Third in the labours of the Disc came on,
> With sturdy step and slow, Hippomedon;
> Artful and strong he pois'd the well-known weight, ⎫
> By Phlegyas warn'd, and fir'd by Mnestheus' fate, ⎬
> That to avoid, and this to emulate. ⎭
> His vigorous arm he try'd before he flung,
> Brac'd all his nerves, and every sinew strung;
> Then with a tempest's whirl and wary eye,
> Pursu'd his cast, and hurl'd the orb on high;
> The orb on high tenacious of its course,
> True to the mighty arm that gave it force,
> Far overleaps all bound, and joys to see
> Its antient lord secure of victory.
> The theatre's green height and woody wall
> Tremble ere it precipitates its fall,
> The ponderous mafs sinks in the cleaving ground,
> While vales and woods and echoing hills rebound.
> As when from Ætna's smoaking summit broke,
> The eyelefs Cyclops heav'd the craggy rock;
> Where Ocean frets beneath the dashing oar,
> And parting surges round the vefsel roar;
> 'Twas there he aim'd the meditated harm,
> And scarce Ulyfses scap'd his giant arm.
> A tyger's pride the victor bore away,
> With native spots and artful labour gay,
> A Shining border round the margin roll'd,
> And calm'd the terrors of his claws in gold.

23. WEST TO GRAY

I AGREE with you that you have broke Statius's head,[1] but it is in like manner as Apollo broke Hyacinth's,[2] you have foiled him infinitely at his own weapon; I must insist on seeing the rest of your translation, and then I will examine it entire, and compare it with the latin, and be very wise and severe, and put on an inflexible face, such as becomes the character of a true

---

[2] This preliminary paragraph was probably a concoction of Mason's.
LETTER 23.—First printed in Mason's *Memoirs*, pp. 10–11.
[1] See Letter 22.
[2] Ovid, *Metam.* x. 174 ff.

son of Aristarchus, of hyper-critical memory. In the mean
while, And calm'd the terrors of his claws in gold,

is exactly Statius—Summos[3] auro mansueverat ungues. I never
knew before that the golden fangs on hammer-cloths were so old
a fashion. Your Hymenêal[4] I was told was the best in the Cambridge Collection[5] before I saw it, and indeed, it is no great
compliment to tell you I thought it so when I had seen it, but
sincerely it pleased me best. Methinks the college bards have
run into a strange taste on this occasion. Such soft unmeaning
stuff about Venus and Cupid, and Peleus and Thetis, and
Zephyrs and Dryads, was never read. As for my poor little
Eclogue, it has been condemned and beheaded by our Westminster judges; an exordium of about sixteen lines absolutely
cut off, and its other limbs quartered in a most barbarous manner. I will send it you in my next as my true and lawful heir,
in exclusion of the pretender,[6] who has the impudence to appear
under my name.

As yet I have not looked into Sir Isaac. Public disputations
I hate; mathematics I reverence; history, morality, and natural
philosophy have the greatest charms in my eye; but who can
forget poetry? they call it idlenefs, but it is surely the most enchanting thing in the world, 'ac dulce otium & pœne omni
negotio pulchrius.'

I am, dear Sir, yours while I am

R. W.

Christ Church, May 24, 1736.

[3] In Statius, *Theb.* vi. 724: 'extremos auro mansueverat ungues.'

[4] On the approaching marriage of Frederick Louis, Prince of Wales, with
the Princess Augusta of Saxe-Gotha, which was solemnized at St. James's
on the evening of Tuesday, 27 April (*Lond. Mag.*, 1736, p. 218). The poem,
in Latin hexameters, is reprinted by Mitford in *Works of Gray* (1835–43), i.
173 ff.

[5] *Gratulatio Academiæ Cantabrigiensis Auspicatissimas Frederici Walliæ Principis
& Augustæ Principissæ Saxo-Gothæ Nuptias Celebrantis.* Cantabrigiæ, Typis
Academicis, 1736. fol. Walpole, Ashton, Dodd, and Lyne, among Gray's
Eton contemporaries, also contributed Latin poems to this collection.
Thomas Wharton, Gray's future correspondent (see Letter 79, n. 8), contri-
buted a poem in Greek hexameters; and Piazza, Gray's Italian teacher (see
Letter 29, n. 4), contributed an Italian poem.

[6] West's poem, in Latin hexameters, was entitled '*Merlinus*; Ecloga'; as
printed in the Oxford *Gratulatio* (see Letter 22, n. 2) it consisted of 46 lines,
signed 'Ricardus West, ex Aede Christi Commensalis'.

24. GRAY TO WALPOLE

D^r S^r   June, 11 [1736][1]—London

IT was hardly worth while to trouble you with a letter, till
I had seen somewhat in Town; not that I have seen anything
now, but what you have heard of before, that is, Atalanta;[2]
there are only four Men, & two women in it;[3] the first is a common Scene of a wood, & does not change at all, till the end of
the last Act, when there appears the temple of Hymen, with
illuminations; there is a row of blue fires burning in order
along the ascent to the temple; a fountain of fire spouts up out
of the ground to the ceiling, & two more crofs each other
obliquely from the sides of the stage; on the top is a wheel, that
whirls always about, & throws out a shower of gold-colour,
silver, & blue fiery rain: Conti[4] I like excefsively in every thing,
but his mouth; which is thus,   ;[5] but this is hardly minded,
when Strada[6] stands by him: Opera's & Plays, and all things
else at present are beat off the Stage, & are forced to yield to
Spring-garden,[7] where last night were above fifteen-hundred

LETTER 24.—First printed by Toynbee (1915), No. 35.
[1] The date of the year is determined by the references to the opera of
Atalanta (see n. 2).
[2] Italian opera by Handel, which was given for the first time on the
occasion of a state visit of the Court to the Opera on 12 May 1736, in honour
of the marriage of Frederick, Prince of Wales, with the Princess Augusta of
Saxe-Gotha. (See Burney, *History of Music*, iv. 395–6.) *Atalanta* was performed for the last time on 9 June, the close of the season, when the Queen
was present. It was perhaps this performance that Gray attended.
[3] 'The singers in this opera were Signor Conti, Signora Strada, Signora
Maria Negri, with Messrs. Beard, Waltz, and Reinhold' (Burney, *loc. cit.*).
[4] Gioacchino Conti (1714–61), called Gizziello, famous soprano, one of
the leading singers of his day. He made his first appearance in London in
Handel's *Ariodante* on 5 May of this year (1736), and took the principal man's
part in *Atalanta*.
[5] Here in the original letter is a sketch of a square cavernous mouth, in
outline like a knuckle-bone. The ugliness of Conti's mouth seems to have
made a strong impression upon Gray. See his letter to John Chute (then
in Florence) six years later, July, 1742 (Letter 112).
[6] Anna Strada del Pô, soprano singer, brought from Italy by Handel in
1729 for the opera in the Haymarket. She remained a member of Handel's
company till she left England in 1738.
[7] Better known by its later name of Vauxhall Gardens. It was established
c. 1661. Early in the eighteenth century the Gardens went out of fashion,
till their popularity was revived under the management of Jonathan Tyers,
who reopened them with a grand entertainment on 7 June 1732, at which
the Prince of Wales was present.

people; I won't say more of it, till I have seen it myself; but as the beauty of the place, when lighted up, and a little musick are the only diversions of it, I don't suppose, it will be an[y]⁸ long time in vogue: I beg your excuse; that I have not yet [execu]⁸ted my commiſsion at Chenevix,⁹ but sometime the next week, I will take care to do my duty; I have also a commiſsion for your Man, (with your leave) that is, to call at Crow's¹⁰ for me, & bid him send me Atalanta¹¹ with all the speed he poſsibly can, which I must owe him for, till I come down again, wᶜʰ won't (I believe) be a vast while: pray, bid Ashton write, & I hope you'll write yourself; Adieu!

Yours ever,
OROZMADES

Addressed: To The Honʳᵃᵇˡᵉ Mʳ Horace Walpole at Kings-College Cambridge
   Postmark: 12 IV

25. GRAY TO WALPOLE

[July 15, 1736]¹

Dear Sʳ

I SYMPATHIZE with you in the Sufferings, which you foresee are coming upon you; we are both at present, I imagine, in no very agreeable situation; for my own part I am under the misfortune of having nothing to do, but it is a misfortune, which, thank my Stars, I can pretty well bear; You are in a Confusion

---

⁸ MS. torn.

⁹ Presumably the shop of Mrs. Chenevix, the toy-woman (see Letter 116, n. 16).

¹⁰ Among the subscribers to the score of *Atalanta* (see n. 11) appears 'Mʳ Crow Sen.ʳ of Cambridge (7 books)'. He was a Cambridge bookseller, payments to whom for binding books are entered in the Pembroke College Library accounts between 1735 and 1741.

¹¹ In the *Gentleman's Magazine* for 1736, among the books published in June, figures 'The Opera of *Atalanta* in score. Composed in Honour of the Happy Nuptials of their Royal Highnesses the Prince & Princess of *Wales*. By Mr. *Handel*'. Burney says (*loc. cit.*): 'Proposals for printing the opera of *Atalanta* in score, by subscription, were published immediately after its first performance; and early in June it was ready to deliver to the subscribers.'

LETTER 25.—First printed in part (in a garbled text) by Mason in *Memoirs*, pp. 25–6; first printed in full by Toynbee (1915), No. 37.

¹ The date is fixed by the reference to the explosion in Westminster Hall (see n. 3), which also points to the letter having been written from London. Gray does not appear to have gone to Burnham till August (see Letter 26).

45

of Wine & Bawdy & Hunting & Tobacco;[2] & heaven be praised, you too can pretty well bear it; while our evils are no more, I believe we sha'nt much repine; I imagine however you'll rather chuse to converse with the living Dead, that adorn the Walls of your Apartments, than with the Dead living, that deck the middles of them, & prefer a picture of Still-life to the realities of a noisy one; &, as I guefs, will learn to imitate them, and for an hour or two at noon, will stick yourself up as formal, as if you had been fixed in your Frame for these hundred years with an upright Pink in one hand, & a great Seal-ring in the other: I know nothing, but that the Judges were all blown up yesterday in Westminster-hall by some unlucky boy, that had affixed a parcel of Squibs & Crackers to several Acts of parliament, whose ruins were scatter'd about the hall with a great noise & displosion;[3] it set the Ld Chancellour[4] a laughing, & frighted every body else out of their senses, and Ld Hardwick[5] order'd the grand Jury to represent it as a libel; yes! I know besides, that I shall be always yours, . . .[6]

26. GRAY TO WALPOLE

[Burnham, Aug. 1736][1]

[   ][2]

I was hinder'd in my last, & so could not give you all the trouble I would have done; the Description of a road, which

---

[2] Walpole was at this time with Sir Robert at Houghton.

[3] 'Wednesday, July 14. A large Paper Parcel was discovered under the Seat of the Counsellors in the Court of Chancery, *Westminster-hall*, then sitting, which being kicked down the Steps, it blew up, and put all present in the utmost Confusion.' The author of the outrage proved to be one Robert Nixon, 'a Nonjuring Clergyman'; he was tried before Lord Hardwicke on 7 Dec. following, and was found guilty (*Gent. Mag.* 1736, p. 746; 1737, p. 121).

[4] Charles Talbot (1685–1737); Solicitor-General, 1726–33; Lord Chancellor (as Baron Talbot of Hensol), 1733–7.

[5] Philip Yorke (1690–1764); Solicitor-General, 1720–4; Attorney-General, 1724–33; created (1733) Baron Hardwicke, and (1754) Earl of Hardwicke; Chief Justice of the King's Bench, 1733–7; Lord Chancellor, 1737–56; High Steward of the University of Cambridge, 1749–64.

[6] Signature torn off (see Letter 1, n. 2).

LETTER 26.—First printed in part (in a garbled text) by Mason in *Memoirs*, pp. 23–5; first printed in full by Toynbee (1915), No. 39.

[1] Mason dates this letter September, 1737; but so far as the month is concerned this is proved to be incorrect by the postmark. The year was almost certainly 1736, since Walpole writes to West on 17 Aug. of that year, no

your Coach-wheels have so often honour'd, it would be need-
lefs to give you; suffice it, that I arrived at Birnam-wood without
the lofs of any of my fine Jewels, & that no little Cacaturient
Gentlewoman made me any reverences by the way; I live with
my Uncle,[3] a great hunter in imagination; his Dogs take up
every chair in the house, so I'm forced to stand at this present
writing, & tho' the Gout forbids him galloping after 'em in the
field, yet he continues still to regale his Ears & Nose with their
comfortable Noise and Stink; he holds me mighty cheap I perceive for walking, when I should ride, & reading, when I should
hunt: my comfort amidst all this is, that I have at the distance
of half a mile thro' a green Lane, a Forest (the vulgar call it a
Common[4]) all my own; at lcast as good as so, for I spy no
human thing in it but myself; it is a little Chaos of Mountains
& Precipices; Mountains it is true, that don't ascend much
above the Clouds, nor are the Declivities quite so amazing, as
Dover-Clitf;[5] but just such hills as people, who love their Necks
as well as I do, may venture to climb, & Crags, that give the
eye as much pleasure, as if they were more dangerous: both Vale
& Hill is cover'd over with most venerable Beeches,[6] & other
very reverend Vegetables, that like most ancient People, are
always dreaming out their old Stories to the Winds

> And, as they bow their hoary Tops, relate
> In murm'ring Sounds the dark Decrees of Fate;
> While Visions, as Poetic eyes avow,
> Cling to each Leaf, & swarm on ev'ry Bough:[7]

doubt shortly after the receipt of this letter, 'Gray is at Burnham' (see
Letter 41 in *Gray–Walpole Correspondence*).
   [2] A piece containing the initial address has been cut out (see Letter 1, n. 2).
   [3] Jonathan Rogers, who had married Gray's aunt, Ann Antrobus. Cole,
writing in 1775, at which time he was Vicar of Burnham, says: 'Mr. Rogers,
his uncle, was an attorney, lived at Britwell, in Burnham Parish, and lies
buried in my church. . . . He lived at an house called Cant's Hall, a small
house, and not far from the common. . . . I think Cant's Hall is in Britwell
division.' (MS. notes, quoted by Mitford in *Works of Gray*, 1836, vol. i, p. cv.)
The lease of this house was left to Ann Rogers by her brother, Robert
Antrobus (d. 1730), in whose will the property is described as 'Goldwins
House and grounds at Cantshill near Burnham' (see *Peterhouse Admission
Book*, p. 200).
   [4] East Burnham Common adjoins the 'Forest', now known as Burnham
Beeches.   [5] *King Lear*, iv. 6 (cf. Letter 31, n. 4).
   [6] 'There are some of the largest beeches I ever saw. The lane to the
common is very romantic, and the scene remarkably diversified for that
county' (Cole MS. notes, *loc. cit.*).
   [7] These lines have not been traced; presumably they are Gray's own.

At the foot of one of these squats me I;[8] il Penseroso, and there grow to the Trunk for a whole morning,

> —the tim'rous Hare, & sportive Squirrel
> Gambol around me—[9]

like Adam in Paradise, but commonly without an Eve, & besides I think he did not use to read Virgil, as I usually do there: in this situation I often converse with my Horace aloud too, that is, talk to you; for I don't remember, that I ever heard you answer me; I beg pardon for taking all the conversation to myself; but it is your own fault indeed. We have old M[r] Southern[10] at a Gentlemans house a little way off, who often comes to see us; he is now 77 year[11] old, & has almost wholly lost his Memory, but is as agreeable, as an old Man can be; at least I persuade myself so, when I look upon him, & think of Isabella[12] & Oroonoko.[13] I shall be in Town in about 3 weeks, I believe; if you direct your letters to London, they will take care to send 'em safe; but I must desire, you would fold 'em with a little more art, for your last had been open'd without breaking the Seal, Adieu,

D[r]   ,[14] yours ever

T: GRAY

They were perhaps suggested by a passage (partly inspired by *Aen.* vi. 283–4) in a Latin poem of West's, written not long before, under the title 'Foliisque Notas et Nomina mandat' (*Gray–Walpole Correspondence*, vol. ii, p. 301):

> 'Nusquam adeo sine Vate suo Nemus: undique sese
> Induere in Versus, et doctum attollere Truncum
> Arbor amat, passimque inolescunt Frondibus ipsis
> Carmina Pastorum, Foliisque sub omnibus haerent.'

Cf. the last stanza of Gray's alcaic ode prefixed to his letter to West from Rome of May, 1740 (Letter 87).

[8] Cradock, quoted by Mitford (*Gray–Mason Correspondence*, p. 486), refers to this as one of the 'affected vulgarisms' in the Letters of Gray.

[9] Perhaps a reminiscence of *Par. Lost*, iv. 340–5.

[10] Thomas Southerne (1660–1746), the dramatist.

[11] Southerne lived to be 86.—Mr. Gray always thought highly of his pathetic powers, at the same time that he blamed his ill taste for mixing them so injudiciously with farce, in order to produce that monstrous species of composition called Tragi-comedy. *Mason.*

[12] The heroine of Southerne's *The Fatal Marriage, or the Innocent Adultery* (1694).

[13] Southerne's *Oroonoko, or the Royal Slave* (1696).

[14] A word here has been scored through, and is undecipherable.

P:S: Regreet Almanzor [15] from me,
Wish Pol: Cutcher [16] joy from me,
Give Cole [17] an humble service from me. [18]

Addressed: To The Hon[ble] M[r] Horace Walpole At Kings-College Cambridge
   Postmark: WINDSOR AV [19]

27. GRAY TO WALPOLE

[Burnham, Sept. 26, 1736][1]

[   ][2]

IT rains, 'tis Sunday, this is the country; three circumstances
so dull in conjunction with the dulnefs of my nature are like
to give birth to an admirable production; I hope you will
receive it, as you would a Michaelmas Goose from a Tenant;
since I send it, not that I believe you have a taste for an awkward fat creature, but because I have no better way of showing
my good-will: your name, I afsure you, has been propagated
in these countries by a Convert of yours, one Cambridge;[3] he

[15] See Letter 2, n. 8.
[16] This individual has not been identified.
[17] William Cole (1714–82), the Cambridge antiquary; he was at Eton
(1726–32) with Gray and Walpole, with the latter of whom he contracted a
friendship which lasted till his death. In Jan. 1733 he was admitted as a
Sizar at Clare Hall; Scholar, 1735; migrated to King's, 1735; B.A., 1737;
M.A., 1740; ordained Deacon, 1744; Priest, 1745; Rector of Hornsey,
1749–51; of Bletchley, 1753–67; Vicar (non-resident) of Burnham, Bucks,
1774–82. After leaving Bletchley he resided at Waterbeach, near Cambridge,
till 1770, when he removed to Milton. He was for twenty years (1762–82)
a regular correspondent of Walpole's, nearly 200 of whose letters to him have
been preserved. He made extensive MS. collections amounting to about
100 folio volumes, which he bequeathed to the British Museum. Included
with these were his *Athenae Cantabrigienses*, which contain biographical details,
not always to be relied upon, of many of his contemporaries, Gray among
them. Cole may perhaps be identified with the individual who was nick-
named 'Plato' by his Etonian friends (see Letter 6, n. 7).
[18] The postscript has been crossed through.
[19] The impression of the date mark is imperfect; the numeral is undecipherable.
   LETTER 27.—First printed in part (in a garbled text) by Mason in
Memoirs, pp. 25–6; first printed in full by Toynbee (1915), No. 43.
   [1] The date of the month is supplied by the postmark; for the date of the
year see Letter 26, n. 1.
   [2] See Letter 1, n. 2.
   [3] This name has been scored through, but is plainly legible. Mason
represents the name by two asterisks. The person in question is Richard
Owen Cambridge (1717–1802), whom Walpole refers to in a letter to Mason
of 10 July 1775, as 'the proprietor of the asterisk', in allusion to Mason's

has brought over his whole family to you; they were before
pretty good Whigs, but now they are absolute Walpolians: we
have hardly any body in the Parish, but knows exactly the
Dimensions of the hall & Saloon at Houghton, & begins to
believe, that the Lanthorn[4] is not quite so great a Consumer of
the fat of the land, as disaffected persons have said: for your
reputation we keep to ourselves that, of your not Hunting, nor
drinking Hogan;[5] e'er a one of which would be sufficient
here to lay your honour in the Dust: I received a little Billet
from my dear Horace, as if he had not heard from me: whereas
I wrote last Sunday; we have not so good an opportunity
here, as I could wish, not lying conveniently for the Post; but
to[morow sennight][6] I hope to be in town, & not long after at
Cambridge.

yours most faithfully
T: G:

P:S: my love to Ashton

Addressed: To The Honᵇˡᵉ Horatio Walpole, Esq of Kings College Cambridge
     Postmark: 27 SE

suppression of his name here and elsewhere. Cambridge, who was a contemporary of Gray and Walpole at Eton, whence he went in 1734 (as a Gentle-
man-commoner) to St. John's College, Oxford, is best known as the author
of the *Scribleriad* (1751), and other poetical pieces, and as a contributor to the
World. Walpole, in whose correspondence his name occurs frequently, in his
letter to Bentley of 5 July 1755 calls him 'Cambridge, the everything'.
    4 A favourite object of Tory satire at the time. *Mason.*—In *Aedes Wal-
polianæ*, in his account of the Hall at Houghton, Walpole says: 'From the
cieling hangs a lantern for eighteen candles, of copper gilt' (*Works of Lord
Orford*, vol. ii, p. 263). Writing to Mann on 25 July 1750, he says: 'My Lord
Chesterfield has bought the Houghton lantern, the famous lantern, that
produced so much Patriot wit; and very likely some of his Lordship's's'; and
in a note he adds: 'In one pamphlet, the noise on this lantern was so
exaggerated, that the author said, on a journey to Houghton, he was carried
first into a glass-room, which he supposed was a porter's lodge, but proved
to be the lantern.'
    5 Otherwise 'hogan-mogan', a strong drink; cf. Dryden, *Wild Gallant*,
i. 2: 'I was damnably drunk with ale, great hogan-mogan ale.' The praises
of 'the *Hogen of Houghton*' are sung in a contemporary ballad entitled
Prosperity to Houghton. The ballad was by Philip Floyd, as Walpole noted on
his copy of the broadsheet (see facsimile in *A Selection of the Letters of Horace
Walpole*, edited by W. S. Lewis, vol. i, p. 127).
    6 Piece cut out (see n. 2); the missing words have been supplied in pencil
by Walpole.

28. GRAY TO WALPOLE
[London, c. Oct. 3, 1736][1]

[   ][2]

THE best News from Cornhill-shire[3] is, that I have a little fever, which denies me the pleasure of seeing either You, or Alexander,[4] or Downing-Street to day, but when that leaves me at my own Disposal, I shall be at yours; Covent-Garden has given me a Sort of Surfeit of M[r] Rich[5] & his Cleverneſs, for I was at the Way of the World, when the Machine broke t'other Night;[6] the House was in Amaze for above a Minute, & I dare say a great many in the Galleries thought it very dextrously perform'd, & that they scream'd as naturally, as heart could wish; till they found it was no jest by their calling for Surgeons; of whom several luckily happen'd to be in the Pit: I stayed to see the poor creatures brought out of the House, & pity poor M[rs]

LETTER 28.—First printed by Toynbee (1915), No. 45.
[1] The date is fixed approximately by the reference to the accident at Covent Garden (see n. 6).
[2] See Letter 1, n. 2.
[3] Gray's father owned a house in Cornhill, where Gray was born, and where his mother and aunt (Mary Antrobus) 'carried on a trade separate from that of Mrs. Gray's husband. . . . They kept a kind of India warehouse on Cornhill under the joint names of Gray and Antrobus' (Mason, *Memoirs*, p. 120). Walpole, on the other hand (who calls Gray's mother Mary Antrobus), and Cole, state that they carried on business in Cornhill as milliners. For the situation of the house see Letter 145, nn. 3, 6.
[4] Delane was playing Alexander, in Lee's *Rival Queens*, at Covent Garden in October of this year (Genest, iii. 503).
[5] See Letter 42, n. 13.
[6] After the performance of Congreve's *Way of the World* at Covent Garden on 1 Oct., there was given 'an Entertainment of Dancing in Grotesque Characters, call'd *The Necromancer, or Harlequin Doctor Faustus*' in which Rich played Harlequin (advt. in *London Daily Post*, 30 Sept. 1736). It was during the latter that the accident witnessed by Gray took place. 'Friday, Oct. 1. This Night, in the Entertainment of Dr. Faustus, at the Theatre-Royal in Covent-Garden, when the Machine, wherein were Harlequin, the Miller's Wife, the Miller, and his Man, was got to the full Extent of its Flying, one of the Wires which held the hind Part of the Car broke first, and then the other broke, and the Machine, and all the People in it, fell down upon the Stage; by which unhappy Accident the young Woman who personated the Miller's Wife had her Thigh broke & her Knee-Pan shatter'd; the Harlequin had his Head bruised and his Wrist strained; the Miller broke his Arm; and the Miller's Man had his Skull so fractured that he is since dead. The Audience was thrown into the greatest Surprize; and nothing was heard but Shrieks and Cries of the utmost Agony, and Horror' (*Lond. Mag.*, 1736, p. 579).

Buchanan⁷ not a little, whom I saw put into a Chair in such a fright, that as she is big with child, I question whether it may not kill her,

I am

Yours ever

T: G:

Addressed: To The Honble Mr Horace Walpole at Chelsea *Postmark:* Penny⁸ Post Paid (date illegible)

29. GRAY TO BIRKETT¹

[London, Oct. 8, 1736]²

S^r

As I shall stay only a fortnight longer in Town, I'll beg you to give yourself the trouble of writing out my Bills, & sending 'em, that I may put myself out of your Debt,³ as soon as I come down: if Piazza⁴ should come to You, you'll be so

---

⁷ The actress, Mrs. Elizabeth Buchanan, whose first appearance was as Calphurnia in *Julius Caesar* at Lincoln's-Inn-Fields on 20 Nov. 1728. In the *Way of the World* her part was Mrs. Fainall. Gray's fears for her life proved founded, for she died in childbed not long after this date. (Genest, iii. 238, 481.)

⁸ So apparently, but the impression is blurred.

LETTER 29.—First printed by Gosse in *Works of Gray*, vol. ii, pp. 3–4; now reprinted from original.

¹ George Birkett (1690–1745), of Peterhouse, Scholar, 1711; B.A., 1711; M.A., 1714; Fellow, 1714–41; Moderator, 1718; Tutor, 1719; Proctor, 1726–7; D.D., 1730; Minister of Little St. Mary's, Cambridge, 1729–40; Rector of Stathern, Leicestershire, 1740–5. He was Gray's Tutor in College.

² The date of the month is supplied by the postmark; the year was probably 1736. Gray says he is staying in London 'only a fortnight longer'; and the Peterhouse records show that he returned to Cambridge about 22 Oct. in that year. In the next letter Birkett writes: 'your Bills have been ready more than 3 Months agoe', and this also fits 1736, as in that year Gray left Cambridge early in June, and had been absent for more than three months.

³ Birkett, as his Tutor, would collect from him the sums due for College charges.

⁴ Hieronimo Bartolommeo Piazza, an apostate Italian priest, who abandoned the Dominican Order, came to England about the year 1720, joined the Anglican communion, and married. In 1722 he published in London a book on the Inquisition, in English and French on opposite pages, with the following title, which throws light on his previous career: '*A Short and True Account of the Inquisition and its Proceeding, As it is practised in Italy, Set forth in some Particular Cases. Whereunto is added, An Extract out of an Authentick Book of Legends of the Roman Church. By* Hierom Bartholomew

S[r]

      As I shall stay only a fortnight longer in Town, I'll beg you to give yourself the trouble of writing out my Bills, & sending 'em, that I may put myself out of your Debt, as soon as I come down: if Piazza should come to You, you'll be so good as to satisfie him; I protest, I forget what I owe him, but he is honest enough to tell you right: my Father & Mother desire me to send their compliments, & I beg you'd believe me S[r]

                your most obed[t] humble Serv[t]

                T: Gray

Facsimile of Letter 29

good as to satisfie him; I protest, I forget what I owe him, but he is honest enough to tell you right: my Father & Mother desire me to send their compliments, & I beg you'd believe me

S^r

your most obed^t humble Servt

T: Gray.

Addressed: To The Revrd Mr George Birkett, Fellow of St Peter's College Cambridge   *Postmark:* 8 oc

30. BIRKETT TO GRAY

[Oct. 1736][1]

S^r

As you stay only a fortnight in Town, I may let you know your Bills have been ready more than 3 Months agoe

Piazza, *an Italian born; formerly a Lector of Philosophy and Divinity, and one of the Delegate Judges of that Court, and now by the Grace of God, a Convert to the Church of* England' (London: Printed by William Bowyer, 1722).

He appears to have settled in Cambridge, where he found employment as a teacher of Italian; and is said to have died there about the year 1745. Walpole, as he records in his *Short Notes of my Life*, learnt Italian of him at Cambridge; as did William Cole. Ashton, writing to West from King's on 4 March 1736, refers to him as 'Walpole's Italian' (see *Gray–Walpole Correspondence*, No. 26). Piazza contributed an Italian poem to the Cambridge *Gratulatio* on the occasion of the marriage of the Prince of Wales in 1736. He there describes himself as 'Assistente Italiano del Regio Professore delle Lingue Moderne'. This was an appointment which was in the personal gift of the Regius Professor, by whom the assistant was paid, and did not imply any official connexion with the University.

It was doubtless under Piazza that Gray was learning Italian 'like any dragon', as he wrote to West in March 1737 (see Letter 37). He subsequently continued his study of Italian at Florence under the Abate Bonducci (see Walpole to Mann, 8 July 1784, n. 2).

LETTER 30.—Draft of letter, with many corrections, now first printed from the original in the Library of Pembroke College, Cambridge. An earlier draft, on the same sheet, runs: 'S^r   As you shall stay only a fortnigh [*sic*] in Town your Bills shall be with you as inclosed. W^t you ow Piazzo I hope may be easily discharged. What I wish you is without Tyrants in y^e... or Rebulicans [*sic*] your

But pretty Mr Gray [*altered from* Day]

I miss spled [*sic*] ...

I w^d doe any service for yr your Uncle Antrobus tho'.'

The words represented by ... are illegible. The last line as far as 'Uncle' has been scored through. The state of the MS. suggests that the writer was fuddled at the time.

[1] The date is determined by that of Gray's letter to which this is the reply.

which Bills I hope you will receive by this. What your indebted[2] to yᵉ Italian Master I do not certainly know. I have
paid a Guinea to Senior Piatzzo, & wtever els upon account is
due shall at proper time be discharged by

your very friend
G B

31. GRAY TO WALPOLE

[London, Oct. 12, 1736][1]

[   ][2]

I BROUGHT my neck safe to town, & I promise you, when I
break it, it shall not be after the Dogs, nor from so mean an
elevation as the Saddle,[3] no, let me fall from Dover-Cliff,[4] or
Leucate's promontory,[5] & if I cannot die like a Hero, let it be
at least like a despairing lover; Mem: I wo'nt swing in a Cam-
brick handkerchief,[6] nor swallow Verdigrease. but however
I that have preserved my neck in the country, have not been
able to do as much by my throat in London; which I made so
sore, coming from Othello, on Wednesday last,[7] that I should
not be easily persuaded even at this present to swallow a bum-
per, tho' it were crown'd with my dear Horace's health; it has
not as yet turn'd to an absolute squinancie,[8] or a fever; but if you
have a mind, I can very easily improve it into either of 'em:
you have imitated your Namesake very happily, I believe; for
I have not the Latin to look at; I wish poor Mʳ Iccius in Ireland

----

[2] Corrected from 'indebtebted'.
LETTER 31.—First printed by Toynbee (1915), No. 44.
[1] The date of the month is supplied by the postmark; that of the year is
determined by Gray's reference to his recent visit to Burnham (see n. 3).
[2] See Letter 1, n. 2.
[3] An allusion to the tastes of his uncle at Burnham, where he had just
been staying (see Letter 26).
[4] 'The dread summit of this chalky bourn,' from which Gloucester flung
himself (as he supposed) (*King Lear*, iv. 6).
[5] 'Leucatae nimbosa cacumina montis' (*Aen.* iii. 274), the modern Cape
Dukato, promontory at the south extremity of the island of Santa Maura
(Leucas), from which unhappy lovers were said to leap into the sea.
[6] Perhaps an allusion to the recent suicide of the Count de Hoyms,
'formerly Prime Minister of State to the late King of Poland, who having
been disgrac'd & confin'd two years in the fortress of Konigstein, hang'd
himself on the 21st of April, at night, with a handkerchief, fasten'd to a hook
in the wall' (*Gent. Mag.*, May 1736, p. 292).
[7] That is, on 6 Oct.; *Othello* had been revived at Drury Lane on the previous night (Genest, iii. 490).   [8] Quinsy.

had taken the poets good advice:[9] pray add my admiration of the first Stanza's to good Mʳ Ashton's, & give him my service for his, & believe me,　　　　　yours ever,

T: GRAY

Addressed: To The Honᵇˡᵉ Mʳ Horace Walpole, of King's College Cambridge
　　Postmark: 13 OC

32. GRAY TO WALPOLE

[　　　　　　　　]¹

HERE am I, a little happy to think, I sha'nt take Degree's; and really, now I know there is no occasion, I don't know but I may read a little Philosophy; it is sufficient to make a thing agreeable, not to have much need of it: such is my humour, but let that paſs: West sup'd with me the night before I came out of town; we both fancied at first, we had a great many things to say to one another; but when it came to the push, I found, I had forgot all I intended to say, & he stood upon Punctilio's and would not speak first, & so we parted: Cole² has been examined by the Proctors, & took Bachelour's degree's, in order (he says) when he is Master of Arts, to aſsist a friend with his Vote & Interest; he told me he would not be puzzled in Philosophy, because he would not expose himself, but desired to be examined in Claſsicks, which he understood: he still talks of having his Leg cut off, & then being married: I have not seen Ashton; he is at Sᵗ Ive's, & I don't know when he comes back; Berkly³ makes a Speech the 5ᵗʰ of November;　　I am,

Dʳ, Dear Horace
　　　　　Yours most truly,
　　　　　　　　　T: G:

[Cambridge] Oct: 27: [1736]⁴
　　when d'ye come

Addressed: To The Honᵇˡᵉ Horatio Walpole, Esq, at the Treasury London
　　Postmark: CAMBRIDGE 29 OC

⁹ Presumably Walpole's imitation of Horace was of 1 *Epist.* xii, which is addressed to Iccius (as is 1 *Odes* xxix). Iccius was managing a friend's estate in Sicily, and Horace encourages him (as a philosopher) to be content with his lot.

LETTER 32.—First printed by Toynbee (1915), No. 46.
¹ See Letter 1, n. 2.
² Cole (see Letter 26, n. 17) took his B.A. degree in October 1736.
³ Samuel Berkley was an Eton contemporary, now at King's, of which he was subsequently Fellow; B.A., 1737; M.A., 1741.
⁴ The date of the year is determined by the reference to Cole (see n. 2).

33. GRAY TO WEST

YOU must know that I do not take degrees, and, after this term, shall have nothing more of college impertinencies to undergo, which I trust will be some pleasure to you, as it is a great one to me. I have endured lectures daily and hourly since I came last, supported by the hopes of being shortly at full liberty to give myself up to my friends and clafsical companions, who, poor souls! though I see them fallen into great contempt with most people here, yet I cannot help sticking to them, and out of a spirit of obstinacy (I think) love them the better for it; and indeed, what can I do else? Must I plunge into metaphysics? Alas, I cannot see in the dark; nature has not furnished me with the optics of a cat. Must I pore upon mathematics? Alas, I cannot see in too much light; I am no eagle. It is very pofsible that two and two make four, but I would not give four farthings to demonstrate this ever so clearly; and if these be the profits of life, give me the amusements of it. The people I behold all around me, it seems, know all this and more, and yet I do not know one of them who inspires me with any ambition of being like him. Surely it was of this place, now Cambridge, but formerly known by the name of Babylon, that the prophet spoke when he said, 'the wild beasts of the desert shall dwell there, and their houses shall be full of doleful creatures, and owls shall build there, and satyrs shall dance there;[1] their forts and towers shall be a den for ever, a joy of wild afses;[2] there shall the great owl make her nest, and lay and hatch and gather under her shadow;[3] it shall be a court of dragons;[4] the screech owl also shall rest there, and find for herself a place of rest'.[5] You see here is a pretty collection of desolate animals, which is verified in this town to a tittle, and perhaps it may also allude to your habitation, for you know all types may be taken by abundance of handles; however, I defy your owls to match mine.

If the default of your spirits and nerves be nothing but the effect of the hyp, I have no more to say. We all must submit to that wayward Queen; I too in no small degree own her sway,

I feel her influence while I speak her power.

LETTER 33.—First printed in Mason's *Memoirs*, pp. 12–14.
[1] Isaiah xiii. 21.   [2] Isaiah xxxii. 14.
[3] Isaiah xxxiv. 15.   [4] Isaiah xxxiv. 13.   [5] Isaiah xxxiv. 14.

But if it be a real distemper, pray take more care of your health, if not for your own at least for our sakes, and do not be so soon weary of this little world: I do not know what refined friendships you may have contracted in the other,[6] but pray do not be in a hurry to see your acquaintance above; among your terrestrial familiars, however, though I say it that should not say it, there positively is not one that has a greater esteem for you than

Yours most sincerely, &c.

Peterhouse, December, 1736.

34. WEST TO GRAY

I CONGRATULATE you on your being about to leave college,[1] and rejoice much you carry no degrees with you. For I would not have had You dignified, and I not, for the world, you would have insulted me so. My eyes, such as they are, like yours, are neither metaphysical nor mathematical; I have, nevertheless, a great respect for your connoisseurs that way, but am always contented to be their humble admirer. Your collection of desolate animals[2] pleased me much; but Oxford, I can assure you, has her owls that match yours, and the prophecy has certainly a squint that way. Well, you are leaving this dismal land of bondage, and which way are you turning your face? Your friends, indeed, may be happy in you, but what will you do with your classic companions? An inn of court is as horrid a place as a college, and a moot case is as dear to gentle dulness[3] as a syllogism. But wherever you go, let me beg you not to throw poetry 'like a nauseous weed away': Cherish its sweets in your bosom, they will serve you now and then to correct the disgusting sober follies of the common law,

---

[6] Perhaps he meant to ridicule the affected manner of Mrs. Rowe's letters of the dead to the living; a book which was, I believe, published about this time. *Mason.*—Mrs. Elizabeth Rowe's (1674–1737) *Friendship in Death, in twenty Letters from the Dead to the Living*, was first published in 1728; third edition, 1733.

LETTER 34.—First printed in Mason's *Memoirs*, pp. 14–16.

[1] I suspect that Mr. West mistook his correspondent; who, in saying he did not take degrees, meant only to let his friend know that he should soon be released from lectures and disputations. It is certain that Mr. Gray continued at college near two years after the time he wrote the preceding letter. *Mason.*

[2] See previous letter.

[3] *Dunciad*, ii. 34: 'gentle Dulness ever loves a joke.'

misce stultitiam consiliis brevem, dulce est desipere in loco;[4] so
said Horace to Virgil, those sons of Anac in poetry, and so say
I to you, in this degenerate land of pigmies,

> Mix with your grave designs a little pleasure,
> Each day of business has its hour of leisure.

In one of these hours I hope, dear sir, you will sometimes
think of me, write to me, and know me yours,

> Ἔξαυδα, μὴ κεῦθε νόῳ, ἵνα εἴδομεν ἄμφω·[5]

that is, write freely to me and openly, as I do to you, and to give
you a proof of it I have sent you an elegy of Tibullus[6] translated. Tibullus, you must know, is my favourite elegiac poet;
for his language is more elegant and his thoughts more natural
than Ovid's. Ovid excells him only in wit, of which no poet had
more in my opinion. The reason I choose so melancholy a
kind of poesie, is because my low spirits and constant ill health
(things in me not imaginary, as you surmise, but too real, alas!
and, I fear, constitutional) 'have tuned my heart to elegies of
woe'; and this likewise is the reason why I am the most irregular
thing alive at college, for you may depend upon it I value my
health above what they call discipline. As for this poor un-
licked thing of an elegy, pray criticise it unmercifully, for I send
it with that intent. Indeed your late translation of Statius[7]
might have deterred me, but I know you are not more able to
excell others, than you are apt to forgive the want of excellence,
especially when it is found in the productions of
Your most sincere friend.
Christ Church, Dec. 22, 1736.

35. GRAY TO WALPOLE

My Dear Horace

I THINK this is the first time, I have had any Occasion to find
fault with S^r R:[s] Male-Administration, and if he should
keep you in town another Week, I don't know whether I shan't

---

[4] *4 Odes*, xii. 27–8.
[5] *Iliad*, i. 363: 'speak it forth, hide it not in thy mind, that we both may
know it.'
[6] Mason omits this elegy, which apparently has not been preserved.
[7] See Letters 22, 22**.
LETTER 35.—First printed by Toynbee (1915), No. 50.

change my Side, & write a Craftsman;[1] I am extreme Sorry,
I could not dine with you last Sunday, but I really was engaged
at Peter-house, & did not know of the honour you intended me,
till night; if it had not been for a great cold I had got, I certainly should have come post to Supper: I engage myself to
drink Tea with you at King's the day after to morrow, for then
we expect you; I mean me, for Ashton is to try not to expect
you then: I believe I shall stay here till February, so pray,
come hither, if that can be any part of a reason for it: the
Moderatour[2] has asked me to make the Tripos-Verses[3] this
year; they say the[4] University has sent a Letter by the Post to
thank my Lord Townsend for the Statue![5] I have had a Letter
from West with an Elegy of Tibullus translated in it,[6] t h u s
l o n g;[7] I have wrote you a letter with 50 I's in it, besides
me's and we's, and I am,

Ever Yours

T: GRAY

Wednesday—[Dec. 29, 1736][8] Cambridge

Addressed: To The Honrble Horace Walpole Esq, at the Treasury, Westminster   *Postmark:* CAMBRIDGE 29 DE

[1] The well-known organ of the Tory opposition, founded in December
1726 by Pulteney and Bolingbroke, in the pages of which Sir Robert Walpole
was for many years systematically denounced.

[2] The Moderators (see Letter 12, n. 6) at this date were James Brown,
Fellow, and afterwards (1770) Master, of Pembroke, later an intimate friend
of Gray's (see Letter 115, n. 1), and Roger Barker, Fellow of Clare.

[3] Latin verses written by undergraduates and distributed with the lists
of successful Tripos candidates every year.   (See Appendix A.)

[4] Gray first wrote 'my', which he smudged out, and altered to 'the'.

[5] The statue of George I by Rysbrack, which was erected in the Senate
House at Cambridge at the expense of Charles, second Viscount Townshend
(1674–1738).   The latter had written on 2 Dec. 1736, offering to bear the
cost of the statue, and a grace accepting the offer, and thanking Lord
Townshend, passed the Senate on 8 Dec.

[6] See previous letter.

[7] Gray has written these two words with the letters far apart.

[8] The date of the year is determined by the references to Lord Townshend
(see n. 5), and to West's letter.

36. GRAY TO WALPOLE

[Cambridge, Jan. 16, 1737][1]

[   ][2]

I HAVE a tast for the works of Cramputius,[3] & his Scraps; if you can fill twelve baskets with such fragments, I have a stomach for 'em all: one should have had a pafsion for Simplicia[4] oneself, if one had lived in those days; she is so open & unreserved in her behaviour: the pleasure of having a mistrefs, that when one made her a compliment, & call'd her Spider; should only cry, ehe! I don't doubt but Portia behaved just s[o][5] when Brutus made love to her; this was reckon'd a Scene of great Gallantry I suppose at that time, & Q: Crafsus Tubero[6] as pretty a fellow with the Women, as the Genie Jonquil:[7] I don't know, whither you have forgot Cambridge, or not; it's plain, you chuse, only to keep it in mind; it seems to be at this time of year, that the humour usually takes you to tell us stories about your coming, but however I would rather be deceived, than hear nothing at all of it; so say something of it pray; every body in Cambridge knows better than I; who remain

yours to command
PATIENT GRISSEL

For god'sake write often, if it be but two Syllables

Addressed: To The Honble Horace Walpole Esq, at the Treasury,[8] Westminster   *Postmark:* CAMBRIDGE 17 IA

LETTER 36.—First printed by Toynbee (1915), No. 24.
    [1] This letter, written from Cambridge on 16 Jan., as the postmark shows, was conjecturally assigned in the *Gray–Walpole Correspondence* to the year 1736. But it appears from the Peterhouse records that in that year Gray did not commence residence till 23 Jan. The date must have been later than 1735 because of the address (see n. 8). Gray was in residence for the whole of January in 1737 and 1738, but as he wrote to Walpole on 15 Jan. 1738, the more likely year is 1737, to which the letter is now assigned.
    [2] See Letter 1, n. 2.
    [3], [4] These characters have not been identified.
    [5] MS. torn.
    [6] This character has not been identified.
    [7] 'Le Génie Jonquille' is a character in *L'Écumoire ou Tanzaï et Néadarné* by Crébillon fils (published in 1734, and translated into English under the title of 'The Skimmer' in 1735), in which he figures as the lover of Néadarné (see Livre iii, chap. 4).
    [8] See Letter 1, n. 8.

37. GRAY TO WEST
Cambridge, March, 1737[1]

*   *   *

I learn Italian like any dragon, and in two months am got through the 16ᵗʰ book of Tafso, whom I hold in great admiration: I want you to learn too, that I may know your opinion of him; nothing can be easier than that language to any one who knows Latin and French already, and there are few so copious and exprefsive.

*   *   *

38. WEST TO GRAY

I HAVE been very ill, and am still hardly recovered. Do you remember Elegy 5th, Book the 3d, of Tibullus, Vos tenet, &c. and do you remember a letter of Mʳ Pope's, in sickness, to Mʳ Steele? This melancholy elegy and this melancholy letter I turned into a more melancholy epistle of my own, during my sickness, in the way of imitation; and this I send to you and my friends at Cambridge, not to divert them, for it cannot, but merely to show them how sincere I was when sick: I hope my sending it to them now may convince them I am no less sincere, though perhaps more simple, when well.

AD AMICOS.
Yes, happy youths, on Camus' sedgy side,
You feel each joy that friendship can divide;
Each realm of science and of art explore,
And with the antient blend the modern lore.
Studious alone to learn whate'er may tend
To raise the genius or the heart to mend;

LETTER 37.—Fragment of letter, first printed in Mason's *Memoirs*, pp. 36–7, n.
[1] Mason adds, that in this same letter Gray tells West 'that his College has set him a versifying on a public occasion (viz. those verses which are called Tripus) on the theme of *Luna est habitabilis*' (see West's letter to Walpole of 18 April 1737, in *Gray–Walpole Correspondence* (No. 57)). In his letter to Walpole of 29 Dec. 1736 (Letter 35) Gray says that he had been asked to make the Tripos verses, and as the verses had to be produced at a Congregation on the Thursday after Mid-Lent Sunday, which in 1737 would be 17 March, it is probable that this letter was written earlier in the year than March, the date assigned to it by Mason. On Tripos verses see Appendix A.
LETTER 38.—First printed in Mason's *Memoirs*, pp. 18–22.

Now pleas'd along the cloyster'd walk you rove,
And trace the verdant mazes of the grove,
Where social oft, and oft alone, ye chuse
To catch the zephyr and to court the muse.
Mean time at me (while all devoid of art
These lines give back the image of my heart)
At me the pow'r that comes or soon or late,
Or aims, or seems to aim, the dart of fate;
From you remote, methinks, alone I stand
Like some sad exile in a desert land;
Around no friends their lenient care to join
In mutual warmth, and mix their heart with mine.
Or real pains, or those which fancy raise,
For ever blot the sunshine of my days;
To sickness still, and still to grief a prey,
Health turns from me her rosy face away.
    Just heav'n! what sin, ere life begins to bloom,
Devotes my head untimely to the tomb;
Did e'er this hand against a brother's life
Drug the dire bowl or point the murd'rous knife?
Did e'er this tongue the slanderer's tale proclaim,
Or madly violate my Maker's name?
Did e'er this heart betray a friend or foe,
Or know a thought but all the world might know?
As yet just started from the lists of time,
My growing years have scarcely told their prime;
Useless, as yet, through life I've idly run,
No pleasures tasted, and few duties done.
Ah, who, ere autumn's mellowing suns appear,
Would pluck the promise of the vernal year;
Or, ere the grapes their purple hue betray,
Tear the crude cluster from the mourning spray.
Stern Power of Fate, whose ebon sceptre rules
The Stygian deserts and Cimmerian pools,
Forbear, nor rashly smite my youthful heart,
A victim yet unworthy of thy dart;
Ah, stay till age shall blast my withering face,
Shake in my head, and falter in my pace;
Then aim the shaft, then meditate the blow,
And to the dead my willing shade shall go.[1]

[1] Here he quits Tibullus; the ten following verses have but a remote
reference to Mr. Pope's letter. *Mason.*

How weak is Man to Reason's judging eye!
Born in this moment, in the next we die;
Part mortal clay, and part ethereal fire,
Too proud to creep, too humble to aspire.
In vain our plans of happiness we raise,
Pain is our lot, and patience is our praise;
Wealth, lineage, honours, conquest, or a throne,
Are what the wise would fear to call their own.
Health is at best a vain precarious thing,
And fair-fac'd youth is ever on the wing;
'Tis like the stream, beside whose wat'ry bed
Some blooming plant exalts his flowry head,
Nurs'd by the wave the spreading branches rise,
Shade all the ground and flourish to the skies;
The waves the while beneath in secret flow,
And undermine the hollow bank below;
Wide and more wide the waters urge their way,
Bare all the roots and on their fibres prey.
Too late the plant bewails his foolish pride,
And sinks, untimely, in the whelming tide.[2]
    But why repine, does life deserve my sigh?
Few will lament my loss whene'er I die.
For those the wretches I despise or hate,
I neither envy nor regard their fate.[3]
For me, whene'er all-conquering Death shall spread
His wings around my unrepining head,
I care not; though this face be seen no more,
The world will pass as chearful as before,
Bright as before the day-star will appear,
The fields as verdant, and the skies as clear;[4]
Nor storms nor comets will my doom declare,
Nor signs on earth, nor portents in the air;
Unknown and silent will depart my breath,
Nor Nature e'er take notice of my death.

[2] 'Youth, at the very best, is but the betrayer of human life in a gentler and smoother manner than age; 'tis like the stream that nourishes a plant upon a bank, and causes it to flourish and blossom to the sight, but at the same time is undermining it at the root in secret.' (Pope's letter, quoted by Mason.)

[3] 'I am not at all uneasy at the thought that many men, whom I never had any esteem for, are likely to enjoy this world after me.' (*Ibid.*)

[4] 'The morning after my exit the sun will rise as bright as ever, the flowers smell as sweet, the plants spring as green.' (*Ibid.*)

Yet some there are (ere spent my vital days)[5]
Within whose breasts my tomb I wish to raise.
Lov'd in my life, lamented in my end,
Their praise would crown me as their precepts mend:
To them may these fond lines my name endear,
Not from the Poet but the Friend sincere.[6]

Christ Church, July 4, 1737.

39. GRAY TO WALPOLE

[Cambridge, July, 1737][1]

My dear Horace

I WAS just going to write to you in opposition to a couple of
very weighty reasons; one, that you did not bid me, &
t'other, that I had nothing to say; but, alas! what are reasons
against one's inclinations, for you know in such a case a feather
at any time will weigh down Lead; but you by instinct knowing
my situation, were so good as to supply me with the cause, tho'
not with materials: if you never were to tell me any fresher piece
of News, than that with which you end your little Modicum,
I should be well enough content, for tho' I heard it every day I
should wonder as much as ever, & it would never be the lefs
agreable for repetition; I rely wholly upon you, my correspondent, for the truth of it, as the only person, who can tell, what
pafses in that little country, where my concerns lie. my
Motions at present (which you ask after the particulars of) are
much like those of a Pendulum, or (Dr Longically[2] speaking)

---

[5] In the original version (scc n. 6) this line ran: 'Yet some there are (ere
sunk in endless night)', which Gray consciously or unconsciously perhaps
had in mind when he wrote the last line of *The Bard*: 'Deep in the roaring
tide he sunk [altered later to "plung'd"] to endless night.'

[6] The text printed by Mason does not give the original version sent by
West, but a version corrected and improved, probably by Gray. See
Appendix C and cf. Letter 106.

LETTER 39.—First printed in part (in a garbled text) and in combination
with a portion of Letter 44 by Mason in *Memoirs*, pp. 34–5; first printed in
full by Toynbee (1915), No. 61.

[1] The date is conjectural and uncertain. Mason dates it August 1738;
but this date seems unlikely. At the end of the letter Gray says he thinks
'to go to town the week after next'; the Peterhouse records show that in 1737
he left Cambridge on or about 28 July (he writes to West from London on
22 Aug.—see Letter 40), whereas in 1738 he was in residence the whole of
July and August, and the first fortnight of September.

[2] Dr. Long, the Master of Pembroke Hall, at this time read lectures in

oscillatory, I swing from Chapell or Hall home, & from home
to chapell or hall; all the strange incidents that happen in my
journeys & returns I shall be sure to acquaint you with; the
most wonderful that I have been able to pick up, as yet, is,
that it rains exceedingly; this has refresh'd the prospect[3] very
agreeably, as the way for the most part lies between green
fields on either hand, terminated with buildings at some distance; Seats, I presume; & they seem of great antiquity: the
roads are very good, being, as I suspect, the work of Julius
Cæsar's army, for they still preserve in many places the appearances of a pavement in pretty good repair, & if they were
not so near home, might perhaps be as much admired as the
Via Appia, that we hear so much cried up: there are at present
several rivulets to be crofsed, & which serve to enliven the view
all round; the country is exceeding fruitful in Ravens, & such
black Cattle. but not to tire you with my travels, You must
know Mr Turner[4] is come down, his list is vastly near being
full, notwishstanding[5] which, & the great cares & duties

experimental philosophy. *Mason.*—Dr. Roger Long (1680–1770), D.D.,
1728; Master of Pembroke 1733–70; Vice-Chancellor, 1733; he was elected
F.R.S. in 1729, and was appointed first Lowndean Professor of Astronomy
and Geometry in 1750. He was the author of an important work on astronomy (unfinished), of which the first two parts were published in 1742 and
1764, and which was completed after his death by his scientific assistant,
Richard Dunthorne (who was also butler of the College), and the mathematician, William Wales. Long was interested also in music and mechanical
inventions. Carter, in his *History of the University of Cambridge* (1753), speaks
of his apartments at the Master's Lodge as being 'stocked with Musical, and
Mathematical Instruments', while in a 'Ground Room' he had a printing
press at which he was printing his astronomical works. In his garden he
contrived waterworks (for 'he is a very great Mechanic') which supplied 'a
beautiful and large Bason', wherein 'he often diverts himself in a Machine
of his own contrivance, to go with the Foot as he rides therein' (pp. 77–8).
In one of the courts of the Hall he erected 'a hollow revolving sphere,
eighteen feet in diameter, representing on its inner surface the apparent
movements of the heavenly bodies' (*D.N.B.*). These inventions explain
Gray's reference to him in Letter 148 as 'Lord of the great Zodiack, the
Glass Uranium, and the Chariot that goes without Horses'.
  [3] All that follows is a humorously hyperbolic description of the quadrangle of Peter-House. *Mason.*
  [4] Shallet Turner, Fellow of Peterhouse, M.A., 1717; LL.D., 1728; Regius
Professor of Modern History, 1735–62; died, 13 Nov. 1762. The references
to his 'list' and 'the great cares and duties' of his office are ironical, as he
never lectured (as neither did Gray himself, when he subsequently held the
same office).
  [5] *Sic.*

attending his office, he says, he thinks to go to Paris every Year. I think too to go to town the week after next,[6] & am

yours eternally

T: GRAY

P.S: I have forgot my English, & can't spell[7]

Addressed: To The Honble Horace Walpole, Esq, at Houghton Hall Norfolk
    Postmark: CAMBRIDGE (date undecipherable).

40. GRAY TO WEST

AFTER a month's expectation of you, and a fortnight's despair, at Cambridge, I am come to town, and to better hopes of seeing you. If what you sent me last[1] be the product of your melancholy, what may I not expect from your more cheerful hours? For by this time the ill health that you complain of is (I hope) quite departed; though, if I were self-interested, I ought to wish for the continuance of any thing that could be the occasion of so much pleasure to me. Low spirits are my true and faithful companions; they get up with me, go to bed with me, make journeys and returns as I do;[2] nay, and pay visits, and will even affect to be jocose, and force a feeble laugh with me; but most commonly we sit alone together, and are the prettiest insipid company in the world. However, when you come, I believe they must undergo the fate of all humble companions, and be discarded. Would I could turn them to the same use that you have done, and make an Apollo of them. If they could write such verses with me, not hartshorn, nor spirit of amber,[3] nor all that furnishes the closet of an apothecary's widow, should persuade me to part with them: But, while I write to you, I hear the bad news of Lady Walpole's death on Saturday night last.[4] Forgive me if the thought of what my poor Horace must feel on that account, obliges me to have done in reminding you that I am

Yours, &c.

London, Aug. 22, 1737.

[6] See n. 1.
[7] Presumably he refers to his having written 'notwishstanding' just above.
LETTER 40.—First printed in Mason's *Memoirs*, pp. 22–3.
[1] His letter of 4 July, enclosing the poem *Ad Amicos* (Letter 38).
[2] Possibly a reminiscence of Cicero, *Pro Archia*, vii. 16: '(haec studia) . . . pernoctant nobiscum, peregrinantur, rusticantur'.
[3] Succinic acid. (*O.E.D.*)
[4] Lady Walpole died on Saturday, 20 Aug. Gray probably heard the news from Ashton.

41. GRAY TO WALPOLE

[London, c. 22 August, 1737][1]

FORGIVE me, my poor dear Horace, if I intrude upon your Grief,[2] sooner pofsibly than I ought; yet hardly soon enough for the Anxiety I am in upon your account; far from having any such confidence in myself, as to imagine any thing I can say should lighten your affliction; I fear your own good Sense, and Resignation to Him, who has spared so long the best of Mothers to you, is hardly able to support you under it; I can the easier imagine the Situation you are in from the fears, which are continually before my eyes, of a like misfortune in my own case;[3] if that were really to happen, I know not the least Shadow of comfort, that could come to me, but what I perhaps might find in my dearest Horace's compafsion, & that pity, he never denies the unhappy: would to God, I might alleviate in some measure his Sorrows, in the part I willingly would bear in them, & in that commiseration, which I should feel for any one in such circumstances, how much more then for him whose friendship has been my greatest joy, & I hope shall continue so many years: for God's sake, as soon as melancholy reflection shall give you any intermifsion, let me hear of your welfare; let me have the pleasure of a line, or the sight of you, as soon as it can be proper: believe, I shall not enjoy a moments ease, till I have some information of your condition; I am, my dearest Walpole, with the greatest truth, your faithful friend, & servant,

T: G:

41*. West to Gray.

[*Oct. or Nov. 1737*]

[In Letter 43 West refers to a letter he wrote to Gray 'above a month ago', to which he had received no answer. The date of Letter 43 is doubtful. If it was written on 3 Dec. 1737, West's unanswered letter would have been written in October; or in November, if Letter 43 were written in January 1738. (See Letter 43, n. 9.)]

LETTER 41.—First printed by Toynbee (1915), No. 64.
[1] The date is determined by the occasion of the letter (see n. 2). Gray had heard the news on 22 Aug. (see Letter 40).
[2] For the loss of his mother, who died in Sir Robert Walpole's house at Chelsea on 20 Aug. 1737. For an account of her death, see Walpole's letter to Charles Lyttelton of 18 Sept. of this year.
[3] Gray lost his own mother on 11 March 1753. See Letter 176.

42. GRAY TO WALPOLE

[London, c. 12 November, 1737][1]

[   ][2]

WE were all here in mighty consternation this morning in imagination that the Queen was dead, not out of a joke, as she died you know a while ago,[3] but seriously gone to the Stygian ferry; however now they say she is only very bad,[4] & in a fair way; as we have been twice bauk'd,[5] she will have much ado to persuade us, that she's dead in earnest & perhaps she will survive her funeral no small time in the breasts of her good subjects: I shall take care to be as sorry, as one of my diminutiveſs ought to be, not for myself, but in charity to my superiours; I saw her a little while ago at the Opera in a green Velvet Sac embroider'd κατὰ the facings & sleeves with Silver, a little French Cap, a long black hood, & her hair in Curls round her face; but you see, Crown'd heads, & heads Mouton-nées, scald heads, & lousy heads, Quack heads & Cane heads must all come together to the Grave,[6] as the famous Abou-saïd[7] has elegantly hinted, in his Persian Madrigals: for my part I shall wear her image long imprinted in my mind, tho' I hope for all this to refresh it frequently, & retouch it from the living Original: I don't know whether I should not debase the dignity of my Subject [after this by][8] telling you anything of Sig^r

LETTER 42.—First printed by Toynbee (1915), No. 66.

[1] The date is determined by the references to Queen Caroline's illness (see n. 4), and by the date of Gray's return to Cambridge (see n. 14).

[2] See Letter 1, n. 2.

[3] A rumour of the Queen's death had been put about in 1731 by certain speculators on the Stock Exchange.

[4] She was taken very ill on 9 Nov.; on 12 Nov. she was dangerously ill, and was discovered to be suffering from a rupture; she received the sacrament on 17 Nov., and died on Sunday night, 20 Nov. (*Gent. Mag.*, 1737, pp. 699–700).

[5] A second false report of the Queen's death had been spread on 25 Aug. of this year, when 'a man on Horseback, in order to pass the Turnpike on the King's private Road from Fulham without paying, pretended he came express from Hampton-Court with an Account of the Queen's Death. The Story spread for a Truth, till the Return of a Messenger sent to Court'—having meanwhile caused heavy losses to speculative dealers in mourning (*Gent. Mag.*).

[6] Cf. Walpole to George Montagu, 28 Oct. 1756: 'as Sir Jonathan Swift said, crowned heads and cane heads, good heads and no heads at all, may all come to disgrace.'

[7] A fictitious authority, the actual author cited being Swift (see n. 6).

[8] Piece cut out; the missing words have been supplied in pencil by Walpole.

Cafarelli,[9] so leaving him, as all the World has done, to screech by himself; we shall descend more gradually, & talk of West, who is just gone to Oxford again: as soon as Ashton told me he was in town, I went to Mr Periam's in Hatton-Garden; but Mr Periam had left his house (& consequently Mrs West, as a Lodger) & was removed to Thavies Inn; at Thavies Inn instead of Mr Periam, I could find nothing but a Note in the key-hole, directing me to Mr Greenaways; but Mr Greenaways key-hole sent me to Mr Herriot; & there I found one of the blood of the Periams, who was so good as to inform me, he knew nothing of the matter; ibi omnis effusus labor:[10] but in a few days more he came to me himself; then I went to supper with him, where he entertain'd me with all the product of his brain, Verses upon Stow, Translations of Catullus, & Homer, Epick Epigrams, & Odes upon the New-Year, Wild Ducks, & Petits Pâtés: we are to write to each other every post, if not oftener: he corresponds with Tozhy Cole, & Quid Prinsep:[11] the transactions of Mr Fleetwood[12] & Rich[13] I defer to my next, or to word of mouth, for I shall be at Cambridge on Tuesday night,[14] tho' I fear my not meeting with you there; I am, S^r,

yours most sincerely,

T: GRAY

[9] Gaetano Majorano, called Caffarelli (1703–83), famous soprano singer, a pupil of Porpora. He came to London in the autumn of this year, but during the whole time of his stay was never in good health nor in good voice, so that the high expectations formed of him were disappointed.

[10] *Georg.* iv. 492.

[11] John Prinsep, a junior Eton contemporary (1731–5) of Gray and Walpole—see Ashton's letters to West of June 1736 in *Gray–Walpole Correspondence* (Nos. 33, 34).

[12] Charles Fleetwood, manager of Drury Lane Theatre. The rivalry between him, as the upholder of the 'legitimate drama', and Rich (see n. 13), the inventor of the pantomime, was the constant theme of the criticasters and poetasters of the day.

[13] John Rich (c. 1682–1761), manager first of the Lincoln's Inn Fields Theatre, and afterwards of Covent Garden. In 1716 he introduced the pantomime, an entertainment which he produced annually till 1760, the year before his death, and in which he invariably, under his stage-name of Lun, played Harlequin. His greatest success was the production in 1728 of Gay's *Beggar's Opera*, which had been refused at Drury Lane, whereby, as was said, 'Gay was made rich, and Rich gay'.

[14] This would be Tuesday, 15 Nov., the day of his return, as shown by the Peterhouse records.

43. WEST TO GRAY

RECEIVING no Answer to my last letter,¹ which I writ above a month ago, I must own I am a little uneasy. The slight shadow of you which I had in town,² has only served to endear you to me the more. The moments I past with you made a strong impression upon me. I singled you out for a friend, and I would have you know me to be yours, if you deem me worthy. —Alas, Gray, you cannot imagine how miserably my time passes away. My health and nerves and spirits are, thank my stars, the very worst, I think, in Oxford. Four-and-twenty hours of pure unalloy'd health together, are as unknown to me as the 400,000 characters in the Chinese vocabulary. One of my complaints has of late been so over-civil as to visit me regularly once a month—jam certus conviva.³ This is a painful nervous headach, which perhaps you have sometimes heard me speak of before. Give me leave to say, I find no physic comparable to your letters. If, as it is said in Ecclesiasticus 'Friendship be the physic of the mind',⁴ prescribe to me, dear Gray, as often and as much as you think proper, I shall be a most obedient patient.

Non ego
Fidis irascar medicis, offendar amicis.⁵

I venture here to write you down a Greek epigram,⁶ which I lately turned into Latin, and hope you will excuse it.

Perspicui puerum ludentem in margine rivi
Immersit vitreæ limpidus error aquæ:

LETTER 43.—First printed in Mason's *Memoirs*, pp. 26–8.
¹ See Letter 41*.
² See Letter 42.
³ Horace, 1 *Epist*. vii. 75.
⁴ West appears to have been thinking of Ecclesiasticus vi. 16, 'A faithful friend is the medicine of life'.
⁵ Horace, 1 *Epist*. viii. 9: Fidis offendar medicis, irascar amicis.
⁶ Of Posidippus or Callimachus (*Anth. Pal.* vii. 170). The Greek original, which is not given by Mason, is as follows:

Τὸν τριετῆ παίζοντα περὶ φρέαρ ᾽Αστυάνακτα
Εἴδωλον μορφᾶς κωφὸν ἐπεσπάσατο.
᾽Εκ δ᾽ ὕδατος τὸν παῖδα διάβροχον ἥρπασε μάτηρ,
Σκεπτομένα ζωᾶς εἴ τινα μοῖραν ἔχει.
Νύμφας δ᾽ οὐκ ἐμίηνεν ὁ νήπιος, ἀλλ᾽ ἐπὶ γούνων
Ματρὸς κοιμηθεὶς τὸν βαθὺν ὕπνον ἔχει.

At gelido ut mater moribundum e flumine traxit
Credula, & amplexu funus inane fovet:
Paullatim puer in dilecto pectore, somno
Languidus, aeternúm lumina composuit.[7]

Adieu! I am going to my tutor's lectures on one Puffendorff,
a very jurisprudent author as you shall read on a summer's day.[8]

Believe me yours, &c.

Christ Church, Dec. 2? [1737][9]

44. GRAY TO WALPOLE

[Cambridge, Dec. 29, 1737][1]

My Dear

I SHOULD say Mr Inspector general of the Exports & Imports,[2]
but that appellation would make but an odd figure in conjunction with the two familiar monosyllables above written,
for, Non bene conveniunt, nec in unâ sede morantur Majestas
& amor,[3] which is being interpreted, Love does not live at the
Custom-house: however by what style, title, or denomination

---

[7] Gray transcribed West's rendering in his copy of the *Anthologia Graeca*
(Stephanus, 1566, p. 220), and added this note, 'Descriptio pulcherrima &
quæ tenuem illum græcorum spiritum mirificè sapit.' (*Mason.*)

[8] *Mids. Night's Dream*, i. 2 (*ad fin.*): '*Quince.* A proper man as one shall see
in a summer's day.'

[9] Mason dated this letter 2 Dec. 1738, an obvious error, as by that date
West had left Oxford. It has been assumed that, as Gray replies on 22 Jan.
1738, the year should be 1737, but it is doubtful if the letter could have been
written on 2 Dec. in that year. West refers to his last letter written 'above
a month ago', but Gray had seen West in London in November (see Letter
42) and West alludes to this meeting. Furthermore Gray, in his reply of
22 Jan., speaks of having received this letter of West's two days before, which
would be scarcely possible of a letter written on 3 Dec. It is possible that
Mason, as he often did, combined parts of two letters, one of which was
written in January, but in the absence of evidence the date must be left
in doubt.

LETTER 44.—First printed in part (in a garbled text) by Mason in *Memoirs*,
pp. 34–5; first printed in full by Toynbee (1915), No. 71.

[1] The date is determined approximately by the references to the recent
death and burial of Queen Caroline (see n. 4) and by the postmark (see n. 12).

[2] In his *Short Notes of my Life* Walpole writes: 'My mother died August
20th, 1737. Soon after, my father gave me the place of Inspector of the
Imports and Exports in the Custom House, which I resigned on his appointing me Usher of the Exchequer, in the room of Colonel William Townshend,
January 29th, 1738.'

[3] Ovid, *Metam.* ii. 846–7.

soever you please to be dignified or distinguish'd hereafter, you'll never get rid of these two words, nor of your christianname: it will stick like a Burr, & you can no more get quitt of it, than St Anthony could of his Pigg: we had no Queen to bury here, so I have no procefsion to tell you of;[4] but we are collecting our flowers, as fast as may be, to strew upon her tomb:[5] Mr Pemberton[6] of Cath: Hall & one Ambrose[7] of Trin: Hall, a blind Man, they say will bear away the bell; both English; Mr Whitehead[8] does not shine vastly this time: the bellman has paid his duty in the following epigram.

> Oh cruel death! how could'st be so unkind
> To snatch the Queen, & leave the King behind?

almost as Laconick, as Mr Conways[9] letter;[10] who has wrought to his sister[11] in the same style, as one would write to the devil whose ancient title has been, Old Boy:,   I am

yours ever

T: GRAY

Addressed: To The Honble Horace Walpole Esq at the Treasury London
Postmark: CAMBRIDGE 30 DE [12]

---

[4] The Queen, who died on 20 Nov., was buried on 17 Dec.

[5] The collection was published in Feb. 1738 under the title, *Pietas Academiæ Cantabrigiensis in Funere Principis Wilhelminæ Carolinæ, & Luctu Augustissimi Georgii II, Brittanniarum, &c. Regis.*

[6] 'Henry Pemberton, A.B., Fellow of Cath. Hall' (B.A., 1734; M.A., 1738), contributed an English poem.

[7] There is no contribution by Ambrose.

[8] William Whitehead, of Clare, B.A., 1739; Fellow, 1742; M.A., 1743; subsequently (1757) Poet Laureate, also contributed an English poem (see Letter 197, n. 9).

[9] This name has been scored through, but is still legible. Hon. Henry Seymour Conway (1721–95), second son of first Baron Conway by his third wife, Charlotte Shorter, sister of Lady Walpole, and thus first cousin of Horace Walpole. He entered the army in 1741. He and his elder brother, Lord Conway (afterwards Earl and Marquis of Hertford), were among Walpole's school-fellows at Eton.

[10] Gray first wrote 'epigram', which he smudged out and altered to 'letter'.

[11] Hon. Anne Seymour Conway (d. 1774), Conway's youngest sister (see Letter 49, n. 2).

[12] So apparently the postmark, but it is too indistinct to be deciphered with certainty.

45. GRAY TO WALPOLE

[Cambridge, Jan. 10, 1738][1]

[   ][2]

I AM in good hopes, that by this time the Eclipse[3] is over with
you, & that your two Satellit's have recover'd their usual
light; the Sublimity of which two metaphors, after you have
taken them out of their pantoufles,[3a] & reduced 'em to their just
value, will be found to amount to my wishes for your health,
& that of your eyes, whose warmth I have been too sensible of,
when they used to shine upon me, not to be very apprehensive
of any damage that might befall 'em: I should have taken care
to write upon Green paper, & dip'd my Pen in Copperas-water,
if you had not afsured me, that they were on the mending hand,
& pretty well able to sustain the whitemaking rays: now as for
the transactions here, you are to be ascertain'd; that the Man
at the Mitre has cut his throat, that one M[r] White[4] of Emanuel
a week ago drown'd himself, but since that has been seen a
few miles of, having the appearance of one that had never
been drown'd; wherefore it is by many conjectured, that he
walketh: D[r] Bouquets verses[5] have been return'd by M[r] Vice-
chancellour[6] to undergo several corrections; the old Man's invention is much [admired as][7] having found out a way to make
bawdy verses upon a Burying:[8] the wind was so high last

LETTER 45.—First printed by Toynbee (1915), No. 72.
[1] The date of the month is supplied by the postmark; that of the year is
determined by the references to the funeral of Queen Caroline, and to the
great gale (see nn. 5, 9).
[2] See Letter 1, n. 2.
[3] This appears to be a reference, not to an actual eclipse, but to some
temporary weakness of Walpole's eyesight. There was an annular eclipse
of the sun on 18 Feb. 1737, which attracted considerable attention, and
Gray's metaphor may have been suggested by the recollection of it.
[3a] Gray is probably repeating a phrase of Walpole's; see Walpole's
letter to George Montagu of 18 May, 1749: 'Take sentiments out of their
pantoufles'.
[4] This individual cannot be identified.
[5] Philip Bouquet (1669–1748), D.D., Fellow of Trinity, Regius Professor
of Hebrew, 1712–48. He contributed four Hebrew stanzas, and a Latin
poem of forty-two lines, to the Cambridge *Pietas* on the occasion of the
funeral of Queen Caroline (17 Dec. 1737) (see Letter 44, n. 5).
[6] William Richardson, Master of Emmanuel.
[7] Piece cut out; the missing words were written in by Walpole.
[8] Dr. Bouquet's poem begins:

'Heu mihi! quod Priami experior mala fata superstes,
    Ut videam teneræ Principis exsequias:

73

night,[9] that I every minute expected to pay you a visit at London perforce, which was the place I certainly should have directed the storm to, if I had been obliged to ride in the Whirlwind:[10] if I don't hear from you this week, I shall be in a thousand Tyrrit's & frights[11] about you; I am, my dear Horace,

y^{rs} most affect:^{tely}

T: GRAY

Addressed: To The Honble Horace Walpole Esq at the Treasury, St James's
Postmark: CAMBRIDGE 11 IA

46. GRAY TO WALPOLE

[   ]¹

THE moving piece of ancient poetry you favour'd me with the sight of, would be sufficient, I must confeſs to deterr me, if I had any ambition of appearing among the Consolatores,² from all pretence to writing at this time; so long as the sad Catastrophe of the beautiful & never-to be enough-lamented Gillian³ dwells upon my memory: those Genius's, my friend, those mighty spirits of antiquity! alas, what are we to 'em? mere tinsel! mere flash! and indeed (not to dwell upon the moral, so feelingly inculcated in this little elegiacal narration, which

Orbatamque Throni Sobolem, Viduique Mariti
    Desertos longa nocte jacere toros.
Ah! quoties voluit collo dare brachia circum?
    Sed toties cupidas lusit imago manus.'

⁹ There was a very violent gale on the evening of 9 Jan. of this year, which did great damage, especially at Bristol (*Gent. Mag.* 1738, p. 49).

¹⁰ Addison's *Campaign*, 292: 'Rides in the whirlwind, and directs the storm'—a line borrowed by Pope in the *Dunciad*, iii. 264.

¹¹ 2 *Hen. IV*, ii. 4: '*Mrs. Quickly.* 'I'll forswear keeping house, afore I'll be in these tirrits and frights.'

LETTER 46.—First printed by Toynbee (1915), No. 73.

¹ See Letter 1, n. 2.

² That is, the contributors to the Cambridge *Pietas* on the occasion of the funeral of Queen Caroline (see Letter 44, n. 5). Gray was not a contributor.

³ The ballad of Gillian, if such there was, has not been traced. One of the pieces (consisting of six stanzas, with refrain) in Thomas D'urfey's *Wit and Mirth* (1719) is entitled 'The Queen's Health: Or, the New Gillian of Croydon'. A chap-book containing 'The Pleasant and delightful history of *Gillian of Croydon*' was published in London in 1727. Possibly Walpole may have borrowed the heroine of this for a ballad of his own composition.

74

'tis impofsible should escape the acutenefs of your penetration)
what can be beyond the elegant simplicity of the language? in
the exordium the poet lays down the groundwork, & foundation, as it were, of that beautiful fabrick he intends to erect; he
does not injudiciously draw his inferences, after he has recounted
the story; at least he does not expatiate much in the end; no!
he leaves the mind then to ruminate at its own leisure, & make
its own applications, when it shall have recover'd itself from
that sorrow, which every virtuous mind must feel after so woful
a tale: he recommends to the ladies of his time a strict ob-
servance of honour & chastity, who, I doubt not, received his
advice with reverence (our modern Females would perhaps
[have laug]⁴h'd at his gravity) he also solcmnly affirms the
truth of it, as well knowing the prevalence of truth over the
mind; from whence his deep insight into Nature is sufficiently
evidenced: at the beginning of his narration, he fixes the place
of his Heroine's habitation in Surry;⁵ he had undoubtedly
observed in Homer, & the imitators of that poet; how much
we are ingaged in the interest of any person, who has the
misfortune of falling in battle, by being told the place of his
birth & abode, as

Υἱὸν⁶ δὲ Στροφίοιο, Σκαμάνδριον, αἵμονα⁶ θήρης, &c⁷:
—'Ορσίλοχόν τε,
Τȣ ῥα πατὴρ μὲν ἔναιεν ἐϋκτιμένῃ⁸ ἐνὶ Φηρῇ,⁹

'tis true, he has not carried it quite so far as Homer in telling
us, whether Gillian loved hunting or not, nor whether her
father's house was well, or ill built; he has showed, as he proceeds, his generous aversion, & contempt for your cockneys &
fluttering beaux of the town, so agreeable to the simplicity of
the age he lived in, & its uncorrupted innocence; by making
this ill-grounded pafsion of Gillian's the cause of all her misfortunes,

—Hinc prima mali labes¹⁰—

I don't wonder at her innocence not being proof against so

---

⁴ Piece cut out (see n. 1); the missing text has been supplied in pencil by
Walpole.
⁵ See n. 3; Croydon is in Surrey.   ⁶ *Sic.*
⁷ *Iliad*, v. 49: 'Skamandrios, son of Strophios, cunning in the chase.'
⁸ *Sic.*
⁹ *Iliad*, v. 542–3: 'And Orsilochos, whose father dwelt in well-built Phere.'
¹⁰ *Aen.* ii. 97: 'Hinc mihi prima mali labes.'

strong allurements as are contain'd in those two unaffected lines,

> He said as how he would her carry
> To London, & her there would marry.

then how feelingly, yet concisely is the main part of the story exprefs'd—

> He did perswade her to his bed,
> And there he got her maidenhead:
> —fulsere ignes, & conscius æther
> Connubiis, summoƈ ulularunt Teastere Nymphæ.[11]

what woman would not consent, when a man swears upon his life? then for the master-stroke,

> She sat down at his door, & cried,
> And broke her heart, & so she died.

I suspect here some small imitation of the celebrated dragon of Wantley (provided that were really elder than this)

> So groan'd, kicked, shit, & died.[12]

[On][13]ly indeed the indecent circumstances are supprefsed, tho' the elegancy is still preserved: pray, excuse these little remarks, which a[re],[14] however ill executed, design'd to make more

---

[11] *Aen.* iv. 167–8 ('ulularunt vertice Nymphæ').
[12] The last line of the ballad of *The Dragon of Wantley*:

> 'Then his head he shak'd, trembled and quaked,
> And down he laid and cry'd;
> First on one knee, then on back tumbled he,
> So groan'd, kickt, shit, and dy'd.'

Gray perhaps read the ballad in the *Collection of Old Ballads, corrected from the best and most antient Copies extant, with Introductions historical and critical* (Lond. 1726–38. 3 vols. 12mo), ascribed to Ambrose Philips, in which it occurs in vol. i, pp. 37–42. More probably, however, the allusion was prompted by the recent performance at the Theatre Royal in Covent Garden of Henry Carey's *The Dragon of Wantley. A Burlesque Opera, . . . moderniz'd from the Old Ballad after the Italian Manner, by Sig. Carini*, an edition of which, with the original ballad prefixed, was published at the same time. The opera was first produced on 26 Oct. 1737, and, after being suspended for a time on account of the death of Queen Caroline (20 Nov.), had a run of sixty-seven nights.
[13] MS. torn.
[14] Partly obliterated by seal.

conspicuous the [ex][14]cellencies of this amiable author, & believe me

your faithful friend, & humble Servt
PHILOGILLIANUS.

Jan: 15—[1738][15] Cambridge.
Addressed: To The Honble Horace Walpole Esq, at the Treasury, St James's.[16]

47. GRAY TO WEST

Glaucias Favonio[1] suo S:

LITERAS, mi Favoni, abs te demum nudiustertiùs, credo, accepi;[2] planè mellitas, nisi fortè quà de ægritudine quadam tuâ dictum: atque hoc sane mihi habitum est non paulò acerbiùs, quod te capitis morbo implicitum efse intellexi; oh morbum mihi quam odiosum! qui de industria id agit, ut ego in singulos menses, Dii boni, quantis jucunditatibus orbarer! quàm ex animo mihi dolendum est, quod

Medio de fonte leporum
Surgit amari aliquid.[3]—

salutem mehercule, nolo, tam parvipendas, atq̅ amicis tam improbè consulas: quanquam tute fortafsis—æstuas angusto limite mundi,[4] viamq̅ (ut dicitur) affectas Olympo,[5] nos tamen non efse tam sublimes, utpote qui hisce in sordibus & fæce diutius paululum versari volumus, reminiscendum est: illæ tuæ Musæ, si te ament modo, derelinqui paulisper non nimis ægrè patientur: indulge, amabo te, plus quam soles, corporis exercitationibus: magis te campus habeat, aprico magis te dedas otio, ut ne id ingenium quod tam cultum curas, diligenter nimis

---

[15] Mason has inserted the date 1737 in the original; this would be correct according to old style (15 Jan. 1737/8); according to new style the date must be 15 Jan. 1738, on account of the reference to the funeral of Queen Caroline, which took place on 17 Dec. 1737.

[16] The letter is endorsed in an uneducated hand:

'send by wm Haselwod
att y[e] Green Dragon
With in beeshops Gate
on wensday be fore
noon'

(See Letter 123, n. 2).

LETTER 47.—T. 9; first printed in Mason's *Memoirs*, pp. 28–9; the letter was transcribed in Gray's Commonplace-book.
[1] Gray addresses him as Favonius in allusion to the name of West (see Letter 2, n. 8).   [2] On the date of West's letter see Letter 43, n. 9.
[3] Lucretius, iv. 1133–4.   [4] Juvenal, *Sat.* x. 169.
[5] Virgil, *Georg.* iv. 562: 'viamque affectat Olympo.'

77

dum foves, officiosarum matrum ritu, interimas. vide, quæso, quàm ἰατρικῶς tecum agimus,

$$—ἤδ᾽ ἐπιθήσω$$
$$φάρμαχ᾽ ἅ κεν παύσῃσι μελαινάων ὀδυνάων·^6$$

si de his pharmacis non satis liquet; sunt festivitates meræ, sunt facetiæ, & risus; quos ego equidem si adhibere nequeo, tamen ad præcipiendum (ut medicorum fere mos est) certè satis sim: id, quod poeticè sub finem epistolæ lusisti, mihi gratifsimum quidem accidit. admodum latinè coctum & conditum tetrasticon[7] Græcam tamen illam ἀφέλειαν mirificè sapit. tu, quod restat, vide sodes, hujus hominis ignorantiam; cum, unde hoc tibi sit depromptum, (ut fatear) prorsus nescio: sane ego equidem nihil in capsis reperio, quo tibi minimæ partis solutio fiat. vale, & me ut soles, ama.

A:D: 11: Kalend: Februar: [Jan. 22, 1738][8]

48. WEST TO GRAY

I OUGHT to answer you in Latin,[1] but I feel I dare not enter the lists with you—cupidum, pater optime, vires deficiunt.[2] Seriously you write in that language with a grace and an Augustan urbanity that amazes me: Your Greek too is perfect in its kind. And here let me wonder that a man, longè græcorum doctissimus, should be at a loss for the verse and chapter whence my epigram is taken. I am sorry I have not my Aldus with me that I might satisfy your curiosity; but he with all my other literary folks are left at Oxford, and therefore you must still rest in suspense. I thank you again and again for your medical prescription. I know very well that those 'risus, festivitates, & facetiæ' would contribute greatly to my cure, but then you must be my apothecary as well as physician, and make

---

[6] *Iliad*, iv. 190–1 (adapted): 'and apply drugs that shall assuage thy dire pangs.'

[7] The epigram of which he had sent Gray a Latin translation (see Letter 43).

[8] The date of the year is determined by that of West's letter of 21 Feb. 1738, which is a reply.

LETTER 48.—First printed in Mason's *Memoirs*, pp. 29–30.

[1] This was written in French, but as I doubted whether it would stand the test of polite criticism so well as the preceding would of learned, I chose to translate so much of it as I thought necessary in order to preserve the chain of correspondence. *Mason.*

[2] Horace, 2 *Sat.* i. 12–13.

up the dose as well as direct it; send me, therefore, an electuary of these drugs, made up secundùm artem, 'et eris mihi magnus Apollo',[3] in both his capacities as a god of poets and god of physicians. Wish me joy of leaving my college, and leave yours as fast as you can. I shall be settled at the Temple very soon.

Dartmouth-Street,[4] Feb. 21, 1737/8.

49. GRAY TO WALPOLE
[Cambridge, Feb. 23, 1738][1]

My best Horace

I CONFESS, I am amazed: of all likely things this is the last I should have believed would come to pafs:[2] however I congratulate you upon being able at this time to talk of Clytemnæstra, & Mrs Porter:[3] I wish, you have not admired this last-mention'd Gentlewoman long enough to catch a little of her art from her, for if I'm not mistaken, you are a very different person behind the Scenes, & whatever face you set upon the matter, I guefs—but perhaps I guefs wrong; I wish I may for your sake; perhaps you are as cool as you would seem: either way I may wish you joy; of your Difsimulation, or Philosophy:

[3] Virgil, *Ecl.* iii. 104.
[4] Dartmouth Street, Westminster, north side of Tothill Street to Great Queen Street (Wheatley's *London*).
LETTER 49.—First printed by Toynbee (1915), No. 76.
[1] The date of the month is supplied by the postmark; that of the year is determined by the reference to Mrs. Porter (see n. 3), and by the fact that Gray (as is indicated by the postmark *Saffron Walden*—one of the regulation postmarks on letters between Cambridge and London) was still at Cambridge, which he left in September 1738 (see Letter 56).
[2] This letter evidently refers to some love-affair, which Walpole had partially confided to Gray—a half-confidence, which evokes from the latter an interesting confession as to his own feelings on the subject of 'the new study . . . the most excellent of all sciences' (viz. the 'art of love'), of which Walpole had become a devotee. It seems to have become an open secret later that he was attached to his first cousin, Hon. Anne Seymour Conway, who in 1755 married John Harris. He was rallied about her by West (see his letter to Walpole of 10 Nov. 1740 in *Gray–Walpole Correspondence*, vol. i, p. 347), and also by his Cambridge tutor, John Whaley, who in a poem addressed to him not long after he left Cambridge writes:
'Flows from thy pen the sweet spontaneous line
While *Seymour's* look supplies the absent nine?'
[3] The famous actress (see Letter 20, n. 8); on 6 April of this year she appeared at Drury Lane as Clytaemnestra in the first performance of Thomson's *Agamemnon*. Walpole must have been discussing the performance by anticipation, presumably in the essay to which Gray refers in his postscript (see n. 7).

79

I long extremely to see you, but till I have that pleasure, me-thinks you might be a little more open in writing; have pity a little upon my curiosity: if you distrust my faith (I won't say Honour; that's for Gentlefolks⁴) and imagine I would shew your letters to any one; yet rely upon my vanity, which won't suffer me to do an ill thing; if you fear the common fate of loose papers, I give you my word to sacrifice to the fire immediately (no small sacrifice, I afsure you) all I shall receive, if you desire it: I don't wonder at the new study you have taken a likeing to; first because it diverts your thoughts from disagreeable objects, next, because it particularly suits your Genius, & lastly, because I believe it the most excellent of all sciences, to which in proportion as the rest are subservient, so great a degree of estimation they ought to gain: would you believe it, 'tis the very thing I would wish to apply to, myself? ay! as simple as I stand here:⁵ but then the Apparatus necefsary to it costs so much; nay, part of it is wholly out of one's power to procure; and then who should pare one, & burnish one? for they would have more trouble & fufs with me, than Cinderaxa's⁶ sisters had with their feet, to make 'em fit for the little glafs Slipper: oh yes! to be sure one must be lick'd; now to lick oneself I take to be altogether impracticable, & to ask another to lick one, would not be quite so civil; Bear I was born, & bear, I believe, I'm like to remain: consequently a little ungainly in my fond-nefses, but I'll be bold to say, you shan't in a hurry meet with a more loving poor animal, than

your faithful Creature,

BRUIN.

P: S: I beg you to continue your Efsay:⁷ & tell Zeph:⁸ when you see him to expect a letter in Rabbinical Hebrew from me, unlefs he writes directly.

Addressed: To The Honble Horace Walpole Esq at the Treasury Sᵗ James
Postmark: SAFFRON WALDEN 24 FE

⁴ See Letter 52, n. 3.
⁵ *Merry Wives of Windsor*, i. 1:
'*Slend.* My cousin Shallow is a justice of peace in his country, simple though I stand here.'
⁶ A variant of Cinderella (it is the name of the cook in William Somer-ville's *Hobbinol*).
⁷ See n. 3. This was probably the 'ingenious paper' referred to in a note from Mrs. Porter to 'her kind and generous friend & Benefactor Mr. Walpole' preserved in the Waller Collection (see *Supplement to the Letters of Horace Walpole*, vol. iii, p. 105). ⁸ Zephyrus, that is West.

50. GRAY TO WALPOLE

[   ]¹

I DID not allow myself time to rejoyce with Ashton upon his good fortune,² till after I had ransacked all his informations, as to you; & with him admired your judgement & conduct;³ for these virtues (I find, you are resolved to shew us) you are as well acquainted with, as we knew you were with their Sisters: what! will no lefs than the whole family serve your turn; sure one of 'em might have contented any moderate stomach! there's Mifs Temperance, Mifs Constance & the rest of 'em; e'er a one, i'gad, a match for an emperour: these, it is well known, or the world much belies you, you have Had; deny it, if you can; and must poor Mifs Prue go to pot too? well, I say no more, but it's too much in all conscience, methinks, for one man to be fit equally for this world, & the next. they tell me you are to be here once more in a little while; dear now, don't let it be much longer. in the mean time have you seen Comus,⁴ & what figure does it make after cutting for the simples?⁵ have you read yourself to sleep with Dᵣ Swift's conversation,⁶ as I did? that confounded Lady Answerall, tho' she says lefs than any body, is the devil to me! pray did you ever see an elephant? I have.

LETTER 50.—First printed by Toynbee (1915), No. 77.
¹ See Letter 1, n. 2.
² Ashton had recently been appointed, through the good offices of Walpole, tutor to the youthful Earl of Plymouth.
³ Early in March of this year Sir Robert Walpole married, as his second wife, Maria Skerrett, who had been his mistress. Horace Walpole had no liking for the match but had accepted it with good temper. This explains Gray's allusions to his 'judgement and conduct' and prudence ('Miss Prue').
⁴ This was an adaptation of Milton's *Comus* for the stage by John Dalton (1709–63), which was produced at Drury Lane on 4 March 1738, the music being composed by Dr. Arne.
⁵ Gray borrowed this phrase from Swift's *Polite Conversation*, Dialogue i:
'*Miss*. I won't quarrel with my bread and butter for all that; I know when I'm well.
Lady Answerall. Well; but, miss ——
Neverout. Ah! dear madam, let the matter fall; take pity on poor miss; don't throw water on a drownded rat.
Miss. Indeed, Mr. Neverout, you should be cut for the simples this morning; say a word more and you had as good eat your nails.'
⁶ *A Complete Collection of Genteel and Ingenious Conversation, according to the most polite Mode and Method, now used at Court, and in the best Companies of England. In three Dialogues.* London, 1738.

if you han't, you never saw an ugly thing. I would not be Aurengzebe for the world; they say, he rid upon one: that's
All.

yours ever,

T: G:

March, 7, [1738][7] Cantab:

Addressed: To The Honble Horace Walpole Esq at the Treasury St James's
Postmark: CAMBRIDGE 10 MR

51. GRAY TO WALPOLE

[   ][1]

THANK God, I had a very good night's rest, and am sufficiently awake to answer your letter, tho', likely to be more dull, than you that write in your sleep: and indeed I do not believe, that you ever are so much asleep, but you can write to a relation, play a sober game at Picquet, keep up a tete á tete conversation, sell a bargain, or perform any of the little offices of life with tolerable spirit; certain I am, there are many people in the world, who in their top spirits are no better eveillés, than you are at four in the morning, reclined upon your pillow. [2]I believe, I partly gueſs [what is] your hopeful branch; I fancy you may find the first letters of both somewhere between H & T inclusive; if I interpret your hieroglyphs aright.[2] as to my journey to London, which you are so good as to preſs, alas! what can I do? if I come, it is for good & all,[3] & I don't know how it is, I have a sort of reluctance to leave this place, un-amiable as it may seem; 'tis true Cambridge is very ugly, she is very dirty, & very dull; but I'm like a cabbage, where I'm stuck, I love to grow; you should pull me up sooner, than any one, but I shall be ne'er the better for transplanting: poor Mr Cornwallis[4] is here, sadly alter'd, so that one can very hardly

[7] The date of the year is determined by the reference to the performance of *Comus* (see n. 4).

LETTER 51.—First printed by Toynbee (1915), No. 78.

[1] See Letter 1, n. 2.

[2-2] The whole of this sentence has been heavily scored through, but is still decipherable, except for the words in square brackets, which are supplied conjecturally. Walpole's letter not having been preserved, the allusion remains unexplained. It is possible that it has reference to a cipher containing the names Horace and Thomas.

[3] Gray remained at Cambridge until the following September (see Letter 56).

[4] Afterwards Archbishop of Canterbury. *Walpole.*—Hon. Frederick

know him; Towers[5] still stands out, & refuses to admit him; so that they have called in their visitours,[6] that is the Vice-chancellour,[7] Dʳ Bently,[8] & Dʳ Ashton;[9] but nothing is yet determined: the Afsizes are just over, I was there; but I a'nt to be transported: Adieu,

yours sincerely

T: GRAY

Cam: March: 20 [1738][10]

Addressed: To The Honᵇˡᵉ Horatio Walpole, Esq at the Treasury Sᵗ James's
Postmark: CAMBRIDGE 20 MR

52. GRAY TO WALPOLE

[Cambridge, March 28, 1738][1]

[   ][2]

YOU can nevcr weary me with repetition of any thing, that makes me sensible of your kindnefs: since that has been the only Idea of any social happinefs that I have ever re-ceived almost, & which (begging your pardon for thinking so

Cornwallis (see Letter 16, n. 5). Cole, whose schoolfellow and contempor-ary at the University he was, says that towards the latter end of his residence he had a stroke of palsy, which took away the use of his right hand, and obliged him to write with his left.
⁵ William Towers, Master of Christ's College, 1723–45. Cornwallis had been elected Fellow on 28 Jan. 1738, but Dr. Towers refused to admit him on the ground that being a peer's son he was not eligible under the statute on the quality of Fellows. Cornwallis appealed to the Vice-Chancellor, who on 24 April 1738, with Dr. Hacket and Dr. Conyers Middleton as assessors, required the Master to admit him, which he did on the following day.
⁶ The visitors of Christ's were 'the Vice-Chancellor with two Senior Doctors in Divinity'.
⁷ William Richardson, D.D., Master of Emmanuel College, 1736–75.
⁸ Dr. Richard Bentley, Master of Trinity, 1700–42; D.D., 1696.
⁹ Dr. Charles Ashton, Master of Jesus, 1701–52, D.D., 1702.
¹⁰ The date of the year is determined by the references to Gray's ap-proaching departure from Cambridge (see n. 3).
LETTER 52.—First printed in part (in a garbled text) by Mason in *Memoirs*, pp. 16–17; first printed in full by Toynbee (1915), No. 28.
¹ Mason dates this letter *Peterhouse*, 23 Dec. 1736; which is certainly wrong so far as the date of the month is concerned, as is proved by the postmark. The allusion to Ashton's departure from Cambridge (cf. Letter 50, n. 2), and to West's possibly being in town, as he probably was at this time in 1738 (see Letter 49, n. 8), point almost certainly to 1738 as the correct date.
² See Letter 1, n. 2.

83

differently from you in such cases) I would by no means have parted with for an exemption from all the uneasinefses mixed with it. but it would be unjust to imagine my taste was any rule for yours, for which reason my letters are shorter & lefs frequent than they would be, had I any materials but myself to entertain you with. love, & brown Sugar must be a poor regale for one of your Goût, & alas! you know I am by trade a Grocer.³ Scandal (if I had any) is a merchandize, you don't profefs dealing in; now & then indeed, & to oblige a friend you may perhaps slip a little out of your Pocket, as a decayed Gentlewoman would a piece of right Mechlin, or a little quantity of run Tea; but this only now & then, not to make a practise of it. Monsters, appertaining to this Climate, you have seen already both wet & dry: so you see within how narrow bounds my Pen is circumscribed; & the whole contents of my share in our Correspondence may be reduced under the two heads of 1: You, 2: I: the first is indeed a subject to expatiate upon, but [you might]⁴ laugh at me for talking of what I do not understand; the second is as tiny, as tiresome, wherefore you shall hear no more of it, till you come to Finis. Ashton was here last night, he goes to morrow, he bid me farewell, & drank a health in Ale & small, to our meeting hereafter in a happy Eternity. Mʳˢ Ward has bought her a silver Chamberpot. Mademoiselle Quimbeau (that was) is weary of her new husband, & has sent a petit billet to a gentleman to pray he would come, & ravish her. there is a curious woman here that spins Glafs, & makes short Aprons, & furbelow'd petticoats of it, a very genteel wear for summer, & discover's⁵ all the motions of the limbs to great advantage. she is a succefsour of Jack, the Aple dumpling Spinner's: my Duck has eat a Snail, &c: & I am

yours eternally
T: G:

³ Mason notes: 'That is, a man who deals only in coarse and ordinary wares: to these he compares the plain sincerity of his own friendship, undisguised by flattery.' But Gray may be speaking literally, in allusion to the 'kind of India warehouse' which Mason says was kept by his mother and aunt in Cornhill (see Letter 28, n. 3). A sense of social inferiority seems implied in this letter, as in letter 49, where he says: 'if you distrust my faith (I won't say Honour; that's for Gentlefolks)'.

⁴ Piece cut out; the missing words have been supplied in pencil by Walpole.

⁵ *Sic.*

P:S: I give you a thousand thanks for your characters. if I knew whither West was in town, I'd write to him.

Addressed: To The Honble Horace Walpole Esq at the Treasury St James's
  Postmark: CAMBRIDGE 29 MR

53. GRAY TO WEST

BARBARAS ædes aditure mecum,[1]
Quas Eris semper fovet inquieta,
Lis ubi latè sonat, et togatum
    Æstuat agmen!

Dulcius quanto, patulis sub ulmi
Hospitæ ramis temerè jacentem
Sic libris horas, tenuicȝ inertes
    Fallere Musâ?

Sæpe enim curis vagor expeditâ
Mente; dum, blandam meditans Camænam,
Vix malo rori, meminive seræ
    Cedere nocti;

Et, pedes quò me rapiunt, in omni
Colle Parnafsum videor videre
Fertilem sylvæ, gelidamcȝ in omni
    Fonte Aganippen.

Risit & Ver me, facilescȝ Nymphæ
Nare captantem, nec ineleganti,
Manè quicquid de violis eundo
    Surripit aura:

Me reclinatum teneram per herbam;
Quà leves cursus aqua cunque ducit,
Et moras dulci strepitu lapillo
    Nectit in omni.

LETTER 53.—First printed in Mason's *Memoirs*, pp. 30–3; the verses were transcribed in Gray's Commonplace-book with the heading 'Ad C. Favonium Aristium' (Aristius Fuscus was the friend to whom Horace addressed the ode 'Integer vitæ', 1 *Odes*, xxii).
  [1] Cf. Horace, 2 *Odes*, vi. In the opening stanza Gray refers to the project he and West had formed of studying law together in the Inner Temple. See Letter 58**, n. 2.

Hæ novo nostrum ferè pectus anno
Simplices curæ tenuere, cœlum
Quamdiú sudum explicuit Favonî
        Purior hora:

Otia et campos nec adhuc relinquo,
Nec magis Phœbo Clytie fidelis;
(Ingruant venti licet, et senescat
        Mollior æstas.)

Namque, seu, lætos hominum labores
Pratacȝ & montes recreante curru,
Purpurâ tractus oriens Eoos
        Vestit, et auro;

Sedulus servo, veneratus orbem
Prodigum splendoris: amœniori
Sive dilectam meditatur igne
        Pingere Calpen;

Usque dum, fulgore magìs magìs jam
Languido circum, variata nubes
Labitur furtim, viridiscȝ in umbras
        Scena recefsit.

O ego felix, vice si (nec unquam
Surgerem rursus) simili cadentem
Parca me lenis sineret quieto
        Fallere letho!

Multà flagranti radiiscȝ cincto
Integris ah! quam nihil inviderem,
Cum Dei ardentes medius quadrigas
        Sentit Olympus?

Ohe! amicule noster, et unde, sodes, tu μουσοπάτακτος[2] adeo
repente evasisti? jam te rogitaturum credo. Nescio hercle, sic
plané habet. Quicquid enim nugarum ἐπὶ σχολῆς inter ambu-
landum in palimpsesto scriptitavi, hisce te maxumè impertiri
visum est, quippe quem probare, quod meum est, aut certè
ignoscere solitum probé novi: bonâ tuâ veniâ sit si fortè videar
in fine subtristior; nam risui jamdudum salutem dixi; etiam
paulè mœstitiæ studiosiorem factum scias, promptumque,
Καινοῖς παλαιὰ δακρύοις στένειν κακά.[3]

---

[2] Term for a poet, used by Cicero, *Epist. ad Quintum Fr.* ii. 10.
[3] 'To bewail old ills with new tears.'—Adapted from a fragment of the
Ἀλέξανδρος of Euripides: παλαιὰ καινοῖς δακρύοις οὐ χρὴ στένειν. *Tovey.*

O lachrymarum fons, tenero sacros
Ducentium ortus ex animo; quater
Felix! in imo qui scatentem
Pectore te, pia Nympha, sensit.

Sed de me satis. Cura ut valeas.

Jun. 1738.

54. GRAY TO ASHTON

My dear Ashton

IT seems you have forgot the poor little tenement in which you so long lodg'd, and have set your heart on some fine Castle in the air: I wish I were Master of the Seat you describe, that I might make your Residence more agreeable; but as it is, I fear you'll hardly meet with common Conveniences.

I deserve you should be angry with me for haveing been so little punctual, in paying my Dues, & returning thanks for your advice some time since. All is at present, mighty well, that is, just as you remember it, & imagin'd it would be: cool enough not to burn, and warm enough not to freeze one, but methinks the Counsel you gave me, was what you did not think proper to make use of in like Circumstances yourself; perhaps you know why the same way of acting should be improper for you, & proper for me: I don't doubt but you have your reasons, & I trust you would not have me do anything wrong.

The account W: gives me of your way of Life[1] is better than I expected: to be sure you must meet daily with little particulars enough to fill a letter, and I should be pleasd with the most minute. Has M^rs L:[2] a pimple upon her Nose? does her Woman love Citron Water?[3] &c: any of these would be a high regale for me. but perhaps you think it telling tales: you know best.

LETTER 54.—First printed by Tovey in *Gray and his Friends*, pp. 37–8; reprinted by Toynbee (1915), No. 80, from Mitford's transcript.

[1] In his capacity as tutor to Lord Plymouth, Ashton was now installed in the house in Hanover Square of Mrs. Lewis, daughter (Anne) and coheiress of Sir Nathan Wright, Bart., of Cranham Hall, Essex, and wife of Thomas Lewis of Harpton Court, Radnor.

[2] Mrs. Lewis.

[3] Cf. Pope, *Rape of the Lock*, iv. 67–9:

'But oh! if e'er thy Gnome could spoil a grace,
Or raise a pimple on a beauteous face,
Like Citron-waters matrons' cheeks inflame . . .'

Have you seen Madame Valmote?[4] naughty Woman! was you at the Christening?[5] is the Princeſs[6] with Child again? was you at the review? have you wrote e'er a Critique on the Accidence? is Despauterius[7] or Linacer[8] most in your favor? but perhaps you think this, tittle-tattle. Well! you know best. Pot-fair[9] is at its height; there's old raffleing. Walpole is gone to Stamford, & to Lynn, but returns in a day or two. I am gone to the Carrier's with this letter, and am

ever yours

T. G.

June 30 [1738][10]—Cambridge.

Addressed: To Mr Ashton, at the Honble Mrs Lewis's, in Hanover Square, London

55. WEST TO GRAY

I RETURN you a thousand thanks for your elegant ode,[1] and wish you every joy you wish yourself in it. But, take my word for it, you will never spend so agreeable a day here as you describe; alas! the sun with us rises only to shew us the

---

[4] Amelia Sophia von Walmoden (1704–65), Hanoverian lady, mistress of George II, who, after the death of Queen Caroline (Nov. 1737), brought her over to England, and installed her in St. James's Palace. In 1739 she was divorced from her husband, and in the following year was created Countess of Yarmouth. 'Monday, June 12. Arriv'd in Town Baron *Valmoute*, Great Chamberlain of *Hanover*, with his Lady, and waited on his Majesty, and met with a most gracious Reception. The Baron's stay here will not be long, but the Lady remains with Baron *Stanberg*, her Brother, Chief Secretary of *Hanover*' (*Gent. Mag.*, 1738, p. 322).

[5] That of George William Frederick (eldest son of Frederick, Prince of Wales), afterwards George III. He was born on 4 June of this year, and was christened in Norfolk House, St. James's Square, on the evening of 21 June, by the Bishop of Oxford.

[6] The Princess of Wales.

[7] Jean Despautère (1460–1520), Flemish grammarian; his *Commentarii Grammatici* were published in 1537.

[8] Thomas Linacre (*c*. 1460–1524), English physician and classical scholar; his *Rudimenta Grammatices*, an elementary Latin grammar in English, composed for the use of the Princess Mary, was first printed *c*. 1524.

[9] An annual fair at Cambridge for the sale of 'horses, cattle, timber, and pottery, beginning on 22 June, and commonly called Midsummer or Pot fair; it is proclaimed by the Heads of the University, and the Mayor and Corporation successively'. (Lewis, *Topog. Dict.*)

[10] The date of the year is determined by the references to the arrival of Madame Walmoden (see n. 4), and to the royal christening (see n. 5).

LETTER 55.—First printed in Mason's *Memoirs*, pp. 33–4.

[1] See Letter 53.

way to Westminster-Hall. Nor must I forget thanking you for your little Alcaic fragment.[1a] The optic Naiads are infinitely obliged to you.

I was last week at Richmond Lodge,[2] with Mr Walpole, for two days, and dined with Cardinal Fleury;[3] as far as my short sight can go, the character of his great art and penetration is very just, he is indeed

Nulli penetrabilis astro.[4]

I go to-morrow to Epsom,[5] where I shall be for about a month. Excuse me, I am in haste, but believe me always, &c.

August 29, 1738.

55*. Gray to Ashton

[*c. Sept. 7, 1738*]

[In his letter to West of 9 Sept. 1738, from Hanover Square (*Gray–Walpole Correspondence*, No. 83), Ashton says: 'A small Piece of Paper light at this House to day with Gray's name attachd to it, & declares he is very well, that Stourbridge fair[1] is full blown, & that he will go to bed at Cambridge but 14 Nights more.'[2]

[1] See Letter 56, n. 1.
[2] Gray was in London on 19 Sept. (see Letter 58).]

56. GRAY TO WEST

I AM coming away all so fast, and leaving behind me, without the least remorse, all the beauties of Sturbridge Fair.[1] Its

[1a] The stanza beginning 'O lachrymarum fons' at the end of Letter 53.
[2] Sir Robert Walpole's eldest son had been appointed Ranger of Richmond Park ('nominally, but my father in reality', says Walpole in his *Reminiscences*, chap. i) in 1725; for the convenience of hunting Sir Robert built a lodge in the New Park, on which he spent £14,000, and to which 'he usually retired on Saturdays and Sundays'.
[3] Sir Robert Walpole. *Mason.*—Cardinal André Hercule de Fleury (1653–1743), First Minister of France from 1726 till his death, during which period he exercised absolute power. The first object of his foreign policy was the maintenance of peace, which was also that of Sir Robert Walpole. Pope, 2 *Sat.* i. 75: 'Peace is my dear delight—not Fleury's more.'
[4] Statius, *Theb.* x. 85.
[5] Where his mother was then residing.
LETTER 56.—First printed in Mason's *Memoirs*, p. 36.
[1] Stourbridge, 1½ miles from Cambridge, was celebrated for its fair, formerly one of the largest in the kingdom, held in September. 'It is proclaimed by the Vice-Chancellor, Doctors, and Proctors of the University of Cambridge, and the Mayor and Aldermen of that borough, and continues more than three weeks.' (Lewis, *Topog. Dict.*)

white bears may roar, its apes may wring their hands, and crocodiles cry their eyes out, all's one for that; I shall not once visit them, nor so much as take my leave. The university has published a severe edict against schismatical congregations, and created half a dozen new little procterlings to see its orders executed, being under mighty apprehensions lest Henley[2] and his gilt tub should come to the Fair and seduce their young ones; but their pains are to small purpose, for lo, after all, he is not coming.

I am at this instant in the very agonies of leaving college, and would not wish the worst of my enemies a worse situation. If you knew the dust, the old boxes, the bedsteads, and tutors that are about my ears, you would look upon this letter as a great effort of my resolution and unconcernedneſs in the midst of evils. I fill up my paper with a loose sort of version of that scene in Pastor Fido[3] that begins, Care selve beati.[4]

[Cambridge] Sept.[5] 1738.

[2] John Henley (1692–1756), an eccentric preacher, commonly known as 'Orator Henley'. He was a Cambridge graduate, and after holding a living in Suffolk, in 1726 he severed his connexion with the Church, and began his 'orations' in a wooden booth in Newport Market. In 1729 he removed to Lincoln's Inn Fields, where, in spite of a prosecution for profaning the clerical character, he continued his 'exhibitions' for many years. He and his 'gilt tub' are celebrated in the *Dunciad* (ii. 2; iii. 199 ff.), where Pope apostrophizes him as, 'Preacher at once, and Zany of thy age'. 'The pulpit of a Dissenter', writes Pope, 'is usually called a Tub; but that of Mr. Orator Henley was covered with velvet, and adorned with gold. . . .' He preached on the Sundays upon Theological matters, and on the Wednesdays upon all other sciences. Each auditor paid one shilling. . . . After having stood some Prosecutions, he turned his rhetoric to buffoonery upon all public and private occurrences.' Sir Robert Walpole turned his talents to account by employing him, at a salary of £100 a year, to ridicule the *Craftsman*, the opposition journal, in a periodical called the *Hyp-Doctor*.

[3] Pastoral tragi-comedy by Battista Guarini (1538–1612), first published in 1590; editions had been published in London in 1728, 1734, and 1736.

[4] Mason's mistake for beate.—This Latin version is extremely elegiac, but as it is only a version I do not insert it . . . and I find amongst his papers an English translation of part of the 4th Canto of Tasso's *Gerusalemme Liberata*, done previously to this, which has great merit. *Mason.* (See Letter 37.)—A translation, dated 1738, of eight stanzas of the 14th (not 4th) Canto of the *Gerusalemme* is in Gray's Commonplace-book (printed in Mitford 1835–43, vol. i, p. 170), and it is probable that this is the version to which Mason refers. Gray also translated the Ugolino episode from the thirty-third Canto of Dante's *Inferno*. (See Toynbee, *Dante in English Literature*, vol. i, pp. 231–4.)

[5] The College books show that Gray left Cambridge in the middle of September.

57. West to Gray

I THANK you again and again for your two last most agreeable letters.[1] They could not have come more a-propos; I was without any books to divert me, and they supplied the want of every thing; I made them my classics in the Country, they were my Horace and Tibullus—Non ita loquor assentandi causâ ut probè nosti si me noris, verum quia sic mea est sententia. I am but just come to Town, and, to shew you my esteem of your favours, I venture to send you by the penny-post, to your Father's,[2] what you will find on the next page; I hope it will reach you soon after your arrival, your boxes out of the waggon, yourself out of the coach, and tutors out of your memory.

Adieu, we shall see one another, I hope, to-morrow.

Elegia.

Quod mihi tam gratæ misisti dona Camænæ,[3]
    Qualia Mænalius Pan Deus ipse velit,
Amplector te, Graie, & toto corde reposco,
    Oh desiderium jam nimis usque meum:
Et mihi rura placent, et me quoqȝ sæpe volentem
    Duxerunt Dryades per sua prata Deæ;
Sicubi lympha fugit liquido pede, sive virentem,
    Magna decus nemoris, quercus opacat humum:
Illuc mane novo vagor, illuc vespere sero,
    Et, noto ut jacui gramine, nota cano.
Nec nostræ ignorant divinam Amaryllida silvæ:
    Ah, si desit amor, nil mihi rura placent.
Ille jugis habitat Deus, ille in vallibus imis,
    Regnat & in Cælis, regnat & Oceano;
Ille gregem taurosqȝ domat, saeviqȝ leonem
    Seminis; ille feros, ultus Adonin, apros:
Quin & fervet amore nemus, ramoqȝ sub omni
    Concentu tremulo plurima gaudet avis.
Duræ etiam in sylvis agitant connubia plantæ,
    Dura etiam & fertur saxa animasse Venus.
Durior & saxis, & robore durior ille est,
    Sincero siquis pectore amare vetat:

LETTER 57.—First printed in Mason's *Memoirs*, pp. 37-9.
[1] Letters 53 and 56.
[2] In Cornhill (see Letter 28, n. 3).
[3] The version from the *Pastor Fido* mentioned in his last letter (see Letter 56, n. 4).

Non illi in manibus sanctum deponere pignus,
    Non illi arcanum cor aperire velim;
Nescit amicitias, teneros qui nescit amores:
    Ah! si nulla Venus, nil mihi rura placent.
Me licet a patriâ longè in tellure juberent
    Externâ positum ducere fata dies;
Si vultus modo amatus adesset, non ego contra
    Plorarem magnos voce querente Deos.
At dulci in gremio curarum oblivia ducens
    Nil cuperem præter posse placere meæ;
Nec bona fortunæ aspiciens, neq̃ munera regum,
    Illa intrà optarem brachia cara mori.

Sept. 17. 1738.[4]

58. GRAY TO WALPOLE

[   ]¹

I HAVE been in town a day or two, & in doubt where to direct to you, till Ashton, whom I saw today, told me you were at Richmond.[2] I have seen him & his Lordling,[3] and am mightily pleased with 'em both; the boy kiſses his eyes out, & had no sooner heard, that I was Mr John Ashton,[4] but he climbed up to the top of my head, & came down again on the other side in half a second. I shall be glad to know when & where I may see you most alone, &

               am Yours ever,
                  T: G:

Tuesday—Night—[September 19, 1738][5]

Addressed: To The Honble Horace Walpole, Junr: Esq at New Park Richmond. *Postmark:* 19 SE

---

[4] Mr. West spent the greatest part of this winter with his mother and sister at Epsom. *Mason* (in *Memoirs*, p. 39.)

LETTER 58.—First printed by Toynbee (1915), No. 86.

[1] See Letter 1, n. 2.

[2] At Sir Robert Walpole's house in New Park (see Letter 55, n. 2).

[3] The Earl of Plymouth (see Letter 54, n. 1).

[4] Ashton's younger brother—he was at Trinity College, Cambridge, of which he subsequently became Fellow; B.A., 1742; M.A., 1746.

[5] The date of the month is supplied by the postmark; that of the year is determined by the reference to Ashton and Lord Plymouth (see n. 3).—Mr. Gray, on his return to Town, continued at his father's house in Cornhill till the March following. *Mason* (in *Memoirs*, p. 39).

58*. GRAY TO WEST

[Dec. 1738][1]

As I know you are a lover of Curiosities, I send you the following, which is a true & faithful Narrative of what pafsed in my Study on Saturday the 16th, instant.[2] I was sitting there very tranquil in my chair, when I was suddenly alarmd with a great hubbub of Tongues. In the street, you suppose? No! in my Study, Sir. In your Study say you? Yes & between my books, which is more. For why should not books talk as well as Crabs & Mice & files & Serpents do in Esop. But as I listend with great attention so as to remember what I heard pretty exactly, I shall set down the whole conversation as methodically as I can, with the names prefixd.

Mad: Sevigné. . Mon cher Aristote! do get a little farther or you'll quite suffocate me.

Aristotle. . *Οὐδέποτε γυνὴ* ? . . I have as much right to be here as you, and I shan't remove a jot.

M. Sevigné. . Oh! the brute! here's my poor Sixth tome[3] is squeezed to death: for God's sake, Bufsy,[4] come & rescue me.

Bufsy Rabutin. . Ma belle Cousine! I would fly to your

LETTER 58*.—First printed by Tovey in *Gray and his Friends* (pp. 154–5); reprinted by Toynbee (1915), No. 139, from Mitford's transcript.

[1] Date conjectural. Mitford dates this letter 1740, in which year Gray was abroad; but from the nature of its contents it is unlikely that it was written while Gray was on his travels. Further, in the letter itself Gray refers to what passed in his study on 'Saturday the 16th, instant'. In 1740 N.S. (the style in use on the Continent) the 16th was a Saturday in Jan., in April, and in July, and it so happens that Gray wrote to West on 15 Jan. (see Letter 78), on 16 April (see Letter 83), and on 16 July (see Letter 91) of that year. The choice lies between a date before Gray left England (in March 1739), and one after he returned. The only month between Sept. 1741 (the date of his return) and 1 June 1742 (the date of West's death) in which the 16th fell on a Saturday was Jan. 1742; to this date, therefore, the letter might belong. But a more likely date is 1738 (in which year the 16th was a Saturday in Sept. and in Dec.), for in Gray's Commonplace-book, among entries probably written in 1738, are references to 'Lettres de Mad: la Marquise de Sevigné a sa fille' (see n. 3), to 'Histoire amoureuse des Gaules, par Bussi Rabutin' (see n. 4), and to Gronovius, all of which are mentioned in this letter. As between Sept. and Dec. in 1738, the sequence of correspondence makes the latter month the more probable.

[2] See n. 1.

[3] A *Recueil des Lettres de Madame la Marquise de Sévigné, à Madame la Comtesse de Grignan, sa fille*, had been published in Paris in six volumes in 1734–7; and another, also in six volumes, in 1738.

[4] Roger de Rabutin (1618–93), Comte de Bussy, Madame de Sévigné's

afsistance. Mais voici un Diable de Strabon qui me tue: I have nobody in my neighbourhood worth conversing with here but Catullus.

Bruyere.[5] . Patience! You must consider we are but books & so can't help ourselves. for my part, I wonder who we all belong to. We are a strange mixture here. I have a Malebranche[6] on one Side of me, and a Gronovius[7] on t'other.

Locke.[8] . Certainly our owner must have very confusd ideas, to jumble us so strangely together. he has afsociated me with Ovid & Ray the Naturalist.[9]

Virgil. . 'Me vero primum dulces ante omnia Musæ
               Accipiant!'[10]

Hen: More.[11] . Of all the Speculations that the Soul of Man can entertain herself withall; there is none of greater Moment than this of her immortality.

Cheyne.[12] . Every Man after fourty is a fool or a Physician.

Euclid. . Punctum est, cujus nulla est—

Boileau. . Peste soit de cet homme avec son Punctum! I wonder any Man of Sense will have a Mathematician in his Study.

Swift. . In short let us get the Mathematicians banishd first; the Metaphysicians and Natural Philosophers may follow them. &c.

Vade Mecum. . Pshaw! I and the Bible are enough for any one's library.

This last ridiculous Egotism made me laugh so heartily that I disturbd my poor books & they talk'd no more.

---

first cousin. His *Histoire Amoureuse des Gaules* was published *c.* 1665; his *Mémoires* in 1696; and his *Lettres* in 1697.

[5] Jean de la Bruyère (1645–96), see Letter 58**, n. 12.

[6] Nicolas Malebranche (1638–1715), French philosopher of the school of Descartes.

[7] Johann Friedrich Gronov (1611–71), German classical scholar.

[8] John Locke (1632–1704).

[9] John Ray (1627–1705), author of *Catalogus Plantarum Angliæ* (1670).

[10] *Georg.* ii. 475, 477.

[11] Henry More (1614–87), Cambridge Platonist. His *Immortality of the Soul, so farre forth as it is demonstrable from the Knowledge of Nature and the Light of Reason*, was published in 1659.

[12] George Cheyne (1671–1743), Scottish physician. His *Essay on Health and Long Life* (1724) begins: 'It is a common saying, That every Man past Forty is either a *Fool* or a Physician.'

58**. WEST TO GRAY

[Epsom, c. Jan. 1739][1]

IMITATION OF HORACE. Lib: I: Ep: 2:

Trojani belli scriptorem, &c:

WHILE haply You (or haply not at all)
Hear the grave Pleadings in the Lawyer's Hall[2]
Or, while You haply Littleton[3] explore,
Turning the learned leaden Pages o'er;
Think me again transported to peruse
The golden Rhapsodies of Milton's Muse:
Who shews us in his high Seraphic Song,
What just, what unjust, what is Right, what Wrong,
With Sense at least, & Evidence as true,
As all our Judges of the Bench could do.
Why thus I think (to Hardwick[4] no Offence)
Give Ear, & with your Coke[5] awhile dispense.

LETTER 58**.—First printed by Tovey in *Gray and his Friends*, pp. 119–23; now reprinted from Gray's transcript in his Commonplace-book.

[1] Date conjectural. Gray notes at the end of his transcript: 'Fav: from Epsome, before I went to France, in 1739.' West was at Epsom during the winter of 1738–9 as appears from the following note of Mason in his *Memoirs* (p. 39): 'Mr. Gray, on his return to Town [Sept. 1738], continued at his father's house in Cornhill till the March following. . . . Mr. West spent the greatest part of the winter with his mother and sister at Epsom, during which time a letter or two more passed between the two friends. But these I think it unnecessary to insert, as I have already given sufficient specimens of the blossoms of their Genius.' From this last remark it may be gathered that other letters of Gray and West in the form of poems belonging to this period were suppressed by Mason.

[2] Westminster Hall (see Letters 55, 89)—Gray left Cambridge in Sept. 1738, without taking a degree, with the intention of studying law in London, where he proposed to join West in the Inner Temple (see Letter 53), a project which was abandoned in consequence of an invitation from Walpole to accompany him on a prolonged tour on the Continent. At the date of this letter this change in Gray's plans had not yet been determined upon, or West had not yet heard of it.

[3] Sir Thomas Littleton (1402–81), judge and author of the famous treatise on 'Tenures', which with the commentary of Sir Edward Coke (see n. 5) long remained the principal authority on English real property law.

[4] Lord Hardwicke, at this date Lord Chancellor (see Letter 25, n. 5).

[5] Sir Edward Coke (1552–1634), judge and author of the famous 'Institutes of the Laws of England'.

The Tale disastrous[6] You remember well,
How Satan tempted, & how Adam fell;
And how He tasted the forbidden Tree,
Seduced by female Curiosity;
How thus our Paradise we lost, & all
The Children perish'd in the Father's Fall.
Nor be that other Tale[7] forgotten here
More moral, tho' less pleasing to the Ear
How in the Desart Wild with Hunger spent
Full forty Days our patient Saviour went.
Then spurning back to Hell the wily Fiend
Taught us on Heaven (Heaven only) to depend,
Hence us redeem'd at our Messiah's cost:
The Cross regaining, what the Apple lost.
Thus, while I read our Epic Bard divine,
My Mind intent with Pleasure Use to joyn,
From either Poem this Instruction draws,
To trust in God, & to obey God's Laws.
    Enough of Sermon: I perceive, you nodd.
You think me mighty wise, & mighty odd:
Your Lips, I see, half verge upon a Smile—
Dear Sir, observe the Horace in my Style.
Just such to Lollius,[8] his misguided Friend,
He knew with decent Liberty to send
Beneath the Critique dext'rous to convey
Advice conceal'd, in the best-natured Way
But You're no Lollius, and no Horace I:
Here is no Room sage Maxims to apply.
Would you not burst outright to hear me say
Satan, my friend, may lead the best astray;
By Nature ill, by Habit worse inclined,
Add Pride, add Envy, add the willful Mind
Still prone to disobey & to deceive,
All men are Adam, & all women Eve.
Thus bad, thus all corrupted, much I fear,
Morality sounds painful to the Ear.
    The Dogs of Night, that murder & that steal,
Outwatch[9] the Watchmen of the publick Weal:

---

[6] *Paradise Lost.*   [7] *Paradise Regained.*
[8] Maximus Lollius, the friend to whom Horace addressed the Epistle imitated by West.
[9] Gray inadvertently wrote 'Outwactch'.

Fools, that We are! less Labour to employ
To save ourselves, than Villains to destroy.
Suppose your Body sick; at any Price
You run to Mead[10] or Hollings[11] for Advice:
This for thy Body: but suppose thy Mind,
For that what Mead or Hollings will you find?
Rise, Sluggard, rise, & quit thy Morning-Bed
E're yet Aurora lifts her rosy Head:
Take Plato down, take Tully, take Bruyére,[12]
Make honest Things, & Studies all thy Care:
At sight of Industry Vice flies away,
As Spectres vanish at the Face of Day.
If ought offensive to the Eye appear
Not long You let the Object be too near:
What hurts the Mind more patient to endure,
For Years together we delay the Cure.
Meanwhile the Time irrevocable flies:
Begin, & have the Spirit to be wise:
Begin, nor do, as did the Rustick Ass
Who stood, & waited till the Stream should pass:
The Stream, Poor fool! You little seem to know,
Flows, as it flow'd, and will for ever flow.
The gay Town-house, the pleasant Country-Seat,
The fertile Meadow, & the Garden neat,
The fruitful Nursery, the tender Wife,
Are Joys Men almost value with their Life:
Yet all these Joys, and more (could more be sent)
Make not the Total of one Word, Content.

[10] Dr. Richard Mead, Physician to George II (see Letter 114, n. 5).

[11] Dr. John Hollings (c. 1683–1739), Physician-General to the Army, and Physician in Ordinary to George II; of Magdalene College, Cambridge; M.D., 1710; F.R.S., 1726; Fellow of Royal College of Physicians, 1726; Harveian Orator, 1734; died May 1739.

[12] Jean de la Bruyère (1645–96), of the Académie Française (1693), author of *Les Caractères*, which was first published in 1688, with the title, *Les Caractères de Théophraste, traduits du grec, avec les caractères et les mœurs de ce siècle*, and went through eight editions, successively remodelled and enlarged, during his lifetime. It is evident, as Tovey points out, that Norton Nicholls was thinking of this line, and attributed it to Gray, when in his *Reminiscences of Gray* he wrote: 'La Bruyére stood high in his estimation. ... I remember part of a line among some juvenile MS. verses in his Commonplace-book of advice to West, in which he recommends to him to rise early and

—read Plato, read Bruyére.'

Not all the Gold of the Peruvian Mine,
Not all the Gems that blaze beneath the Line,
Can cure a Fever, or one Care expell:
Possessions make not the Possessour well.
The Man, who lives in Hope, or lives in Fear,
In nougt He has can tast the Joy sincere:
Sooner shall Handel give the Deaf delight,
And Rafael's Pencil charm the Blind to Sight.
First cleanse the Vessel, e're the Wine you pour;
T'will else be Vinegar, & Wine no more.
Obvious to Sense the Allegory lies:
Would you be happy, be but only wise.
Reject all Pleasures of the Sense: they're vain.
Each Hour of Pleasure has it's Hour of Pain.
Bound thy mad Wishes; fix on something sure:
The Harpy Avarice is ever poor.
May none but Vilain's, be with Envy curst!
Of all the Vices 'tis the Vice the worst:
Scarce all the Tortures of the Damn'd in Hell
The Pangs of wretched Envy can excell.
Sore shall He smart & most severely pay,
Who lets his Passion o'er his Reason sway:
Oft, to his Scorn, shall his unguarded Rage
Act o'er the Part of Cassius on the Stage
Reprove his Friend, upbraid, insult, resent,
Rave like one wild, grow sorry, & repent.[13]
Oh, if you'd live in gentle Peace with all
Restrain the boiling Fury of thy Gall:
Oh! early wise it's growing force restrain;
Like the Steed, curb it: like the Lyon, chain.
    Youth, Youth 's the Season for Instruction fit.
The Colt's young Neck is pliant to the Bit.
The young Hawk listens to the Master's Sound,
The Whelp unlash'd was never yet a Hound.
Now, Boy, 's the time. my gentle Boy, draw nigh:
Come with thy blushing Front, & open Eye
Now, while thy Breast is, as the Current, clear,
Unruffled, unpolluted, & sincere:
Now fair & honest all thy Hours employ,
For know, the Man is grafted on the Boy.

[13] A reference to Shakespeare's *Julius Cæsar*, iv. 3.

The Cask once season'd keeps the Flavour long.
Adieu! thus ends my moralizeing Song.
   Abrupt I finish: my hard Task is o'er:
Forgive me, Pope! I'll imitate no more.

59. GRAY TO MRS. GRAY[1]

Amiens, April 1, N.S. 1739.

As we made but a very short journey to-day, and came to our inn early, I sit down to give you some account of our expedition. On the 29th (according to the style here)[2] we left Dover at twelve at noon, and with a pretty brisk gale, which pleased everybody mighty well, except myself who was extremely sick the whole time; we reached Calais by five: The weather changed, and it began to snow hard the minute we came into the harbour, where we took the boat, and soon landed. Calais is an exceeding old, but very pretty town, and we hardly saw any thing there that was not so new and so different from England, that it surprized us agreeably. We went the next morning to the great Church, and were at high Mafs (it being Easter Monday). We saw also the Convent of the Capuchins, and the Nuns of St. Dominic; with these last we held much conversation, especially with an English Nun, a Mrs. Davis, of whose work I sent you, by the return of the Pacquet, a letter-case to remember her by. In the afternoon we took a Post-chaise (it still snowing very hard) for Boulogne, which was only eighteen miles further. This chaise is a strange sort of conveyance, of much greater use than beauty, resembling an ill-shaped chariot, only with the door opening before instead of the side; three horses draw it, one between the shafts, and the other two on each side, on one of which the postillion rides, and drives too:[3] This vehicle will, upon occasion, go fourscore miles a-day, but Mr. Walpole, being in no hurry, chooses to

LETTER 59.—First printed in Mason's *Memoirs*, pp. 41–3.
   [1] Gray left Dover for his tour with Walpole to France and Italy on Sunday, 29 March (New Style = 18 March Old Style) and was abroad until the beginning of September 1741.
   [2] 'New Style' (according to the reformed calendar instituted by Pope Gregory XIII in 1582) was not adopted in England till 1752. Gray's letters from France and Italy were dated by the New Style: letters to him from England must have been dated by the Old Style.
   [3] This was before the introduction of Post-chaises here, else it would not have appeared a circumstance worthy notice. *Mason.*

make easy journeys of it, and they are easy ones indeed; for the motion is much like that of a sedan, we go about six miles an hour, and commonly change horses at the end of it: It is true they are no very graceful steeds, but they go well, and through roads which they say are bad for France, but to me they seem gravel walks and bowling-greens; in short it would be the finest travelling in the world, were it not for the inns, which are mostly terrible places indeed. But to describe our progreſs somewhat more regularly, we came into Boulogne when it was almost dark, and went out pretty early on Tuesday morning; so that all I can say about it is, that it is a large, old, fortified town, with more English in it than French. On Tuesday we were to go to Abbéville, seventeen leagues, or fifty-one short English miles; but by the way we dined at Montreuil, much to our hearts' content, on stinking mutton cutlets, addle eggs, and ditch water. Madame the hosteſs made her appearance in long lappets of bone lace and a sack of linsey-woolsey. We supped and lodged pretty well at Abbéville, and had time to see a little of it before we came out this morning. There are seventeen convents in it, out of which we saw the chapels of the Minims and the Carmelite Nuns. We are now come further thirty miles to Amiens, the chief city of the province of Picardy. We have seen the cathedral, which is just what that of Canterbury must have been before the reformation. It is about the same size, a huge Gothic building, beset on the outside with thousands of small statues, and within adorned with beautiful painted windows, and a vast number of chapels dreſsed out in all their finery of altar-pieces, embroidery, gilding, and marble. Over the high altar is preserved, in a very large wrought shrine of maſsy gold, the reliques of St. Firmin, their patron saint. We went also to the chapels of the Jesuits and Ursuline Nuns, the latter of which is very richly adorned. To-morrow we shall lie at Clermont, and next day reach Paris. The country we have paſsed through hitherto has been flat, open, but agreeably diversified with villages, fields well-cultivated, and little rivers. On every hillock is a wind-mill, a crucifix, or a Virgin Mary dreſsed in Flowers, and a sarcenet robe; one sees ⟨not⟩⁴ many people or carriages on the road; now and then indeed you meet a strolling friar, a country-man with his great muff, or a woman riding astride on a little aſs, with short petticoats, and a great head-dreſs of blue wool. * * *

    ⁴ Mason omits 'not'.

60. GRAY TO WEST

Paris, April 12, 1739.

ENFIN donc me voici à Paris.[1] Mr. Walpole is gone out to supper at Lord Conway's,[2] and here I remain alone, though invited too. Do not think I make a merit of writing to you preferably to a good supper; for these [eight][2a] days we have been here, have actually given me an aversion to eating in general. If hunger be the best sauce to meat, the French are certainly the worst cooks in the world; for what tables we have seen have been so delicately served, and so profusely, that, after rising from one of them, one imagines it impofsible ever to eat again. And now, if I tell you all I have in my head, you will believe me mad, mais n'importe, courage, allons! for if I wait till my head grow clear and settle a little, you may stay long enough for a letter. Six days have we been coming hither, which other people do in two; they have not been disagreeable ones; through a fine, open country, admirable roads, and in an easy conveyance; the inns not absolutely intolerable, and images quite unusual presenting themselves on all hands. At Amiens we saw the fine cathedral, and eat paté de perdrix; pafsed through the park of Chantilly by the Duke of Bourbon's palace, which we only beheld as we pafsed; broke down at Lusarche; stopt at St. Denis, saw all the beautiful monuments of the Kings of

LETTER 60.—First printed in Mason's *Memoirs*, pp. 44–7.

[1] In *Short Notes of my Life* Walpole writes: 'In 1739, March 10th [the date is obviously wrong: see Letter 59, n. 1], I set out on my travels with my friend Mr Thomas Gray, and went to Paris. From thence, after a stay of about two months, we went with my cousin Henry Conway to Rheims, in Champagne, stayed there three months; and passing by Geneva, where we left Mr Conway, Mr Gray and I went by Lyons to Turin, over the Alps, and from thence to Genoa, Parma, Placentia, Modena, Bologna, and Florence. There we stayed three months, chiefly for the sake of Mr Horace Mann, the English Minister.'

[2] Francis Seymour Conway (1718–94), second Baron Conway; afterwards (1750) Earl, and (1793) Marquis of Hertford; Ambassador at Paris, 1763–5; Viceroy of Ireland, 1765–6. He was Horace Walpole's first cousin, and brother of Henry Seymour Conway (afterwards Field-Marshal Conway) (see n. 4).

[2a] A correction of 'three' in Mason's text which must have been a mistake or a misprint (perhaps by a misreading of 8 as 3. Cf. Letters 71, 81). Gray says below that they reached Paris on Saturday. As the letter is dated 12 April (Sunday), and Gray says that they dined with Lord Holderness on one day, and with Lord Waldegrave on another, and went to the Comédie Française on two others, besides visiting churches and palaces, it is evident that they must have arrived on Saturday, 4 April, and had consequently been in Paris eight days.

France, and the vast treasures of the abbey, rubies, and emeralds as big as small eggs, crucifixes, and vows, crowns and reliquaries, of inestimable value; but of all their curiosities the thing the most to our tastes, and which they indeed do the justice to esteem the glory of their collection, was a vase of an entire onyx, measuring at least five inches over, three deep, and of great thicknefs. It is at least two thousand years old, the beauty of the stone and sculpture upon it (representing the mysteries of Bacchus) beyond exprefsion admirable; we have dreamed of it ever since. The jolly old Benedictine, that showed us the treasures, had in his youth been ten years a soldier; he laughed at all the reliques, was very full of stories, and mighty obliging. On Saturday evening we got to Paris, and were driving through the streets a long while before we knew where we were. The minute we came, voila Milors Holdernefse,[3] Conway, and his brother;[4] all stayed supper, and till two o'clock in the morning, for here nobody ever sleeps; it is not the way: Next day go to dine at my Lord Holdernefse's, there was the Abbé Prevôt,[5] author of the Cleveland,[6] and several other pieces much esteemed: The rest were English. At night we went to the Pandore; a spectácle literally, for it is nothing but a beautiful piece of machinery of three scenes. The first represents the chaos, and by degrees the separation of the elements. The second, the temple of Jupiter, and the giving of the box to Pandora. The third, the opening of the box, and all the mischiefs that ensued. An absurd design, but executed in the highest perfection, and that in one of the finest theatres in the world; it is the grande sale des machines in the Palais des Tuileries. Next day dined at Lord Waldegrave's;[7] then to the opera. Imagine to yourself for the drama four acts[8] entirely

[3] Robert D'Arcy (1718–78), fourth Earl of Holdernesse (1722); Ambassador at Venice, 1744–6; Minister at The Hague, 1749–51; Secretary of State, 1751–61, in the Pelham and Pitt Ministries (save for a few days in 1757); Governor to the Prince of Wales, 1771–6. In 1754 he presented Mason to the living of Aston, in Yorkshire, and appointed him his Chaplain (see Letter 144, n. 33).   [4] Hon. Henry Seymour Conway (see Letter 44, n. 9).

[5] Antoine-François Prévost d'Exiles (1697–1763), best known as the author of *Manon Lescaut* (1731).

[6] *Le Philosophe anglois, ou Histoire de Monsieur Cleveland, fils naturel de Cromwell, écrite par lui-mesme, et traduite de l'anglois* (8 vols., 1731–9). An English translation was published in 1734.

[7] James Waldegrave (1684–1741), first Earl Waldegrave, Ambassador in Paris, 1730–40.

[8] The French opera has only three acts, but often a prologue on a different

unconnected with each other, each founded on some little history, skilfully taken out of an ancient author, e.g. Ovid's Metamorphoses, &c., and with great addreſs converted into a French piece of gallantry. For instance, that which I saw, called the Ballet de la Paix, had its first act built upon the story of Nereus.[9] Homer having said he was the handsomest man of his time,[10] the poet, imagining such a one could not want a mistreſs, has given him one. These two come in and sing sentiment in lamentable strains, neither air nor recitative; only, to one's great joy, they are every now and then interrupted by a dance, or (to one's great sorrow) by a chorus that borders the stage from one end to the other, and screams, past all power of simile to represent. The second act was Baucis and Philemon.[11] Baucis is a beautiful young shepherdeſs, and Philemon her swain. Jupiter falls in love with her, but nothing will prevail upon her; so it is all mighty well, and the chorus sing and dance the praises of Constancy. The two other acts were about Iphis and Ianthe,[12] and the judgment of Paris. Imagine, I say, all this transacted by cracked voices, trilling divisions upon two notes and a half, accompanied by an orchestra of humstrums, and a whole house more attentive than if Farinelli[13] sung, and you will almost have formed a just notion of the thing.[14] Our astonishment at their absurdity you can never conceive; we had enough to do to expreſs it by screaming an hour louder than the whole dramatis personæ. We have also seen twice the Comedie Françoise; first, the Mahomet Second,[15] a tragedy that has had a great run of late; and the thing itself does not want

subject, which (as Mr. Walpole informs me, who saw it at the same time) was the case in this very representation. *Mason.*

   [9] 'Nereus' in Mason's text should obviously be 'Nireus'.

   [10] *Iliad*, ii. 673–4: 'Nireus the most beauteous of all the Greeks that came up to Troy, after the noble son of Peleus.'

   [11] Ovid, *Metam.* viii. 620 ff.   [12] Ovid, *Metam.* ix. 666 ff.

   [13] Carlo Broschi, called Farinelli (1705–82), famous soprano singer. He sang in London during the three years 1734–6, his first appearance being in *Artaserse*, the music of which was composed by his brother Riccardo Broschi (see Letter 20, n. 5).

   [14] Our author's sentiments here seem to correspond entirely with those which J. J. Rousseau afterwards published in his famous Lettre sur la Musique Françoise. In a french letter also, which Mr. Gray writ to his friend soon after this, he calls their music 'des miaulemens & des heurlemens effroyables, melés avec un tintamarre du diable; voilà la musique Françoise en abregé'. *Mason* (see Letter 61*).

   [15] By Jean-Baptiste Sauvé de la Noue (1701–61); this tragedy had been produced for the first time on 23 Feb. of this year.

its beauties, but the actors are beyond measure delightful. Mademoiselle Gaufsin[16] (Mr. Voltaire's Zara[17]) has with a charming (though little) person the most pathetic tone of voice, the finest exprefsion in her face, and most proper action imaginable. There is also a Dufrêne,[18] who did the chief character, a handsome man and a prodigious fine actor. The second we saw was the Philosophe marié,[19] and here they performed as well in comedy; there is a Mademoiselle Quinault,[20] somewhat in Mrs. Clive's[21] way, and a Monsieur Grandval,[22] in the nature of Wilks,[23] who is the genteelest thing in the world. There are several more would be much admired in England, and many (whom we have not seen) much celebrated here. Great part of our time is spent in seeing churches and palaces full of fine pictures, &c., the quarter of which is not yet exhausted. For my part, I could entertain myself this month merely with the common streets and the people in them. * * *

61. GRAY TO ASHTON

Dear Ashton,

YOU and West have made us happy to night in a heap of letters, & we are resolvd to repay you tenfold. Our English perhaps may not be the best in the World, but we have the Comfort to know that it is at least as good as our French. So to begin. Paris is a huge round City, divided by the Seine, a very near relation (if we may judge from the resemblance) of your old acquaintance, that ancient river, the river Cam. Along it on either side runs a key of perhaps as handsome buildings, as any in the World. the view down which on either

[16] Jeanne-Catherine Gaussin (1711–67); she made her first appearance in 1731, and did not quit the stage till 1763.
[17] *Zaïre*, Voltaire's masterpiece (see Letter 20, n. 13).
[18] Abraham-Alexis Quinault Dufresne (1693–1741); he is described as being endowed with 'une taille noble et haute, des yeux éloquens, un organe enchanteur'.
[19] By Philippe Néricault Destouches (1680–1754); it was first produced in 1727.
[20] Jeanne-Françoise Quinault (c. 1700–83), sister of Dufresne (see n. 18).
[21] Catherine Raftor (1711–85), wife (1732) of George Clive, a barrister, commonly known as Kitty Clive.
[22] François-Charles Grandval (1710–84).
[23] Robert Wilks (c. 1665–1732), chiefly distinguished as a comedian, though he played many tragic parts with success.
LETTER 61.—First printed by Tovey in *Gray and his Friends*, pp. 39–41; reprinted by Toynbee (1915), No. 89, from Mitford's transcript.

hand from the Pont Neuf is the charming'st Sight imaginable. There are infinite Swarms of inhabitants & more Coaches than Men. The Women in general dref̄sd in Sacs, flat Hoops of 5 yards wide nosegays of artificial flowers, on one shoulder, and faces dyed in Scarlet up to the Eyes. The Men in bags,[1] roll-upps,[2] Muffs and Solitaires.[3] our Mornings have been mostly taken up in Seeing Sights: few Hotels or Churches have escapd us, where there is anything remarkable as to building, Pictures or Statues.

Mr Conway is as usual, the Companion of our travels, who, till we came, had not seen anything at all; for it is not the fashion here to have Curiosity. We had at first arrival an inundation of Visits pouring in upon us, for all the English are acquainted, and herd much together & it is no easy Matter to disengage oneself from them, so that one sees but little of the French themselves.

To be introduced to the People of high quality, it is absolutely necef̄sary to be master of the Language, for it is not to be imagind that they will take pains to understand anybody, or to correct a stranger's blunders. Another thing is, there is not a House where they don't play, nor is any one at all acceptable, unlef̄s they do so too . . a profef̄sed Gamester being the most advantageous Character a Man can have at Paris. The Abbés indeed & Men of learning are a People of easy accef̄s enough, but few English that travel have knowledge enough to take any great Pleasure in their Company, at least our present Set of travellers have not. We are, I think to remain here no longer than Ld Conway stays, and then set out for Rheims, there to reside a Month or two, & then to return hither again. this is our present design & very often little hanker-ings break out, so that I am not sure, we shall not come back tomorrow.

We are exceedingly unsettled & irresolute, don't know our own Minds for two Moments together, profef̄s an utter aversion for all Manner of fatigue, grumble, are ill natured & try to bring ourselves to a State of perfect Apathy in which ⟨we⟩ are

---

[1] Bag-wigs.
[2] Otherwise called rolling-hose—'stockings of which the tops could be rolled up or down on the leg.' (*O.E.D.*)
[3] 'A loose neck-tie of black silk, sometimes secured to the bag of the wig behind, and in front either falling loosely or secured by a brooch.' (*Cent. Dict.*)

so far advanced, as to declare we have no Notion of caring for any mortal breathing but ourselves. In short I think the greatest *evil* ⟨that⟩ could have happen'd to us, is our liberty, for we are not at all capable to determine our own actions.

My dear Ashton I am ever

Yours sincerely

T: G:

Paris—Hotel de Luxembourg. Rue des petits Augustins
    April 21. N.S. [1739]

61*. Gray to West

[Paris, April or May, 1739]

[In a note to Gray's letter to West of 12 April 1739 from Paris (Letter 60, n. 14) Mason mentions (*Memoirs*, p. 46) 'a French letter, which Mr. Gray writ to his friend soon after this' (see Letter 60, n. 14). This letter, which was no doubt the first of the two letters in French to West mentioned by Mason in his letter to Walpole of 28 June 1773 (see *Walpole–Mason Correspondence*, vol. i, pp. 82, 85–6, 87, is not extant). For the second letter, see below, Letter 63**.]

62. GRAY TO WEST

Paris, [c. May 15, and] May 22, 1739.

AFTER the little particulars aforesaid I should have proceeded to a journal of our transactions for this week past, should have carried you post from hence to Versailles, hurried you

LETTER 62.—First printed in Mason's *Memoirs*, pp. 47–50. The text of this letter is manifestly garbled; it is evidently a clumsy combination by Mason of portions of two different letters, the date of the latter of which he has attached to the whole. It is clear from Walpole's letter to West from Paris, [May] 1739 (see Letter 90 in *Gray–Walpole Correspondence*) that he and Gray paid two visits to Versailles. Walpole speaks of their having been there on 'Wednesday', and of their going there again 'next Sunday', which, from the reference to the installation of the 'Knights of the Holy Ghost', we know from Gray's letter to have been Whitsunday, i.e. 17 May. 'Wednesday', therefore, must have been 13 May, and Walpole's letter must have been written on Friday, 15 May; otherwise, if he had been writing on Thursday, instead of 'Wednesday' he would have said 'yesterday', and if on Saturday, instead of 'next Sunday' he would have said 'to-morrow'. Walpole's letter to West, therefore, describes what he and Gray saw at Versailles on Wednesday, 13 May, which, with a difference of detail, is exactly what Mason's garbled text of this letter makes Gray tell West they saw on Saturday, 16 May, *after their arrival at Versailles at 8 o'clock in the evening*—a manifest impossibility, seeing that the sights included the apartments, the gardens, and the Trianon.

The first part of this letter (with the exception of the passage as to their

through the gardens to Trianon, back again to Paris, so away to Chantilly. But the fatigue is perhaps more than you can bear, and moreover I think I have reason to stomach your last piece of gravity. Supposing you were in your soberest mood, I am sorry you should think me capable of ever being so difsipé, so evaporé, as not to be in a condition of relishing any thing you could say to me. And now, if you have a mind to make your peace with me, arouse ye from your megrims and your melancholies, and (for exercise is good for you) throw away your night-cap, call for your jack-boots, and set out with me, last Saturday evening, for Versailles—and so at eight o'clock, pafsing through a road speckled with vines, and villas, and hares, and partridges, we arrive at the great avenue, flanked on either hand with a double row of trees about half a mile long, and with the palace itself to terminate the view; facing which, on each side of you is placed a semi-circle of very handsome buildings, which form the stables. These we will not enter into, because you know we are no jockies. Well! and is this the great front of Versailles? What a huge heap of littlenefs![1] it is composed, as it were, of three courts, all open to the eye at once, and gradually diminishing till you come to the royal apartments, which on this side present but half a dozen windows and a balcony. This last is all that can be called a front, for the rest is only great wings. The hue of all this mafs is black, dirty red, and yellow; the first proceeding from stone changed by age; the second, from a mixture of brick; and the last, from a profusion of tarnished gilding. You cannot see a more disagreeable tout-ensemble; and, to finish the matter, it is all stuck over in many places with small busts of a tawny hue between every window. We pafs through this to go into the garden, and here the case is indeed altered; nothing can be vaster and more magnificent than the back front; before it a very spacious terrace spreads itself, adorned with two large basons; these are bordered and lined (as most of the others) with white marble, with handsome statues of bronze reclined on their edges. From

arrival at Versailles on Saturday evening, which Mason conveyed presumably from Gray's letter of 22 May) is no doubt the 'panegyric' referred to by Walpole, and was written probably about the same time as his, after their visit on the Wednesday. The last part, beginning, 'Here then we walk by moonlight', is no doubt a portion of the letter written by Gray on 22 May, after their second visit.

[1] Pope, *Moral Essays*, iv. 109 (of Timon's Villa): 'Lo, what huge heaps of littleness around!'

hence you descend a huge flight of steps into a semi-circle formed by woods, that are cut all round into niches, which are filled with beautiful copies of all the famous antique statues in white marble. Just in the midst is the bason of Latona; she and her children are standing on the top of a rock in the middle, on the sides of which are the peasants, some half, some totally changed into frogs, all which throw out water at her in great plenty. From this place runs on the great alley, which brings you into a complete round, where is the bason of Apollo, the biggest in the gardens. He is rising in his car out of the water, surrounded by nymphs and tritons, all in bronze, and finely executed, and these, as they play, raise a perfect storm about him; beyond this is the great canal, a prodigious long piece of water, that terminates the whole: All this you have at one coup d'œil in entering the garden, which is truly great. I cannot say as much of the general taste of the place; every thing you behold savours too much of art; all is forced, all is constrained about you; statues and vases sowed every where without distinction; sugar-loaves and minced-pies of yew; scrawl-work of box, and little squirting jets-d'eau, besides a great samenefs in the walks, cannot help striking one at first sight, not to mention the silliest of labyrinths, and all Æsop's fables in water; since these were designed in usum Delphini only. Here then we walk by moonlight, and hear the ladies and the nightingales sing. Next morning, being Whitsunday, make ready to go to the Installation of nine Knights du Saint Esprit, Cambis is one:[2] high mafs celebrated with music, great croud, much incense, King,[3] Queen,[4] Dauphin,[5] Mesdames,[6] Cardinals, and Court: Knights arrayed by his majesty; reverences before the altar, not bows, but curtsies; stiff hams; much tittering among the ladies; trumpets, kettle-drums and fifes. My dear West, I am vastly delighted with Trianon, all of us with Chantilly; if you would know why, you must have patience, for I can hold my pen no longer, except to tell you that I saw Britannicus[7] last Night; all

[2] Louis-Dominique, Comte de Cambis, French Ambassador in London, where he died, 12 Feb. 1740.
[3] Louis XV, now in the twenty-fourth year of his reign.
[4] Marie Leszczynska (d. 1768).
[5] Louis (d. 1765), now in his tenth year, father of Louis XVI.
[6] The daughters of Louis XV, of whom the eldest, Louise-Élisabeth, and the only one who married, was in her fifteenth year.
[7] By Racine; first produced in 1669. It was on this play that Gray modelled his tragedy of *Agrippina*, which he did not complete, and of which

the characters, particularly Agrippina and Nero, done to perfection; to-morrow Phædra and Hippolitus.[8] We are making
you a little bundle of petites pieces; there is nothing in them,
but they are acting at present; there are too Crebillon's Letters,[9]
and Amusemens sur le langage des Bêtes, said to be of one
Bougeant,[10] a Jesuit; they are both esteemed, and lately come
out. This day se'nnight we go to Rheims.

63. GRAY TO ASHTON

My Dear Ashton

I SHALL not make you any excuses, because I can't: I shall
not try to entertain you with descriptions, for the same
reason; & moreover, because I believe you don't care for them.
so that you can have no occasion to wonder at my brevity,
when you consider me, as confined to the narrow bounds of the
history of We, quatenus We. which I continue.

Our tête à tête conversations, that you enquire after, did
consist lefs in words, than in looks & signs, & to give you a
notion of them, I ought to send you our pictures; tho' we should
find it difficult to set for 'em in such attitudes, as we very
naturally fall into, when alone together. at present Mr Conway,
who lives with us, joins to make them a little more verbose,
& every thing is mighty well. on Monday next we set out for
Rheims, (where we expect to be very dull;) there to stay a
month or two; then we crofs Burgundy, & Dauphiny, & so go
to Avignon, Aix, Marseilles, &c: the weather begins to be
violently hot already even here, & this is our ingenious contrivance, as the summer increases, to seek out cool retreats
among the scorch'd rocks of Provence; I will not promise, but

only a fragment has been preserved.—The *Britannicus* of M. Racine, I know
was one of Mr. Gray's favourite plays; and the admirable manner in which
I have heard him say that he saw it represented at Paris by Mademoiselle
Dumesnil, seems to have led him to choose the death of Agrippina for this
his first and only effort in the drama. *Mason.* (See Letter 101, n. 8.)

   [8] Racine's *Phèdre*; first produced in 1677.

   [9] *Lettres de la Marquise de*** au Comte de****, by Claude-Prosper-Jolyot de
Crébillon (1707–77).

   [10] Guillaume-Hyacinthe Bougeant (1690–1743); his *Amusement philoso-
phique sur le Langage des Bêtes* was published in this year.

   LETTER 63.—First printed by Tovey in *Gray and his Friends*, pp. 41–5,
from Mitford's transcript; reprinted by Toynbee (1915), No. 92, from the
original.

that if next winter bid fair for extreme cold, we shall take a trip to Muscovy. you in the mean time will be quietly enjoying the temperate air of England under your own vine, & under your own (at least under Mrs Lewis's)[1] Fig-tree; & I don't doubt but the fruits of your leisure will turn to more account, than those of our laborious peregrination, and while our thoughts are rambling about, & changeing situation oftener than our bodies, you will be fixing your attention upon some weighty truth, worthy a Sage of your honour's magnitude. the end of your researches, I mean whatever your profound contemplation brings to light, I should be proud to be acquainted with; whither it please to be invoked under the appellation of Sermon, Vision, Eſsay, or discourse: in short, on whatever head you chuse to be loquacious (Wall on Infant-Baptism[2] excepted) a diſsertation will be very acceptable, & received with a reverence due to the hand it comes from.

We have seen here your Gustavus Vasa,[3] that had raised the general expectation so high long ago. a worthy piece of prohibited marchandise in truth! the town must have been extreme mercifully disposed; if, for the sake of ten innocent lines, that may peradventure be pick'd out, it had consented to spare the lives of the ten thousand wicked ones, that remain. I don't know what condition your Stage is in, but the French is in a very good one at present; among the rest they have a Mad^lle Duminie,[4] whose every look & gesture is violent Nature; she is Paſsion itself incarnate: I saw her the other night do the Phædra of Racine in a manner; which affected me so strongly, that, as

---

[1] See Letter 54, n. 1.

[2] *The History of Infant Baptism* (Lond. 1705, 2 vols. 8vo), by William Wall (1647–1728).

[3] *Gustavus Vasa, the Deliverer of his Country*, a tragedy by Henry Brooke (c. 1703–83). After five weeks' rehearsal, the play had been announced for performance at Drury Lane, when it was suddenly prohibited by the Lord Chamberlain under Sir Robert Walpole's Licensing Act of 1737. It was then, as a protest, published by subscription, by which the author is said to have cleared over £1,000. The tragedy was subsequently produced with success at Dublin under the title of *The Patriot*.

[4] So Gray wrote. The actress in question, Marie-Françoise Dumesnil (1711–1803), had made her first appearance at the Théâtre Français two years before. She remained on the stage for nearly forty years, during which time she was a great favourite with the public. Mme du Deffand, however, judged her severely. Writing to Horace Walpole, who was a great admirer of the actress, in 1769, she says: 'Je revis hier *Hamlet* . . . votre Mlle Dumesnil est abominable, elle fait de grands cris, et puis elle débride dix ou douze vers de suite, comme si elle parlait à l'oreille.'

you see, I can't help prattling about her even to you, that do not care two-pence.

You have got My Ld Conway there among ye; what do people think about him, & his improvements? you poſsibly see him sometimes, for he visits at Mrs Conduit's. is he charming, & going to be married, like Mr Barrett? pray, write to me, & persuade West to do the same, who unleſs you rouse him, & preach to him, what a sin it is to have the vapours, & the dismals, will neglect himself; I won't say, his friends; that I believe him incapable of. I again recommend him to your care, that you may nourish him, & cherish him, & administer to him some of that cordial spirit of chearfulneſs, that you used to have the Receipt of. my Compliments to my Lord.[4] Good night,

Yours ever

T: G:

Paris—May 29. N: S: Friday-night. [1739]

63*. West to Gray

[June, 1739]

[Gray, in a letter (Letter 131) to Walpole, which may be dated 8 Feb. 1747, mentions in a list of West's poems 'A Translation from Pro-pertius . . . (sent to me at Rheims)'. The translation (which is printed by Tovey in *Gray and his Friends*, pp. 127–8) was transcribed by Gray in his Commonplace-book with a note: 'Fav: June 1739'. This must have been sent to Gray in a letter no longer extant.]

63**. Gray to West

[Rheims, June 1739]

[In a letter to Walpole of 28 June 1773, at the time when he was engaged on his *Memoirs of Gray*, Mason enclosed two letters of Gray to West, written in French, and asked Walpole's advice as to their being printed. Walpole was against it, on the ground that the French was 'neither correct nor elegant'. 'The first', he wrote on 5 July, 'I well remember: the second you may be sure I never saw before. . . . If you print them, I have no objection to your inserting the passage you have marked for reprobation, and which alludes to me. You see how easily [? misprint for 'early'] I had disgusted him; but my faults were very trifling, and I can bear their being known, and for-give his displeasure. I still think I was as much to blame as he was; and as the passage proves what I have told you, let it stand, if you

---

[4] Ashton's pupil, Lord Plymouth.

publish the whole letter.' Mason eventually decided to print neither. 'I have followed your advice', he wrote on 16 July, 'with respect to the two French letters, and instead of printing either of them, have inserted one to his mother [namely, Letter 64], which will preserve the chain of correspondence.' The second letter consequently, which like the first (Letter 61*) has not been traced, is conjecturally assigned to this place. It was probably the letter referred to by Walpole in his letter to West of 18 June from Rheims (*Gray–Walpole Correspondence*, No. 93) in which he says:

'How I am to fill up this letter is not easy to divine. I have consented that Gray shall give you an account of our situation and proceedings. . . . I had prepared the ingredients for a description of a ball, and was just ready to serve it up to you, but he has plucked it from me.']

64. GRAY TO MRS. GRAY

Rheims,[1] June 21, N.S. 1739.

WE have now been settled almost three weeks in this city, which is more considerable upon account of its size and antiquity, than from the number of its inhabitants, or any advantages of commerce. There is little in it worth a stranger's curiosity, besides the cathedral church, which is a vast Gothic building of a surprising beauty and lightneſs, all covered over with a profusion of little statues, and other ornaments. It is here the Kings of France are crowned by the Archbishop of Rheims, who is the first Peer, and the Primate of the kingdom: The holy veſsel made use of on that occasion, which contains the oil, is kept in the church of St. Nicasius[2] hard by, and is believed to have been brought by an angel from heaven at the coronation of Clovis, the first christian king. The streets in

LETTER 64.—First printed in Mason's *Memoirs*, pp. 50–2.

[1] Miss Berry notes on Walpole's letter to West of 18 June: 'Mr. Walpole was now removed to Rheims, where, with his cousin Henry Seymour Conway and Mr. Gray, he resided three months, principally to acquire the French language.' Walpole and Gray left Paris for Rheims on Monday, 1 June (see Letter 63). In his *Journal* for 1739–41* Gray notes, under Rheims: 'staid 3 Months here—lodged at Monsr Hibert's, Rue St Dennis, June, July, August, 1739.'

[2] In his *Journal* Gray notes that 'the holy vial brought from heaven to anoint Clovis' was preserved in the Church St. Remi, 'the Patron of the city'.

---

* A small pocket-book, 'France and Italy 1739–1741', in the possession of Sir John Murray, contains notes made by Gray of his stay at Rheims and of his journey from Rheims to Florence. It is quoted as *Journal* in the notes to the letters that follow. Part of it was printed by Gosse, *Works of Gray*, vol. i, pp. 237–46.

general have but a melancholy aspect, the houses all old; the
public walks run along the side of a great moat under the ramparts, where one hears a continual croaking of frogs; the country
round about is one great plain covered with vines, which at this
time of the year afford no very pleasing prospect, as being not
above a foot high. What pleasures the place denies to the sight,
it makes up to the palate; since you have nothing to drink but
the best champaigne in the world, and all sort of provisions
equally good. As to other pleasures, there is not that freedom
of conversation among the people of fashion here, that one sees
in other parts of France; for though they are not very numerous
in this place, and consequently must live a good deal together,
yet they never come to any great familiarity with one another.
As my Lord Conway had spent a good part of his time among
them, his brother, and we with him, were soon introduced into
all their afsemblies: As soon as you enter, the lady of the house
presents each of you a card, and offers you a party at quadrille;
you sit down, and play forty deals without intermifsion, except-
ing one quarter of an hour, when every body rises to eat of
what they call the gouter, which supplies the place of our tea,
and is a service of wine, fruits, cream, sweetmeats, crawfish and
cheese. People take what they like, and sit down again to play;
after that, they make little parties to go to the walks together,
and then all the company retire to their separate habitations.
Very seldom any suppers or dinners are given; and this is the
manner they live among one another; not so much out of any
aversion they have to pleasure, as out of a sort of formality
they have contracted by not being much frequented by people
who have lived at Paris. It is sure they do not hate gaiety any
more than the rest of their country-people, and can enter into
diversions, that are once proposed, with a good grace enough;
for instance, the other evening we happened to be got together
in a company of eighteen people, men and women of the best
fashion here, at a garden in the town to walk; when one of the
ladies bethought herself of asking, Why should not we sup here?
Immediately the cloth was laid by the side of a fountain under
the trees, and a very elegant supper served up; after which
another said, Come, let us sing; and directly began herself:
From singing we insensibly fell to dancing, and singing in a
round; when somebody mentioned the violins, and immediately
a company of them was ordered: Minuets were begun in the
open air, and then came country-dances, which held till four

o'Clock next morning; at which hour the gayest lady there proposed, that such as were weary should get into their coaches,
and the rest of them should dance before them with the music
in the van; and in this manner we paraded through all the
principal streets of the city, and waked every body in it. Mr.
Walpole had a mind to make a custom of the thing, and would
have given a ball in the same manner next week, but the women
did not come into it; so I believe it will drop, and they will
return to their dull cards, and usual formalities. We are not to
stay above a month longer here, and shall then go to Dijon,
the chief city of Burgundy, a very splendid and very gay town;
at least such is the present design.

65. Gray and Walpole to Ashton

My dear Ashton,

THE exceeding Slowneſs and Sterility of me, & this Place &
the vast abundance & volubility of Mr Walpole & his Pen
will sufficiently excuse to you the shortneſs of this little matter.
He insists that it is not him, but his Pen that is so volubility,
& so I have borrowd it of him; but I find it is both of 'em that
is so volubility, for tho I am writing as fast, as I can drive, yet
he is still chattering in vast abundance. I have desired me to
hold his tongue, pho, I mean him, & his, but his Pen is so used
to write in the first Person, that I have screwd my finger &
thumb off, with forcing it, into the third. After all this confusion of Persons, & a little stroke of Satyr upon me the Pen
returns calmly back again into the old *I*, & *me*, as if nothing
had happend to tell you how much I am tired, & how crofs
I am, that this cursed Scheme of Mefsrs. Selwyn[1] & Montague[2]
should have come acroſs all our Measures,[3] & broke in upon the
whole year, which, what with the Month we have to wait for
them, & the Month they are to stay here, will be entirely slipt

LETTER 65.—First printed by Tovey in *Gray and his Friends*, pp. 45–7; reprinted by Toynbee (1915), No. 96, from Mitford's transcript. Gray obviously
wrote the first paragraph of the letter.

[1] George Augustus Selwyn (1719–91), the well-known wit, second son of
Colonel John Selwyn, of Matson, Gloucestershire, a lifelong friend of Walpole from their school-days at Eton till his death.

[2] George Montagu (d. 1780), eldest son of Brigadier Edward Montagu,
and nephew of the second Earl of Halifax. His friendship with Walpole
dated from Eton, and lasted till within ten years of his death, when a breach
arose which was never repaired.

away, at least, the agreable Part of it, and if we journey at all, it will be thro' dirty roads, & falling leaves.

The Man, whose arguments you have so learnedly stated,[4] & whom you did not think fit to honour with a Confutation, we from thence conceive to be one, who does us honour, in thinking us fools, & so you see, I lay my Claim to a share of the glory; we are not vastly curious about his Name, first because it don't signify, 2dly because we know it already: it is either S^r T: G: himself, or your friend Mr Fenton, if it's them we don't care, & if it is not, we don't care neither, but if you care to convince the Man, whoever he be, that we are in some points not altogether fools, you might let him know that we are most sincerely

Yours

Rheims—July. [1739]   H W.   ℡

Addressed: To Mr Ashton at Mrs Lewes's Hanover Square London. Franc à Paris. pour l'Angleterre

66. GRAY TO ASHTON

Rheims. 25 Aug. N: S [1739]

My dear Ashton,

I AM not so ignorant of Pain myself as to be able to hear of anothers Sufferings, without any Sensibility to them, especially when they are those of One, I ought more particularly to feel for; tho' indeed the goodneſs of my own Constitution, is in some Sense a Misfortune to me, for as the health of everybody I love seems much more precarious than my own, it is but a melancholy prospect to consider myself as one, that may poſsibly in some years be left in the World, destitute of the advice or good Wishes of those few friends, that usd to care for me, and without a likelihood or even a desire of gaining any new ones. this letter will, I hope, find you perfectly recoverd, & your own painful experience will, for the future, teach you not to give so much in to a sedentary Life, that has [I] fear been the Cause of your illneſs. Give my duty to your Mind, & tell

[3] In his letter to West of 20 July 1739 (*Gray–Walpole Correspondence*, No. 95) Walpole writes: 'This is the day that Gray and I intended for the first of a southern circuit; but as Mr Selwyn and George Montagu design us a visit here, we have put off our journey for some weeks.'

[4] Ashton's letter is not extant and the allusions to 'S^r T: G:' and 'Mr Fenton' lack explanation.

LETTER 66.—First printed by Tovey in *Gray and his Friends*, pp. 47–8; reprinted by Toynbee (1915), No. 97, from Mitford's transcript.

115

her she has taken more care of herself, than of my tother poor friend, your Body, & bid her hereafter remember how nearly *her* Welfare is connected with *his:* tell her too, that she may pride herself in her great family, & despise him for being a poor Mortal, as much as she pleases, but that he is her wedded husband, & if he suffers, she must smart for it. my inferences you will say, don't follow very naturally, nor have any great relation to what has been said, but they are as follows.

Meſsʳˢ Selwin and Montague have been here these 3 weeks, are by this time pretty heartily tired of Rheims, & return in about a week. The day they set out for England, we are to do the same for Burgundy, in our way only as it is said to Provence, but People better informd conceive that Dijon will be the end of our expedition. for me, I make everything that does not depend on me, so indifferent to me, that if it be to go to the Cape of good Hope I care not: if you are well enough, you will let me know a little of the history of West who does not remember there is such a Place as Champagne in the world.

Your's ever
T. G.

Addressed: To Mʳ Ashton at Mʳˢ Lewes's in Hanover Square London Franc a Paris. pour l'Angleterre franc jusqu'a Paris.

67. GRAY TO PHILIP GRAY[1]

Dijon, Friday, Sept. 11, N. S. 1739.

WE have made three short days journey of it from Rheims hither,[2] where we arrived the night before last: The road we have paſsed through has been extremely agreeable; it runs through the most fertile part of Champaigne by the side of the river Marne, with a chain of hills on each hand at some distance, entirely covered with woods and vineyards, and every now and

LETTER 67.—First printed in Mason's *Memoirs*, pp. 53–4.

[1] See Genealogical Table.

[2] In his *Journal*, under the heading 'From Rheims to Dijon', Gray says their route was by Verzenay, Sillery, Châlons sur Marne (where they dined 'à la Poste'), Vitry le François, St. Dizier ('an ugly old town, with suburbs bigger than itself', where they lay 'au Lion d'or'), Joinville, Vignoris (where they dined), Langres ('a small city on a high hill', where they lay 'au Cerf volant'), and the village of Thil, where they entered Burgundy; from here 'thro' a fine fertile plain by an Avenue of Lime-trees', they came to Dijon ('the Capital of the Dutchy, a very small, but beautiful City, of an oval form, full of People of Quality, & a very agreable Society', where they stayed '4 Days—a la Croix d'or').

then the ruins of some old castle on their tops; we lay at
St. Dizier the first night, and at Langres the second, and got
hither the next evening time enough to have a full view of this
city in entering it: It lies in a very extensive plain covered with
vines and corn, and consequently is plentifully supplied with
both. I need not tell you that it is the chief city of Burgundy,
nor that it is of great antiquity; considering which one should
imagine it ought to be larger than one finds it. However, what
it wants in extent, is made up in beauty and cleanlinefs, and
in rich convents and churches, most of which we have seen.
The palace of the States is a magnificent new building, where
the Duke of Bourbon is lodged when he comes every three years
to hold that Afsembly, as governour of the Province. A quarter
of a mile out of the town is a famous Abbey of Carthusians,
which we are just returned from seeing. In their chapel are
the tombs of the ancient Dukes of Burgundy, that were so
powerful, till at the death of Charles the Bold, the last of them,
this part of his dominions was united by Lewis XI. to the crown
of France. To-morrow we are to pay a visit to the Abbot of
the Cistercians, who lives a few leagues off, and who uses to
receive all strangers with great civility; his Abbey is one of the
richest in the kingdom; he keeps open house always, and lives
with great magnificence. We have seen enough of this town
already to make us regret the time we spent at Rheims; it is
full of people of condition, who seem to form a much more
agreeable society than we found in Champaigne; but as we
shall stay here but two or three days longer, it is not worth
while to be introduced into their houses. On Monday or Tuesday we are to set out for Lyons,[3] which is two days journey
distant, and from thence you shall hear again from me.

68. Gray to West

Lyons, Sept. 18, N. S. 1739.

SCAVEZ vous bien, mon cher ami, que je vous hais, que je vous
deteste? voila des termes un peu forts; et that will save me,
upon a just computation, a page of paper and six drops of ink;

[3] From Dijon, Gray records in his *Journal*, their road was through Nuys
[Nuits] and Beaune, Châlons sur Saône, Mâcon (where they lay), Ville-
franche, and so to Lyons, on approaching which they had 'a charming View
of the Fauxbourgs of that City, the Saône, & the little Mountains about it,
cover'd with Convents, Houses, & Gardens of the Bourgeois'.
LETTER 68.—First printed in Mason's *Memoirs*, pp. 54–6.

which, if I confined myself to reproaches of a more moderate
nature, I should be obliged to employ in using you according
to your deserts. What! to let any body reside three months at
Rheims, and write but once to them? Please to consult Tully
de Amicit. page 5, line 25, and you will find it said in exprefs
terms, 'Ad amicum inter Remos relegatum mense uno quin-
quies scriptum esto;'[1] nothing more plain, or lefs liable to false
interpretations. Now because, I suppose, it will give you pain
to know we are in being, I take this opportunity to tell you
that we are at the ancient and celebrated Lugdunum,[2] a city
situated upon the confluence of the Rhône and Saône (Arar,
I should say) two people, who, though of tempers extremely
unlike, think fit to join hands here, and make a little party to
travel to the Mediterranean in company; the lady comes gliding
along through the fruitful plains of Burgundy, incredibili lenitate, ita ut oculis in utram partem fluat judicari non pofsit;[3] the
gentleman runs all rough and roaring down from the mountains
of Switzerland to meet her; and with all her soft airs she likes
him never the worse; she goes through the middle of the city
in state, and he pafses incog. without the walls, but waits for
her a little below. The houses here are so high, and the streets
so narrow, as would be sufficient to render Lyons the dismallest
place in the world, but the number of people, and the face of
commerce diffused about it, are, at least, as sufficient to make
it the liveliest: Between these two sufficiencies, you will be in
doubt what to think of it; so we shall leave the city, and proceed to its environs, which are beautiful beyond exprefsion; it is
surrounded with mountains, and those mountains all bedroped
and bespeckled with houses, gardens, and plantations of the

[1] A fictitious quotation.
[2] In his *Journal*, under 'Lions', Gray notes: 'lodged a l'Hotel de Bourgogne, près de la Grande Place. a fortnight. Principal quarters of that
great city lie in a Peninsula formed by the confluence of the Rhône, &
Saône. a Stone bridge of 18 Arches laid over the first, which runs with
extreme rapidity, & is full of Islands, joins this, & the Fauxbourg de
la Guillotiere: another stone bridge, & 3 wooden ones over the Saône con-
nect it with the rest of the City, & Suburbs, which lie mostly on the
declivity of several very steep hills. the streets are generally extreme
narrow, & the houses high, but the whole enliven'd by its great Populous-
nefs & Commerce. the best prospects are from the Chartreuse, & Ste Marie
de Fourviere.'
[3] Caesar, *De Bello Gallico*, i. 12: 'Flumen est Arar, quod per fines Æduorum
et Sequanorum in Rhodanum influit, incredibili lenitate, ita ut oculis, in
utram partem fluat, judicari non possit.

rich Bourgeois, who have from thence a prospect of the city in the vale below on one hand, on the other the rich plains of the Lyonnois, with the rivers winding among them, and the Alps, with the mountains of Dauphiné, to bound the view. All yesterday morning we were busied in climbing up Mount Four-viere, where the ancient city stood perched at such a height, that nothing but the hopes of gain could certainly ever persuade their neighbours to pay them a visit: Here are the ruins of the Emperors' palaces, that resided here, that is to say, Augustus and Severus; they consist in nothing but great maſses of old wall, that have only their quality to make them respected. In a vineyard of the Minims are remains of a theatre; the Fathers, whom they belong to, hold them in no esteem at all, and would have showed us their sacristy and chapel instead of them: The Ursuline Nuns have in their garden some Roman baths, but we having the misfortune to be men, and heretics, they did not think proper to admit us. Hard by are eight arches of a most magnificent aqueduct, said to be erected by Antony, when his legions were quartered here: There are many other parts of it dispersed up and down the country, for it brought the water from a river many leagues off in La Forez. Here are remains too of Agrippa's seven great roads which met at Lyons; in some places they lie twelve feet deep in the ground: In short, a thousand matters that you shall not know, till you give me a description of the Païs de Tombridge, and the effect its waters have upon you.

69. West to Gray and Walpole

Moi R West.

COMME nous avons entendu par notre fidel & bon ami Thomas Ashton,[1] que vous, Tho. Gray & Hor. Walpole, nos anciens & bienaimez alliés, vous êtes fachés un peu, de ce que nous n'avons pas ecrit ce long tems, ni à l'un ni l'autre, & que vous le considerez tous deux comme un contrevention de nôtre amitié, Nous de notre bonne volunté promettons pour le futur

---

LETTER 69.—First printed by Toynbee (1915), No. 100.

[1] In a letter to West of 25 Aug. (No. 98 in *Gray–Walpole Correspondence*) Ashton wrote: 'Our friends on the other side of the water salute thee, but they complain as much of the want of thy letters as I do, of the want of thyself' (see Letter 66, *ad fin.*).

d'être plus exacts en nôtre correspondance, &, parceque nous avons envie de continuer la paix & la tranquilité, qui ont été de tout tems entre nous trois,[2] nous sommes resolus en plein conseil de vous demander pardon, &, au lieu que nous pouvions nous plaindre de vous à nôtre tour, & rejetter la faute sur vous, á la mode Espagnole, nous au contraire, pour donner à l'Europe un exemple de nôtre moderation, avouons que nous sommes coupables, & vous prions, de nous continuer vôtre amitié, & correspondance.

Signé.   Moi RW.

Soussigné.   Grimalkin, premier Chat.

I hope this silly, unmeaning thing won't be open'd & stop't at the post.

Adieu! Mes chers —

Temple. Sept\[r\]. 24. [1739]

Addressed: To Horace Walpole Esq\[r\]. au soin de Monsieur Alexander, Banquier, à Paris, France *Stamped:* RJ

70. WEST TO GRAY

Temple, Sep. 28. 1739.

IF wishes could turn to realities, I would fling down my law books, and sup with you to-night. But, alas, here am I doomed to fix, while you are fluttering from city to city, and enjoying all the pleasures which a gay climate can afford. It is out of the power of my heart to envy your good fortune, yet I cannot help indulging a few natural desires; as for example, to take a walk with you on the banks of the Rhône, and to be climbing up mount Fourviere;

Jam mens prætrepidans avet vagari:

Jam læti studio pedes vigescunt.[1]

However, so long as I am not deprived of your correspondence, so long shall I always find some pleasure in being at home. And, setting all vain curiosity aside, when the fit is over, and my reason begins to come to herself, I have several other powerful motives which might easily cure me of my restless inclinations: Amongst these, my Mother's ill state of health is not the least;

---

[2] West originally wrote 'deux'.

LETTER 70.—First printed in Mason's *Memoirs*, pp. 56-8.

[1] Catullus, xlvi. 7–8.

which was the reason of our going to Tunbridge, so that you cannot expect much description or amusement from thence. Nor indeed is there much room for either; for all diversions there may be reduced to two articles, gaming and going to church. They were pleased to publish certain Tunbrigiana this season; but such ana! I believe there were never so many vile little verses put together before. So much for Tunbridge: London affords me as little to say. What! so huge a town as London? Yes, consider only how I live in that town. I never go into the gay or high world, and consequently receive nothing from thence to brighten my imagination. The busy world I leave to the busy; and am resolved never to talk politics till I can act at the same time. To tell old stories, or prate of old books, seems a little musty; and toujours Chapon bouilli, won't do. However, for want of better fare, take another little mouthful of my poetry.

> O meæ jucunda comes quietis!
> Quæ ferè ægrotum solita es levare
> Pectus, et sensim ah! nimis ingruentes
>   Fallere curas:
>
> Quid canes? quanto Lyra dic furore
> Gesties, quando hâc reducem sodalem
> Glauciam[2] gaudere simul videbis
>   Meque sub umbrâ?

71. GRAY TO MRS. GRAY
Lyons, Oct. 13, N. S. 1739.

IT is now almost five weeks since I left Dijon, one of the gayest and most agreeable little cities of France, for Lyons, its reverse in all these particulars. It is the second in the kingdom in bigneſs and rank, the streets excefsively narrow and nasty; the houses immensely high and large; (that, for instance, where we are lodged, has twenty-five rooms on a floor, and that for five stories) it swarms with inhabitants like Paris itself, but chiefly a mercantile people, too much given up to commerce, to think of their own, much lefs of a stranger's diversions. We have no acquaintance in the town, but such English as happen to be

---

[2] He gives Mr. Gray the name of Glaucias frequently in his Latin verse, as Mr. Gray calls him Favonius. *Mason.*
LETTER 71.—First printed in Mason's *Memoirs*, pp. 58–60.

paſsing through here, in their way to Italy and the South, which at present happen to be near thirty in number. It is a fortnight since we set out from hence upon a little excursion to Geneva. We took the longest road, which lies through Savoy, on purpose to see a famous monastery, called the grand Chartreuse,[1] and had no reason to think our time lost. After having travelled [two][2] days very slow (for we did not change horses, it being impoſsible for a chaise to go post in these roads) we arrived at a little village, among the mountains of Savoy, called Echelles; from thence we proceeded on horses, who are used to the way, to the mountain of the Chartreuse: It is six miles to the top; the road runs winding up it, commonly not six feet broad; on one hand is the rock, with woods of pine-trees hanging over head; on the other, a monstrous precipice, almost perpendicular, at the bottom of which rolls a torrent, that sometimes tumbling among the fragments of stone that have fallen from on high, and sometimes precipitating itself down vast descents with a noise like thunder, which is still made greater by the echo from the mountains on each side, concurs to form one of the most solemn, the most romantic, and the most astonishing scenes I ever beheld: Add to this the strange views made by the craggs and cliffs on the other hand; the cascades that in many places throw themselves from the very summit down into

¹ In his *Journal* Gray gives the following account of this excursion: 'Journey to Geneva, thro' Dauphiné, and Savoy. 5 Days, (en Voiture) & a half. First night at La Verpillier, a poor Village. 2ᵈ Day enter'd Savoy at Pont-Beauvoisin, lay at Echelles. the road runs over a Mountain, which gives you the first tast of the Alps, in it's magnificent rudeneſs, & steep precipices: set out from Echelles on horseback to see the Grande Chartreuse. the way to it up a vast mountain, in many places the road not 2 yards broad; on one side the rock hanging over you, & on the other a monstrous precipice. in the bottom runs a torrent, called Les Guiers morts, that works its way among the rocks with a mighty noise, & frequent Falls. you here meet all the beauties so savage & horrid a place can present you with; Rocks of various & uncouth figures, Cascades pouring down from an immense height out of hanging Groves of Pine-Trees, & the solemn Sound of the Stream, that roars below, all concur to form one of the most poetical Scenes imaginable: this continues for 2 leagues, & then (within a little of the Mountain's top) you come to the Convent itself, which is only considerable for it's situation, & bigneſs.' On revisiting the Chartreuse (which is about thirty-seven miles from Grenoble) in August 1741, after his parting from Walpole, Gray wrote in the visitors' book his famous Alcaic ode, 'Oh tu, severi relligio loci'.

² Mason: 'seven'; evidently a mistake for 'two' (perhaps by a misreading of 7 for 2), inasmuch as Gray says in his *Journal* that they lay at Échelles the second day (see n. 1).

the vale, and the river below; and many other particulars impofsible to describe; you will conclude we had no occasion to repent our pains. This place St. Bruno chose to retire to, and upon its very top founded the aforesaid Convent, which is the superior of the whole order. When we came there, the two fathers, who are commifsioned to entertain strangers, (for the rest must neither speak one to another, nor to any one else) received us very kindly; and set before us a repast of dried fish, eggs, butter, and fruits, all excellent in their kind, and extremely neat. They prefsed us to spend the night there, and to stay some days with them; but this we could not do, so they led us about their house, which is, you must think, like a little city; for there are 100 fathers, besides 300 servants, that make their clothes, grind their corn, prefs their wine, and do every thing among themselves: The whole is quite orderly and simple; nothing of finery, but the wonderful decency, and the strange situation, more than supply the place of it. In the evening we descended by the same way, pafsing through many clouds that were then forming themselves on the mountain's side. Next day we continued our journey by Chamberry, which, though the chief city of the Dutchy, and residence of the king of Sardinia,[3] when he comes into this part of his dominions, makes but a very mean and insignificant appearance; we lay at Aix, once famous for its hot baths, and the next night at Annecy; the day after, by noon, we got to Geneva. I have not time to say any thing about it, nor of our solitary journey back again. * * *

72. GRAY TO PHILIP GRAY

Lyons, Oct. 25, N. S. 1739.

IN my last I gave you the particulars of our little journey to Geneva: I have only to add, that we stayed about a week, in order to see Mr. Conway settled there: I do not wonder so many English choose it for their residence; the city is very small, neat, prettily built, and extremely populous; the Rhône runs through the middle of it, and it is surrounded with new fortifications, that give it a military compact air; which, joined to the happy, lively countenances of the inhabitants, and an exact discipline always as strictly observed as in time of war, makes the little republic appear a match for a much greater

[3] Charles Emmanuel III, King of Sardinia, 1730–73.
LETTER 72.—First printed in Mason's *Memoirs*, pp. 60–2.

power; though perhaps Geneva, and all that belongs to it, are not of equal extent with Windsor and its two parks. To one that has pafsed through Savoy, as we did, nothing can be more striking than the contrast, as soon as he approaches the town. Near the gates of Geneva runs the torrent Arve, which separates it from the King of Sardinia's dominions; on the other side of it lies a country naturally, indeed, fine and fertile; but you meet with nothing in it but meager, ragged, bare-footed peasants, with their children, in extreme misery and nastinefs; and even of these no great numbers: You no sooner have crofsed the stream I have mentioned, but poverty is no more; not a beggar, hardly a discontented face to be seen; numerous, and well-drefsed people swarming on the ramparts; drums beating, soldiers, well cloathed and armed, exercising; and folks, with businefs in their looks, hurrying to and fro; all contribute to make any person, who is not blind, sensible what a difference there is between the two governments, that are the causes of one view and the other. The beautiful lake, at one end of which the town is situated; its extent; the several states that border upon it; and all its pleasures, are too well known for me to mention them. We sailed upon it as far as the dominions of Geneva extend, that is, about two leagues and a half on each side; and landed at several of the little houses of pleasure, that the inhabitants have built all about it, who received us with much politenefs. The same night we eat part of a trout, taken in the lake, that weighed thirty-seven pounds; as great a monster as it appeared to us, it was esteemed there nothing extra-ordinary, and they afsured us, it was not uncommon to catch them of fifty pounds; they are drefsed here, and sent post to Paris upon some great occasions; nay, even to Madrid, as we were told. The road we returned through was not the same we came by: We crofsed the Rhône at Seyfsel, and pafsed for three days among the mountains of Bugey, without meeting with any thing new: At last we came out into the plains of La Brefse, and so to Lyons again. Sir Robert has written to Mr. Walpole, to desire he would go to Italy; which he has resolved to do; so that all the scheme of spending the winter in the South of France is laid aside, and we are to pafs it in a much finer country. You may imagine I am not sorry to have this oppor-tunity of seeing the place in the world that best deserves it: Besides as the Pope[1] (who is eighty-eight, and has been lately

               [1] Clement XII.

at the point of death) cannot probably last a great while, perhaps we may have the fortune to be present at the election of a new one, when Rome will be in all its glory. Friday next we certainly begin our journey; in two days we shall come to the foot of the Alps, and six more we shall be in pafsing them. Even here the winter is begun; what then must it be among those vast snowy mountains where it is hardly ever summer? We are, however, as well armed as pofsible against the cold, with muffs, hoods, and masks of bever, fur-boots, and bear skins. When we arrive at Turin, we shall rest after the fatigues of the journey. * * *

73. GRAY TO MRS. GRAY

Turin, Nov. 7, N. S. 1739.

I AM this night arrived here, and have just set down to rest me after eight days tiresome journey: For the three first we had the same road we before past through to go to Geneva; the fourth we turned out of it, and for that day and the next travelled rather among than upon the Alps; the way commonly running through a deep valley by the side of the river Arc, which works itself a pafsage, with great difficulty and a mighty noise, among vast quantities of rocks, that have rolled down from the mountain tops. The winter was so far advanced, as in great measure to spoil the beauty of the prospect, however, there was still somewhat fine remaining amidst the savagenefs and horror of the place: The sixth we began to go up several of these mountains; and as we were pafsing one, met with an odd accident enough: Mr. Walpole had a little fat black spaniel,[1] that he was very fond of, which he sometimes used to set down, and let it run by the chaise side. We were at that time in a very rough road, not two yards broad at most; on one side was a great wood of pines, and on the other a vast precipice; it was noon-day, and the sun shone bright, when all of a sudden, from the wood-side, (which was as steep upwards, as the other part was downwards) out rushed a great wolf, came close to the head of the horses, seized the dog by the throat,

LETTER 73.—First printed in Mason's *Memoirs*, pp. 63–5.
[1] This dog, called 'Tory', had been given to Walpole in Paris by Lord Conway (see Walpole's letter to Cole of 10 Dec. 1775). Walpole describes the above incident to West in his letter of 11 Nov. 1739 (No. 104 in *Gray–Walpole Correspondence*).

and rushed up the hill again with him in his mouth. This was done in lefs than a quarter of a minute; we all saw it, and yet the servants had not time to draw their pistols, or do any thing to save the dog. If he had not been there, and the creature had thought fit to lay hold of one of the horses; chaise, and we, and all must inevitably have tumbled above fifty fathoms perpendicular down the precipice. The seventh we came to Lanebourg,[2] the last town in Savoy; it lies at the foot of the famous mount Cenis, which is so situated as to allow no room for any way but over the very top of it. Here the chaise was forced to be pulled to pieces, and the baggage and that to be carried by mules: We ourselves were wrapped up in our furs, and seated upon a sort of matted chair without legs, which is carried upon poles in the manner of a bier, and so begun to ascend by the help of eight men. It was six miles to the top, where a plain opens itself about as many more in breadth, covered perpetually with very deep snow, and in the midst of that a great lake of unfathomable depth, from whence a river takes its rise, and tumbles over monstrous rocks quite down the other side of the mountain. The descent is six miles more, but infinitely more steep than the going up; and here the men perfectly fly down with you, stepping from stone to stone with incredible swiftnefs in places where none but they could go three paces without falling. The immensity of the precipices, the roaring of the river and torrents that run into it, the huge craggs covered with ice and snow, and the clouds below you and about you, are objects it is impofsible to conceive without seeing them; and though we had heard many strange descriptions of the scene, none of them at all came up to it. We were but five hours in performing the whole, from which you may judge of the rapidity of the men's motion. We are now got into Piedmont, and stopped a little while at La Ferriere, a small village about three quarters of the way down, but still among the clouds, where we began to hear a new language spoken round about us; at last we got quite down, went through the Pás de Suse, a narrow road among the Alps, defended by two fortrefses, and lay at Bofsolens: Next evening through a fine avenue of nine miles in length, as straight as a line, we arrived at this city,[3] which, as

---

[2] Lanslebourg, about 10 miles NE. of Mont Cenis, on the right bank of the Arc.

[3] In his *Journal* Gray writes: 'Turin—a week—à l'Auberge Royale. The Straitnefs of the Streets, which in the new quarter are wholly laid

you know, is the capital of the Principality, and the residence of the King of Sardinia. * * *[4] We shall stay here, I believe, a fortnight, and proceed for Genoa, which is three or four days journey to go post. I am, &c.

74. GRAY TO WEST

Turin, Nov. 16, N. S. 1739.

AFTER eight days journey through Greenland, we arrived at Turin. You approach it by a handsome avenue of nine miles long, and quite strait. The entrance is guarded by certain vigilant dragons, called Douaniers, who mumbled us for some time. The city is not large, as being a place of strength, and consequently confined within its fortifications; it has many beauties and some faults; among the first are streets all laid out by the line, regular uniform buildings, fine walks that surround the whole, and in general a good lively clean appearance: But the houses are of brick plaistered, which is apt to want repairing; the windows of oiled paper, which is apt to be torn; and every thing very slight, which is apt to tumble down. There is an excellent Opera, but it is only in the Carnival: Balls every night, but only in the Carnival: Masquerades, too, but only in the Carnival. This Carnival lasts only from Christmas to Lent; one half of the remaining part of the year is pafsed in remembering the last, the other in expecting the future Carnival. We cannot well subsist upon such slender diet, no more than upon an execrable Italian Comedy, and a Puppet-Show, called Rap-

out by the line, as it contributes much to the beauty of this City, so it makes it appear much smaller, than it really is, for at your first entrance you see quite through it. the Strada del Po is near ½ a mile long, with a handsome *Corridore* ["Arcade" written over] on both sides from one end to the other, & is terminated by a fine Doric Gate, that leads to the Po, which runs not a quarter of a mile from the Town. . . the buildings here in general are of brick, either plaister'd, or intended to be so (for in those, that are not, the holes of the scaffolding are all left unstopt) & generally of some regular order, 4 Story high, for the length of whole streets: the windows are oil'd Paper, which is often torn, & has a very ill effect to the eye. Many great houses; the Architecture but indifferent, but altogether makes a good appearance enough.'

4 * * * That part of the letter here omitted, contained only a description of the city; which, as Mr. Gray has given it to Mr. West in the following letter, and that in a more lively manner, I thought it unnecessary to insert. A liberty I have taken in other parts of this correspondence, in order to avoid repetitions. *Mason.*

LETTER 74.—First printed in Mason's *Memoirs*, pp. 65–8.

presentazione d'un' anima dannata, which, I think, are all the present diversions of the place; except the Marquise de Cavaillac's Conversazione, where one goes to see people play at Ombre and Taroc,[1] a game with 72 cards all painted with suns, and moons, and devils and monks. Mr. Walpole has been at court; the family are at present at a country palace, called La Venerie. The palace here in town is the very quintefsence of gilding and looking-glafs; inlaid floors, carved pannels, and painting, wherever they could stick a brush. I own I have not, as yet, any where met with those grand and simple works of Art, that are to amaze one, and whose sight one is to be the better for: But those of Nature have astonished me beyond exprefsion. In our little journey up to the Grande Chartreuse,[2] I do not remember to have gone ten paces without an exclamation, that there was no restraining: Not a precipice, not a torrent, not a cliff, but is pregnant with religion and poetry. There are certain scenes that would awe an atheist into belief, without the help of other argument. One need not have a very fantastic imagination to see spirits there at noon-day: You have Death perpetually before your eyes, only so far removed, as to compose the mind without frighting it. I am well persuaded St. Bruno was a man of no common genius, to choose such a situation for his retirement; and perhaps should have been a disciple of his, had I been born in his time. You may believe Abelard and Heloïse were not forgot upon this occasion: If I do not mistake, I saw you too every now and then at a distance among the trees; il me semble, que j'ai vu ce chien de visage là quelque part. You seemed to call to me from the other side of the precipice, but the noise of the river below was so great, that I really could not distinguish what you said; it seemed to have a cadence like verse. In your next you will be so good to let me know what it was. The week we have since pafsed among the Alps, has not equalled the single day upon that mountain, because the winter was rather too far advanced, and the weather a little foggy. However, it did not want its beauties; the savage rudenefs of the view is inconceivable without seeing it: I reckoned in one day, thirteen cascades, the least of which was, I dare say, one hundred feet in height. I had Livy in the chaise with me, and beheld his 'Nives cœlo propè immistæ, tecta informia imposita rupibus, pecora jumentaque torrida

---

[1] A contemporary description of the game of taroc or *minchiate* is given by C. de Brosses, *Lettres Familières*, XLIV.)   [2] See Letter 71, n. 1.

frigore, homines intonsi & inculti, animalia inanimaque omnia rigentia gelu; omnia confragosa, præruptaque'.[3] The creatures that inhabit them are, in all respects, below humanity; and most of them, especially women, have the tumidum guttur,[4] which they call goscia. Mont Cenis, I confefs, carries the per-mifsion mountains have of being frightful[5] rather too far; and its horrors were accompanied with too much danger to give one time to reflect upon their beauties. There is a family of the Alpine monsters I have mentioned, upon its very top, that in the middle of winter calmly lay in their stock of provisions and firing, and so are buried in their hut for a month or two under the snow. When we were down it, and got a little way into Piedmont, we began to find 'Apricos quosdam colles, rivosque prope sylvas, & jam humano cultu digniora loca'.[6] I read Silius Italicus too, for the first time; and wished for you according to custom. We set out for Genoa in two days time.[7]

75. GRAY TO WEST

Genoa, Nov. 21, 1739.

> Horridos tractus, Boreæą linquens
> Regna Taurini fera, molliorem
> Advehor brumam, Genuæą amantes
>   Littora soles.

AT least if they do not, they have a very ill taste; for I never beheld any thing more amiable. Only figure to yourself a vast semicircular bason, full of fine blue sea, and vefsels of all sorts and sizes, some sailing out, some coming in, and others at anchor; and all round it palaces and churches peeping over one another's heads, gardens and marble terrases full of orange and cyprefs trees, fountains, and trellis-works covered with vines,

---

[3] Livy, xxi. 32.

[4] Goitre—Juvenal, *Sat.* xiii. 162: 'Quis tumidum guttur miratur in Alpibus?'

[5] A phrase, as Mason notes, borrowed from Madame de Sévigné: 'Guille-ragues disoit hier que Pellisson abusoit de la permission qu'ont les hommes d'être laids' (*à Mme de Grignan*, 5 janv. 1764).

[6] Livy, xxi. 37.

[7] Their route from Turin, as Gray notes in his *Journal*, was through Moncalieri, Asti (a small city where they lay), Alessandria, Novi ('the first Town in the Genoese State', where they lay), over the mountains by the road over 'the highest of 'em called the Bouquet', then through the plain, where they had to cross a torrent above 20 times, and so into the City of Genoa.

LETTER 75.—First printed in Mason's *Memoirs*, pp. 68–70.

which altogether compose the grandest of theatres.[1] This is the first coup d'oeil, and is almost all I am yet able to give you an account of, for we arrived late last night. To-day was, luckily, a great festival, and in the morning we resorted to the church of the Madonna delle Vigne, to put up our little orisons; (I believe I forgot to tell you, that we have been sometime converts to the holy Catholic church) we found our Lady richly drefsed out, with a crown of diamonds on her own head, another upon the child's, and a constellation of wax lights burning before them: Shortly after came the Doge, in his robes of crimson damask, and a cap of the same, followed by the Senate in black. Upon his approach began a fine concert of music, and among the rest two eunuchs' voices, that were a perfect feast to ears that had heard nothing but French operas for a year. We listened to this, and breathed nothing but incense for two

---

[1] In his *Journal*, after mentioning the approach to Genoa through 'the magnificent Fauxbourg', which 'is a little mile long with many noble Villas on either hand, with their gardens & marble decorations', Gray continues: 'there is a sort of Terrace here in use, that I have not before seen; on the top of their high walls next the street, runs a row of marble Columns of a regular order; between 'em are Statues, or Orange trees placed, & on them rests a frame of Trellis-work, which is cover'd with Vines, or Jefsamine; these have a noble effect, as have the Porticoes, that many of their houses are flanked with; they are usually even with the 2d Story, supported by tall pillars of white Marble; & Balustrades of the same, with cielings of Stucco, white figures on a grey ground: they look cool, & stately. the Gates are commonly lofty arches, thro' which you have a view of the Vestibule, the square area surrounded by the galleries, upon which the apartments open, with double flights of steps, that lead up into them, & another opposite arch, that discovers to you either the gardens behind, or a Nich with a Statue, & Fountain; or some piece of painting in perspective to represent one or the other. this is the general form of their palaces both without, & within the City, & some of them are wholly built of marble. . . . the City surrounds its Port, which is semicircular, entirely, & appears from the Sea, like a most stately Theatre, it's houses, & palaces, Churches, & Porticoes gradually riseing one above another, & intermix'd with Gardens, & Terrafses full of Oranges, Vines, Lemon, & Cyprefs-Trees. the declivity of its situation, tho' it adds much to the beauty of the prospect, is a great inconvenience in reality; the streets being all too narrow, & too steep to admit of Coaches; however they are always clean, & well-paved. . . . at the Western gate is a very high Watch-tower, & from hence runs a handsome Terrace along by the Sea-side for a great way; here Coaches can drive, & enjoy a noble view of a part of the City with that beautiful Bay, which is usually cover'd with Vefsels of all Sizes. . . . The 2 noblest Streets in Genoa, are those called the Strade Nuova, & Balbi. they are neither of them very long, or wide; but have on each side 6 or 7 of the most beautiful palaces.' Gray notes that at Genoa they stayed, 'alla Sta Martha, a week'.

hours. The Doge is a very tall, lean, stately, old figure, called Costantino Balbi;[2] and the Senate seem to have been made upon the same model. They said their prayers, and heard an absurd white friar preach, with equal devotion. After this we went to the Annonciata, a church built by the family Lomellini, and belonging to it; which is, indeed, a most stately structure, the inside wholly marble of various kinds, except where gold and painting take its place. From hence to the Palazzo Doria. I should make you sick of marble, if I told you how it was lavished here upon the porticoes, the balustrades, and terrases, the lowest of which extends quite to the sea. The inside is by no means answerable to the outward magnificence; the furniture seems to be as old as the founder of the family.[3] There great imbofsed silver tables tell you, in bas-relief, his victories at sea; how he entertained the Emperor Charles, and how he refused the sovereignty of the Commonwealth when it was offered him; the rest is old-fashioned velvet chairs, and gothic tapestry. The rest of the day has been spent, much to our hearts' content, in cursing French music and architecture, and in singing the praises of Italy. We find this place so very fine, that we are in fear of finding nothing finer. We are fallen in love with the Mediterranean sea, and hold your lakes and your rivers in vast contempt. This is

'The happy country where huge lemons grow,'

as Waller says;[4] and I am sorry to think of leaving it in a week for Parma, although it be

The happy country where huge cheeses grow.

76. Gray to Mrs. Gray

Bologna, Dec. 9, N. S. 1739.

OUR journey hither has taken up much lefs time than I expected. We left Genoa (a charming place, and one that deserved a longer stay) the week before last; crofsed the moun-

---

[2] Doge, 1738–40.
[3] The famous admiral, Andrea Doria (1466–1560).
[4] *Battle of the Summer Islands*, i. 5–6:
    Bermuda, walled with rocks, who does not know?
    That happy island where huge lemons grow . . .
LETTER 76.—First printed in Mason's *Memoirs*, pp. 70–2.

tains, and lay that night at Tortona,[1] the next at St. Giovanni, and the morning after came to Piacenza. That city, (though the capital of a Dutchy) made so frippery an appearance, that instead of spending some days there, as had been intended, we only dined, and went on to Parma; stayed there all the following day, which was pafsed in visiting the famous works of Corregio in the Dome, and other churches. The fine gallery of pictures, that once belonged to the Dukes of Parma, is no more here; the King of Naples[2] has carried it all thither, and the city had not merit enough to detain us any longer, so we proceeded through Reggio to Modena; this, though the residence of its Duke, is an ill-built melancholy place, all of brick, as are most of the towns in this part of Lombardy: He himself lives in a private manner, with very little appearance of a court about him; he has one of the noblest collections of paintings in the world, which entertained us extremely well the rest of that day and a part of the next; and in the afternoon we came to Bologna:[3] So now you may wish us joy of being in the dominions

---

[1] In his *Journal* Gray says they did not enter Tortona (see n. 3); presumably they passed the night outside the city.

[2] Charles of Bourbon, son of Philip V of Spain, King of Naples, or of the Two Sicilies, 1735–59; King of Spain, as Charles III, 1759–88.

[3] The journey from Genoa to Bologna is described as follows in Gray's *Journal*: 'Nov: 28 1739. Left Genoa; crofs'd the mountains again, & came to Tortona. this City is one of the K: of Sardinia's last acquisitions, & strongly fortified. 'tis on an eminence. we did not enter it, for the gates were shut. The vast plains of Lombardy were now begun; lay at Castel St Giovanni. Pafsed the famous river, Trebia; the country on this side of it, where Scipio incamped, after Hannibal had crofsed the Po, is still, as Livy has described it, Loca altiora, collesq impeditiores equiti, the more remarkable, as the rest is a huge, & very level plain. it was at this time so narrow, & so shallow a stream, that we crofsed without a ferry in the Chaise; but the vast broad, & stony Channel of it, tho' then dry, was a sufficient intimation of it's bignefs at certain seasons . . . on the other side of it is a naked plain for a little while, & beyond that Willows, & Shrubs: here was the Scene of that Battle. there are in that plain some vestigia of an Aqueduct, 8 or 10 great ruinous mafses of Brick, on which the Arches seem to have rose. pofsibly it convey'd the water of that river to Placentia. we dined at that City, which makes a very mean appearance . . . pafsed thro' Borgo St Dennino . . .; ferried over the R: Taro, & arrived very late at night at Parma, which is 5 little miles further. stayed there one day. The City, being all built of Brick (like the others in this part of Lombardy) & that not plaister'd, has but a smoky, & melancholy appearance; there are few, or no good buildings: it is large, & the little R: Parma runs thro' the middle of it. . . . Pafsed the River Lenza (anciently Nigella) over a very long bridge, which goes acrofs the whole channel of it: the Stream itself one might jump

of his Holineſs. This is a populous city, and of great extent:
All the streets have porticoes on both sides, such as surround
a part of Covent-Garden, a great relief in summer-time in such
a climate; and from one of the principal gates to a church of
the Virgin, [where is a wonder-working picture, at three miles
distance] runs a corridore of the same sort, lately finished, and,
indeed, a most extraordinary performance. The churches here
are more remarkable for their paintings than architecture, being
mostly old structures of brick; but the palaces are numerous,
and fine enough to supply us with somewhat worth seeing from
morning till night. The country of Lombardy, hitherto, is one
of the most beautiful imaginable; the roads broad, and exactly
straight, and on either hand vast plantations of trees, chiefly
mulberries and olives, and not a tree without a vine twining
about it and spreading among its branches. This scene, indeed,
which must be the most lovely in the world during the proper
season, is at present all deformed by the winter, which here is
rigorous enough for the time it lasts; but one still sees the
skeleton of a charming place, and reaps the benefit of its product, for the fruits and provisions are admirable; in short you
find every thing, that luxury can desire, in perfection. We have
now been here a week, and shall stay some little time longer.
We are at the foot of the Apennine mountains; it will take up
three days to croſs them, and then we shall come to Florence,
where we shall paſs the Christmas. Till then we must remain
in a state of ignorance as to what is doing in England, for our
letters are to meet us there: If I do not find four or five from
you alone, I shall wonder.

over . . . paſsed thro' Reggio without stopping; the country all hereabouts,
& quite to Bologna is as fertile, & well-cultivated as poſsible, & must in
summer afford the most beautiful view in the world; the fields are regularly
planted with rows of Elms, Mulberry, & *Olive Trees*, & Vines running up
every one of them; between them is Corn sown, & the hedges are many of
them kept cut, as in a Garden; the roads are commonly quite strait, & very
broad for leagues together; we came in the afternoon to Modena. That
City makes at least as bad an appearance as Parma, & much in the same
kind; only that here are Portico's running along all the Streets, which add
somewhat to the view, & keep it clean. stayed there one day. . . . The
Beauty of the Country rather increases, than diminishes, as you go from
hence to Bologna; but it is a beauty still of the same nature.'

77. GRAY TO MRS. GRAY

Florence, Dec. 19, N. S. 1739.

WE spent twelve days at Bologna,[1] chiefly (as most travellers do) in seeing sights; for as we knew no mortal there, and as it is no easy matter to get admiſsion into any Italian house, without very particular recommendations, we could see no company but in public places; and there are none in that city but the churches. We saw, therefore, churches, palaces, and pictures from morning to night; and the 15th of this month set out for Florence,[2] and began to crofs the Apennine mountains; we travelled among and upon them all that day, and, as it was but indifferent weather, were commonly in the middle of thick clouds, that utterly deprived us of a sight of their beauties: For this vast chain of hills has its beauties, and all the vallies are cultivated; even the mountains themselves are many of them so within a little of their very tops. They are not so horrid as the Alps, though pretty near as high; and the whole road is admirably well kept, and paved throughout, which is a length of fourscore miles, and more: We left the Pope's dominions, and lay that night in those of the Grand Duke[3] at Fiorenzuola,[4] a paltry little town, at the foot of Mount Giogo, which is the highest of them all. Next morning we went up it; the post-house is upon its very top, and usually involved in clouds, or half-buried in the snow. Indeed there was none of the last at the time we were there, but it was still a dismal habitation. The descent is most exceſsively steep, and the turnings very

LETTER 77.—First printed in Mason's *Memoirs*, pp. 72–4.

[1] Of Bologna, where they stayed '12 Days, al Pelegrino', Gray says in his *Journal* : 'That City does not at all strike the eye upon entering it, but rather has a mean & dirty appearance. very few of the Streets are without a Portico on each side, which, tho' irregular, is undoubtedly an ornament: but in general the buildings (some Palaces excepted) are very old, & being of Brick, the whole has an air of Melancholy.'

[2] In his *Journal* Gray records: 'To Florence . . 2 Days. Begun to paſs the Apennine. cloudy damp weather. road paved, & *admirably kept*; what one could see of the prospect leſs savage than the Alps, & agreeable enough; lay at Fiorenzuola, a paltry, & ill-provided *Village*. next morning crofs'd the Giogo, vastly steep, & dangerous, particularly the descent. view of the plains of Florence in comeing down from the mountains very beautiful! many olive, & Lemon Trees.'

[3] Francis II, of Lorraine (1708–65), Grand Duke of Tuscany, 1737–65, husband of Maria Theresa; Emperor, as Francis I, 1745–65.

[4] In Tuscany, near the source of the Santerno.

short and frequent; however, we performed it without any danger, and in coming down could dimly discover Florence, and the beautiful plain about it, through the mists; but enough to convince us, it must be one of the noblest prospects upon earth in summer. That afternoon we got thither; and Mr. Mann,[5] the resident, had sent his servant to meet us at the gates, and conduct us to his house. He is the best and most obliging person in the world. The next night we were introduced at the Prince of Craon's[6] afsembly (he has the chief power here in the Grand Duke's absence). The Princefs,[7] and he, were extremely civil to the name of Walpole, so we were asked to stay supper, which is as much as to say, you may come and sup here whenever you please; for after the first invitation this is always understood. We have also been at the Countefs Suarez's,[8] a favourite of the late Duke,[9] and one that gives the first movement to every thing gay that is going forward here. The news is every day expected from Vienna of the Great Duchefs's[10] delivery; if it be a boy, here will be all sorts of balls, masquerades, operas, and illuminations; if not, we must wait for the Carnival, when all those things come of course. In the mean time it is impofsible to want entertainment; the famous gallery, alone, is an amusement for months; we commonly pafs

[5] Horace, afterwards Sir Horace, Mann (1701–86), second son of Robert Mann, a London merchant. He was in 1737 appointed assistant to the Minister at the Court of Tuscany, and in 1740 became Minister, and held the post until his death. He was created a Baronet, 1755; died unmarried at Florence, aged 85, Nov. 1786, having never revisited England since taking up his appointment. Walpole and Mann, whose families were connected, became intimate friends, and when the former returned to England they began a correspondence, which continued uninterruptedly for forty-five years (during which they never met), until Mann's death. During their stay in Florence (at least for part of the time), Walpole and Gray resided in Mann's house (see Letter 90, n. 7).

[6] Marc de Beauvau (1679–1754), Prince de Craon, whom Walpole describes as 'a good-natured simple old man, poor and extravagant, loves piquet, the Princess, and baubles'. He and the Princess at this time were resident in Florence, where the Prince was at the head of the Council of Regency.

[7] Anne-Marguerite de Ligniville (d. 1772), Princesse de Craon, formerly the favourite mistress of Leopold, last Duke of Lorraine, by whom she had twenty children. The Duke married her to M. de Beauvau, and prevailed on the Emperor to make him a Prince of the Empire.

[8] She figures frequently (as Madame Suares) in Walpole's early letters to Mann.   [9] Giovanni Gastone, the last Medicean Grand-Duke, 1723-37.

[10] Maria Theresa; the child was a boy, who in 1765, on his father's death, became Emperor as Joseph II.

two or three hours every morning in it, and one has perfect leisure to consider all its beauties. You know it contains many hundred antique statues, such as the whole world cannot match, besides the vast collection of paintings, medals, and precious stones, such as no other prince was ever master of; in short, all that the rich and powerful house of Medicis has in so many years got together.[11] And besides this city abounds with so many palaces and churches, that you can hardly place yourself any where without having some fine one in view, or at least some statue or fountain, magnificently adorned; these undoubtedly are far more numerous than Genoa can pretend to; yet, in its general appearance, I cannot think that Florence equals it in beauty. Mr. Walpole is just come from being presented to the Electreſs Palatine Dowager;[12] she is a sister of the late Great Duke's; a stately old lady, that never goes out but to church, and then she has guards, and eight horses to her coach. She received him with much ceremony, standing under a huge black canopy, and, after a few minutes talking, she aſsured him of her good will, and dismiſsed him: She never sees any body but thus in form; and so she paſses her life, poor woman! * * *

78. GRAY TO WEST

Florence, Jan. 15, 1740.

I THINK I have not yet told you how we left that charming place Genoa: How we croſsed a mountain, all of green marble, called Buchetto:[1] How we came to Tortona, and waded through the mud to come to Castel St. Giovanni, and there eat

[11] He catalogued and made occasional short remarks on the pictures, &c., which he saw here, as well as at other places, many of which are in my possession, but it would have swelled this work too much if I had inserted them. *Mason.*—Some of these notes were printed by Mitford 1835–43, vol. iv, pp. 225–305; others, by Tovey in *Gray and his Friends*, pp. 203–60.

[12] Anna Maria Luisa (1667–1743), the last of the House of Medici. She was daughter of the Grand Duke Cosimo III, and sister of Giovanni Gastone (see n. 6); she married Johann Wilhelm, Elector Palatine, 1690–1716, after whose death she returned to reside in Florence (see Walpole's letter to Mann of 3 March 1743). Walpole refers to Gray's account of this visit in his letter to Mark Noble of 22 March 1787 (see *Supplement to the Letters of Horace Walpole*, vol. iii, p. 335, and note).

LETTER 78.—First printed in Mason's *Memoirs*, p. 75.

[1] In the Ligurian Apennines.—In the account of their journey from Turin to Genoa, in his *Journal*, Gray notes: 'the Bouquet, over which the road winds, supplies Genoa with that beautiful Marble, speckled with Green,

mustard and sugar with a dish of crows' gizzards: Secondly, how we paſsed the famous plains

> Quà Trebie glaucas salices intersecat undâ,
>   Arvaque Romanis nobilitata malis.
> Visus adhuc amnis veteri de clade rubere
>   Et suspirantes ducere mæstus aquas;
> Maurorumque ala, & nigræ increbrescere turmæ,
>   Et pulsa Ausonidum ripa sonare fugâ.[2]

Nor, thirdly, how we paſsed through Piacenza, Parma, Modena, entered the territories of the Pope; stayed twelve days at Bologna; croſsed the Apennines, and afterwards arrived at Florence. None of these things have I told you, nor do I intend to tell you, till you ask me some questions concerning them. No not even of Florence itself, except that it is as fine as poſsible, and has every thing in it that can bleſs the eyes. [3]But, before I enter into particulars, you must make your peace both with me and the Venus de Medicis, who, let me tell you, is highly and justly offended at you for not inquiring, long before this, concerning her symmetry and proportions. * * *[3]

78.* West to Gray
[Feb. or March 1740]

[West wrote a letter to Gray, which Mason thought 'too bizarre for the Public'. The letter must have been written in February or March, as Gray's reply was written in March or April (see Letter 78.**]

78.** Gray to West
[March or April 1740]

[From Mason's correspondence with Walpole in July 1773 (*Walpole– Mason Correspondence*, vol. i, pp. 87 ff.) we learn that there were two letters of Gray written in Italian, which Mason (after submitting them to Walpole) did not print. The first of these was in reply to a letter of West (Letter 78*). In Gray's letter there were verses 'Te dea etc', which Mason thought very beautiful, and an allusion to the Venus de Medici, 'which occasioned a very pretty Latin elegy of West's, which he sent him in return' (see Letter 84). Walpole was not pleased with Gray's Italian letter and suggested that Mason

White, & Black, which you see in their Churches, & Palaces: the Rocks, as you go along, appear all of that hue, & huge rough blocks of it frequently are seen at the doors of little Villages, that lie hereabouts.'
    [2] The river Trebbia, which falls into the Po near Piacenza, was the scene of the defeat of the Romans by Hannibal, 218 B.C. Mason cannot have copied Gray's text correctly. Gray probably wrote Trebiæ (not Trebie) and unda (not undâ) in line 1, and alæ (not ala) in line 5.
    [3–3] This last paragraph is an addition of Mason's. See Letter 78**.

might mention Gray's having spoken of the Venus to West without producing his letter. Mason followed Walpole's advice, and interpolated in Gray's letter to West of 15 Jan. a reference to the Venus (see Letter 78, n. 3). Gray's letter was probably written in March or April, as West's reply (see Letter 84) was written in April.]

79. GRAY TO WHARTON

Proposals for printing by Subscription, in

THIS LARGE
LETTER[1]

The Travels of T: G: GENT: which will consist of the following Particulars.

CHAP: 1:

THE Author arrives at Dover; his conversation with the Mayor of that Corporation; sets out in the Pacquet-Boat, grows very sick; the Author spews, a very minute account of all the circumstances thereof: his arrival at Calais; how the inhabitants of that country speak French, & are said to be all Papishes; the Author's reflexions thereupon.

2.

How they feed him with Soupe, & what Soupe is. how he meets with a Capucin; & what a Capucin is. how they shut him up in a Post-Chaise, & send him to Paris; he goes wondring along dureing 6 days; & how there are Trees, & Houses just as in England. arrives at Paris without knowing it.

3.

Full account of the river Seine, & of the various animals & plants its borders produce. Description of the little Creature, called an Abbé, its parts, & their uses; with the reasons, why they will not live in England, & the methods, that have been used to propagate them there. a Cut of the Inside of a Nunnery; it's Structure, wonderfully adapted to the use of the animals, that inhabit it: a short account of them, how they propagate without the help of a Male, & how they eat up their own young ones, like Cats, and Rabbets. supposed to have both Sexes in themselves, like a Snail. Diſsection of a Dutcheſs with Copper-Plates, very curious.

LETTER 79.—First printed by Mitford (1816), vol. ii, pp. 71–7; now reprinted from original.

[1] Gray wrote these words in large capitals to indicate the type in which his imaginary work was to be printed.

4.

Goes to the Opera; grand Orchestra of Humstrums, Bag-pipes, Salt-boxes, Tabours, & Pipes. Anatomy of a French Ear, shewing the formation of it to be entirely different from that of an English one, & that Sounds have a directly contrary effect upon one & the other. Farinelli[1a] at Paris said to have a fine manner, but no voice. Grand Ballet, in which there is no seeing the dance for Petticoats. Old Women with flowers, & jewels stuck in the Curls of their grey Hair; Red-heel'd Shoes & Roll-ups[2] innumerable, Hoops, & Paniers immeasurable, Paint unspeakable. Tables, wherein is calculated with the utmost exactnefs, the several Degrccs of Red, now in use, from the riseing blush of an Advocate's Wife to the flameing Crimson of a Princefs of the blood; done by a Limner in great Vogue.

5.

The Author takes unto him a Taylour. his Character. how he covers him with Silk, & Fringe, & widens his figure with buckram a yard on each side; Wastcoat, & Breeches so strait, he can neither breath, nor walk. how the Barber curls him en Bequille, & à la negligee, & ties a vast Solitaire[3] about his Neck; how the Milliner lengthens his ruffles to his finger's ends, & sticks his two arms into a Muff. how he cannot stir, & how they cut him in proportion to his Clothes.

6.

He is carried to Versailles; despises it infinitely. a difsertation upon Taste. goes to an Installation in the Chappel-royal. enter the King, & 50 Fiddlers Solus. Kettle-Drums, & Trumpets, Queens, & Dauphins, Princefses, & Cardinals, Incense, & the Mafs. Old Knights, makeing Curtsies; Holy-Ghosts, & Fiery-tongues.

7.

Goes into the Country to Rheims in Champagne. stays there 3 Months, what he did there (he must beg the reader's pardon, but) he has really forgot.

8.

Proceeds to Lyons. Vastnefs of that City. Can't see the Streets for houses.[4] how rich it is, & how much it stinks. Poem

---

[1a] See Letter 60, n. 13.   [2] See Letter 61, n. 2.   [3] See Letter 61, n. 3.
[4] Mitford quotes from Walpole's *Fugitive Pieces* (vol. i, p. 222): 'When one

upon the Confluence of the Rhône, & the Saône, by a friend of the Author's; very pretty!

9.

Makes a journey into Savoy, & in his way visits the Grande Chartreuse; he is set astride upon a Mule's back, & begins to climb up the Mountain. Rocks & Torrents beneath; Pine-trees, & Snows above; horrours, & terrours on all sides. the Author dies of the Fright.

10.

He goes to Geneva. his mortal antipathy to a Presbyterian, & the cure for it. returns to Lyons. gets a surfeit with eating Ortolans, & Lampreys; is advised to go into Italy for the benefit of the air. . . .

11.

Sets out the latter end of November[5] to crofs the Alps. he is devoured by a Wolf, & how it is to be devoured by a Wolf. the 7th day he comes to the foot of Mount Cenis. how he is wrap'd up in Bear Skins, & Bever-Skins, Boots on his legs, Caps on his head, Muffs on his hands, & Taffety over his eyes; he is placed on a Bier, & is carried to heaven by the savages blind-fold. how he lights among a certain fat nation, call'd Clouds;[6] how they are always in a Sweat, & never speak, but they fart. how they flock about him, & think him very odd for not doing so too. he falls flump into Italy.

12.

Arrives at Turin; goes to Genoa, & from thence to Placentia; crofses the River Trebia: the Ghost of Hannibal appears to him; & what it, & he, say upon the occasion. locked out of

is misled by a proper name, the only use of which is to direct, one feels like the countryman, who complained—"That the houses hindered him from seeing Paris." The thing becomes an obstruction to itself.' And from *Menagiana* (vol. i, p. 13): 'Mons. le Duc de M. disoit, que les maisons de Paris etoient si hautes, qu'elles empechoient de voir la ville.'

⁵ A slip for October; they reached Turin on 7 Nov. (see Letter 73).

⁶ In his letter to West from Turin of 11 Nov. 1739 Walpole writes: 'At the foot of mount Cenis we were obliged to quit our chaise, which was taken all to pieces and loaded on mules; and we were carried in low arm-chairs on poles, swathed in beaver bonnets, beaver gloves, beaver stockings, muffs, and bear-skins. When we came to the top, behold the snows fallen! and such quantities, and conducted by such heavy clouds that hung glouting, that I thought we could never have waded through them.'

Parma in a cold winter's night: the author by an ingenious stratagem gains admittance. despises that City, & proceeds thro' Reggio to Modena. how the Duke, & Dutchefs lye over their own Stables, & go every night to a vile Italian Comedy. despises them, & it; & proceeds to Bologna.

13.

Enters into the Dominions of the Pope o' Rome. meets the Devil, & what he says on the occasion. very publick, & scandalous doings between the Vines & the Elm-trees, & how the Olive-trees are shock'd thereupon. Author longs for Bologna-Sausages, & Hams; & how he grows as fat as a Hog.

14.

Observations on Antiquities. the Author proves, that Bologna was the ancient Tarentum; that the Battle of Salamis, contrary to the vulgar opinion, was fought by Land, & that not far from Ravenna. that the Romans were a Colony of the Jews,[7] & that Eneas was the same with Ehud.

15.

Arrival at Florence. is of opinion, that the Venus of Medicis is a modern performance, & that a very indifferent one, & much inferiour to the K: Charles at Chareing-Crofs. Account of the City, & Manners of the Inhabitants. a learned Difsertation on the true Situation of Gomorrah. . . .

And here will end the first part of these instructive & entertaining Voyages. the Subscribers are to pay 20 Guineas; 19 down, & the remainder upon delivery of the book. N:B: A few are printed on the softest Royal Brown Paper for the use of the Curious. . . . .

My Dear, dear Wharton[8]
(Which is a dear more than I give any body else. it is very odd to begin with a Parenthesis, but) You may think me a Beast, for not haveing sooner wrote to you, & to be sure a Beast I am. now when one owns it, I don't see what you have left to say. I take this opportunity to inform you (an opportunity

---

[7] See Letter 85.
[8] Of Old-Park, near Durham. With this gentleman Mr. Gray contracted an acquaintance very early; and though they were not educated together at Eton, yet afterwards at Cambridge, when the Doctor was Fellow of Pem-

I have had every week this twelvemonth) that I am arrived
safe at Calais, & am at present at Florence, a city in Italy in
I don't know how many degrees N: latitude. under the Line I
am sure it is not, for I am at this instant expireing with Cold.
You must know, that not being certain what circumstances of
my History would particularly suit your curiosity, & knowing
that all I had to say to you would overflow the narrow limits
of many a good quire of Paper, I have taken this method of
laying before you the contents, that you may pitch upon what
you please, & give me your orders accordingly to expatiate
thereupon: for I conclude you will write to me; won't you? oh!
yes, when you know, that in a week I set out for Rome, & that
the Pope is dead,[9] & that I shall be (I should say, God willing;
& if nothing extraordinary intervene; & if I'm alive, & well;
& in all human probability) at the Coronation of a new one.
now as you have no other correspondent there, & as if you do
not, I certainly shall not write again (observe my impudence)
I take it to be your interest to send me a vast letter, full of all
sorts of News, & Bawdy, & Politics, & such other ingredients,

---

broke Hall, they became intimate friends, and continued so to the time of
Mr. Gray's death. *Mason.*—Thomas Wharton (1717–94), physician, Gray's
most intimate friend, was the eldest of the three sons of Robert (1690–1752),
Mayor of Durham, second son of Thomas (1652–1714), physician, eldest son
of the celebrated physician and anatomist, Dr. Thomas Wharton (1614–73),
Fellow, and for many years Censor, of the Royal College of Physicians, the
friend of Isaac Walton and Elias Ashmole. Thomas, the friend of Gray (who
was his senior by a year or more, but of the same standing in the University),
was admitted as a Pensioner at Pembroke College, Cambridge (with which
he had an hereditary connexion, his great-grandfather and uncle having both
been members of the College) in 1734; B.A., 1738; elected Fellow, 1739;
M.A., 1741; M.D., 1752. He vacated his Fellowship in 1747, on his marriage
to Margaret Wilkinson, of Cross Gate, Durham, by whom he had three
sons and five daughters (see Genealogical Tables). He succeeded to the
estate of Old-Park (which had been acquired by his great-great-grand-
father in 1620) on the death of his father in 1752. Gray, as the address of
this letter shows, had become intimate with him during his first period of
residence at Peterhouse; and the friendship was renewed after Gray's return
to College in 1742, when he found Wharton in residence at Pembroke.
Wharton continued to reside (at irregular intervals) until Oct. 1746, when
he left Cambridge, after which he and Gray were separated for five years
(see Letter 166, n. 7). They met again in Cambridge in April 1752, and
afterwards were often together in London, and at Wharton's home at Old-
Park. Wharton, who became a Fellow of the Royal College of Physicians
in 1754, and was Censor in 1757, practised as a physician in London between
1752 and 1758, when he went to reside at Old-Park.
   9 Clement XII (Lorenzo Corsini, elected in 1730) died 6 Feb. 1740.

as to you shall seem convenient with all decent expedition. only do not be too severe upon the Pretender;[10] &, if you like my Style, pray say so. this is à la Françoise; & if you think it a little too foolish, & impertinent; you shall be treated alla Toscana with a thousand Signoria Illustrifsima's. in the mean time I have the honour to remain

Your lofing Frind tell Deth. T: GRAY

Florence. March. 12. N: S: [1740].

P:S: This is à l'Angloise. I don't know where you are; if at Cambridge, pray let me know all how, & about it; and if my old friends Thompson, or Clark[11] fall in your way, say I am extremely theirs. but if you are in town, I entreat you to make my best Compliments to Mrs. Wharton.[12] Adieu, Yours Sincerely a second time.

80. GRAY TO MRS. GRAY

Florence, March 19, 1740.

THE Pope is at last dead, and we are to set out for Rome on Monday next. The Conclave is still sitting there, and likely to continue so some time longer, as the two French Cardinals are but just arrived, and the German ones are still expected. It agrees mighty ill with those that remain inclosed: Ottoboni[1]

---

[10] For the reason, see Letter 81 *ad fin.*

[11] These were presumably contemporaries of Gray at Peterhouse, in which case the former was John Thompson, a Yorkshireman, educated at Bradford, who was admitted Pensioner of Peterhouse in June 1732; B.A., 1735; M.A., 1739; and elected Ramsay Fellow, and later Parke Fellow. Clark was John Clerke, son of Thomas Clerke, Rector of Beckenham, Kent (born in 1717), who was admitted Pensioner of St. Catharine's in April 1734 and migrated to Peterhouse in Nov. 1735; he was (like Gray) Cosin and Hale Scholar; B.A., 1738; Fellow, 1740; M.A., 1742; M.D., 1753; d. 1790. He practised for many years as a physician at Epsom. A letter to him from Gray, dated 12 Aug. 1760, was printed by Mason (see Letter 318). On the death of his wife (27 April 1757) Gray wrote the epitaph beginning, 'Lo! where this silent Marble weeps', which is inscribed on the tablet to her memory in the Church of Beckenham, Kent (see Letter 266). Gray visited him at Epsom in 1763 (see Letter 373, n. 2).

[12] Presumably Wharton's mother, who is mentioned in Gray's letter to him of 26 Dec. 1754 (Letter 194 *ad fin.*).

LETTER 80.—First printed in Mason's *Memoirs*, pp. 77–8.

[1] Cardinal Pietro Ottoboni, created Cardinal by Alexander VIII in 1689. He had a celebrated collection of cameos and intaglios, which was dispersed after his death (see Walpole to West, 7 May 1740).

is already dead of an apoplexy; Altieri[2] and several others are said to be dying, or very bad: Yet it is not expected to break up till after Easter. We shall lie at Sienna the first night, spend a day there, and in two more get to Rome. One begins to see in this country the first promises of an Italian spring, clear unclouded skies, and warm suns, such as are not often felt in England; yet, for your sake, I hope at present you have your proportion of them, and that all your frosts, and snows, and short-breaths are, by this time, utterly vanished. I have nothing new or particular to inform you of; and, if you see things at home go on much in their old course, you must not imagine them more various abroad. The diversions of a Florentine Lent are composed of a sermon in the morning, full of hell and the devil; a dinner at noon, full of fish and meager diet; and, in the evening, what is called a Conversazione, a sort of afsembly at the principal people's houses, full of I cannot tell what: Besides this, there is twice a week a very grand concert. * * *

81. GRAY TO MRS. GRAY

Rome, April 2, N. S. 1740.

THIS is the [eighth][1] day since we came to Rome, but the first hour I have had to write to you in. The journey from Florence cost us four days, one of which was spent at Sienna, an agreeable, clean, old city, of no great magnificence, or extent; but in a fine situation, and good air. What it has most considerable is its cathedral, a huge pile of marble, black and white laid alternately, and laboured with a gothic nicenefs and delicacy in the old-fashioned way. Within too are some paintings and sculpture of considerable hands. The sight of this, and some collections that were showed us in private houses, were a sufficient employment for the little time we were to pafs there; and the next morning we set forward on our journey through a country very oddly composed; for some miles you have a continual scene of little mountains cultivated from top to bottom with rows of olive-trees, or else elms, each of which has its vine twining about it, and mixing with the branches; and corn sown

[2] See Letter 85, n. 8.
LETTER 81.—First printed in Mason's *Memoirs*, pp. 78–81.
[1] Mason 'third', evidently a mistake for 'eighth' (perhaps by a misreading of 3 for 8). Walpole, writing to West from Rome on 26 Mar., says 'we are this instant arrived'; consequently 2 April was the eighth day since they came to Rome. Cf. Letter 60, n. 2 a.

between all the ranks. This, diversified with numerous small houses and convents, makes the most agreeable prospect in the world: But, all of a sudden, it alters to black barren hills, as far as the eye can reach, that seem never to have been capable of culture, and are as ugly as uselefs. Such is the country for some time before one comes to Mount Radicofani, a terrible black hill, on the top of which we were to lodge that night. It is very high, and difficult of ascent; and at the foot of it we were much embarrafsed by the fall of one of the poor horses that drew us. This accident obliged another chaise, which was coming down, to stop also; and out of it peeped a figure in a red cloak, with a handkerchief tied round its head, which, by its voice and mien, seemed a fat old woman;[2] but, upon its getting out, appeared to be Senesino,[3] who was returning from Naples to Sienna, the place of his birth and residence. On the highest part of the mountain is an old fortrefs, and near it a house built by one of the Grand Dukes for a hunting-seat, but now converted into an inn: It is the shell of a large fabrick, but such an inside, such chambers, and accommodations, that your cellar is a palace in comparison; and your cat sups and lies much better than we did; for, it being a saint's eve, there was nothing but eggs. We devoured our meager fare; and, after stopping up the windows with the quilts, were obliged to lie upon the straw beds in our clothes. Such are the conveniences in a road, that is, as it were, the great thoroughfare of all the world. Just on the other side of this mountain, at Ponte-Centino, one enters the patrimony of the church; a most delicious country, but thinly inhabited. That night brought us to Viterbo, a city of a more lively appearance than any we had lately met with; the houses have glafs windows, which is not very usual here, and most of the streets are terminated by a handsome fountain. Here we had the pleasure of breaking our fast on the leg of an old hare and some broiled crows. Next morning, in descending Mount Viterbo, we first discovered (though at near thirty miles distance) the cupola of St. Peter's, and a little after began to enter on an old Roman pavement, with now and then a ruined tower, or a sepulcher on each

---

[2] See Walpole's letter to West, of 23 March 1740, from Radicofani.
[3] Francesco Bernardi (*c.* 1680–*c.* 1750), known as Senesino, from Siena, his birthplace, famous soprano; he was one of the Italian singers engaged by Handel for his opera company in London, where he sang on numerous occasions between 1720 and 1735.

hand. We now had a clear view of the city, though not to the best advantage, as coming along a plain quite upon a level with it; however, it appeared very vast, and surrounded with magnificent villas and gardens. We soon after crofsed the Tiber, a river that ancient Rome made more considerable than any merit of its own could have done: However, it is not contemptibly small, but a good handsome stream; very deep, yet somewhat of a muddy complexion. The first entrance of Rome is prodigiously striking. It is by a noble gate, designed by Michel Angelo, and adorned with statues; this brings you into a large square, in the midst of which is a vast obelisk of granite, and in front you have at one view two churches of a handsome architecture, and so much alike that they are called the twins; with three streets, the middlemost of which is one of the longest in Rome. As high as my expectation was raised, I confefs, the magnificence of this city infinitely surpafses it. You cannot pafs along a street but you have views of some palace, or church, or square, or fountain, the most picturesque and noble one can imagine. We have not yet set about considering its beauties, ancient and modern, with attention; but have already taken a slight transient view of some of the most remarkable. St. Peter's I saw the day after we arrived, and was struck dumb with wonder. I there saw the Cardinal d'Auvergne,[4] one of the French ones, who, upon coming off his journey, immediately repaired hither to offer up his vows at the high altar, and went directly into the Conclave; the doors of which we saw opened to him, and all the other immured Cardinals came thither to receive him. Upon his entrance they were clofcd again directly. It is supposed they will not come to an agreement about a Pope till after Easter, though the confinement is very disagreeable. I have hardly philosophy enough to see the infinity of fine things, that are here daily in the power of any body that has money, without regretting the want of it; but custom has the power of making things easy to one. I have not yet seen his majesty of Great-Britain,[5] &c. though I have the two boys in the gardens of the Villa Borgese, where they go a-shooting almost every day; it was at a distance, indeed, for we did not choose to meet them, as you may imagine. This letter (like all those the English send, or receive) will pafs through the hands

---

[4] Henri Oswald de la Tour d'Auvergne Bouillon (1671–1747), Archbishop of Tours, 1719; of Vienne, 1721; created Cardinal by Clement XII in 1737   [5] The Old Pretender (see Letter 85, n. 12).

of that family, before it comes to those it was intended for. They do it more honour than it deserves; and all they will learn from thence will be, that I desire you to give my duty to my father, and wherever else it is due, and that I am, &c.

82. GRAY TO MRS. GRAY

Rome, April 15, 1740. Good Friday.

TO-DAY I am just come from paying my adoration at St. Peter's to three extraordinary reliques, which are exposed to public view only on these two days in the whole year, at which time all the confraternities in the city come in procefsion to see them. It was something extremely novel to see that vast church, and the most magnificent in the world, undoubtedly, illuminated (for it was night) by thousands of little crystal lamps, disposed in the figure of a huge crofs at the high altar, and seeming to hang alone in the air. All the light proceeded from this, and had the most singular effect imaginable as one entered the great door. Soon after came one after another, I believe, thirty procefsions, all drefsed in linen frocks, and girt with a cord, their heads covered with a cowl all over, only two holes to see through left. Some of them were all black, others red, others white, others party-coloured; these were continually coming and going with their tapers and crucifixes before them; and to each company, as they arrived and knelt before the great altar, were shown from a balcony at a great height, the three wonders, which are, you must know, the head of the spear that wounded Christ; St. Veronica's handkerchief, with the miraculous imprefsion of his face upon it; and a piece of the true crofs, on the sight of which the people thump their breasts, and kifs the pavement with vast devotion. The tragical part of the ceremony is half a dozen wretched creatures, who with their faces covered, but naked to the waist, are in a side-chapel disciplining themselves with scourges full of iron prickles; but really in earnest, as our eyes can testify, which saw their backs and arms so raw we should have taken it for a red satin doublet torn, and shewing the skin through, had we not been convinced of the contrary by the blood which was plentifully sprinkled about them. It is late; I give you joy of Port-Bello[1], and many other things, which I hope are all true. * * * *

LETTER 82.—First printed in Mason's *Memoirs*, pp. 82–3.
[1] See Letter 83, n. 4.

83. WALPOLE AND GRAY TO WEST

Rome, April 16, 1740. N.S.

I'LL tell you, West, because one is amongst new things, you think one can always write new things. When I first came abroad, every thing struck me, and I wrote its history; but now I am grown so used to be surprised, that I don't perceive any flutter in myself when I meet with any novelties; curiosity and astonishment wear off, and the next thing is, to fancy that other people know as much of places as one's self; or, at least, one does not remember that they do not. It appears to me as odd to write to you of St. Peter's, as it would do to you to write of Westminster-abbey. Besides, as one looks at churches, &c. with a book of travels in one's hand, and sees everything particularized there, it would appear transcribing, to write upon the same subjects. I know you will hate me for this declaration; I remember how ill I used to take it when anybody served me so that was travelling.—Well, I will tell you something, if you will love me: You have seen prints of the ruins of the temple of Minerva Medica; you shall only hear its situation, and then figure what a villa might be laid out there. 'Tis in the middle of a garden: at a little distance are two subterraneous grottos, which were the burial-places of the liberti of Augustus. There are all the niches and covers of the urns with the inscriptions remaining; and in one, very considerable remains of an ancient stucco ceiling with paintings in grotesque. Some of the walks would terminate upon the Castellum Aquæ Martiæ, St. John Lateran, and St. Maria Maggiore, besides other churches; the walls of the garden would be two aqueducts, and the entrance through one of the old gates of Rome. This glorious spot is neglected, and only serves for a small vineyard and kitchen-garden.

I am very glad that I see Rome while it yet exists: before a great number of years are elapsed, I question whether it will be worth seeing. Between the ignorance and poverty of the present Romans, every thing is neglected and falling to decay; the villas are entirely out of repair, and the palaces so ill kept, that half the pictures are spoiled by damp. At the villa Ludovisi is a large oracular head of red marble, colossal, and with vast foramina for the eyes and mouth:—the man that showed the palace said

LETTER 83.—First printed in *Works of Lord Orford*, vol. iv, pp. 444–6.

it was *un ritratto della famiglia*. The cardinal Corsini[1] has so thoroughly pushed on the misery of Rome by impoverishing it, that there is no money but paper to be seen. He is reckoned to have amassed three millions of crowns. You may judge of the affluence the nobility live in, when I afsure you, that what the chief princes allow for their own eating is a testoon a day; eighteen pence: there are some extend their expense to five pauls, or half a crown: cardinal Albani[2] is called extravagant for laying out ten pauls for his dinner and supper. You may imagine they never have any entertainments: so far from it, they never have any company. The princesses and duchesses particularly lead the dismallest of lives. Being the posterity of popes, though of worse families than the ancient nobility, they expect greater respect than my ladies the countesses and marquises will pay them; consequently they consort not, but mope in a vast palace with two miserable tapers, and two or three monsignori, whom they are forced to court and humour, that they may not be entirely deserted. Sundays they do issue forth in a vast unwieldy coach to the Corso.

In short, child, after sunset one passes one's time here very ill; and if I did not wish for you in the mornings, it would be no
• compliment to tell you that I do in the evening. Lord! how many English I could change for you, and yet buy you wondrous cheap! And then French and Germans I could fling into the bargain by dozens. Nations swarm here. You will have a great fat French cardinal garnished with thirty abbés roll into the area of St. Peter's, gape, turn short, and talk of the chapel of Versailles. I heard one of them say t'other day, he had been at the *Capitale*. One asked of course how he liked it—*Ah! il y a assez de belles choses.*

Tell Asheton I have received his letter, and will write next post; but I am in a violent hurry and have no more time; so Gray finishes this delicately——

Not so delicate; nor indeed would his conscience suffer him to write to you, till he received de vos nouvelles, if he had not

---

[1] Neri Maria Corsini, created Cardinal by Clement XII in 1730; see C. de Brosses (*Lettres Familières*, LI): 'Le gouvernement est entre ses foibles mains: il a mis les finances surtout en pitoyable état. Le peuple crie hautement de la rareté et du mauvais titre de l'argent, se plaint du transport de l'espèce à Florence.'

[2] Annibales Albani (d. 1751), created Cardinal by Clement XI in 1711.

the tail of another person's letter to use by way of evasion. I sha'n't describe, as being in the only place in the world that deserves it; which may seem an odd reason—but they say as how it's fulsome, and every body does it (and I suppose every body says the same thing); else I should tell you a vast deal about the Coliseum, and the Conclave, and the Capitol, and these matters. A-propos du Colisée, if you don't know what it is, the prince Borghese will be very capable of giving you some account of it, who told an Englishman that asked what it was built for: 'They say 'twas for Christians to fight with tigers in.' We are just come from adoring a great piece of the true crofs, St. Longinus's spear, and St. Veronica's handkerchief; all which have been this evening exposed to view in St. Peter's. In the same place, and on the same occasion last night, Walpole saw a poor creature naked to the waist discipline himself with a scourge filled with iron prickles, till he had made himself a raw doublet, that he took for red satin torn, and showing the skin through. I should tell you, that he fainted away three times at the sight, and I twice and a half at the repetition of it. All this is performed by the light of a vast fiery crofs, composed of hundreds of little crystal lamps, which appears through the great altar under the grand tribuna, as if hanging by itself in the air. All the confraternities of the city resort thither in solemn procefsion, habited in linen frocks, girt with a cord, and their heads covered with a cowl all over, that has only two holes before to see through. Some of these are all black, others parti-coloured and white: and with these masqueraders that vast church is filled, who are seen thumping their breast, and kifsing the pavement with extreme devotion. But methinks I am describing:—'tis an ill habit; but this, like everything else, will wear off. We have sent you our compliments by a friend of yours, and correspondent in a corner, who seems a very agreeable man; one Mr. Williams:[3] I am sorry he staid so little a

[3] This is supposed to be the John Williams who had been secretary to West's father, and who after the death of the latter (1726) is said to have carried on a liaison with West's mother, and eventually (after West's death) to have married her.* 'Mr. Gray said, the cause of the disorder, a consumption, which brought Mr. West to an early grave, was the fatal discovery which he made of the treachery of a supposed friend, and the viciousness of a mother whom he tenderly loved; this man, under the mask of friendship

* The Mrs. Williams mentioned in the *Delany Correspondence* (v. 144–5) was probably West's mother, not his sister as there suggested.

while in Rome. I forget Porto Bello[4] all this while; pray let
us know where it is, and whether you or Asheton had any hand
in the taking of it. Duty to the admiral. Adieu!

Ever yours,
T. GRAY.

84. WEST TO GRAY

ELEGIA.[1]

[April, 1740][2]

ERGO desidiæ videor tibi crimine dignus;
  Et meritò: victas do tibi sponte manus.
Arguor & veteres nimium contemnere Musas,
  Irata et nobis est Medicæa Venus.[3]
Mene igitur statuas & inania saxa vereri!
  Stultule! marmoreâ quid mihi cum Venere?
Hìc veræ, hìc vivæ Veneres, & mille per urbem,
  Quarum nulla queat non placuisse Jovi.
Cedite Romanæ formosæ et cedite Graiæ,[4]
  Sintque oblita Helenæ nomen et Hermionæ!
Et, quascunque refert ætas vetus, Heroinæ:
  Unus honor nostris jam venit Angliasin.
Oh quales vultus, Oh quantum numen ocellis!
  I nunc & Tuscas improbe confer opes.
Ne tamen hæc obtusa nimis præcordia credas,
  Neu me adeo nullâ Pallade progenitum:
Testor Pieridumque umbras & flumina Pindi
  Me quoque Calliopes semper amasse choros;
Et dudum Ausonias urbes, & visere Graias
  Cura est, ingenio si licet ire meo:

to him and his family, intrigued with his mother, and robbed him of his
peace of mind, his health, and his life' (Norton Nicholls, *Reminiscences of
Gray*, in Appendix Z). A still more sinister story was recorded by Dyce, who
stated, on the authority of Mitford, 'that West's death was hastened by
mental anguish, there having been good reason to suspect that *his mother
poisoned his father*' (see Gosse, *Works of Gray*, vol. ii, p. 113).

  [4] On the Isthmus of Panama; taken from the Spaniards by Admiral
Vernon, 20 Nov. 1739.

  LETTER 84.—First printed in Mason's *Memoirs*, pp. 76–7.
  [1] The letter which accompanied this little elegy is not extant. *Mason.*
  [2] The date is supplied by Gray's note ('Fav: sent from London to Florence.
April—1740') on his transcript of the poem in his Commonplace-book.
  [3] See Letter 78**.
  [4] Propertius, 2 *Eleg.* xxv. 66 : 'Cedite Romani scriptores, cedite Graii.'

151

Sive est Phidiacum marmor,[5] seu Mentoris æra,[6]
    Seu paries Coo nobilis e calamo;[7]
Nec minus artificum magna argumenta recentûm
    Romanique decus nominis & Veneti:
Quà Furor & Mavors & sævo in Marmore vultus,
    Quàque et formoso mollior ære Venus.
Quàque loquax spirat fucus, vivique labores,
    Et quicquid calamo dulciùs ausa manus:
Hìc nemora, et solâ mærens Melibœus in umbrâ,
    Lymphaque muscoso prosiliens lapide;
Illìc majus opus, faciesque in pariete major
    Exurgens, Divûm & numina Cœlicolûm;
O vos fælices, quibus hæc cognoscere fas est,
    Et totâ Italiâ, quà patet usque, frui!
Nulla dies vobis eat injucunda, nec usquam
    Norîtis quid sit tempora amara pati.

85. WALPOLE AND GRAY TO ASHTON

Rome, May 14, 1740. N.S.

BOILEAU's Discord dwelt in a College of Monks.[1] At present
the Lady is in the Conclave. Cardinal Corsini[2] has been
interrogated about certain Millions of Crowns that are absent
from the Apostolic Chamber; He refuses giving Account, but
to a Pope: However he has set several Arithmeticians to work,
to compose Summs, & flourish out Expenses, which probably
never existed. Cardinal Cibo[3] pretends to have a Banker at
Genoa, who will prove that he has received three Millions on
the Part of the Eminent Corsini. This Cibo is a madman, but
set on by others. He had formerly some great office in the
government, from whence they are generally rais'd to the

[5] Sculpture by Phidias.
[6] Chased vases by Mentor.
[7] Paintings by Apelles, the most famous of which (Venus rising from
the sea) was painted for a temple at Cos, his reputed birthplace.
    LETTER 85.—First printed by Tovey in *Gray and his Friends*, pp. 49–54;
now reprinted from original.
    [1] *Lutrin*, i. 25 ff.:

        Quand la Discorde encor toute noire de crimes,
        Sortant des Cordeliers pour aller aux Minimes, &c.

    [2] See Letter 83, n. 1.
    [3] Camillo Cibo (d. 1743), of the princely house of Massa Carrara;
created Cardinal by Benedict XIII in 1729.

Cardinalate. After a time, not being promoted as he expected, he resign'd his Post, and retir'd to a Mountain where He built a most magnificient Hermitage. There He inhabited for two years, grew tir'd, came back and received the Hat.

Other feuds have been between Card. Portia[4] and the Faction of Benedict the Thirteenth,[5] by whom He was made Cardinal. About a month ago, he was within three Votes of being Pope. he did not apply to any Party, but went gleaning privately from all & of a sudden burst out with a Number; but too soon, & that threw Him quite out. Having been since left out of their Meetings, he ask'd one of the Benedictine Cardinals the reason; who replied, that he never had been their Friend, & never should be of their assemblies; & did not even hesitate to call him Apostate. This flung Portia into such a Rage that He spit blood, & instantly left the Conclave with all his Baggage. But the great Cause of their Antipathy to Him, was His having been one of the Four, that voted for putting Coscia[6] to Death; Who now regains his Interest, & may prove somewhat disagreable to his Enemies; Whose Honesty is not abundantly heavier than His Own. He met Corsini t'other Day, & told Him, He heard His Eminence had a mind to his Cell: Corsini answer'd He was very well contented with that He had. Oh, says Coscia, I don't mean here in the Conclave; but in the Castle S^t. Angelo.

With all these Animosities, One is near having a Pope. Card. Gotti,[7] an Old, inoffensive Dominican, without any Relations, wanted yesterday but two voices; & is still most likely to succeed. Card. Altieri has been sent for from Albano, whither he was retir'd upon account of his Brother's Death,[8] & his own Illness; & where He was to stay till the Election drew nigh. There! there's a sufficient Competency of Conclave News, I think.

We have miserable Weather for the Season; Coud You think I was writing to You by my fireside at Rome in the middle of

---

[4] Leandro (d. 1740), of the family of the Counts Porzia, created Cardinal in 1728.

[5] Pietro Francesco Orsini, Pope Benedict XIII, 1724–30.

[6] Niccolà Coscia (d. 1755), Archbishop of Benevento, created Cardinal by Benedict XIII in 1725.

[7] Vincenzio Luigi Gotti (d. 1742), Patriarch of Jerusalem, created Cardinal by Benedict XIII in 1728.

[8] Giovanni Battista Altieri (d. 1740), Archbishop of Tyre, created Cardinal by Benedict XIII in 1724; and Lorenzo Altieri (d. 1741), created Cardinal by Alexander VIII in 1690.

May? the Common People say tis occasion'd by the Pope's Soul, which cannot find Rest.

How goes your War? We are persuaded here of an additional one with France, Lord! it will be dreadfull to return thro Germany. I don't know who cooks up the News, here, but we have some Strange Peice every day. One that is much in Vogue, & would not be disagreable for US, is, that the Czarina[9] has clap'd the Marquis de la Chetardie[10] in Prison. One must hope till some Months hence tis all contradicted.

I am balancing in great Uncertainty, whether to go to Naples or stay here; You know 'twoud be provoking to have a Pope chosen just as One's Back was turn'd: and if I wait, I fear the Heats may arrive. I don't know what to do.

We are going to-night to a Great Assembly, at One of the Villas just out of the City, whither all the English are invited;[11] amongst the rest, M^r. Stuard and his two Sons.[12] There is one lives with Him call'd Lord Dunbar,[13] Murray's[14] brother, who wou'd be his Minister, if he had any Occasion for One. I meet him frequently in public places, & like Him. He is very sensible, very agreable & well bred.

Good night, Child: by the way I have had no letters from England, these two last Posts.

Yrs ever.

I am by trade a Finisher of Letters. don't you wonder at the Conclave? instead of being immured, every one in his proper hutch, as one used to imagine: they have the liberty of skuttleing out of one hole into another, & might breed, if they were young enough. I do afsure you every thing one has heard say of Italy is a Lye, & am firmly of opinion, that no mortal was

---

[9] Anne, Empress of Russia (1730–40).

[10] Joachim Jacques Trotti (1705–59), Marquis de la Chétardie; Ambassador to Russia, 1739–42. He was the lover of Elizabeth, daughter of Peter the Great. Her accession to the throne (1741) was largely due to his intrigues. The report of his imprisonment was unfounded.

[11] See Letter 86, *ad fin.*

[12] James Edward Stuart (the Old Pretender), Charles Edward Stuart (the Young Pretender), and Henry Benedict Stuart (afterwards Cardinal of York).

[13] Hon. James Murray (*c.* 1690–1770), second son of fifth Viscount Stormont, titular Earl of Dunbar (1721).

[14] Hon. William Murray (1705–93), fourth son of fifth Viscount Stormont (see Letter 120, n. 25).

ever here before us. I am writeing to prove there never was any such people as the Romans, that this was antiently a Colony of the Jews, and that the Coliseum was built on the model of Solomon's Temple. our people have told so many Stories of them, that they don't believe any thing we say about ourselves; Porto Bello is still said to be impregnable[15] & it is reported the Dutch have declared War against us. the English Court here brighten up on the News of our Conquests, & conclude all the contrary has happen'd. you do not know perhaps, that we have our little good fortune in the Mediterranean, where Adm^l. Haddock has overturn'd certain little Boats carrying troops to Majorca, drown'd a few hundreds of them, & taken a little Grandee of Spain, that commanded the expedition: at least so they say at Naples:[16] I'm very sorry, but methinks they seem in a bad condition. is West dead to the World in general, or only so to me? for you I have not the impudence to accuse; but you are to take this, as a sort of reproof, & I hope you will demean yourself accordingly. you are hereby authorized to make my very particular compliments to My L^d. Plymouth, & return him my thanks de l'honneur de son souvenir. so I finish my Postscript with

Yours Ever T:G:

86. GRAY TO WEST

Tivoli, May 20, 1740.

THIS day being in the palace of his Highnefs the Duke of Modena,[1] he laid his most serene commands upon me to write to Mr. West, and said he thought it for his glory, that I should draw up an inventory of all his most serene pofsefsions for the said West's perusal.—Imprimis, a house, being in circumference a quarter of a mile, two feet and an inch; the said house containing the following particulars, to wit, a great room. Item, another great room; item, a bigger room; item, another room; item, a vast room; item, a sixth of the same; a seventh ditto; an eighth as before; a ninth as abovesaid; a tenth (see No. 1.); item, ten more such, besides twenty besides, which, not to be too particular, we shall pafs over. The said rooms contain

---

[15] See Letter 83, n. 4.
[16] An exaggerated report—Admiral Haddock had merely captured two Spanish transports with soldiers from Majorca. (*Gent. Mag.*, 1740, p. 199.) LETTER 86.—First printed in Mason's *Memoirs*, pp. 83–7.
[1] Francis III (of Este), Duke of Modena, 1737–80.

nine chairs, two tables, five stools, and a cricket. From whence we shall proceed to the garden, containing two millions of superfine laurel hedges, a clump of cyprefs trees, and half the river Teverone, that pifses into two thousand several chamber-pots. Finis.—Dame Nature desired me to put in a list of her little goods and chattels, and, as they were small, to be very minute about them. She has built here three or four little mountains, and laid them out in an irregular semi-circle; from certain others behind, at a greater distance, she has drawn a canal, into which she has put a little river of hers, called Anio; she has cut a huge cleft between the two innermost of her four hills, and there she has left it to its own disposal; which she has no sooner done, but, like a heedlefs chit, it tumbles headlong down a declivity fifty feet perpendicular, breaks itself all to shatters, and is converted into a shower of rain, where the sun forms many a bow, red, green, blue and yellow. To get out of our metaphors without any further trouble, it is the most noble sight in the world. The weight of that quantity of waters, and the force they fall with, have worn the rocks they throw themselves among into a thousand irregular craggs, and to a vast depth. In this channel it goes boiling along with a mighty noise till it comes to another steep, where you see it a second time come roaring down (but first you must walk two miles farther) a greater height than before, but not with that quantity of waters; for by this time it has divided itself, being crofsed and opposed by the rocks, into four several streams, each of which, in emulation of the great one, will tumble down too; and it does tumble down, but not from an equally elevated place; so that you have at one view all these cascades intermixed with groves of olive and little woods, the mountains rising behind them, and on the top of one (that which forms the extremity of one of the half-circle's horns) is seated the town itself. At the very extremity of that extremity, on the brink of the precipice, stands the Sybils' temple, the remains of a little rotunda, surrounded with its portico, above half of whose beautiful Corinthian pillars are still standing and entire; all this on one hand. On the other, the open Campagna of Rome, here and there a little castle on a hillock, and the city itself on the very brink of the horizon, indistinctly seen (being 18 miles off) except the dome of St. Peter's; which, if you look out of your window, wherever you are, I suppose, you can see. I did not tell you that a little below the first fall, on the side of the rock, and hanging over that torrent, are little ruins which they shew you for Horace's house, a curious situation to observe the

> Præceps Anio, & Tiburni lucus, & uda
> Mobilibus pomaria rivis.[2]

Mæcenas did not care for such a·noise, it seems, and built him a house (which they also carry one to see) so situated that it sees nothing at all of the matter, and for any thing he knew there might be no such river in the world. Horace had another house on the other side of the Teverone, opposite to Mæcenas's; and they told us there was a bridge of communication, by which 'andava il detto Signor per trastullarsi coll' istefso Orazio'. In coming hither we crofsed the Aquæ Albulæ, a vile little brook that stinks like a fury, and they say it has stunk so these thousand years. I forgot the Piscina of Quintilius Varus, where he used to keep certain little fishes. This is very entire, and there is a piece of the aqueduct that supplied it too; in the garden below is old Rome, built in little, just as it was, they say. There are seven temples in it, and no houses at all: They say there were none.

May 21.

We have had the pleasure of going twelve miles out of our way to Palestrina. It has rained all day as if heaven and us were coming together. See my honesty, I do not mention a syllable of the temple of Fortune, because I really did not see it; which, I think, is pretty well for an old traveller. So we returned along the Via Prænestina, saw the Lacus Gabinus and Regillus, where, you know, Castor and Pollux appeared upon a certain occasion.[3] And many a good old tomb we left on each hand, and many an Aqueduct,

> Dumb are whose fountains, and their channels dry.

There are, indeed, two whole modern ones, works of Popes, that run about thirty miles a-piece in length; one of them conveys still the famous Aqua Virgo to Rome, and adds vast beauty to the prospect. So we came to Rome again, where waited for us a splendidifsimo regalo of letters; in one of which came You, with your huge characters and wide intervals, staring. I would have you to know, I expect you should take a handsome crow-quill when you write to me, and not leave room for a pin's point

---

[2] Horace, 1 *Odes*, vii. 13–14.
[3] At the battle of the Lake Regillus, when the Romans defeated the Latins, 498 B.C. (Livy, ii. 19; Cicero, *Nat. Deor.* ii. 2, § 6).

in four sides of a sheet royal. Do you but find matter, I will find spectacles.

I have more time than I thought, and I will employ it in telling you about a Ball that we were at the other evening. Figure to yourself a Roman villa; all its little apartments thrown open, and lighted up to the best advantage. At the upper end of the gallery, a fine concert, in which La Diamantina, a famous virtuosa, played on the violin divinely, and sung angelically; Giovannino and Pasqualini (great names in musical story) also performed miraculously. On each side were ranged all the secular grand monde of Rome, the Ambaſsadors, Princeſses, and all that. Among the rest Il Serenisſimo Pretendente (as the Mantova gazette calls him) displayed his rueful length of person, with his two young ones,[4] and all his ministry around him. 'Poi nacque un grazioso ballo,' where the world danced, and I sat in a corner regaling myself with iced fruits, and other pleasant rinfrescatives.

87. GRAY TO WEST

Rome, May 1740.

MATER rosarum, cui teneræ vigent
 Auræ Favonî, cui Venus it comes
  Lasciva, Nympharum choreis
   Et volucrum celebrata cantu!
Dic, non inertem fallere quâ diem
Amat sub umbrâ, seu sinit aureum
  Dormire plectrum, seu retentat
   Pierio Zephyrinus[1] antro
Furore dulci plenus, & immemor
Reptantis inter frigora Tusculi
  Umbrosa, vel colles amici
   Palladiæ superantis Albæ.
Dilecta Fauno, & capripedum choris
Pineta, testor vos, Anio minax
  Quæcunque per clivos volutus
   Præcipiti tremefecit amne,

---

[4] See Letter 85, n. 12.

LETTER 87.—First printed in Mason's *Memoirs*, pp. 87–92; (Gray transcribed the verses in his Commonplace-book).

[1] Rich[d]. West. *Walpole*.—He intitled this ode 'Ad C. Favonium Zephyrinum', and writ it immediately after his journey to Frescati and the cascades of Tivoli, which he describes in the preceding letter. *Mason*.

Illius altum Tibur, & Æsulæ
Audîſse sylvas nomen amabiles,
Illius & gratas Latinis
Naiasin ingeminâſse rupes:
Nam me Latinæ Naiades uvidâ
Vidêre ripâ, quà niveas levi
Tam sæpe lavit rore plumas
Dulcè canens Venusinus ales;[2]
Mirum! canenti conticuit nemus,
Sacriϙ fontes, et retinent adhuc
(Sic Musa juſsit) saxa molles
Docta modos, veteresque lauri.
Mirare nec tu me citharæ rudem
Claudis laborantem numeris: loca
Amœna, jucundumque ver in-
-compositum docuere carmen;
Hærent sub omni nam folio nigri
Phœbea luci (credite) somnia,[3]
Argutiusque & lympha & auræ
Nescio quid solito loquuntur.

I am to-day just returned from Alba, a good deal fatigued; for you know the Appian[4] is somewhat tiresome. We dined at Pompey's;[5] he indeed was gone for a few days to his Tusculan, but, by the care of his Villicus, we made an admirable meal. We had the dugs of a pregnant sow, a peacock, a dish of thrushes, a noble scarus just fresh from the Tyrrhene, and some conchylia

---

[2] In a copy of this ode in Gray's handwriting, which belonged to Horace Walpole, and is now in the Waller Collection, these last lines read:

> quâ niveas lavit
> Tam sæpe plumas rore puro
> Et gelido Venusinus ales.

[3] Cf. *Aen.* vi. 283–4:

> Ulmus opaca ingens quam sedem Somnia vulgo
> Vana tenere ferunt, foliisque sub omnibus hærent;

and see Letter 26, n. 17.

[4] Mitford quotes Statius, 2 *Silv.* ii. 12: 'Appia longarum teritur regina viarum.'

[5] However whimsical this humour may appear to some readers, I chose to insert it, as it gives me an opportunity of remarking that Mr. Gray was extremely skilled in the customs of the ancient Romans; and has catalogued, in his common place book, their various eatables, wines, perfumes, cloathes, medicines, &c. with great precision, referring under every article to passages in the Poets and Historians where their names are mentioned. *Mason.*

of the Lake with garum sauce: For my part I never eat better
at Lucullus's table. We drank half a dozen cyathi a-piece of
ancient Alban to Pholoë's[6] health; and, after bathing, and playing an hour at ball, we mounted our efsedum again, and proceeded up the mount to the temple. The priests there entertained us with an account of a wonderful shower of birds eggs,
that had fallen two days before, which had no sooner touched
the ground, but they were converted into gudgeons; as also that
the night past a dreadful voice had been heard out of the
Adytum, which spoke Greek during a full half hour, but no
body understood it. But quitting my Romanities, to your great
joy and mine, let me tell you, in plain English, that we come
from Albano. The present town lies within the inclosure of
Pompey's Villa in ruins. The Appian way runs through it, by
the side of which, a little farther, is a large old tomb, with five
pyramids upon it, which the learned suppose to be the burying-
place of the family, because they do not know whose it can be
else. But the vulgar afsure you it is the sepulchre of the Curiatii,
and by that name (such is their power) it goes. One drives to
Castel Gondolfo, a house of the Pope's, situated on the top of
one of the Collinette, that forms a brim to the bason, commonly
called the Alban lake. It is seven miles round; and directly
opposite to you, on the other side, rises the Mons Albanus, much
taller than the rest, along whose side are still discoverable (not
to common eyes) certain little ruins of the old Alba longa. They
had need be very little, as having been nothing but ruins ever
since the days of Tullus Hostilius. On its top is a house of the
Constable Colona's, where stood the temple of Jupiter Latialis.
At the foot of the hill Gondolfo, are the famous outlets of the
lake, built with hewn stone, a mile and a half under ground.
Livy, you know, amply informs us of the foolish occasion of this
expence,[7] and gives me this opportunity of displaying all my
erudition, that I may appear considerable in your eyes. This
is the prospect from one window of the palace. From another
you have the whole Campagna, the City, Antium, and the
Tyrrhene sea (twelve miles distant) so distinguishable, that you
may see the vefsels sailing upon it. All this is charming. Mr.
Walpole says, our memory sees more than our eyes in this

---

[6] Horace, 1 *Odes*, xxxiii. 7; &c.
[7] The *emissarium* for draining the Alban Lake is said to have been con-
structed during the siege o Veii by the Romans, 406–396 B.C. (Livy, v. 15–
17, 19).

country. Which is extremely true; since, for realities, Windsor, or Richmond Hill, is infinitely preferable to Albano or Frescati. I am now at home, and going to the window to tell you it is the most beautiful of Italian nights, which, in truth, are but just begun (so backward has the spring been here, and every where else, they say.) There is a moon! there are stars for you! Do not you hear the fountain? Do not you smell the orange flowers? That building yonder is the Convent of S. Isidore; and that eminence, with the cyprefs trees and pines upon it, the top of M. Quirinal. This is all true, and yet my prospect is not two hundred yards in length. We send you some Roman inscriptions to entertain you. The first two are modern, transcribed from the Vatican library by Mr. Walpole.

> Pontifices olim quem fundavere priores,
>   Præcipuâ Sixtus perficit arte tholum;[8]
> Et Sixti tantum se gloria tollit in altum,
>   Quantum se Sixti nobile tollit opus:
> Magnus honos magni fundamina ponere templi,
>   Sed finem cæptis ponere major honos.
>
> Saxa agit Amphion, Thebana ut mœnia condat:
>   Sixtus & immensæ pondera molis agit.[9]
> Saxa trahunt ambo longè diversa: sed arte
>   Hæc trahit Amphion; Sixtus & arte trahit.
> At tantum exsuperat Dircæum Amphiona Sixtus,
>   Quantum hic exsuperat cætera saxa lapis.

Mine is ancient, and I think not lefs curious. It is exactly transcribed from a sepulchral marble at the villa Giustiniani. I put stops to it, when I understand it.

> DIS Manibus
> Claudiæ, Pistes
> Primus Conjugi
> Optumae, Sanctae,
> Et Piae, Benemeritate.
>
> Non æquos, Parcae, statuistis stamina vitæ.
> Tam bene compositos potuistis sede tenere.
> Amifsa est conjux. cur ego & ipse moror?
> Si · bella · efse · mî · iste · mea · vivere · debuit ·
> Tristia contigerunt qui amifsâ conjuge vivo.
> Nil est tam miserum, quam totam perdere vitam.

[8] The dome of St. Peter's was finally completed in 1590, under Sixtus V (Pope 1585–90).
[9] Sixtus erected the obelisk in the Piazza of St. Peter's in 1586.

Nec vita enasci dura peregistis crudelia pensa, sorores,
Ruptaque deficiunt in primo munere fusi.
O nimis injustæ ter denos dare munus in annos,
Deceptus · grautus · fatum · sic · prefsit · egestas ·
Dum vitam tulero, Primus Pistes lugea conjugium.[10]

88. GRAY TO MRS. GRAY

Naples, June [14], 1740.

OUR journey hither was through the most beautiful part of the finest country in the world; and every spot of it, on some account or other, famous for these three thousand years past.[1] The season has hitherto been just as warm as one would wish it; no unwholesome airs, or violent heats, yet heard of:

[10] Mason presumably reproduced the punctuation inserted by Gray; the blunders in lines 5, 9, 15, were no doubt due to carelessness on the part of Mason. The inscription is given as under in *Corpus Inscriptionum Latinarum: Inscriptiones Urbis Romae Latinae*. Vol. vi, Pars iii, p. 1783, No. 15546. *Cippus marmoreus. In villa Iustiniana . . . Nunc in Museo Vaticano.*

> DIIS MANIBVS
> CLAVDIAE · PISTES
> PRIMVS · CONIVGI
> OPTVMAE · SANCTAE
> ET · PIAE · BENEMERITAE
>
> NON · AE·QVOS · PAR·CAE STA·TV·IS·TIS · STA·MINA VITAE ·
> TAM · BE·NE · COM·PO·SI·TOS · PO·TVIS·TIS · SEDE · TENE·RE
> A·MIS·SA · EST · CON·IVNX · CVR · EGO · ET · IP·SE MO·ROR
> SI · FELIX · ES·SEM · PIS·TE · ME·A · VI·VE·RE · DE·BV·IT
> TRISTIA CONTIGERVN · QVI · A·MIS·SA · CON·IV·GE · VI·VO
> NIL · EST · TAM · MISE·RVM · QVAM · TO·TAM · PER·DE·RE · VI·TAM
> NEC · VI·TAE · NAS·CI · DVRA · PER·EGIS·TIS · CRV·DE·LI·A · PEN·SA · SORORES
> RVP·TA·QVE · DE·FICI·VNT · IN · PRI·MO · MV·NE·RE · FV·SI
> O · NIMIS · INIVS·TAE · TER · DE·NOS · DA·RE · MV·NVS · IN · AN·NOS
> DECEPTVS GRA·VI·VS · FATVM · SIC · PRES·SIT · EGES·TAS
> DVM · VI·TAM · TV·LE·RO · PRI·MVS · PIS·TES · LVGE·A · CONIVGIVM

LETTER 88.—First printed in Mason's *Memoirs*, pp. 92–4. Mason dates this letter 17 June; but 17 is almost certainly a mistake of his, or a misprint, for 14, for Gray speaks here of having been at Portici (Herculaneum) 'to-day', which is shown by Walpole's letter to West describing the same visit (No. 122 in *Gray–Walpole Correspondence*) to have been 14 June; further, Gray himself in notes headed 'The Environs of Naples, June 16 NS 1740' (the date is the date when the notes were written) gives an account of Portici which he had then seen (see his *Notes of Travel*, printed in Tovey's *Gray and his Friends*, pp. 235 ff.).

[1] Mr. Gray wrote a minute description of every thing he saw in this tour from Rome to Naples; as also of the environs of Rome, Florence, &c. But as these papers are apparently only memorandums for his own use, I do not think it necessary to print them, although they abound with many uncommon remarks, and pertinent classical quotations. The reader will please to observe throughout this section, that it is not my intention to give Mr. Gray's Travels, but only extracts from the Letters which he writ during his travels.

The people call it a backward year, and are in pain about their corn, wine, and oil; but we, who are neither corn, wine, nor oil, find it very agreeable. Our road was through Velletri, Cisterna, Terracina, Capua, and Aversa, and so to Naples. The minute one leaves his Holinefs's dominions, the face of things begins to change from wide uncultivated plains to olive groves and well-tilled fields of corn, intermixed with ranks of elms, every one of which has its vine twining about it, and hanging in festoons between the rows from one tree to another. The great old fig-trees, the oranges in full bloom, and myrtles in every hedge, make one of the delightfullest scenes you can conceive; besides that, the roads are wide, well-kept, and full of pafsengers, a sight I have not beheld this long time. My wonder still increased upon entering the city, which I think, for number of people, outdoes both Paris and London. The streets are one continued markct, and thronged with populace so much that a coach can hardly pafs. The common sort are a jolly lively kind of animals, more industrious than Italians usually are; they work till evening; then take their lute or guitar (for they all play) and walk about the city, or upon the sea-shore with it, to enjoy the fresco. One sees their little brown children jumping about stark-naked, and the bigger ones danc-ing with castanets, while others play on the cymbal to them. Your maps will show you the situation of Naples; it is on the most lovely bay in the world, and one of the calmest seas: It has many other beauties besides those of nature. We have spent two days in visiting the remarkable places in the country round it, such as the bay of Baiæ, and its remains of antiquity; the lake Avernus, and the Solfatara, Charon's grotto, &c. We have been in the Sybils' cave and many other strange holes under ground (I only name them, because you may consult Sandy's travels);[2] but the strangest hole I ever was in, has been to-day at a place called Portici, where his Sicilian Majesty[3] has a country-seat. About a year ago, as they were digging, they discovered some parts of ancient buildings above thirty feet deep in the ground: Curiosity led them on, and they have been digging ever since; the pafsage they have made, with all its turnings and windings, is now more than a mile long. As you walk you see parts of an

Mason.—See Letter 77, n. 11. The papers mentioned by Mason are notes of travel in France and Italy, some owned by Sir John Murray, some in the Eton College Library. See the preceding note.

    [2] For Sandys' Travels see Letter 94, n. 2.   [3] See Letter 76, n. 2.

amphitheatre, many houses adorned with marble columns, and incrusted with the same; the front of a temple, several arched vaults of rooms painted in fresco. Some pieces of painting have been taken out from hence, finer than any thing of the kind before discovered, and with these the King has adorned his palace; also a number of statues, medals, and gems; and more are dug out every day. This is known to be a Roman town,[4] that in the Emperor Titus's time was overwhelmed by a furious eruption of Mount Vesuvius, which is hard by. The wood and beams remain so perfect that you may see the grain; but burnt to a coal, and dropping into dust upon the least touch. We were to-day at the foot of that mountain, which at present smokes only a little, where we saw the materials that fed the stream of fire, which about four years since ran down its side. We have but a few days longer to stay here; too little in conscience for such a place. * * *

89. WEST TO GRAY

Bond-street, June 5, 1740

I LIVED at the Temple till I was sick of it: I have just left it, and find myself as much a lawyer as I was when I was in it. It is certain, at least, I may study the law here as well as I could there. My being in chambers did not signify to me a pinch of snuff. They tell me my father was a lawyer, and, as you know, eminent in the profession;[1] and such a circumstance must be of advantage to me. My uncle[2] too makes some figure in Westminster hall; and there's another advantage: Then my grandfather's[3] name would get me many friends. Is it not strange that a young fellow, that might enter the world with so many

---

[4] Herculaneum—see Walpole's account of it in his letter to West, from Naples, of 14 June 1740 (No. 122 in *Gray–Walpole Correspondence*).

LETTER 89.—First printed in Mason's *Memoirs*, pp. 97–9. 5 June, Old Style, is the equivalent of 16 June, New Style. This letter is therefore later than Letter 88, which should be dated June [14].

[1] Richard West (d. 1726), who is described as having been 'eminent for legal and constitutional learning', was Lord Chancellor of Ireland (May 1725–Dec. 1726). His son was ten years old at the time of his death.

[2] Thomas Burnet (1694–1753), third son of Bishop Burnet, West's maternal grandfather; he was made a serjeant-at-law in 1736, and was appointed King's serjeant in 1740; in 1741 he was appointed a judge of the Court of Common Pleas; he was knighted in 1745.

[3] In a note on an early letter of West's to him Walpole states that West was 'Only Son of Ld Chancellor West of Ireland, by Elizabeth, Daughter to Dr Burnet Bishop of Salisbury' (*Gray-Walpole Correspondence* No. 18, preliminary note).

advantages, will not know his own interest? &c. &c.—What
shall I say in answer to all this? For money, I neither dote upon
it nor despise it; it is a necessary stuff enough. For ambition, I
do not want that neither; but it is not to sit upon a bench. In
short, is it not a disagreeable thing to force one's inclination,
especially when one's young? not to mention that one ought to
have the strength of a Hercules to go through our common law;
which, I am afraid, I have not. Well! but then, say they, if one
profession does not suit you, you may choose another more to
your inclination. Now I protest I do not yet know my own
inclination, and I believe, if that was to be my direction, I
should never fix at all: There is no going by a weathercock.—I
could say much more upon this subject; but there is no talking
tête-à-tête cross the Alps. O the folly of young men, that never
know their own interest! they never grow wise till they are
ruined! and then nobody pities them, nor helps them.—Dear
Gray! consider me in the condition of one that has lived these
two years without any person that he can speak freely to. I
know it is very seldom that people trouble themselves with the
sentiments of those they converse with; so they can chat about
trifles, they never care whether your heart aches or no. Are you
one of these? I think not. But what right have I to ask you this
question? Have we known one another enough, that I should
expect or demand sincerity from you? Yes, Gray, I hope we
have; and I have not quite such a mean opinion of myself, as
to think I do not deserve it.—But, Signor, is it not time for me
to ask something about your further intentions abroad? Where
do you propose going next? an in Apuliam? nam illò si adve-
neris, tanquam Ulysses, cognosces tuorum neminem. Vale. So
Cicero prophesies in the end of one of his letters[4]—and there
I end.

'Yours, &c.[5]

90. GRAY TO PHILIP GRAY

Florence, July [10], 1740.

AT my return to this city, the day before yesterday, I had
the pleasure of finding yours dated June the 9th. The

[4] To L. Valerius (*Epist. ad Fam.* i. 10).

[5] Mason notes that 'this letter was written apparently in much agitation
of mind, which Mr. West endeavours to conceal by an unusual carelessness
of manner'. West's trouble was no doubt on account of his mother (see
Letter 83, n. 3).

LETTER 90.—First printed in Mason's *Memoirs*. pp. 95-7. Mason dates

period of our voyages, at least towards the south, is come, as you wish. We have been at Naples, spent nine or ten days there, and returned to Rome, where finding no likelihood of a Pope yet these three months, and quite wearied with the formal afsemblies, and little society of that great city, Mr. Walpole determined to return hither to spend the summer, where he imagines he shall pafs his time more agreeably than in the tedious expectation of what, when it happens, will only be a great show. For my own part, I give up the thoughts of all that with but little regret; but the city itself I do not part with so easily, which alone has amusements for whole years. However, I have pafsed through all that most people do, both ancient and modern; what that is you may see, better than I can tell you, in a thousand books. The Conclave we left in greater uncertainty than ever; the more than ordinary liberty they enjoy there, and the unusual coolnefs of the season, makes the confinement lefs disagreeable to them than common, and, consequently, maintains them in their irresolution. There have been very high words, one or two (it is said) have come even to blows; two more are dead within this last month, Cenci[1] and Portia;[2] the latter died distracted; and we left another (Altieri)[3] at the extremity: Yet nobody dreams of an election till the latter end of September. All this gives great scandal to all good catholics, and every body talks very freely on the subject. The Pretender (whom you desire an account of) I have had frequent opportunities of seeing at church, at the corso, and other places; but more particularly, and that for a whole night, at a great ball given by Count Patrizii to the Prince and Princefs Craon,[4] (who were come to Rome at that time, that he might receive from the hands of the Emperor's minister there the order of the golden fleece) at which he and his two sons were present. They are good fine boys, especially the younger, who has the more spirit of the two, and both danced incefsantly all night long. For him,

this letter 16 July, which, as Gray says that they returned to Florence 'the day before yesterday', would give 14 July as the date of their return. Mason's date must be wrong, since Walpole begins a letter to Conway at Radicofani, half-way on their journey, on 5 July, and dates the continuation of it from Florence on 9 July. Assuming that they had reached Florence the day before, i.e. on 8 July, then Gray's letter would have been written on 10 July, which may have been misread by Mason, or misprinted, as 16.

[1] Serafino Cenci (d. 1740), Archbishop of Benevento, created Cardinal by Clement XII in 1734.   [2] See Letter 85, n. 4.

[3] See Letter 85, n. 8.   [4] See Letter 77. nn. 6, 7.

he is a thin ill-made man, extremely tall and aukward, of a most unpromising countenance, a good deal resembling King James the Second, and has extremely the air and look of an idiot, particularly when he laughs or prays. The first he does not often, the latter continually. He lives private enough with his little court about him, consisting of Lord Dunbar,[5] who manages every thing, and two or three of the Preston Scotch Lords, who would be very glad to make their peace at home.

We happened to be at Naples on Corpus Christi Day, the greatest feast in the year, so had an opportunity of seeing their Sicilian Majesties to advantage. The King walked in the grand procefsion, and the Queen[6] (being big with child) sat in a balcony. He followed the Host to the church of St. Clara, where high mafs was celebrated to a glorious concert of music. They are as ugly a little pair as one can see: She a pale girl, marked with the small-pox; and he a brown boy with a thin face, a huge nose, and as ungain as pofsible.

We are settled here with Mr. Mann in a charming apartment;[7] the river Arno runs under our windows, which we can fish out of. The sky is so serene, and the air so temperate, that one continues in the open air all night long in a slight nightgown without any danger; and the marble bridge is the resort of every body, where they hear music, eat iced fruits, and sup by moon-light; though as yet (the season being extremely backward every where) these amusements are not begun. You see we are now coming northward again, though in no great haste; the Venetian and Milanese territories, and either Germany or the South of France, (according to the turn the war may take) are all that remain for us, that we have not yet seen; as to Loretto, and that part of Italy, we have given over all thoughts of it.

91. GRAY TO WEST
Florence, July 16, 1740.

YOU do yourself and me justice, in imagining that you merit, and that I am capable of sincerity.[1] I have not a thought,

[5] See Letter 85, n. 13.

[6] Maria Amelia, of Saxony, eldest daughter of Frederick Augustus II, King of Poland; she married Charles, King of the Two Sicilies, in 1738.

[7] Mann was lodged in the 'Casa Manetti in Via de' Santi Apostoli by the Ponte di Trinità' (see Walpole's letter to Miss Berry of 29 Nov. 1790). Walpole wrote to Conway on 9 July: 'I am lodged with Mr Mann. . . . I have a *terreno* all to myself with an open gallery on the Arno'.

LETTER 91.—First printed in Mason's *Memoirs*, pp. 99–102.

[1] See West's letter to Gray of 5 June (Letter 89).

or even a weaknefs, I desire to conceal from you; and consequently on my side deserve to be treated with the same opennefs of heart. My vanity perhaps might make me more reserved towards you, if you were one of the heroic race, superior to all human failings; but as mutual wants are the ties of general society, so are mutual weaknefses of private friendships, supposing them mixt with some proportion of good qualities; for where one may not sometimes blame, one does not much care ever to praise. All this has the air of an introduction designed to soften a very harsh reproof that is to follow; but it is no such matter: I only meant to ask, Why did you change your lodging? Was the air bad, or the situation melancholy? If so, you are quite in the right. Only, is it not putting yourself a little out of the way of a people, with whom it seems necefsary to keep up some sort of intercourse and conversation, though but little for your pleasure or entertainment, (yet there are, I believe, such among them as might give you both) at least for your information in that study, which, when I left you, you thought of applying to? for that there is a certain study necefsary to be followed, if we mean to be of any use in the world, I take for granted; disagreeable enough (as most necefsities are) but, I am afraid, unavoidable. Into how many branches these studies are divided in England, every body knows; and between that which you and I had pitched upon, and the other two, it was impofsible to balance long. Examples shew one that it is not absolutely necefsary to be a blockhead to succeed in this profefsion. The labour is long, and the elements dry and unentertaining; nor was ever any body (especially those that afterwards made a figure in it) amused, or even not disgusted in the beginning; yet, upon a further acquaintance, there is surely matter for curiosity and reflection. It is strange if, among all that huge mafs of words, there be not somewhat intermixed for thought. Laws have been the result of long deliberation, and that not of dull men, but the contrary; and have so close a connexion with history, nay, with philosophy itself, that they must partake a little of what they are related to so nearly. Besides, tell me, Have you ever made the attempt? Was not you frighted merely with the distant prospect? Had the Gothic character and bulkinefs of those volumes (a tenth part of which perhaps it will be no further necefsary to consult, than as one does a dictionary) no ill effect upon your eye? Are you sure, if Coke[2] had been printed

----

[2] See Letter 58**, n. 5.

by Elzevir, and bound in twenty neat pocket volumes, instead
of one folio, you should never have taken him up for an hour,
as you would a Tully, or drank your tea over him? I know how
great an obstacle ill spirits are to resolution. Do you really
think, if you rid ten miles every morning, in a week's time you
should not entertain much stronger hopes of the Chancellorship,
and think it a much more probable thing than you do at present?
The advantages you mention are not nothing; our inclinations
are more than we imagine in our own power; reason and resolution determine them, and support under many difficulties. To
me there hardly appears to be any medium between a public
life and a private one; he who prefers the first, must put himself
in a way of being serviceable to the rest of mankind, if he has
a mind to be of any consequence among them: Nay, he must
not refuse being in a certain degree even dependent upon some
men who already are so. If he has the good fortune to light on
such as will make no ill use of his humility, there is no shame in
this: If not, his ambition ought to give place to a reasonable
pride, and he should apply to the cultivation of his own mind
those abilities which he has not been permitted to use for others'
service. Such a private happinefs (supposing a small compe-
tence of fortune) is almost always in every one's power, and the
proper enjoyment of age, as the other is the employment of
youth. You are yet young, have some advantages and opportunities, and an undoubted capacity, which you have never
yet put to the trial. Set apart a few hours, see how the first year
will agree with you, at the end of it you are still the master;
if you change your mind, you will only have got the knowledge
of a little somewhat that can do no hurt, or give you cause of
repentance. If your inclination be not fixed upon any thing
else, it is a symptom that you are not absolutely determined
against this, and warns you not to mistake mere indolence for
inability. I am sensible there is nothing stronger against what
I would persuade you to, than my own practice; which may
make you imagine I think not as I speak. Alas! it is not so; but
I do not act what I think, and I had rather be the object of your
pity, than you should be that of mine; and, be afsured, the
advantage I may receive from it, does not diminish my concern
in hearing you want somebody to converse with freely, whose
advice might be of more weight, and always at hand. We have
some time since come to the southern period of our voyages; we
spent about nine days at Naples. It is the largest and most

populous city, as its environs are the most deliciously fertile country, of all Italy. We sailed in the bay of Baiæ, sweated in the Solfatara, and died in the grotta del Cane, as all strangers do; saw the Corpus Christi procefsion, and the King and the Queen,[4] and the city underground,[5] (which is a wonder I reserve to tell you of another time) and so returned to Rome for another fortnight; left it (left Rome!) and came hither for the summer. You have seen an Epistle to Mr. Ashton,[6] that seems to me full of spirit and thought, and a good deal of poetic fire. I would know your opinion. Now I talk of verses, Mr. Walpole and I have frequently wondered you should never mention a certain imitation of Spencer, published last year by a namesake of yours,[7] with which we are all enraptured and enmarvailed.

92. WALPOLE AND GRAY TO WEST

Florence, July 31, 1740. N.S.

Dear West,

I HAVE advised with the most notable antiquarians of this city on the meaning of *Thur gut Luetis*. I can get no satisfactory interpretation. In my opinion 'tis Welsh. I don't love offering conjectures on a language in which I have hitherto made little proficiency, but I will trust you with my explication. You know the famous Aglaughlan, mother of Cadwalladhor, was renowned for her conjugal virtues, and grief on the death of her royal spouse. I conclude this medal was struck in her regency, by her express order, to the memory of her lord, and that the inscription *Thur gut Luetis* means no more than *her dear Llewis* or *Llewellin*.[1]

---

[4] See Letter 90, n. 6.
[5] Herculaneum (see Letter 88).
[6] *An Epistle from Florence to Thomas Ashton Esq.*, *Tutor to the Earl of Plimouth.* It was first printed in Dodsley's *Collection* (vol. ii, pp. 305 ff.) in 1748 (see Gray's letter to Walpole of that year—Letter 144). Walpole subsequently printed it among his *Fugitive Pieces* (see *Works of Lord Orford*, vol. i, pp. 4–16).
[7] Gilbert West (1703–56); his imitation of Spenser (*A Canto of the Faery Queen*) was published in 1739, and afterwards (in 1748) reprinted in Dodsley's *Collection* (vol. ii, pp. 63–87) under the title of 'On the Abuse of Travelling'.
LETTER 92.—First printed in *Works of Lord Orford*, vol. iv, pp. 450–2.
[1] The words are not Welsh, and no explanation of them has been offered.

In return for your coins I send you two or three of different kinds. The first is a money of one of the kings of Naples; the device, a horse; the motto, *Equitas regni*. This curious pun is on a coin in the Great Duke's collection, and by great chance I have met with a second. Another is, a satirical medal struck on Lewis XIV.; 'tis a bomb, covered with flower-deluces, bursting; the motto, *Se ipsissimo*. The last, and almost the only one I ever saw with a text well applied, is a German medal with a rebellious town besieged and blocked up; the inscription, *This kind is not expelled but by fasting.*

Now I mention medals, have they yet struck the intended one on the taking of Porto Bello? Admiral Vernon[1a] will shine in our medallic history. We have just received the news of the bombarding Carthagena,[2] and the taking Chagre.[3] We are in great expectation of some important victory obtained by the squadron under sir John Norris;[4] we are told the Duke[5] is to be of the expedition: is it true?[6] All the letters too talk of France's suddenly declaring war; I hope they will defer it for a season, or one shall be obliged to return through Germany.

The Conclave still subsists, and the divisions still increase; it was very near separating last week, but by breaking into two popes; they were on the dawn of a schism. Aldovrandi[7] had thirty-three voices for three days, but could not procure the requisite two more; the Camerlingo[8] having engaged his faction to sign a protestation against him, and each party were inclined to elect. I don't know whether one should wish for a schism or not; it might probably rekindle the zeal for the church in the powers of Europe, which has been so far decaying.

On Wednesday we expect a third she-meteor. Those learned

[1a] Admiral Edward Vernon (1684–1757). Nearly fifty medals commemorating the capture of Porto Bello (see Letter 83, n. 4) were struck.

[2] Unsuccessfully bombarded by Admiral Vernon, 6–9 March 1740.

[3] A small fort, on the Isthmus of Panama, taken by Admiral Vernon, 24 March 1740.

[4] Admiral Sir John Norris (1660–1749), Lord of the Admiralty, 1718–29.

[5] Prince William Augustus (1721–65), second son of King George II; cr. Duke of Cumberland, 1726; Commander-in-Chief at Fontenoy, 1745; at Culloden, 1746; resigned all his military commands after the signature of the Convention of Klosterzeven (1757).

[6] 'Monday, July 14. Sir John Norris in the "Victory", on board of which was also the Duke of Cumberland, sailed from St. Helen's with his squadron of 20 men of war.' (*Gent. Mag.*, 1740, p. 356.)

[7] Cardinal Pompeo Aldovrandi (d. 1752).

[8] Cardinal Annibale Albani, the Pope's Chamberlain.

luminaries the Ladies P[omfret]⁹ and W[alpole]¹⁰ are to be joined by the Lady M[ary] W[ortley] M[ontagu].¹¹ You have not been witness to the rhapsody of mystic nonsense which these two fair ones debate incessantly, and consequently cannot figure what must be the issue of this triple alliance: we have some idea of it. Only figure the coalition of prudery, debauchery, sentiment, history, Greek, Latin, French, Italian, and metaphysics; all, except the second, understood by halves, by quarters, or not at all. You shall have the journals of this notable academy. Adieu, my dear West!

Yours ever,

HOR. WALPOLE.

Though far unworthy to enter into so learned and political a correspondence, I am employed pour barbouiller une page de 7 pouces et demie en hauteur, et 5 en largeur; and to inform you that we are at Florence, a city of Italy, and the capital of Tuscany: the latitude I cannot justly tell, but it is governed by a prince called Great-duke; an excellent place to employ all one's animal sensations in, but utterly contrary to one's rational powers. I have struck a medal upon myself: the device is thus O, and the motto *Nihilifsimo,* which I take in the most concise manner to contain a full account of my person, sentiments, occupations, and late glorious succefses. If you choose to be annihilated too, you cannot do better than undertake this journey. Here you shall get up at twelve o'clock, breakfast till three, dine till five, sleep till six, drink cooling liquors till eight, go to the bridge till ten, sup till two, and so sleep till twelve again.

Labore fefsi venimus ad larem nostrum,
Desideratoque acquiescimus lecto:

⁹ Henrietta Louisa Jeffreys (d. 1761), daughter and heiress of second Baron Jeffreys; m. (1720) Thomas Fermor, first Earl of Pomfret. Walpole frequently ridicules her affectation of learning.
¹⁰ Margaret Rolle, Baroness Walpole, afterwards Countess of Orford; only daughter and heiress of Samuel Rolle, of Heanton Satchville, Devonshire; m. 1 (1724), Robert Walpole, Lord Walpole, eldest son of the Prime Minister (whom he succeeded in 1745 as second Earl of Orford); 2 (1751), Hon. Sewallis Shirley, son of first Earl Ferrers, from both of whom she was separated.
¹¹ Lady Mary Pierrepont (d. 1762), daughter of Evelyn Pierrepont, Duke of Kingston, by his first wife, Lady Mary Fielding; m. (1712) Edward Wortley-Montagu. Miss Berry represents the three names by initials only.

Hoc est, quod unum est, pro laboribus tantis.
O quid solutis est beatius curis? [12]

We shall never come home again; a universal war is just upon
the point of breaking out; all outlets will be shut up. I shall be
secure in my nothingnefs, while you, that will be so absurd as to
exist, will envy me. You don't tell me what proficiency you
make in the noble science of defence. Don't you start still at the
sound of a gun? Have you learned to say Ha! ha! and is your
neck clothed with thunder?[13] Are your whiskers of a tolerable
length? And have you got drunk yet with brandy and gun-
powder? Adieu, noble captain![14]

93. GRAY TO MRS. GRAY

Florence, Aug. 21, N.S. 1740.

IT is some time since I have had the pleasure of writing to you,
having been upon a little excursion crofs the mountains to
Bologna. We set out from hence at sunset, pafsed the Apennines
by moon-light, travelling incefsantly till we came to Bologna
at four in the afternoon next day. There we spent a week agreeably enough, and returned as we came. The day before yesterday arrived the news of a Pope; and I have the mortification of
being within four days journey of Rome, and not seeing his
coronation, the heats being violent, and the infectious air now
at its height. We had an instance, the other day, that it is not
only fancy. Two country fellows, strong men, and used to the
country about Rome, having occasion to come from thence
hither, and travelling on foot, as common with them, one died
suddenly on the road; the other got hither, but extremely weak,
and in a manner stupid; he was carried to the hospital, but died
in two days. So, between fear and lazinefs, we remain here, and
must be satisfied with the accounts other people give us of the

---

[12] Catullus, xxxi, *Ad Sirmionem Pæninsulam*:

O quid solutis est beatius curis?
Cum mens onus reponit, ac peregrino
Labore fessi venimus larem ad nostrum,
Desideratoque acquiescimus lecto.
Hoc est, quod unum est pro laboribus tantis.

Gray is quoting from memory, but the impossible first line may be due
to a mistake of Miss Berry or the printer.

[13] Job xxxix. 25.

[14] West had thoughts of entering the army.

LETTER 93.—First printed in Mason's *Memoirs*, pp. 103–4.

matter. The new Pope is called Benedict XIV. being created Cardinal by Benedict XIII.[1] the last Pope but one. His name is Lambertini, a noble Bolognese, and Archbishop of that city.[2] When I was first there, I remember to have seen him two or three times; he is a short, fat man, about sixty-five years of age, of a hearty, merry countenance, and likely to live some years. He bears a good character for generosity, affability, and other virtues; and, they say, wants neither knowledge nor capacity. The worst side of him is, that he has a nephew or two; besides a certain young favourite, called Melara, who is said to have had, for some time, the arbitrary disposal of his purse and family. He is reported to have made a little speech to the Cardinals in the Conclave, while they were undetermined about an election, as follows: 'Most eminent Lords, here are three Bolognese of different characters, but all equally proper for the Popedom. If it be your pleasures, to pitch upon a Saint, there is Cardinal Gotti;[3] if upon a Politician, there is Aldrovandi;[4] if upon a Booby, here am I.' The Italian is much more expreſsive, and, indeed, not to be translated; wherefore, if you meet with any body that understands it, you may show them what he said in the language he spoke it. 'Emin[fsimi]. Sigr[i]. Ci siamo tré, diversi sì, mà tutti idonei al Papato. Si vi piace un Santo, c' è l'Gotti;[5] se volete una testa scaltra, e Politica, c' è l'Aldrovandé;[6] se un Coglione, eccomi!' Cardinal Coscia[7] is restored to his liberty, and, it is said, will be to all his benefices. Corsini[8] (the late Pope's nephew) as he has had no hand in this election, it is hoped, will be called to account for all his villanous practices. The Pretender, they say, has resigned all his pretensions to his eldest boy, and will accept of the Grand Chancellorship, which is thirty thousand crowns a-year; the pension he has at present is only twenty thousand. I do not affirm the truth of this last article; because, if he does, it is neceſsary he should take the

---

[1] See Letter 85, n. 5.

[2] Prospero Lambertini, created Cardinal in 1726; Pope 1740–58.— 'Bolonois, archevêque de Bologne, bonhomme, uni, facile, aimable et sans morgue, chose rare en ceux de son espèce; goguenard et licencieux dans ses discours; exemplaire et vertueux dans ses actions; plus d'agrément dans l'esprit que d'étendue dans le génie; savant surtout dans le droit canon; passe pour pencher vers le jansénisme; estimé et aimé dans son corps, quoique sans morgue, ce qui est singulier.' (C. de Brosses, *Lettres Familières*, LI.)

[3] See Letter 85, n. 7.
[4] *Sic.* See Letter 92, n. 7.
[5] So Mason; read 'c'è'l Gotti'.
[6] So Mason.
[7] See Letter 85, n. 6.
[8] See Letter 83, n. 1.

ecclesiastical habit, and it will sound mighty odd to be called his Majesty the Chancellor.——So ends my Gazette.

93*. West to Gray
[*Aug. 1740*]

[In his letter to West of 25 Sept. (Letter 94) Gray refers to 'a very diminutive letter', which West had written, in reply to a letter of Gray, which West described as his 'serious letter' (Letter 91 of 16 July). West's letter is not extant.]

94. GRAY TO WEST
Florence, Sept. 25, N.S. 1740.

WHAT I send you now, as long as it is, is but a piece of a poem.[1] It has the advantage of all fragments, to need neither introduction nor conclusion: Besides, if you do not like it, it is but imagining that which went before, and came after, to be infinitely better. Look in Sandy's Travels[2] for the history of Monte Barbaro, and Monte Nuovo.[3]

*   *   *

LETTER 94.—First printed in Mason's *Memoirs*, pp. 105–9.
[1] A copy of a slightly different version of this poem in Gray's handwriting was among the Walpole MSS. in the Waller Collection.
[2] George Sandys (1598–1644) published an account of his travels, under the title of *The Relation of a Journey begun an. Dom. 1610, in Four Books*, in 1615.
[3] Mason quotes (with some errors of transcription): 'West of Cicero's villa stands the eminent Gaurus, a stony and desolate mountain, in which are diverse obscure caverns, choaked almost with earth, where many have consumed much fruitless industry in searching for treasure. The famous Lucrine Lake extended formerly from Avernus to the aforesaid Gaurus: But is now no other than a little sedgy plash, choaked up by the horrible and astonishing eruption of the new mountain; whereof, as oft as I think, I am easy to credit whatsoever is wonderful. For who here knows not, or who elsewhere will believe, that a mountain should arise, (partly out of a lake and partly out of the sea) in one day and a night, unto such a height as to contend in altitude with the high mountains adjoining? In the year of our Lord 1538, on the 29th of September, when for certain days foregoing the country hereabout was so vexed with perpetual earthquakes, as no one house was left so entire as not to expect an immediate ruin; after that the sea had retired two hundred paces from the shore, (leaving abundance of fish, and springs of fresh water rising in the bottom) this mountain visibly ascended, about the second hour of the night, with an hideous roaring, horribly vomiting stones and such store of cinders as overwhelmed all the building thereabout, and the salubrious baths of Tripergula, for so many ages celebrated; consumed the vines to ashes, killing birds and beasts: the fearful inhabitants of Puzzol flying through the dark with their wives and children; naked, defiled, crying out, and detesting their calamities. Manifold mischiefs have they

Nec procul infelix se tollit in æthera Gaurus,
Prospiciens vitreum lugenti vertice pontum:
Tristior ille diu, & veteri desuetus olivâ
Gaurus, pampineæcჳ eheu jam nescius umbræ;
Horrendi tam sæva premit vicinia montis,
Attonitumცჳ urget latus, exuritცჳ ferentem.
    Nam fama est olim, mediâ dum rura silebant
Nocte, Deo victa, & molli perfusa quiete,
Infremuifse æquor ponti, auditamცჳ per omnes
Latè tellurem surdùm immugire cavernas:[4]
Quo sonitu nemora alta tremunt; tremit excita tuto
Parthenopæa sinu, flammantiscჳ ora Vesevi.
At subitò se aperire solum, vastoscჳ recefsus
Pandere sub pedibus, nigrâცჳ voragine fauces;
Tum[5] piceas cinerum glomerare sub æthere nubes
Vorticibus rapidis, ardenticჳ imbre procellam.
Præcipites fugere feræ, percჳ avia longè
Sylvarum fugit pastor, juga per deserta,
Ah, miser! increpitans saepè altâ voce per umbram
Nequicquam natos, creditცჳ audire sequentes.
Atque ille excelso rupis de vertice solus
Respectans notascჳ domos, & dulcia regna,
Nil usquàm videt infelix præter mare tristi
Lumine percufsum, & pallentes sulphure campos,
Fumumცჳ, flammascჳ, rotatacჳ turbine saxa.
    Quin ubi detonuit fragor, & lux reddita cælo;
Mæstos confluere agricolas, pafsucჳ videres
Tandem iterum timido deserta requirere tecta:
Sperantes, si forte oculis, si fortè darentur
Uxorum cineres, miserorumve ofsa parentum,
(Tenuia, sed tanti saltem solatia luctus)
Unâ colligere, & justâ componere in urnâ.
Uxorum nusquam cineres, nusquam ofsa parentum
(Spem miseram!) afsuetosve Lares, aut rura videbunt.

suffered by the barbarous, yet none like this which Nature inflicted.——This
new mountain, when newly raised, had a number of issues; at some of them
smoking and sometimes flaming; at others disgorging rivulets of hot waters;
keeping within a terrible rumbling; and many miserably perished that
ventured to descend into the hollowness above. But that hollow on the top
is at present an orchard, and the mountain throughout is bereft of its terrors.' (Bk. iv, pp. 275, 277–8.)
    4 Waller MS.: 'Tellurem late surdum mugire cavernas'.
    5 Waller MS.: 'Et'.

Quippe ubi planities campi diffusa jacebat;
Mons novus: ille supercilium, frontemcʒ favillâ
Incanum ostentans, ambustis cautibus, æquor
Subjectum, stragemcʒ suam, mæsta arva, minaci
Despicit imperio, solocʒ in littore regnat.
　Hinc infame loci nomen, multoscʒ per annos
Immemor antiquæ laudis, nescire labores
Vomeris, & nullo tellus revirescere cultu.
Non avium colles, non carmine matutino
Pastorum resonare; adeò undique dirus habebat
Informes latè horror agros,[6] saltuscʒ vacantes.
Sæpius et[7] longè detorquens navita proram
Monstrabat digito littus, sævæcʒ revolvens
Funera narrabat noctis, veteremcʒ ruinam.
　Montis adhuc facies manet hirta atcʒ aspera saxis:
Sed furor extinctus jamdudum, & flamma quievit,
Quæ nascenti aderat, seu forté bituminis atri
Defluxere olìm rivi, atque effæta lacuna
Pabula sufficere ardori, virescʒ recusat;
Sive in visceribus meditans[8] incendia jam nunc
(Horrendùm) arcanis glomerat genti efse futuræ
Exitio, sparsos tacituscʒ recolligit ignes.
Raro per clivos haud[9] secius ordine vidi
Canescentem oleam: longum post tempus amicti
Vite virent tumuli;[10] patriamcʒ revisere gaudens
Bacchus in afsuetis tenerum caput exerit[11] arvis
Vix tandem, infidocʒ audet se credere cœlo.

There was a certain little ode[12] set out from Rome, in a letter
of recommendation to you, but pofsibly fell into the enemies'
hands, for I never heard of its arrival. It is a little impertinent
to enquire after its welfare; but you, that are a father, will
excuse a parent's foolish fondnefs. Last post I received a very
diminutive letter:[13] It made excuses for its unentertainingnefs,
very little to the purpose; since it afsured me, very strongly, of
your esteem, which is to me the thing; all the rest appear but as

---

[6] Waller MS.: 'informes tam durus habebat Horror agros late circum'.
[7] Waller MS.: 'hoc'.　　　　　　[8] Waller MS.: 'meditata'.
[9] Waller MS.: 'Per clivos raro nec'.
[10] Waller MS.: 'colles' altered to 'tumuli'.
[11] Waller MS.: 'exserit'.
[12] The Alcaic ode ('Mater rosarum') sent with Letter 87.
[13] See Letter 93*.

the petits agrémens, the garnishing of the dish. P. Bougeant,[14] in his Langage des Bêtes, fancies that your birds, who continually repeat the same note, say only in plain terms, 'Je vous aime, ma chere; ma chere, je vous aime;' and that those of greater genius indeed, with various trills, run divisions upon the subject; but that the *fond*, from whence it all proceeds, is 'toujours je vous aime'. Now you may, as you find yourself dull or in humour, either take me for a chaffinch or nightingale; sing your plain song, or show your skill in music, but in the bottom let there be, toujours, toujours de l'Amitié.

As to what you call my serious letter;[15] be afsured, that your future state is to me entirely indifferent. Do not be angry, but hear me; I mean with respect to myself. For whether you be at the top of Fame, or entirely unknown to mankind; at the Council-table, or at Dick's coffee-house;[16] sick and simple, or well and wise; whatever alteration mere accident works in you, (supposing it utterly impofsible for it to make any change in your sincerity and honesty, since these are conditions sine quâ non) I do not see any likelihood of my not being yours ever.

95. GRAY TO PHILIP GRAY

Florence, Oct. 9, 1740.

THE beginning of next spring is the time determined for our return at furthest; pofsibly it may be before that time. How the interim will be employed, or what route we shall take, is not so certain. If we remain friends with France, upon leaving this country we shall crofs over to Venice, and so return through the cities north of the Po to Genoa; from thence take a felucca to Marseilles, and come back through Paris. If the contrary fall out, which seems not unlikely, we must make the Milanese, and those parts of Italy, in our way to Venice; from thence pafs through the Tirol into Germany, and come home by the Low-Countries. As for Florence, it has been gayer than ordinary for this last month, being one round of balls and entertainments, occasioned by the arrival of a great Milanese Lady; for the only thing the Italians shine in, is their reception of strangers. At such times every thing is magnificence: The more remarkable,

---

[14] See Letter 62, n. 10. [15] Letter 91.

[16] On the south side of Fleet St., near Temple Bar. It was a favourite resort of West's (see Walpole to West, and West to Ashton in *Gray–Walpole Correspondence*, Nos. 90 and 135). Gray also frequented it (see Letter 99).

LETTER 95.—First printed in Mason's *Memoirs*, pp. 109–11.

as in their ordinary course of life they are parsimonious, even to a degree of nastinefs. I saw in one of the vastest palaces in Rome (that of Prince Pamfilio) the apartment which he himself inhabited, a bed that most servants in England would disdain to lie in, and furniture much like that of a soph¹ at Cambridge, for convenience and neatnefs. This man is worth 30,000*l.* sterling a year. As for eating, there are not two Cardinals in Rome that allow more than six paoli, which is three shillings a day, for the expence of their table;² and you may imagine they are still lefs extravagant here than there. But when they receive a visit from any friend, their houses and persons are set out to the greatest advantage, and appear in all their splendour; it is, indeed, from a motive of vanity, and with the hopes of having it repaid them with interest, whenever they have occasion to return the visit. I call visits going from one city of Italy to another; for it is not so among acquaintance of the same place on common occasions. The new Pope has retrenched the charges of his own table to a sequin (10s.) a meal. The applause which all he says and does meets with, is enough to encourage him really to deserve fame. They say he is an able and honest man; he is reckoned a wit too. The other day, when the Senator of Rome came to wait upon him, at the first compliments he made him the Pope pulled off his cap: His Master of the Ceremonies, who stood by his side, touched him softly, as to warn him that such a condescension was too great in him, and out of all manner of rule: Upon which he turned to him and said, 'Oh! I cry you mercy, good Master, it is true, I am but a Novice of a Pope; I have not yet so much as learned ill manners.' * * *

96. Gray to Philip Gray

Florence,¹ Jan. 12, 1741.

WE still continue constant at Florence, at present one of the dullest cities in Italy. Though it is the middle of the Carnival there are no public diversions; nor is masquerading

---

¹ Short for 'sophister', a student in his second or third year.
² See Walpole's remarks in Letter 83.
Letter 96.—First printed in Mason's *Memoirs*, pp. 111–13.
¹ Between the date of this and the foregoing letter the reader will perceive an interval of full three months: as Mr. Gray saw no new places during this period, his letters were chiefly of news and common occurrences, and are therefore omitted. *Mason.*

permitted as yet. The Emperor's[2] obsequies are to be celebrated publickly the 16th of this month; and after that, it is imagined every thing will go on in its usual course. In the mean time, to employ the minds of the populace, the Government has thought fit to bring into the city in a solemn manner, and at a great expence, a famous statue of the Virgin called the Madonna dell'Impruneta,[3] from the place of her residence, which is upon a mountain seven miles off. It never has been practised but at times of public calamity; and was done at present to avert the ill effects of a late great inundation,[4] which it was feared might cause some epidemical distemper. It was introduced a fortnight ago in procefsion, attended by the Council of Regency, the Senate, the Nobility, and all the Religious Orders, on foot and bare-headed, and so carried to the great church, where it was frequented by an infinite concourse of people from all the country round. Among the rest I paid my devotions almost every day, and saw numbers of people pofsefsed with the devil, who were brought to be exorcised. It was indeed in the evening, and the church-doors were always shut before the ceremonies were finished, so that I could not be eye-witnefs of the event; but that they were all cured is certain, for one never heard any more of them the next morning. I am to-night just returned from seeing our Lady make her exit with the same solemnities she entered. The show had a finer effect than before; for it was dark; and every body (even those of the mob that could afford it) bore a white-wax flambeau. I believe there were at least five thousand of them, and the march was near three hours in pafsing before the window. The subject of all this devotion is supposed to be a large Tile with a rude figure in bas-relief upon it. I say supposed, because since the time it was found (for it was found in the earth in ploughing) only two people have seen it; the one was, by good luck, a saint; the other was struck blind for his presumption. Ever since she has been covered with seven veils; neverthelefs, those who approach her tabernacle cast their eyes down, for fear they should spy her through all her

---

[2] Charles VI (Emperor, 1711) died 20 Oct. 1740.

[3] 'This is probably the miraculous image of Santa Maria dell' Impruneta, which is housed in the Church of that name on the San Miniato side of the Arno a few miles from Florence. . . . The image is miracle-working by tradition, and in former times was carried on occasions of distress to the city of Florence.' (Mr. Alfred E. Hamill in *Notes and Queries*, vol. 165, Nov. 18, 1933, p. 358.)

[4] See Walpole's letter to West of Nov. 1740.

veils. Such is the history, as I had it from the Lady of the house where I stood to see her pafs; with many other circumstances; all which she firmly believes, and ten thousand beside.

We shall go to Venice in about six weeks, or sooner. A number of German troops are upon their march into this State, in case the King of Naples thinks proper to attack it. It is certain he has asked the Pope's leave for his troops to pafs through his country. The Tuscans in general are much discontented, and foolish enough to wish for a Spanish government, or any rather than this. * * * *

96.* Gray to West

[*c. April, 1741*]

[In his letter to West from Florence of 21 April 1741 (Letter 97) Gray refers to a previous letter he had written to him, criticizing his tragedy of *Pausanias*.]

96.** West to Gray

[*April, 1741*]

[In his letter to West of 21 April 1741 (Letter 97) Gray speaks of having just received a letter from West.]

97. GRAY TO WEST

Florence, April 21, 1741.

I KNOW not what degree of satisfaction it will give you to be told that we shall set out from hence the 24th of this month, and not stop above a fortnight at any place in our way. This I feel, that you are the principal pleasure I have to hope for in my own country. Try at least to make me imagine myself not indifferent to you; for I must own I have the vanity of desiring to be esteemed by somebody, and would choose that somebody should be one whom I esteem as much as I do you. As I am recommending myself to your love, methinks I ought to send you my picture (for I am no more what I was, some circumstances excepted, which I hope I need not particularize to you); you must add then, to your former idea, two years of age, reasonable quantity of dullnefs, a great deal of silence, and something that rather resembles, than is, thinking; a confused notion of many strange and fine things that have swum before my eyes for some time, a want of love for general society, indeed an inability to it. On the good side you may add a sensibility for what others feel, and indulgence for their faults or weaknefses, a love of truth, and detestation of every thing else. Then you are to deduct a little

LETTER 97.—First printed in Mason's *Memoirs*, pp. 113–16.

impertinence, a little laughter, a great deal of pride, and some spirits. These are all the alterations I know of, you perhaps may find more. Think not that I have been obliged for this reformation of manners to reason or reflection, but to a severer school-mistrefs, Experience. One has little merit in learning her lefsons, for one cannot well help it; but they are more useful than others, and imprint themselves in the very heart. I find I have been harangueing in the style of the Son of Sirach,[1] so shall finish here, and tell you that our route is settled as follows: First to Bologna for a few days, to hear the Viscontina[2] sing; next to Reggio, where is a Fair. Now, you must know, a Fair here is not a place where one eats ginger-bread or rides upon hobby-horses; here are no musical clocks, nor tall Leicestershire women; one has nothing but masquing, gaming, and singing. If you love operas, there will be the most splendid in Italy, four tip-top voices, a new theatre, the Duke and Duchefs in all their pomps and vanities. Does not this sound magnificent? Yet is the city of Reggio but one step above Old Brentford.[2a] Well; next to Venice by the 11th of May, there to see the old Doge[3] wed the Adriatic Whore. Then to Verona, so to Milan, so to Marseilles, so to Lyons, so to Paris, so to West, &c. in sæcula sæculorum. Amen.

Eleven months, at different times, have I pafsed at Florence; and yet (God help me) know not either people or language. Yet the place and the charming prospects demand a poetical farewell, and here it is.

> *   *   Oh Fæsulæ amœna
> Frigoribus juga, nec nimiùm spirantibus auris!
> Alma quibus Tusci Pallas decus Apennini
> Efse dedit, glaucâque suâ canescere sylvâ!
> Non ego vos posthàc Arni de valle videbo
> Porticibus circum, & candenti cincta coronâ
> Villarum longé nitido consurgere dorso,
> Antiquamve Ædem, et veteres præferre Cuprefsus
> Mirabor, tectisque super pendentia tecta.

[1] Jesus the son of Sirach, the alleged author of Ecclesiasticus.

[2] Caterina Visconti; she afterwards sang in England (see Walpole's letters to Mann of 11 Sept., 5, 12, and 23 Nov. 1741).

[2a] See Boswell's *Life of Johnson*, vol. iv, p. 186: 'When Dr. Adam Smith was expatiating on the beauty of Glasgow, he (Johnson) 'had cut him short by saying, "Pray, Sir, have you ever seen Brentford?"' Brentford may have passed into a proverb.

[3] Luigi Pisani, Doge of Venice, 1735–41; he died within two months (17 June) of the date of this letter, aged 78.

I will send you, too, a pretty little Sonnet of a Sig.ʳ. Abbate Buondelmonte,[4] with my imitation of it.

> Spefso Amor sotto la forma
> D'amistà ride, e s'asconde:
> Poi si mischia, e si confonde
> Con lo sdegno, e col rancor.
> In Pietade ei si trasforma;
> Par trastullo, e par dispetto:
> Mà nel suo diverso aspetto
> Sempr' egli è l'istefso Amor.

> Lusit amicitiæ interdum velatus amictu,
>   Et benè compositâ veste fefellit Amor.
> Mox iræ afsumsit cultus, faciemque minantem,
>   Inque odium versus, versus & in lacrymas:
> Ludentem fuge, nec lacrymanti, aut crede furenti;
>   Idem est difsimili semper in ore Deus.

Here comes a letter from you.—I must defer giving my opinion of Pausanias till I can see the whole, and only have said what I did in obedience to your commands.[5] I have spoken with such freedom on this head, that it seems but just you should have your revenge; and therefore I send you the beginning not of an Epic Poem, but of a Metaphysic one.[6] Poems and Metaphysics (say you, with your spectacles on) are inconsistent things. A metaphysical poem is a contradiction in terms. It is true, but I will go on. It is Latin too to increase the absurdity. It will, I suppose, put you in mind of the man who wrote a treatise of Canon Law in Hexameters. Pray help me to the description of a mixt mode, and a little Episode about Space.[7]

[4] Giuseppe Maria Bondelmonti (1713–57), of the ancient family of that name.

[5] See Letters 96,* 96.**

[6] The beginning of the first book of a didactic poem, *De Principiis Cogitandi*. The fragment which he now sent contained the first fifty-three lines. *Mason.*—The poem, which is addressed 'Ad Favonium', was first printed by Mason (*Memoirs*, pp. 160–9). The opening lines of the fourth book, containing an invocation to West after his death, were sent by Gray to Walpole in 1747 (see Letter 131, n. 20).

[7] This is the last extant letter which Gray wrote from Italy. Mason, at the beginning of the Section in his *Memoirs* concerned with Gray's travels (p. 40), gave an explanation, in words dictated to him by Walpole: 'I shall only further say to forewarn the reader of a disappointment, that this

98. Gray to Chute

[Dover—c. Sept: 1: O:S: 1741]

[In his letter to Chute of 7 Sept. 1741 (Letter 99) Gray addresses him as 'suavifsime Chutî! whom I wrote to from Dover'. The letter was no doubt written on the day Gray landed at Dover on his way to London, which Mason says he reached about 1 Sept.]

99. GRAY TO CHUTE[1]

My Dear S^r

I COMPLAIN no more. You have not forgot me. Mrs Dick, to whom I resorted for a Dish of Coffee, instead thereof produced unto me from between her fat Breasts your kind Letter, big with another no lefs kind from our poor mangled Friend[2] to

correspondence is defective towards the end, and includes no description either of Venice or its territory; the last places which Mr. Gray visited. This defect was occasioned by an unfortunate disagreement between him and Mr. Walpole, . . .: this therefore occasioned their separation at Reggio. Mr. Gray went before him to Venice.' At the end of the Section (p. 116) Mason adds: 'When Mr. Gray left Venice, which he did the middle of July following, he returned home through Padua, Verona, Milan, Turin, and Lyons. From all of which places he writ either to his Father or Mother with great punctuality: But merely to inform them of his health and safety; about which (as might be expected) they were now very anxious, as he travelled only with a "Laquais de Voyage".' See Appendix D. Mason presumably destroyed Gray's letters to his father and mother. Gray must have written also to West, but no letters survive.

LETTER 99.—First printed (in modified text) by Chaloner Chute in *History of the Vyne*, pp. 86–9; now reprinted from original.

¹ John Chute (1701–76), the last descendant in the male line of Chaloner Chute, Speaker of the House of Commons (1659), was the tenth and youngest child of Edward Chute (1658–1722), of the Vyne, in Hampshire, his mother being Katherine Keck, widow of Ferdinand Tracy. He was educated at Eton, and after his father's death lived chiefly abroad until 1746, when he returned to England. On the death of his brother Anthony in 1754 he succeeded to the family estates, and thenceforth resided at the Vyne until his death. Walpole and Gray made his acquaintance at Florence in 1740, while they were staying with Mann. After Gray parted from Walpole at Reggio in 1741 he spent two months with Chute at Venice. On his return to England Chute became very intimate with Walpole, and renewed his friendship with Gray, who on more than one occasion was his guest at the Vyne. It seems probable that there was a breach in their friendship in 1758 (see Letter 228, n. 1).

² Horace Mann, who, as Chute notes, 'was at this time much tried by illness, which he bore most patiently'. Walpole refers to his 'violent illness' in his letter to Mann from Paris in August of this year. It involved a serious operation—hence Gray's phrase.

whom I now addreſs myself (you don't take it ill) & let him
know, that as soon as I got hither, I took wing for the Strand to
see a certain Acquaintance of his[3] (for I then knew not whether
he were dead, or alive) & get some News of him. I was so
struck with the great resemblance between them,[4] that it made
me cry out. he is a true Eagle, but a little tamer, & a little fatter
than the Eagle Resident: I told him so, but he did not seem to
think it so great a Compliment, as I did. his Wife[5] had miscarried but was quite well again; his house half pulled down,
but riseing again more magnificent from its Ruins. he received
me, as became a Bird of his Race, & suffer'd himself to be
careſsed without giveing me one Peck, or Scratch. the only
bad thing I know of him, is, that he wears a Frock, & a Bob-
Wigg. may I charge you, my dear Mr Chute (I give you your
great Name for want of a little tiny one) with my Compliments
to Dr Cocchi,[6] Benevoli[7] (tho' I hate him) & their Patient.
particularly to this last for recovering so soon, & so much to my
Satisfaction. I think one may call him dear Creature, & be
fond in Security under the Sanction of your Cover. I carried
his Mus:^m Flor:^{m8} to Commiſsioner Haddock,[9] who is Liddel's[10]
Uncle. that Gentleman had left Paris, haveing been elected for

---

[3] His twin brother, Galfridus (d. 1756), sometime M.P. for Maidstone;
he was the youngest of the three sons of Robert Mann, Deputy-Treasurer
of Chelsea Hospital, and was in business with his eldest brother Edward as
an army clothier.

[4] As was Walpole; he writes to Mann, 18 Sept. 1748: 'Your brother Gal
is extremely a favourite with me: I took to him for his resemblance to you,
but am grown to love him upon his own fund'.

[5] She was a virago. Walpole speaks of her 'infernal temper', and calls her
'Tisiphone', and 'a little white fiend'. (See his letters to Mann of 5 Feb.,
18 March, 16 Dec. 1756; and 3 Sept. 1757.)

[6] This was Antonio Cocchi (d. 1758), described by Walpole as 'a learned
physician and author of Florence; a particular friend of Mr. Mann'. He
came from Florence to attend Walpole during his serious illness at Reggio in
May of this year, after Gray had left for Venice.

[7] Another physician (see Letter 112).

[8] These were the earliest volumes of the *Museum Florentinum, exhibens insigni-
ora vetustatis monumenta, quæ Florentiæ sunt in thesauro mediceo, cum observationibus
Anton. Franc. Gorii* (Florentiæ, 1731–66, 12 vol., fol. max.). Vols. i–ii com-
prised engraved gems; vol. iii, statues; vols. iv–vi, coins. Vols. vii–x (portraits
of painters in the Imperial Gallery at Florence); vols. xi–xii (supplement to
the foregoing by Abate Anton. Pazzi), were published later.

[9] Richard Haddock (d. 1751), Comptroller of the Navy, 1733–49; he
was elder brother of Vice-Admiral Nicholas Haddock (see Letter 85, n. 16).

[10] Presumably Richard Liddell (d. 1746), who was returned in May of
this year for Bossiney (Cornwall).

some place in this Parliament, & (tho' it is like to be contro-
verted) took that opportunity to return to England for a time,
but is now gone, I think to Spaw. Adieu! M^r M: * * *
* * * *¹¹

Nunc ad te totum me converto, suavifsime Chutî! whom I
wrote to from Dover.¹¹ᵃ if this be London, Lord send me to
Constantinople. either I, or it are extremely odd. the Boys
laugh at the depth of my Ruffles, the immensity of my Bagg, &
the length of my Sword. I am as an Alien in my native land,
yea! I am as an Owl among the small birds. it rains, every
body is discontented, & so am I. you can't imagine how morti-
fieing it is to fall into the hands of an English Barber. Lord, how
You or Polleri would storm in such a Case. don't think of
comeing hither without Lavaur,¹² or something equivalent to
him (not an elephant).¹³ the Natives are alive, & flourishing.
the fashion is a grey frock with round Sleeves, Bob-wig, or a
Spencer, plain Hat with enormous Brims, & shallow Crown,
cock'd as bluff, as pofsible, Muslin-Neckcloth twisted round,
rumpled, & tuck'd into the breast; all this with a certain
Safaring¹³ᵃ Air, as if they were just come back from Cartagena.¹⁴
if my pockets had any thing in them, I should be afraid of every
body I met. look in their face, they knock you down; speak to
them, they bite off your Nose. I am no longer ashamed in
publick, but extremely afraid. if ever they catch me among 'em,
I give them leave to eat me. so much for drefs, as to Politicks,
every body is extreme angry with all that has been, or shall be
done: even a Victory at this time would be look'd upon as a
wicked attempt to please the Nation. the Theatres open not
till tomorrow, so you will excuse my giveing no account of them

---

¹¹ A sentence here of rather more than half a line, beginning (apparently)
'don't', has been scored through, and is undecipherable.
¹¹ᵃ This letter has not been preserved (see Letter 98)
¹² Probably a French barber employed by Chute.
¹³ There are several versions of this malapropism. Pinkerton in his *Walpoliana* gives the following, among other anecdotes of Lord William Poulet,
on the authority of Walpole: 'Lord William Poulet, though often Chairman
of Committees of the House of Commons, was a great dunce, and could
scarce read. . . . A gentleman writing to desire a fine horse he had, offered
him any *equivalent*. Lord William replied, that the horse was at his service,
but he did not know what to do with an *elephant*' (vol. i, pp. 17–18).
¹³ᵃ Gray put a curved stroke over the 'a'; possibly he meant 'Seafaring'.
¹⁴ In Colombia, S. America, the attempted capture of which by Admiral
Vernon and General Wentworth in March–April of this year had ended in
disastrous failure.

tonight. now I have been at home, & seen how things go there, would I were with you again, that the Remainder of my Dream might at least be agreeable. as it is, my prospect can not well be more unpleasing; but why do I trouble your Goodnature with such considerations? be afsured, that when I am happy (if that can ever be) your Esteem will greatly add to that happinefs, & when most the contrary, will always alleviate, what I suffer. many, many thanks for your kindnefs; for your travels, for your News, for all the trouble I have given, & must give you. omit nothing, when you write, for things that were quite indifferent to me at Florence, at this distance become interesting. humble Service to Polleri; obliged for his harmonious Salutation, I hope to sec some Scratches with his black Claw in your next. Adieu! I am most sincerely, & ever Your's

T G:

London—Sept: 7: O:S: [1741]

P:S: Nobody is come from Paris yet.[15]

Addressed: A Mons:ʳ Monsieur Chute, Gentilhomme Anglois chez Mons:ʳ Ubaldini nel Corso de' Tintori à Florence.

99.* Conway to Gray

[*Sept. 1741*]

[In an undated letter to Henry Conway (see Letter 44, n. 9), which was probably written not long after his arrival in England on 14 Sept. 1741, Horace Walpole says: 'Before I thank you for myself, I must thank you for that excessive good nature you showed in writing to poor Gray. I am less impatient to see you, as I find you are not the least altered, but have the same tender friendly temper you always had.'

As Gray had returned to England on 1 Sept., Conway's letter to him (which has not been preserved) was presumably written between that date and the date of Walpole's letter, that is to say, in the first half of September.]

100. WEST TO GRAY

I WRITE to make you write, for I have not much to tell you. I have recovered no spirits as yet; but, as I am not displeased with my company, I sit purring by the fire-side in my arm-chair

---

15 Meaning, no doubt, Walpole, who had made a stay in Paris towards the end of August on his way home. He arrived in London a week after the date of this letter, on 14 Sept.

LETTER 100.—First printed in Mason's *Memoirs*, pp. 121–2.

with no small satisfaction. I read too sometimes, and have begun Tacitus, but have not yet read enough to judge of him; only his Pannonian sedition in the first book of his annals, which is just as far as I have got, seemed to me a little tedious. I have no more to say, but to desire you will write letters of a handsome length, and always answer me within a reasonable space of time, which I leave to your discretion.

Popes,[1] March 28, 1742.

P.S. The new Dunciad![2] qu'en pensez vous?

101. GRAY TO WEST

[c. 1 April 1742][1]

I TRUST to the country, and that easy indolence you say you enjoy there, to restore you your health and spirits; and doubt not but, when the sun grows warm enough to tempt you from your fire-side, you will (like all other things) be the better for his influence. He is my old friend, and an excellent nurse, I afsure you. Had it not been for him, life had often been to me intolerable. Pray do not imagine that Tacitus, of all authors in the world, can be tedious. An annalist, you know, is by no means master of his subject; and I think one may venture to say, that if those Pannonian affairs are tedious in his hands, in another's they would have been insupportable. However, fear not, they will soon be over, and he will make ample amends. A man, who could join the *brilliant* of wit and concise sententiousnefs peculiar to that age, with the truth and gravity of better times, and the deep reflection and good sense of the best moderns, cannot choose but have something to strike you. Yet what I admire in him above all this, is his detestation of tyranny,

---

[1] David Mitchell's, Esq; at Popes, near Hatfield, Hertfordshire; at whose house he died the 1st of June following. *Mason.*—It seems probable that West and Gray had both been in town during the winter. West now begins a correspondence after their parting.

[2] The fourth book of the *Dunciad* had been published this month (March 1742), under the title of *The New Dunciad: as it was found in the year MDCCXLI, with the Illustrations of Scriblerus and Notes Variorum.*

LETTER 101.—First printed in Mason's *Memoirs*, pp. 122–3.

[1] The date must be either the end of March or the beginning of April, as the letter answers West's of 28 March, and West's answer to it is dated 4 April.

and the high spirit of liberty that every now and then breaks out, as it were, whether he would or no. I remember a sentence in his Agricola that (concise as it is) I always admired for saying much in a little compaſs. He speaks of Domitian, who upon seeing the last will of that General, where he had made him Coheir with his Wife and Daughter, 'Satis constabat lætatum eum, velut honore, judicioque: tam cæca & corrupta mens afsiduis adulationibus erat, ut nesciret a bono patre non scribi hæredem, nisi malum principem'.²

As to the Dunciad,³ it is greatly admired: the Genii of Operas and Schools,⁴ with their attendants, the pleas of the Virtuosos and Florists,⁵ and the yawn of dulneſs in the end,⁶ are as fine as anything he has written. The Metaphysicians' part⁷ is to me the worst; and here and there a few ill-exprefsed lines, and some hardly intelligible.

I take the liberty of sending you a long speech of Agrippina;⁸ much too long, but I could be glad you would retrench it. Aceronia, you may remember, had been giving quiet counsels. I fancy, if it ever be finished, it will be in the nature of Nat. Lee's Bedlam Tragedy,⁹ which had twenty-five acts and some odd scenes.

102. WEST TO GRAY

Popes, April 4, 1742.

I OWN in general I think Agrippina's speech too long; but how to retrench it, I know not:¹ But I have something else to say, and that is in relation to the style, which appears to me too

---

² Cap. xliii, *ad fin.*　　　　　　³ See Letter 100, n. 2.
⁴ Bk. iv, ll. 45 ff.　　　　　　⁵ Bk. iv, ll. 347 ff.
⁶ Bk. iv, ll. 605 ff.　　　　　　⁷ Bk. iv, ll. 239 ff.

⁸ The speech herewith sent to Mr. West was the concluding one of the first scene of a tragedy, which I believe was begun the preceding winter. *Mason.* (See Letters 62, n. 7; 102, n. 1.)

⁹ Nathaniel Lee (*c.* 1653–92), the dramatist, became insane, and while in Bedlam is said to have written a tragedy in five-and-twenty acts.

LETTER 102.—First printed in Mason's *Memoirs*, pp. 136–7.

¹ Mason claims to have obviated the objection against the length of Agrippina's speech, 'not by retrenching, but by putting part of it into the mouth of Aceronia, and by breaking it in a few other places'. 'Originally', he adds, 'it was one continued speech from the line, "Thus even grave and undisturbed Reflection", to the end of the scene; which was undoubtedly too long for the lungs of any actress.' Unhappily, Mason's garbled version, with its ridiculous interpolations, is the only text of *Agrippina* that has been preserved.

antiquated. Racine was of another opinion; he no where gives
you the phrases of Ronsard: His language is the language of
the times, and that of the purest sort; so that his French is
reckoned a standard. I will not decide what style is fit for our
English stage; but I should rather choose one that bordered upon
Cato,[2] than upon Shakespear. One may imitate (if one can)
Shakespear's manner, his surprizing strokes of true nature, his
expressive force in painting characters, and all his other beauties;
preserving at the same time our own language. Were Shakespear alive now, he would write in a different style from what
he did. These are my sentiments upon these matters: Perhaps
I am wrong, for I am neither a Tarpa,[3] nor am I quite an Aristarchus.[4] You see I write freely both of you and Shakespear;
but it is as good as writing not freely, where you know it is
acceptable.

I have been tormented within this week with a most violent
cough; for when once it sets up its note, it will go on, cough after
cough, shaking and tearing me for half an hour together; and
then it leaves me in a great sweat, as much fatigued as if I had
been labouring at the plough. All this description of my cough
in prose, is only to introduce another description of it in verse,
perhaps not worth your perusal; but it is very short, and besides
has this remarkable in it, that it was the production of four
o'clock in the morning, while I lay in my bed tossing and cough-
ing, and all unable to sleep.——

> Ante omnes morbos importunissima tussis,
> Quâ durare datur, traxitque sub ilia vires:
> Dura etenim versans imo sub pectore regna,
> Perpetuo exercet teneras luctamine costas,
> Oraque distorquet, vocemque immutat anhelam:
> Nec cessare locus: sed saevo concita motu
> Molle domat latus, & corpus labor omne fatigat:
> Unde molesta dies, noctemque insomnia turbant.
> Nec Tua, si mecum Comes hic jucundus adesses,
> Verba juvare queant, aut hunc lenire dolorem
> Sufficiant tua vox dulcis, nec vultus amatus.[5]

[2] Addison's tragedy, first produced at Drury Lane in 1713.
[3] Spurius Maecius Tarpa, literary censor under Augustus.
[4] The great critic of antiquity (fl. 156 B.C.).
[5] In Gray's copy in his Commonplace-book he notes: 'Fav: April 4 Wrote
in the Country after his severe Illness, which left behind it a continual
Hectic & Cough.'

Do not mistake me, I do not condemn Tacitus: I was then inclined to find him tedious: The German sedition sufficiently made up for it; and the speech of Germanicus, by which he reclaims his soldiers, is quite masterly. Your New Dunciad I have no conception of. I shall be too late for our dinner if I write any more.

Yours.

103. GRAY TO WEST

London, [8] April, Thursday[1] [1742].

YOU are the first who ever made a Muse of a Cough; to me it seems a much more easy task to versify in one's sleep, (that indeed you were of old famous for)[2] than for want of it. Not the wakeful nightingale (when she had a cough) ever sung so sweetly. I give you thanks for your warble, and wish you could sing yourself to rest. These wicked remains of your illneſs will sure give way to warm weather and gentle exercise; which I hope you will not omit as the season advances. Whatever low spirits and indolence, the effect of them, may advise to the contrary, I pray you add five steps to your walk daily for my sake; by the help of which, in a month's time, I propose to set you on horseback.

I talked of the Dunciad as concluding you had seen it; if you have not, do you choose I should get and send it you? I have myself, upon your recommendation, been reading Joseph Andrews.[3] The incidents are ill laid and without invention; but the characters have a great deal of nature, which always pleases even in her lowest shapes. Parson Adams is perfectly well; so is Mrs. Slipslop, and the story of Wilson; and throughout he shews himself well read in Stage-Coaches, Country Squires, Inns, and Inns of Court. His reflections upon high people and low people, and miſses and masters, are very good. However

LETTER 103.—First printed in Mason's *Memoirs*, pp. 138–41.
[1] This must be 8 April.
[2] Jacob Bryant (1715–1804), a schoolfellow of West's, in a letter written in 1798 (printed in Mitford's Life of Gray in *Gray's Poetical Works*, 1847, pp. lx ff.), says: 'This is, I believe, founded in truth; for I remember some who were of the same house mentioning that he often composed in his dormant state, and that he wrote down in the morning what he had conceived in the night.' See also West's letter to Walpole of 1 June 1736 in *Gray–Walpole Correspondence*, p. 77.
[3] Fielding's novel, which had been published in the previous February.

the exaltedneſs of some minds (or rather as I shrewdly suspect their insipidity and want of feeling or observation) may make them insensible to these light things, (I mean such as characterize and paint nature) yet surely they are as weighty and much more useful than your grave discourses upon the mind,[4] the paſsions, and what not. Now as the paradisaical pleasures of the Mahometans consist in playing upon the flute and lying with Houris, be mine to read eternal new romances of Marivaux[5] and Crebillon.[6]

You are very good in giving yourself the trouble to read and find fault with my long harangues. Your freedom (as you call it) has so little need of apologies, that I should scarce excuse your treating me any otherwise; which, whatever compliment it might be to my vanity, would be making a very ill one to my understanding. As to matter of stile, I have this to say: The language of the age is never the language of poetry; except among the French, whose verse, where the thought or image does not support it, differs in nothing from prose. Our poetry, on the contrary, has a language peculiar to itself; to which almost every one, that has written, has added something by enriching it with foreign idioms and derivatives: Nay sometimes words of their own composition or invention. Shakespear and Milton have been great creators this way; and no one more licentious than Pope or Dryden, who perpetually borrow expreſsions from the former. Let me give you some instances from Dryden, whom every body reckons a great master of our poetical tongue.——Full of *museful mopeings*—unlike the *trim* of love—a pleasant *beverage*—a *roundelay* of love—stood silent in his *mood*—with knots and *knares* deformed—his *ireful mood*—in

---

[4] He seems here to glance at Hutchinson, the disciple of Shaftesbury: of whom he had not a much better opinion, than of his master. *Mason*.—Mason no doubt means Francis Hutcheson (1694–1746), at this time Professor of Moral Philosophy at Glasgow. (See Letter 115, n. 5.)

[5] Pierre Carlet de Chamblain de Marivaux (1688–1763), the author of many comedies and novels, the most famous of which was *La Vie de Marianne* (see Letter 112, n. 31).

[6] See Letter 62, n. 9. According to Mason, it was Crébillon's *Égarements du Cœur et de l'Esprit* (published in 1736) that Gray especially admired. *Le Sopha*, for which Gray confesses his partiality in his letter to Chute of 24 May 1742, was published in 1740. (See Letter 109, n. 7.) Some twenty years later than this Walpole, writing to Gray from Paris (19 Nov. 1765), says: 'Crébillon is entirely out of fashion, and Marivaux a proverb: *marivauder* and *marivaudage* are established terms for being prolix and tiresome.' (See Letter 417.)

proud *array*—his *boon* was granted—and *disarray* and shameful
rout—*wayward* but wise—*furbished* for the field—the *foiled dodderd*
oaks—*disherited*—*smouldring* flames—*retchlefs* of laws—*crones* old
and ugly—the *beldam* at his side—the *grandam-hag*—*villanize* his
Father's fame.——But they are infinite: And our language not
being a settled thing (like the French) has an undoubted right
to words of an hundred years old, provided antiquity have not
rendered them unintelligible. In truth, Shakespear's language
is one of his principal beauties; and he has no lefs advantage
over your Addisons and Rowes in this, than in those other great
excellencies you mention. Every word in him is a picture. Pray
put me the following lines into the tongue of our modern
Dramatics:

> But I, that am not shaped for sportive tricks,
> Nor made to court an amorous looking-glafs:
> I, that am rudely stampt, and want love's majesty
> To strut before a wanton ambling nymph:
> I, that am curtail'd of this fair proportion,
> Cheated of feature by difsembling nature,
> Deform'd, unfinish'd, sent before my time
> Into this breathing world, scarce half made up—[7]

And what follows. To me they appear untranslatable; and if
this be the case, our language is greatly degenerated. However,
the affectation of imitating Shakespear may doubtlefs be carried
too far; and is no sort of excuse for sentiments ill-suited, or
speeches ill-timed, which I believe is a little the case with me.
I guefs the most faulty exprefsions may be these—*silken* son of
dalliance[8]—*drowsier* pretensions—wrinkled *beldams*—*arched* the
hearer's brow and *riveted* his eyes in *fearful extasie*. These are
easily altered or omitted: and indeed if the thoughts be wrong
or superfluous, there is nothing easier than to leave out the
whole. The first ten or twelve lines are, I believe, the best;[9]
and as for the rest, I was betrayed into a good deal of it by
Tacitus; only what he has said in five words, I imagine I have
said in fifty lines: Such is the misfortune of imitating the
inimitable. Now, if you are of my opinion, una litura may do

[7] *Richard III*, i. 1 (*ad init.*).

[8] In the third speech of Agrippina—an echo, as Tovey points out, of
Pope's 'silken sons' in the *Dunciad* (iv. 292), and Shakespare's 'silken
dalliance' in *Henry V* (Act ii, l. 2).

[9] The lines which he means here are from—*thus ever grave and undisturb'd*
reflection—to *Rubellius lives*. For the part of the scene, which he sent in his
former letter, began there. *Mason.*

the busineſs better than a dozen; and you need not fear unravelling my web. I am a sort of spider; and have little else to
do but spin it over again, or creep to come other place and spin
there. Alas! for one who has nothing to do but amuse himself,
I believe my amusements are as little amusing as most folks.
But no matter; it makes the hours paſs, and is better than ἐν
ἀμαθίᾳ καὶ ἀμᴂσίᾳ καταβιῶναι.[10] Adieu.

104. WEST TO GRAY

[c. 12] April[1] [1742]

To begin with the conclusion of your letter, which is Greek,
I desire that you will quarrel no more with your manner of
passing your time. In my opinion it is irreproachable, especially
as it produces such excellent fruit; and if I, like a saucy bird, must
be pecking at it, you ought to consider that it is because I like
it. No una litura I beg you, no unravelling of your web, dear
Sir! only pursue it a little further, and then one shall be able
to judge of it a little better. You know the crisis of a play is in
the first act; its damnation or salvation wholly rests there. But
till that first act is over, every body suspends his vote; so how
do you think I can form, as yet, any just idea of the speeches
in regard to their length or shortness? The connexion and
symmetry of such little parts with one another must naturally
escape me, as not having the plan of the whole in my head;
neither can I decide about the thoughts whether they are
wrong or superfluous; they may have some future tendency
which I perceive not. The style only was free to me, and there
I find we are pretty much of the same sentiment: For you say
the affectation of imitating Shakespear may doubtless be
carried too far; I say as much and no more. For old words we
know are old gold, provided they are well chosen. Whatever
Ennius[2] was, I do not consider Shakespear as a dunghill in the
least: On the contrary, he is a mine of antient ore, where all our

---

[10] Tovey refers to Aelian, who states (*Var. Hist.* vii. 15) that the Myti-
lenaeans imposed this penalty on their revolted allies, that their children
should not be educated (γράμματα μὴ μανθάνειν, μηδὲ μουσικὴν διδάσκεσθαι),
considering it the heaviest of punishments to be condemned to pass one's
life in a state of ignorance and grossness (πασῶν κολασέων βαρυτάτην εἶναι
ταύτην, ἐν ἀμουσίᾳ καὶ ἀμαθίᾳ καταβιῶναι ἡγησάμενοι).

LETTER 104.—First printed in Mason's *Memoirs*, pp. 142–4.

[1] The letter is in reply to Gray's letter of 8 April (Letter 103).

[2] Virgil, who borrowed from Ennius, is reported to have said, 'lego
aurum in stercore Ennii'.

great modern poets have found their advantage. I do not know how it is, but his old expressions have more energy in them than ours, and are even more adapted to poetry; certainly, where they are judiciously and sparingly inserted, they add a certain grace to the composition; in the same manner as Poussin[3] gave a beauty to his pictures by his knowledge in the antient proportions: But should he, or any other painter, carry the imitation too far, and neglect that best of models Nature, I am afraid it would prove a very flat performance. To finish this long criticism: I have this further notion about old words revived, (is not this a pretty way of finishing?) I think them of excellent use in tales; they add a certain drollery to the comic, and a romantic gravity to the serious, which are both charming in their kind; and this way of charming Dryden understood very well. One need only read Milton to acknowledge the dignity they give the Epic. But now comes my opinion that they ought to be used in Tragedy more sparingly, than in most kinds of poetry. Tragedy is designed for public representation, and what is designed for that should certainly be most intelligible. I believe half the audience that come to Shakespear's plays do not understand the half of what they hear.—But finissons enfin.—Yet one word more.—You think the ten or twelve first lines the best, now I am for the fourteen last;[4] add, that they contain not one word of antientry.

I rejoice you found amusement in Joseph Andrews. But then I think your conceptions of Paradise a little upon the Bergerac.[5] Les Lettres du Seraphim R. a Madame la Cherubinesse de Q. What a piece of extravagance would there be!

And now you must know that my body continues weak and enervate. And for my animal spirits, they are in perpetual fluctuation: Some whole days I have no relish, no attention for any thing; at other times I revive, and am capable of writing a long letter, as you see; and though I do not write speeches, yet I translate them. When you understand what speech, you will own that it is a bold and perhaps a dull attempt. In three words, it is prose, it is from Tacitus, it is of Germanicus.[6] Peruse, perpend, pronounce.

[3] Nicolas Poussin (1594–1665).

[4] He means the conclusion of the first scene. *Mason.*

[5] Cyrano de Bergerac (1620–55); he was the author of *Histoires Comiques des États et Empires de la Lune et du Soleil*, to which Swift is said to have been indebted in *Gulliver's Travels.*

[6] Mason omits this translation. The speech in question was probably that in *Annals*, i. 42–3.

105. GRAY TO WEST

My Dear West   [London, April 23, 1742.][1]

I SHOULD not have fail'd to answer your Letter immediately,
but I went out of town for a little while, wch hinder'd me. its
length (beside the Pleasure naturally accompanying a long
letter from you) affords me a new one, when I think it is a kind
of Symptom of the Recovery of your Health, & flatter myself
that your bodily Strength returns in proportion. pray do not
forget to mention the Progreſs you make continually. as to
Agrippina, I begin to be of your opinion, & find myself (as
Women are of their children) leſs enamour'd of my Productions
the older they grow. she is laid up to sleep,[2] till next Summer:
so bid her Good night. I think you have translated Tacitus
very justly, that is freely, & accommodated his thoughts to the
Turn & Genius of our Language. which at the same time I
commend your Judgement, is no commendation of the English
tongue, which is too diffuse, & daily grows more & more
enervate, & one shall never be more sensible of this, than in
turning an Author like Tacitus. I have been trying it in some
parts of Thucydides (who has a little resemblance of him in his
Conciseneſs) & endeavour'd to do it closely, but found it produced mere Nonsense. if you have any inclination to see what
figure he makes in Italian, I have a Tuscan translation of
Davanzati,[3] much-esteem'd in Italy; & will send you the same

LETTER 105.—First printed in part in Mason's *Memoirs*, pp. 145–6 (without the translation of Propertius); now first printed in full from original.

[1] The date of the year has been inserted by Mason; that of the month is
supplied by the postmark.

[2] He never after awakened her; and I believe this was occasioned by the
strictures which his friend had made on his dramatic style; which (though he
did not think them well founded, as they certainly were not) had an effect
which Mr. West, we may believe, did not intend them to have. I remember
some years after I was also the innocent cause of his delaying to finish his fine
ode on the progress of Poetry. I told him, on reading the part he shewed me,
that 'though I admired it greatly, and thought that it breathed the very spirit
of Pindar, yet I suspected it would by no means hit the public taste.' Finding
afterwards that he did not proceed in finishing it, I often expostulated with him
on the subject; but he always replied 'No, you have thrown cold water upon
it.' I mention this little anecdote, to shew how much the opinion of a friend,
even when it did not convince his judgment, affected his inclination. *Mason.*

[3] Bernardo Davanzati (1529–1606), a Florentine; his translation of the
Annals was published in 1596–1600. Gray had his translation of the whole
of Tacitus published posthumously in 1637, as appears from a Catalogue of
Gray's library (in the Pierpont Morgan Library).

1742　　　　　　　　　　　　　　　　　　17

My Dear West

p. 145. mem. Letter printed, Verses not —

I should not have fail'd to answer your Letter immediately, but I went out of town for a little while, wch hinder'd me. it's length (beside the Pleasure naturally accompanying a long letter from you) affords me a new one, when I think it is a kind of symptom of the Recovery of your Health, & flatter myself that your bo:dily strength returns in proportion. pray do not forget to mention the Progress you make continually. as to Agrippina, I begin to be of your opinion, & find myself (as Women are of their children) less enamour'd of my Productions the older they grow. she is laid up to sleep, till next Summer: so bid her Good-night. I think you have tran:slated Tacitus very justly, that is freely, & accommodated his thoughts to the Turn & Genius of our Language: which at the same time I commend your Judgement, is no commendation of the English tongue, which is too diffuse, & daily grows more & more enervate, & one shall never be more sensible of this, than in turning an Author like Tacitus. I have been trying it in some parts of Thucydides (who has a little resemblance of him in his Conciseness) & endeavour'd to do it closely, but found it produced mere Nonsense. if you have any inclination to see what figure he makes in Italian, I have a Tuscan Translation of Davanzati, much-esteem'd in Italy, & will send you the same Speech you sent me: that is, if you care for it. in the mean time accept of Propertius.

Facsimile of Letter 105

Speech you sent me: that is, if you care for it. in the mean time
accept of Propertius.[4]

LIB: 2: ELEG: 1 :

To Mecænas

You ask, why thus my Loves I still rehearse?
Whence the soft Strain & ever-melting Verse?
From Cynthia all, that in my Numbers shines;
She is my Genius, she inspires the Lines,
No Phœbus else, no other Muse I know:
She tunes my easy Rhime, & gives the Lay to flow.
If the loose Curls around her Forehead play,
Or lawlefs o'er their Ivory Margin stray:
If the thin Coan Web her Shape reveal,
And half disclose the Limbs it should conceal.
Of those loose Curls, that ivory Front I write;
Of the dear Web whole Volumes I indite:
Or if to Musick she the Lyre awake,
That the soft Subject of my Song I make;
And sing, with what a carelefs Grace she flings
Her artful Hand acrofs the sounding Strings.
If sinking into Sleep she seem to close
Her languid Lids, I favour her Repose
With lulling Notes, & thousand Beauties see,
That Slumber brings to aid my Poetry.
When lefs averse, & yielding to Desires
She half accepts, & half rejects my Fires:
While to retain the envious Lawn she tries,
And struggles to elude my longing Eyes:
The fruitful Muse from that auspicious Night
Dates the long Iliad of the amorous Fight.
In brief whate'er she do, or say, or look
'Tis ample Matter for a Lover's Book
And many a copious Narrative you'll see,
Big with th' important Nothing's History.
    Yet would the Tyrant Love permit me raise
My feeble Voice to sing the Victor's Praise,
To paint the Hero's Toil, the Ranks of War,
The laurel'd Triumph, & the sculptured Car:
No Giant-Race, no Tumult of the Skies,

---

[4] A copy of this poem is in Gray's Commonplace-book with variants of
no great importance.

No Mountain-Structure in my Verse should rise;
No Tale of Thebes, or Ilium there should be,
Nor how the Persian trod th' indignant Sea,
Nor Marius' Cimbrian Wreaths would I relate,
Nor lofty Carthage struggleing with her Fate:
Here should Augustus great in Arms appear,
And thou, Mecænas, be my second Care:
Here Mutina from Flames & Famine free
And there th' ensanguin'd Wave of Sicily,
And sceptred Alexandria's captive Shore,
And sad Philippi red with Roman Gore.
Then, while the vaulted Skies loud Io's rend,
In golden Chains should loaded Monarchs bend;
And hoary Nile with pensive Aspect seem
To mourn the Glories of his sevenfold Stream:
The long-contended World's old Discords cease,
And Actium's Terrours grace the Pomp of Peace;
While Beaks, that late in fierce Encounter met,
Move thro' the sacred Way, & vainly threat.
Thee too the Muse should consecrate to Fame,
And with his Garlands weave thy ever-faithful Name.
But nor Callimachus' enervate Strain
May tell of Jove, & Phlegra's blasted Plain;
Nor I with unaccustom'd Vigour trace
Back to its Source divine the Julian Race.
Sailors to tell of Seas & Winds delight,
The Shepherd of his Flocks, the Soldier of the Fight,
A milder Warfare I in verse display,
Each in his proper Art should wast the Day:
Nor thou my gentle Calling disapprove,
To die is glorious in the Bed of Love.
Happy the Youth, & not unknown to Fame,
Whose heart has never felt a second Flame.
Oh, might that envied Happinefs be mine,
To Cynthia all my Wishes I confine
Or if, alas! it be my fate to try
Another Love, the quicker let me die.[5]

[5] This and the three preceding lines are Gray's adaptation of two lines,
which Scaliger took from another elegy (ii. 3, 45–6) and inserted in the
text of this elegy. He was followed by Broekhuyzen (see Letters 106, n. 2,
and 107, n. 2). The lines as printed by Scaliger are:
> His saltem ut tenear jam finibus: aut mihi siquis
> Venerit alter amor, acrius ut moriar.

But she, the Mistrefs of my Faithful Breast,
Has oft the Charms of Constancy confest,
Condemns her fickle Sex'es fond Mistake,
And hates the Tale of Troy for Helen's Sake.
Me from myself the soft Enchantrefs stole,
Ah, let her ever my Desires controul,
Or if I fall, the Victim of her Scorn,
From her loved Doors may my pale Coarse be born.
The Power of Herbs can other Harms remove,
And find a Cure for every Ill, but Love.
The Lemnian's Hurt Machaon could repair,
Heal the slow Chief, & send again to War.
To Chiron Phœnix owed his long-lost Sight,
And Phœbus' Son restored Androgeon to the Light.
Here Skill is vain, even Magick here must fail,
The powerful Mixture, & the Midnight Spell.
The Hand, that can my captive Heart release,
And to this Bosom give its wonted Peace,
May the long Thirst of Tantalus allay,
And drive th' infernal Vulture from his Prey.
For Ills unseen what remedy is found,
Or who can probe the undiscover'd Wound?
The Bed avails not, or the Leeche's care,
Nor changeing Skies can hurt, nor sultry Air,
'Tis hard th' elusive Symptoms to explore,
Today the Lover walks, tomorrow is no more:
A Train of mourning Friends attend his Pall,
And wonder at the sudden Funeral.
When then my Fates, that breath they gave, shall claim,
When the short Marble shall preserve a Name,
A little Verse, my All that shall remain;
Thy pafsing Courser's slacken'd Speed detain,
(Thou envied Honour of thy Poet's Days,
Of all our Youth th' Ambition & the Praise!)
Then to my quiet Urn awhile draw near,
And say, (while o'er the place you drop a Tear)
Love & the Fair were of his Life the Pride,
He lived, while She was kind, & when she frown'd, he died.
                                        Vale.

Addressed: To Richard West Esq, at David Mitchell's Esq of Popes near
Hatfield Hartfordshire   *Postmark:* 24 AP

106. WEST TO GRAY

Popes, May 5, 1742

WITHOUT any preface I come to your verses,[1] which I read over and over with excessive pleasure, and which are at least as good as Propertius. I am only sorry you follow the blunders of Broukhusius,[2] all whose insertions are nonsense. I have some objections to your antiquated words, and am also an enemy to Alexandrines; at least I do not like them in Elegy. I like your Elegy extremely, so extremely, that I long to shew you some little errors you are fallen into by following Broukhusius: for example, your thirty first lines are most intelligibly soft and pretty: but pray what sense do you affix to your six Broukhusian lines, that begin at happy youth and end at—let me die? * * *[3] Were I with you now, and Propertius with your verses lay upon the table between us, I could discuss this point in a moment; but there is nothing so tiresome as spinning out a criticism in a letter; doubts arise, and explanations follow, till there swells out at least a volume of undigested observations: and all because you are not with him whom you want to convince. Read only the letters between Pope and Cromwell[4] in proof of this; they dispute without end. Are you aware now that I have an interest all this while in banishing Criticism from our correspondence? Indeed I have; for I am going to write down a little Ode (if it deserves the name) for your perusal, which I am afraid will hardly stand that test. Nevertheless I leave you at your full liberty; so here it follows.

LETTER 106.—First printed in part (in a garbled text) in Mason's *Memoirs*, pp. 146–8.   [1] See Letter 105 *ad fin.*

[2] Jan van Broekhüyzen (1649–1707), Dutch classical scholar, published a critical edition of Propertius in 1702, and in the passage to which West refers followed Scaliger's text (see Letter 105, n. 5).

[3] This paragraph (from 'I like') is here printed from a fragment of the original formerly in the possession of Col. W. F. Prideaux, who published it in *Notes and Queries* (9th Ser. iv. 531–2). Mason omitted the latter half of the paragraph, and printed as the beginning: 'But, after all, I admire your translation so extremely, that I cannot help repeating I long to shew you some little errors' &c.; and he added the following note: 'I have omitted here a paragraph or two, in which different lines of the Elegy were quoted, because I had previously omitted the translation of it.'

[4] Henry Cromwell, a man about town, more than thirty years Pope's senior, with whom he corresponded between 1707 and 1711. *The Familiar Letters to Henry Cromwell* were published in 1726 (by Pope's own connivance, as was afterwards proved) by Edmund Curll, the bookseller (1675–1747).

ODE.

Dear Gray, that always in my heart
Possessest far the better part,
What mean these sudden blasts that rise
And drive the Zephyrs from the skies?
O join with mine thy tuneful lay,
And invocate the tardy May.

Come, fairest Nymph, resume thy reign!
Bring all the Graces in thy train!
With balmy breath, and flowery tread,
Rise from thy soft ambrosial bed;
Where, in elysian slumber bound,
Embow'ring myrtles veil thee round.

Awake, in all thy glories drest,
Recall the Zephyrs from the west;
Restore the sun, revive the skies,
At mine, and Nature's call, arise!
Great Nature's self upbraids thy stay,
And misses her accustom'd May.

See! all her works demand thy aid;
The labours of Pomona fade:
A plaint is heard from ev'ry tree;
Each budding flow'ret calls for thee;
The Birds forget to love and sing;
With storms alone the forests ring.

Come then, with Pleasure at thy side,
Diffuse thy vernal spirit wide;
Create, where'er thou turn'st thy eye,
Peace, Plenty, Love, and Harmony;
Till ev'ry being share its part,
And Heav'n and Earth be glad at heart.[5]

107. GRAY TO WEST

London, May 8, 1742.

I REJOICE to see you putting up your prayers to the May: She cannot choose but come at such a call. It is as light and genteel as herself. You bid me find fault; I am afraid I cannot;

[5] This text, as printed by Mason, does not give the original version sent by West, but a version, corrected and improved, probably by Gray. See Appendix C and cf. Letter 38. It was in reply to this Ode that Gray wrote his own *Ode on the Spring* (see Letter 125, n. 4).

however I will try. The first stanza (if what you say to me in it did not make me think it the best) I should call the worst of the five (except the fourth line). The two next are very picturesque, Miltonic, and musical; her bed is so soft and so snug that I long to lie with her. But those two lines 'Great Nature' are my favourites. The exclamation of the flowers is a little step too far.[1] The last stanza is full as good as the second and third; the last line bold, but I think not too bold. Now, as to myself and my translation, pray do not call names. I never saw Broukhusius in my life. It is Scaliger[2] who attempted to range Propertius in order; who was, and still is, in sad condition.* * *[3] You see, by what I sent you, that I converse, as usual, with none but the dead: They are my old friends, and almost make me long to be with them. You will not wonder therefore, that I, who live only in times past, am able to tell you no news of the present. I have finished the Peloponnesian war[4] much to my honour, and a tight conflict it was, I promise you. I have drank and sung with Anacreon for the last fortnight, and am now feeding sheep with Theocritus. Besides, to quit my figure, (because it is foolish) I have run over Pliny's Epistles and Martial ἐκ παρέργ8; not to mention Petrarch, who, by the way, is sometimes very tender and natural. I must needs tell you three lines in Anacreon, where the expreſsion seems to me inimitable. He is describing hair as he would have it painted.

> "Ελικας δ' ἐλευθέρ8s μοι
> Πλοκάμων ἄτακτα συνθεὶς
> 'Αφὲς ὡς θέλ8σι κεῖσθαι.[5]

Gueſs, too, where this is about a dimple.

> Sigilla in mento impreſsa Amoris digitulo
> Vestigio demonstrant mollitudinem.

LETTER 107.—First printed in Mason's *Memoirs*, pp. 148–50.
[1] See Appendix C.
[2] Joseph Justus Scaliger (1540–1609), the great scholar; he published an edition of Propertius in 1577. Gray was right in attributing the insertion to Scaliger (see Letter 105, n. 5).
[3] Here some criticism on the Elegy is omitted. *Mason.*
[4] In Thucydides.
[5] The passage occurs in Ode xxix: 'Setting in careless array the wanton tendrils of thy tresses, let them lie as they list.'

108. WEST TO GRAY

Popes, May 11, 1742.

YOUR fragment is in Aulus Gellius;[1] and both it and your Greek delicious. But why are you thus melancholy? I am so sorry for it, that you see I cannot forbear writing again the very first opportunity; though I have little to say, except to expostulate with you about it. I find you converse much with the dead, and I do not blame you for that; I converse with them too, though not indeed with the Greek. But I must condemn you for your longing to be with them. What, are there no joys among the living? I could almost cry out with Catullus[2] 'Alphene immemor, atque unanimis false sodalibus!' But to turn an accusation thus upon another, is ungenerous; so I will take my leave of you for the present with a 'Vale et vive paullisper cum vivis.'[3]

108.* Gray to Chute

[*c. 20 May, 1742*]

[In the letter to Chute of 24 May (Letter 109) Gray says: 'I had wrote to you but a few days ago.']

109. GRAY TO CHUTE

My Dear S^r

THREE Days ago, as I was in the Coffee-house very deep in Advertisements, a Servant came in, & waked me (as I thought) with the Name of Mr Chute, for half a minute I was not sure, but that it was You transported into England by some strange Chance the Lord knows how; till he brought me to a Coach that seem'd to have lost its way by looking for a Needle in a Bottle of Hay, in it was a Lady,[1] who said she was not You,

LETTER 108.—First printed in Mason's *Memoirs*, p. 150.

[1] Not in Aulus Gellius, but, as Mitford points out, in Nonius Marcellus. The passage occurs in the *Compendiosa Doctrina*, Lib. ii. *De Honeste sed Nove Dictis*: 'Mollitudinem, pro mollitiem. [2] xxx. 1.

[3] This is West's last extant letter; he died at Popes, near Hatfield, on the following 1 June. In Gray's Commonplace-book at Pembroke College, Cambridge, are transcripts of two translations from Catullus by West, to which Gray has appended the note: 'Fav: Wrote, May 11, 1742'. These translations (which are printed by Tovey in *Gray and his Friends*, pp. 167–8), doubtless accompanied the above letter, but were omitted by Mason, who must have omitted also a portion of the letter relating to them. It seems probable that there were other letters written by West before his death, which Mason did not print. See preliminary note to Letter 110, and Letter 131, n. 16.

LETTER 109.—First printed by Mitford in *Works of Gray* (1835–43), vol. ii, pp. 183–8; now reprinted from original.

[1] Perhaps Chute's sister-in-law, Mrs. Francis Chute (see Letter 122, n. 8).

but only a near relation, & was so good to give me a Letter, with which I return'd to my Den in order to prey upon it. I had wrote to you but a few days ago,[2] & am glad of so good an Excuse to do it again, wch I may the better do, as my last was all out, & nothing to the Purpose, being design'd for a certain Mr Chute at Rome, & not him at Florence.

I learn from it that I have been somewhat smarter, than I ought, but (to shew you with how little Malice) I protest I have not the least Idea what it was: my Memory would be better, did I read my own Letters so often, as I do yours. you must attribute it to a sort of kittenish Disposition, that scratches, where it means to carefs; however I don't repent neither; if 'tis that, has made you write. I know, I need not ask pardon, for you have forgiven me: nay, I have a good Mind to complain myself. how could you say, that I design'd to hurt you, because I knew you could feel? I hate the thoughts of it, & would not for the world wound any thing, that was sensible. 'tis true, I should be glad to scratch the Carelefs, or the Foolish, but no armour is so impenetrable, as Indifference & Stupidity, and so I may keep my Claws to myself. for another Instance of the shortnefs of my Memory would you believe, I have so little knowledge of the Florentine History, as not to guefs, who the Lady-Errant is you mention? sure it can't be the R:^di 3 & her faithful Swain, or may be M. G:^di 4 & the little Abbé. what you do there so long, I have no Conception. if you stay at other Places in proportion, I despair of ever seeing you again. 'tis true indeed Mr Mann is not every where. I am shock'd to think of his Sufferings,[5] but he of all Men was born to suffer with a good Grace. he is a Stoick without knowing it, & seems to think Pain a Pleasure: I am very sorry to complement him upon such an Occasion, & wish with all my Heart he were not so pleased. I much fear his Books are gone already; but if not, to be sure he shall have Middleton,[6] & the Sofa.[7] it seems most people here are not

---

[2] The letter is not extant (see Letter 108*).

[3] The Marchesa Riccardi. Walpole, in his letter to Mann of 15 July 1745, speaks of having received many civilities from her at Florence.

[4] Mann, in a letter to Walpole of 17 Sept. 1741, in an account of the dismissal of certain *cicisbeos* by their mistresses, says: 'Madame Gondi has turned off the poor pale-faced Abbé'.   [5] See Letter 98, n. 2.

[6] Conyers Middleton's *History of the Life of M. Tullius Cicero*, 2 vols., 4to, was published by subscription in 1741. It was reprinted in 3 vols. 8vo in 1742, and this edition was sent to Mann (see Letter 112, n. 22).

[7] *Le Sopha, Conte moral*, by Crébillon fils, published in 1740. In the post-

such admirers of it, as I was: but I won't give up an inch of it for all that. did I tell you about Mr Garrick,[8] that the Town are horn-mad after; there are a dozen Dukes of a night at Goodmans-fields[9] sometimes, & yet I am stiff in the opposition.[10] our fifth Opera was the Olympiade,[11] in which they retain'd most of Pergolesi's[12] Songs. & yet 'tis gone already, as if it had been a poor thing of Galuppi's.[13] two nights did I enjoy it all alone, snugg in a Nook in the Gallery, but found no one in those regions had ever heard of Pergolesi, nay, I heard several affirm it was a Composition of Pescetti's:[14] now there is a 6th sprung up by the name of Cefalo & Procri.[15] my Lady of Queensbury[16]

script to his letter to Mann of 11 Feb. 1742 Walpole writes: 'We have at last got Crébillon's *Sofa*: Lord Chesterfield received three hundred, and gave them to be sold at White's. It is admirable! except the beginning of the first volume, and the last story, it is equal to anything he has written.'

[8] David Garrick on 19 Oct. 1741 made his famous appearance at Goodman's Fields in the part of Richard III, which at once established his reputation—'the patent houses were deserted, and a string of carriages thronged the route from Temple Bar to Goodman's Fields' (*D.N.B.*).

[9] Goodman's Fields was a large open space lying between the Minories and Church Lane, Whitechapel; the theatre was in what is now Great Alie Street. (Wheatley's *London*.)

[10] Walpole, writing to Mann two days later, expresses the like opinion: 'All the run is now after Garrick, a wine-merchant, who is turned player, at Goodman's Fields. He plays all parts, and is a very good mimic. His acting I have seen, and may say to you, who will not tell it again here, I see nothing wonderful in it; but it is heresy to say so: the Duke of Argyll says, he is superior to Betterton.'

[11] The *Olimpiade* was an opera of Metastasio's written to celebrate the birthday of the Empress Elizabeth, wife of the Emperor Charles VI, in 1733. It was first performed in London at the King's Theatre, on 20 April 1742, the music being a pasticcio, mostly by Pergolesi, but partly by D. Scarlatti and others.

[12] Giovanni Battista Pergolesi (1710–36), a native of Jesi; the year before his death he composed the *Olimpiade*, 'the music of which was in his happiest vein', for performance in Rome, where it was a complete failure. His last work was the celebrated *Stabat Mater* (see Letter 214, n. 21).

[13] Baldassare Galuppi (1706–85), a Venetian; he composed upwards of fifty operas.

[14] Giovanni Battista Pescetti (*c.* 1704–*c.* 1766), native of Venice, where he died; he spent some years in England, being director of Covent Garden in 1739, and of the Haymarket in 1740. Walpole mentions a new opera of his in his letter to Mann of 22 Jan. 1742.

[15] The name of the composer of this opera, which was only performed three times, is unknown. The music was not printed, and the libretto apparently has not survived.

[16] Lady Catherine Hyde (1701–77), second daughter of fourth Earl of

is come out against my Lady of Marlborough;[17] & she has her Spirit too, & her Originality, but more of the Woman, I think, than t'other; as to the Facts it don't signify two pence, who's in the right; the manner of fighting, & character of the Combatants is all: 'tis hoped old Sarah will at her again. a Play of Mr Glover's,[18] I am told, is prepareing for the stage call'd Boadicea:[19] it is a fine Subject, but I have not an extreme Opinion of him. the Invalides at Chelsea intend to present Ranelagh-Gardens,[20] as a Nusance,[20a] for breaking their first Sleep with the sound of Fiddles: it opens, I think, tonight.[21] Mefsieurs the Commons are to ballot for 7 Persons tomorrow, commifsion'd to state the publick accounts, & they are to be such, who have no places, nor are anyways dependent on the King. the Committee have petition'd for all Papers relateing to the Convention:[22] a bill has pafs'd the lower House for indemnifying all, who might subject themselves to Penalties by revealing any transaction with regard to the Conduct of My Ld Orford,[23] & tomorrow the Lords are summon'd about it.[24]

Clarendon, and wife (1720) of Charles Douglas, third Duke of Queensberry; noted for her beauty (which she retained till her death), her wit, and her eccentricities. She was the 'Kitty' of Prior's *Female Phaëton*, to which Walpole added a stanza (see his letter to Mann of 26 April 1771).

[17] Sarah Jennings (d. 1744), widow (at this time eighty-two) of John Churchill, first Duke of Marlborough. She had just published her *Memoirs* in the shape of *An Account of the Conduct of the Dowager Duchess of Marlborough, From her first coming to Court, To the Year 1710. In a Letter from Herself to My Lord ——*, which provoked numerous pamphlets in reply, one of which presumably emanated from the Duchess of Queensberry.

[18] Richard Glover (1712–85), best known as the author of *Leonidas*.

[19] It was not till December 1753 that *Boadicea* appeared, when it was performed for nine nights at Drury Lane, two editions of it being published by Dodsley in the same month.

[20] So called from the ground on which they were laid out having been the property of the first Earl of Ranelagh; they were close to Chelsea Hospital, the present gardens of which are (in part) on the site.

[20a] 'To present as a nuisance' is to lay an information against someone for allowing a public nuisance (*O.E.D.*).

[21] Walpole (who, of course, uses old style) writes to Mann on 26 May 1742: 'Two nights ago Ranelagh Gardens were opened at Chelsea'; the date of this letter consequently is fixed as 24 May 1742, O.S. (See n. 35.)

[22] This was the Convention of Madrid with Spain, signed on 14 Jan. 1739; it had been debated in the Commons in the following March, when Walpole's majority fell to 28.

[23] Sir Robert Walpole had been created Earl of Orford on 9 Feb. of this year.

[24] The Indemnity Bill was passed in the Commons on 13 May but was thrown out in the Lords by a large majority on 25 May (see Walpole to Mann, 13 and 26 May 1742).

the Wit of the times consists in Satyrical Prints, I believe, there
have been some Hundreds within this Month; if you have any
hopeful young Designer of Caricaturas, that has a political
Turn, he may pick up a pretty Subsistance here: let him paſs
thro' Holland to improve his Taste by the way. we are all very
sorry for poor Queen Hungary;[25] but we know of a second
Battle (wᶜʰ perhaps you may never hear off, but from me) as
how Prince Lobbycock[26] came up in the Nick of Time, & cut
120,000 of 'em all to pieces, & how the King of Pruſsia narrowly
scaped aboard a Ship, & so got down the Dannub to Wolf-in-
Bottle,[27] where Mʳ Mallyboyce[28] lay incamp'd, & how the
Hannoverians with Prince Hissy-Castle[29] at their head, fell upon
the French Mounseers, & took him away with all his Treasure,
among which is Pitt's Diamond,[30] & the Great Cistern.[31] all this

[25] Maria Theresa had been proclaimed Queen of Hungary in June of the
previous year; the Austrians under Prince Charles of Lorraine had just
been defeated at Chotusitz by Frederick the Great (17 May).
[26] That is, the Austrian general, Prince George Christian Lobkowitz
(1702–53).   [27] Wolfenbüttel, about ten miles south of Brunswick.
[28] Jean Baptista François Desmarets (1682–1762), Marquis de Maillebois,
Maréchal de France.
[29] Frederick, Hereditary Prince, afterwards (1760) Landgrave of Hesse-
Cassel; he married, in 1740, Mary, fourth daughter of George II, and died in
1785. He had recently been appointed Generalissimo of the allied forces
(see Walpole to Mann, 25 Feb. 1742).
[30] A diamond weighing 410 carats, which had been bought in India in
1701 for £20,400 by Thomas Pitt (grandfather of the Earl of Chatham), then
Governor of Madras, and sold by him in 1717 to the Regent Duc d'Orléans,
on behalf of Louis XV, for £135,000. Some incidents in the previous history
of the diamond suggested Pope's lines:

> Asleep and naked as an Indian lay,
> An honest factor stole a gem away;
> He pledg'd it to the knight: the knight had wit,
> So kept the di'mond, and the rogue was bit.

('Moral Essays Epist. to Lord Bathurst', ll. 361–4), the last line of which
originally ended 'and was rich as Pitt'. Gray refers to the Pitt diamond
again in connexion with Pitt's acceptance of a pension in 1761 (see Letters
346 and 353).
[31] The Great Cistern was made by Charles Kandler from a design by
Henry Jernegan in 1734–5. It was too big to find a private purchaser and
a Government lottery was held to dispose of it, the profits being devoted
to the fund for building Westminster Bridge. It passed into the possession
of the Tsar (see W. J. Cripps, *Old English Plate*, sixth edition, p. 344).
Cisterns (of silver, copper, or pewter) used to be part of the outfit of a
dining-room, being used apparently for rinsing plates, forks, &c., during a
meal.

is firmly believed here, & a vast deal more; upon the Strength of which we intend to declare War with France.

You are so obligeing as to put me in mind of our last Years little expeditions;[31a] alas! S[r], they are past, & how many Years will it be, at the rate you go on, before we can pofsibly renew them in this Country? in all probability I shall be gone first on a long Expedition to that undiscover'd Country, from whose bourn no Traveller returns; however (if I can) I will think of you, as I sail down the *River of Eternity*. I can't help thinking, that I should find no difference almost between this world & t'other (for I converse with none but the dead here) only indeed I should receive, nor write no more Letters (for the Post is not very well regulated) if you see the King of Naples, pray talk with him on this Subject, for I see he is upon Settleing one between his country & Constantinople, & I take this to be but a little more difficult.

My Dab of Musick & Prints you are very good to think of sending with your own; to which I will add a farther Trouble by desireing you to send me some of the Roots of a certain Flower, w[ch] I have seen at Florence, it is a huge white Hyacynth tinged with Pink (M[r] M: knows what I mean, by that same token that they grow sometimes in the fat Gerina's [32] *Boosom*) I mean, if they bear a reasonable Price, w[ch] you will judge of for me: but don't give yourself any pains about[33] it, for if they are not easily had, & at an easy Rate, I am not at all eager for them: do you talk of *strumming*? ohime! who have not seen the face of a *Haspical*,[34] since I came home; no; I have hanged up my Harp on the Willows; however I look at my Musick now & then, that I may not forget it, for when you return, I intend to sing a Song of Thanksgiving & praise the Lord with a chearful Noise of many-stringed Instruments. Adieu! dear S[r], I am sincerely Yours
                                                                                          T G:

[May 24 O:S: 1742][35] London. Not forgetting my Kifs Hands to
  Mr Whithed[36]

Addressed :[37] A Monsieur Mons:[r] Chute Gentilhomme Anglois chez Mons:[r] Mann, Resident de Sa Majesté Britannique a la Cour Toscane Florence Par Hollande

  [31a] See Appendix D.
  [32] This was no doubt the 'Madame Gerini, a good fat creature', of Mann's letter to Walpole of 12 Aug. 1742.
  [33] From this point to the end of the letter is in another hand, a note intimating that 'the centre of this page is torn and lost, but 'tis copied below'.

110. GRAY TO WEST

London, May 27, 1742.

MINE, you are to know, is a white Melancholy, or rather Leucocholy for the most part; which though it seldom laughs or dances, nor ever amounts to what one calls Joy or Pleasure, yet is a good easy sort of a state, and ça ne laiſse que de s'amuser. The only fault of it is insipidity; which is apt now and then to give a sort of Ennui, which makes one form certain little wishes that signify nothing. But there is another sort, black indeed, which I have now and then felt, that has somewhat in it like Tertullian's rule of faith, Credo quia impoſsibile est; for it believes, nay, is sure of every thing that is unlikely, so it be but frightful; and, on the other hand, excludes and shuts its eyes to the most poſsible hopes, and every thing that is pleasurable; from this the Lord deliver us! for none but he and sunshiny weather can do it. In hopes of enjoying this kind of

34 Corruption of harpsichord. Goldsmith, thirty years later, in *She Stoops to Conquer* (Act iv), makes Tony Lumpkin speak of 'the haspicholls'.

35 The copy has 'March O.S. London'. This is obviously wrong as Gray's reference to the opening of Ranelagh Gardens 'tonight' fixes the date as 24 May 1742, O.S. (see n. 21).

36 Francis Whithed (1719–51), of Southwick Park, near Fareham, in Hampshire; his name was originally Thistlethwayte, but he had taken that of Whithed on succeeding to the estate of an uncle. Walpole and Gray had made his acquaintance and that of his cousin, John Chute, at Florence in 1740. He returned to England with Chute in September 1746, and entered Parliament in the following July as member for Southampton county. He died at the Vyne in March 1751 to the great grief of Chute, who regarded him almost as a son. Gray was at Venice with Chute and Whithed after he parted from Walpole at Reggio in 1741.

37 The address has been cut off; it is now copied from the cover, which was found in the hands of a bookseller.

LETTER 110.—First printed in Mason's *Memoirs*, pp. 151–5. It seems likely that in this instance, as in many others, Mason has combined parts of two or more letters. Gray and West were exchanging letters in April at intervals of three or four days; and so they continued to do at the beginning of May. But after West's letter of 11 May (Letter 108) Mason prints what professes to be Gray's reply, and dates it 27 May. The gap of sixteen days is unlikely; it is probable that other letters were written by both Gray and West in the interval, and it may be conjectured that Mason has combined part of a letter of Gray's about 15 May, referring to his melancholy, written in answer to West's letter, and parts of one or more later letters, one of which may have been written on 27 May; Gray says that he is going into the country, and there is other evidence (see the postscript to Letter 111) that it was about this date that he went to Stoke.

weather, I am going into the country[1] for a few weeks, but shall be never the nearer any society; so, if you have any charity, you will continue to write. My life is like Harry the fourth's supper of Hens. 'Poulets a la broche, Poulets en Ragôut, Poulets en Hâchis, Poulets en Fricasées.'[2] Reading here, Reading there; nothing but books with different sauces. Do not let me lose my desert then; for though that be Reading too, yet it has a very different flavour. The May seems to be come since your invitation; and I propose to bask in her beams and drefs me in her roses.

Et Caput in vernâ semper habere rosâ.[3]

I shall see Mr. * * and his Wife, nay, and his Child too, for he has got a Boy. Is it not odd to consider one's Cotemporaries in the grave light of Husband and Father? There is my Lords * * and * * *, they are Statesmen:[4] Do not you remember them dirty boys playing at cricket? As for me, I am never a bit the older, nor the bigger, nor the wiser than I was then: No, not for having been beyond sea. Pray how are you?

I send you an inscription for a wood joining to a park of mine; (it is on the confines of Mount Cithæron, on the left hand as you go to Thebes) you know I am no friend to hunters, and hate to be disturbed by their noise.

᾿Αζόμενος πολυθήρον ἐκηβόλȣ ἄλσος ἀνάσσας
τᾶς δεινᾶς τεμένη λεῖπε, κυναγὲ, θεᾶς

[1] Upon a visit to his relations at Stoke. *Mason.*—Gray's uncle, Jonathan Rogers (see Letter 26, n. 3), was then residing at West End Cottage, Stoke, where, sometime after his death in October 1742, Mrs. Gray and her sister, Mary Antrobus, retired to live with his widow. The house, much enlarged and altered, is now known as Stoke Court.

[2] Gray here associates with Henry IV of France a story of which there are several well-known variants. One of these is given by Boccaccio in the *Decameron* (i. 5), where it is related how the Marchioness of Monferrato entertained the King of France at a supper which consisted of nothing but chicken served in various ways. Another form of the story gave rise to the proverbial expression 'toujours perdrix'. (See *Notes and Queries*, 11th Ser. x. 194, 236.)

[3] Propertius, 3 *Eleg.* iii. 44.

[4] Lord Sandwich, Lord Halifax. Qr. both at Eton in mine and Mr. Gray's time, and early in the Ministry. *Cole.* (MS. note quoted by Mitford, 1835–43, vol. i, p. cvi)—John Montagu (1718–92), fourth Earl of Sandwich; and George Montagu Dunk (1716–71), second Earl of Halifax. Neither of them had held office at the date of Gray's letter.

Μᾰνοι ἄρ ἔνθα κύνων ζαθέων κλαγγεῦσιν ὑλαγμοὶ,
ἀνταχεῖς Νυμφᾶν ἀγροτερᾶν κελάδῳ.

Here follows also the beginning of an Heroic Epistle; but you must give me leave to tell my own story first, because Historians differ. Mafsinifsa was the son of Gala King of the Mafsyli; and, when very young at the head of his father's army, gave a most signal overthrow to Syphax, King of the Masæsylians, then an ally of the Romans. Soon after Asdrubal, son of Gisgo the Carthaginian General, gave the beautiful Sophonisba, his daughter, in marriage to the young prince. But this marriage was not consummated on account of Mafsinifsa's being obliged to hasten into Spain, there to command his father's troops, who were auxiliaries of the Carthaginians. Their affairs at this time began to be in a bad condition; and they thought it might be greatly for their interest, if they could bring over Syphax to themselves. This in time they actually effected; and to strengthen their new alliance, commanded Asdrubal to give his daughter to Syphax. (It is probable their ingratitude to Mafsinifsa arose from the great change of affairs, which had happened among the Mafsylians during his absence; for his father and uncle were dead, and a distant relation of the royal family had usurped the throne.) Sophonisba was accordingly married to Syphax: and Mafsinifsa, enraged at the affront, became a friend to the Romans. They drove the Carthaginians before them out of Spain, and carried the war into Africa, defeated Syphax, and took him prisoner; upon which Cirtha (his capital) opened her gates to Lælius and Mafsinifsa. The rest of the affair, the marriage, and the sending of poison, every body knows.[5] This is partly taken from Livy,[6] and partly from Appian.[7]

SOPHONISBA MASSINISSÆ.

EPISTOLA.

Egregium accipio promifsi Munus amoris,
    Inque manu mortem jam fruitura fero:
Atque utinam citius mandafses, luce vel unâ;
    Transieram Stygios non inhonesta lacus.

---

[5] Masinissa married Sophonisba, but the Romans demanded her surrender; whereupon Masinissa, to spare her the humiliation of captivity, sent her a bowl of poison with which she put an end to her life.

[6] Livy, xxix. 23; xxx. 3–15.   [7] *Pun.* 10, 27, 28.

Victoris nec pafsa toros, nova nupta, mariti,
  Nec fueram fastus, Roma superba, tuos.
Scilicet hæc partem tibi, Mafsinifsa, triumphi
  Detractam, hæc pompæ jura minora suæ
Imputat, atque uxor quod non tua prefsa catenis,
  Objecta & sævæ plausibus urbis eo:
Quin tu pro tantis cepisti præmia factis,
  Magnum Romanæ pignus amicitiæ!
Scipiadæ excuses, oro, si tardius utar
  Munere. Non nimiùm vivere, crede, velim.
Parva mora est, breve sed tempus mea fama requirit:
  Detinet hæc animam cura suprema meam.
Quæ patriæ prodefse meæ Regina ferebar,
  Inter Elisæas gloria prima nurus,
Ne videar flammæ nimis indulsifse secundæ,
  Vel nimis hostiles extimuifse manus.
Fortunam atque annos liceat revocare priores,
  Gaudiaque heu! quantis nostra repensa malis.
Primitiasne tuas meministi atque arma Syphacis
  Fusa, & per Tyrias ducta trophæa vias?
(Laudis at antiquæ forsan meminifse pigebit,
  Quodque decus quondam causa ruboris erit.)
Tempus ego certe memini, felicia Pœnis
  Quo te non puduit solvere vota deis;
Mæniaque intrantem vidi: longo agmine duxit
  Turba salutantum, purpureique patres.
Fæminea ante omnes longe admiratur euntem
  Hæret & aspectu tota caterva tuo.
Jam flexi, regale decus, per colla capilli,
  Jam decet ardenti fuscus in ore color!
Commendat frontis generosa modestia formam,
  Seque cupit laudi surripuifse suæ.
Prima genas tenui signat vix flore juventas,
  Et dextræ soli credimus efse virum.
Dum faciles gradiens oculos per singula jactas,
  (Seu rexit casus lumina, sive Venus)
In me (vel certè visum est) conversa morari
  Sensi; virgineus perculit ora pudor.
Nescio quid vultum molle spirare tuendo,
  Credideramque tuos lentius ire pedes.
Quærebam, juxta æqualis si dignior efset,
  Quæ poterat visus detinuifse tuos:

Nulla fuit circum æqualis quæ dignior efset,
   Afseruitque decus conscia forma suum.
Pompæ finis erat. Totâ vix nocte quievi:
   Sin premat invitæ lumina victa sopor,
Somnus habet pompas, eademque recursat imago;
   Atque iterum hesterno munere victor ades.

            *   *   *   *8

110*. Gray to West

[*c. June 3, 1742*]

[In his letter to Ashton of 17 June 1742 (Letter 111) Gray mentions having received back unopened a letter he had recently written to West, which was the first intimation he had of West's death. This letter doubtless accompanied the *Ode on the Spring* (see Letter 125, n. 4).]

111. GRAY TO ASHTON

My dear Ashton,

THIS melancholy day is the first that I have had any notice of my Lofs in poor West, and that only by so unexpected a Means as some Verses publishd in a Newspaper (they are fine & true & I believe may be your own).¹ I had indeed some reason to suspect it some days since from receiving a letter of my own² to him sent back unopen'd. The stupid People had put it no Cover, nor thought it worth while to write one Line to inform me of the reason, tho' by knowing how to direct, they must imagine I was his friend. I am a fool indeed to be surprizd at meeting with Brutishnefs or want of Thought among Mankind; what I would desire is, that you would have the goodnefs

---

⁸ It seems much to be regretted that the author did not finish this poem. But I believe he never proceeded further with it. *Mason.*—Mitford, who prints this poem in his *Works of Thomas Gray*, 1835–43, vol. i, pp. 200–4, draws attention to the numerous classical reminiscences throughout the piece. He also remarks upon Gray's metrical irregularities.

LETTER 111.—First printed by Tovey in *Gray and his Friends*, pp. 170–1; reprinted by Toynbee (1915), No. 153, from Mitford's transcript.

¹ A copy of the lines by Ashton was enclosed by Walpole in a letter to Mann at the beginning of July (see Mrs. Toynbee's *Letters of Horace Walpole*, vol. i, p. 248). A slightly different version is printed by Tovey (*op. cit.*, pp. 171–2) from a transcript by Gray in his Commonplace-book.

² See Letter 110*.

to tell me, what you know of his death, more particularly as soon as you have any Leisure; my own Sorrow does not make me insensible to your new Happinefs,[3] which I heartily congratulate you upon, as the means of Quiet, and Independence, & the Power of exprefsing your benevolence to those you love. neither my Misfortune, nor my joy shall detain you longer at a time, when doubtlefs you are a good deal employd; only believe me sincerely yours

T. GRAY.

P.S. Pray do not forget my impatience,—especially if you do not happen to be in London. I have no one to enquire of but yourself. 'tis now three weeks, that I have been in the Country, but shall return to Town in 2 days.

June 17——Stoke. 1742.

112. GRAY TO CHUTE AND MANN

*   *   *   *   *

*   *   *   *   *

*   *   *   *   *[1]

Jews-Harp. ask Mr Whithed, whither when he goes to Heaven, he does not expect to see all his favourite Hens, all his dear little Pouts,[2] untimely Victims of the Pot & the Spit, come pipping & gobbling in a melodious Voice about him. I know, he does, there's nothing so natural. Poor Conti![3] is he going to be a Cherub? I remember here (but he was not ripe then) he had a very promiseing Squeak with him, & that his Mouth, when open, made an exact Square.[4] I have never been at Ranelagh Gardens since they were open'd[5] (for what does it signify to me?) but they do not succeed. People see it once or twice & so they go to Vaux-Hall. well, but is not it a very

---

[3] This presumably refers to Ashton's nomination to the Crown living of Aldingham, in North Lancashire, as the result of an application by Walpole to Henry Pelham on Ashton's behalf (see his letter to Pelham of 17 May 1742).

LETTER 112.—First printed by Mitford in *Works of Gray* (1835–43), vol. ii, pp. 176–80; now reprinted from original.

[1] The first half-sheet of the letter has been torn off and lost.

[2] Pouts or Poults are young birds. See Letter 124, n. 5.

[3] See Letter 24, n. 4.

[4] See Letter 24, n. 5.

[5] 24 May of this year (1742)—see Letter 109, n. 21.

great Design, very new, finely lighted? well, yes, aye, very
fine truly; & so they yawn, & go to Vaux-Hall. & then it's
too hot, & then it's too cold, & here's a Wind, & there's a
Damp; & so the Women go to Bed, & the Men to a Bawdy[6]-
House. you are to take Notice, that in our Country Delicacy
& Indelicacy amount to much the same thing, the first will not
be pleased with any Thing, & the other cannot: however to
do us Justice, I think, we are a reasonable, but by no means
a pleasurable People, & to mend us we must have a Dash of
the French, & Italian. yet I don't know how, Travelling does
not produce its right Effect—I find, I am talking; but You
are to attribute it to my haveing at last found a Pen, that
writes.

You are so good, 'tis a shame to scold at you, but you never
till now certified me, that you were at Casa Ambrosio.[7] I did
not know in what Light to consider you. I had an Idea, but did
not know wherc to put it, for an Idea must have a Place per
campeggiar bene. You were an Intaglia[8] unset, a Picture without a Frame. but now all is well; tho' I am not very sure yet,
whither you are above Stairs, or on the Ground-floor; but by
your mentioning the Terrazzino,[9] it must be the latter. do the
Frogs of Arno sing as sweetly, as they did in my Days? do you
sup al fresco? Have you a Mugherino[10] Tree & a *Nanny*? I fear,
I don't spell this last Word right: pray, ask M[r] M.; oh dear!
I fear I am a Blunderer about Hyacynths,[11] for to be sure, they
can't be taken out of the Ground till they have done blooming,
& they are perhaps just now in Flower. that you may know my
Place,[12] I am just going into the Country[13] for one easy fortnight,
& then in earnest intend to go to Cambridge to Trinity Hall.[14]

---

[6] This word is scored through, but is still legible.
[7] Apparently Chute was not living with Mann in the Casa Manetti (see
Letter 90, n. 7), but had quarters of his own in the Casa Ambrosio.
[8] *Sic.*
[9] Chute dates a letter to Walpole on 24 June of this year from 'Charming
Terrazzino, Casa Ambrosio, Florence'.
[10] *Jasminum sambac*, the Arabian sweet-scented white jasmine. 'Nanny'
may possibly have been a nickname for a housekeeper. (So Walpole called
his housekeeper at Strawberry Hill.) [11] See Letter 109.
[12] See above: 'an Idea must have a Place per campeggiar bene'.
[13] No doubt to Stoke, where he had been in June (see Letter 111).
[14] Gray had left Cambridge in Sept. 1738; he was now about to return for
the purpose of taking a degree in law (see Appendix F). The intention
here expressed of going to Trinity Hall (a college founded especially for
the study of law) was not carried out, as he went back to Peterhouse.

my sole Reason (as you know) is to look, as if[14a]—and when I feel
it go against my Stomach, I remember it was Your Prescription, and so it goes down: look upon me then, my Dear S^r, in
my proper Light, & consider how necefsary it is to me to hear
from You, as often as you can bestow an Hour upon me; I
flatter myself, your Kindnefs will try to get the better of your
Indolence, when you reflect how cruelly alone I must be in the
midst of that Crowd!

   The Remainder of this Page I hope you will pardon me, if I
dedicate to my good Mr Mann. S^r, I had the pleasure of receive-
ing Your good dear Letter, & only defer'd thanking You till
now, that I might be able to execute your little Commifsion
first, the Contents of which I send to your Brother[15] along with
this Letter. but first let me enquire, how you do. alas! S^r, you
may call 'em, Benevoli, or whatever soft Names you please, but
I much fear they don't understand their businefs like our people
with a thousand Consonants. I perfectly believe Dr Cocchi's[16]
good Intentions, but he is not the Executioner himself, & here
it is not sufficient to wish well; if it were I'm sure my Wishes are
fervent enough to be felt even at Florence in spight of all the
Lakes,[17] & Seas, & Enemies, that lie betwixt us. they are daily
employ'd for your Happinefs, & will, I hope, be of more Use to
You, than they have been to myself. the Books, I send you, are
the Etat de la France,[18] 3 Vol: Fol:° upon my Word an excellent
book. he is a sensible, knowing, Englishman, only had the
Misfortune to be born in France. Life of Mahomet,[19] by the
same Author, it is famous: you are desired to make no reflections, nor draw Consequences, when you read it. Ld Burleigh's
Papers[20]—seem very curious, & well enough chose. by the way,

[14a] Gray means that he wished to look as if he were preparing for the legal
profession, although he had no intention of following it. See Mason, *Memoirs*,
p. 120 (quoted in Appendix F). He must have discussed his plans, when he
was with Chute a year before.
[15] Galfridus (see Letter 99, n. 3).
[16] Mann's two physicians (see Letter 99, nn. 6, 7).
[17] The original word has been almost obliterated, and 'Lakes' has been
written in above it by a later hand; from the faint indications still remaining this, and not 'Lands', seems to be what Gray wrote.
[18] *État de la France, dans lequel on voit tout ce qui regarde le gouvernement
ecclésiastique, politique, etc.* The author was Henri de Boulainvilliers, Comte
de Saint-Saire, a voluminous writer, commonly known as the Comte de
Boulainvilliers (1658–1722).
[19] An 8vo edition of his *Vie de Mahomed* was published in London in 1730.
[20] The first instalment of the *Collection of State Papers* of William Cecil

they have lately publish'd Thurlow's Papers[21] here in 7 Vol: folio, out of which it would be hard to collect a Pocket-Volume worth haveing. Dr Middleton's Cicero, 3 Vol:[22] & a Letter on the Catholick Religion[23] worth your reading. Philip de Comines, 5 Vol:[24] the Louvre Edition[25] is much more splendid, but wants the Supplement, & Notes, wch are here. W:^{n} on the M:^{s} [26] a very impudent fellow: his Dedications will make you laugh. Ludlow's Memoirs, 3 Vol:[27] as unorthodox in Politics, as the other in Religion. 2 lyttel Bookys tocheing Kyng James, the fyrst: very rare . .[28] Le Sopha,[29] de Crebillon—Collect: of Plays,[30] 10 Vol: there are none of Shakespear, because you had better have all his Works together.—they come to about £7 18s. 6d. the whole Cargo. you will find among them 3 Parts of Marianne,[31] for Mr Chute. if he has them already, how can

(1520–98), Lord Burghley, Queen Elizabeth's famous Secretary of State, covering the period 1541–70, which was edited by Samuel Haynes (Lond., fol., 1740).

[21] A *Collection of State Papers* of John Thurloe (1616–68), Cromwell's Secretary of State, edited, with Life, by Thomas Birch (Lond., 7 vols., fol., 1742).

[22] See Letter 109, n. 6.

[23] A fourth edition of his *Letter from Rome, showing an Exact Conformity between Popery and Paganism*, first published in 1729, had been issued, with the addition of a Prefatory Discourse and Postscript, in 1741.

[24] Philippe de Commynes (c. 1445–c. 1511), author of *Mémoires*, in two parts, covering the years 1464–83, and 1494–5. Gray refers probably to the Brussels edition of 1723 in 5 vols., 8vo, comprising the additions.

[25] Edited by Denys Godefroy, and printed at the Imprimerie Royale du Louvre, Paris, 1649, one vol., fol.

[26] *Six Discourses on the Miracles, and two Defences of them*, by Thomas Woolston (Lond., 2 vols., 8vo, 1727–30). Each of the *Discourses* had a dedication, satirical or impudent, addressed to one of the Bishops: the first *Defence of His Discourses* had a comic dedication to the Queen, the second, which was dedicated to the Lord Chief Justice, is not obviously satirical.

[27] *Memoirs, with a Collection of original Papers* of Edmund Ludlow (c. 1617–92), the regicide (Vevay, 3 vols., 8vo, 1698–9; and Lond., 1721–2).

[28] Mitford suggests that these may be Sir Anthony Weldon's *Court and Character of K. James, written and taken by Sir A. W. being an Eye and Eare Witnesse* (Lond., 12mo, 1650), and Sir William Sanderson's *Aulicus Coquinariae, or a Vindication in Answer to a Pamphlet entitled 'The Court and Character of King James'* (Lond., 12mo, 1650).

[29] See Letter 109, n. 7.

[30] Probably a miscellaneous assortment of plays.

[31] *La Vie de Marianne, ou les Avantures de Madame la Comtesse de * * **. Par Monsieur de Marivaux (see Letter 103, n. 5), appeared in 12 *Parties* between 1731 and 1743.

I help it? why would he make no mention of Mad:^lle de Thevire³² to me?

And now let me congratulate you, as no longer a Min:³³ but, far del Mondo!³⁴ veramente un Ministrone,³⁵ & King of the Mediterranean. pray your Majesty, give Orders to your Men of War, if they touch at Naples, to take care of the Parma Collection,³⁶ & be sure, don't let them bombard Genoa. if you can bully the Pope out of the Apollo Belvedere, well & good: I'm not against it. I'm enchanted with your good Sister, the Queen of Hungary;³⁷ as old as I am, I could almost fight for her myself. see what it is to be happy; every body will fight for those, that have no occasion for them. pray, take care to continue so; but whither you do, or not, I am truly

The Parliament's up, & all the World are   Yours
made Lords, & Secretaries, & Commiſsioners.³⁸   T G:

July . . London. [1742].³⁹

³² This should be Mlle de Tervire (the Religieuse, whose history occupies the last three sections of the book).

³³ Minister, perhaps with a glance at 'Mini', Walpole's pet name for Mann.

³⁴ Gray's expression 'far del mondo!' was no doubt an inexact reproduction (by a foreigner) of the familiar exclamation 'poſsar (=può fare) il mondo!', the equivalent of the literary 'potenza del mondo!', 'by all the powers!' (Information from Professor Cesare Foligno.)

³⁵ 'A great minister.' English ships were now in command of the Mediterranean.

³⁶ In his letter to his mother of 9 Dec. 1739, from Bologna (Letter 76), Gray writes: 'The fine Gallery of Pictures that once belonged to the Dukes of Parma, is no more here; the King of Naples has carried it all thither'.

³⁷ The French under Marshal Belleisle in Prague, which they had taken in the previous year, were at this time besieged and hard pressed by the Austrians. Walpole wrote to Mann on 24 June: 'They say there came an express last night, of the taking of Prague and the destruction of some thousand French. It is really amazing, the fortune of the Queen!' But the news was premature, the French held out till December, when they evacuated the city with disastrous losses.

³⁸ Parliament was prorogued in the second week of July—on the 13th Pulteney became Earl of Bath; the next day Walpole sent Mann a list of the preferments.

³⁹ From the allusions to public events and to Gray's intended return to Cambridge, the year is obviously 1742.

113. GRAY TO CHUTE

My dear S^r

WHAT do You chuse I should think of a whole Year's Silence? have you absolutely forgot me, or do you not reflect, that it is from yourself alone I can have any Information concerning You? I do not find myself inclined to forget you: the same Regard for your Person, the same Desire of seeing you again I felt when we parted still continues with me as fresh as ever. don't wonder then if in spite of Appearances I try to flatter myself with the Hopes of finding Sentiments something of the same kind however buried in some dark Corner of your Heart, & perhaps more than half extinguish'd by long Absence, & various Cares of a different Nature. I will not alarm your Indolence with a long Letter. my Demands are only three, & may be answer'd in as many Words. how You do? where You are? & When You return? if you chuse to add anything further it will be a Work of Superer—I will not write so long a Word entire, least I fatigue your Delicacy, & you may think it incumbent on you to answer it by another of equal Dimensions. You believe me, I hope, with great Sincerity Yours

T G.

PS: For ought I know You may be in England. my very true Compliments (not such as People make to one another) wait upon Mr Whithed.¹ he will be the most travel'd Gentleman in Hampshire.

Oct: 25. Cambridge [1743 or 1744]²

114. GRAY TO WHARTON

My dear Wharton

IT is a long Time, since I ought to have return'd you my Thanks for the Pleasure of your Letter; I should say, the

LETTER 113.—First printed by Mitford in *Works of Gray* (1835–43), vol. ii, pp. 188–9; now reprinted from original.   ¹ See Letter 109, n. 36.

² The date is conjectural: it is after Gray's return to Cambridge in 1742, when he returned to Peterhouse as a Fellow-commoner, and might be 1743 or 1744.

LETTER 114.—First printed in part (in a garbled text) in Mason's *Memoirs*, pp. 173–5; first printed in full by Mitford (1816), vol. ii, pp. 141–3; now reprinted from original.

This letter was dated 1742 by Mason; that the correct date is 1743 is proved by the references to Gray's degree, and to the Pembroke Jubilee (see notes 3 and 13).

Prodigy of your Letter, for such a Thing has not happen'd above twice within this last Age to mortal Man, & no one here can conceive what it may portend. Mr Trollope,[1] I suppose, has told you, how I was employed a part of the Time; how by my own indefatigable Application for these ten Years past, & by the Care & Vigilance of that worthy Magistrate, the Man-in-Blew[2] (who, I'll afsure you, has not spared his Labour, nor could have done more for his own Son) I am got half way to the Top of Jurisprudence,[3] & bid as fair as another Body to open a case of Impotency[4] with all Decency & Circumspection. you see my Ambition: I do not doubt, but some 30 Years hence I shall convince the World & You, that I am a very pretty young Fellow, & may come to shine in a Profefsion perhaps the noblest in the World, next to Man-Midwifery. as for yours: if your Distemper & You can but agree about going to London, I may reasonably expect in a much shorter Time to see you in your three-corner'd Villa, doing the honours of a well-furnish'd Table with as much Dignity, as rich a Mien, & as capacious a

---

[1] William Trollope, of Pembroke; B.A., 1727; M.A., 1730; Fellow, 1731. From several of Gray's references to him he appears to have been more or less of an invalid. Gray after his return to Peterhouse in 1742 was on terms of intimate friendship with him; and under his sponsorship borrowed books from the Pembroke Library. He went out of residence in 1746, but resided for a few weeks in the next year, when he was appointed President; after which he ceased to reside. He died 3 May 1749. Trollope has been credited with the authorship of the poem on 'The Characters of the Christ-Cross Row', believed by Walpole to be Gray's (see Letter 139, n. 12).

[2] A Servant of the Vice-Chancellor's for the time being, usually known by the name of Blue Coat, whose business it is to attend Acts for Degrees, &c. *Mason.*—Gray refers to him again in his account to Wharton (in Letter 150) of the installation of the Duke of Newcastle as Chancellor. This official was the University Marshal, who was appointed by the Vice-Chancellor. The Marshal in 1743 was Robert Hibble, the vouchers for whose new blue (or purple) coat in June 1744, amounting to £3 18s. od., for materials and making, are preserved in the Cambridge Registry. It appears that his salary as Marshal was paid quarterly at £13 15s. od. (See 'The Man-in-Blew', by Dr. H. P. Stokes, in *Cambridge Review*, 6 May 1927.)

[3] That is to say, he had qualified for the degree of Bachelor of Civil Law. He had been admitted LL.B. designate on 16 Dec. of this year (1743), and became full LL.B. in 1744. See Appendix F.

[4] Such a case would be tried in the Ecclesiastical Court, which was open only to Advocates who had taken the degree of Doctor of Civil Law at Oxford or Cambridge. Gray, as a Bachelor, would be half-way to the Doctorate. (See Appendix F.)

Belly as D^{r}Mead.⁵ methinks I see D^{r}Askew⁶ at the lower End
of it, lost in Admiration of your goodly Person & Parts, cramming down his Envy (for it will rise) with the Wing of a Phea-
sant, & drowning it in neat Burgundy. but not to tempt your
Asthma too much with such a Prospect, I should think you
might be almost as happy, & as great as this, even in the Country. but you know best; & I should be sorry to say anything,
that might stop you in the Career of Glory. far be it from me to
hamper the Wheels of your gilded Chariot. go on, S^{r}Thomas; &
when you die (for even Physicians must die) may the Faculty in
Warwick Lane⁷ erect your statue in S^{r}John Cutler's⁸ own Niche.

As to Cambridge it is, as it was, for all the World; & the
People are, as they were; & M^{r}Trollope is as he was, that is,
half ill, half well. I wish with all my Heart they were all better,
but what can one do? there is no News, only I think I heard a
Whisper, as if the Vice-Chancellour⁹ should be with Child:
(but I beg you not to mention this, for I may come into trouble

⁵ Richard Mead (1673–1754), the leading English physician of his day
who, as Johnson said, 'lived more in the broad sunshine of life than almost
any man'. (Boswell, *Life*, vol. iii, p. 355.)

⁶ This no doubt was Anthony Askew (1722–72), son of a well-known
physician of Newcastle, Dr. Adam Askew (1697–1773); he was at this time
studying for the medical profession at Emmanuel College, and did not take
his M.D. degree till 1750; but Gray, who is forecasting the future, calls him
'D^{r}Askew' by anticipation, just as below he bestows on Wharton himself the
prospective title (which he never attained) of 'Sir Thomas'. Anthony
Askew, who was elected F.R.S. in 1749, and Fellow of the College of
Physicians in 1753, became eventually better known as a classical scholar
and book-collector than as a physician. As north-countrymen, and both
studying for the same profession, he and Wharton (whose junior he was by
five years) were probably friends, which would account for Gray's mention
of him as likely to envy Wharton's (expected) success.

⁷ In Warwick Lane (leading from Newgate Street to Paternoster Row)
from 1674 to 1825 was the old College of Physicians built by Wren.

⁸ Sir John Cutler (c. 1608–93), a wealthy London merchant, notorious
for his avarice, which has been immortalized by Pope in *Moral Essays*
(iii. 315–34). He was none the less a liberal benefactor of the College of
Physicians, the anatomical theatre of which, named after him 'Theatrum
Cutlerianum', was erected at his expense. In a niche on the outside of the
building was placed a full-length statue of him, with a eulogistic inscription
beneath; but after his death the College obliterated the inscription and
removed the statue, in consequence, it is said, of an exorbitant demand on
the College made by his executors—hence Gray's allusion to Cutler's empty
niche.

⁹ William George, D.D. (d. 1756), Provost of King's, 1743–56; he had
been head master of Eton while Gray and Horace Walpole were there;
in 1748 he was appointed Dean of Lincoln.

about it) there is some Suspicion, that the Profeſsor of Mathematicks[10] had a Hand in the thing. Dr Dickens[11] says the University will be obliged to keep it, as it was got, in Magistratu.

I was going to tell you, how sorry I am for your Illneſs. but, I hope, it is too late to be sorry now: I can only say, that I really w a s very sorry. may you live a hundred Christmases, & eat as many Collars of Brawn stuck with Rosemary. Adieu, I am sincerely Yours

T G:

Dec: 27 [1743] Cambridge . . Won't You come to the Jubilee?[12] Dr Long[13] is to dance a Saraband & Hornpipe of his own Invention without lifting either Foot once from the Ground.

Addressed: To Thomas Wharton, Esq, at Alderman Wharton's on the Market-Place in the City of Durham *Postmark:* CAMBRIDGE

115. GRAY TO WHARTON

YOU write so feelingly to little Mr Brown,[1] & represent your abandon'd Condition in Terms so touching, that, what

[10] John Colson (1680–1760), F.R.S., 1713; Lucasian Professor of Mathematics (1739–60), in succession to Saunderson, the blind professor. Cole describes him as 'an old bachelor . . . an humourist and peevish'.

[11] Francis Dickins, LL.D., Fellow of Trinity Hall, Regius Professor of Civil Law, 1714–55. Horace Walpole records in his *Short Notes of my Life*: 'I went to lectures in civil law to Dr Dickens, of Trinity Hall.'

[12] The Jubilee was the celebration of what was thought to be the four-hundredth anniversary of the foundation of Pembroke Hall by Marie de Châtillon, daughter of Guy de Châtillon, Comte de Saint Pol, widow of Aymer de Valence, Earl of Pembroke. The date of foundation accepted at the present day is 1347, but during Gray's lifetime it was held to have been 1343. This appears, not only from the statement in 'the case of the Fellows of Pembroke' in their dispute in 1747 with Dr. Long that 'the College was founded in the year 1343' (see Appendix F), but also from the title of a poem by Christopher Smart, a member of the College, which has recently come to light, 'A Secular Ode on the Jubilee at Pembroke College, Cambridge, in 1743'. It appears from the College records that Wharton did not attend the Jubilee celebration, which no doubt was held on the following New Year's Day, on the occasion of the Foundress's Feast, that date for the Feast being prescribed by the ancient statutes of the College. (See 'The Jubilee at Pembroke Hall in 1743', by Leonard Whibley, in *Blackwood's Magazine*, Jan. 1927.)

[13] See Letter 39, n. 2.

LETTER 115.—First printed in part (in a garbled text) in Mason's *Memoirs*, pp. 177–9; first printed in full by Mitford (1816), vol. ii, pp. 148–50; now reprinted from original.

[1] James Brown (1709–84), son of James Brown, citizen and goldsmith of

Gratitude could not effect in several Months, Compaſsion has brought about in a few Days, & broke that strong Attachment, or rather Allegiance, w ch I & all here owe to our sovereign Lady & Mistreſs, the President of Presidents, & Head of Heads (if I may be permitted to pronounce her Name, that ineffable Octogrammaton) the Power of LAZINESS.¹ᵃ you must know she had been pleased to appoint me (in Preference to so many old Servants of hers, who had spent their whole Lives in qualifying themselves for the Office) Grand Picker of Straws, & Push-Pin-Player in ordinary to her Supinity (for that is her Title) the first is much in the Nature of Ld President of the Council, & the other, like the Groom-Porter, only without the Profit. but, as they are both Things of very great Honour in this Country, I consider'd with myself the Load of Envy attending such great Charges, & besides (between you & I) I found myself unable to support the Fatigue of keeping up the Appearance, that Persons of such Dignity must do, so I thought proper to decline it, & excused myself as well as I could: however as you see such an Affair must take up a good deal of Time, & it has always been the Policy of this Court to proceed slowly, like the Imperial, & that of Spain, in the Dispatch of Busineſs; so that you will the easier forgive me, if I have not answer'd your Letter before.

You desire to know, it seems, what Character the Poem² of your young Friend bears here. I wonder to hear you ask the

London, a Grecian from Christ's Hospital, was admitted as a Sizar at Pembroke College, Cambridge, in 1726; B.A., 1730; M.A., 1733; Fellow, 1735; ordained Priest 1735; Vicar of Shepreth, Cambs., 1737; President (i.e. Vice-Master) of Pembroke, 15 May 1749; Proctor, 1750–1; Master, 21 Dec. 1770–84; D.D., 1771; Vice-Chancellor, 1771–2; Vicar of Stretham in Isle of Ely, 1771 (see Letter 540). He was a small man, precise in manner, and of a resolute courage. Gray writes in Letter 120: He 'wants nothing, but a Foot in height and his own Hair, to make him a little old Roman', and there are many other playful allusions to his diminutive stature. Cole describes him as 'a very worthy man, a good scholar, small and short-sighted'. He probably made Gray's acquaintance when an undergraduate (see Appendix B), and he was his sponsor when Gray was admitted as a Fellow-commoner at Pembroke (see Appendix E, n. 7). He was a loyal friend and admirer of Gray throughout his life. He was joint-executor with Mason of Gray's will, and was present at his burial at Stoke-Poges. He was with him to the last during his brief illness (see his letters to Wharton and Nicholls in Appendix W).

¹ᵃ See Letter 149: 'the Spirit of Lazyness (the Spirit of the Place)'.

² Pleasures of the Imagination. *Mason.*—The author Mark Akenside (1721–70) was the son of a butcher of Newcastle-upon-Tyne. After studying

Opinion of a Nation, where those who pretend to judge, don't judge at all; & the rest (the wiser Part) wait to catch the Judgement of the World immediately above them, that is, Dick's Coffee-House,[3] & the Rainbow:[4] so that the readier Way would be to ask Mrs This & M^rs T'other, that keeps the Bar there. however to shew you I'm a Judge, as well as my Countrymen, tho' I have rather turn'd it over, than read it, (but no matter: no more have they) it seems to me above the middleing, & now & then (but for a little while) rises even to the best, particularly in Description. it is often obscure, & even unintelligible, & too much infected with the Hutchinson-Jargon.[5] in short it's great fault is that it was publish'd at least 9 Years too early.[6] and so methinks in a few Words, a la Mode du Temple,[7] I have very pertly dispatch'd what perhaps may for several Years have employd a very ingenious Man worth 50 of myself. here is a small poem, call'd the Enthusiast,[8] wch is all pure Description, & as they tell me by the same Hand. is it so, or not? Item, a more bulky one upon Health, wrote by a Physician:[9] do you

first theology, and then medicine at Edinburgh, he returned to Newcastle for two years, and finished his poem on the *Pleasures of the Imagination*. This he took to Dodsley at the end of 1743, and it was published anonymously on 16 Jan. 1744. He graduated in medicine at Leyden and having settled in London became a prosperous physician. Wharton had probably got to know him in Newcastle. In a letter to Mason, c. 28 Nov. 1758 (Letter 284*), Gray says of Wharton: 'he pretends no friendship, & has but a slight acquaintance with the Doctor' (i.e. Akenside).

  [3] See Letter 94, n. 16.

  [4] The Rainbow Coffee-House, in Fleet Street, near the Inner Temple Gate, originally established in 1657 by James Farr, a barber.

  [5] Gray means Francis Hutcheson (see Letter 103, n. 4), who in 1726 and 1728 published anonymously *Four Essays*, viz. 'Inquiry concerning Beauty, Order, Harmony, Design'; 'Inquiry concerning Moral Good and Evil'; 'Essay on the Nature and Conduct of the Passions and Affections'; and 'Illustrations upon the Moral Sense'; which led to his appointment in 1729 to the Professorship of Moral Philosophy at Glasgow. His best-known work, *A System of Moral Philosophy*, was not published till 1755, nine years after his death.

  [6] In defiance, that is, of the Horatian precept: 'Si quid tamen olim Scripseris . . . nonum . . . prematur in annum' (*Ars Poet.* 386–8).

  [7] An allusion to the youthful lawyer-critics of the Inns of Court who frequented the coffee-houses near the Temple (see Letter 144, n. 22a).

  [8] *The Enthusiast, or the Lover of Nature*, a poem in blank verse, was published anonymously by Dodsley on 7 March, 1744. The author was Joseph Warton (1722–1800), at that date a young Oxford graduate (see Letter 129, n. 18).

  [9] John Armstrong, M.D. (1709–79), author of *The Art of Preserving Health*, a didactic poem in four books in blank verse, published in 1744.

know him? Master Tommy Lucretius[10] (since you are so good to enquire after the Child) is but a puleing Chitt yet, not a bit grown to speak off, I believe, poor Thing! it has got the Worms, that will carry it off at last. oh Lord! I forgot to tell you, that M*r* Trollope[11] & I are in a course of Tar-Water,[12] he for his Present, and I for my future Distempers: if you think it will kill me, send away a Man & Horse directly, for I drink like a Fish. I should be glad to know how your [   ][13] goes on, & give you Joy of it.

You are much in the Right to have a Taste for Socrates, he was a divine Man. I must tell you by Way of the News of the Place, that the other Day M*r* Fraigneau[14] (entering upon his Profeſsorship) made an Apology for him an Hour long in the Schools, & all the World, except Trinity-College, brought in Socrates Guilty. Adieu, D*r* Sir, & believe me

Your Friend & Servant,
T G.

Cambridge . . Thursday Ap: 26. [1744][15]

Addressed: To Thomas Wharton Esq, at M*r* Alderman Wharton's of Durham By Caxton Bag[16] *Postmark:* CAMBRIDGE

[10] His own poem *De Principiis Cogitandi* (see Letter 97, n. 6).
[11] See Letter 114, n. 1.
[12] George Berkeley (1685–1753), Bishop of Cloyne (1734), published in 1744 his *Siris*, containing 'Philosophical Reflections and Inquiries concerning the Virtues of Tar-water, and divers other subjects connected together and arising one from another'. Walpole writes to Mann on 29 May 1744: 'We are now mad about tar-water, on the publication of a book . . . written by D*r* Berkeley, Bishop of Cloyne. The book contains every subject from tar-water to the Trinity. A man came into an apothecary's shop the other day, "Do you sell tar-water?"—"Tar-water!" replied the apothecary, "why, I sell nothing else!" ' [13] Word obliterated.
[14] William Fraigneau (1717–88), of Huguenot extraction, Fellow of Trinity, Regius Professor of Greek at Cambridge from 1744 to 1750.
[15] The letter is endorsed by Wharton, '26 April 1746', but it was written in 1744, as the references to Fraigneau's inaugural lecture and to Akenside show (see n. 14).
[16] *Cantabrigia Depicta*, in a list of the Posts from Cambridge, has: '*North Post* by *Caxton*, sets out every Night at *Ten* except *Sunday*; and returns every Forenoon, except *Sunday*.' Caxton was a stage on the North Road not far from Cambridge (see Letter 117, n. 8).

116. GRAY TO WHARTON

I AM not lost: here am I at Stoke, whither I came on Tuesday,[1] & shall be again in Town on Saturday,[2] & at Cambridge on Wednesday or Thursday.[3] you may be curious to know what has past.[4] I wrote a Note the Night I came,[5] & immediately received a very civil Answer. I went the following Evening[6] to see *the Party* (as Mrs. Foible[7] says) was something abash'd at his Confidence: he came to meet me, kifs'd me on both Sides with all the Ease of one, who receives an Acquaintance just come out of the Country, squatted me into a Fauteuil, begun to talk of the Town & this & that & t'other, & continued with little Interruption for three Hours, when I took my Leave very indifferently pleased, but treated with wondrous Good-breeding. I supped with him next night (as he desired) Ashton was there, whose Formalities tickled me inwardly, for he I found was to be angry about the Letter I had wrote him.[8] however in going home together our Hackney-Coach jumbled us into a Sort of Reconciliation:[9] he hammer'd out somewhat like an Excuse; &

LETTER 116.—First printed by Mitford (1816), vol. ii, pp. 144–6; now reprinted from original.

This letter, which is dated by Gray (at the end) simply 'Stoke. Thursday', has been endorsed by Wharton: 'Mr Gray, 16 Nov. 1744 or 1745'; but 16 Nov. (which is the date of the postmark) in 1744 was a Friday, and in 1745 it was a Saturday. The correct date is certainly 14 Nov. 1745, which was a Thursday: this agrees with the other dates mentioned in the letter, and is confirmed by the Peterhouse records, which show that Gray was absent from Cambridge from 7 Nov. to 21 Nov. in 1745. That the year was 1745 is confirmed by Gray's letter to Chute of 12 Oct. 1746 (Letter 124).

[1] 12 Nov.   [2] 16 Nov.   [3] 20 or 21 Nov.

[4] That is, between himself and Walpole on the occasion of their first meeting and reconciliation after their quarrel. See Appendix D.

[5] Thursday, 7 Nov., the date of his arrival in London from Cambridge.

[6] 8 Nov. Walpole was in the house in Arlington Street, which had been left to him by his father.

[7] Congreve, *Way of the World*, iii. 1: '*Lady Wishfort.* O Foible, where hast thou been? what hast thou been doing? *Foible.* Madam, I have seen the Party.'

[8] Tovey plausibly suggests that the letter in question was one written by Gray to Ashton from abroad, which contained expressions reflecting upon Walpole, to whom they were communicated by Ashton, who was thus instrumental in bringing about the actual breach between Gray and Walpole (see *Gray and his Friends*, pp. 6–12). See Appendix D.

[9] *Spectator*, No. 132: 'The coach jumbled us insensibly into some sort of familiarity'.

I received it very readily, because I cared not two pence, whither it were true or not. so we grew the best Acquaintance imaginable, & I set[10] with him on Sunday some Hours alone, when he inform'd me of abundance of Anecdotes much to my Satisfaction, & in short open'd (I really believe) his Heart to me with that Sincerity, that I found I had still lefs Reason to have a good Opinion of him, than (if pofsible) I ever had before. next Morning[11] I breakfasted alone with M^r W: when we had all the Eclaircifsement I ever expected, & I left him far better satisfied, than I had been hitherto. when I return, I shall see him again. such is the Epitome of my four Days.[12] M^r & Mrs Simms & Mad^lle Nanny[13] have done the Honours of Leaden Hall[14] to a Miracle, & all joyn in a Compliment to the Doctor. your Brother[15] is well, the Books are in good Condition. Mad^me Chenevix[16] has frightened me with Ecritoires she asks three

---

[10] 'Set' (for 'sit' or 'sat') has instances quoted in the *O.E.D.* as late as the nineteenth century. It is described as now being 'dialect or vulgar'. Gray uses it also in Letters 135, 382.

[11] Monday, 11 Nov.   [12] In London, 8–11 Nov.

[13] Probably, as Tovey suggests, the people at Wharton's lodgings in town, somewhere near the College of Physicians.

[14] At that time 'a very large building of free-stone, containing within it three large courts or yards, all encompassed with buildings', which was pulled down c. 1880. Leadenhall, then as now, was the great market for all poultry brought into London for sale, besides being a general provision market.

[15] Wharton's youngest brother Jonathan, third son of Robert Wharton (1690–1752), of Old Park, Durham. Jonathan, who resided in Boswell Court, Carey Street, Lincoln's Inn (see Letter 353, and address of Letter 463), was presumably a solicitor. He married a Miss Mary Wilson, and died childless in 1768. (See Genealogical Table.)

[16] 'The toy-woman à la mode,' as Walpole calls her in his letter to Mann of 5 June 1747, from whom he bought the remainder of her lease of the 'little rural bijou' at Twickenham, which by successive additions and reconstructions eventually developed into the famous 'Gothic Castle' of Strawberry Hill. Mrs. Chenevix was sister of the no less noted toy-woman at Bath, Mrs. Bertrand. Her shop, according to an advertisement in the *Daily Journal* for 24 May 1733, quoted by Austin Dobson, was at that time 'against Suffolk Street, Charing Cross'. In a paper contributed to the *World* of 19 Dec. 1754, Walpole says: 'Mrs Chenevix has not more insinuation when she sells a snuff-box of papier-maché, or a bergemot toothpick-case, than a highwayman when he begs to know if you have no rings nor bank-bills'. In a *Common Place Book of Verses, Stories, Characters, Letters, &c.* (in the collection of Earl Waldegrave) Walpole describes her as 'a toywoman at Charing Cross, famous for her high prices and fine language'. Her shop was reckoned one of the sights of London (see Walpole's letter to Mann of 15 Sept. 1746).

Guinea's for, that are not worth three half pence: I have been in several Shops & found nothing pretty. I fear it must be bespoke at last.

the Day after I went you received a little Letter directed to me, that seems wrote with a Skewer. please to open it, & you'll find a receipt of Dan: Adcock for ten Pound, wch I will beg you to receive of Gillham[17] for me. if the Letter miscarried, pray take care the Money is paid to no one else. I expect to have a Letter from you when I come to Town, at your Lodgeings. . . .[18] Adieu, S^r, I am sincerely Yours

T G:

Stoke. Thursday. [Nov. 14, 1745][19]

Addressed: To Thomas Wharton Esq, Fellow of Pembroke College Cambridge *Postmark:* 16 NO

117. GRAY TO WALPOLE

Dear S^r

YOU are so good to enquire after my usual Time of comeing to Town; it is at a Season, when even You, the perpetual Friend of London, will I fear hardly be in it, the Middle of June: and I commonly return hither in September, a Month, when I may more probably find you at home.[1] I do not imagine that any Thing farther can be done with Mr Turner,[2] but You only, who saw the Manner of his promiseing, can judge of that. what he calls the College, is the Master[3] & his Party of

17 Otherwise Gillam, the Cambridge–London carrier patronized by Gray (see Letter 347, n. 1).

18 A whole line of the MS. has here been obliterated.

19 See initial note.

LETTER 117.—First printed in part in *Works of Lord Orford*, 1798, vol. v, pp. 383–4; first printed in full by Toynbee (1915), No. 154.

1 Gray refers to the summer vacation, which he usually spent at Stoke.

2 Shallet Turner, of Peterhouse, Regius Professor of Modern History (see Letter 39, n. 4). What follows evidently refers to a Fellowship election at Peterhouse. The Probationer Fellow elected on this occasion (probably in April) was Pyers Libanus, B.A., 1744; M.A., 1748 (grandson of John Libanus of Peterhouse, an exile from Bohemia 'religionis causa'), who, having completed the year of probation, was confirmed as Foundation Fellow on 14 April of the following year.

3 John Whalley, Fellow of Pembroke, 1721; Master of Peterhouse, 1733–48; D.D., 1737; Regius Professor of Divinity, 1742.

Fellows, among wch he himself has been reckon'd latterly: but, I know, it must be from some other Influence, than that of the Master merely, if he vote with them; wch if Mr Brudenel[4] could stand, might very likely be made Use of (as he is nearly related to several People of Condition) but he is disqualified at present in every Sense. 'tis likely indeed he is intended for next Year, & Mr Turner has had some Application made already, by his knowing anything about him; but he mistakes the Time.

Our Defeat to be sure is a rueful Affair for the Honour of the Troops,[5] but the Duke[6] is gone, it seems, with the Rapidity of a Cannon-Bullet to undefeat us again. the Common-People in Town at least know how to be afraid: but We are such *uncommon* People here as to have no more Sense of Danger, then if the Battle had been fought when & where the Battle of Cannæ was. the Perception of these Calamities and of their Consequences, that we are supposed to get from Books, is so faintly imprefs'd, that we talk of War, Famine, & Pestilence with no more Apprehension, than of a broken Head, or of a Coach overturn'd between York & Edinburgh. I heard three People, sensible middle-aged Men (when the Scotch were said to be at Stamford, & actually were at Derby[7]) talking of hireing a Chaise to go to Caxton,[8] (a Place in the high Road) to see the Pretender & the Highlanders, as they pafsed.

I can say no more for Mr Pope, (for what You keep in Reserve may be worse than all the Rest) it is natural to wish the finest Writer, one of them, we ever had should be an honest Man. it is for the Interest even of that Virtue, whose Friend he profefs'd himself, & whose Beauties he sung, that he should

---

[4] George Bridges Brudenell, admitted Pensioner of Peterhouse in April 1743. He was the eldest son of James Brudenell, the grandson of Robert, second Earl of Cardigan, and was thus cousin of George, fourth Earl (afterwards Duke of Montagu). He was not qualified for a Fellowship at this time, as he had not yet taken his degree. He was subsequently for many years M.P. for Rutland.

[5] General Hawley was defeated at Falkirk on 17 Jan. by the forces of the Young Pretender. 'The very same dragoons ran away at Falkirk, that ran away at Preston Pans' (Walpole to Mann, 28 Jan. 1746).

[6] The Duke of Cumberland, who had been appointed Commander-in-Chief to replace General Hawley, and had 'gone post to Edinburgh, where he hoped to arrive to-night' (Walpole, *loc. cit.*).

[7] On 4 Dec. 1745.

[8] About ten miles from Cambridge, on the road to Huntingdon and the north.

not be found a dirty Animal.[9] but however this is Mr Warburton's[10] Buſineſs, not mine, who may scribble his Pen to the Stumps & all in vain, if these Facts are so. it is not from what he told me about himself[11] that I thought well of him, but from a Humanity & Goodneſs of Heart, ay, & Greatneſs of Mind, that runs thro his private Correspondence, not leſs apparent than are a thousand little Vanities & Weakneſses mixed with those good Qualities, for no body ever took him for a Philosopher.

If you know anything of Mr Mann's State of Health & Happiness, or the Motions of Mr Chute[12] homewards, it will be a particular Favour to inform me of them, as I have not heard this half year from them.

I am sincerely Yours

T GRAY.

Cambr: Febr: 3–1746

118. GRAY TO WALPOLE

[Cambridge, March 28, 1746][1]

Dear S^r

I HAVE expected some time what You tell me. if T:[2] can be prevail'd upon to stay away it is all I desire: for he is mistaken in imagineing that will leave still an Equality among the Fellows. it is all an idle Tale the Master for his own Interest would propagate about the Party of his Antagonists. whatever

---

[9] This no doubt refers to Pope's lines (in *Moral Essays*, ii. 115 ff.) on 'Atossa' (the Duchess of Marlborough), which Bolingbroke published this year on a sheet with a note stating that the Duchess had paid Pope £1,000 for their suppression—'he took the money, yet the world sees the verses'.

[10] William Warburton (1698–1779), subsequently (1759) Bishop of Gloucester, Pope's literary executor (see Letter 272, n. 15).

[11] Pope died 30 May 1744; there is nothing to fix the date of Gray's interview with him.

[12] Chute returned to England in the following September (see Letter 122).

LETTER 118.—First printed by Toynbee (1915), No. 155.

[1] The date of the month is supplied by the postmark; that of the year is determined by the reference to the election at Peterhouse discussed in the previous letter.

[2] Presumably Shallet Turner (see Letter 117, n. 2).

some of the People who give us their Vote may have been I may confidently affirm no one so young as my Friend[3] can be more rationally [4]& zealously well-affected to the Government than he. the Hurry I write in does not permit to return you the Thanks I ought for your stedfastnefs & resolution in obligeing me.   I am Yours sincerely

                                         T: GRAY

Addressed: To The Hon[ble] Horace Walpole Esq at his House in Arlington-Street Westminster *Postmark:* ROYSTON[5] 29 MR

119. GRAY TO WALPOLE

My dear S[r]

I COULD make You abundance of Excuses, as indeed I have Reason: but they would be bad & false ones, such as my Respect for you will not permit me to use. attribute then this long Interval of Silence to whatever Motive you please besides; only don't imagine it Neglect, or Want of Sensibility to the many Exprefsions of Kindnefs you bestow'd upon me in your last Letter. my Sentiments are nothing alter'd since that Time, however tardy I may have been in telling you so: I well remember how little you love Letters, where all the Materials are drawn out of oneself; yet such mine must have been from a Place, where nothing ever happens but Trifles, that it would be mere Impertinence to think of entertaining You with. however I am apt to suspect you have been a little angry, for D[r] Middleton tho' often with you in Town, did not bring me the least Compliment to shew you remember'd me. do you mean to continue so, or shall You see me the lefs willingly next week, when I mean to call at your Door some Morning? I hope you are still in Town. believe me D[r] S[r] very sincerely Yours   T GRAY

Cambridge—July 7 [1746][1]

3 This may have been Henry Tuthill; see Appendix G, n. 5.
4 From this point the writing shows signs of haste.
5 The stamp was not inked, but the impress is legible. The post to London went on three days a week by Royston and three days by Saffron Walden. The letters were sometimes stamped at these places and not at Cambridge.
   LETTER 119.—Now first printed from the original. The last three lines were printed in facsimile in Pinkerton's *Walpoliana*. The letter is endorsed, no doubt by Pinkerton: 'Original letter from Mr. Gray the Poet to Mr. Walpole, given me by Mr. W.'
   1 The date of the year is conjectural, but the College records show that Gray was in residence on 7 July 1746 and left Cambridge about 13 July. Walpole was in Arlington Street on 7 July 1746. The tone of the letter suggests that it was written not very long after Gray's reconciliation with Walpole.

120. GRAY TO WHARTON

My Dear Wharton

I AM just returned hither[1] from Town, where I have past better than a Fortnight, (including an Excursion that I made to Hampton Court, Richmond, Greenwich & other Places) & am happily met by a letter from You, [one from Tuthill],[2] & another from Trollope.[3] as I only run over Dr Andrew's[4] Answers hastily in a Coffee House, all I could judge was that they seem'd very unfavourable on the whole to our Cause,[5] & threw every thing into the Hands of a Visitour, for wch Reason I thought they might have been conceal'd, till the Attorney-General's[6] Opinion arrived, wch will perhaps raise the Spirits of such, as the other may have damp'd a little; or leave Room at least to doubt whether the Matter be so clear on the Master's

---

LETTER 120.—First printed by Mitford (1816), vol. ii, pp. 151–6; now reprinted from original.

[1] Stoke.

[2] The words, which have been obliterated in the original, were supplied by Mitford. Here and in the manuscripts of many letters of Gray to Wharton (Letter 148 is an exception) the name of Tuthill, or the abbreviation T, has been more or less completely obliterated. Mitford in all the passages restored the name without comment. From the context, or on other grounds, his restorations can generally be accepted, and they are inserted, within brackets, in the text of subsequent letters. In his preface to the *Correspondence of Gray and Norton Nicholls* (1843), Mitford remarks: 'When Mason returned the Wharton Correspondence, it was found that he not only had taken the greatest liberties with the text, but had cut out the names of several persons mentioned; in that mutilated state the manuscript was lent to the present Editor. The name of *Mr. Tuthill* was in almost all cases erased (p. viii, n.)'.

The Tuthill here in question was Henry Tuthill, who had graduated B.A. from Peterhouse in 1743, and been ordained Deacon in 1744, and five weeks before the date of this letter (on 5 July 1746) had migrated to Pembroke Hall. He graduated M.A. from Pembroke in 1747, was ordained Priest, 1748; and was elected to a Fellowship on 2 March 1748/9, of which he was deprived on 2 Feb. 1757. (See Appendix G.)

[3] See Letter 114, n. 1.

[4] John Andrew (d. 1747), of Trinity Hall; LL.D., 1711; Fellow, 1705–47; Judge of the Consistory Court of London, 1739–47 (see n. 5).

[5] This was the case of the Fellows of Pembroke against the Master in the matter of the veto claimed and exercised by him in the election of Fellows. (See Appendix H.) In referring to 'our cause' Gray regards himself as allied in interest with the Fellows of Pembroke. (Cf. Letters 121, 135, 143.)

[6] Sir Dudley Ryder (1691–1756), Solicitor-General, 1733–7; Attorney-General, 1737–54; Chief Justice of King's Bench, 1754–6.

Side as Andrew would have it. You can't suppose, that I was in the least uneasy about Mr Brown's[7] Fortitude, who wants nothing, but a Foot in height & his own Hair, to make him a little old Roman: with two dozen such I should not hesitate to face an Army of Heads, tho' they were all as tall as Dr Adams.[8] I only wish every body may continue in as good a Disposition as they were; & imagine, if pofsible, Roger[9] will be Fool enough to keep them so. I saw Trollope for about an Hour in London; & imagineing he could not be left in the dark as to your Consultations, I mention'd, that I had cast an Eye over Andrew's Paper, & that it was not so favourable as we hoped. he spoke however with Horrour of going to Law; with great Pafsion of the Master; & with Pleasure of himself for quitting a Place, where he had not found a Minute's Ease in I know not how long: yet I perceive his Thoughts run on nothing else, & he trembled while he spoke. he writes to me here on the same Subject; & after abusing Roger, he adds, Whartoni rubro hæc subscribe libello.[10]

My Evenings have been chiefly spent at Ranelagh & Vaux-Hall, several of my Mornings, or rather Noons, in Arlington-Street,[11] & the rest at the Tryal of the Lords.[12] the first Day I was not there, & only saw the Ld High-Steward's Parade in going: the second & third [13][* * * * * * * * Peers were all in their Robes * * * * * * * * by their wearing Bag-Wigs & Hats instead of Coronets.[14] My Lord H: Steward[15] was the least part][13] of the Shew, as he wore only his Baron's Robe, & was always asking the Heralds what he should do next, & bowing or smileing about to his Acquaintance. as to his Speech you see it; People hold it very cheap, tho' several Incorrectnefses

---

[7] See Letter 115, n. 1.

[8] Dr. John Adams, Master of Sidney-Sussex College, who died two days after the date of this letter.

[9] That is, Dr. Roger Long, Master of Pembroke (see Letter 39, n. 2).

[10] Horace, 1 *Sat.* x. 92 (100): 'I, puer, atque meo citus haec subscribe libello'.

[11] At Walpole's house (see Letter 116, n. 6).

[12] The trial of the rebel Lords in Westminster Hall, which began on 28 July and ended on 1 Aug.—For a more detailed account see Walpole's letter to Mann of that day.

[13-13] MS. torn—text partly restored in another hand.

[14] Peers wear their coronets at Coronations, never at State Trials.

[15] Philip Yorke (1690–1764), Baron Hardwicke (1733) (see Letter 25, n. 5).

have been alter'd in the printed Copy.[16] Kilmarnoch[17] spoke in Mitigation of his Crime near half an Hour with a decent Courage, & in a strong, but pathetic, Voice. his Figure would prejudice people in his Favour being tall & genteel: he is upwards of 40, but to the Eye not above 35 Years of Age. what he said appears to lefs Advantage, when read. Cromartie[18] (who is about the same Age a Man of lower Stature, but much like a Gentleman) was sinking into the Earth with Grief & Dejection. with Eyes cast down & a Voice so low, that no one heard a Syllable, that did not sit close to the Bar, he made a short Speech to raise Compafsion. it is now, I see, printed; & is reckon'd extremely fine. I believe, you will think it touching & well-exprefsed: if there be any Meannefs in it, it is lost in that Sorrow he gives us for so numerous & helplefs a Family. Lady-Cromartie[19] (who is said to have drawn her Husband into these Circumstances) was at Leicester-House[20] on Wednesday with four of her Children; the Princess saw her, & made no other answer than by bringing in her own Children & placeing them by her; w^ch (if true) is one of the prettiest Things I ever heard. she was also at the Duke's,[21] who refused to admit her: but she waited till he came to his Coach & threw herself at his Knees, while her Children hung upon him, till he promised her all his Interest could do; & before on several Occasions he has been heard to speak very mildly of Cromartie, & very severely of Kilmarnoch. so if any be spared, it will probably be the former, tho' he had a pension of 600£ a-Year from the Government, & the Order for giveing Quarter to no Englishman was found in his Pocket.[22] as to Balmerino[23] he never had any Hopes

16 The High Steward's speech, says Walpole, was 'very long and very poor, with only one or two good passages'.
17 William Boyd (1704–56), fourth Earl of Kilmarnock (1717); he was beheaded on Tower Hill on 18 Aug. following.
18 George Mackenzie (1703–66), third Earl of Cromarty (1731); he was sentenced to death, but was reprieved, and received a conditional pardon in 1749.
19 Isabel (d. 1769), daughter of Sir William Gordon, Bart., of Invergordon.
20 The residence of Frederick, Prince of Wales.
21 The Duke of Cumberland.
22 Walpole says: 'If Lord Cromartie had pleaded *not guilty*, there was ready to be produced against him a paper signed with his own hand, for putting the English prisoners to death.'
23 Arthur Elphinstone (1688–1746), sixth Lord Balmerino (or Balmerinoch) (1746); he pleaded not guilty, but was sentenced to death, and beheaded with Lord Kilmarnock on Tower Hill on 18 Aug.

from the Beginning: he is an old soldier-like Man of a vulgar Manner & Aspect, speaks the broadest Scotch, & shews an Intrepidity, that some ascribe to real Courage, & some to Brandy. You have heard perhaps, that the first Day (while the Peers were adjourned to consider of his Plea, & he left alone for an Hour & half in the Bar) he diverted himself with the Ax, that stood by him, played with its Tafsels & tryed the Edge with his Finger: & some Lord, as he pafsed by him, saying he was surprised to hear him alledge anything so frivolous, & that could not pofsibly do him the least Service: he answer'd, that as there were so many Ladies present, he thought it would be uncivil to give them no Amusement. the D: of Argyle²⁴ telling him how sorry & how astonish'd he was to see him engaged in such a Cause. My Lord (says he) for the two Kings & their Rights I cared not a Farthing, wᶜʰ prevailed: but I was starveing; & by God if Mahomet had set up his Standard in the Highlands, I had been a good Mufselman for Bread, & stuck close to the Party, for I must eat. the Sollicitor-General²⁵ came up to speak to him too; & he turns about to old Williamson.²⁶ Who is that Lawyer, that talks to me? My Lᵈ, it is Mʳ Murray. Ha! Mʳ Murray, my good Friend (says he, & shook him by the Hand) & how does your good Mother?²⁷ oh, she was of admirable Service to us; we should have done nothing without her in Perthshire. he recommends (he says) his Peggy²⁸ ('tis uncertain * * * * the Favour of the Government, for she has * * * *²⁹

²⁴ Archibald Campbell (1682–1761), third Duke of Argyll (1743); he was a staunch Hanoverian.

²⁵ Hon. William Murray (1705–93), fourth son of fifth Viscount Stormont; afterwards (1756) Baron Mansfield, and (1776) Earl of Mansfield; he was Solicitor-General, 1742–54; Attorney-General, 1754–6; Lord Chief Justice of the King's Bench, 1756–88. His elder brother, James, a well-known Jacobite, who had been created Earl of Dunbar by the Old Pretender in 1721, was in Rome when Walpole and Gray were there in 1740 (see Letter 85, n. 13).

²⁶ Colonel Williamson, Lieutenant of the Tower, who had charge of the prisoners. Balmerino complained of his brutality (see Walpole to Mann, 16 and 21 Aug. 1746).

²⁷ Margery Scott, only child of David Scott, of Scotstarvet, co. Fife; she was no longer alive at this time, having died at Scone on 8 April of this year, a fact of which Balmerino must have been ignorant.

²⁸ Margaret, daughter of Captain John Chalmers; she was in the Tower with her husband (Walpole to Mann, 1 and 12 Aug. 1746). In response to a letter written on her behalf by Balmerino the day before his execution the Old Pretender sent her £60 in 1747; she died in 1765.

²⁹ Piece cut out of MS.

³⁰[I have been diverted with an Account of old Lovat³¹ in his Confinement at]³⁰ Edinburgh. there was a Captain Maggett, that is obliged to lie in the Room every Night with him. when first he was introduced to him, he made him come to his Bedside where he lay in a hundred flannel Wastcoats and a furr'd Night-gown, took him in his Arms, & gave him a long Embrace, that absolutely suffocated him. he will speak nothing but French; insists upon it, that Maggett is a Frenchman & calls him, Mon cher Capitaine Magot (You know *Magot* is a Monkey) at his Head lie two Highland Women & at his feet two Highland Men. by his Bedside is a Close-Stool to wch he rises two or three times in a Night, & always says, Ah, mon cher Capitaine Magot! vous m'excuserez, mais la Nature demande que je chie! he is to be impeached by the House of Commons, because not being actually in Arms, it would otherwise be necefsary, that the Jury of Invernefs should find a Bill of Indictment against him, wch it is very sure they would not do. when the Duke return'd to Edinburgh they refused to admit Kingston's light Horse & talked of their Privileges. but they came in Sword in Hand, & replied, that when the Pretender was at their Gates, they had said nothing of their Privileges. the Duke rested some Hours there, but refused to see the Magistracy.

I believe you may think it full Time, that I close my Budget of Stories: Mr. W: I have seen a good deal, & shall do a good deal more, I suppose, for he is looking for a House somewhere about Windsor³² dureing the Summer. all is mighty free, &

³⁰⁻³⁰ Text inserted by another hand from mutilated page of MS.

³¹ Simon Fraser (*c.* 1667–1747), eleventh Baron Lovat; he intrigued with both sides, and was induced to join the Jacobites in '45 by the promise from the Old Pretender of the Dukedom of Fraser, though he was nearly 80. He escaped from Culloden, but was captured some weeks later and brought to London and imprisoned in the Tower. He was taken to the House of Lords on 18 Dec. to hear the articles of impeachment, and was then allowed till 13 Jan. to prepare for trial. He was found guilty of high treason on 18 March, sentence of death was passed on the following day, and he was beheaded on Tower Hill on 9 April 1747. His confinement at Edinburgh must have been while he was on his way as a prisoner from Fort William to London. His trial and execution are described by Walpole in his letters to Mann of 20 March and 10 April 1747.

³² Walpole writes to George Montagu on 5 Aug. 1746: 'If you can find me out any clean, little house in Windsor, ready furnished. . . . I shall be glad to take it for three or four months'; on 11 Aug. he announces that he has taken the house of one Mr. Jordan, 'within the precincts of the Castle at Windsor' (*Short Notes*) (see also letter to Mann of 21 Aug. 1746).

even friendly. more than one could expect. you remember a
Paper in the Museum on Mefsage-Cards[33] w[ch] he told me was
Fielding's, & asked my Opinion about: it was his own, & so was
the Advertisement on Good-Breeding,[34] that made us laugh so.
Mr. A:[35] I have had several Conversations with, & do really
believe he shews himself to me such as he really is: I don't tell
you, I like him ever the better for it; but that may be my Fault,
not his. the Pelhams[36] lie very hard at his Stomach: he is not
40 yet, but he is 31, he says, & thinks it his Duty to be married.[37]
one Thing of that Kind is just broke off; she had 12000[£ in][37a]
her own Hands. this a profound Secret, but I not conceiving
that he told it m[e as] such, happen'd to tell it to Stonhewer,[38]

[33] 'A SCHEME for Raising a Large Sum of Money for the Use of the
Government, By laying a TAX on MESSAGE-CARDS and NOTES'; first published
in No. ii of the *Museum*, where it is signed 'Descartes'; reprinted in *Works
of Lord Orford*, 1798, vol. i, pp. 132–9.

[34] 'ADVERTISEMENT. *This Day is published, in Ten Volumes in Folio*, THE
HISTORY OF GOOD-BREEDING, From the Creation of the World, To the Present
Times: As set forth in FORMS and CEREMONIES. And appointed to be used in
CHURCHES, VISITS, CORONATIONS, &c. Collected from the best Authors; As
Baker's Chronicle, the *Compleat Dancing-Master*, the *Law of Nations*, the *Mar-
grave's Monitor*, the *Constable's Guide*, *Picart's Religious Ceremonies*, *&c*. The
Whole adapted to the meanest Capacities, Whether Peeresses, Lords,
Chamberlains, Embassadors, Bishops, Justices of the Peace, Gentlemen
Ushers, Barbers, or Chamber-Maids. In this Great Print, PRAY LET US.
By the Author of the *Whole Duty of Man*'; first published in No. v of
the *Museum*, May 1746; reprinted in *Works of Lord Orford*, 1798, vol. i,
pp. 141–5.

[35] Ashton.

[36] Henry Pelham, Prime Minister, and his brother, the Duke of Newcastle,
Secretary of State for the South. Ashton no doubt had been hoping for
further preferment. After his nomination by Pelham to the Crown living of
Aldingham in 1742 (see Letter 111, n. 3) he did not receive another living
until 1749 (see Letter 14, n. 3).

[37] He did not marry till 1760 (see Letter 14, n. 3).

[37a] MS. torn; text here and below restored conjecturally.

[38] Richard Stonhewer (for so, and not Stonehewer, his name is spelt by
Stonhewer himself in letters and in his will, and by Gray) (c. 1728–1809),
son of Rev. Richard Stonhewer (d. 29 Oct. 1769), Rector of Houghton-
le-Spring, Durham; he was educated at Kepyer in that parish, and at
Trinity College, Cambridge (his father's College), where he was admitted
Pensioner on 4 Nov. 1745; he matriculated 1745–6, and graduated B.A.
in 1749–50, being eighth in the Tripos list; in Oct. 1751 he was elected
Fellow of Peterhouse, and proceeded M.A. in 1753, in the same year as
his pupil, the Earl of Euston, afterwards (1757) third Duke of Grafton, also
a member of Peterhouse, whose intimate friend he subsequently became.
In 1755 he was appointed Historiographer to his Majesty (see Letter 196,
n. 3), and in 1756 Knight Harbinger (he is entered in the *Court and*

who told it Lyne,[39] who told it Asht: again, all i[n the] Space of three Hours. whereby I incurr'd a Scolding; so pray don't let me fall under [a] second, & lose all my Hopes of riseing in the Church. he is still, as I said, resolute to m[arry] out of Hand; only two things he is terrified at, lest she should not breed, & lest she should love him: I comforted him by saying, there was no Danger of either.

the Muse, I doubt, is gone,[39a] & has left me in far worse Company: if she returns, you will hear of her. You see I have left no Room for a Catalogue,[40] wch is a Sort of Policy, for its hardly poſsible my Memory should supply one: I will try by next Time, wch will be soon, if I hear from you. if your Curiosity require any more Circumstances of these Tryals * * * will see * * * find some gr * * * * * [41] my best Compliments to the Little

City Register for 1757, as holding this office). He seems to have received some further preferment in 1759, possibly the post of interpreter of Oriental Languages, which he is known to have held a year or two later (see Letter 294, n. 19). When Grafton in 1765 became Secretary of State for the North he appointed Stonhewer under-secretary. On 15 Aug. 1766 he was appointed private secretary to the Duke of Grafton, then First Lord of the Treasury, and in January 1767 Commissioner of Excise. It was due to his influence with Grafton, then Prime Minister, that Gray was appointed in July 1768 to the Regius Professorship of Modern History at Cambridge.

Gray must have become acquainted with Stonhewer sometime before this date, probably soon after he came into residence at Trinity, through the introduction of Wharton. Their relations became intimate—in his letter to Stonhewer on the death of his father (see Letter 507) Gray calls him 'my best friend', and by his will he left him £500 stock and one of his diamond rings, a similar bequest being made to Wharton.

Stonhewer was also intimate with Mason (see Letter 144, n. 33), who left to Stonhewer Gray's manuscripts and books. The three volumes of Gray's Commonplace-book, as well as portraits of Gray and Mason, Stonhewer bequeathed to Pembroke College. Cole says of Stonhewer: 'He was one of the prettiest Figures of a Man I ever saw, & was as pretty a scholar'.

³⁹ Richard Lyne (1715–67), Gray's senior at Eton by a year, was admitted at King's, as a Scholar, in 1733; graduated B.A., 1737–8, M.A., 1741; D.D., 1764; elected Fellow, 1737. He was for a time Assistant Master at Eton, and Fellow, in 1752; Rector of Abbot's Ripton, Hunts., 1744–67; Chaplain to the King, 1744–67; Rector of Eynesbury, Hunts., 1750–67.

³⁹ᵃ Gray had presumably told Wharton of some poem that he had begun (see Letter 121, n. 11).

⁴⁰ That is, of books for the Pembroke College Library; he sent a list with the next letter.

⁴¹ Strip torn out of MS.

Man of the World.[42] Adieu, my dear Wharton; believe me very truly Yours

T GRAY.

Stoke . . Sunday. [Aug. 10, 1746].[43]

Addressed: [To] [Th]omas Wharton Esq, Fellow of [Pem]broke Hall Cambridge *Postmark:* 13 AV

121. GRAY TO WHARTON

My Dear Wharton

WHAT can one say to these Things? if it had been in the Power of Lawyers to interpret into Common-Sense Statutes made by old Monks, or Monk-directed old Women, we might have hoped for a more favourable Answer to our Queries?[1] as it is, I fear they may have done more Hurt than Good: all I know, is this, that I should rejoyce poor [T:][2] had some Place to rest the Sole of his Foot in; & I flatter myself You will never omitt anything in your Power to support his little Interest among a People, with whom You first raised it. I would gladly know the Time of your Audit, for I would be at Cambridge by that Time, if I could. Mr. W:[3] has taken a House in Windsor & I see him usually once a Week; but I think, that will hardly detain me beyond the Time I proposed to myself. he is at present gone to Town to perform the disagreeable Task of presenting & introduceing about a young Florentine, the Marquis Rinuccini,[4] who comes recommended to him. the D: is here at his Lodge[5] with three Whores & three Aid-de Camps; & the Country swarms with People. he goes to Races,

---

[42] James Brown (see Letter 115, n. 1).

[43] The year is obviously 1746; as the postmark is 13 August (Wednesday), and the letter is dated Sunday, no doubt it was written on 10 August.

LETTER 121.—First printed in part (in a garbled text) in Mason's *Memoirs*, pp. 181–2; first printed in full by Mitford (1816), vol. ii, pp. 156–64; now reprinted from original.

[1] See Letter 120, n. 5, and Appendix H.

[2] T: has been scored through, but is still legible (see Letter 120, n. 2).

[3] Walpole (see Letter 120, n. 32).

[4] The Marquis Folco Rinuncini, whose father 'had been envoy in England, and Prime Minister to John Gaston, the last Great Duke [of Tuscany]'; he had come with a letter of introduction from Mann (see Walpole to Mann, 15 Sept. 1746).

[5] The Duke of Cumberland, as Ranger of Windsor Forest and Great Park, had a lodge in the Park (see Walpole to Conway, 3 Oct. 1746).

& they make a Ring about him, as at a Bear-baiting; and no Wonder, for they do the same at Vaux-hall and Ranelagh. at this last, somebody was telling me they heard a Man lamenting to some Women of his Acquaintance, & saying, how he had been up close to him, & he never repented of anything so much in his Life, as that he did not touch him.

I am not altogether of your Opinion, as to your Historical Consolation in time of Trouble. a calm Melancholy it may produce, a stiller Sort of Despair (& that only in some Circumstances & on some Constitutions) but I doubt no real Content or Comfort can ever arise in the human Mind, but from Hope. Old Balmerino when he had read his Paper to the People, pull'd off his Spectacles, spit upon his Handkerchief, & wiped them clean for the Use of his Posterity; & that is the last Page of his History. have you seen Hogarth's Print of Ld Lovat?[6] it is admirable.

I can not help thinking if I had been near you, I should have represented the Horror of the Thing in such a Light, as that you should never have become a Prey to Mr Davie.[7] I know, that he'll get you up in a Corner some Day, & pick your bones & John[7a] will find nothing of you, but such a little Heap, as a Cat that is a good Mouser leaves, the Head & the Tail piled together. my Concern for you produced a Vision, not such a one as you read in the Spectators, but actually a Dream. I thought I was in t'other World and confined in a little Apartment much like a Cellar, enlighten'd by one Rush-Candle that burn'd blue. on each Side of me sate (for my Sins) Mr Davie & my friend M^r A:;[8] they bow'd continually & smiled in my

---

[6] Walpole in his *Anecdotes of Painting in England* describes this as 'Simon lord Lovat, drawn from the life and etched in aquafortis by William Hogarth, 1746'. Mitford quotes the following from Nichols's *Life of Hogarth* (1781): 'Mr Walpole once invited Gray the Poet, and Hogarth to dine with him, but what with the reserve of the one, and a want of colloquial talents in the other, he never passed a duller time than between those representations of Tragedy and Comedy; being obliged to rely entirely on his own efforts to support conversation (p. 97)'.

[7] This was probably Alexander Davie, of Sidney Sussex, M.A., 1717, who is mentioned in Wordsworth's *Social Life at the Universities in the Eighteenth Century* (p. 619) as one of the reputed authors of *The Academic*, a pamphlet on the Regulations of 1750 (see Letter 143, n. 3)

[7a] Presumably Wharton's servant in college, and perhaps the same man as 'your John' in Gray's letter to Wharton of 12 Dec. 1757 (Letter 258).

[8] Ashton.

Face, and while one fill'd me out very bitter Tea, the other sweetened it with a vast deal of brown Sugar: alltogether it much resembled Syrup of Buckthorn. in the corner sat [Tuthill][9] very melancholy, in Expectation of the Tea-Leaves.

I take it very ill you should have been in the twentieth Year of the War, & yet say nothing of the Retreat from before Syracuse:[10] is it, or is it not the finest Thing you ever read in your Life? and how does Xenophon, or Plutarch agree with you? for my Part I read Aristotle; his Poeticks, Politicks, and Morals, tho' I don't well know, wch is which. in the first Place he is the hardest Author by far I ever meddled with. then he has a dry Concisenefs, that makes one imagine one is perusing a Table of Contents rather than a Book: it tasts for all the World like chop'd Hay, or rather like chop'd Logick; for he has a violent Affection to that Art, being in some Sort his own Invention; so that he often loses himself in little trifleing Distinctions & verbal Niceties, & what is worse leaves you to extricate yourself as you can. thirdly he has suffer'd vastly by the Transcribblers, as all Authors of great Brevity necefsarily must. fourthly and lastly he has abundance of fine uncommon Things, wch make him well worth the Pains he gives one. you see what you have to expect. this & a few autumnal Verses[11] are my Entertainments dureing the Fall of the Leaf. notwithstanding wch my Time lies heavy on my Hands, & I want to be at home again.

I have just received a Visit from A:,[12] he tells me we have certainly [a Peace][13] with Spain very far advanced, w^ch 'tis likely will produce a general one[14] & that the King, when he has finish'd it, is determined to pafs the rest of his Days at Windsor. wch to me is strange, however it comes from the Pelhamites. I send you here a Page of Books:[15] enough I

[9] See Letter 120, n. 2.

[10] At the end of the seventh book of Thucydides.

[11] Tovey (*Gray's English Poems*, pp. 128 ff.) doubts Mason's statement (*Memoirs*, p. 157) that 'the *Elegy in a Country Churchyard* was begun if not concluded in 1742', and taking this passage in connexion with Gray's reference to 'the Muse' (see Letter 120, n. 39ᵃ) thinks that the 'autumnal Verses' can only belong to the *Elegy*, which, he supposes, was now being begun. (See Appendix I.)

[12] Ashton (see Letter 120, n. 36).   [13] MS. torn.

[14] Negotiations for peace had been opened at Breda, but proved abortive; peace was at length concluded at Aix-la-Chapelle, 18 Oct. 1748.

[15] The lists were apparently extracted by Gray from an 'Alphabetical Catalogue' of some 900 books compiled by him, which is in one of his notebooks now in the Pierpont Morgan Library, New York. The College does

imagine to chuse out of, considering the State of your Coll: Finances. the best Editions of ancient Authors should be the first Things, I reckon, in a Library: but if you think otherwise, I will send a Page of a different Kind. pray write soon, & think me very faithfully

Yours T G:

Sept: 11. 1746. Stoke . . . Say many good Things to Mr Brown from me.

ANCIENTS.

 1. Aristophanes, Kusteri. Amst: Fol: 1710.
 2. Aristotelis Opera, ed: Du-Val. 4v. Fol: Paris, 1654. Gr: Lat: (Fabricius likewise recommends the Ed:^{n} of Sylburgius, all Greek, 1587. 5 V: 4to. apud Wechelios).
 3. Arrian. Jac: Gronovii. Lugd: Bat: 1704.
 4. Apollonius Rhodius. Hoelzlinii. Elzev: 1641. 8vo.
 5. Arati, atq Eratosthenis Fragmenta. Oxon: 8vo. 1672.
 6. Aristidis Opera, ed: S: Jebb. 2 V: 4to. Oxon: 1722–30.
 7. M: Aurelius, Gatakeri. Ultraject: Fol: 1698.
 8. Ammianus Marcellinus, H: Valesii. Par: 1681. Fol:
 9. Ausonius, Tollii. Amst: Blaeu. 1671. 8vo.
 10. Antonini Itinerarium. Varior: Wesselingii. 4to. 1735.
 11. Bertii Theatr:^{m} Geographicum. Fol: Amst: 1618. Elzev: (it contains the best Edition of Ptolemy, by M: Servetus).
 12. Boethius. Varior: Basil: 1650. Fol:
 13. Corpus Oratorum Græc:, H: Stephani. Fol: 1575.
 14. Q: Curtius, Snakenburgi. 1724. 4to.
 15. Cassiodori Opera. Garretti. Rothomagi, 1679. 2 V: Fol:
 16. Diodorus Siculus. the last new Ed:^{n} in 2 V: Fol:^{o}
 17. Dionysius Halicarn:, Hudsoni. 2 V: Fol: Oxon: 1704.
 18. Dio Prusæensis. Morelli. Paris. 1604. Fol:^{o}
 19. Dicæarchi Fragmenta. H: Steph: Genevæ. 1589. 8vo.
 20. Dio Cassius. Hanoviæ. 1606. Fol:
 21. Epistolæ Græc: antiquæ . . . a Caldorina Societate. Fol: Aurel. Allobrogum. 1606.
 22. Ennii Fragmenta. Hesselii. 4to. 1707. Amst:
 23. Festus, de Verborum Significatione, Dacerii, in Us: Delphini. 4to. Par: 1618.
 24. Florus. Varior: 1692. 8vo.

not seem to have acted on Gray's suggestion or to have made any large purchase of books at this time.

25. Geoponica, Cassiani Bassi. ed: P: Needham. Cantab: 1704. 8vo.

26. Aulus Gellius, Oiselii &c: 1706. 4to.

27. Gemistius Pletho. Fol: 1540. Basil:

28. Himerius & Polemo. H: Stephani. 4to. 1567.

29. Hesiodus. Grævii. Amst: 8vo—1667.

30. Historiæ Augustæ Scriptores. Varior: ap: Hackios. 2 V: 8vo. 1670–1.

31. Hierocles. Mer: Casauboni. 8vo. Lond: 1665.

32. Hist: Byzantinæ Scriptores. Par: & Romæ. from 1645 to 1702. (I think, including Banduri's Antiquities, there are 30 vol: Fol:°)

33. Harpocration, Jac: Gronovii. 1696. Lug: Bat: 4to.

34. Isocrates. H: Wolfii. ap: H: Steph: 1693. Fol:°

35. Josephus, Hudsoni. 2 V: 1726. Amst: Fol:

36. Libanius. Morelli. 2 V: Fol: Paris. 1606–27.

37. Libanii Epistolæ. Fol: 1738. Amst:

38. Lycophron, Potteri. Oxon: Fol: 1697.

39. Livius, Creverii. 6 V: 4to. Par:

40. Lucanus, Oudendorpii. 2 V: 4to. 1728.

41. Macrobius. J: F: Gronovii. 1670. 8vo. Lug: Bat: (unfinish'd)

42. Nicander. G: Morelli. Par: 4to. 1557.

43. Oppian, Riterhusii. Lug: Bat: 1597.

44. Pausanias, Kuhnii. Lipsiæ. 1696. Fol:

45. Pomponius Mela, Jac. Gronovii. 8vo. 1722.

46. Plinii Hist: Naturalis, Harduini. Par: 5 V: 4to. 1685 & republish'd. ib: 3 V: Fol: 1723.

47. Polybius. Varior: 3 V: 8vo. 1670. Amst:

48. Philostratorum Opera, Olearii. Lips: Fol:° 1709.

49. Philo Judæus, ed: Mangey. 2 V: Fol: 1742. Lond:

50. Pollucis Onomasticon. Varior: Fol: 2 V: 1706.

51. Prudentius. N: Heinsii. Amst: Elz: 1667. 12mo.

52. Palladius, de Brachmanibus. Ed: Bisse. 4to. 1665. Lond.

53. Plautus. 2 V: Gronovii &c: 8vo. 1684. Amst:

54. Panegyrici Veteres. in Us: Delphini. 4to. 1677. Par:

55. Poetæ Minores, ed: P. Burmanni. 2 V: 4to. 1731. Lug: Bat:

56. Plinii Epistolæ, Cortii & Var: 1734. 4to. Amst:

57. Excerpta ex Polybio &c: H: Valesii. 4to. 1634. Par:

58. Rutilii Itinerarium, Grævii. 1687: 8vo. Amst:

59. Sophocles, P: Stephani. 4to. 1603.

60. Suetonius, Grævii. 1691. 4to. & 1703. Pitisci. 2 V: 4to. Leov:^{diae} 1714. (I don't know, wch is the best Edition.)
61. Stephanus Byzantinus, Ab: Berkelii. 1688. Fol: L: Bat:— Lucæ Holstenii Notæ. Amst: Fol:
62. Sidonius, Sirmondi. 1652. Par: 4to & cum Oper:^{bus} Sirmondi.
63. Synesius, Petavii. Par: 1640. Fol:
64. Symmachus. J: Parei. Neap: Nemetum. 1617. 8vo.
65. Silius Italicus, Drakenburgi. Ultraj: 1717. 4to.
66. Senecæ Tragediæ, Schroderi. 4to. Delf: 1728.
67. Themistius, Harduini. Par: Fol: 1684.
68. Theocritus. Varior: 1604. 4to. ap: Commelin:
69. Thucydides, Dukeri. Fol:
70. Valerius Flaccus Burmanni. L: Bat: 1724. 4to.
71. Aurelius Victor, Arntzenii. 1733. 4to.
72. Valerius Maximus. Torrentii. 4to. L: Bat: 1726.
73. Xenophon, Leunclavii. Fol: 1625. Par: & the three Vol: that Hutchinson has publish'd. 4to Oxon:

ANTIQUARIES. GRAMMARIANS. &C:

Bonanni, delle antiche Siracuse. 2 V: Palermo. 1717.
Boissard, Antiquitates Urb: Romanæ. 3 V: Fol: Francof:
Bergier, Hist: des Grands Chemins de l'Emp: Romaine. 2 V: 4to. Brux: 1728.
Bellori, Vet: Philosophorum &c: Imagines. 1685. Fol: Romæ.
Du Cange, Glossarium Latinitatis mediæ vel infimæ. 3 V: Fol:
——————— Græcum, ejusd: ætatis. 3 V: Fol: 1678. Par: both republish'd in 1733.
Ang: Caninius de Hellenismo, ed: a T: Crenio. 1700. L: Bat: 8vo.
Dodwell, de vet: Græc: & Rom: Cyclo cum Annal: Thucydi[deis et] Xenophonteis. Oxon: 4to. 1701.
—————— Annales Statiani, Velleiani, Quintilianei.[16]
—————— Prælectiones, in Schol: Camdenianâ. Ox: 1692. 8.[16]
—————— Exercitationes, de Ætate Phalaridis & Pythagoræ. 170[4][16]
Fabretti Inscriptiones. 1691. Rom: Fol:
Fabricii Bibl: Græca, V: 14. 4to. 1708. (this I believe you have.)
—————— ca Latina.[17] 3 V: 8vo. 1721.
—————— Antiquaria. 4to. 1713.

[16] MS. torn.   [17] That is, Bibliotheca Latina.

Fabretti, de Aquæductibus Rom: 4to. 1680. Romæ.
Fabretti, de Columnâ Trajani, &c: 1685. Fol: Romæ.
Gruteri Inscriptiones, ed: Grævii. 4 V: Fol: 1708.
Salengre, Thesaurus Antiq: Roman:^{arum}. 3 V: 1716. Fol:
     Hagæ.
Muratori, Thesaurus Antiq: 2 V: Fol: 173 . . . .
Gyraldi (Lilii) Opera, ed: Jensii. Fol: 1696. L: Bat:
Goldasti Epistolæ Philologicæ. 8vo. Lipsiæ.
Heineccii Antiq:^{um} Rom:^{æ} Jurisprudentiæ Syntagma. 2 V:
     8vo. 1724.
Hankius, de Byzantin: Scriptoribus. 1677. Lips: 4to.
Heindreich, de Carthagin: Republicâ. Francof: ad Oderum.
Loydii, Series Olympiadum &c: Fol: Oxon: 1700.
Martinii Lexicon Philologicum. ed: Grævii. 2 V: Fol: 1701.
     Amst:
Montfaucon, Palæographia Græca. 1708. Fol: Par:
Notitia Dignitatum utriusq Imperii, a P: Labbæo. 1651.
     Par: 8vo. (this may perhaps be in the Byzant: Collec-
     tion.)
Palmerii Græcia Antiqua. 1678. 4to. L. Bat: (unfinish'd.)
Petavius, de Doctrina Temporum. 2 V: 1703. Fol:
Streinnius, de Rom. Familiarum Stemmatibus. Fol: 1659. Par:
Ursinus, Vet: Imagines & Elogia. 1570. Fol: Romæ.
——— de Familiis Romanis. 1577. ibid:
Vaillant, Ptolemæorum Hist:^{a} 1701. Fol: Amst: Seleuci-
     darum. 4to. Par: 1681. Arsacidarum—

Addressed: To Thomas Wharton Esq, Fellow of Pembroke Hall Cambridge
   Postmark: 13 SE

122. GRAY TO CHUTE

MY God! Mr Chute in England?[1] what & have you seen
him? and did he say nothing to you? not a Word of
me! such was my Conversation, when I first heard News so

LETTER 122.—First printed by Mitford in *Works of Gray* (1835–43),
vol. iii, pp. 19–20; now reprinted from original.
   [1] In his letter to Mann of 2 Oct. 1746 from Windsor, Walpole writes: 'By
your own loss you may measure my joy at the receipt of the dear Chutes
[meaning John Chute and Francis Whithed, whom he sometimes spoke of
as the 'Chuteheds']. I strolled to town one day last week, and there I found
them!' In the same letter he says they had gone 'chez eux', i.e. to Whithed's
place at Southwick Park, near Fareham.

surprising, with a Person,[2] that (when I reflect) it is indeed no great Wonder You did not much interrogate concerning me, as you knew nothing of what has past of late.[3]

But let me ask you yourself, have a few Years totally erased me from your Memory? You are generous enough perhaps to forget all the Obligations I have to you, but is it Generosity to forget the Person you have obliged too? while I remember myself, I can not but remember you; & consequently can not but wonder, when I find no where one Line, one Syllable, to tell me you are arrived. I will venture to say, there is no body in England however nearly connected with you, that has seen you with more real Joy & Affection than I shall. You are, it seems, gone into the Country whither (had I any Reason to think you wish'd to see me) I should immediately have follow'd you: as it is, I am returning to Cambridge; but with Intention to come back to Town again, whenever you do; if you will let me know the Time, & Place.

I readily set M^r Wh:^d4 free from all Imputations. he is a fine young Personage in a Coat all over Spangles just come over from the Tour of Europe to take Pofsefsion, & be married:[5] & consequently can't be supposed to think of any Thing, or remember any body. but You ——! however I don't altogether clear him. he might have said something to one, who remembers him when he was but a Pout.[6] neverthelefs I desire my hearty Gratulations to him, & say I wish him more Spangles, & more Estates, & more Wives. Adieu! my dear S^r, I am ever

Yours
T GRAY.

London—Oct: [c. 6[7] 1746] .. To T:G: of Peterhouse, Cambridge.

[2] Walpole.
[3] Chute would have been chary of mentioning Gray to Walpole, knowing that they had quarrelled, and not yet having learned of their reconciliation (see Letter 116).   [4] Whithed.
[5] Chaloner Chute (*History of the Vyne*, pp. 100–1) notes: 'A portrait of Francis Whithed at the Vyne by Rosalba shows him much as this letter describes him, "a fine young personage in a coat all over spangles". The picture is matched by a portrait, also by Rosalba, of Margaret, daughter and heiress of John Nichol, of Southgate, Middlesex. Not long before Whithed's death Chute had arranged for him to marry Miss Nichol (see Walpole's letter to Mann of 1 April 1751, quoted in Letter 165, n. 1).
[6] See Letter 124, n. 5.
[7] The letter must have been written in the first week of October, as Gray found Chute's reply on his return to Cambridge on 10 Oct. (see Letter 125, *ad init.*).

P:S: My Compliments to Mrs Chute[8] (who once did me the Honour to write to me) & say, I give her Joy very sincerely of your Return.

Addressed: To John Chute Esq at Mr Whithed's of Southwick near Fareham in Hampshire[9]

123. GRAY TO WHARTON

[8 Oct. 1746][1]

My Dear Wharton,

THIS is only to entreat you would order mes Gens to clean out the Appartments, spread the Carpets, air the Beds, put up the Tapestry, unpaper the Frames, &c: fit to receive a great Potentate, that comes down in the Flying Coach drawn by Green Dragons[2] on Friday the 10th Instant. as the Ways are bad, & the Dragons a little out of Repair (for they don't actually fly; but only go, like a lame Ostrich, something between a Hop & a Trot) it will probably be late when he lands, so he would not chuse to be known, & desires there may be no Bells, nor Bonfires: but as Persons incog: love to be seen, he will slip into the Coffee

---

[8] A note on the margin of the original states this to be 'Mrs Francis Chute'. This lady was the widow of John Chute's brother, Francis (see Walpole's note on his letter to Mann of 7 Aug. 1745), who had died in the summer of 1745. She was probably the 'near relation' of John Chute mentioned by Gray in Letter 109. It has been conjectured that it was she who helped to bring about the reconciliation of Gray and Walpole (see Appendix D).

[9] The address is no longer with the original.

LETTER 123.—First printed in part (in a garbled text) in Mason's *Memoirs*, pp. 173–5; first printed in full by Mitford (1816), vol. ii, pp. 143–4; now reprinted from original.

[1] The letter is endorsed '8 Oct. 44 or 45'. But the Peterhouse books show that Gray was in residence there on 8 Oct. both in 1744 and 1745; whereas in 1746 he commenced residence on 10 Oct., which was Friday, the day of his intended arrival, as announced in this letter.

[2] This humorous description was no doubt prompted by the fact that the stage-coach in which Gray proposed to return to Cambridge started from the *Green Dragon* in Bishopsgate Street, as appears from the following announcement, under the head of *Coaches*, in *Cantabrigia Depicta*:

'*Stage-Coach for Four Passengers at 10s each,* Sets out from the *Red-Lion* in the *Petty-Cury* at Seven in the Morning on *Tuesdays, Thursdays,* and *Saturdays,* from *Midsummer* to *Christmas,* to the *Green-Dragon* in *Bishopsgate-street;* from whence it returns at the same Hour on *Mondays, Wednesdays,* and *Fridays.* The other half Year it sets out from the *Blue-Boar* in *Cambridge,* inns at the *Green-Dragon* aforesaid: and returns to the *Blue-Boar.*' The *Green Dragon* was No. 86 Bishopsgate Street (see also Letter 46, n. 16).

House. is Mr Trollope⁴ among you? good lack! he will pull off
my Head for never writeing to him. oh Conscience! Conscience!⁵

Addressed: To Thomas Wharton Esq, Fellow of Pembroke Hall Cambridge
Postmark: [o]c 8

124. GRAY TO CHUTE

My Dear S^r

YOU have not then forgot me, & I shall see you again: it
suffices, & there needed no other Excuse. I loved You too
well not to forgive you without a Reason; but I could not but
be sorry for myself.

You are lazy (you say) & listlefs & gouty & old, & vex'd and
perplex'd: I am all that (the Gout excepted) & many Things
more, that I hope you never will be: so that what you tell me on
that Head est trop flateux¹ pour moi: our Imperfections may at
least excuse, & perhaps recommend us to one another: methinks
I can readily pardon Sicknefs & Age & Vexation for all the
Depredations they make within & without, when I think they
make us better Friends & better Men, wch I am persuaded is
often the Case. I am very sure, I have seen the best-temper'd
generous tender young Creatures in the World, that would have
been very glad to be sorry for People they liked, when under any
Pain, and could not; merely for Want of knowing rightly, what
it was, themselves.

I find Mr Walpole then made some Mention of me to you.
yes, we are together again. it is about a Year, I believe, since
he wrote to me to offer it, & there has been (particularly of late)
in Appearance the same Kindnefs & Confidence almost as of
old. what were his Motives I can not yet guefs: what were mine,
you will imagine, & perhaps blame me.² however as yet I
neither repent, nor rejoice overmuch: but I am pleased. he is
full, I afsure you, of your Panegyric. never any body had half
so much Wit as Mr Chute³ (wch is saying every thing with him,
you know) & Mr W.^d is the finest young Man, that ever was

⁴ See Letter 114, n. 1.
⁵ The rest has been cut away.
LETTER 124.—First printed by Mitford in *Works of Gray* (1835–43),
vol. iii, pp. 21–2; now reprinted from original.
¹ *Sic.*
² Gray seems to imply that Chute had thought Walpole so much in the
wrong, when they quarrelled, that Gray ought not to have accepted his
overtures.
³ Walpole says of Chute in his letter to Mann of 2 Oct. 1746: 'I don't

imported.[4] I hope to embrace this fine Man (if I can) & thank him heartily for being my Advocate, tho' in vain: he is a good Creature, & I am not sure but I shall be tempted to eat a Wing of him with Sellery-Sauce[5]—I am interrupted. whenever I know of your Time, I will be in Town presently. I can not but make M[rs] Chute[6] my best Acknowledgements for takeing my Part. Heaven keep you all! I am, my best M[r] Chute, very faithfully Yours

T G:

Cambr:[ge] Oct: 12. Sunday. [1746]

Addressed: To John Chute Esq at M[r] Whithed's of Southwick near Fareham in Hampshire *Postmark:* CAMBRIDGE 13 OC

125. GRAY TO WALPOLE

My Dear S[r]

I FOUND (as soon as I got hither) a very kind Letter from M[r] Chute, from whence I have Reason to hope we may all meet in Town about a Week hence. You have probably been there, since I left you, & consequently have seen the M[r] Barry[1] you desired some Account of: yet as I am not certain of this, & should be glad to know whether we agree about him; I will neverthelefs tell you what he is, & the Imprefsion he made upon me. he is upwards of six Foot in Height, well & proportionably

know how he will succeed here, but to me he has more wit than anybody I know'; and again, on 4 Nov. of the same year: 'M[r] Chute has absolutely more wit, knowledge, and good nature, than, to their great surprise, ever met together in one man'; thirty years later (27 May 1776), a few days after Chute's death, he writes: 'His wit and quickness illuminated everything. . . . The vigour of his mind was strong as ever; his powers of reasoning clear as demonstration; his rapid wit astonishing as at forty, about which time you and I knew him first'.

  [4] In the above-quoted letter to Mann of 2 Oct. Walpole speaks of Whithed as 'a very pretty gentleman'.

  [5] There must have been a jest on Whithed's name. 'Whitehead' was a name given to partridges when newly hatched (*O.E.D.*), and partridge with celery sauce is a dish in Verrall's *Cookery* (see Letter 330, n. 23). It is part of the same jest that Gray talks of Whithed 'when he was but a Pout' (Letter 122; and cf. Letter 112).

  [6] See Letter 122, n. 8.

  LETTER 125.—First printed by Toynbee (1915), No. 157.

  [1] Spranger Barry (1719–77), a Dublin silversmith, who had taken to the stage in Dublin two years before. He made his first appearance in London as Othello at Drury Lane on 4 Oct. of this year, and speedily became a formidable rival of Garrick. Gray's account of his voice and person is borne out by other contemporary observers.

made, treads well, & knows what to do with his Limbs; in short a noble graceful Figure: I can say nothing of his Face, but that it was all Black, with a wide Mouth & good Eyes. his Voice is of a clear & pleasing Tone, something like Delane's,[2] but not so deep-mouth'd, not so like a Paſsing Bell. when high strained, it is apt to crack a little, & be hoarse: but in its common Pitch, & when it sinks into any softer Paſsion, particularly expreſsive & touching. in the first Scenes, especially where he recounts to the Senate the Progreſs of his Love, & the Means he used to win Desdemona, he was quite mistaken, & I took a Pique against him: instead of a Cool Narration he flew into a Rant of Voice & Action, as tho' he were relating the Circumstances of a Battle that was fought yesterday. I expected nothing more from him, but was deceived: in the Scenes of Rage & Jealousy he was seldom inferior to Quin:[3] in the Parts of Tenderneſs & Sorrow far above him. these latter seem to be his peculiarly: his Action is not very various, but rarely improper, or without Dignity: & some of his Attitudes are really fine. he is not perfect to be sure; but I think may make a better Player than any now on the Stage in a little while. however to see a Man in one Character, & but once, is not sufficient: so I rather ask your Opinion by this, than give you mine.

I annex (as you desired) another Ode.[4] all it pretends to with you is, that it is mine, & that you never saw it before, & that it is not so long as t'other.

> Lo, where the rosie-bosom'd Hours,
> Fair Venus' Train, appear,
> Disclose the long-expecting Flowers,
> And wake the purple Year!
> The Attic Warbler pours her Throat
> Responsive to the Cuckow's Note,

---

[2] See Letter 20, n. 7.　　　　　　　[3] See Letter 3, n. 17.
[4] The *Ode on the Spring* ('the other' being no doubt that *On a Distant Prospect of Eton College*), originally called by Gray *Noontide, an Ode*. The poem was written in 1742, and was sent to West after his death (no doubt with Letter 110), as appears from a note appended by Gray to his transcript in the Pembroke MSS.: 'at Stoke, the beginning of June 1742 sent to Fav: not knowing he was then Dead'. It was first printed (with the title *Ode*) in 1748 in Dodsley's *Collection of Poems by several Hands* (vol. ii, pp. 265 ff.), in which were also included the *Ode on a Distant Prospect of Eton College* (vol. ii, pp. 261 ff.) (see Letter 139, n. 1) and the *Ode on the Death of a Favourite Cat* (vol. ii, pp. 267 ff.) (see Letter 134, n. 3). It is the first of the *Six Poems* with the designs of Bentley, published in 1753 (see Letter 161, n. 2).

The untaught Harmony of Spring:
While whisp'ring Pleasure as they fly
Cool Zephyrs thro' the clear blue Sky
Their gather'd Fragrance fling

Where'er the Oak's thick Branches stretch
A broader browner Shade;
Where'er the rude & mofs-grown Beech
O'ercanopies the Glade;
Beside some Water's rushy Brink
With me the Muse shall sit, & think
(At Ease reclined in rustic State)
How vain the Ardour of the Crowd,
How low, how indigent the Proud,
How little are the Great![6]

          —a Bank
Oercanopied with luscious Woodbine
  Shakesp: Mids: Night's Dream[5]

Still is the toiling Hand of Care:
The panting Herds repose.
Yet hark, how thro' the peopled Air
The busy Murmur glows!
The Insect-Youth are on the Wing
Eager to tast the honied Spring,
And float amid the liquid Noon:
Some lightly o'er the Current skim,
Some shew their gayly-gilded Trim
Quick-glanceing to the Sun.

      Nare per æstatem liqui-
       dam. Virg:[7]

To Contemplation's sober Eye
Such is the Race of Man:
And they that creep, & they that fly,
Shall end where they began.
Alike the Busy & the Gay
But flutter thro' Life's little Day,
In Fortune's varying Colours drest:
Brush'd by the Hand of rough Mischance,
Or chill'd by Age, their airy Dance
They leave, in Dust to rest.

   [5] Act ii, Sc. 1.
   [6] These two lines were printed in this form in Dodsley's *Collection*; Gray afterwards altered them to
        How low, how little are the Proud
        How indigent the Great!
in which form they appear in the *Six Poems*. Mason states that Gray made the correction 'on account of the point of *little* and *great*'.
   [7] *Georg.* iv. 59.

Methinks I hear in Accents low
The sportive Kind reply,
Poor Moralist! & what art Thou?
A solitary Fly!
Thy Joys no glittering Female meets,
No Hive hast thou of hoarded Sweets,
No painted Plumage to display:
On hasty Wings thy Youth is flown;
Thy Sun is set; thy Spring is gone:
We frolick, while 'tis May.

My Compliments to Ashton. Adieu, I am sincerely
Yours

T G:

Camb: Oct: 20. [1746]⁸

126. GRAY TO CHUTE

Cambridge . . Sunday [Nov. 23, 1746]¹

Lustrifsimo

IT is doubtlefs highly reasonable, that two young Foreigners come into so distant a Country to acquaint themselves with strange Things should have some Time allowed them to take a View of the King (God blefs him) & the Ministry, & the Theatres, & Westminster Abbey & the Lyons,² & such other Curiosities of the Capital City: you civilly call them Difsipations; but to me they appear Employments of a very serious Nature, as they enlarge the Mind, give a great Insight into the Nature & Genius of a People, keep the Spirits in an agreeable Agitation, and (like the True Artificial Spirit of Lavender) amazingly fortify & corroborate the whole nervous System. but as all Things sooner or later must pafs away, & there is a certain Period, when (by the Rules of Proportion) one is to grow weary of every Thing: I may hope at length a Season will arrive, when you will be tired of forgetting me. 'tis true you have a long

⁸ The date of the year has been inserted in the original by Mason.
    LETTER 126.—First printed (in modified text) by Chaloner Chute in *History of the Vyne*, pp. 102–4, now reprinted from original.
    ¹ The date is determined by the postmark, 24 No (the day after the letter was written): 23 Nov. was a Sunday in 1746, which is obviously the year.
    ² At the Tower of London.

Journey to make first, a vast Series of Sights to paſs thro'. let me see! you are at Lady Brown[3] already. I have set a Time, when I may say, oh! he is now got to the Waxwork in Fleet-street:[4] there is nothing more but Cupid's Paradise,[5] & the Hermaphrodite from Guinea, & the Original Basilisk Dragon, & the Buffalo from Babylon, & the New Chimpanzee,[6] & then I. have a Care, you had best, that I come in my Turn: you know in whose Hands I have deposited my little Interests. I shall infallibly appeal to my *best invisible* Friend[7] in the Country.

I am glad Castalio[8] has justified himself & me to You. he seem'd to me more made for Tenderneſs, than Horrour, & (I have Courage again to insist upon it) might make a better Player than any now on the Stage. I have not alone received (thank you) but almost got thro' Louis Onze.[9] 'tis very well, methinks, but nothing particular. what occasion'd his

---

[3] Margaret, daughter of Hon. Robert Cecil, second son of third Earl of Salisbury; she married Sir Robert Brown (d. 1760), first Baronet (1732), at one time Paymaster of the Works, and formerly a merchant at Venice and British Resident there. Lady Brown, who died in 1782 at the age of 86, was a patroness of foreign singers. She is stated by Dr. Burney (*History of Music*, iv. 671) to have been 'one of the first persons of fashion who had the courage at the risk of her windows to have concerts on a Sunday evening'. Writing to Mann on 13 Feb. 1743 Walpole says of one Ceretesi, a Florentine recently arrived in England: 'I am literally waiting for him now, to introduce him to Lady Brown's Sunday night; it is the great mark for all travelling and travelled calves'. Gray was acquainted with her (see Letter 154*).

[4] Fleet Street was famous for its wax-work exhibitions, the most cele-brated of which was that of the 'ingenious Mrs Salmon', mentioned in Nos. 28 and 31 of Addison's *Spectator*.

[5] No doubt the place of public resort at Bermondsey known as 'Cupid's Gardens'—'What is now a straw-yard skirting the river was once the City Ranelagh, called *Cupid's Gardens*, and the trees, now black with mud, were the bowers under which the citizens loved, on the summer evenings, to sit beside the stream, drinking their sack and ale' (Thornbury and Walford's *Old and New London*, vol. vi, p. 116).

[6] In Chambers's *Cyclopaedia* (1753), art. 'Chimpanzee', it is stated: 'In the year 1738 we had one of these creatures brought over into England by the captain of a ship in the Guinea trade'.

[7] Possibly Mrs. Francis Chute (see Letter 122, n. 8).

[8] Character in Otway's *Orphan*; the part had been played at Drury Lane on 15, 17–20 Nov. of this year by Spranger Barry (see Letter 125, n. 1).

[9] *Histoire de Louis Onze*, 2 vols., 1745, with *Pièces Justificatives*, 1746, by Charles Pinot Duclos (1704–72), subsequently (1750) Historio-grapher of France in succession to Voltaire.

Castration[10] at Paris, I imagine, were certain Strokes in Defence of the Gallican Church & its Liberties—a little Contempt cast upon the Popes, & something here & there on the Conduct of the great Princes. there are a few Instances of Malice against our Nation, that are very foolish.

My Companion,[11] whom you salute, is (much to my Sorrow) only so now & then. he lives 20 Miles off at Nurse, & is not so meagre as when you first knew him, but of a reasonable Plumposity. he shall not fail being here to do the Honours, when you make your publick Entry. heigh-ho! when that will be, chi sá? but, mi lusinga il dolce sogno!—I love Mr Whithed, & wish him all Happinefs. Farewell, my dear S^r, I am ever Yours

T G:

Commend me kindly to Mr Walpole.

Addressed: To John Chute Esq at the House of Francis Whithed Esq in New Bond Street Westminster   *Postmark:* CAMBRIDGE 24 NO

127. GRAY TO WHARTON

My Dear Wharton

I WOULD make you an Excuse (as indeed I ought) if they were a Sort of Thing I ever gave any Credit to myself in these Cases, but I know they are never true. nothing so silly as

[10] The book was censured by an Arrêt du Conseil, and its republication was prohibited until 'plusieurs endroits contraires, non seulement aux droits de la couronne sur différentes provinces du royaume, mais au respect avec lequel on doit parler de ce qui regarde la religion ou les règles des mœurs, et la conduite des principaux membres de l'église', had been excised.

[11] This was probably Nicholas Bonfoy (d. 1775), of Abbott's Ripton (or Rippon), near Huntingdon, about twenty miles from Cambridge, whom Walpole and Gray met in Paris in 1739 (see Walpole's letter to West from Paris, 21 April 1739). In making the grand tour Bonfoy would naturally, like other English, visit Florence in due course, where he would have the opportunity of renewing relations with Walpole and Gray, and of making the acquaintance of Chute. After his return to Cambridge Gray, as may be gathered from his letters, became intimate with Bonfoy and his mother, and frequently visited them at Abbott's Ripton.

Bonfoy was admitted Pensioner at Pembroke in 1725, and was admitted at Gray's Inn in 1724; he was appointed Serjeant-at-Arms in the House of Commons, 1762 (see Letter 547, n. 7).

LETTER 127.—First printed in part (in a garbled text) in Mason's *Memoirs*, pp. 180–1; first printed in full by Mitford (1816), vol. ii, pp. 164–7; now reprinted from original.

Indolence, when it hopes to disguise itself: every one knows it by it's Saunter; as they do his Majesty (God blefs him) at a Masquerade by the Firmnefs of his Tread, & the Elevation of his Chin. however somewhat I had to say, that has a little Shadow of Reason in it. I have been in Town (I suppose you know) flaunting about at publick Places of all kinds with my two Italianized Friends.[1] the World itself has some Attraction in it to a Solitary of six Years standing; & agreeable well-meaning People of Sense (thank Heaven there are so few of them) are my peculiar Magnet. it is no Wonder then, if I felt some Reluctance at parting with them so soon; or if my Spirits, when I return'd back to my Cell, should sink for a time, not indeed to Storm & Tempest, but a good deal below Changeable. besides Seneca says (and my Pitch of Philosophy does not pretend to be much above Seneca)[2] Nunquam mores, quos extuli, refero. aliquid ex eo, quod composui, turbatur: aliquid ex his, quæ fugavi, redit. and it will happen to such as we, mere Imps of Science. well it may, when Wisdom herself is forced often—in sweet retired Solitude

> To plume her Feathers, & let grow her Wings,
> That in the various Bustle of Resort
> Were all too ruffled & sometimes impair'd.[3]

It is a foolish Thing, that one can't only not live as one pleases, but where & with whom one pleases, without Money. Swift somewhere says, that Money is Liberty;[4] & I fear money is Friendship too & Society, & almost every external Blefsing. it is a great tho' ill-natured, Comfort to see most of those, who have it in Plenty, without Pleasure, without Liberty, & without Friends.

Mr Brown (who I afsure you holds up his Head & his Spirits very notably) will give you an Account of your College Proceedings, if they may be so call'd, where nothing proceeds at all.

[1] Chute and Whithed; Walpole had been with them for he wrote to Mann a few days before, on 5 Dec., 'the Chutes and I deal extremely together'. The College books show that Gray was absent from Cambridge from c. 30 Oct. to c. 15 Nov.; in his letter to Wharton of 27 Dec. (Letter 129) he refers to this visit to London as 'my Dissipation de quinze jours'.

[2] Seneca, *Epist.* vii, *ad init.*

[3] Milton, *Comus*, 378–80 (adapted).

[4] See Swift's letter to Pope of 16 July 1728, quoted by Mitford 1835–43, vol. iii, p. 24, n.

only the last Week Roger⁵ was so wise to declare ex motu proprio, that he took Mʳ Delaval⁶ (who is now a Fell: Commoner) into his own Tuition. this raised the dirty Spirit of his Friend, Mʳ May⁷ (now Tutor in Francis's⁸ Room) against him, & even gentle Mʳ Peele,⁹ (who never acts but in Conjunction) together with Mʳ Brown (who pretended to be mighty angry, tho' in reality heartily glad) and they all came to an Eclaircisement in the Parlour. they abused him pretty reasonably, & it ended in threatening them as usual with a Visitor. in short they are all as rude as may be, leave him at Table by himself, never go into the Parlour, till he comes out; or if he enters, when they are there, continue sitting even in his own Magisterial Chair. May bickers with him publickly about twenty paltry Matters, & Roger t'other Day told him he was impertinent. what would you have more? you see they do as one would wish. if you were here all would be right. I am surprised not to hear you mention, when that will be; pray give an Account of yourself. I am very sincerely Yours

                                                           T G:

P:S: When I went to Town Part of my Errand was to sell a little Stock I had, to pay off Birkett's¹⁰ old Debt now at Xmas, but it was so low, I should have lost near 12 per Cent, & so it

---

⁵ Dr. Roger Long, Master of Pembroke.

⁶ This was John Blake (afterwards Hussey) Delaval (1728–1808), second son of Francis Blake Delaval, of Seaton Delaval and Ford, co. Northumberland, and elder brother of Edward Hussey Delaval (see Letter 163, n. 12). He was created a Baronet in 1761; an Irish Peer as Baron Delaval, in 1783; and a Peer of Great Britain in 1786. He was M.P. for Berwick, 1765–74, 1780–6. On the death of his eldest brother, Sir Francis Blake Delaval, K.B., in 1771 he succeeded to the family estates. During his brief residence at Pembroke (for the abrupt termination of which see Gray's letter to Wharton of 27 Dec. 1746—Letter 129) Christopher Smart (see Letter 135, n. 8) was his private tutor. In 1751 Smart at the request of his former pupil wrote a prologue and epilogue for a performance 'by several persons of quality' of *Othello* at Drury Lane, the parts of Othello and Iago being played by Francis Blake Delaval and John Blake Hussey Delaval. (See *Poems of C. Smart*, 1791, vol. i, p. xx.)

⁷ Samuel May, of Pembroke; B.A., 1737; M.A., 1740; Fellow, 1740; Proctor, 1759–60; Vicar of Waresley, Hunts., 1746–72; d. 1787.

⁸ John Francis, of Pembroke; B.A., 1729; M.A., 1732; Fellow, 1733; President, 1746; Vicar of Waresley, Hunts., 1745–6; of Soham, Cambs., 1746–82.

⁹ John Peele, of Pembroke; B.A., 1741; M.A., 1744; Fellow, 1743; Vicar of Tilney All Saints, Norfolk, 1749–1805.

¹⁰ Gray, as an undergraduate, was under Birkett's tutorship (see Letter 29, n. 1). Gray had probably let some of his bills run on since he

continues. if you think of being here near that Time, & find
it not inconvenient to you to lend me 40£, you will save me the
Money I mention. (as I remember you once offer'd) but if any
Inconvenience attend it, you must imagine I don't by any
Means desire it; & you need not be at the Trouble of any
Excuse, as I well know, nothing but the not being able would
hinder your doing it immediately. let me know, because other-
wise I have another Journey to make to Town.

Dec: 11 . . Cambridge.

Addressed: To Dʳ Thomas Wharton at Durham By Caxton Bag *Postmark:*
CAMBRIDGE

128. GRAY TO WALPOLE
Cambridge, Dec. [22] Monday [1746].¹

THIS comes du fond de ma cellule to salute Mr. H. W. not
so much him that visits and votes, and goes to White's and
to court; as the H. W. in his rural capacity, snug in his tub on
Windsor-hill,² and brooding over folios of his own creation:³
him that can slip away, like a pregnant beauty (but a little
oftener), into the country, be brought to bed perhaps of twins,
and whisk to town again the week after with a face as if nothing
had happened. Among the little folks, my godsons and daughters, I can not choose but enquire more particularly after the
health of one; I mean (without a figure) the Memoires:⁴ Do
they grow? Do they unite, and hold up their heads, and drefs

returned to Cambridge in 1742. He was now a graduate Fellow-commoner,
but a Fellow-commoner of whatever standing did not pay cook's and
butler's charges &c. directly; these would be collected by the tutor (see
Appendix E).

LETTER 128.—First printed in *Works of Lord Orford*, vol. v, pp. 389–90.

¹ The date of the year is determined by the references to Lord Lovat, to
Sir Charles Hanbury Williams, and to the opera *Mitridate* (see nn. 5, 7, 8).
From the allusion to the impeachment of Lord Lovat (see n. 5) it seems
probable that the date of the month was Monday, 22 Dec.

² In the previous August Walpole had taken a house at Windsor (see
Letter 120, n. 32). In a letter to Conway of 3 Oct. he refers to it as 'my little
tub of forty pounds a year'.

³ At the beginning of November Walpole had written 'an Epilogue to
Tamerlane on the suppression of the Rebellion', which was spoken by Mrs.
Pritchard in the character of the Comic Muse at Covent Garden Theatre
on 4 and 5 Nov., and was printed by Dodsley the next day (*Short Notes*).

⁴ In his *Short Notes* Walpole records, under the year 1751, 'About this time
I began to write my *Memoirs*'; but it is evident from this and a subsequent
remark of Gray's (see Letter 130, n. 9) that he must have planned them some
years before.

themselves? Do they begin to think of making their appearance in the world, that is to say, fifty years hence, to make posterity stare, and all good people crofs themselves? Has Asheton (who will then be lord bishop of Killaloe, and is to publish them) thought of an *aviso al lettore* to prefix to them yet, importing, that if the words church, king, religion, ministry, &c. be found often repeated in this book, they are not to be taken literally, but poetically, and as may be most strictly reconcileable to the faith then established;—that he knew the author well when he was a young man; and can testify upon the honour of his function, that he said his prayers regularly and devoutly, had a profound reverence for the clergy, and firmly believed everything that was the fashion in those days?

When you have done impeaching my lord Lovat,[5] I hope to hear *de vos nouvelles*, and moreover, whether you have got colonel Conway[6] yet? Whether sir C. Williams[7] is to go to Berlin? What sort of a prince Mitridate[8] may be?—and whatever other tidings you choose to refresh an anchoret with. *Frattanto* I send you a scene in a tragedy:[9] if it don't make you cry, it will make you laugh; and so it moves some pafsion, that I take to be enough. Adieu, dear sir! I am

Sincerely yours,
T. Gray.

[5] See Letter 120, n. 31. On 18 Dec. he appeared in the House of Lords to hear the articles of impeachment.

[6] He was in Scotland, where he had been acting as Aide-de-Camp to the Duke of Cumberland. The Duke had come south in July, and had left for The Hague on 30 Nov., but Conway had found an attraction in the person of Lady Ailesbury (the 'Scotchwoman' of Walpole's letter to Conway of 24 Oct.), whom he married in the following year.

[7] Sir Charles Hanbury Williams (1708–59), at this time M.P. for Monmouthshire. Walpole writes to Mann on 5 Dec., 'Sir Charles Williams is talked of for going to Berlin, but it is not yet done'; and on 25 Dec., 'Sir Charles Williams has kissed hands, and sets out for Dresden in a month'. He was not appointed to Berlin till 1749.

[8] '1746. *Mitridate,* an opera entirely by the new composer Terradellas, was brought out, 2 Dec., and had a run of ten nights' (Burney, *Hist. of Music,* iv. 455). The Prince of Wales was a patron of the opera at this time. 'We have operas, but no company at them; the Prince and Lord Middlesex, *impresarii*' (Walpole to Mann, 5 Dec.).

[9] The first scene in Mr. Gray's unfinished tragedy of *Agrippina*, published in Mr. Mason's edition of his works. Berry.—Gray had sent a speech from this scene to West in April 1742 (see Letter 101, n. 8).

129. GRAY TO WHARTON

My Dear Wharton.

I HAVE received your Bill, & am in Confusion to hear, you have got in Debt yourself in Order to bring me out of it: I did not think to be obliged to you so much, nor on such Terms: but imagined you would be here, & might easily spare it.¹ the Money shall be repaid as soon as ever it is wanted, & sooner if the Stocks rise a little higher. my Note you will find at the End of my Letter, wᶜʰ you ought to have, ἐάν τι κατὰ τὸ ἀνθρώπινον συμβαίνῃ:² the rest of my Acknowledgements are upon Record, where they ought to be, with the rest of your Kindnefses. the Bill was paid me here; I suppose there is no Likelihood of its being stop'd in Town.

It surprises me to hear you talk of so much Businefs, & the Uncertainty of your Return; & what not? sure you will find Time to give me an Account of your Transactions, & your Intentions. for your Ears, don't let 'em think of marrying you! for I know if you marry at all, you will *be married*. I mean, pafsively. & then (besides repenting of what you were not guilty of) you will never go abroad, never read any thing more, but Farriery-Books, and Justice-Books, & so either die of a Consumption; or live on, & grow fat, wᶜʰ is worse. for me & my Retirement (for you are in the Right to despise my Difsipation de quinze Jours)³ we are in the midst of Diog: Laertius & his Philosophers, as a Prœmium to the Series of their Works, & those of all the Poets & Orators, that lived before Philip of Macedon's Death: & we have made a great Chronological Table⁴ with our own Hands, the Wonder & Amazement of

---

LETTER 129.—First printed in part (in a garbled text) in Mason's *Memoirs*, p. 205; first printed in full by Mitford (1816), vol. ii, pp. 167–9; now reprinted from original.

¹ Gray had asked for a loan of £40 (see Letter 127, *ad fin.*), supposing that Wharton would be returning into residence at Pembroke, where his expenses would be small. Wharton went out of residence in the previous October, and did not return.

² 'Should that befall which is the lot of man', otherwise, 'in the event of my decease'; perhaps a reminiscence of Polybius, ἄν τι συμβῇ περὶ ἡμᾶς ἀνθρώπινον (iii. 5, 8).

³ His visit to London to see Chute and Whithed (see Letter 127, n. 1).

⁴ This laborious work was formed much in the manner of the President Henault's 'Histoire de France'. Every page consisted of nine columns; one for the Olympiad, the next for the Archons, the third for the public affairs of Greece, the three next for the Philosophers, and the three last for Poets,

Mr Brown; not so much for Publick Events, tho' these too have a Column afsign'd them, but rather in a literary Way, to compare the Times of all great Men, their Writeings & Transactions. it begins at the 30th Olympiad, & is already brought down to the 113th; that is, 332 Years. our only Modern Assistants, are Marsham,[5] Dodwell,[6] & Bentley.[7] [Tuthill][8] continues quiet in his Læta Paupertas, & by this Time (were not his Friends of it) would have forgot there was any such Place as Pembroke in the World. All Things there are just in Statu quo; only the Fellows, as I told you, are grown pretty rudish to their Sovereign in general,[9] for Francis is now departed. poor dear Mr Delaval[10] indeed has had a little Misfortune. Intelligence was brought, that he had with him a certain Gentlewoman properly call'd Nell Burnet, (but whose Nom de Guerre was Capt:^{n} Hargraves) in an Officer's Habit, whom he had carried all about to see Chappels & Libraries, & make Visits in the Face of Day. the Master raised his Pofse-Comitatus in Order to search his Chambers, & after long Feeling & Snuffleing about the Bed, he declared they had certainly been there. wch was very true, & the Captain was then locked up in a Cupboard there, while his Lover stood below in Order to convey him out at Window, when all was over. however they took Care not to discover her, tho' the Master affirm'd; had he but caught her, he would soon have known, whether it was a Man, or a Woman. upon this Mr Del: was desired to cut out his Name, & did so:

Historians, and Orators. I do not find it carried further than the date above-mentioned. *Mason.*—Charles Jean François Hénault (1685–1770), had published in this year (1746) a second edition of his *Nouvel Abrégé Chronologique de l'Histoire de France* (first published in 1744); it is not improbable that Gray took the idea of his Chronological Table from it. He commends it in Letter 154. Some of Gray's notes for this Table are preserved in the Pembroke library.

⁵ Sir John Marsham (1602–5), author of *Chronicus Canon Ægyptiacus, Ebraicus, Græcus, cum Disquisitionibus historicis et criticis.* Lond. 1672, fol.

⁶ Henry Dodwell, the elder (1641–1711), published *De Veteribus Graecorum Romanorumque Cyclis Dissertationes* in 1701, and *Annales Thucydidei et Xenophontei* in 1702.

⁷ Richard Bentley (1662–1742), D.D., Master of Trinity College, Cambridge; his famous *Epistola de Johanne Malela Antiocheno*, pointing out the errors in the Greek chronicle of John Malelas of Antioch, addressed to Dr. John Mill, Principal of St. Edmund Hall, was first printed as an appendix to Mill's edition of the chronicle published at Oxford in 1691, and was reprinted at Cambridge in 1713.   ⁸ See Letter 120, n. 2.

⁹ See Letter 127.   ¹⁰ See Letter 127, n. 6.

next Day D^r L: repented, & wrote a Paper to testify he never knew any Hurt of him, wch he brought to Dr Whaley,[11] who would have directly admitted him here, if Stuart[12] had not absolutely refused. he was offer'd about at several Colleges, but in vain. then D^r L: call[ed][13] two Meetings to get him re-admitted there, but every one was inexorable & so he has lost his Pupil,[14] who is gone, I suppose, to lie with his Aunt Price.[15] Trollope continues in Dev'reux-Court:[16] all our Hopes are now in the Commencement.[17]

Have you seen the Works of two young Authors, a Mr Warton[18] & a Mr Collins,[19] both Writers of Odes? it is odd enough, but each is the half of a considerable Man, & one the Counter-Part of the other. the first has but little Invention, very poetical choice of Expression, & a good Ear. the second, a fine Fancy, model'd upon the Antique, a bad Ear, great Variety of Words, & Images with no Choice at all. they both deserve to last some Years, but will not. Adieu! dear S^r I am very sincerely Yours

T G:

Dec: 27 [1746][20] I was 30 Year old yesterday. what is it o'clock by you?

---

[11] John Whalley, Master of Peterhouse (see Letter 117, n. 3).

[12] Charles Stuart, Fellow of Peterhouse; B.A., 1738; M.A., 1742.

[13] MS. frayed.   [14] See Letter 127.

[15] As his mother's maiden name was Apreece (see Letter 163, n. 13), this was presumably either a sister-in-law, or an unmarried sister of hers.

[16] Devereux Court, Strand, leading into Essex Street; here was Tom's Coffee-house, a well-known resort of men of letters.

[17] Commencement was the great ceremony when the full degrees of Master or Doctor were conferred, at the end of the academical year. The first Tuesday in July was Commencement Day. Gray apparently hoped that most of the Fellows would be in Cambridge for the occasion, and that a fresh effort on behalf of Tuthill might then be made.

[18] Joseph Warton (1722–1800), of Oriel College, Oxford; B.A., 1744; subsequently head master of Winchester, 1766–93; and editor of Pope's works. His *Odes on Several Occasions* was published by Dodsley on 4 Dec. 1746; and a second edition on 9 Jan. 1747.

[19] William Collins (1721–59), of Magdalen College, Oxford; B.A., 1743; he was a friend and school-fellow of Joseph Warton at Winchester, and proposed to bring out a joint volume of odes with him, but the project fell through. His own volume, *Odes on Several Descriptive and Allegoric Subjects*, which included the *Ode to Evening*, was published in December 1746 by Millar, with the date 1747 on the title-page. It met with little success, and Collins is said to have burnt the unsold copies in disgust.

[20] Date of year supplied by Wharton.

130. GRAY TO WALPOLE

January, 1747.

IT is doubtlefs an encouragement to continue writing to you, when you tell me you answer me with pleasure:[1] I have another reason which would make me very copious, had I any-thing to say; it is, that I write to you with equal pleasure, though not with equal spirits, nor with like plenty of materials: please to subtract then so much for spirit, and so much for matter; and you will find me, I hope, neither so slow, nor so short, as I might otherwise seem. Besides, I had a mind to send you the remainder of Agrippina, that was lost in a wildernefs of papers. Certainly you do her too much honour: she seemed to me to talk like an *Oldboy*,[1a] all in figures and mere poetry, instead of nature and the language of real pafsion. Do you remember *Approchez-vous, Neron*[2]——Who would not rather have thought of that half line than all Mr. Rowe's[3] flowers of elo-quence? However, you will find the remainder here at the end in an outrageous long speech: it was begun above four years ago (it is a misfortune you know my age, else I might have added), when I was very young. Poor West put a stop to that tragic torrent[4] he saw breaking in upon him:—have a care, I warn you, not to set open the flood-gate again, lest it should drown you and me and the bishop[5] and all.

I am very sorry to hear you treat philosophy and her followers like a parcel of monks and hermits, and think myself obliged to vindicate a profefsion I honour, bien que je n'en tienne pas boutique (as mad. Sevigné says).[6] The first man that ever bore thc namc, if you remember, used to say, that life was like the

LETTER 130.—First printed in *Works of Lord Orford*, vol. v, pp. 384–6.

[1] Walpole had obviously replied to Gray's letter of 22 Dec. 1764 (Letter 128).

[1a] Colonel Oldboy is a character in the comic opera *Lionel and Clarissa*, which was being performed at Covent Garden about this time.

[2] 'Approchez-vous, Néron, et prenez votre place'—words spoken by Agrippina to her son at the commencement of the second scene of the fourth act of Racine's *Britannicus*. Gray and Walpole had seen *Britannicus* acted in Paris in May 1739 (see Letter 62 *ad fin.*).

[3] Nicholas Rowe (1674–1718), Poet Laureate and dramatist, whose best-known tragedy, *The Fair Penitent*, was first produced in 1703.

[4] See Letter 105, n. 2.

[5] No doubt, Ashton, the prospective 'Lord Bishop of Killaloe' (see Letter 128).

[6] 'Il se trouvera à la fin que moi, qui ne lève point boutique de philo-sophie, je l'exercerai plus qu'eux tous' (*a Mad. de Grignan*, 21 Sept. 1689).

Olympic games[7] (the greatest public aſsembly of his age and country), where some came to show their strength and agility of body, as the champions; others, as the musicians, orators, poets, and historians, to show their excellence in those arts; the traders, to get money; and the better sort, to enjoy the spectacle, and judge of all these. They did not then run away from society for fear of its temptations: they paſsed their days in the midst of it: conversation was their buſineſs: they cultivated the arts of persuasion, on purpose to show men it was their interest, as well as their duty, not to be foolish, and false, and unjust; and that too in many instances with succeſs: which is not very strange; for they showed by their life that their leſsons were not impracticable; and that pleasures wcrc no temptations, but to such as wanted a clear perception of the pains annexed to them. But I have done preaching à la Grecque. Mr. Ratcliffe[8] made a shift to behave very rationally without their instructions, at a season which they took a great deal of pains to fortify themselves and others against: one would not desire to lose one's head with a better grace. I am particularly satisfied with the humanity of that last embrace to all the people about him. Sure it must be somewhat embarraſsing to die before so much good company!

You need not fear but posterity will be ever glad to know the absurdity of their ancestors: the foolish will be glad to know thcy wcrc as foolish as thcy, and thc wiſe will bc glad to find

[7] The reference is to the saying of Pythagoras, as quoted by Cicero (*Tusc. Quæst.* v. 3): 'similem sibi videri vitam hominum, et mercatum eum, qui haberetur maximo ludorum apparatu totius Græciæ celebritate, nam ut illic alii corporibus exercitatis gloriam et nobilitatem coronæ peterent: alii emendi, aut vendendi quæstu et lucro ducerentur: esset autem quoddam genus eorum, idque vel maxime ingenuum, qui nec plausum, nec lucrum quærerent, sed visendi causa venirent, studioseque perspicerent, quid ageretur, et quo modo'. The saying is also recorded by Diogenes Laertius in his life of Pythagoras.

[8] Charles Radcliffe (1693–1746), brother of the third Earl of Derwentwater (beheaded in 1716), who but for the attainder would have been fifth Earl of Derwentwater. He had been sentenced to death after the rebellion of 1715, but escaped from Newgate. In Nov. 1745 he was captured on board the *Soleil* privateer, and sent to the Tower; he was tried and condemned to death (21 Nov. 1746) under his former sentence, and beheaded on Tower Hill (8 Dec.). 'Mr. Ratcliffe, preceded by the sheriffs, the divine, and some friends, ascended the scaffold, after having taken leave of them with great serenity and calmness of mind. . . . He behaved with the greatest fortitude and coolness of temper, and was by no means terrified at the approach of death' (*Univ. Chron.*).

themselves wiser. You will please all the world then; and if you recount miracles you will be believed so much the sooner.[9] We are pleased when we wonder; and we believe because we are pleased. Folly and wisdom, and wonder and pleasure, join with me in desiring you would continue to entertain them: refuse us if you can. Adieu, dear sir!

T. GRAY.

131. GRAY TO WALPOLE

I HAD been absent from this Place a few Days, & at my Return found Cibber's Book[1] upon my Table: I return you my Thanks for it, & have already run over a considerable Part, for who could resist Mʳˢ Lætitia Pilkington's[2] Recommendation? (by the Way is there any such Gentlewoman, or has somebody put on the Style of a scribbleing Woman's Panegyric to deceive & laugh at Colley?) he seems to me full as pert & as dull as usual. there are whole Pages of Common-Place Stuff, that for Stupidity might have been wrote by Dʳ Waterland[3] or any other grave Divine, did not the flirting saucy Phrase give them at a Distance an Air of Youth & Gayety. it is very true, he is often in the right with regard to Tully's Weaknefses; but was there any one that did not see them? those, I imagine, that would find a Man after God's own Heart, are no more likely to trust the Doctor's Recommendation, than the Player's. & as to Reason & Truth: would they know their own Faces, do you think? if they look'd in the Glafs, & saw themselves so bedizen'd

[9] An allusion to Walpole's *Memoirs* (see Letter 128, n. 4).
LETTER 131.—First printed in part by Mason in *Memoirs*, pp. 182–5; first printed in full by Toynbee (1915), No. 162.
[1] Colley Cibber (see Letter 20, n. 10); his book *The Character and Conduct of Cicero considered from the History of his Life*, by the Rev. Dr. Middleton, was published in January of this year.
[2] An Irish adventuress (1712–50), in whom Cibber interested himself. In her *Memoirs*, published in 1748, she writes: 'Mr. Cibber was writing the Character and Conduct of Cicero consider'd: and did me the Honour to read it to me: ... This gave me an opportunity of writing a poem to him' (ed. 1754, vol. iii, p. 82—quoted by Tovey). Her recommendatory verses were on a loose sheet, inserted at the beginning of Cibber's book (see Letter 132 *ad fin.*).
[3] Daniel Waterland (1683–1740), Master of Magdalene College, Cambridge (1713), who had been engaged in a controversy with Conyers Middleton over Matthew Tindal's *Christianity as old as the Creation* (1730), which he attacked in *Scripture Vindicated* (1730–2).

in tatter'd Fringe & tarnish'd Lace, in French Jewels, & dirty Furbelows, the frippery of a Stroller's Wardrobe?

Litterature (to take it in its most comprehensive Sense, & include every Thing, that requires Invention, or Judgement, or barely Application & Industry) seems indeed drawing apace to its Diſsolution; & remarkably since the Beginning of the War. I should be glad to know why, if any one will tell me. for I believe there may be natural Reasons discoverable enough without haveing Recourse to St John, or St Alexander's[4] Revelations. I remember to have read Mr Spence's pretty Book,[5] tho' (as he then had not been at Rome for the last Time) it must have increased greatly since that in Bulk. if you ask me what I read; I protest I don't remember one Syllable; but only in general, that they were the best-bred Sort of Men in the World, just the Kind of *Frinds* one would wish to meet in a fine Summer's Evening, if one wish'd to meet any at all. the Heads & Tails of the Dialogues, publish'd separate in 16mo, would make the sweetest Reading in Natiur for young Gentlemen of Family & Fortune, that are learning to dance: I am told, he has put his little Picture before it.[6] I rejoyce to hear, there is such a Crowd of dramatical Performances comeing upon the Stage. Agripp:^{na} [7] can stay very well, she thanks you; & be damn'd at Leisure: I hope in God you have not mention'd, or shew'd to any Body that Scene (for trusting in it's Badneſs, I forgot to caution you concerning it) but I heard the other Day, that I was writeing a Play, & was told the Name of it, wch no body here could know, I'm sure. the Employment you propose to me, much better

---

[4] Gray's allusion is ironical, but no satisfactory explanation has been suggested to identify St. Alexander and his Revelations.

[5] Dodsley on 5 Feb. published Spence's *Polymetis: or an Enquiry concerning the Agreement between the Works of the Roman Poets and the Remains of the Antient Artists*, his collections for which had been commenced in 1732 under the title of *Noctes Florentinæ*. Gray, as appears from Letter 132 *ad in.*, had seen a portion of the work in manuscript. Joseph Spence (1699–1768), Fellow of New College, Oxford, 1720; B.A. 1724; ordained, 1724; M.A. 1727; Professor of Poetry, in succession to Thomas Warton, 1728–38; Regius Professor of Modern History, 1742–68. Besides his *Polymetis*, his best-known work is his collection of literary *Anecdotes*, published after his death. Spence was travelling in Italy with Lord Lincoln (afterwards Duke of Newcastle) at the same time as Walpole and Gray, and Gray must have seen him in Venice (see Appendix D).

[6] Spence's portrait, engraved by G. Vertue from a painting by Isaac Whood, is prefixed to the first edition (1747) of *Polymetis*.

[7] See Letter 130.

suits my Inclination. but I much fear our Joynt-Stock would hardly compose a small Volume:[8] what I have, is leſs considerable than you would imagine; & of that little we should not be willing to publish all. there is an Epistle, ad Amicos[9] (that is, to us all at Cambridge) in English, of above fourscore Lines: the Thoughts are taken from Tibullus, & from a Letter of Mʳ Pope's in Prose. it begins

> While You, where Camus rolls his sedgy Tide &c:

2. An Imitation of Horace, Trojani belli scriptorem &c:[10] about 120 Lines, wrote to me. begins

> While haply You (or haply not at all)
> Hear the grave Pleadings in the Lawyer's Hall &c:

3. A Translation from Propertius.[11] L: 3. El. 15 . . . 50 Lines. begins . . (sent to me at Rheims)

> Now prostrate, Bacchus, at thy Shrine I bend &c:

4. An Elegy, Latin. 34 Lines.[12] begins, Quod mihi tam gratæ &c:

5. Another, sent to Florence. 36 Lines.[13]—Ergo desidiæ videor &c:

6, 7, 8, 9, 10, 11. Translation from Posidippus, an Epigram[14] . . Some Lines; on the hard Winter:[15] long Verse . . on himself, a little before his Death.[16] long Verse. 2 Imitations of Catullus' Basia. English.[17] a little Ode of 5 Stanza's, to the Spring.[18]

This is all I can any where find. You, I imagine, may have a good deal more.[19] I should not care, how unwise the ordinary Sort of Readers might think my Affection for him provided those few, that ever loved any Body, or judged of any thing rightly, might from such little Remains be moved to consider, what he would have been; & to wish, that Heaven had granted him a longer Life, & a Mind more at Ease. I can't help fancy-

---

[8] The task which Mr. Walpole had recommended to him, was that of printing his own and Mr. West's Poems in the same volume. *Mason.*—See Appendix C.

[9] See Letter 38.   [10] See Letter 58**.   [11] See Letter 63*.
[12] See Letter 57.   [13] See Letter 84.   [14] See Letter 43.
[15] Printed by Tovey in *Gray and his Friends*, p. 137.
[16] This poem may have been in one or other of West's letters written in May 1742 and is no longer extant. See Letter 108, n. 3.
[17] See Letter 108, n. 3.   [18] See Letter 106.
[19] For other pieces by West, not included in Gray's list, see *Gray–Walpole Correspondence*, vol. ii, pp. 301–22. A complete list of West's poems and translations, so far as they have been preserved, is given in *Gray–Walpole Correspondence*, vol. ii, pp. 323–6.

ing, that if you could find out Mrs West, & ask her for his Papers of that kind (Ashton might do it in your Name) she would be ready enough to part with them, & we might find something more: at least it would be worth while to try; for she had 'em in a great Box altogether, I well know.

I send you a few Lines, tho' Latin (wch you don't like) for the sake of the Subject. it makes Part of a large Design,[20] & is the Beginning of the fourth Book, wch was intended to treat of the Paſsions. excuse the 3 first Verses: you know Vanity (with the Romans) is a poetical License.

Hactenus haud segnis Naturæ arcana retexi
Musarum interpres, primusq; Britanna per arva
Romano liquidum deduxi flumine rivum.
  Cum Tu opere in medio, spes tanti & causa laboris,
Linquis, & æternam fati te condis in umbram!
Vidi egomet duro graviter concuſsa dolorc
Pectora, in alterius non unquám lenta dolorem;
Et languere oculos vidi & pallescere amantem
Vultum, quo nunquam Pietas nisi rara, Fidesq;,
Altus amor Veri, & purum spirabat Honestum.
Visa tamen tardi demúm inclementia morbi
Ceſsare est, reducemq; iterúm roseo ore Salutem
Speravi, atq; uná tecum, dilecte Favonî,
Credulus heu longos, ut quondam, fallere Soles.
Heu spes nequicquam dulces, atq; irrita vota,
Heu mæstos Soles, sine te quos ducere flendo
Per desideria, & questus jam cogor inanes!
  At tu, sancta anima, & nostri non indiga luctûs
Stellanti templo, sinceriq; ætheris igne
Unde orta es, fruere. atq; oh si secura, nec ultrá
Mortalis, notos olím miserata labores
Respectes, tenuesq; vacet cognoscere curas:
Humanam si forté altâ de sede procellam
Contemplere, metus, stimulosq; cupidinis acres,
Gaudiaq; & gemitus, parvoq; in corde tumultum
Irarum ingentem, & sævos sub pectore fluctus:
Respice & has lachrymas, memori quas ictus amore
Fundo; quod poſsum, proptér lugere sepulchrum
Dum juvat, & mutæ vana hæc jactare favillæ.

[20] The *De Principiis Cogitandi,* of which he had sent the commencement to West in 1741 (see Letter 97, n. 6).

P: S: My Love to the Chutheds.[21] pray tell 'em I am learning Whisk,[22] & have sent one of my old Gowns to be made up into full-bottom'd Hoods . . . Compliments to M^rs Tr—cy[23] . . . Adieu, S^r, I am

Yours ever

T G:

Cambr: Sunday—[Feb. 8, 1747][24]

132. GRAY TO WALPOLE

[c. Feb. 15, 1747][1]

I HAVE abundance of Thanks to return You for the Entertainment Mr Spence's Book has given me, wch I have almost run over already; & I much fear (see what it is to make a Figure) the Breadth of the Margin, & the Neatnefs of the Prints, wch are better done than one could expect, have prevail'd upon me to like it far better, than I did in Manuscript. for I think, it is not the very genteel Deportment of Polymetis, nor the lively Wit of Mysagetes, that have at all corrupted me.

There is one fundamental Fault, from whence most of the little Faults throughout the whole arise. he profefses to neglect the Greek Writers, who could have given him more Instruction on the very Heads he profefses to treat, than all the others put together. who does not know, that upon the Latine, the Sabine, & Hetruscan Mythology (wch probably might themselves at a remoter Period of Time owe their Origin to Greece too) the

---

[21] Familiar name used by Gray and Walpole for John Chute (see Letter 99, n. 1) and his friend Francis Whithed (see Letter 109, n. 36).

[22] Whist had become the rage a few years before. Walpole, writing to Mann on 9 Dec. 1742 (the year in which Hoyle's *Short Treatise on Whist* was first printed), says: 'Whisk has spread an universal opium over the whole nation; it makes courtiers and Patriots sit down to the same pack of cards.' A seventh edition of Hoyle's book was published this year (1747).

[23] No doubt Mrs. Tracy, a connexion of John Chute, whose father had married (1686) Katherine Keck, widow of Ferdinand Tracy (see Letter 225, n. 3).

[24] The date of the year (which has been inserted in the original by Mason) and that of the month are determined by the references to Cibber's book and to Spence's *Polymetis* (see nn. 1, 5). 8 February was Sunday in 1747.

LETTER 132.—First printed in part (in a garbled text) by Mason in *Memoirs*, pp. 185–7; first printed in full by Toynbee (1915), No. 163.

[1] Mason dated 'Cambridge, 1747'. From the reference to Spence's *Polymetis* (see Letter 131, n. 5) and to Middleton's book (see n. 5) it may be conjectured that the letter was written about the middle of February.

Romans ingrafted almost the whole Religion of Greece to make
what is call'd their own? it would be hard to find any one Circumstance, that is properly of their Invention. in the ruder
Days of the Republick the picturesque Part of their Religion
(wch is the Province he has chose, & would be thought to confine himself too) was probably borrowed entirely from the
Tuscans, who, as a wealthy & tradeing People, may be well
supposed, & indeed are known, to have had the Arts flourishing
in a considerable Degree among them. what could inform him
here, but Dionysius Halic: (who exprefsly treats of those Times
with great Curiosity & Industry) & the Remains of the first
Roman Writers? the former he has neglected as a Greek; & the
latter he says were but little acquainted with the Arts, & consequently are but of little Authority. in the better Ages, when
every Temple & publick Building in Rome was peopled with
imported Deities & Hero's, & when all the Artists of Reputation
they made Use of were Greeks, what Wonder, if their Eyes grew
familiarised to Grecian Forms & Habits (especially in a Matter
of this kind, where so much depends upon the Imagination) &
if those Figures introduced with them a Belief of such Fables,
as first gave them Being, & drefs'd them out in their various
Attributes. it was natural then; & (I should think) necefsary,
to go to the Source itself, the Greek Accounts of their own
Religion. but, to say the Truth, I suspect he was little conver-
sant in those Books & that Language, for he rarely quotes any
but Lucian, an Author that falls in every Bodie's Way, & who
lived at the very extremity of that Period he has set to his
Enquiries, later than any of the Poets he has meddled with, &
for that Reason ought to have been regarded, as but an indifferent Authority, especially being a Syrian too. as he says
himself; his Book, I think, is rather a Beginning than a perfect
Work; but a Beginning at the wrong End: for if any body should
finish it by enquireing into the Greek Mythology, as he pro-
poses; it will be necefsary to read it backward.

There are several little Neglects, that any one might have
told him of, I minded in reading it hastily, as P: 311, a Discourse about Orange-Tree's occasion'd by Virgil's, inter odoratum lauri nemus.[2] where he fancies the Roman Laurus to be
our Laurel: tho' undoubtedly the Bay-tree, wch is *odoratum*, &
(I believe) still call'd Lauro, or Alloro, at Rome. & that the

---

[2] *Aen.* vi. 658.

Pomum[3] Medicum in the Georgick is the Orange: tho' Theo-phrastus, whence Virgil borrow'd it, or even Pliny whom he himself quotes, might convince him, it is the Cedrato, wch he has often tasted at Florence. P: 144. is an Account of Domeni-chin's[4] Cardinal Virtues, & a Fling at the Jesuits; neither of wch belong to them. the Painting is in a Church of the Barna-biti, dedicated to St Carlo Borroméo, whose Motto is Humilitas. P: 151. in a Note he says, the old Romans did not *regard Fortune as a Deity*. tho' Serv: Tullius (whom she was said to be in Love with; nay, there was actually an Affair between them) founded her Temple in Foro Boario. by the Way her Worship was Greek; & this King was educated in the Family of Tarquin: Priscus, whose Father was a Corinthian. so it is easy to conceive, how early the Religion of Rome might be mixed with that of Greece .. &c: &c:

Dr Midd:^{n} has sent me to day a Book on the Roman Senate,[5] the Substance of a Dispute between Ld Hervey[6] & Him, tho' it never *interrupted their Friendship*,[7] he says, & I dare say not ... Mrs Læt: Pilkington is a Name under certain recommendatory Verses in the Front of Cibber's Book,[8] that seem designed to laugh at him. they were in a loose Sheet, not sow'd in. how does your Comedy[9] succeed? I am told, very well. Adieu! I am
Yours ever
T G:

My Respects to the Chutheds. I am much their's, tho' to no Purpose.

---

[3] The reference is to the 'malum felix' of *Georg.* ii. 127. Neither the laurel nor the orange was naturalized in Europe in Virgil's time.

[4] Zampieri Domenichino (1581–1641), of Bologna, a pupil of Annibale Caracci.

[5] Conyers Middleton's *Treatise on the Roman Senate* was published in February this year (see Letter 135, n. 18).

[6] John Hervey (1696–1743) (the Sporus of Pope), eldest surviving son of John Hervey, first Earl of Bristol; he entered the House of Lords as Baron Hervey of Ickworth in 1733. To him Middleton dedicated his *Life of Cicero*, and his *Treatise on the Roman Senate* contained 'the substance of several letters addressed to the late Lord Hervey concerning the manner of elect-ing senators'.

[7] If this is an allusion to his difference with Walpole, it is proof of the renewal of their cordial relations.   [8] See Letter 131, nn. 1, 2.

[9] Gray may have known that Walpole was writing the farce, which was published in *Old England*, No. 224, of 16 May 1747, with the title *Terræfilius or Harlequin Candidate*.

133. GRAY TO WALPOLE

Cambridge [c. Feb. 22], 1747.

As one ought to be particularly careful to avoid blunders in a compliment of condolence, it would be a sensible satisfaction to me (before I testify my sorrow, and the sincere part I take in your misfortune) to know for certain, who it is I lament. I knew Zara and Selima,[1] (Selima, was it? or Fatima) or rather I knew them both together; for I cannot justly say which was which. Then as to your handsome Cat, the name you distinguish her by, I am no lefs at a lofs, as well knowing one's handsome cat is always the cat one likes best; or, if one be alive and the other dead, it is usually the latter that is the handsomest. Besides, if the point were never so clear, I hope you do not think me so ill-bred or so imprudent as to forfeit all my interest in the surviver: Oh no! I would rather seem to mistake, and imagine to be sure it must be the tabby one that had met with this sad accident. Till this affair is a little better determined, you will excuse me if I do not begin to cry:

'Tempus inane peto, requiem, spatiumque doloris.'[2]

Which interval is the more convenient, as it gives time to rejoice with you on your new honors.[3] This is only a beginning; I

LETTER 133.—First printed in Mason's *Memoirs*, pp. 188–9, as one letter with the following. As Cole (in a note printed by Mitford, *Works of Gray*, 1835–43, vol. i, p. cvii) pointed out, Mason clumsily joined parts of two letters. The absurdity of his combination is obvious, as, in the first part, Gray asks the name of the cat and other particulars to enable him to write the poem lamenting her death; in the second part he sends the completed poem. The date of 1 March, which Mason gave to the combination, may be taken as the date of the second letter; the first letter may be assumed to have been written about a week before, within a few days of Walpole's election to the Royal Society, see n. 3.

[1] This is not what Gray wrote, as appears from the following passage in a letter of Mason to Edward Bedingfield (now in the Henry E. Huntington Library), written on 22 Dec. 1773, while he was engaged on his *Memoir of Gray*, in the revision of which he was greatly indebted to Bedingfield: 'I have sent a letter lately rec^d from Mr Walpole about the Ode on the Cat wch as it has more humour in it than that to Dr Wharton, I wish to have it inserted in its stead. but there is an idle allusion in it to scripture; I wish you would alter it in the print tho I did not care to erase the MS. read 'I knew Zara and Selima,' instead of 'Zara I know & Selima I know'.'

[2] *Aen.* iv. 433–4: 'Tempus inane peto, requiem spatiumque furori,
          Dum mea me victam doceat fortuna dolere.'

[3] Mr. Walpole was about this time elected a Fellow of the Royal Society. *Mason.*—His election took place on 19 Feb. 1746/7.

reckon next week we shall hear you are a Free-Mason, or a Gormogon[4] at least.

134. GRAY TO WALPOLE

[March 1,[1] 1747].

*   *   *   *   *   *   *   *

Heigh ho! I feel (as you to be sure have done long since) that
I have very little to say, at least in prose.[2] Somebody will be
the better for it; I do not mean you, but your Cat, feuë Mademoiselle Selime, whom I am about to immortalise for one week
or fortnight, as follows.[3]

*   *   *   *   *   *   *   *

*   *   *   *   *   *   *   *

There's a Poem for you, it is rather too long for an Epitaph.

135. GRAY TO WHARTON

My Dear Wharton

You ask me, what I would answer in case any one should ask
me a certain Question concerning You.[1] In my Conscience,

---

[4] Pseudo-Chinese—a member of a society imitating the Freemasons,
founded early in the 18th century. (*O.E.D.*) Gray evidently had in mind
Dunciad, iv. 570 ff., where Pope speaks of those who

        Shine in the dignity of F.R.S.
        Some, deep Free-Masons . . .
        Some Botanists, or Florists at the least,
        Or issue Members of an Annual feast.
        Nor past the meanest unregarded, one
        Rose a Gregorian, one a Gormogon.

LETTER 134.—First printed in Mason's *Memoirs*, pp. 188–9, as one letter
with the preceding.

[1] For the date see Letter 133, preliminary note.

[2] The opening sentence can scarcely have been the beginning of a letter.
Mason may have inserted it to form the join with the previous letter, and
may have omitted other matter.

[3] Mason notes that 'the 4th Ode in the Collection of his Poems was
inserted after these asterisks'. This was the *Ode on the Death of a Favourite Cat
Drowned in a Tub of Gold Fishes* (see Letter 135). Gosse, *Works of Gray*,
vol. i, p. 11, says that 'a manuscript of this poem . . . exists in a letter to
Walpole dated March 1, 1747'. As the letter is only preserved in Mason's
text, this is an obvious blunder, and the variants, quoted by Gosse and other
editors, 'of the Walpole MS.', appear to be the readings of the text as it was
printed in Dodsley's *Collection* (see Letter 125, n. 4).

LETTER 135.—First printed in part (in a garbled text) in Mason's
Memoirs, p. 206; first printed in full by Mitford (1816), vol. ii, pp. 179–82;
now reprinted from original.   [1] As to his getting married.

I should say, Yes; & the readier as I have had a Revelation about it: 'twas in a Dream that told me you had taken a Fancy to one of the four last Letters in the Alphabet. I think it can't be X, nor Z (for I know of no female Zeno, or Xenophon) it may be Y perhaps, but I have somehow a secret Partiality for W.[2] am I near it, or no? by this Time I suppose, 'tis almost a done Thing. there is no struggling with Destiny, so I acquiesce. thus far only I should be glad to know with Certainty, whither it be likely [you][3] should continue in Statu Quo,[4] till the Commencement[5] (wch I dont conceive) for o[therwise][3] I should think it rather better for [T:][6] to give up his Pretensions with a good Grace, than to wait the Pleasure of those dirty Cubs, who will infallibly prefer the first that offers of their own People. but I submit this to your Judgement, who (as you first made him a Competitor) ought to determine at what Time he may most decently withdraw. I have some Uneasiness too on Brown's Account, who has sacrificed all his Interests with so much Frankness, & is still so resolute to do every Thing for us without Reserve, that I should see him with great Concern under the Paw of a fell Visitor, & exposed to the Insolence of that old Rascal, the Master. Tr:^pe[7] (if you remember) would engage himself no longer than the end of this Year? 'tis true he has never said any thing since, tending that Way; but he is not unlikely to remember it at a proper Time. and as to Sm:,[8] he must

---

[2] The lady was Margaret, eldest daughter of Anthony Wilkinson, of Cross Gate, Durham. See Genealogical Table.

[3] MS. torn, where the letter had been sealed—text restored conjecturally.

[4] As soon as Wharton married he would cease to be a Fellow of Pembroke.

[5] At the beginning of July, when there might be a College meeting (see Letter 129, n. 17).

[6] T. (for Tuthill) has been scored through. See Letter 120, n. 2.

[7] See Letter 114, n. 1.

[8] Christopher Smart, the poet (1722–71), admitted from Durham School at Pembroke as Sizar, 1739; Craven University Scholar for Classics, 1742; B.A. 1743–4; M.A. 1747; Fellow, 1745. While still an undergraduate he wrote the Tripos Verses on three occasions, as well as the *Secular Ode on the Jubilee at Pembroke Hall* (Letter 114, n. 12), and in 1743 published his translation into Latin Verse of Pope's *Ode on St. Cecilia's Day*. After his election to a fellowship he held various College offices, and in 1746 was private tutor to John Blake Delaval (afterwards Lord Delaval) during his brief College career (Letter 127, n. 6).

He had entered the College with an allowance of £40 a year, from the Duchess of Cleveland, which was continued, after her death, by the Duke (Letter 143, n. 6), but through drink and extravagant living he got into debt (Letter 143). He was treated with generosity by the College, but he

necefsarily be abîmé, in a very short Time. his Debts daily increase (you remember the State they were in, when you left us) Addison,[9] I know, wrote smartly to him last Week; but it has had no Effect, that signifies. only I observe he takes Hartshorn from Morning to Night lately: in the mean time he is amuseing himself with a Comedy[10] of his own Writeing, wch he makes all the Boys of his Acquaintance act, & intends to borrow the Zodiack Room,[11] & have it performed publickly.[12] our Friend Lawman, the mad Attorney, is his Copyist;[13] & truly the Author himself is to the full as mad as he. his Piece (he says)

was incapable of economy, and in 1749 he gave up his academic career and went out of residence. In 1750, and for three years in succession, and in 1755, he was awarded the Seatonian Prize for an English poem on a sacred subject. Meanwhile he had begun his literary career in London, and in 1752 or 1753 he married Miss Anna Maria Carnan, step-daughter of John Newbery, the bookseller. The marriage was kept secret but came to the knowledge of the College in November 1753, and at the end of the year he vacated his fellowship, but was given 'leave to keep his name on the College books without any expense, so long as he continues to write for the premium left by Mr. Seaton'. Within a little while his name went off the books and his connexion with the College ceased. For his subsequent madness and confinement see Letter 286, n. 6.

9 Smart's old tutor, Leonard Addison (1699–1772), B.A. 1720; Fellow of Pembroke, 1722; M.A. 1723; President, 1736; Proctor, 1736–7; D.D. 1753; Vicar of Waresley, Hunts., 1735–45; of Saxthorpe, Norf., 1744–72; Rector of Causton, and of Salle, Norf., 1747–72.

10 Some account of the play *A Trip to Cambridge or the Grateful Fair* is given in *The Life of Christopher Smart*, prefixed to the 1791 edition of his *Poems*, pp. xii–xvi. Among the actors, besides Smart himself, were John Gordon, afterwards Precentor of Lincoln (mentioned in Letter 372 as a friend of Smart), John Randall, organist of Pembroke and later of King's, and Professor of Music (see Letter 499), and Richard Forester, afterwards Fellow of Pembroke (see Letter 220, n. 10). Richard Stonhewer (see Letter 120, n. 38) was prompter.

11 Perhaps the room of the Zodiac Club, a literary society, so called from its consisting of twelve members denominated from the twelve signs, which was established in the University in Dec. 1725 (see Cooper's *Annals of Cambridge*, iv. 187).

12 'After many disappointments in attempting to get an old play-house at Hunnibun's the coach-maker's, and afterwards the Free-School in Free-School-Lane, the play was acted [in April 1747] in Pembroke College-Hall; the parlour of which made the Green Room' (see *Life of Smart* prefixed to the 1791 ed. of his *Poems*, p. xiv).

13 This may be the same individual as the copyist of whom Gray says in his letter to Walpole of 8 Oct. 1751 (Letter 161): 'We have a Man here that writes a good Hand; but he has two little Failings, that hinder my recommending him to you. he is lousy, & he is mad: he sets out this Week for Bedlam.'

is inimitable, true Sterling Wit, & Humour by God; & he can't hear the Prologue without being ready to die with Laughter. he acts five Parts himself, & is only sorry, he can't do all the rest. he has also advertised a Collection of Odes;[14] & for his Vanity & Faculty of Lyeing, they are come to their full Maturity. all this, you see, must come to a Jayl, or Bedlam,[15] & that without any help, almost without Pity. by the Way now I talk of a Jayl, please to let me know, when & where you would have me pay my own Debts.[16]

Chapman[17] (I suppose you know) is warm in his Mastership. soon after his Accefsion I was to see him: there was a very brillant[17a] (Cambridge) Afsembly, Middleton,[18] Rutherforth,[19] Heberden,[20] Robinson,[21] Coventry,[22] & various others. he did the Honours with a great Deal of comical Dignity, afsisted

[14] The advertisement has not been traced. In a letter with the date '7th of Janry 1747-8' printed by Sir E. Gosse, in the *Times Literary Supplement* of 27 May 1926, Smart asks Dodsley to advertise his 'Proposals'. 'Proposals for *Printing by Subscription*, a Collection of Original Poems, by Christopher Smart, M.A., Fellow of *Pembroke Hall*, in the University of Cambridge' were printed at the end of the first edition of Smart's Seatonian Prize poem for 1750; and these same 'Proposals' were advertised in the *General Evening Post* of 4 Aug. 1750 (see letter of G. T. Gray in *Times Lit. Supp.*, 1 July 1926). The first collected edition of Smart's *Poems on Several Occasions* was issued in 1752.

[15] As is well known, it came to both (see n. 8).   [16] See Letter 129.

[17] Thomas Chapman (1717–60), Scholar of Christ's, 1734; B.A. 1738; M.A. 1741; Fellow of Christ's, 1741–6; Master of Magdalene, 1746–60; Prebendary of Durham, 1750. He was the author of an *Essay on the Roman Senate*. Cole called him conceited and overbearing. For his marriage, see Letter 149; and for his death (on 9 June 1760), Letters 313, 317, 318, 321.

[17a] The old form of the word generally out of use in Gray's time.

[18] Conyers Middleton (1683–1750) had for some years held an assured position in Cambridge. He was chief Librarian of the University. His *Life of Cicero*, published in 1741 (see Letter 109, n. 6), brought him wealth and reputation. He had a house in Cambridge, 'the only easy place one could find to converse in', as Gray described it (Letter 154), and a country house a few miles out where he spent his summers. He had recently published his *Treatise on the Roman Senate* (Letter 132, n. 5) and was still active in theological controversy.

[19] Thomas Rutherforth (1712–71), of St. John's; B.A. 1730; M.A. 1733; Fellow, 1733–52; D.D. 1745; Regius Professor of Divinity, 1756–71. In 1765 he was a possible candidate for the Mastership of St. John's (see Letter 399). Mason in Letter 288 (25 Jan. 1759) calls him 'that saintly Butcher.'

[20] William Heberden (1710–1801), of St. John's, the distinguished physician and scholar; B.A. 1728; M.A. 1732; Fellow, 1731–52; M.D. 1739; a friend of Gray and Mason. He attended Dr. Johnson in his last illness.

[21] There is no clue to the identity of this Robinson, who is not to be confounded with Gray's friend, Billy Robinson (see Letter 304, n. 4).

[22] Henry Coventry (c. 1710–52), Fellow of Magdalene College, Cam-

by a Bedmaker in greasy Leather Breeches & a Livery, & now he is gone to Town to get Preferment. but what you'll wonder at & what delights me, Coventry is his particular Confident (tho' very disagreeably to himself) he can't open his Door, but he finds the Master there, who comes to set[23] with him at all Hours, & brings his Works with him, for he is writeing a great Book on the Roman Constitution. well, upon the Strength of this I too am grown very great with Coventry, & to say the Truth (bateing his Nose,[24] & another Circumstance, w[ch] is nothing to me) he is the best Sort of Man in this Place. M:[n] [25] has publish'd a small Oct:[vo] on the Roman Senate, well enough, but nothing of very great Consequence, & is now gone to be inducted into a Sine-Cure (not £100 a-Year)[26] that S[r] J: Frederick[27] gave him. what's worse, for the Sake of this little nasty Thing (I am told) he is determined to supprefs a Work,[28] that would have made a great Noise, or publish it all mangled & disfigured, & this when he has (I am afsured) near 700£ a-year of his own already, & might live independent, & easy, and speak his Mind in the Face of the whole World Clerical and Laïcal. such a Passion have some Men to lick the Dust, & be trampled upon. the Fellow-Com[mo]ners[29] (the Bucks) are run mad, they set Women upon their Heads in the Streets at [noon][30]day, break open Shops, game in the Coffee-houses on Sundays, & in short act after my [own][30] Heart.[31]

My Works are not so considerable as you imagine. I have read Pausania[s and Athe]næus[31a] all thro', & Æschylus again.

bridge; B.A. 1729; M.A. 1733; nephew of fifth Earl of Coventry. He was the author of *A Dialogue between Philemon and Hydaspes on false Religion* (1736–44) (see Walpole to Montague, 30 May 1736.)

[23] See Letter 116, n. 10.

[24] Cole, who had met Coventry frequently in the society of Conyers Middleton and Horace Walpole, remarks: 'He used to dress remarkably gay, with much gold lace, had a most prominent Roman nose, and was much of a gentleman'.   [25] Middleton (see Letter 132, n. 5).

[26] The rectory of Hascombe in Surrey, worth no more than £50 a year.

[27] Sir John Frederick (1678–1755), first Baronet of Hampton, Middlesex.

[28] This may have been *A Free Inquiry into the Miraculous Powers which are supposed to have subsisted in the Christian Church from the earliest ages*, published in 1749, an *Introductory Discourse* to which was published in 1747.

[29] MS. torn—On the status of Fellow-commoners, see Appendix H.

[30] MS. torn, where the letter had been sealed—text restored conjecturally.

[31] For the growth of disorder in the University about this time, see Wordsworth, *Social Life at the English Universities in the Eighteenth Century*, pp. 72 ff.; and Winstanley, *The University of Cambridge in the Eighteenth Century*, pp. 17–18, 199 ff.   [31a] MS. torn.

I am now in Pindar[32] & Lysias: for I take Verse and Prose together, like Bread & Cheese. the Chronology[33] is growing daily. the most noble of my Performances latterly is a Pôme on the uncommon Death of M^r W:^{s}[34] Cat. wch being of a proper Size & Subject for a Gentleman in your Condition to peruse (besides that I flatter myself, Miſs —— will give her Judgement upon it too), I herewith send you. it won't detain you long.

On a favourite Cat, call'd Selima, that fell into a China Tub[35]
     with Gold-Fishes in it & was drown'd

> 'Twas on a lofty Vase's Side,
> Where China's gayest Art had dyed
> The azure Flowers that blow:
> Demurest of the Tabby Kind,
> The pensive Selima reclined
> Gazed on the Lake below.

> Her conscious Tail her Joy declared.
> The fair round Face, the snowy Beard,
> The Velvet of her Paws,
> Her Coat, that with the Tortoise vyes,
> Her Ears of Jett, & Emerald Eyes
> She saw, & purr'd Applause.

[32] There is a record of Gray's studies in a notebook now in the British Museum (MS. Add. 36817). This contains notes in his handwriting on Pindar, dated 20 March, and notes on Aristophanes dated 20 June of this year, together with Greek genealogies, which were probably intended for his Chronological Tables. On the fly-leaf there is an inscription stating that the manuscript was the gift of Richard Stonhewer to T. J. Mathias in the year 1806. A notebook of Gray's in the Pierpont Morgan Library has notes on Athenaeus dated 4 Jan. 1747 and notes on Lysias dated 20 March 1747.

[33] See Letter 129, n. 4.

[34] It appears from a passage in an unpublished letter of Mason to Edward Bedingfield, written on 22 Dec. 1773, that Mason originally intended to make use of this letter, and printed it accordingly, but subsequently replaced it by Gray's letter to Walpole, as having 'more humour in it' (see Letter 133, n. 1).

[35] Mr. Walpole, since the death of Mr. Gray, has placed the China vase in question on a pedestal at Strawberry Hill, with the four [*corr.* six] lines of the Ode for its inscription: "'Twas on *this* Vase's lofty [*corr.* lofty Vase's] side', &c. *Mason* (*Poems*), p. 74.—'The large blue and white china tub in which Mr. Walpole's cat was drowned' stood on a pedestal in the cloister near the entrance. (See *Description of Strawberry Hill*, in *Works of Lord Orford*, vol. ii, p. 400.) It is now in possession of Lord Derby at Knowsley.

Still had she gazed, but 'midst the Tide
Two angel-Forms were seen to glide,
The Genii of the Stream:
Their scaly Armour's Tyrian Hue
Thro' richest Purple to the View
Betray'd a golden Gleam.

The haplefs Nymph with Wonder saw.
A Whisker first, & then a Claw,
With many an ardent Wish,
She stretch'd in vain to reach the Prize.
What female Heart can Gold despise?
What Cat's averse to Fish?

Presumptuous Maid! with Eyes intent
Again she stretch'd, again she bent
Nor knew the Gulph between.
Malignant Fate sate by, & smiled.
The slippery Verge her Feet beguiled:
She tumbled headlong in.

Eight Times emergeing from the Flood
She mew'd to ev'ry watry God
Some speedy Aid to send
No Dolphin came, no Nereïd stirr'd,
Nor cruel Tom, nor Harry heard.
A Fav'rite has no Friend!

From hence, ye Beauties, undeceiv'd
Know, one false Step is ne'er retrieved,
And be with Caution bold.   .
Not all, that strikes your wand'ring Eyes,
And heedlefs Hearts is lawful Prize,
Nor all, that glisters, Gold.[36]

[Adieu][37] my dear S^r, I am ever Yours,

T G:

Cambr: March [17].[38] Tuesday-Night.

[36] If the text printed in Dodsley's *Collection* (see Letter 134, n. 3) is that of
the original version sent to Walpole, Gray had made some small changes in
the poem, most of which he adopted when he printed it in the edition of the
Six Poems with Bentley's designs (see Letter 170, n. 1ª).   [37] MS. frayed.
[38] As this presumably is the letter referred to by Gray in his letter to
Wharton of 26 March (Letter 136), the date is probably Tuesday, 17 March.

Trollope[39] is in Town still at his Lodgeings, & has been very ill. Brown wrote a month ago to Hayes[40] & Christoph[n]:[41] but has had no Answer, whither or no, they shall be here at the Commencement.[42] can you tell? Morley[43] is going to be married to a grave & stayed Maiden of 30 Years old with much Pelf, & his own Relation. poor Soul!

Addressed: To D[r] Thomas Wharton of Durham *Postmark:* CAMBRIDGE

136. GRAY TO WHARTON

My Dear Wharton

I PERCEIVE, that mine[1] did not reach you, till the Day after you had wrote your little Letter. if you have time to give the Gentleman (before he goes to Town) my Note indorsed by You, or will send it to your Brother, the Money[2] shall be paid in Town at the Day you mention. the rest of my Questions are all sufficiently answer'd by the News you tell me (not but that I knew it before) what can one say to a Person in such Circumstances? I need not say, how much Happineſs I wish you: if that be the Way to it, I rejoice to see you with your Boots on. it would be cruel to detain you long at present; when you have any Leisure, I hope you will let me a little more into the Matter. the Old Maids give you heartily Joy, & hug themselves in their Virginity. Carlyon[3] is in your Room, & I can't well go, &

[39] See Letter 114, n. 1.
[40] Thomas Hayes of Pembroke, B.A. 1735; Fellow, 1736; M.A. 1739; M.D. 1747.
[41] Preston Christopherson, a native of Addington, near Penrith, was admitted as Sizar at St. John's in 1731; B.A. 1735; M.A. 1739; Grindal Fellow of Pembroke, 25 April 1737. Grindal Fellowships were restricted to natives of Cumberland and certain other northern counties (hence members of other Colleges were often chosen).
[42] See Letter 129, n. 17.
[43] Perhaps William Morley, of Peterhouse, B.A. 1733.
LETTER 136.—First printed by Mitford (1835–43), vol. iii, p. 45; now reprinted from original.
[1] Letter 135.
[2] The amount of his loan from Wharton (see Letter 129).
[3] Three brothers Carlyon were admitted to Pembroke between 1734 and 1738. The one mentioned here was probably Thomas Carlyon, B.A. 1739–40; M.A. 1744. He was the second son of Thomas Carlyon of Tregrehan, near St. Austell, and was for fifty-one years rector of St. Just in Roseland, Cornwall, where he died at the age of 76 in Jan. 1793. He is said to have been a friend and correspondent of Gray (see Introduction).

strip him:[4] I reckon he will not remain long here. Adieu, & think me

Yours ever

[Thursday], March 26 [1747].[5] Camb:ge   T G

Addressed: To Dr Thomas Wharton, of Durham   *Postmark:* CAMBRIDGE

137. GRAY TO WHARTON
My dear Wharton

I HIGHLY approve of your travelling Nuptials, & only wonder you don't set forth on Easter-Day,[1] rather than stay to be dish'd up there, & put to Bed by a whole Heap of prurient Relations. I don't conceive what one can do with such People, but run away from them. my very Letter blushes to think it must speak with you at a Time when there is but one Person you can properly have any Thing to say to.

However, tho' I have not the Pleasure of knowing Mr Wilkinson,[2] my new Relation, much lefs of knowing how good a Charioteer he is: yet I will readily trust him with my Neck to carry to Stilton,[3] or where he pleases. if I arrive there in a shatter'd Condition, I hope the Lady you belong to will receive me the more graciously, as a Person, that had an Ambition to break a Limb, or two in her Service. but you must desire him (as you say) to invite me.

You shall receive the Money,[4] as soon as you get to Town. my Aunt[5] has it in her Hands: when I see you, I shall learn your

---

4 Wharton probably wanted to remove his belongings.

5 Date of year supplied by Wharton.

LETTER 137.—First printed by Mitford (1835–43), vol. iii, p. 46; now re-printed from original.

1 Easter Day in 1747 was 19 April. Wharton was married on 20 April (see Surtees' *Durham*, vol. iii, p. 300). He vacated his fellowship on his marriage.

2 This was no doubt William Wilkinson, eldest son (b. 1727) of Anthony Wilkinson, of Cross Gate, Durham, and brother of Wharton's bride (see Letter 135, n. 2). He was a Fellow-commoner of Trinity, where he had matriculated in 1746; he was admitted at the Inner Temple in 1745; became High Sheriff of Northumberland in 1757; died in 1768. Gray calls Wilkinson 'my new Relation' in accordance with his habit, of which numerous instances occur in this correspondence, of playfully adopting the relations and friends of those to whom he was attached.

3 In Hunts., about twelve miles north of Huntingdon, on the Great North Road. Gray was to be driven there from Cambridge by Wilkinson to meet Wharton and his bride on the way to London for their honeymoon.

4 See Letter 136, n. 2.

5 Probably Mrs. Olliffe (see Letter 145, n. 8).

Direction, & she shall come & pay it. I won't trouble you with long Letters at present. Adieu I am sincerely Yours

T G:

P:S: My Compliments!

[c. April 10, 1747]⁶

Addressed: To Dʳ Thomas Wharton of Durham By Caxton Bag *Postmark:* CAMBRIDGE

138. GRAY TO WALPOLE

I AM not dead, neither sleep I so sound, as not to feel the Jog you give me, or to forget that I ought to have wrote before. but I have been on the Confines of that Land, where all Things are forgotten; & return'd from thence with a Lofs of Appetite & of Spirits, that has made me a very silly Gentleman, & not worth your Correspondence. however I am tolerable well again, & came post hither on Friday¹ to see my Mother [   ]² she was then at the Extremity, but is far better at present: I have no Businefs to regale you with all [t]his,³ but it is only by Way of Excuse. on Monday next I hope to return home, & in my Way (probably on Tuesday Morning) to call at your Door, & that of the Chuteheds,⁴ if pofsible.

I am obliged to you for transcribeing Voltaire & Mʳ Lyttleton.⁵ the last has six good prettyish Lines. the other I do not much admire

Ni sa Flute, ni son Epée.⁶

---

⁶ Wharton endorsed the letter 'March or April 1747'; as Gray had written to Wharton as lately as 26 March (Letter 136), and had apparently heard from him since then, this letter was probably written about the above date.

LETTER 138.—First printed by Toynbee (1915), No. 161.

¹ 8 May.   ² Piece cut out.   ³ MS. torn.   ⁴ See Letter 131, n. 21.

⁵ George Lyttelton (1709–73), son of Sir Thomas Lyttelton, fourth Baronet, of Hagley Park, Worcestershire; Chancellor of the Exchequer, 1755–6; created (1756) Baron Lyttelton. The poem in question (which Walpole must have seen in manuscript, as it was not published until November, see Letter 142, n. 1) was his *Monody* to the memory of his wife, who died on 19 Jan. of this year.

⁶ M. Roger Martin has suggested that the poem, which Walpole had transcribed, was *Stances* VII, one of many short poems which Voltaire addressed to Frederick the Great, between 1740 and 1747. Their general theme is the union in the great monarch of the poet, the artist, and the warrior. *Stances* VII is a farewell on leaving Berlin (dated 2 Dec. 1740), and contains the following stanza:

Adieu, vous dont l'auguste main,
Toujours au travail occupée,
Tient, pour l'honneur du genre humain
La plume, la lyre et l'épée.

the Thought is Martial's, & many others after him; & the Verses frippery enough, as his easy Poetry usually is. nobody loves him better than I in his grander Style.

Adieu, Dear S^r, I am ever

Yours

T GRAY

Stoke. [May 13, 1747]⁷

Addressed: To the Honble Horace Walpole Esq at his House in Arlington-Street Westminster *Postmark:* WINDSOR⁸ 13 MA

139. GRAY TO WALPOLE

[c. 15 June 1747].¹

WHEN I received the testimonial of so many considerable personages to adorn the second page of my next edition, and (adding them to the Testimonium Autoris de seipso) do relish and enjoy all the conscious pleasure resulting from six pennyworths of glory, I cannot but close my satisfaction with a sigh for the fate of my fellow-labourer in poetry, the unfortunate Mr. Golding,² cut off in the flower or rather the bud of his

Gray's 'Ni sa Flute, ni son Epée' might be an adaptation of the last line, with the derisive substitution of 'flute' for 'lyre' (Frederick's flute-playing was mocked at). Gray says that the thought in Voltaire is Martial's. There are (as M. Martin points out) various epigrams in praise of Domitian, which Gray might have had in mind. Epigram viii. 82. 3–4 (*rebus pariter Musisque vacare*) has the suggestion that the Emperor could at once govern the State and honour the Muses.

⁷ The date of the month is supplied by the postmark; that of the year is determined by the reference to Lyttelton's *Monody* (see n. 5).

⁸ The stamp was not inked, but the impress is legible. The Peterhouse records show that Gray was absent at this date.

LETTER 139.—First printed in Mitford's *Correspondence of Thomas Gray and the Rev. Norton Nicholls* (1843), pp. 217–21. Mitford transcribed from the original letter to Walpole. In a note to the *Walpole–Mason Correspondence*, vol. i, p. 412, Mitford states that 'a few omissions deemed necessary were made in printing the poem', and adds that 'Gray's MS. copy was destroyed by the gentleman who bought it at Strawberry Hill.

¹ The date is determined by the reference to Gray's *Ode on a Distant Prospect of Eton College* which was published by Dodsley (in folio, price sixpence) on 30 May 1747, and the letter was probably written about 15 June (see n. 2).

² It is possible that Mr. Golding, who had evidently written a poem on Windsor and had recently died, should be identified with William Goldwin who died on 1 June 1747. Gray was often uncertain about names (or Mitford might have made a mistake in transcribing). William Goldwin was born at Windsor (where he was buried); he was a scholar of Eton and King's; B.A.

282

honours, who had he survived but a fortnight more, might have been by your kind offices[3] as much delighted with himself, as I. Windsor and Eton might have gone down to posterity together, perhaps appeared in the same volume,[4] like Philips[5] and Smith,[6] and we might have set at once to Mr. Pond[7] for the frontispiece, but these, alas! are vain reflections. To return to myself. Nay! but you are such a wit! sure the gentlemen an't so good, are they? and don't you play upon the word. I promise you, few take to it here at all,[8] which is a good sign (for I never knew anything liked here, that ever proved to be so any where else,) it is said to be mine, but I strenuously deny it, and so do all that are in the secret, so that nobody knows what to think; a few only of King's College gave me the lie, but I hope to demolish them; for if *I* don't know, who should? Tell Mr. Chute, I would not have served him so, for any brother in Christendom, and am very angry. To make my peace with the noble youth[9] you mention, I send you a Poem that I am sure they will read (as well as they can) a masterpiece—it is said, being an admirable

1705; M.A. 1708; Fellow of King's, 1703–10; Master of Bristol Grammar School, 1709–17; Vicar of St. Nicholas, Bristol, 1717–47. He published (among other poems) *Musae Juveniles* (1706), and *A Poetical Description of Bristol* (1712). The *Gentleman's Magazine*, vol. xvii, 1747, p. 396, printed *An anatomical Epitaph on an invalid, written by himself*, and referred to him as the 'learned, facetious and Rev. Wm. Goodwin' [*sic*], who 'left several other pieces of the like kind'. His associations with Windsor and Eton would explain his writing a poem on Windsor, and the date of his death would fit with Gray's allusions, if we suppose him writing about 15 June.

   [3] It is probable, as has generally been assumed, that Walpole arranged with Dodsley the publication of the *Eton Ode*, as he did afterwards for other poems of Gray's. He may also have arranged for the publication of the poem on Windsor. This has not been traced, and it is possible that its publication was dropped after the death of the author.

   [4] It seems to have been a custom, attested by many examples, for the works of Smith and Philips, although printed for different booksellers, and at different dates, to be bound in one volume. It is such an association that Gray suggests might have united 'Windsor and Eton' had 'the unfortunate Mr Golding ' survived.

   [5] John Philips (1676–1709), author of the *Splendid Shilling* and *Cyder*, had for his closest friend at Christ Church Edmund Smith.

   [6] Edmund Smith (1672–1710), author of a tragedy, *Phædra and Hippolytus*, which was printed in 1710, together with *A Poem to the Memory of Mr. John Philips*.

   [7] Arthur Pond (c. 1705–58), painter and engraver, especially noted for his portraits.

   [8] For Gray's opinion of his critics at Cambridge see Letter 245.

   [9] Probably Whithed.

improvement on that beautiful piece called Pugna Porcorum,[10]
which begins

Plangite[11] porcelli Porcorum pigra propago;

but that is in Latin, and not for their reading, but indeed, this
is worth a thousand of it, and unfortunately it is not perfect,
and it is not mine.[12]

THE CHARACTERS OF THE CHRIST-CROSS ROW,
BY A CRITIC, TO M^{rs} ——.

*　　　　　*　　　　　*[12a]

Great D draws near—the Dutchefs sure is come,
Open the doors of the withdrawing-room;
Her daughters deck'd most daintily I see,
The Dowager grows a perfect double D.
E enters next, and with her Eve appears.
Not like yon Dowager deprest with years;
What Ease and Elegance her person grace,
Bright beaming, as the Evening-star, her face;
Queen Esther next—how fair e'en after death,
Then one faint glimpse of Queen Elizabeth;
No more, our Esthers now are nought but Hetties,
Elizabeths all dwindled into Betties;
In vain you think to find them under E,
They're all diverted into H and B.

[10] *Pugna Porcorum per P. Porcium poetam Paracelses pro Potore*, Parisiis, 1589;
the work (a 12mo of 8 pp.) consists entirely of words beginning with 'p'.

[11] 'Plaudite', not 'Plangite', is actually the first word of the poem.

[12] In a letter to Walpole of 20 March 1773, Mason speaks of William
Trollope, Fellow of Pembroke (see Letter 114, n. 1), as 'the author of the
poem on the Alphabet, from which and from Gray's, a more perfect copy
might be taken of that whimsical yet clever production' (*Gray–Walpole
Correspondence*, vol. i, p. 65). Walpole replied on 27 May, 'I return you
Mr Trollop's verses, of which many are excellent, and yet I cannot help thinking the best were Gray's, not only as they appear in his writing, but as they
are more nervous and less diffuse than the others'. Mitford (*Correspondence of
Gray and Norton Nicholls*, p. 218) quotes the following note, written and signed
by Walpole on his copy of the verses: 'Gray would never allow the foregoing
Poem to be his, but it has too much merit, and the humour and versification
are so much in his style, that I cannot believe it to be written by any other
hand.' On the other hand Gray writes 'it is not mine', and it is hard to
believe that he would have praised the 'masterpiece', as he did, if it had
been his own composition. The most likely conclusion is that Trollope
wrote the poem and that Gray made improvements and additions.

[12a] The asterisks no doubt indicate the omissions which Mitford deemed
necessary (see preliminary note).

284

F follows fast the fair—and in his rear,
See Folly, Fashion, Foppery, straight appear,
All with fantastic clews, fantastic clothes,
With Fans and Flounces, Fringe and Furbelows.
Here Grub-street Geese presume to joke and jeer,
All, all, but Grannam Osborne's Gazetteer.[13]
High heaves his hugenefs H, methinks we see,
Henry the Eighth's most monstrous majesty,
But why on such *mock* grandeur should we dwell,
H mounts to Heaven, and H descends to Hell.

      *   *   *

As H the Hebrew found, so I the Jew,
See Isaac, Joseph, Jacob, pafs in view;
The walls of old Jerusalem appear,
See Israel, and all Judah thronging there.

      *   *   *

P pokes his head out, yet has not a pain;
Like Punch, he peeps, but soon pops in again;
Pleased with his Pranks, the Pisgys call him Puck,
Mortals he loves to prick, and pinch, and pluck;
Now a pert Prig, he perks upon your face,
Now peers, pores, ponders, with profound grimace,
Now a proud Prince, in pompous Purple drest,
And now a Player, a Peer, a Pimp, or Priest;
A Pea, a Pin, in a perpetual round,
Now seems a Penny, and now shews a Pound;
Like Perch or Pike, in Pond you see him come,
He in plantations hangs like Pear or Plum,
Pippin or Peach; then perches on the spray,
In form of Parrot, Pye, or Popinjay.
P, Proteus-like all tricks, all shapes can shew,
The Pleasantest Person in the Christ-Crofs row.

      *   *   *

As K a King, Q represents a Queen,
And seems small difference the sounds between;
K, as a man, with hoarser accent speaks,
In shriller notes Q like a female squeaks;

[13] The *Daily Gazetteer* in which Francis Osborne defended Sir Robert Walpole's administration against the attacks of the *Craftsman* (see Letter 35, n. 1). Osborne was frequently referred to by his opponents as 'Mother Osborne'.

Behold K struts, as might a King become,
Q draws her train along the Drawing-room,
Slow follow all the quality of State,
Queer Queensbury[14] only does refuse to wait.

*　　　　　　*　　　　　　*

Thus great R reigns in town, while different far,
Rests in retirement, *little* Rural R;
Remote from cities lives in lone Retreat,
With Rooks and Rabbit burrows round his seat—
S, sails the Swan slow down the Silver stream.

*　　　　　　*　　　　　　*

So big with Weddings, waddles W,
And brings all Womankind before your view;
A Wench, a Wife, a Widow, and a W—e,
With Woe behind, and Wantonnefs before.

When you and Mr Chute can get the remainder of *Mariane*,[15]
I shall be much obliged to you for it—I am terribly impatient.

140. GRAY TO WALPOLE

I CAME to Town the Day, that you went out of it, & am now
at Stoke very hot, & very well, thank 'ye. I embrace your
Invitation, & shall be glad to make you a Visit at Strawberry-
Hill.[1] the Week I leave to you; it is indifferent to me, what

---

14 Lady Catherine Hyde (d. 1777), second daughter of fourth Earl of
Clarendon; married (1720) Charles Douglas, third Duke of Queensberry.
She was noted for her beauty (which she retained till her death), and for her
eccentricities, which bordered upon insanity. She was the 'Kitty' of Prior's
poem *The Female Phaethon*. Gay, whom she took under her protection, for
many years lived under her roof. It was for soliciting subscriptions at St.
James's for the second part of the *Beggar's Opera*, after the performance had
been forbidden by the Duke of Grafton as Lord Chamberlain, that her
dismissal from Court in 1728, to which Gray here alludes, was due. A draft
of her letter to the King on this occasion was among the Walpole MSS. in
the Waller Collection (see *Gray–Walpole Correspondence*, vol. ii, p. 83, n. 14).
　The Duchess was received at Court again in this year (see Walpole to
Mann, 26 June 1747).
　15 Marivaux's novel (see Letter 112, n. 31).
　LETTER 140.—First printed by Toynbee (1915), No. 165.
　1 Walpole had removed here from Windsor a few months before (see
letters to Mann, 5 June; and to Conway, 8 June 1747): 'In May, 1747, I
took a small house near Twickenham, for seven years. I afterwards bought
it, by Act of Parliament, it belonging to minors. . . . In one of the deeds I
found it was called Strawberry Hill.' (*Short Notes*.)

Time next Month it shall be: Mr Walpole & Comp: will settle it among them. you must inform me what Place on the Windsor Road is nearest Twickenham, for I am no Geographer: there I will be at the appointed Day, & from thence you must fetch me.

Nicolini with a whole Coach-full of the Chattichees[2] has been at Cambridge in an Equipage like that of Destiny & his Comrades in the Roman Comique.[3] they said they had been in the Meridional Parts of Great-Britain, & were now visiting the Oriental. your Friend Dr Middleton has married really a pretty kind of Woman[4] both in Figure & Manner, wch is strange methinks. Adieu, I am

Yours ever

T GRAY.

Wednesday [August, 1747][5]

141. GRAY TO WALPOLE

IF I am mistaken, You will have the Trouble of reading a few unnecefsary Lines: but I imagine a Letter[1] I wrote to you (about a Week after I received yours) has never come to your Hands. it was to say that I should be glad to make you a Visit as you propose, & left it to you what Time this Month it should be: only desired, that you would inform me a little beforehand, & tell me (who am too fine a Person to know where any English

---

[2] Panciatici, and Nicolini, and Pandolfini, Florentines then in England. *Walpole.* Nicolini and Pandolfini had been friends of Walpole in Florence (see his letter to Mann, of 15 Sept., 1746).

[3] By Paul Scarron (1610–60) the reference is to the description in the first chapter of the *Roman Comique* of the 'charrette pleine de coffres, de malles, et de gros paquets . . . qui faisoient comme une pyramide', belonging to a troupe of strolling actors, the 'nom de théâtre' of whose leader was 'le Destin'.

[4] His 3^d. wife. *Walpole.*—Middleton's second wife had died in April 1745. His third wife, whom he married in 1750, when he was sixty-four, was Anne, daughter of John Powell of Boughrood, near Radnor.

[5] That this letter was written in August is evident from the fact that Gray talks of visiting Walpole 'next month', while in the following letter (dated 9 Sept.), in which he refers to the present letter, he talks of the visit as for 'this month'. The date of the year is determined by the reference to the 'Chattichees' (see n. 2). The actual date was probably Wednesday, 19 or 26 August 1747. The College records point to Gray having left Cambridge on 16 Aug. or a day or two earlier.

LETTER 141.—First printed by Toynbee (1915), No. 166.

[1] Letter 140.

Place lies) whither Hounslow or Brentford be nearest Twickenham, where I would be on a certain Day, & you must fetch me
from thence. Adieu! I am

Yours ever

T GRAY.

Stoke, at Mrs Rogers's.²
Wednesday—Sept: 9. [1747]³

Addressed: To The Honble Horace Walpole Esq at his House in Arlington
Street Westminster *Postmark:* WINDSOR⁴ 11 SE

142. GRAY TO WALPOLE

Nov. Tuesday, Cambridge [1747]¹

IT is a misfortune to me to be at a distance from both of you
at present.² A letter can give one so little idea of such
matters! * * * * I always believed well of his heart and temper,
and would gladly do so still. If they are as they should be, I
should have expected every thing from such an explanation;
for it is a tenet with me (a simple one, you'll perhaps say), that
if ever two people, who love one another, come to breaking, it
is for want of a timely eclaircifsement, a full and precise one,
without witnefses or mediators, and without reserving any one
disagreeable circumstance for the mind to brood upon in
silence.

I am not totally of your mind as to Mr. Lyttleton's Elegy,³
though I love kids and fawns⁴ as little as you do. If it were all

---

² His aunt (Ann Antrobus), the widow of Jonathan Rogers who died in
1742 (see Letter 110, n. 1).   ³ See Letter 140, n. 5.
⁴ The stamp was not inked, but the impress is legible.

LETTER 142.—First printed in *Works of Lord Orford*, vol. v, pp. 388–9.
¹ The date of the year is determined by the reference to Lyttelton's
Monody, which was announced in the *Gentleman's Magazine* for November
1747 (vol. xvii, p. 548) as published in that month. Tuesdays in November
1747 were the 3rd, 10th, 17th, and 24th.
² It seems probable that Ashton is the person here referred to. He and
Walpole came to a final breach in 1750 (see Walpole to Mann, 25 July 1750,
'I have long had reason to complain of his behaviour; in short, my father is
dead, and I can make no bishops. He has at last quite thrown off the mask';
see also letter to Mann of 22 Dec. 1750, *ad fin.*). (See Letter 153, n. 5.)
³ See Letter 138, n. 5.
⁴ Cf. Stanza VI:

Sweet babes, who, like the little playful fawns,
Were wont to trip along these verdant lawns
By your delighted Mother's side,
Who now your infant steps shall guide?

288

like the fourth stanza,[5] I should be excefsively pleased. Nature and sorrow, and tendernefs, are the true genius of such things; and something of these I find in several parts of it (not in the orange-tree):[6] poetical ornaments are foreign to the purpose; for they only show a man is not sorry;—and devotion worse; for it teaches him, that he ought not to be sorry, which is all the pleasure of the thing. I beg leave to turn your weathercock the contrary way. Your Epistle[7] I have not seen a great while, and doctor M.[8] is not in the way to give me a sight of it: but I remember enough to be sure all the world will be pleased with it, even with all its *faults upon its head*, if you don't care to mend them. I would try to do it myself (however hazardous), rather than it should remain unpublished. As to my Eton Ode,[9] Mr. Dodsley is *padrone*.[10] The second[11] you had, I suppose you do not think worth giving him: otherwise, to me it seems not worse than the former. He might have Selima[12] too, unlefs she be of

And Stanza XI:
>   Ev'n for the kid or lamb that pour'd its life
>   Beneath the bloody knife
>   Her gentle tears would fall.

[5] Stanza IV:
>   In vain I look around
>   O'er all the well-known ground
>   My Lucy's wonted footsteps to descry;
>   Where oft we us'd to walk,
>   Where oft in tender talk
>   We saw the summer sun go down the sky;
>   Nor by yon fountain's side
>   Nor where its waters glide
>   Along the valley, can she now be found:
>   In all the wide-stretch'd prospect's ample bound
>   No more my mournful eye
>   Can aught of her espy,
>   But the sad sacred earth where her dear relics lie.

[6] In Stanza XIII:
>   The verdant orange lifts its beauteous head:
>   From every branch the balmy flow'rets rise,
>   On every bough the golden fruits are seen;
>   With odours sweet it fills the smiling skies.

[7] From Florence, to Thomas Asheton. *Berry*.—See Letter 144, n. 22.

[8] Conyers Middleton (see Letter 135, n. 18).

[9] *Ode on a Distant Prospect of Eton College*. Dodsley had published it (see Letter 139, n. 1).

[10] To publish in his collection of poems. *Berry*.—See Letter 144, n. 2.

[11] The Ode to Spring. *Berry*.—See Letter 125, n. 4.

[12] The Ode on Mr. Walpole's cat drowned in the tub of gold-fish. *Berry*.—See Letter 134, n. 3.

too little importance for his patriot-collection; or perhaps the *connections* you had with her may interfere. *Che so io?* Adieu! I am yours ever,

T. G.

143. GRAY TO WHARTON

My Dear Wharton

I REJOICE to hear you are safe arrived, tho' drawn by *four wild Horses*, like People one reads of in the Book of Martyrs. yet I can not chuse but lament your Condition, so coop'd up in the Elvet-House[1] with Spirits & Hobgoblins about you, & Pleasure at one Entrance quite shut out; you must so much the more set open all the other Avenues to admit it, open your Folio's, open your De L'Isle,[2] & take a Prospect of that World, wch the cruel Architect has hid from your corporeal Eyes, & confined 'em to the narrow Contemplation of your own *Backside*, & Kitchen Garden. Mr Keene[3] has been here, but is now gone to Town

LETTER 143.—First printed by Mitford (1816), vol. ii, pp. 183–6; now reprinted from original.

[1] Wharton's first residence in Durham after his marriage. The house was perhaps the property of the Wilkinson family, as John Wilkinson (d. 1734), Mrs. Wharton's uncle, is described as 'of Elvet'. As regards the situation, Tovey prints (vol. iii, p. 353) the following note from a Durham correspondent: 'There are two streets here, Old Elvet and New Elvet. Old Elvet is still a good street, New Elvet is a slum, but had fine houses once, and I think Wharton may have lived there. A house in one part of the street would be quite shut in at the back and with no view in front—just what one gathers from Gray's letter.'

[2] Claude Delisle (1644–1720), geographer and historian; author of *Atlas Historique et Géographique* (Paris, 1718), and *Abrégé de l'Histoire Universelle* (7 vols., Paris, 1731).

[3] Edmund Keene (1714–81), scholar of Caius, 1730–4; B.A. 1734; M.A. 1737; Fellow, 1736–9; Fellow of Peterhouse, 1739; Master, 1749–54; D.D. 1749; Vice-Chancellor, 1749–51; Rector of Stanhope, co. Durham, 1740–70; Bishop of Chester, 1752–71; Bishop of Ely, 1771–81. In 1764 he was offered, but refused, the primacy of Ireland (see Letter 401).

When (in Dec. 1752) Keene was talked of for preceptor to the Prince of Wales, Walpole wrote to Mann: 'Keene, Bishop of Chester, is a man that will not prejudice his fortune by any ill-placed scruples. My father gave him a living of seven hundred pounds a year to marry one of his natural daughters: he took the living [that of Stanhope]; and my father dying soon after, he dispensed with himself from taking the wife, but was so generous as to give her very near one year's income of the living. He then was the Duke of Newcastle's tool at Cambridge, which university he has half turned Jacobite, by cramming down new ordinances to carry measures of that Duke; and being rewarded with the bishopric, he was at dinner at the Bishop of Lin-

for a little While, & returns to paſs the Winter with us. we are tolerably gracious, & he speaks mighty well of you: but when I look upon his countenance & his Ways, I can never think of bestowing [Tuthill][4] upon him (tho' it were never so advantagious, & they both had a Mind to it) and so I have said nothing to either of them. I found, he had no Hopes of your Petition;[5] & believe, you are right in thinking no farther of it. your Mention of Mr Vane,[6] reminds me of poor Smart[7] (not that I, or any other Mortal, pity him) about three Weeks ago he was arrested here at the Suit of a Taylor in London for a Debt of about 50£ of three Years standing. the College had about 28£ due to him in their Hands, the rest (to hinder him from going to the Castle,[8] for he could not raise a Shilling) Brown, May, & Peele,[9] lent him upon his Note. upon this he remain'd confined to his Room, lest his Creditors here should snap him; & the Fellows went round to make out a List of

coln's when he received the nomination. He immediately rose from the table, took his host into another room, and begged he would propose him to a certain great fortune, to whom he had never spoke, but for whom he now thought himself a proper match.' The lady, whom he married in May 1753, was the only daughter and heiress of a wealthy retired linen draper in Cheapside.

It was during Keene's Vice-Chancellorship that the new regulations 'for restoring good order and discipline in the University' were passed (26 June 1750), after having 'caused great heats and animosities in the University' (see Cooper's *Annals*, vol. iv, pp. 278–81, where the regulations are printed in full; see also Wordsworth's *Social Life at the English Universities in the Eighteenth Century*, pp. 65 ff.: and Winstanley's *University of Cambridge in the Eighteenth Century*, pp. 199 ff.). The apparent intimacy between Keene and Wharton hinted at in this letter (see also Letters 148, 150) was probably due to the fact that Keene's living of Stanhope was only about twenty miles from Durham, where he and Wharton would often meet. Gray had no liking for him, but kept on good terms with him (see Letter 148).

4 See Letter 120, n. 2.

5 There is nothing to show what this refers to.

6 Henry Vane (c. 1705–58), eldest son of Gilbert Vane, second Baron Barnard, whom he succeeded as third Baron in 1753; in 1754 he was created Earl of Darlington, and in 1755 was appointed Joint-Paymaster of the Forces (see Letter 211). Smart's father, a native of Durham, had been steward to Vane's uncle, William Vane, second son of the first Baron Barnard, hence the connexion between Vane and Smart. The latter had an allowance of £40 a year made to him by the Duchess of Cleveland (d. 1742), which was continued to him by the Duke, Vane's brother-in-law (see Letter 311, n. 4).

7 See Letter 135, n. 8.

8 In *Cantabrigia Depicta* it is stated that of the Castle 'there are now but few Remains, except the Gateway, which serves for the County-Gaol'.

9 Fellows of Pembroke (see Letter 127, nn. 7, 9).

his Debts, wch amount in Cambridge to above 350£. that they might come the readier to some Composition, he was advised to go off in the Night, & lie hid somewhere or other. he has done so, & this has made the Creditors agree to an Afsignment of 50£ per ann: out of his Income, wch is above 140£, if he lives at Cambridge (not else). but I am apprehensive, if this come to the Ears of Mr Vane he may take away the 40£ hitherto allowed him by the Duke of Cleveland;[10] for before all this (last Summer) I know they talk'd of doing so, as Mr Smart (they said) was settled in the World. if you found an Opportunity, pofsibly you might hinder this (wch would totally ruin him now) by representing his Absurdity in the best Light it will bear: but at the same Time they should make this a Condition of its Continuance; that he live in the College, soberly, & within Bounds, for that upon any Information to the Contrary it shall be absolutely stop'd. this would be doing him a real Service, tho' against the Grain: yet I must own, if you heard all his Lies, Impertinence, & Ingratitude in this Affair, it would perhaps quite set you against him, as it has his only Friend (Mr Addison)[11] totally. & yet one would try to save him, for Drunkennefs is one great Source of all this, & he may change it. I would not tell this Matter in the North,[12] were I you, till I found it was known by other Means. we have had an Opinion from the Attor:^ny General[13] in a manner directly contrary to the former. he does not seem to have been clear then; so that he may pofsibly not be so now. the Kings-Bench (he says) can take no Cognizance of it; the Visitor must do all, & he is the Vice-Chancellor[14] by K: James's Charter, wch is good. this is sad indeed, & the Fellows, before they acquiesce in it, seem desirous of consulting Dr Lee,[15] who is well acquainted with College-Matters.

[10] William Fitzroy (1698–1774), third and last Duke of Cleveland (1730) of the first creation. Vane married (1725) his sister Grace, eldest daughter of the second Duke. The Duchess, who gave Smart the allowance (see n. 6), was Henrietta Finch, daughter of Daniel, sixth Earl of Winchelsea.

[11] See Letter 135, n. 9.

[12] Vane's seat at Raby Castle was within twenty miles of Wharton's residence at Durham.

[13] Gray now reverts to the case of the Fellows of Pembroke against the Master (see Appendix H).

[14] At this time Francis Sawyer Parris, D.D., Master of Sidney Sussex.

[15] George Lee (1700–58) was younger brother of Sir William Lee, Chief Justice of the King's Bench. Lee, who migrated (1720) from Clare College, Cambridge, to Christ Church, Oxford, became D.C.L. in 1729, and in the

Have you seen Lyttelton's Monody[16] on his Wife's Death? there are Parts of it too stiff & poetical; but others truly tender & elegiac, as one would wish. Dodsley is publishing three Miscellaneous Volumes;[17] some new, many that have been already printed. Lyttelton, Nugent,[18] and G: West[19] have given him several Things of theirs. M^r W: has given him three Odes of mine[20] (wch you have seen before) & one of Mr West's (my Friend, who is dead) wch in Spite of the Subject is excellent: it is on the late Queen's Death.[21] there is a Mr Archibald Bower,[22] a Scotchman bred in Italy, Profeſsour in three Universities there, & of the Inquisition. he was employed by the Court of Rome to write a History of the Popes. as he searched into the Materials, his Eyes were open'd: he came to England, has changed his Religion, & continues his Work in our Language under the Patronage of Mr Pitt, the Yorks, &c: the Preface is come out with the Proposals,[23] & promises exceeding well. doubtleſs there is no part of History more curious, if it be well perform'd.

My best wishes wait upon Mrs. Wharton, and ——.[24] my Compliments to Miſs Wharton,[25] & to King Harry, the

same year was admitted advocate at Doctors' Commons. He was Dean of Arches and Judge of the Prerogative Court of Canterbury from 1751 till his death, having been knighted in 1752.

[16] See Letters 138, n. 5; 142, nn. 4–6.

[17] See Letter 144, n. 2.   [18] See Letter 144, nn. 18, 19.

[19] See Letter 91, n. 7.   [20] See Letter 142, nn. 9–12.

[21] See Letter 144, n. 34.

[22] Archibald Bower (1686–1766), educated at the Scots College at Douay, was admitted a Jesuit at Rome in 1706, and afterwards studied divinity there, 1717–21; in 1726 he came to England, and joined the English Church; in 1745 he was readmitted Jesuit, but again left the Society in 1747. In 1754, after the publication of the first three volumes of his *History of the Popes* (1748–53), he was accused of being secretly a member of the Roman Church, though professing himself to be a Protestant, and became involved in a war of pamphlets to refute charges brought against him by Sir Henry Bedingfield and John Douglas (afterwards Bishop of Salisbury). An account of this 'most curious history' is given by Walpole (who was strongly prejudiced in Bower's favour) in his letter to Mann of 23 Feb. 1756.

[23] These were issued on 25 March 1747; the work itself was published in seven volumes, 1748–66.

[24] This dash, which comes at the end of the line in the original, is not the expletive stroke with which Gray usually fills a blank space next the margin; it is something more than that, and besides is followed by a full stop. Gray no doubt intended a veiled reference to the parents' hopes of progeny.

[25] No doubt his eldest sister, Catherine, afterwards (1752) Mrs. Ettrick (see Letter 401, n. 1).

8th—26. Brown will write; [he's the . . . little man and always . . .]27 Adieu, I am ever

Yours,
T G:

Nov: 30 . . Cambridge [1747].28

P:S: I said something to Stonhewer,29 who (I believe) will do what he can. he is now in London.

143*. Gray to Whalley

[*c. Dec. 1747*]

[In his letter to Walpole of Jan. 1748 (Letter 144) Gray says that he had written a letter to Dr. Whalley (see Letter 117, n. 3) to rebuke him for calling him 'a kind of Atheist'. This letter, to which Gray refers again in his letter to Wharton of 19 Aug. 1748 (Letter 146), is not extant.]

144. GRAY TO WALPOLE

[Jan. or Feb., 1748]1

I AM obliged to you for Mr. Dodsley's book,2 and, having pretty well looked it over, will (as you desire) tell you my opinion of it. He might, methinks, have spared the Graces3 in his

---

26 Perhaps his next brother, Richard, who later was Mayor of Durham (see Letter 213, n. 1).

27 About three-quarters of a line in the MS. has been obliterated, and is now undecipherable. Mitford apparently was able to decipher and restore to the text the words in the brackets.

28 So endorsed by Wharton.   29 See Letter 120, n. 38.

LETTER 144.—First printed in part in *Works of Lord Orford*, vol. v, pp. 393–7; the remainder first printed by Toynbee (1915), No. 168 (see nn. 40, 44).

1 The date is determined by the reference to Dodsley's book (see n. 2) which was published on 15 Jan. 1748; this letter, therefore, was probably written at the end of January, or early in February.

2 *A Collection of Poems, By several Hands. In Three Volumes.* London: Printed for R. Dodsley. M.DCC.XLVIII.—Robert Dodsley (1703–64), author and bookseller, originally a footman, started as a bookseller at the Tully's Head in Pall Mall in 1735, when he published, among others, for Pope, Akenside, Young, Johnson, and Goldsmith. About 1755 he took his younger brother, James, into partnership, in whose favour he retired in 1759. He died while on a visit to Joseph Spence at Durham in 1764.

3 Two editions of the first three volumes were published in 1748. The earlier has a vignette of the Three Graces on the title-page; the vignette on the title-page of the second and later editions is Apollo and the Nine Muses. The page references in the notes to this letter are to the first edition.

294

frontispiece, if he chose to be œconomical, and drefsed his authors in a little more decent raiment—not in whited-brown paper and distorted characters, like an old ballad. I am ashamed to see myself;[4] but the company keeps me in countenance: so to begin with Mr. Tickell.[5] This is not only a state-poem (my ancient aversion), but a state-poem on the peace of Utrecht.[6] If Mr. Pope had wrote a panegyric on it, one could hardly have read him with patience: but this is only a poor short-winded imitator of Addison, who had himself not above three or four notes in poetry; sweet enough indeed, like those of a German flute, but such as soon tire and satiate the ear with their frequent return. Tickell has added to this a great poverty of sense, and a string of transitions that hardly become a school-boy. However, I forgive him for the sake of his ballad,[7] which I always thought the prettiest in the world. All there is of M. Green[8] here has been printed before: there is a profusion of wit every where; reading would have formed his judgment, and harmonized his verse, for even his wood-notes often break out into strains of real poetry and music. The Schoolmistrefs[9] is excellent in its kind, and masterly; and (I am sorry to differ from you, but) London[10] is to me one of those few imitations, that have all the ease and all the spirit of an original. The same man's verses at the opening of Garrick's theatre[11] are far from bad. Mr. Dyer[12] (here you will despise me highly) has more of poetry in his imagination, than almost any of our number; but

---

[4] His *Eton Ode, Ode on the Spring,* and *Ode on the Death of a Favourite Cat* (vol. ii, pp. 261–4, 265–7, 267–9); the name of the author is not given.

[5] Thomas Tickell (1686–1740), deputy Professor of Poetry at Oxford in 1711, during the absence of Joseph Trapp, the first Professor.

[6] The first piece in the *Collection* (vol. i, pp. 5–23), the poem *On the Prospect of Peace,* first published in 1712, which was praised by Addison as 'a noble performance' in the *Spectator* for 30 Oct. 1712 (No. 523).

[7] *Colin and Lucy* (vol. i, pp. 24–7).

[8] Matthew Green (1696–1737); six pieces of his are included (vol. i, pp. 28 ff.), viz. *The Spleen* (his last poem, first published posthumously in 1737); *An Epigram*; *The Sparrow and Diamond*; *Jove and Semele*; *The Seeker*; and *On Barclay's Apology for the Quakers.*

[9] By William Shenstone (1714–63); in vol. i, pp. 211 ff. (first published in 1742).

[10] By Samuel Johnson (1709–84); in vol. i, pp. 101 ff. (an imitation of the third satire of Juvenal, first published in 1738).

[11] *Prologue spoken by Mr. Garrick at the Opening of the Theatre Royal, Drury Lane* (in October, 1747) (vol. iii, pp. 150 ff.).

[12] John Dyer (c. 1700–58); two pieces of his are included (vol. i, pp. 72 ff.), viz. *Grongar Hill* (1727), and *The Ruins of Rome* (1740).

rough and injudicious. I should range Mr. Bramston[13] only a step or two above Dr. King,[14] who is as low in my estimation as in yours. Dr. Evans[15] is a furious madman; and Pre-existence[16] is nonsense in all her altitudes. Mr. Lyttelton[17] is a gentle elegiac person: Mr. Nugent[18] sure did not write his own ode.[19] I like Mr. Whitehead's[20] little poems, I mean the Ode on a tent, the Verses to Garrick, and particularly those to Charles Townshend, better than any thing I had seen before of him. I gladly paſs over H. Brown,[21] and the rest, to come at you. You know I was of the publishing side, and thought your reasons against it none; for though, as Mr. Chute said extremely well, the *still small voice* of Poetry was not made to be heard in a crowd; yet Satire will be heard, for all the audience are by nature her friends; especially when she appears in the spirit of Dryden, with his strength, and often with his versification; such as you have caught in those lines on the royal unction, on the papal dominion, and convents of both sexes, on Henry VIII.

[13] James Bramston (c. 1694–1744); represented by two pieces (vol. i, pp. 115 ff.), *The Art of Politics* (a burlesque imitation of the *Ars Poetica* of Horace, 1729), and *The Man of Taste* (1733).

[14] William King, D.C.L. (1663–1712), author of the *Dialogues of the Dead* (1699), an attack upon Bentley; represented here (vol. i, pp. 223 ff.) by *The Art of Cookery, in imitation of Horace's Art of Poetry* (1708).

[15] Abel Evans, D.D. (1679–1737), author of (vol. i, p. 238) *The Apparition; a Dialogue betwixt the Devil and a Doctor concerning the Rights of the Christian Church* (1710).

[16] *Pre-Existence, a Poem in Imitation of Milton*, anonymous (vol. i, p. 268).

[17] George Lyttelton (see Letter 138, n. 5); represented (vol. ii, pp. 1 ff.) by *The Progress of Love; in Four Eclogues* (1732).

[18] Robert Nugent (1702–88), later (1767) Baron Nugent and Viscount Clare (in Ireland), and (1776) Earl Nugent. His second and third marriages, to two wealthy widows, gave rise to Walpole's term 'to Nugentize'.

[19] His ode (vol. ii, p. 203) addressed to William Pulteney (afterwards Earl of Bath), first published in 1739. Walpole, who in a letter to Montagu (25 July 1748) speaks of this poem as Nugent's 'glorious Ode on religion and liberty', in his *Memoires of the Last Ten Years of the Reign of George the Second*, writes: 'Nugent had lost the reputation of a great poet, by writing works of his own, after he had acquired fame by an ode that was the joint production of several others'; and he adds in a note: 'It was addressed to Lord Bath, upon the author's change of his religion; but was universally believed to be written by Mallet, who was tutor to Newsham, Mr. Nugent's son, and improved by Mr. Pultney himself and Lord Chesterfield.'

[20] William Whitehead (see Letter 44, n. 8); his *Ode to a Gentleman on his pitching a Tent in his Garden*, and the verses to Garrick and to Charles Town-shend are in vol. ii (pp. 244 ff.).

[21] Isaac Hawkins Browne (1705–60), author of *A Pipe of Tobacco*, in imitation of Pope, Swift, Thomson, &c. (vol. ii, pp. 276 ff.).

and Charles II. for these are to me the shining parts of your Epistle.[22] There are many lines I could wish corrected, and some blotted out, but beauties enough to atone for a thousand worse faults than these. The opinion of such as can at all judge, who saw it before in Dr. Middleton's hands, concurs nearly with mine. As to what any one says, since it came out; our people (you must know) are slow of judgement; they wait till some bold body saves them the trouble, and then follow his opinion; or stay till they hear what is said in town, that is at some bishop's table, or some coffee-house about the Temple. When they are determined, I will tell you faithfully their verdict.[22a] As for the Beauties,[23] I am their most humble servant. What shall I say to Mr. Lowth,[24] Mr. Ridley,[25] Mr. Rolle,[26] the reverend Mr. Brown,[27] Seward,[28] &c.? If I say, Meſsieurs! this is not the thing; write prose, write sermons, write nothing

---

[22] *An Epistle from Florence to T. A. Esq., Tutor to the Earl of P* . . . (vol. ii, pp. 305 ff.); reprinted in *Works of Lord Orford*, vol. i, pp. 4–16. It was written in 1740, and was highly praised by Gray at the time (see Letter 91 *ad fin.*).

[22a] An allusion to what Gray elsewhere calls criticism 'à la mode du Temple' (see Letter 115, n. 7).

[23] *The Beauties: An Epistle to Mr. Eckardt the Painter* (vol. ii, pp. 321 ff.); reprinted in *Works of Lord Orford*, vol. i, pp. 19–24. This piece was written in July 1746, and printed in the following September. A third piece by Walpole, not mentioned by Gray, was also included in the *Collection*, viz. *The Epilogue to Tamerlane* (vol. ii, p. 325) (see Letter 128, n. 3).

[24] Walpole, in a manuscript note in his copy of Dodsley (now in the British Museum), states that the *Choice of Hercules* (vol. iii, p. 1) was by 'the Revᵈ Mr. Lowth, since Bp. of Oxford and London', i.e. Robert Lowth, Professor of Poetry at Oxford, 1741–51 (see Letter 209, n. 5); and he adds that 'part of this poem has been set to music by Handel, and was first printed in Spence's *Polymetis*' (see Letter 131, n. 5).

[25] Glocester Ridley (1702–74), Fellow of New College, Oxford, 1724–34; B.C.L. 1729; D.D. 1767; Prebendary of Salisbury, 1766–74; he is represented by two pieces (vol. iii, pp. 18–54), viz. *Psyche* and *Jovi Eleutherio, or an Offering to Liberty*.

[26] Author of *Life burthensome, an Epistle* (vol. iii, pp. 58 ff.).

[27] John Brown (1715–66), of St. John's College, Cambridge; M.A. 1739; D.D. 1755; subsequently well known as the author of *An Estimate of the Manners and Principles of the Times* (see Letter 237, n. 3); two pieces of his are included in the *Collection* (vol. iii, pp. 99–136), viz. *Honour* (1743), and an *Essay upon Satire*. He was also the author of two tragedies, *Barbarossa*, produced at Drury Lane in 1754 (see Letter 194, n. 6), and *Athelstane*, produced in 1756. For a further account of him see Letters 424 and 427 and Appendix R.

[28] Thomas Seward (1708–90), Canon of Lichfield, father of Anna Seward (see Letter 209, n. 6); author of *The Female Right to Literature* and three other poems (vol. ii, pp. 295–304).

at all; they will disdain me, and my advice. What then would
the sickly peer[29] have done, that spends so much time in admiring everything that has four legs, and fretting at his own
misfortune in having but two; and cursing his own politic head
and feeble constitution, that won't let him be such a beast as he
would wish? Mr. S. Jenyns[30] now and then can write a good
line or two—such as these—

> Snatch us from all our little sorrows here,
> Calm every grief, and dry each childish tear, &c.

I like Mr. Aston Hervey's fable;[31] and an ode[32] (the last of
all) by Mr. Mason,[33] a new acquaintance of mine, whose

[29] Lord Hervey. *Berry.*—John Hervey, eldest son of first Earl of Bristol
(see Letter 132, n. 6). Throughout his life he suffered from bad health, and
had what Walpole describes as 'a coffin-face' (to Mann, 7 Jan. 1742). The
reference is to Hervey's two *Epistles to Mr. Fox* in Dodsley's *Collection* (vol.
iii, pp. 240 ff.).

[30] Soame Jenyns (1704–87), M.P. for Cambridgeshire; ten pieces by him
are included in the *Collection* (vol. iii, pp. 153 ff.). The couplet quoted by
Gray comes from the last, *An Essay on Virtue* (p. 206). In 1757 he published
A Free Enquiry into the Nature and Origin of Evil (see Letter 237, n. 4).

[31] A slip of Gray's—*The Female-Drum: or, the Origin of Cards. A Tale.
Addrest to the Honourable Miss Carpenter* (vol. iii, p. 232), according to Walpole
(see n. 24), was by 'the Hon. and Rev. Mr. Hervey Aston' (the Rev. Henry
Hervey, fifth son of the first Earl of Bristol, assumed the name of Aston on
his marriage in 1730 to Catherine, heiress to Sir Thomas Aston, of Aston,
Cheshire). Miss Carpenter, Walpole notes, was 'afterwards Countess of
Egremont'.

[32] *Ode to a Water Nymph* (vol. iii, pp. 330–3) (see Letter 312, n. 22).

[33] William Mason (1724–97) (see Genealogical Table), the friend, literary
executor, and biographer of Gray, whose acquaintance he had made in the
previous year (1747), and by whom he was familiarly called 'Scroddles'.
He had been admitted to St. John's College, Cambridge, in 1742, and
graduated B.A. in 1745–6. In 1747, largely through the recommendation
of Gray, he was nominated to a Fellowship in Pembroke College, but the
Master prevented his election till March 1749. He was ordained Deacon
17 Nov., and Priest 24 Nov. 1754, and three days later was instituted
Rector of Aston, Yorkshire, on the presentation of the Earl of Holdernesse,
a distant connexion (see Letter 181, n. 3), who appointed him domestic
Chaplain, and whose private secretary he appears to have been for a time
at the beginning of that year (see Letter 184, n. 4). He was subsequently
Chaplain to the King, 1757–60, 1761–72; Canon Residentiary and Precentor
of York, 1762. He became acquainted with Horace Walpole in 1754 (see
Letter 188 *ad fin.*), or perhaps earlier (see Letter 159), and was on terms
of intimacy with him until 1784, when a political difference put an end to
their friendship for some years. Mason was the author of a number of plays,
satires, and poems, many of which underwent a minute revision at the
hands of Gray before publication. His *Musaeus*, a monody to the memory

Musæus too seems to carry with it the promise at least of something good to come. I was glad to see you distinguished who poor West was, before his charming ode,[34] and called it anything rather than a Pindaric. The town is an owl, if it don't like Lady Mary,[35] and I am surprised at it: we here are owls enough to think her eclogues[36] very bad; but that I did not wonder at. Our present taste is sir T. Fitz-Osborne's Letters.[37] I send you a bit of a thing for two reasons: first, because it is one of your favourites, Mr. M. Green;[38] and next, because I would do justice. The thought on which my second ode[39] turns is manifestly stole from hence:—not that I knew it at the time,

of Pope, written in 1744, had been published in the previous year (1747). At the beginning of Section IV of his *Memoirs* Mason writes: 'It was not till about the year 1747 that I had the happiness of being introduced to the acquaintance of Mr. Gray. Some very juvenile imitations of Milton's juvenile poems, which I had written a year or two before, and of which the Monody on Mr. Pope's death was the principal, he then, at the request of one of my friends, was so obliging as to revise. The same year, on account of a dispute which had happened between the master and fellows of Pembroke Hall, I had the honour of being nominated by the Fellows to fill one of the vacant Fellowships. I was at this time scholar of St. John's College, and Batchelor of Arts, personally unknown to the gentlemen who favoured me so highly; therefore that they gave me this mark of distinction and preference was greatly owing to Mr. Gray, who was well acquainted with several of that society, and to Dr. Heberden, whose known partiality to every, even the smallest degree of merit, led him warmly to second his recommendation.'

[34] His *Monody on the Death of Queen Caroline* (vol. ii, pp. 269 ff.), written in 1737; it is described as 'By Richard West, Esq.; Son to the Chancellor of Ireland, and Grandson to Bishop Burnet'. The poem is reprinted in Tovey's *Gray and his Friends*, pp. 110 ff. Tovey notes that the stanza of Gray's *Elegy*, 'The boast of heraldry, the pomp of power' &c. is evidently reminiscent of the following lines of West's *Monody*:

> Ah me! what boots us all our boasted power,
> Our golden treasure, and our purpled state?
> They cannot ward th' inevitable hour,
> Nor stay the fearful violence of Fate.

[35] Lady Mary Wortley-Montagu (see Letter 92, n. 11).

[36] *Six Town Eclogues* (vol. iii, pp. 274 ff.); they had been printed (not for the first time) in the previous year, and published by Dodsley at the instance of Walpole, who writing to Mann (24 Nov. 1747) says of them, 'they don't please, though so excessively good'.

[37] *Letters on Several Subjects*, by Sir Thomas Fitzosborne, a pseudonym of William Melmoth (1710–99), the translator of the letters of Pliny, and of Cicero *Ad Familiares*. The first volume of 'Fitzosborne's Letters', which had appeared in 1742, was reissued, together with a second volume, in this year.

[38] See n. 8.

[39] The *Ode on the Spring* (see Letter 125, n. 4).

but, having[40] seen this many Years before, to be sure it imprinted itself on my Memory, & forgetting the Author, I took it for my own. the Subject was the Queen's Hermitage.[41]

*   *

Tho' yet no Palace grace the Shore
To lodge the Pair you[42] should adore;
Nor Abbies great in Ruins rise,
Royal Equivalents for Vice:
Behold a Grott in Delphic Grove
The Graces & the Muses love,
A Temple from Vain-Glory free;
Whose Goddefs is Philosophy;
Whose Sides such licensed Idols[43] crown,
As Superstition would pull down:
The only Pilgrimage I know,
That Men of Sense would chuse to go.
W^ch sweet Abode, her wisest Choice,
Urania cheers with heavenly Voice:
While all the Virtues gather round
To see her consecrate the Ground.
    If Thou, the God with winged Feet,
In Council talk of this Retreat;
And jealous Gods Resentment shew
At Altars raised to Men below:
Tell those proud Lords of Heaven, 'tis fit
Their House our Heroes should admit.
While each exists (as Poets sing)
A lazy, lewd, immortal, Thing:

[40] The remainder of the letter, from this point, is printed from the original.

[41] This was a 'subterraneous building, adorned with astronomical figures and characters' (*Gent. Mag.*, 1735, p. 331), and fitted with a library, which had been erected in the royal gardens at Richmond by Queen Caroline; she called it 'Merlin's Cave', by which name it is several times referred to by Pope (*Imitations of Horace*, 2 Epist. i. 355; 2 Epist. ii. 139). Green's poem was first printed privately in 1732. Gray subsequently made acknowledgement of his indebtedness to Green in a note attached to the first line of the fourth stanza of his *Ode*.

[42] Speaking to the Thames. *Gray's note.*

[43] The four Busts. *Gray.*—A poem, *In Richmond Gardens*, printed in the *London Magazine* for 1738 (p. 38), mentions the busts:

Next to my view the *Hermitage* appears
*   *   *   *
Within on curious marble carv'd compleat,
Majestic *Boyle* claims a superior seat.
Newton and *Locke*, *Clarke*, *Wollaston* appear,
Drest with the native robes they us'd to wear.

    They must, or grow in Disrepute,
    With Earth's first Commoners recruit.
        Needlefs it is in Terms unskill'd
    To praise, whatever Boyle shall build.
    Needlefs it is the Busts to name
    Of Men, Monopolists of Fame;
    Four Chiefs adorn the modest Stone
    For Virtue, as for Learning, known.
    The thinking Sculpture helps to raise
    Deep Thoughts, the Genii of the Place:
    To the Mind's Ear, & inward Sight,
    There Silence speaks, & Shade gives Light:
    While Insects from the Threshold preach,
    And Minds disposed to Musing teach;
    Proud of strong Limbs & painted Hues
    They perish by the slightest Bruise
    Or Maladies begun within
    Destroy more slow Life's frail Machine:
    From Maggot-Youth thro' Change of State
    They feel like us the Turns of Fate;
    Some born to creep have lived to fly,
    And changed Earth's Cells for Dwellings high:
    And some, that did their six Wings keep,
    Before they died, been forced to creep.
    They Politicks, like ours, profefs:
    The greater prey upon the lefs.
    Some strain on Foot huge Loads to bring,
    Some toil incefsant on the Wing:
    Nor from their vigorous Schemes desist
    Till Death; & then are never mist.
    Some frolick, toil, marry, increase,
    Are sick & well, have War & Peace,
    And broke with Age in half a Day
    Yield to Succefsors, & away.

                    *   *

[44]Please to tell Mr Chute, that I never borrow'd any Life of
Mahomet (if that be his Meaning) having read Boulainvillers[45]
long ago: but that I have Du Clos' Louis Onze,[46] & will send
it him, if you will be so good as to send me Directions both to
Mr Whithed; & Mr Chute (per se) at his Lodgeings, wch I would

---

[44] The remainder of the letter from this point (except the signature), and
the postscript were omitted by Miss Berry.
[45] See Letter 112, nn. 18, 19.
[46] *Histoire de Louis Onze* (1745), by Charles Pinot Duclos (1704–72).

be glad to know for more Reasons than this. I hear Lamb-Pye[47] is dead, & could have wished to be told the Consequences: but both You & He, I doubt, will grow to regard me in the Light of a *Miscellaneous Writer*. Adieu, I am

Yours ever

T G:

P:S: If You chance to see a Letter of mine in any body's Hand, this is the History of it. Dr Whalley,[48] who has hated me ever since that Affair of Mr Turner,[49] thought fit to intimate to a large Table full of People, that I was a Kind of Atheist. I wrote to him partly to laugh at, & partly to reprove him for his Malice; & (as what he said was publick) I shew'd my Letter to several of those, who had heard him; & threaten'd (not in earnest, you may imagine) to have it hawk'd about Streets. they took me literally, & by Way of Anticipation my Letter has been consign'd to one Etoffe[50] (a Fiend of a Parson, that you

---

[47] Who this was does not appear.
[48] Master of Peterhouse (see Letter 117, n. 3).
[49] Shallet Turner, Regius Professor of Modern History (see Letter 117, n. 2).
[50] Of the Rev. Henry Etough, or Etoffe, Cole has left a lively description (Brit. Mus. *Add.* 5829, *fol.* 184; 5868, *fol.* 48). He was 'a pimping, tale-bearing dissenting teacher, who by adulation and flattery, and an everlasting fund of news and scandal, made himself agreeable to many of prime fortune, particularly Sir Robert Walpole'. He 'thought it more to the purpose to come over to the established Church, where better company, and better preferment were to be met with. He used to be much at Cambridge, when I resided there and was a busy, impertinent meddler in everyone's affairs'. Cole also mentions his 'tale-bearings and whisperings among the Heads, such as Dr. Whaley [*sic*], Bishop Keene etc.'

To his mischief-making activities Gray refers also in Letters 164, 165. His resentment against this 'Fiend of a Parson' found expression in an epigram which he wrote under a drawing of Etough, which Mason had made. The date of the epigram is approximately determined by a letter of Cole's to Granger of 11 Dec. 1769, in which he states that Mason's drawing was made 'twenty years ago. The verses were also wrote at the same time'. (*Letters between the Rev. James Granger and many of the most eminent Literary men of his time*, 1805, p. 331). Gray's verses, as transcribed by Mason, in Gray's Commonplace-book, are as follows:

> Such Tophet was; so looked the grinning Fiend
> Whom many a frighted Prelate called his friend.
> Our Mother-Church with half-averted sight
> Blushed as she blesst her griesly proselyte:
> Hosannahs rang thro Hells tremendous borders,
> And Satan's self had thoughts of taking orders.

Caricature of the Rev. Henry Etough
from an engraving of a drawing by William Mason

know) to shew about here, & to carry to Town, if any one will read it. he makes Criticisms on it, & has found out a false Spelling, I'm told. Adieu!

145. GRAY TO WHARTON

My Dear Wharton

THO' I have been silent so long; do not imagine, I am at all lefs sensible to your Kindnefs, w^{ch} (to say the Truth) is of a Sort,[1] that however obvious & natural it may seem, has never once occur'd to any of my good Friends in Town, where I have been these seven Weeks. their Methods of Consolation were indeed very extraordinary: they were all so sorry for my Lofs,[2]

with a note: 'after l. 2 addition to the first copy

I saw them bow and while they wish'd him dead

With $\begin{Bmatrix} \text{servile} \\ \text{civil} \end{Bmatrix}$ simper nod the mitred head.'

In 1769 Michael Tyson (see Letter 534, n. 4) made an etching of Mason's drawing, with the six lines of 'the first copy' below the portrait. There are some small changes in the text. For further details see 'The Poet Gray and the Rev. Henry Etough', by John Beresford, in the *Times Literary Supplement*, 22 July 1926; and 'Gray's Satirical Poems', by Leonard Whibley, in the *Times Literary Supplement*, 9 Oct. 1930.

LETTER 145.—First printed in part (in a garbled text) in Mason's *Memoirs*, pp. 189–90; first printed in full by Mitford (1816), vol. ii, pp. 186–9; now reprinted from original.

[1] The offer of a loan (see Letter 146, n. 2), which Gray ultimately accepted (Letter 149, *ad fin.*).

[2] The destruction by fire of the house in Cornhill where he was born, and where Mrs. Gray and her sister had carried on their business (see Letter 28, n. 3). Although the house was insured in Mrs. Gray's name, and payment on account of the loss was made to her, it appears that Gray had the benefit and responsibility of ownership.

The following account of the fire in which the house was burned is given in the *Gentleman's Magazine* for 1748 (vol. xviii, p. 138):

'Friday March 25. About 1 in the morning, a fire broke out at Mr *Eldridge's* (who with his wife, two daughters, and a journeyman were burnt, and his lodger Mr *Cook*, kill'd by jumping out of window) a peruke-maker in Exchange Alley, Cornhill; which burnt with great fury for 10 hours, and consumed almost all the houses in the said alley, and *Birchin Lane*, with the stately row of buildings in *Cornhill*, from *Change Alley* to St. *Michael's Alley*, among which were several noted coffee-houses and taverns, five booksellers and many other valuable shops in *Cornhill*. Some accounts make the number of houses destroy'd 160, but by the plan just published it appears to be no more than 80, and 14 or 15 damaged'.

A more detailed account is given in the *London Magazine* for 1748 (pp. 139–

that I could not chuse but laugh. one offer'd me Opera-Tickets, insisted upon carrying me to the Grand-Masquerade, desired me to sit for my Picture.[3] others asked me to their Concerts, or Dinners & Suppers at their Houses; or hoped, I would drink Chocolate with them, while I stayed in Town. all my Gratitude (or if you please, my Revenge) was to accept of every Thing they offer'd me: if it had been but a Shilling, I would have taken it. thank Heaven, I was in good Spirits; else I could not have done it. I profited all I was able of their Civilities, & am returned into the Country loaded with their Bontés & Politeſses, but richer still in my own Reflexions, wch I owe in great Measure to them too. suffer a great Master[4] to tell them you for me in a better Manner

> Aux sentimens de la Nature,
> Aux plaisirs de la Verité,
> Preferant le goût frelaté
> Des plaisirs, qu'a fait l'imposture[5]
> Ou qu'inventa[5] la vanité;
> Voudrois-je partager ma vie
> Entre les jeux de la folie,
> Et l'ennui de l'oisiveté,
> Et trouver la melancolie
> Dans le sein de la volupté? &c:

Your Friendship has interested itself in my Affairs so naturally, that I can not help troubleing you with a little Detail of them. the House I lost was insured for 500£, & with the Deduction of 3 per C^t they paid me 485£, with wch I bought, when Stocks

40), to which is prefixed 'A New & Correct Plan of all the Houses destroyed and damaged in the Fire which began in Exchange-Alley Cornhill on Friday March 25, 1748'. A number of names are given on this plan (see Illustration).

     [3] The friend, who 'insisted upon carrying me to the Grand-Masquerade, desired me to sit for my Picture', was no doubt Walpole. In his letter to Mann of 29 April 1748, Walpole refers to 'the most magnificent masquerade that ever was seen: it was by subscription at the Haymarket: everybody who subscribed five guineas had four tickets'. The picture must have been the portrait of Gray painted by Eckhardt for Walpole. The only other evidence of the date of its painting is in Walpole's letter to Cole of 10 Sept. 1771, where he says it was 'painted soon after the publication of the Ode on Eton'. The painting has hitherto been dated 1747: Gray's reference shows that it was a year later.

     [4] Jean-Baptiste-Louis Gresset (1709–77); the lines come from his poem, *La Chartreuse* (1734), in which he describes his cell in the College of Louis-le-Grand at Paris, where he was educated (see n. 15).

     [5] Gresset wrote 'que fait' and 'qu'invente'.

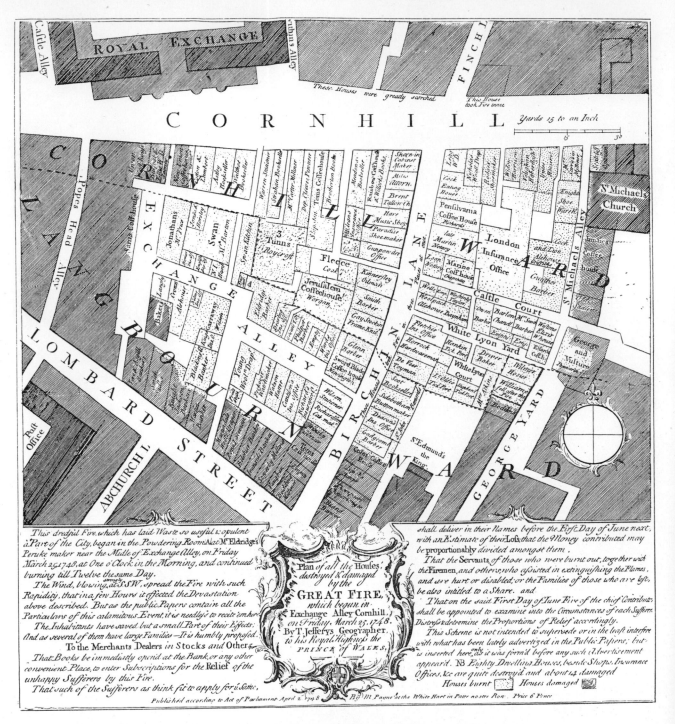

Plan of the great fire in the City, on March 25, 1748

published by M. Payne

were lower, 525£. the Rebuilding will cost 590, & other Expences, that necefsarily attend it, will mount that Summ to 650.[6] I have an Aunt[6a] that gives me 100£; & another,[7] that I hope will lend me what I shall want: but if (contrary to my Expectation) I should be forced to have recourse to your Afsistance: it can not be for above 50£; & that, about Xmas next when the Thing is to be finish'd. and now, my dear Wharton, why must I tell you a Thing so contrary to my own Wishes, & to yours, I believe? it is impofsible for me to see you in the North, or to enjoy any of those agreeable Hours I had flatter'd myself with. I must be in Town several Times dureing the Summer; in August particularly, when half the Money is to be paid: the Relation,[8] that used to do Things for me, is from Illnefs now quite incapable; & the good People here would

---

[6] The following interesting account of the transaction with the insurance office is given in *The London Assurance: A Chronicle*, by Bernard Drew:
'When the devastating fire on March 25th, 1748, broke out in Cornhill and the lanes and alleys adjacent we learn from the *London Magazine* for the period in question that "no publick Office has been burnt except The London Assurance who had time to save their effects and have suffered only in the loss of their house". The Corporation, however, had an interest in another building not a stone's throw from their own. This was No. 41 Cornhill, the birth-place in 1716 of the poet Thomas Gray. . . . The house was insured with the London Assurance for £500 and an entry in the Corporation's cash book exactly three weeks after the fire in Cornhill records the payment of £485 to Dorothy Gray (the poet's mother) in settlement of the claim. When we consider that the fire occurred on March 25th, and the cheque was signed by April 14th, we get some idea of the promptitude of The London Assurance in meeting its liabilities. . . . It may appear curious at first sight that Mrs. Gray was only paid £485 on a £500 policy, but it is possible that the premises were not totally destroyed, or, on the other hand, that a three per cent. reduction was made for a speedy settlement. . . . We know from Gray's letters that the house destroyed cost £650 to rebuild, from which it would appear that M[rs] Gray was considerably underinsured. The tenant, at the time the premises were burnt, appears to have been one Sarrazine, a milliner.* . . . To-day the building is No. 39 Cornhill, and is occupied by the Union Discount Co. of London, Ltd., while a tablet on the wall records the fact that Gray was born in a house which once stood upon that site' (pp. 124–6).
[6a] Probably Mrs. Rogers, with whom his mother and maiden aunt, Mary Antrobus, were living at Stoke, in the house where Gray was now staying.
[7] Presumably Mrs. Olliffe (see Letter 271, n. 3).
[8] In Letter 137 Gray tells Wharton that his Aunt will pay money due to him. This may have been Mrs. Olliffe and she may have been the Relation mentioned here.

---

* The last house on the west side of the Cornhill end of St. Michael's Alley is marked on the plan (see Illustration), among the houses that were burnt, as having been in the occupation of 'M[rs] Sarrazin Milliner'.

think me the most carelefs & ruinous of Mortals, if I should
think of such a Journey at this Time. the only Satisfaction I can
pretend to, is that of hearing from you; & particularly about
this Time, I was bid to expect good News.[9]
Your Opinion of Diodorus is doubtlefs right; but there are
Things in him very curious, got out of better Authors now lost.
do you remember the Egyptian History, & particularly the
Account of the Gold-Mines?[10] my own Readings have been
cruelly interrupted. what I have been highly pleased with is
the new Comedy from Paris, by Grefset; Le Mechant,[11] one of
the very best Drama's I ever met with. if you have it not, buy
his Works altogether in two little Volumes.[12] they are collected
by the Dutch Booksellers, & consequently there is some Trash;
but then there are the Ver-vert,[13] the Epistle to P: Bougeant,[14]
the Chartreuse[15] that to his Sister,[16] an Ode on his Country,[17]

9 Of the arrival of a little Wharton, 'the little Doctress' of Letter 146.
10 The passage occurs in Lib. iii, cap. 12.
11 '*Le Méchant, Comédie*. En cinq Actes en vers. Représentée par les
Comédiens Ordinaires du Roi aux mois d'Avril & Mai 1747, & remise au
Théâtre aux mois de Novembre & Décembre de la même année.' It is in
vol. ii, pp. 177–353, of the 1748 Amsterdam edition of Gresset's works (see
n. 12).
12 *Les Œuvres de M^r. Gresset*. A Amsterdam, Aux Depens de la Compagnie.
MDCCXLVII. 2 vols. 12mo.
13 '*Ver-Vert*, à Madame de ***, Abbesse de **' (vol. i, pp. 9–44). This
is the history, in four cantos, written in 1733, of a parrot in the convent of
the Visitandines at Nevers, who on account of his reputation for piety was
invited by the sisterhood at Nantes to pay them a visit. During the journey,
however, he picked up so much bad language:—
> Il entonna tous les horribles mots
> Qu'il avoit su raporter des bateaux:
> Jurant, sacrant d'une voix dissolue
> Faisant passer tout l'Enfer en revue,
> Les B. les F. voltigeoient sur son bec—

that he was sent back to Nevers in disgrace. Here he did penance, and at
last died in the odour of sanctity of a surfeit of comfits.
In his *Reminiscences of Gray* Norton Nicholls records that Gray 'disliked
French poetry in general; but was much pleased with Gresset, and extremely
with his poem of the Vert-Vert'.
14 '*Epitre au Pere Bougeant, Jesuite*. A C**. 20 November 1736' (vol. i,
pp. 146–75).
15 '*La Chartreuse*. Epitre A M.D.D. N' (vol. i, pp. 66–100).
16 '*Epitre à ma Sœur*' (vol. i, pp. 180–91). Mason, *Poems*, p. 82, referring to
Gray's fragmentary ode *On the Pleasure arising from Vicissitude*, states: 'I have
heard Mr. Gray say that M. Gresset's "Epitre a ma Sœur" gave him the first
idea of this Ode'.
17 '*Odes: L'Amour de la Patrie*' (vol. i, pp. 310–69).

& another on Mediocrity;[18] & the Sidnei,[19] another Comedy, wch have great Beauties. there is a Poem by Thomson,[20] the Castle of Indolence, with some good Stanzas. Mr. Mason is my Acquaintance:[21] I liked that Ode[22] very much, but have found no one else, that did. he has much Fancy, little Judgement, & a good deal of Modesty. I take him for a good & well-meaning Creature; but then he is really *in Simplicity a Child*,[23] & loves every body he meets with: he reads little or nothing, writes abundance, & that with a Design to make his Fortune by it. there is now, I think, no Hopes of the Pembroke Busine∫s[24] coming to any-thing. [My poor Tuthill][25] will be in a Manner destitute (even of a Curacy) at Midsummer.[26] I need not bid you think of him, if any probable Means offer of doing him Good: I fear, he was not made to think much for himself. pray, let me hear from you soon. I am at Mrs Rogers's of Stoke near Windsor, Bucks.

[18] 'Odes: *La Médiocrité*' (vol. i, pp. 358–63).

[19] '*Sidnei*, *Comédie*, Représentée, pour la première fois, en 1745 par les Comédiens ordinaires du Roi' (vol. ii, pp. 107–76).

[20] James Thomson (1700–48); he died a few weeks later, on 27 Aug. *The Castle of Indolence: An Allegorical Poem*, in Spenserian stanzas, had been published in May.

[21] It is strange that Gray should write as if Wharton had never heard of Mason. Eight months before Mason had been nominated to a fellowship at Pembroke (see Letter 144, n. 33), and Wharton must have been kept informed of College news.

[22] Ode to a Water Nymph, published about this time in Dodsley's Miscellany. *Mason.*—He adds the following personal note: 'On reading what follows, many readers, I suspect, will think me as simple as ever, in forbearing to expunge the paragraph: But as I publish Mr. Gray's sentiments of authors, as well living as dead, without reserve, I should do them injustice, if I was more scrupulous with respect to myself. My friends, I am sure, will be amused with this and another passage hereafter of a like sort. My enemies, if they please, may sneer at it; and say (which they will very truly) that twenty-five years have made a very considerable abatement in my general philanthropy. Men of the world will not blame me for writing from so prudent a motive, as that of making my fortune by it; and yet the truth, I believe, at the time was that I was perfectly well satisfied, if my publications furnished me with a few guineas to see a Play or an Opera.' *Memoirs*, p. 190.

[23] A reminiscence of Pope's *Epitaph on Mr. Gay*, in Westminster Abbey, 1732:

In Wit, a Man; Simplicity, a Child.

[24] See Appendix H.

[25] See Letter 120, n. 2. The three lines that follow are lightly scored through in MS.

[26] In September, however, Tuthill was ordained priest and admitted to the curacy of Brampton, Hunts. See Appendix G.

my thanks, & best Compliments to Mrs Wharton, & your Family. does that Name include any body, that I am not yet acquainted with? Adieu, I am ever

Truly Yours

T Gray.

June. 5 . . . 1748.

146. Gray to Wharton

Stoke. Aug. 19 [1748]

My Dear Wharton

After having made my Compliments to the Godmothers of the little Doctrefs,[1] who are to promise & vow for her that she shall understand, & be grateful some twelve or fifteen Years hence I congratulate Mrs Wharton & your family on this Occasion, & doubtlefs desire nothing more than to see you all the next Summer, tho' as to Promises, I dare not; lest some unlucky Event again come acrofs, & put the Performance out of my Power. I am not certain whether I shall be obliged to have recourse to your Afsistance[2] or no about Christmas: but if I am, I will be sure to give you Notice in due Time.

I am glad you have had any Pleasure in Grefset: he seems to me a truly elegant & charming Writer. the Mechant is the best Comedy I ever read.[3] Edward[4] I could scarce get thro': it is puerile; tho' there are good Lines; such as this, for Example

Le jour d'un nouveau regne est le jour des ingrats.

LETTER 146.—First printed in part (in a garbled text) in Mason's *Memoirs*, p. 191; first printed in full by Mitford (1816), vol. ii, pp. 190–2; now reprinted from original.

[1] Wharton's first child, his daughter Mary, the 'Lady Mary' of Letter 390; more usually 'Miss Wharton' (see Letters 420, 459, 519, &c. and Genealogical Table. From Gray's message of compliment to the godmothers it may be inferred that he was godfather.

[2] By way of loan, towards the cost of rebuilding the house in Cornhill (see Letter 145).

[3] See Letter 145, n. 11.

[4] The play in question was '*Edouard III. Tragédie.* Représentée pour la première fois, sur le Théâtre de la Comédie Françoise, le 22 Janvier 1740'. It is in vol. ii, pp. 1–106, of the 1748 Amsterdam edition of Gresset's works (see Letter 145, n. 12). The quotation comes from Act iii, Sc. 7:

De la Cour un instant change toute la face;
Tout vole à la faveur, tout quite la disgrace:
Ceux mêmes qu'il servit ne le défendront pas:
Le jour d'un nouveau règne est le jour des ingrats.

but good Lines will make any thing rather than a good Play. however you are to consider, this is a Collection made by the Dutch Booksellers. many Things unfinish'd or wrote in his Youth, or design'd not for the World, but to make a few Friends laugh, as the Lutrin vivant,[5] &c: there are two noble Verses, wch as they are in the middle of an *Ode to the King*,[6] may perhaps have escaped you.

> Le Cri d'un peuple heureux est la seule Eloquence,
> Qui sçait parler des Rois.

wch is very true, & should have been a Hint to himself not to write Odes to the King at all.

My Squabble with the Profeſsor[7] I did not think worth mentioning to you. my Letter was by no means intended as a Composition, & only design'd to be shew'd to some, who were Witneſses to the Impertinence, that gave Occasion for it: but he was Fool enough by Way of Revenge to make it mighty publick.

I don't wonder your Mr Bolby[8] disapproves M^r [·][9] Conduct at Rome: it was indeed very unlike his own. but when every body there of our Nation was base enough either to enter into an actual Correspondence with a certain most serene Person,[10] or at least to talk careleſsly & doubtfully on what was then transacting at home, sure it was the Part of a Man of Spirit to declare his Sentiments publickly & warmly. he was so far from making a Party, that he & M^r . . .[11] were the only Persons, that were of that Party. as to his Ends in it; from his first Return to England he has always frequented the Pr—ces Court, & been

---

[5] *'Le Lutrin Vivant.* A Mr. l'Abbé de Segonzac' (vol. i, pp. 47–56). The 'living lectern' was a choir-boy, whose breeches had been patched with some leaves of a book of offices containing part of the mass of the patron saint; while he was acting as lectern he was attacked by a wasp in a tender part, with direful consequences.

[6] *'Ode sur la Convalescence du Roi'* (vol. i, pp. 364–9), in celebration of the recovery in 1744 of Louis le Bien-Aimé from putrid fever at Metz. The quotation comes from Stanza xxi.

[7] Dr. Whalley, Master of Peterhouse, and Regius Professor of Divinity (see PS. to Letter 144).

[8] This was probably Thomas Bowlby (Boulby or Bouldby), who later (in 1754) married Lady Mary Powis (*née* Brudenell), eldest daughter of third Earl of Cardigan, and sister of the last Duke of Montagu.

[9] Scored through in MS. Gray here wrote an initial only.

[10] The Old Pretender.

[11] Scored through in MS. Gray here wrote the full name, which is indecipherable. There is no clue to the identity of the individual in question.

the open Friend of Mr. H: W:[12] w[ch] could certainly be no Way
to recommend himself to the Ministry: unlefs you suppose his
Views were very distant indeed.

I should wish to know (when you can find Time for a Letter)
what you think of my young Friend, St:[r] [13] & what Company
he is fall'n into in the North. I fill up with the Beginning of a
Sort of Efsay.[14] what Name to give it I know not, but the Subject
is, the Alliance of Education & Government; I mean to shew that
they must necefsarily concur to produce great & useful Men.

> As sickly Plants betray a niggard Earth,
> Whose flinty Bosom starves her generous Birth,
> Nor genial Warmth, nor genial Juice retains
> Their Roots to feed, & fill their verdant Veins.
>
>   And as in Climes, where Winter holds his Reign,
> The Soil, tho' fertile, will not teem in vain,
> Forbids her Gems to swell, her Shades to rise,
> Nor trusts her Blofsoms to the churlish Skies.
>
>   So draw Mankind in vain the vital Airs,
> Unform'd, unfriended, by those kindly Cares,
> That Health & Vigour to the Soul impart,
> Spread the young Thought, & warm the opening Heart.
>
>   So fond Instruction on the growing Powers
> Of Nature idly lavishes her Stores:
> If equal Justice with unclouded Face
> Smile not indulgent on the rising Race,
> And scatter with a free, tho' frugal, Hand
> Light golden Showers of Plenty o'er the Land.
> But gloomy Sway have fix'd her Empire there ⎫
> To check their tender Hopes with chilling Fear, ⎬
> And blast the vernal Promise of the Year. ⎭

[12] Gray had recently been staying at Strawberry Hill (see Walpole to
Montague, 11 Aug. 1748 *ad fin.*).   [13] See Letter 120, n. 38.
[14] This is the fragmentary poem called by Gray's editors *The Alliance of
Education and Government*. The 57 lines sent in this letter are followed in the
manuscript of the Wharton letters by a transcript in Wharton's hand of
50 more lines. The 107 lines are in Gray's Commonplace-book, with the
title 'Essay 1st'.   They are all that Gray wrote of the philosophic poem
which he projected. He left notes for parts, which were never written (see
Mason, *Memoirs*, pp. 200 ff.).

Gibbon (*Decline and Fall* (Bury), vol. iii, p. 332, n. 131) wrote: 'Instead of
compiling tables of chronology and natural history, why did not Mr. Gray
apply the powers of his genius to finish the philosophic poem of which he
has left such an exquisite specimen?' Gray gave his own answer to the same
question when it was put by Norton Nicholls (see Appendix Z).

This spacious animated Scene survey
From where the rowling Orb, that gives the Day,
His sable Sons with nearer Course surrounds
To either Pole, and Life's remotest Bounds:
How rude soe'er th'exteriour Form we find,
Howe'er Opinion tinge the varied Mind;
Alike to all the Kind impartial Heav'n
The Sparks of Truth & Happinefs has given.
With Sense to feel, with Mem'ry to retain,
They follow Pleasure, & they fly from Pain.
Their Judgement mends the Plan their Fancy draws,
Th' Event presages, & explores the Cause.
The soft Returns of Gratitude they know,
By Fraud elude, by Force repell the Foe,
While mutual Wishes, mutual Woes endear
The social Smile & sympathetic Tear.
Say then, thro' Ages by what Fate confined
To different Climes seem diff'rent Souls afsign'd?
Here measured Laws & philosophic Ease
Fix & improve the polish'd Arts of Peace:
There Industry & Gain their Vigils keep,
Command the Winds, & tame th'unwilling Deep,
Here Force & hardy Deeds of Blood prevail:
There languid Pleasure sighs in every Gale.
Oft o'er the trembling Nations from afar
Has Scythia breath'd the living Cloud of War:
And where the Deluge burst, with sweepy Sway
Their Arms, their Kings, their gods were roll'd away,
As oft have ifsued, Host impelling Host,
The blue-eyed Myriads[15] from the Baltic Coast,
The prostrate South to the Destroyer yields
Her boasted Titles & her golden Fields;
With grim Delight the Brood of Winter view
A brighter Day & Skies of azure Hue
Catch the new Fragrance of the breathing Rose,
And quaff the pendent Vintage, as it grows.

   *   *   *

I desire your Judgement upon so far, before I proceed any farther. Adieu! I am,

        Ever Yours
          T G.

[15] Gray substituted 'Myriads' for 'Nations', which he originally wrote.

Pray shew it to no one (as it is a Fragment) except it be
St:ʳ who has seen most of it already, I think.

Addressed: To Dr Thomas Wharton, at Durham   *Postmark:* 22 AV

147. GRAY TO COLE

[c. 1748]¹

Mʳ. GRAY desires Mʳ. Cole would lend him the 2ᵈ V: of yᵉ
Biogr: Britann: ;² & inform him, what is the Number of yᵉ
Book wᶜʰ the Master of Bennet³ wants out of yᵉ King's Library.⁴

147*. GRAY TO CHUTE

[c. 1748 ?]¹

My Dear Sʳ

I WAS yesterday told, that Turner (the Profeſsor of Modern
History here) was dead in London.² if it be true; I conclude,

LETTER 147.—Now first printed from the original.
  ¹ Date conjectural; it must have been between 1748, the year of the
publication of the second volume of the *Biographia Britannica* (see n. 2), and
1750, the year of the death of the Master of Benet (see n. 3).
  ² *Biographia Britannica; or the Lives of the most eminent Persons of Great Britain
and Ireland.* Lond. 1747–66, 7 vols. fol.
  ³ Edmund Castle, Public Orator, 1726, Master of Benet (otherwise
Corpus Christi), 1745–50.
  ⁴ Cole has written on this note: 'My worthy Friend, poor Mʳ. Gray of
Pembroke, his Hand Writing. The Mʳ. of Benet here mentioned was my
worthy Friend Mr. Castle.
  I had stuck this in a MS. vol. as a Specimen of Mʳ. Gray's writing.'
  LETTER 147*.—First printed in *History of the Vyne*, pp. 114–15; now reprinted from original.
  ¹ This letter, which is without indication of date in the original, has
hitherto been connected with Gray's letter to Wharton of 4 Dec. 1762
(Letter 363) and assigned, therefore, to November 1762. The letter to
Wharton refers to the death of Professor Turner; this letter states that Gray
had heard of Turner's death the day before; both refer to Gray's hopes of
succeeding him. But a comparison of the two letters shows that they could
not have been written on the same occasion.
  Turner died 13 Nov. 1762. In the letter to Wharton Gray relates that
having left Wharton, he had made a leisurely journey to London, where he
'found Professor Turner had been dead above a fortnight'; he had stayed
some days in London, before returning to Cambridge, which he did about
25 Nov. (see Letter 363, n. 1). If the letter to Chute had been written
in 1762, it could not have been written later than the middle of November;
but at that time, as we know from the letter to Wharton, Gray was travelling
in the north of England and did not hear of Turner's death until his arrival

it is now too late to begin asking for it: but we had (if you remember) some Conversation on that Head at Twickenham; & as you have probably found some Opportunity to mention it to Mʳ W: since, I would gladly know his Thoughts about it. what he can do, he only can tell us: what he will do, if he can, is with me no Question. if he could find a proper Channel; I certainly might ask it with as much, or more Propriety, than any one in this Place. if any thing were done, it should be as private as poſsible; for if the People, who have any Sway here, could prevent it, I think they would most zealously. I am not sorry for writing you a little interested Letter: perhaps it is a Stratagem: the only one I had left, to provoke an Answer from you, & revive our—Correspondence, shall I call it? there are many particulars relating to you, that have long interested me more than twenty Matters of this Sort, but you have had no Regard for my Curiosity: and yet it is something, that deserves a better Name! I don't so much as know your Direction, or that of Mʳ Whithed. Adieu! I am ever

Yours
T GRAY.

Addressed: To John Chute Esq

in London. The two letters cannot be made to fit the same event. There is another piece of evidence, which is also decisive. At the end of the letter to Chute, Gray refers to Whithed; this can only be Chute's friend, Francis Whithed: but he died in March 1751 (see Letter 160, n. 2). The letter must have been written, on a false report of Turner's death, while Whithed was alive, therefore before March 1751, and not earlier than May 1747, when Walpole bought Strawberry Hill (see Letter 140, n. 1), as Gray reminds Chute of a conversation which they had had at Twickenham. It appears from Walpole's letters to Montagu and Mann of August 1748, that Gray and Chute had recently been with him. The letter is, conjecturally and without any certainty, dated in that year, but it must be recognized that it may have been written at some other date between the limits mentioned. But whichever of the possible years be the date of the letter, it is a surprise to find Gray and his friends canvassing his succession to the Regius Professorship at this early stage of his career. What has hitherto been accepted as the earliest indication of his pretensions to the Professorship does not occur till 1759, in a passage at the end of his letter to Brown of 28 May in that year (see Letter 294).

² Dr. Shallet Turner, of Peterhouse (see Letter 39, n. 4). It was a false report, see n. 1.

148. GRAY TO WHARTON

My Dear Wharton

SHALL I be expeditious enough to bring you the News of the
Peace, before you meet with it in the Papers? not the Peace
of Aix la Chapelle,[1] Mother of Proclamations & of Fireworks,
that lowers the Price of Oranges & Malaga-Sack,[2] & enhaunces
that of Poor-Jack[3] and barrel'd Cod:[4] no, nor the Peace between
Adil-Shah & the Great Mogol;[5] but the Peace of Pembroke[6]
sign'd between the high & mighty Prince Roger, surnamed
the Long, Lord of the great Zodiack, the Glafs Uranium, &
the Chariot that goes without Horses,[7] on the one Part;
& the most noble James Brown,[8] the most serene Theophilus
Peele,[9] and the most profound Nehemiah May,[10] &c: on the
other.

In short without farther Preliminaries Knowles,[11] Mason,[12] &
Tuthill[13] are elected, and the last of them is actually here on the
Spot, as you will shortly hear from himself. the Negotiations,

LETTER 148.—First printed in part (in a garbled text) in Mason's
Memoirs, pp. 201–3; first printed in full by Mitford (1816), vol. ii, pp. 192–5;
now reprinted from original.

[1] Walpole writes to Mann on 29 April 1748: 'The preliminaries of the
Peace are actually signed by the English, Dutch, and French. . . . Spain is
not mentioned, but France answers for them.' The actual treaty was signed
on 18 Oct. 1748.

[2] On the prospect of peace with Spain.

[3] 'The sort of Cod that is caught near the Shore, and on the Coast of
Newfoundland and dryed, is called Poor-Jack' (quot. in *O.E.D.* from
Collins's *Salt and Fishery*, c. 1682).

[4] One of the conditions of the Peace was the restoration to France of
Louisbourg, capital of Cape Breton, the staple industry of which was the
Cod-fishery.

[5] In 1747 Nadir Shah was assassinated, and was succeeded by his nephew
Ali, who assumed the title of Adil Shah. There seems to be no record of the
treaty between Adil Shah (who reigned only for a few months), and the
Mogul Emperor, to which Gray refers.

[6] This was the settlement of the dispute between the Master and Fellows
of Pembroke as to the veto claimed by the former (see Appendix H).

[7] See Letter 39, n. 2.   [8] See Letter 115, n. 1.

[9] See Letter 127, n. 9. Peele was called John and the name Theophilus
is facetious.

[10] See Letter 127, n. 7. Nehemiah is a facetious substitute for Samuel.

[11] Thomas Knowles, of Pembroke, B.A. 1744; M.A. 1747; Fellow, 1749;
D.D. 1753.   [12] See Letter 144, n. 33.

[13] See Letter 120, n. 2. Here and elsewhere in this letter the name Tuthill
is left without erasure or obliteration.

that preceded this wonderful Event, are inexplicable. the Succefs of the Affair was extremely uncertain but the very Night before it, & had come to nothing, if Browne fixed & obstinate as a little Rock had not resisted the Sollicitations of Smith,[14] & Smart,[15] almost quarrel'd with Peele and May, & given up, as in a Huff, the Liveing of Tylney,[16] to wch he had that Morning been presented. I say, this seem'd to them to be done in a Huff, but was in reality a Thing he had determined to do, be the Event of the Election what it would. they were desirous of electing two, as the Master proposed, Knowles & Mason, or Mason & Gaskarth,[17] for they were sure he would never admit Tuthill, as he had so often declared it. however, I say, Brown continued stedfast, that all three should come in, or none at all; & when they met next day, he begun by resigning Tylney, & then desired the Master would either put an End to their long Disputes himself, as they intreated him; or else they would refer the whole to a Visitor, & did conjure him to call one in, as soon as pofsible. the rest did not contradict him, tho' the Proposal was much against their real Inclinations. so Roger believing them unanimous (after some few Pribbles & Prabbles)[18] said, well then, if it be for ye Good of ye College—but you intend Knowles shall be Senior?—To be sure, Master—Well then—& so they proceeded to Election & all was over in a few Minutes. I do believe, that Roger despairing now of a Visitor to his Mind, & advised by all his Acquaintance (among whom I reckon Keene,[19] whose Acquaintance I have cultivated

[14] John Smith, of Pembroke, B.A. 1741; M.A. 1744; Fellow, 1741.

[15] See Letter 135, n. 8.

[16] Tilney All Saints, a few miles from King's Lynn. In the *Registrum Magnum* of Pembroke are the following entries (for the year 1748/9):
'March 1, 1748. Mr Brown was presented to the Vicarage of Tilney void by the death of Dr Whalley and the seal ordered to be set to such presentation.
'March 2, 1748. Mr Brown declin'd making use of the presentation to Tilney given the day before.
'Mr Knowles, Dr Mason, Mr Tuthill nominated and elected fellows (each with five votes)
'March 16. Mr Peele presented to the Vicarage of Tilney.'

[17] Joseph Gaskarth, Sizar of Pembroke, 1744; son of Joseph Gaskarth, of Hill Top, Cumberland (mentioned in Gray's Journal in the Lakes of 2 Oct. 1769—see Letter 506); B.A. 1748; Fellow, 8 Nov. 1749; M.A. 1751; he held a lectureship from 1751, and was Senior Treasurer from 1753.

[18] *Merry Wives of Windsor*, i. 1: *Sir Hugh Evans*. 'It were a goot motion if we leave our pribbles and prabbles.'

[19] See Letter 143, n. 3.

with the same Views you mention'd in your Letter to Brown) to finish the Matter, had been for some Months determined to do so, but not till he made a last Effort. he made it indeed, but not having Sagacity enough to find out, how near carrying his Point he was; being ignorant of the Weakneſs of a Part of his College, & they not cunning, or perhaps not dishonest enough, to discover it to him, he thought he had miſs'd his Aim, & so gave it up without farther Struggling. I hope you will be glad to see so good an End of an Affair you give Birth to: Brown is quite happy, & we vastly glad to be obliged to the only Man left among them, that one would care to be obliged to. there are two more Fellowships remain to be filled up at the Commencement. by the Way Tuthill has been just holding a Candle—not to the Devil, but to the Master, as he was reading some Papers in Hall; and the Boys peep'd in at the Screens to see it, & to laugh.

Keene is most sadly *implicated* in the beginning of his Reign about an Election,[20] & I am of his Cabinet-Council, hitherto for the Reasons you[21] wot of, & now because I can't help it. but I am rather tired of College-Details (as I doubt not, you are) & so I leave this Story to be recorded by the Annalists of Peterhouse; & let Historians of equal Dignity tell of the Triumphs of Chappy,[22] the Installations,[23] the Visitations, & other memorable Events, that distinguish & adorn his glorious Reign.

You ask for some Account of Books. the principal I can tell you of is a Work of the Presid:ᵗ Montesquieu's,[24] the Labour of

[20] Keene had been elected Master of Peterhouse, in succession to Dr. Whalley, on 31 Dec. 1748; the disputed election was to a Fellowship. 'Implicated' was no doubt Keene's own expression (see Letter 149, n. 4).

[21] MS. 'yot'.

[22] Dr. Chapman, Master of Magdalene, and Vice-Chancellor (see Letter 135, n. 17).

[23] The Duke of Newcastle had been elected Chancellor of the University, in succession to the Duke of Somerset, who had been Chancellor for nearly sixty years, on 14 Dec. 1748. Gray refers to his coming installation, which took place 1 July 1749 (see Letter 150).

[24] Charles de Secondat, Baron de la Brède et de Montesquieu (1689–1755); Président à Mortier of the Parlement of Bordeaux, 1716; member of the Académie Française, 1727; besides the *Esprit des Lois*, the first edition of which (that mentioned by Gray) appeared at Geneva in 1748 (see n. 25), he published (anonymously) in 1721 the celebrated *Lettres Persanes*, and in 1734 *Considérations sur les Causes de la Grandeur et de la Décadence des Romains*. Of the *Esprit des Lois* Walpole writes to Mann (10 Jan. 1750) that he thinks it 'the best book that ever was written—at least I never learned half so much from all I ever read. There is as much wit as useful knowledge'; and (on

20 Years. it is call'd, L'Esprit des Loix, 2 V: 4to, printed at Geneva.[25] he lays down the Principles on wch are founded the three Sorts of Government, Despotism, the limited Monarchic, & the Republican, & shews how from thence are deduced the Laws & Customs, by wch they are guided & maintained; the Education proper to each Form, the influences of Climate, Situation, Religion, &c: on the Minds of particular Nations, & on their Policy. the Subject (you see) is as extensive as Mankind; the Thoughts perfectly new,[26] generally admirable, as they are just, sometimes a little too refined: in short there are Faults, but such as an ordinary Man could never have committed: the Style very lively & concise (consequently sometimes obscure) it is the Gravity of Tacitus (whom he admires) temper'd with the Gayety & Fire of a Frenchman.

The Time of Night will not suffer me to go on, but I will write again in a Week. my best Compliments to Mrs Wharton, & your Family. I am ever

Most sincerely Yours

T GRAY.

March 9. [1748–9][27] Thursday, Cambridge.

149. GRAY TO WHARTON

April 25 [1749].[1] Cambridge

My dear Wharton

I PERCEIVE, that Second Parts are as bad to write, as they can be to read; for this, wch you ought to have had a Week after the first, has been a full Month in coming forth. the Spirit of Lazynefs (the Spirit of the Place),[1a] begins to pofsefs even me,

25 Feb).: 'In what book in the world is there half so much wit, sentiment, delicacy, humanity?'

[25] 'De L'Esprit des Loix *Ou du Rapport que les Loix doivent avoir avec la Constitution de chaque Gouvernement, les Mœurs, le Climat, la Religion, le Commerce,* &c. *à quoi l'Auteur a ajouté* Des recherches nouvelles sur les Loix Romaines touchant les Successions, sur les Loix Françoises, & sur les Loix Féodales. A Genève, Chez Barillot & Fils.' The work was published in 2 vols., 4to, without the name of the author, and without date.

[26] Gray originally wrote 'knew'.

[27] Date of year supplied by Wharton.

LETTER 149.—First printed in part (in a garbled text) in Mason's *Memoirs*, pp. 204–5; first printed in full by Mitford (1816), vol. ii, pp. 196–9; now reprinted from original.

[1] Date of year supplied by Wharton.

[1a] See Letter 115 *ad init.*

that have so long declaimed against it: yet has it not so prevail'd, but that I feel that Discontent with myself, that *Ennuy*, that ever accompanies it in its Beginnings. Time will settle my Conscience, Time will reconcile me to this languid Companion: we shall smoke, we shall tipple, we shall doze together. we shall have our little Jokes, like other People, and our long Stories; Brandy will finish what Port begun; & a Month after the Time you will see in some Corner of a London Even:ng Post, Yesterday, died the Revnd Mr John Grey, Senior-Fellow of Clare-Hall, a facetious Companion, & well-respected by all that knew him.[2] his death is supposed to have been occasion'd by a Fit of an Apoplexy, being found fall'n out of Bed with his Head in the Chamber-Pot.

I am half ashamed to write University News to you, but as perhaps you retain some little Leven of Pembroke Hall, your nursing Mother, I am in hopes you will not be more than half-ashamed to read it. Pembroke then is all harmonious & delight-ful since the Pacification:[3] but I wish you would send them up some Boys, for they are grown extremely thin[3a] from their late long Indisposition. Keene's *Implications*[4] have ended queerly, for contrary to all Common-Sense Peter Nourse[5] & two others have joined Rogers,[6] & brought in a shameful low Creature by a Majority. the Master appeals to the Visitor against their Choice, as of a Person not qualified. he has received the Appeal, & (I suppose) will put in Brocket[7] (Dr Keene's Man) by main

[2] Tovey notes that in the announcement of Gray's death in the *Annual Register* for 1771 he actually was described as Rev. Dr Thomas Grey, LL.B.'
[3] See Letter 148, n. 6.
[3a] From the College records it appears that in 1748 only one pensioner was admitted, and in 1749 two sizars; after that the numbers went up a little, but there were many vacant rooms.
[4] See Letter 148, n. 20.
[5] Peter Nourse, of St. John's, B.A. 1733; M.A. 1736; Fellow of Peter-house, 1736; Vicar of Cherry Hinton, Cambs., 1739–49; Minister of Little St. Mary, Cambridge, 1750; d. 1758.
[6] Thomas Rogers, of Peterhouse; B.A. 1740; M.A. 1743; Fellow, 1741–50; Vicar of Ellington, Hunts., 1746–81; d. 1781.
[7] Lawrence Brockett, of Trinity, Scholar, 1744; B.A. 1747; Fellow, 1749; M.A. 1750; Tutor, 1751–3; B.D. 1761; Professor of Modern History, 1762–8 (see Letter 364 *ad fin.*), to which chair he was nominated by Lord Bute, to whose son-in-law, Sir James Lowther (1736–1806), afterwards (1784) first Earl of Lonsdale (see Letter 475, n. 7), he had been private tutor. He was a candidate for the Mastership of Trinity in 1768 (see Letter 467). He was killed by a fall from his horse, 24 July 1768 (see Letters 480, 481). It was in succession to Brockett that Gray was appointed Professor by

Force. Chapman[8] is at present in Town in waiting; he has just married a Miſs Barnwell, Niece to one D[r] Barnwell,[9] who was Minister of Trompington, with 2000£, a plain Woman, & about his own Age. I hear, that when he sent to Leicester-House[10] to know, when the Prince would be waited upon with the Book of Verses on the Peace[11] the Prince appointed no Day at all; but order'd the Verses to be sent, & left there. the Design of receiving the University at New-Castle House[12] is said to be alter'd; the Duke intending to come hither, (I imagine) after the Parliament is risen. Roſse's[13] Epistles of Tully ad Familiares will come out in about a Week. it is in two handsome 8[vo] Volumes with an Introd:[tion] & Notes in English,[14] but no Translation, dedicated to L[d] Gower.[15] now I am come to Books, there is a new Edition of Montesquieu's Work (w[ch] I mention'd

the Duke of Grafton. Gray's anticipation that the Visitor (the Bishop of Ely) would make Brockett a Fellow of Peterhouse was not fulfilled.

[8] See Letter 135, n. 17. He had been appointed Chaplain to the King in the previous year, and was at this time Vice-Chancellor.

[9] John Barnwell, of Trinity, B.A. 1705; M.A. 1708; Fellow, 1707; D.D. 1728. He was Vicar of Trumpington, 1732–46.

[10] The residence of Frederick, Prince of Wales, in Leicester Fields (Leicester Square). The house had been bought in 1718 by George II when Prince of Wales, after he had quarrelled with his father, and had been ordered to leave St. James's.

[11] *Gratulatio Academiæ Cantabrigiensis de reditu serenissimi Regis Georgii II post pacem et libertatem Europæ feliciter restitutam Anno M.DCC. XLVIII.* Cantabrigiæ, Typis Academicis. M.DCC. XLVIII. fol. Among the authors were William Mason, B.A. of St. John's College; Christopher Smart, M.A., Fellow of Pembroke Hall, and William Whitehead, M.A. of Clare Hall—the future Poet Laureate.

[12] In Lincoln's Inn Fields (see Letter 148, n. 23).

[13] John Ross (in his early life he spelt his name Rosse) (1719–92), of St. John's, B.A. 1741; M.A. 1744; Fellow, 1744–70; D.D. 1756; Chaplain to the King, 1757; Vicar of Frome, Somerset, 1760–92; Canon of Durham, 1769–78; Bishop of Exeter, 1778–92. He was a friend of Gray, who (according to Nichols, *Literary Anecdotes*, vol. ii, p. 184) assisted him in a pamphlet which he wrote against Markland. Ross was a candidate for the Mastership of Trinity in 1768 (see Letter 467), and later in the same year was talked of for the Deanery of Ely (see Letters 489, 490). It appears from Gray's letter to Robinson of 10 Oct. 1763 (Letter 380) that Gray had been invited by Rosse to pay him a visit at Frome.

[14] *Marci Tullii Ciceronis Epistolarum ad Familiares Libri xvi.* Edidit, et Commentario Anglico illustravit Joannes Ross, A.M. Coll. D. Joan. Cant. Socius. Cantabrigiae. Typis Academicis excudebat J. Bentham. A. M.DCC.XL.IX. 2 vols. 8vo.

[15] John Leveson Gower (1694–1754), second Baron (1709) and first Earl Gower (1746).

to you before) publishing in 2V 8ᵛᵒ.¹⁶ have you seen old Crebillon's¹⁷ Catilina, a Tragedy, wᶜʰ has had a prodigious Run at
Paris? historical Truth is too much perverted in it, wᶜʰ is
ridiculous in a Story so generally known: but if you can get over
this, the Sentiments & Versification are fine, & most of the
Characters (particularly the principal one) painted with great
Spirit. observe, if you chuse to send for it, not to have Brindley's
Edition, wᶜʰ is all false Prints, but Vaillant's.¹⁸ there is a Work
publishing in Denmark by Subscription (4 Guineas) Travels in
Egypt by Capt: Norden.¹⁹ he was once in England (as Tutor
to a young Count Daniskiold, hereditary Admiral of Denmark)
& known to many Persons for a Man of Sense, & that understood
Drawing extremely well: accordingly it is the Plates, that raise
it to such a price, & are said to be excellent. the Author himself is dead, & his papers are publish'd by the Academy at
Copenhagen. Mʳ Birch,²⁰ the indefatigable, has just put out a
thick 8ᵛᵒ of original Papers of Q: Elizabeth's Time. there are

¹⁶ See Letter 148, n. 24. This new edition of the *Esprit des Lois* was published in London in this year.

¹⁷ Prosper Jolyot de Crébillon (1674–1762), dramatist, father of the
Crébillon whose romances Gray so much admired (see Letter 103, n. 6).
He had recently produced *Catilina*, which was performed for the first time on
12 Dec. 1748.

¹⁸ In the *Gentleman's Magazine* for Jan. 1749 editions of *Catilina* are announced as published by Brindley and Dodsley. Vaillant was an importer
of French books: no edition of *Catilina* with his imprint has been traced.

¹⁹ *Voyage d'Egypte et de Nubie*, Par Mr. Frederic Louis Norden, Capitaine
des Vaisseaux du Roi. *Ouvrage enrichi de Cartes & de Figures dessinées sur les
lieux, par l'Auteur même*. A Copenhague, De l'Imprimerie de la Maison
Royale des Orphelins. MDCCLV. 2 tom. fol.
Friderik Ludvig Norden (1708–42), an officer in the Danish navy, was
sent to Egypt in 1737 by King Christian VI of Denmark with a commission
to write an account of his travels. The work was published after his death
as above.

²⁰ Thomas Birch (1705–66), F.R.S. and F.S.A. 1735; D.D. 1753; 'a
worthy, good-natured soul, full of industry and activity, and running about
like a young setting-dog in quest of anything, new or old, and with no parts,
taste, or judgement' (Walpole to Cole, 5 Feb. 1780). In 1742 he published
the *Thurloe Papers* in 7 vols., fol., 'out of which', wrote Gray to Mann
(Letter 112), 'it would be hard to collect a pocket volume worth having'.
The work here in question was 'An Historical View of the Negotiations
between the Courts of *England*, *France*, and *Brussels*, from the Year 1592 to
1617. By Thomas Birch. M.A. F.R.S. And Rector of the United-Parishes of
St. Margaret-Pattens and *St. Gabriel-Fenchurch* London: Printed for A. Millar,
opposite to *Katherine-Street*, in the Strand. M.DCC.XLIX.' (8vo).
Gray possessed and annotated a copy of this work, to which he refers again
in his letter to Wharton of 25 March 1756 (Letter 214).

many curious Things in it, particularly Letters from Sʳ Rob:
Cecil (Salisbury)²¹ about his Negotiations with Henry the 4ᵗʰ
of France; the Earl of Monmouth's²² odd Account of Q:
Elizabeth's Death, several Peculiarities of James 1ˢᵗ & Pr:
Henry, &c: and above all an excellent Account of the State of
France with Characters of the King, his Court, & Ministry, by
Sʳ G: Carew,²³ Ambaſsador there. this, I think, is all new
worth mentioning, that I have seen or heard of, except a
natural History of Peru in Spanish, printed at London,²⁴ by
Don —— something, a Man of Learning, sent thither by the
Court on Purpose.

I shall venture to accept of a Part of that kind Offer you once
made me²⁵ (for my Finances are much disorder'd this Year) by
desiring you to lend me twenty Guineas. the sooner you can do
this, the more convenient it will be to me, & if you can find a
Method to pay it here; still more so. but if any thing should
happen, that may defer it, or make this Method troublesome:
then I will desire you to make it payable in Town after the
first Week in June, when I shall be obliged to go thither.

I want to hear from you, to know of your Health & that of
your Family. my best Compliments to Mʳˢ Wharton, Mʳ
Brown comes & throws in his *little comps* too, & we are both
very truly

Yours
T G: i: b:²⁶

Addressed: To Dʳ Thomas Wharton at Durham By Caxton *Postmark:*
CAMBRIDGE

²¹ Robert Cecil (c. 1563–1612), first Earl of Salisbury (1605), Principal
Secretary of State, 1596–1612. His 'Negotiations' occupy pp. 1–411 of
Birch's volume.

²² Robert Carey (c. 1560–1639), first Earl of Monmouth (1626). His
account of the death of Queen Elizabeth is given on pp. 205–13 of Birch's
volume.

²³ Sir George Carew (d. 1612), Ambassador to France, 1605–9. His
'Relation', after remaining in manuscript for nearly 150 years, was communicated by Lord Hardwicke to Birch, by whom it was published in the
volume (pp. 413–528) referred to by Gray (see n. 20).

²⁴ The work in question must have been *Observaciones Astronomicas y Phisicas
hechas en el Reyno del Peru* (Madrid, 1748, fol.) by Juan George. No copy with
a London imprint is known, and it is unlikely that a book written in Spanish
would have been printed in London; possibly Gray wrote London by a slip
for Madrid.   ²⁵ See Letter 145, n. 1.

²⁶ That is, James Brown—a playful allusion, like his '*little comps*', to
Brown's diminutive stature (see Letter 115, n. 1).

150. GRAY TO WHARTON

My Dear Wharton

I PROMISED Dr Keene[1] long since to give you an Account of our Magnificences here,[2] but the News-Papers & he himself in Person have got the Start of my Indolence, so that by this Time you are well acquainted with all the Events, that adorned that Week of Wonders. thus much I may venture to tell you, because it is probable no body else has done it, that our Friend Chappy's[3] Zeal & Eloquence surpaſsed all Power of Description. Vesuvio in an Eruption was not more violent than his

LETTER 150.—First printed in part (in a garbled text) in Mason's *Memoirs*, pp. 206–7; first printed in full by Mitford (1816), vol. ii, pp. 200–2; now reprinted from original.

[1] See Letter 143, n. 3.

[2] The Duke of Newcastle's installation as Chancellor of the University. *Mason.*—Cooper, in *Annals of Cambridge*, under the year 1749, gives the following account of the ceremony: 'The installation of the Duke of Newcastle as Chancellor of the University took place at Cambridge on the 1st of July. The University being assembled in the Senate House, a deputation was sent to his Grace, who was at Clare Hall, whence, preceeded by the Bedels and several Doctors he came to the Senate House, at the steps of which he was met by Dr Chapman the Vicechancellor, who walked up the Senate House at his left hand. They then ascended the chair of state, the Duke standing at the left hand thereof, and the Vicechancellor on the right. A band of music having performed a short overture, the Vicechancellor made a congratulatory speech in English. Then he presented the Duke with the patent of office, which was read aloud by the Senior Proctor. The Vicechancellor then presented the book of statutes, and taking the Duke's right hand in his own, the Senior Proctor administered the oath of office. He was then seated by the Vicechancellor in the chair of State. Mr Yonge the Public Orator having made a Latin oration, the Duke returned his thanks to the University for the honour conferred on him. Then was performed the Installation Ode, written by William Mason M.A. fellow of Pembroke Hall, and set to music by Boyce. . . . [Here follows Mason's ode.] The proceedings, in the Senate House being concluded, the Chancellor and University went in procession to Trinity College, where in the hall was a splendid dinner, 800 dined in the hall and the Master's lodge. . . . On Sunday, the 2d of July, the Chancellor attended both services at Great St. Mary's Church. . . . On the 3d of July, honorary degrees were conferred. . . the Commencement was on the 4th of July, and on the 5th, the Chancellor left Cambridge' (vol. iv, pp. 268 ff.).

Walpole writes to Mann, 25 June 1749: 'Saturday, Sunday, and Monday next, are the banquets at Cambridge, for the instalment of the Duke of Newcastle as Chancellor. The whole world goes to it: he has invited, summoned, pressed the entire body of nobility and gentry from all parts of England. His cooks have been there these ten days. . . .'

[3] Dr. Chapman, the Vice-Chancellor.

322

The Duke of Newcastle and his Cook.

Caricature of the Duke of Newcastle and his cook Clouet

from an engraving in the British Museum

Utterance, nor (since I am at my Mountains) Pelion with all its Pine-trees in a Storm of Wind more impetuous than his Action. and yet the Senate-house still stands, & (I thank God) we are all safe and well at your Service. I was ready to sink for him, & scarce dared to look about me, when I was sure it was all over: but soon found I might have spared my Confusion, for all People join'd to applaud him: every thing was quite right; & I dare swear, not three People here but think him a Model of Oratory. for all the Duke's little Court came with a Resolution to be pleased; & when the Tone was once given the University, who ever wait for the Judgement of their Betters, struck into it with an admirable Harmony. for the rest of the Performances they were (as usual) very ordinary. every one, while it lasted, was very gay, & very busy in the Morning, & very owlish & very tipsy at Night. I make no Exceptions from the Chancellour to Blew-Coat.⁴ Mason's Ode⁵ was the only Entertainment, that had any tolerable Elegance; & for my own Part I think it (with some little abatements) uncommonly well on such an Occasion. pray let me know your Sentiments, for doubtlefs you have seen it. the Author of it grows apace into my good Graces, as I know him more: he is very ingenious with great Good-Nature & Simplicity. a little vain, but in so harmlefs & so comical a Way, that it does not offend one at all; a little ambitious, but withall so ignorant in the World & its Ways, that this does not hurt him in one's Opinion. so sincere & so undisguised, that no Mind with a Spark of Generosity would ever think of hurting him, he lies so open to Injury. but so indolent, that if he can not overcome this Habit, all his good Qualities will signify nothing at all. after all I like him so well, I could wish you knew him.

[Tuthill],⁶ who was here at the Installation & in high Spirits, will come to settle in Cambridge at Michaelmas. and I have hopes, that these two with Brown's afsistance may bring Pembroke into some Esteem: but then there is no making

---

⁴ The University Marshal (see Letter 114, n. 2).

⁵ 'An Ode performed in the Senate House at Cambridge, July 1, 1749, at the Installation of his Grace Thomas Holles Duke of Newcastle, Chancellor of the University. By Mʳ Mason, Fellow of Pembroke-Hall. Set to Musick by Mʳ Boyce, Composer to his Majesty.'

The ode was reprinted in Dodsley's *Collection of Poems* (vol. iv, pp. 269 ff.); it was not included in the editions of Mason's Collected Works until that published in 1797 (vol. iii, p. 9).

⁶ See Letter 120, n. 2.

Bricks without Straw. they have no Boys at all,⁶ᵃ & unless you can send us a Hamper or two out of the North to begin with, they will be like a few Rats straggling about an old deserted Mansion-House.

I should be glad (as you will see Keene often⁷) if you could throw in a Word, as of your own head merely, about a Fellowship for Stonhewer. he has several times mention'd it himself, as a Thing he would try to bring about either at Queen's or Christ's, where he has interest: but I know not how, it has gone off again, & we have heard no more lately about it. I know it is not practicable here at Peter-house, because of his County;⁸ & tho' at Pembroke we might poſsibly get a Majority, yet Roger⁹ is an animal, that might play over again all his old Game, & with a better appearance than before. you would therefore oblige me, if you would sound him upon this subject, for it is Stonhewer's Wish, & (I think) would be an Advantage to him, if he had a Reason for continuing here some time longer. if you can get Keene to be explicit about it (but it must seem to be a Thought entirely of your own) I will desire you to let me know the Result. my best Wishes, Dear Sʳ, ever attend on you, & Mʳˢ Wharton. I am most sincerely & unalterably

Yours

T G:

Aug: 8 [1749]¹⁰ Cambridge

151. GRAY TO MRS. GRAY

Cambridge, Nov. 7, 1749.

THE unhappy news I have just received from you equally surprises and afflicts me.¹ I have lost a person I loved very much, and have been used to from my infancy; but am much

---

⁶ᵃ See Letter 149, n. 3ᵃ.   ⁷ See Letter 143, n. 3 *ad fin.*

⁸ In the Peterhouse Statutes there was a restriction that not more than two Fellows should be elected from any one county. The two Fellowships open to natives of Durham (Stonhewer's county) were filled at the time. He was however elected in Oct. 1751 Ramsey Fellow. This was a bye-Fellowship not subject to the restriction.

⁹ Roger Long, Master of Pembroke; the allusion is to his claim to exercise a veto on elections to fellowships (see Appendix H).

¹⁰ Date of year supplied by Wharton.

LETTER 151.—First printed in Mason's *Memoirs*, pp. 207–8.

¹ The death of his aunt, Mrs. Mary Antrobus, who died the 5th of November, and was buried in a vault in Stoke churchyard near the chancel door, in which also his mother and himself (according to the direction in his will) were afterwards buried. *Mason.*

more concerned for your lofs, the circumstances of which I forbear to dwell upon, as you must be too sensible of them yourself; and will, I fear, more and more need a consolation that no one can give, except He who has preserved her to you so many years, and at last, when it was his pleasure, has taken her from us to himself: and perhaps, if we reflect upon what she felt in this life, we may look upon this as an instance of his goodnefs both to her, and to those that loved her. She might have languished many years before our eyes in a continual increase of pain, and totally helplefs; she might have long wished to end her misery without being able to attain it; or perhaps even lost all sense, and yet continued to breathe; a sad spectacle to such as must have felt more for her than she could have done for herself. However you may deplore your own lofs, yet think that she is at last easy and happy; and has now more occasion to pity us than we her. I hope, and beg, you will support yourself with that resignation we owe to him, who gave us our being for our good, and who deprives us of it for the same reason. I would have come to you directly, but you do not say whether you desire I should or not; if you do, I beg I may know it, for there is nothing to hinder me, and I am in very good health.

152. GRAY TO WALPOLE

Sunday, Nov: 12 [1749].[1] Cambridge.

Dear S^r,

I HOPE in God it is your Uncle,[2] or his Son[3] (for News-Papers are apt to confound ye) but from the Circumstances I fear it must be you, that have had so very narrow an Escape from Death. excuse me, if I am sollicitous to know how you are after such a Surprise; & whether you have really met with no considerable Hurt from this Accident. or was it an Accident, & did they only mean to rob you?[4]

LETTER 152.—First printed by Toynbee (1915), No. 169.

[1] The date of the year is determined by the reference to Walpole's 'accident' (see n. 4).

[2] Horatio Walpole (1698–1757), younger brother of Sir Robert, afterwards (1756) Baron Walpole of Wolterton; he was Horace Walpole's god-father.

[3] Horatio Walpole (1723–1809), eldest son of the preceding, whom he succeeded (1757) as second Baron Walpole of Wolterton; he was at this time M.P. for King's Lynn.

[4] In his *Short Notes* Walpole writes: 'One night in the beginning of November, 1749, as I was returning from Holland House by moonlight,

I sincerely rejoice at your Deliverance, & hope soon to tell you so in Town; but in the mean time should be glad to know from yourself how it happen'd; & how it feels, when one returns back from the very Brink of Destruction. believe me, my dear S^r, ever

Yours,

T GRAY.

Addressed: To The Honble Horace Walpole Esq in Arlington Street London
    Postmark: CAMBRIDGE 13 NO

153. GRAY TO WALPOLE

Stoke, June 12, 1750.

Dear Sir,

As I live in a place, where even the ordinary tattle of the town arrives not till it is stale, and which produces no events of its own, you will not desire any excuse from me for writing so seldom, especially as of all people living I know you are the least a friend to letters spun out of one's own brains, with all the toil and constraint that accompanies sentimental productions. I have been here at Stoke a few days (where I shall continue good part of the summer); and having put an end to a thing,[1] whose beginning you have seen long ago,[2] I immediately send

about ten at night, I was attacked by two highwaymen in Hyde Park, and the pistol of one of them going off accidentally, razed the skin under my eye, left some marks of shot on my face, and stunned me. The ball went through the top of the chariot, and if I had sat an inch nearer to the left side, must have gone through my head.'

A long account of the robbery appeared in *The London Evening Post* for 9–11 Nov. 1749.

The identity of the robbers was disclosed when Maclean was taken in July of the following year, and in the course of his examination before Justice Lediard confessed to this and numerous other robberies, at the same time giving evidence against his confederate Plunket, who however escaped being taken. (See Walpole's letter to Mann of 2 Aug. 1750; and also his paper in *The World* for Dec. 1754, from which letter it appears that it was Maclean who so nearly shot him through the head.)

James Maclaine or Maclean, who was known as the 'gentleman highway-man', was the second son of a Scottish Presbyterian minister, and brother of the well-known divine, Alexander Maclaine, translator of Mosheim's *Ecclesiastical History.* He was tried at the Old Bailey, and executed at Tyburn on 3 Oct. 1750, being then in his twenty-sixth year. Walpole refused to appear against him and in consequence, as he wrote to Mann (20 Sept. 1750), was 'honourably mentioned in a Grub ballad'.

LETTER 153.—First printed in *Works of Lord Orford*, vol. v, p. 386.
    [1] This was the Elegy in the church-yard. *Berry.*
    [2] Walpole stated that he had seen the beginning of the *Elegy* some four

it you.[3] You will, I hope, look upon it in the light of a *thing with an end to it*; a merit that most of my writings have wanted, and are like to want, but which this epistle I am determined shall not want, when it tells you that I am ever

Yours,
T. GRAY.

Not that I have done yet; but who could avoid the temptation of finishing so roundly and so cleverly in the manner of good queen Anne's days? Now I have talked of writings; I have seen a book, which is by this time in the prefs, against Middleton (though without naming him), by Asheton.[4] As far as I can judge from a very hasty reading, there are things in it new and ingenious, but rather too prolix, and the style here and there savouring too strongly of sermon. I imagine it will do him credit. So much for other people, now to *self* again. You are desired to tell me your opinion, if you can take the pains, of these lines. I am once more

Ever Yours.

154. GRAY TO WHARTON

My dear Wharton   Stoke—Aug: 9 1750

ARISTOTLE says (one may write Greek to you without Scandal) that Οἱ τόποι οὐ διαλύουσι τὴν φιλίαν ἁπλῶς, ἀλλὰ τὴν ἐνέργειαν· ἐὰν δὲ χρόνιος ἡ ἀπουσία γένηται καὶ τῆς φιλίας δοκεῖ λήθην ποιεῖν· ὅθεν εἴρηται Πολλὰς δὴ φιλίας ἀπροσηγορία διέλυσεν.[1]

years before this. He wrote to Mason on 1 Dec. 1773: '*The Churchyard* was, I am persuaded, posterior to West's death at least three or four years. . . . At least I am sure that I had the twelve or more first lines from himself above three years after that period'. (*Walpole–Mason Correspondence*, vol. i, p. 109). See Appendix I.

[3] The copy sent to Walpole was presumably sent to Dodsley when the *Elegy* was printed in Feb. 1751 (see Letter 157).

[4] It was the publication of this book which brought about the final rupture between Walpole and Ashton—'He has at last quite thrown off the mask, and in the most direct manner, against my will, has written against my friend Dr Middleton . . . I have forbid him my house' (Walpole to Mann, 25 July 1750). (See Letter 142, n. 2.) The book in question was *A Dissertation on 2 Peter i. 19, in which it is shewn that the interpretation of this passage . . . as it is proposed by the author* of the 'Grounds and Reasons of the Christian Religion' is not probably the sense of the Author*. By Thomas Ashton: London. 1750.

LETTER 154.—First printed in part (in a garbled text) in Mason's *Memoirs*, pp. 209–10; first printed in full by Mitford (1816), vol. ii, pp. 205–7; now reprinted from original.

[1] 'Difference of place does not put an end to friendship absolutely, but

---

* Anthony Collins (1676–1729).

but Aristotle may say whatever he pleases. I do not find myself at all the worse for it. I could indeed wish to refresh my Ἐνέργεια a little at Durham by a Sight of you, but when is there a Probability of my being so happy? it concerned me greatly when I heard the other Day, that your Asthma continued at Times to afflict you, & that you were often obliged to go into the Country to breath. you cannot oblige me more than by giving me an Account of the State both of your Body & Mind; I hope the latter is able to keep you chearful & easy in spite of the Frailties of its Companion. as to my own it can do neither one, nor the other; & I have the Mortification to find my spiritual Part the most infirm Thing about me. You have doubtlefs heard of the Lofs I have had in Dr. Middleton,[2] whose House was the only easy Place one could find to converse in at Cambridge. for my Part I find a Friend so uncommon a Thing, that I can not help regretting even an old Acquaintance, wch is an indifferent Likenefs of it, & tho' I don't approve the Spirit of his Books, methinks 'tis pity the World should lose so rare a Thing as a good Writer.[3] my Studies can not furnish a Recommendation of many new Books to you. there is a Defense de l'Esprit des Loix[4] by Montesquieu himself. it has some lively Things in it, but is very short, & his Adversary[5] appears to be so mean a Bigot, that he deserved no Answer. there are 3 V: in 4to of, Histoire du Cabinet du Roi,[6] by Mefs: Buffons,[7] &

only to the active exercise of it. If, however, the absence be prolonged it seems to beget forgetfulness of the friendship itself; whence the saying: Want of intercourse has ended many a friendship' (from *Ethics*, viii. 5). Wharton was evidently a competent Greek scholar (see Letter 23, n. 5).

[2] See Letter 135, n. 18. He had died on 28 July.

[3] Mr. Gray used to say, that good writing not only required great parts, but the very best of those parts. *Mason.*

[4] See Letter 148, n. 24. The *Défense de l'Esprit des Loix* was issued at Geneva in 12mo in 1750 by Barillot et fils, the publishers of the original work.

[5] The Jansenist Abbé Fontaine de La Roche (1688–1761); his attack was anonymous.

[6] *Histoire Naturelle, Générale et Particulière, avec la Description Du Cabinet du Roi.* A Paris, De l'Imprimerie Royale. M.DCCXLIX. 3 vols. 4to. The work was eventually completed in forty-four volumes in 1804. Gray announces to Wharton the arrival of vol. vii in April 1760 (see Letter 311); of vols. ix and x in January 1762 (see Letter 353); of vols. xi and xii in July 1764 (see Letter 390); of vol. xiii in March 1766 (see Letter 420); and of vol. xiv in August 1766 (see Letter 423).

[7] Georges Louis Leclerc, Comte de Buffon (1707–88), Keeper of the Jardin du Roi and of the Cabinet du Roi (1739), member of the Académie Française (1753), and F.R.S.

D'Aubenton.[8] the first is a Man of Character, but (I am told) has hurt it by this Work. it is all a Sort of Introduction to Natural History. the weak Part of it is a Love of System,[9] wch runs thro' it, the most contrary Thing in the World to a Science, entirely grounded upon Experiments, & that has nothing to do with Vivacity of Imagination. there are some microscopical Observations, that seem'd curious to me, on those Animalcula to wch we are supposed to owe our Origin; & wch he has discover'd of like Figure in Females not pregnant, & in almost every Thing we use for Nourishment, even Vegetables, particularly in their Fruits & Seeds. not that he allows them to be animated Bodies, but *Molecules organisées.* if you ask what that is, I can not tell; no more than I can understand a new System of Generation wch he builds upon it. but what I was going to commend is a general View he gives of the Face of the Earth, follow'd by a particular one of all known Nations, their peculiar Figure & Manners, wch is the best Epitome of Geography I ever met with, & wrote with Sense, & Elegance: in short these Books are well worth turning over. the Memoires of the Abbé de Mongon[10] in 5 V: are highly commended, but I have not seen them. he was engaged in several Embassies to Germany, England, &c: during the Course of the late War. The Presid: Henault's Abregé Chronol:^{ique} de l'Hist: de France[11] I believe I have before mention'd to you, as a very good Book of its Kind.

You advised me in your last to be acquainted with [Keene][12] & we are accordingly on very good & civil Terms: but to make us love one another (I reckon) you hardly proposed. I always

[8] Louis Jean Marie Daubenton (1716–1800), collaborator of Buffon, by whom he was appointed in 1745 to the post of Keeper and Demonstrator of the natural history museum of the Jardin du Roi. He was responsible for the descriptive and anatomical portions of the work. His collaboration with Buffon did not extend beyond the first fifteen volumes.

[9] Tovey quotes Buffon's remark to Mme Necker: 'Vous pourriez croire que c'est l'amour de la gloire qui m'attire dans le désert et me met la plume à la main, c'est le seul amour de l'ordre qui m'a déterminé.'

[10] The Abbé Charles Alexandre de Montgon (1690–1770), the agent in France of Philip V of Spain. His *Mémoires* were published in eight volumes, 1745–53.

[11] See Letter 129, n. 4. Walpole gives an account of the *Abrégé* in his letter to Mann of 10 Jan. 1750; and of Hénault himself in his letter from Paris to Conway of 6 Oct. 1765.

[12] Name scored through in MS., but still legible. In writing to Wharton of Tuthill's election to a Fellowship (Letter 148), Gray alludes to Keene having advised Roger Long 'to finish the matter', presumably by giving up his opposition to the election of Mason and Tuthill.

placed the Service he did me [about Tuthill][13] to your Account. this latter has done him some Service, about his Regulations.[14] if you will give me the Pleasure of a Letter, while I continue here, it will be a great Satisfaction to me. I shall stay a Month longer. my best Wishes to M[rs] Wharton & your Family. I am

Ever Yours

T GRAY.

Do not imagine I have forgot my Debts, I hope to repay them this Year.

154*. LADY SCHAUB TO GRAY

[Stoke, September 1750][1]

LADY SCHAUB'S[2] compliments to Mr. Gray; she is sorry not to have found him at home, to tell him that Lady Brown[3] is very well.

---

[13] See Letter 120, n. 2.

[14] See Letter 143, n. 3 *ad fin.*

LETTER 154*.—Reprinted from Mason's *Memoirs*, p. 211 (quoted in n. 1). In the sale of Gray's manuscripts and books in 1851, 'Lady Schaub's note, the autograph of the Long Story and Miss Speed's complimentary letter' (Letter 155) were included with other manuscripts in Lot. 53. They were also (in a separate lot, No. 227) in the sale of 1854.

[1] The date is inferred from Mason's account (*Memoirs*, p. 211) :

'About this time [summer of 1750] M[r] Gray had put his last hand to his celebrated Elegy in the Country Church-yard, and had communicated it to his friend M[r] Walpole [see Letter 153], whose good taste was too much charmed with it to suffer him to withhold the sight of it from his acquaintance; accordingly it was shewn about for some time in manuscript, (as M[r] Gray intimates in the subsequent letter to D[r] Wharton) [see Letter 156] and received with all the applause it so justly merited. Amongst the rest of the fashionable world, for to these only it was at present communicated, Lady Cobham, who now lived at the mansion-house at Stoke-Poges [see Letter 155, n. 4], had read and admired it. She wished to be acquainted with the author; accordingly her relation Miss Speed [see Letter 155, n. 1] and Lady Schaub, then at her house, undertook to bring this about by making him the first visit. He happened to be from home, when the Ladies arrived at his Aunt's solitary mansion; and, when he returned, was surprized to find, written on one of his papers in the parlour where he usually read, the [above] note: This necessarily obliged him to return the visit, and soon after induced him to compose a ludicrous account of this little adventure for the amusement of the Ladies in question. He wrote it in ballad measure, and entitled it a Long Story.'

The *Elegy* had been completed before the middle of June (see Letter 153); the *Long Story*, in spite of Gray's note in his Commonplace-book dating it 'August 1750', cannot have been completed earlier than the middle of September because of the reference in stanza 30 to an incident of the trial

330

155. Miss Speed[1] to Gray

Sir,

I AM as much at a loss to bestow the Commendation due to your performance[2] as any of our modern Poets would be to

of the highwayman, James Maclean (see Letter 152, n. 4), which took place on 13 Sept. The stanza runs:

> But soon his rhetorick forsook him,
> When he the solemn hall had seen;
> A sudden fit of ague shook him,
> He stood as mute as poor *Macleane*.

The last line is an unmistakable allusion to the sorry figure cut by the highwayman after the verdict of guilty had been pronounced, when, instead of making the expected speech, he could only falter out, 'I cannot speak, my Lord'.

Gray was at Stoke from early in June throughout the summer of 1750, and stayed on till late in the autumn. As in a note to the *Long Story* he says of Maclean: he was 'A famous highwayman hanged the week before', and as the execution took place on 3 Oct., the poem was presumably finished about 10 Oct., Lady Schaub's visit having probably been made some time in September.

[2] Horace Walpole, in a MS. note in his copy of Maty's *Memoirs of the Earl of Chesterfield* (1777), says Lady Schaub 'was a French widow of Nismes, and a Protestant, and remarried to Sir Luke Schaub. She is one of the heroines in Gray's *Long Story*' (see Letter 155, n. 2). Sir Luke Schaub was a Swiss, a native of Basle. He had been secretary to Lord Cobham (see Letter 155, n. 4) when he was ambassador at Vienna in 1715, and was afterwards secretary to the first Earl of Stanhope. He was knighted in 1720, and in the following year was sent as ambassador to Paris, in which capacity he remained till 1724. He died in 1758.

Lady Schaub had the reputation of being 'very gallant'. Horace Walpole, in the account of Sir Thomas Robinson's ball in his letter to Mann of 2 Nov. 1741, mentions among the pretty women there 'a Lady Schaub, a foreigner, who, as Sir Luke says, *would* have him: as the town says, Lord Chomley *will* have her'. She had apartments for many years in Hampton Court Palace, where she died in 1793 (*D.N.B.*).

[3] The lady in question was no doubt Margaret, wife of Sir Robert Brown (see Letter 126, n. 3).

LETTER 155.—First printed by Tovey in *Gray and his Friends*, p. 197; now reprinted from Mitford's transcript.

[1] The daughter of Samuel Speed (1682–1731), Lieut.-Colonel in Gore's Regiment of Dragoons, by his wife Cardonnel Jones, daughter of Richard Jones, of Brentford, Middlesex; she was born and baptized at Holyrood, 8 Jan. 1728. After the death of her only surviving brother, Lieut.-Colonel Samuel Speed (b. 1716), who was killed in action at Bergen-op-Zoom in 1747, she resided with Lady Cobham (see n. 3), whose niece she was, according to Walpole (see his notes on the PS. to his letter to Mann of 18 Sept. 1777). She inherited a large fortune from Lady Cobham (see n. 3 and Letter 313), and it was rumoured that she and Gray were going

[Note 2 on p. 333.

imitate them; Every body that has seen it, is charm'd and Lady

to make a match (see Letters 313 and 321); but about the end of 1761 (see Letter 353, n. 12) she married Joseph Marie de Viry, Baron de la Perrière, afterwards Comte de Viry, Sardinian Minister at The Hague, London and Paris (see Letters 353 and 420). She died in Savoy in 1783, as she was about to visit England (see Walpole to Lady Ossory, 30 Jan. 1783).

The following recollections of Gray and Miss Speed were communicated to the editor of Gray's *Poetical Works*, published by John Sharpe in 1821, by Admiral Sir John Thomas Duckworth (1748–1817), whose father, Rev. Henry Duckworth, became Vicar of Stoke in 1756. The Admiral says 'that he and his elder brother at that time, when they were about eight or ten years of age, were regularly and frequently invited, with their father and mother, to dine at "the Great House". . . . He likewise remembers that he was then used to accompany his father in his visits to Mᵣ Gray and his aunt Mᵣˢ Rogers, at West End; that he has often been at home when those visits were returned; and that on these occasions, the author of the *Ode to Eton College* would frequently take pleasure in gratifying the young Etonian by the gift of a shilling, or half a crown. . . . He relates that he has "more than once" been an eyewitness of the potent effect wrought by the exuberant spirits of the "witty amazon" [Miss Speed], in prevailing upon the poet, instead of being conducted by a muse, or mounted on his Pegasus, to trust himself to her guidance, along the parish lanes, in a butcher's cart' (pp. 67–8).

An interesting 'Portrait of Henrietta Jane Speed, Countess de Viry', written after her death by the second Earl Harcourt, is printed in the *Harcourt Papers* (viii. 1–3): 'She was daughter of Colonel Speed, and lineally descended from the geographer of that name [John Speed, c. 1552–1629]; at the death of her father, when she was very young, she was received into the family of Viscount Cobham, her relation, and educated under the care of himself, and of the Viscountess, his wife; who at her death bequeathed the whole of her large fortune to Miss Speed. Mme de Viry possessed the most brilliant parts, she was good humoured, full of vivacity, and had an inexhaustible fund of original and engaging wit; strong sense, united with observation, and penetration the most acute, more than supplied the want of literary knowledge, for which she had not the least relish; and, without having ever given herself the trouble of learning anything, she appeared to know everything. . . . Her person was tall, but not slender, her complexion dark, and, although she had no pretensions to beauty, yet an easy and graceful air, with fine eyes and teeth, united to render her altogether extremely pleasing. . . . She was as incapable of the feeling of affection as of those of hatred or dislike; she would extract entertainment even from folly and insipidity, and no company displeased her, but she really loved nobody. . . . Yet, such was the fascinating power she derived from her invariable good humour and vivacity, and the witty playfulness of her conversation, that to live with her in intimacy without becoming attached to her was impossible. . . . She died [on her husband's estate in Savoy] of an apoplexy occasioned by excessive corpulency.'

A second letter from Miss Speed to Gray, written in 1759, has been preserved (see Letter 300). It was at her request that Gray wrote the song beginning 'Thyrsis when we parted', &c. 'to an old air of Geminiani, the

Cobham[3] was the first, tho' not the last that regretted the loss
of the 400 stanzas;[4] all I can say is, that your obliging inclina-

thought from the French' (see Walpole's *Memoir of Gray*, in Appendix Y, and
his letter to Lady Ailesbury of 28 Nov. 1761); and the verses beginning:
'With beauty, with pleasure, surrounded' (see Tovey, *Gray's English Poems*,
p. 262).

A letter from her (as Comtesse de Viry) to Walpole, with some verses by
Voltaire, written from Madrid in 1771, is printed in *Supplement to the Letters
of Horace Walpole*, vol. iii, pp. 221–2. When Mason's *Memoirs* of Gray were
published (1775) she wrote to reproach Walpole with having forgotten his
promise to send her a copy (see his letter to her of April, 1776).

[2] The *Long Story*, the two 'heroines' of which were Lady Cobham's guest,
Lady Schaub (see Letter 154*, n. 2), and Miss Speed. Of the former Gray
says (in stanza 7):

> The first came cap-a-pee from France
> Her conqu'ring destiny fulfilling,
> Whom meaner beauties eye askance,
> And vainly ape her art of killing.

The portrait of Miss Speed, to whose 'great deal of wit' Walpole bears
witness (see *Letters*, vol. ix, p. 453, n. 3; vol. x, p. 112, n. 5), follows in the next
stanza:

> The other Amazon kind Heaven
> Had arm'd with spirit, wit, and satire:
> But *Cobham* had the polish given
> And tip'd her arrows with good-nature.

> To celebrate her eyes, her air—
> Coarse panegyricks would but teaze her.
> Melissa is her Nom de Guerre.
> Alas, who would not wish to please her!

The *Long Story* was one of the poems with the designs of Richard Bentley
published by Dodsley in March 1753 (*Designs by Mr R. Bentley, for Six Poems
by Mr T. Gray*) (see Letter 161, n. 2). In the illustration to the poem Bentley's drawing has two figures which may be taken to be portraits of Lady
Schaub and Miss Speed, while Gray is represented as hidden by the Muses.

[3] Dowager Viscountess Cobham, widow of Field-Marshal Sir Richard
Temple, Bart., of Stowe, Bucks., first Viscount Cobham (d. 1749). She was
the daughter (Anne) of Edmund Halsey, of Southwark and Stoke Poges,
M.P. for Buckingham, 1717–22 (one of the founders of the famous brewery
in Park Street, Southwark, which afterwards passed to the Thrales, and from
them to the firm of Barclay and Perkins), who purchased the Manor House
at Stoke Poges about the year 1720 from the Gayer family (see Letter 169,
n. 3). Lady Cobham died 20 March 1760, leaving to Miss Speed, as Gray
informs Wharton (see Letter 313) 'at least 30,000£ with a house in Town,
plate, jewels, china, and old-japan infinite'. Walpole, writing to Mann on
11 Dec. 1760, says that Miss Speed had bought Chute's London house for
£3,000.

[4] Before the last stanza of the poem Gray inserted '[*Here 500 Stanzas are
lost*]'.

tion in sending it has fully answerd; as it not only gave us amusement the rest of the Evening, but always will, on reading it over. Lady Cobham and the rest of the Company hope to have yours' tomorow at dinner.

I am your oblig'd & obedient
HENRIETTA JANE SPEED.

Sunday [October 1750].[5]

156. GRAY TO WHARTON

My dear Wharton

YOU are apprised by this time (I don't doubt) that your Mr Spencer[1] is chose at Pembroke. I received, while I was at Stoke, a Letter from [Tuthill],[2] wherein were these Words 'Spencer will, I am almost persuaded, be chose at this Audit, & perhaps without a Quarrel. I shall vote for him with great Pleasure, because I believe he may justly claim it, & because I believe Dr Wharton would, if he knew of our Election, desire it, for *he* was maintain'd by his Mr Wilkinson.'[3] Dr Long did not make any Resistance, when he saw how it would go, so Chapman[4] had little Occasion for his *effectual Interest*. oh, by the Way I give you joy of that agreeable Creature, who has got one of your Prebends of 400£ a Year,[5] & will visit you soon, with that dry Piece of Goods, his Wife.[6]

Of my House[7] I can not say much: I wish I could! but for

[5] This must be the probable date, as the *Long Story* was not completed until the second week of October (see Letter 154*, n. 1).

LETTER 156.—First printed in part (in a garbled text) in Mason's *Memoirs*, p. 221; first printed in full by Mitford (1816), vol. ii, pp. 227–9; now reprinted from original.

[1] Richard Spenser, of Trinity, Scholar, 1749; B.A. 1750; M.A. 1753; Rector of Rawreth, Essex, 1755–62; d. 1762. A native of Kirkby Stephen, Westmorland, and educated at Durham, he was elected Fellow of Pembroke on 13 Nov. 1750, on Archbishop Grindal's foundation (see Letter 135, n. 41).

[2] See Letter 120, n. 2.

[3] See Letter 137, n. 2. Wilkinson was of the same school and college as Spenser.

[4] Master of Magdalene (see Letter 135, n. 17).

[5] Chapman had been made a Prebendary of Durham on 12 Dec. of this year.   [6] See Letter 149.

[7] The house he was rebuilding in Cornhill. *Mason.*—This seems to be a mistake, as the Cornhill house was to have been finished by Christmas 1748 (see Letter 145). The reference is probably to Gray's house at Wanstead (see Letter 196, n. 9).

my Heart it is no lefs yours than it has long been; & the last Thing in the World, that will throw it into Tumults, is a fine Lady.[8] the Verses[9] you so kindly try to keep in countenance were wrote to divert that particular Family, & succeeded accordingly. but, being shew'd about in Town, are not liked there at all. Mrs French,[10] a very fashionable Personage, told M^r W:[11] that she had seen a Thing by a Friend of his, wch she did not know what to make of, for it aim'd at every Thing, & meant nothing. to wch he replied, that he had always taken her for a Woman of Sense, & was very sorry to be undeceived. On the other hand the Stanza's,[11] wch I now enclose to you, have had the Misfortune by M^r W:^s Fault[12] to be made still more publick, for wch they certainly were never meant, but it is too late to complain. they have been so applauded, it is quite a Shame to repeat it. I mean not to be modest; but I mean, it is a Shame for those, who have said such superlative Things about them, that I can't repeat them. I should have been glad, that you & two or three more People had liked them, wch would have satisfied my ambition on this Head amply. I have been this Month in town, not at Newcastle-House, but diverting myself among my gay Acquaintance; & return to my Cell with so much the more Pleasure. I dare not speak of my future Excursion to Durham for fear—but at present it is my full Intention.

His Prufsian Majesty[13] has published the *Suite des Memoires*[14] pour servir a l'Histoire de la Maison de Brandebourg, wch includes a very free Account of his Grandfather's[15] Life, who was the first King of that House, Reflections on the gradual Advance in Science, Commerce, &c: of his Subjects, & on their

---

[8] Miss Henrietta Speed (see Letter 155, n. 1).

[9] The *Long Story* (see Letter 154*, n. 1).

[10] This was presumably the wife of Jeffery French (d. 1754), for whom see Walpole's letters to Mann of 6 Jan. 1743 and to Montagu of 30 May 1751. Boswell, *Life*, vol. iv, p. 48, alludes to 'the house of Mrs. French in London, well known for her elegant assemblies, and bringing eminent people together'.

[11] Elegy in a Country Church-yard. *Mason.*

[12] For Walpole's part in making the *Elegy* public see Letter 154*, n. 1.

[13] Frederick II ('the Great'), King of Prussia, 1740–86, eldest son of Frederick William I, 1713–40.

[14] *Suite des Mémoires pour servir a l'Histoire de Brandebourg, contenant le Règne de Frederic I. Avec quelques autres pieces Interessantes.* Imprimè Pour la Satisfaction du Public. 1750.

[15] Frederick I, Elector of Brandenburg (1688), King of Prussia, 1701–13.

Changes in Religion. it is much in Voltaire's Manner.[15a] the Book itself is at present hard to be got, but you may see a good Extract of it in the Mercure historique,[16] a Work publish'd monthly: whether it is that for Oct: or Sept:[r] I can not justly say. there is also an Account of the History of Crusades, w[ch] seem's to be Voltaire's,[17] & promises well. I hear talk of a Pamphlet, call'd, Voix du Sage & du Peuple,[18] ascribed to Montesquieu; & a Book, styled only *Lettres*, by the Procureur General, Fleury,[19] on the Power of the Clergy in France, but have not seen either of them, being very scarce as yet. M[r] de Buffon[20] has discover'd the Speculum of Archimedes, w[ch] burns at 200 Foot distance;[21] and a Chymist in

*   *   *   *   *   *   *

*   *   *   *   *   *   *[22]

You mention Stonhewer. I should be glad to know whether he frequents you? whether you find him improved? & what sort of Life he leads among your Country-folks? Brown,[23] who has been in the midst of Tumults & Mutinies lately[24] [and

[15a] Voltaire denied doing any thing more to the book than correcting the grammar.

[16] No extract from the *Suite des Mémoires* is to be found in the *Mercure Historique* for 1750.

[17] *Histoire des Croisades* (which formed part of chapters 53–8 of Voltaire's *Essai sur les Mœurs*) was originally published in the *Mercure* in 1750 and 1751.

[18] This was by Voltaire—'La Voix du Sage et du Peuple. A Amsterdam chez Le Sincère. 1750', 16 pp. 8vo (see Bengesco, *Bibliographie de Voltaire*, vol. ii, pp. 54–5).

[19] The book entitled *Lettres*: *Ne repugnate vestro bono*, London 1750 (but really published in Paris) was attributed to the elder Joly de Fleury, Pro-curateur-Général, 1717–46 (whose son succeeded him in this office), but it is known to have been written by Daniel Bargeton (1675–1750). It was suppressed 'par arrêt du Conseil' in June 1750.

[20] See Letter 154, n. 7.

[21] Tovey quotes from Gibbon: 'Without any previous knowledge of Tzetzes or Anthemius, the immortal Buffon imagined and executed a set of burning-glasses, with which he could inflame planks at the distance of two hundred feet. (Supplément à l'Hist. Naturelle, tom. i, pp. 399–483, quarto edition.)' (*Decline and Fall*, chap. xl, note, ed. Bury, vol. iv, p. 243.) As appears from an entry in his Commonplace-book, Gray read about Buffon's burning-glasses in the *Mémoires de l'Académie des Sciences*.

[22] Piece cut away.

[23] He was at this time Proctor (see Letter 115, n. 1).

[24] This is an allusion to the affair of the Westminster Club, in which Brown had been involved in his official capacity as Senior Proctor. The following account is given in Cooper's *Annals of Cambridge* (vol. iv, p. 282): 'On the 17th of November [1750] forty-six gentlemen of the University

Tuthill, desire their][25] best Compliments to you. mine ever wait on Mrs Wharton. Adieu, believe me

Most truly Yours.

Dec: 18. [1750].[26]   Cambridge.

ELEGY, WRITTEN IN A COUNTRY-CHURCHYARD

The Curfeu tolls the Knell of parting Day,
The lowing Herd wind slowly o'er the Lea,
The Ploughman homeward plods his weary Way,
And leaves the World to Darkneſs & to me.
Now fades the glimm'ring Landscape on the Sight,
And all the Air a solemn Stillneſs holds:
Save where the Beetle wheels his droning Flight,
Or drowsy Tinkleings lull the distant Folds:

who had been educated at Westminster School, met together at the Tuns tavern, according to custom, to celebrate the accession of Queen Elizabeth, the foundress of that school, Thomas Francklin, M.A., fellow of Trinity College, and Regius Professor of Greek, was in the chair. At 11 o'clock, as the company were about to disperse, James Brown, M.A., fellow of Pembroke, the Senior Proctor, entered the room. Some confusion ensued, and shortly afterwards Mr Brown preferred a complaint against Professor Francklyn, Samuel Crew, M.A., fellow of Trinity College, Thomas Ansell, LL.B., fellow of Trinity Hall, Mr Vane, fellow-commoner of Peterhouse, and Mr Vernon, fellow-commoner of Trinity College, for insulting and interrupting him in the execution of his office of Proctor. The case (which excited very great interest) was heard before the Vicechancellor and Heads, partly in the Law Schools and partly in the Senate House, on the 24th, 27th, and 29th of November, on which latter day the Court decided that the accused were guilty of the charges against them, and they were reprimanded by the Vicechancellor. Such of them as were in statu pupillari were also fined 6s 8d each, all the defendants were condemned in the expenses of the Court, and Mr Ansell, for his rude contemptuous and disobedient behaviour to the Vicechancellor during his defence, was suspended from his degree. Mr Ansell appealed from this sentence, but the Vicechancellor decided it was a case in which no appeal could be allowed. During the investigation of this case, the scholars behaved so riotously in the Vicechancellor's court, that sixteen pro-proctors were appointed, by grace of the Senate, to preserve order'. The right of appeal became a subject of contention: see Letter 163, n. 14, and for a detailed account of the whole proceedings, see Winstanley's *University of Cambridge in the Eighteenth Century*, pp. 211 ff.

25 See Letter 120, n. 2.

26 Wharton inserted the date 1751, which was afterwards altered to 1750. The references to Spenser's election as Fellow (n. 1), to Chapman's appointment as Prebendary of Durham (n. 5), and to the affair of the Westminster Club (n. 24), show that 1750 is the correct date.

Save that from yonder ivy-mantled Tower
The mopeing Owl does to the Moon complain
Of such, as wand'ring near her secret Bower
Molest her ancient solitary Reign.
    Beneath those rugged Elms, that Yewtree's Shade,
Where heaves the Turf in many a mould'ring Heap,
Each in his narrow Cell for ever laid,
The rude Forefathers of the Hamlet sleep.
    The breezy Call of incense-breathing Morn,
The Swallow twitt'ring from the straw-built Shed,
The Cock's shrill Clarion, & the ecchoing Horn,
No more shall rowse them from their lowly Bed.
    For them no more the blazing Hearth shall burn,
Or busy Huswife ply her Evening Care.
No Children run to lisp their Sire's Return,
Nor climb his Knees the envied Kiſs to share.
    Oft did the Harvest to their Sickles yield,
Their Furrow oft the stubborn Glebe has broke,
How jocund did they drive their Team a-field!
How bow'd the Woods beneath their sturdy Stroke!
    Let not Ambition mock their useful Toil,
Their homely Joys, & Destiny obscure;
Nor Grandeur hear with a disdainful Smile
The short & simple Annals of the Poor.
    The Boast of Heraldry, the Pomp of Power,
And all that Beauty, all that Wealth e'er gave,
Awaits alike th' inevitable Hour.
The Paths of Glory lead but to the Grave.
    Forgive, ye Proud, th' involuntary Fault,
If Memory to These no Trophies raise,
Where thro' the long-drawn Ile & fretted Vault
The pealing Anthem swells the Note of Praise.
    Can storied Urn or animated Bust
Back to its Mansion call the fleeting Breath?
Can Honour's Voice provoke the silent Dust,
Or Flatt'ry sooth the dull cold Ear of Death?
    Perhaps in this neglected Spot is laid
Some Heart, once pregnant with celestial Fire,
Hands, that the Reins of Empire might have sway'd,
Or waked to Extasy the living Lyre;
    But Knowledge to their Eyes her ample Page
Rich with the Spoils of Time did ne'er unroll:

338

Chill Penury repreſs'd their noble Rage,
And froze the genial Current of the Soul.
  Full many a Gem of purest Ray serene
The dark unfathom'd Caves of Ocean bear:
Full many a Flower is born to blush unseen,
And waſt it's Sweetneſs on the desert Air.
  Some Village-Hambden, that with dauntleſs Breast
The little Tyrant of his Fields withstood,
Some mute inglorious Milton here may rest,
Some Cromwell, guiltleſs of his Country's Blood.
  Th' Applause of list'ning Senates to command,
The Threats of Pain & Ruin to despise,
To scatter Plenty o'er a smiling Land,
And read their Hist'ry in a Nation's Eyes,
  Their Lot forbad: nor circumscribed alone
Their growing Virtues, but their Crimes confined;
Forbad to wade thro' Slaughter to a Throne,
Or shut the Gates of Mercy on Mankind,
  The struggling Pangs of conscious Truth to hide,
To quench the Blushes of ingenuous Shame,
Or heap the Shrines of Luxury & Pride
With Incense, kindled at the Muse's Flame.
  Far from the madding Crowd's ignoble Strife,
Their sober Wishes never learn'd to stray:
Along the cool sequester'd Vale of Life
They kept the noiseleſs Tenour of their Way.
  Yet ev'n these Bones from Insult to protect
Some frail Memorial still erected nigh,
With uncouth Rhymes & shapeleſs Sculpture deck'd,
Implores the paſſing Tribute of a Sigh.
  Their Name, their years, spell'd by th' unletter'd Muse,
The Place of Fame & Elegy supply;
And many a holy Text around She strews
That teach the rustic Moralist to die.
  For who to dumb Forgetfulneſs a Prey
This pleasing anxious Being e'er resign'd,
Left the warm Precincts of the chearful Day,
Nor cast one longing lingering Look behind?
  On some fond Breast the parting Soul relies,
Some pious Drops the closing Eye requires:
Ev'n from the Tomb the Voice of Nature cries,
And in our Ashes glow their wonted Fires.

For Thee, who mindful of th' unhonour'd Dead
Dost in these Lines their artlefs Tale relate,
If chance by lonely Contemplation led
Some kindred Spirit shall enquire thy Fate;
    Haply some hoary-headed Swain may say,
'Oft have we seen him at the Peep of Dawn
'Brushing with hasty Steps the Dews away
'To meet the Sun upon the upland Lawn.

    'There, at the Foot of yonder nodding Beech,
'That wreathes its old fantastic Roots so high
'His listlefs Length at Noontide would he stretch
'And pore upon the Brook, that babbles by.

    'Hard by yon Wood, now smiling as in Scorn
'Mutt'ring his wayward Fancies would he rove
'Now drooping woeful-wan, like one forlorn,
'Or crazed with Care, or crofs'd in hopelefs Love.

    'One Morn I mifs'd him on the custom'd Hill,
'Along the Heath, & near his fav'rite Tree:
'Another came, nor yet beside the Rill,
'Nor up the Lawn, nor at the Wood was he.

    'The next with Dirges due in sad Array
'Slow thro' the Churchway-Path we saw him born.
'Approach & Read, for thou canst read, the Lay
'Graved on the Stone beneath yon aged Thorn.

Epitaph.

    Here rests his Head upon the Lap of Earth
A Youth, to Fortune & to Fame unknown:
Fair Science frown'd not on his humble Birth,
And Melancholy mark'd him for her own.

    Large was his Bounty & his Soul sincere,
Heaven did a Recompence as largely send:
He gave to Misery all he had, a Tear;
He gain'd from Heav'n ('twas all he wish'd) a Friend.

    No farther seek his Merits to disclose,
Or draw his Frailties from their dread Abode,
(There they alike in trembling Hope repose)
The Bosom of his Father & his God.

157. GRAY TO WALPOLE

My dear S[r]   [Cambridge, Feb. 11. 1751][1]

As you have brought me into a little Sort of Distreſs, you must aſsist me, I believe, to get out of it, as well as I can. yesterday I had the Misfortune of receiving a Letter from certain Gentlemen (as their Bookseller expreſses it) who have taken the *Magazine of Magazines*[1a] into their Hands. they tell me, that an *ingenious* Poem, call'd, *Reflections* in a Country-Churchyard, has been communicated to them, w[ch] they are printing forthwith: that they are inform'd, that the *excellent* Author of it is I by name, & that they beg not only his *Indulgence*, but the *Honor of his Correspondence*, &c: as I am not at all disposed to be either so indulgent, or so correspondent, as they desire; I have but one bad Way left to escape the Honour they would inflict upon me. & therefore am obliged to desire you would make Dodsley print it immediately (w[ch] may be done in leſs than a Week's time)[2] from your Copy, but without my Name, in what Form is most convenient for him, but in his best Paper & Character. he must correct the Preſs himself, & print it without any Interval between the Stanza's, because the Sense is in some Places continued beyond them; & the Title must be, Elegy, wrote in a Country Church-yard. if he would add a Line or two to say it came into his Hands by Accident,[3] I should like

LETTER 157.—First printed in part (in a garbled text) by Mason, in *Memoirs*, p. 222; first printed in full by Toynbee (1915), No. 171.

[1] The date of the month is supplied by the postmark; that of the year (which has been inserted in the original by Mason) is determined by the reference to the publication of the *Elegy* (see n. 2).

[1a] *The Magazine of Magazines*, the enterprise of William Owen, had first appeared in 1750. The February number of its second volume appeared on 16 Feb., a day later than Dodsley's edition (see n. 2), and announced the *Elegy* as by 'M[r] *Gray* of *Peterhouse, Cambridge*', so that Gray's authorship was made known from the first.

[2] It was actually published by Dodsley four days after the date of the letter on 15 Feb. 1751, as a 4to pamphlet, price sixpence. For a full discussion of the circumstances of publication and for an account of textual variations see F. G. Stokes, *An Elegy written in a Country Church Yard by Thomas Gray*, Oxford, 1929.

[3] In the *Advertisement* prefixed to the first edition the Editor (i.e. Walpole) says: 'The following Poem came into my Hands by Accident, if the general Approbation with which this little Piece has been spread, may be call'd by so slight a Term as Accident. It is this Approbation which makes it unnecessary for me to make any Apology but to the Author: As he cannot but

it better. if you think fit, the 102^d Line may be read

Awake, & faithful to her wonted Fires.[4]

but if this be worse than before; it must go, as it was. in the 126th, for *ancient*[5] Thorn, read *aged*.

If you behold the Mag: of Mag:[s] in the Light that I do, you will not refuse to give yourself this Trouble on my Account, wch you have taken of your own Accord before now. Adieu, S^r, I am

Yours ever

T G:

If Dodsley don't do this immediately, he may as well let it alone.

Addressed: To The Honble Horace Walpole, Esq in Arlington Street London
   Postmark: CAMBRIDGE 12 FE

158. GRAY TO WALPOLE

Ash-Wednesday [Feb. 20], Cambridge, 1751.

My dear Sir,

You have indeed conducted with great decency my little *misfortune*: you have taken a paternal care of it, and ex-prefsed much more kindnefs than could have been expected from so near a relation. But we are all frail; and I hope to do as much for you another time. Nurse Dodsley has given it a pinch or two in the cradle, that (I doubt) it will bear the marks of as long as it lives. But no matter: we have ourselves suffered under her hands before now;[1] and besides, it will only look the more

feel some Satisfaction in having pleas'd so many Readers already, I flatter myself he will forgive my communicating that Pleasure to many more.'

4 In Stanza 23—the line so appeared in the first edition. Gray made a slip in inserting the comma after 'Awake', and put the blame on Bentley in his letter to Walpole of 3 March (Letter 159, n. 9). The comma was omitted in the third edition.

5 The lines referred to as the 102nd and 126th are actually the 92nd and 116th. There can be little doubt that when he wrote this letter Gray had before him the holograph copy of the *Elegy* in his Commonplace-book, in which he has himself numbered every tenth line, and in so doing has inad-vertently omitted 90, and passed from 80 to 100.

LETTER 158.—First printed in *Works of Lord Orford*, vol. v, p. 387.

1 Gray probably alludes to the printing of his three Odes and of some of Walpole's verses in Dodsley's *Collection of Poems* in 1748 (see Letters 142, 144).

carelefs, and by *accident*[2] as it were. I thank you for your advertisement, which saves my honour, and in a manner *bien flatteuse pour moi*, who should be put to it even to make myself a compliment in good English.

You will take me for a mere poet, and a fetcher and carrier of singsong, if I tell you that I intend to send you the beginning of a drama,[3] not mine, thank God, as you'll believe, when you hear it is finished, but wrote by a person whom I have a very good opinion of. It is (unfortunately) in the manner of the ancient drama, with choruses, which I am, to my shame, the occasion of; for, as great part of it was at first written in that form, I would not suffer him to change it to a play fit for the stage, as he intended, because the lyric parts are the best of it, and they must have been lost. The story is Saxon, and the language has a tang of Shakespeare, that suits an old-fashioned fable very well. In short, I don't do it merely to amuse you, but for the sake of the author, who wants a judge, and so I would lend him *mine*: yet not without your leave, lest you should have us up to dirty our stockings at the bar of your house for wasting the time and politics of the *nation*. Adieu, sir!

I am ever yours,
T. GRAY.

159. GRAY TO WALPOLE

Cambridge, March 3, 1751.

ELFRIDA (for that is the fair one's name) and her author[1] are now in town together. He has promised me, that he will send a part of it to you some morning while he is there; and (if you shall think it worth while to descend to particulars) I should be glad you would tell me very freely your opinion about it; for he shall know nothing of the matter, that is not fit for the ears of a *tender* parent—though, by the way, he has ingenuity and merit enough (whatever his drama may have) to bear hearing his faults very patiently. I must only beg you not to show it, much lefs let it be copied; for it will be published, though not as yet.[2]

---

2 See the *Advertisement* in n. 3 to Letter 157.
3 This was the Elfrida of Mr. Mason. *Berry.*—See Letter 165*.
LETTER 159.—First printed in *Works of Lord Orford*, vol. v, pp. 387–8.
1 Mason (see Letter 158, n. 3). It seems probable that Mason made Walpole's acquaintance at this time. See Letter 144, n. 33.
2 It was published in March 1752.

I do not expect any more editions,[3] as I have appeared in more magazines than one.[4] The chief errata were *sacred* bower for *secret*;[5] *hidden* for *kindred*[6] (in spite of dukes and clafsicks);[7] and *frowning* as in scorn for *smiling*.[8] I humbly propose, for the benefit of Mr. Dodsley and his matrons, that take *awake*[9] for a verb, that they should read *asleep*, and all will be right. Gil Blas[10] is the Lying Valet[11] in five acts. The Fine Lady[12] has half-a-dozen good lines dispersed in it. Pompey is the hasty production of a Mr. Coventry[13] (cousin to him you knew),[14] a young clergyman: I found it out by three characters, which once made part of a comedy that he showed me of his own writing. Has that miracle of *tendernefs and sensibility* (as she calls it) lady Vane[15] given you any amusement? Peregrine, whom she uses as a vehicle, is very poor indeed with a few exceptions. In the last volume is a character of Mr. Lyttelton,

---

[3] Of the Elegy in the church-yard. *Berry.*—As a matter of fact, as Gray notes on the Pembroke MS., it 'went thro' four Editions; in two months; and afterwards a fifth, 6th, 7th, and 8th, 9th, and 10th, and 11th'.

[4] It was published in the *Magazine of Magazines* for February (vol. ii, p. 160); it also appeared in the *London Magazine* for March (vol. xx, pp. 134–5), but as this was not published till the first week of April, Gray was probably jesting on the title of the *Magazine of Magazines*.

[5] In Stanza 3.

[6] In Stanza 24.

[7] This allusion has not been explained.

[8] In Stanza 27.

[9] In Stanza 23; see Letter 157, n. 4.

[10] By Edward Moore (1712–57), afterwards editor of the *World* (1753–7); *Gil Blas* had been produced at Drury Lane on 2 Feb. of this year, and ran for nine nights. Gray implies that Moore had plagiarized Garrick's play, and spun it out into a full-length comedy.

[11] Adapted by Garrick from Motteux's *Novelty*; first produced in 1741.

[12] Miss Berry: 'The fine lady'. The reference apparently is to *The Modern Fine Lady* (1750) of Soame Jenyns (see Letter 144, n. 30).

[13] Francis Coventry (d. 1759), of Magdalene College, Cambridge; B.A. 1748; M.A. 1752; his satirical romance, *Pompey the Little, or the Adventures of a Lapdog*, was published this year. He was Vicar of Edgware.

[14] Henry Coventry (see Letter 135, n. 22).

[15] Frances Anne Hawes (1713–88), daughter of a South Sea Director; she married, first (1732) William Hamilton (d. 1734), second son of the fourth Duke of Hamilton; secondly (1735) William Vane, second Viscount Vane (d. 1789). Smollett, whose *Adventures of Peregrine Pickle* was published this year, in consideration of a handsome fee, inserted as chapter 88 of his novel her *Memoirs of a Lady of Quality*. 'My Lady Vane has literally published the Memoirs of her own life, only suppressing part of her lovers, no part of the success of the others with her: a degree of profligacy not to be accounted for' (Walpole to Mann, 13 March 1751).

under the name of Gosling Scrag, and a parody of part of his Monody,[16] under the notion of a pastoral on the death of his grandmother. I am ever yours,

T. GRAY.

160. GRAY TO WALPOLE

Cambridge . . April 16 [1751][1]

I AM ashamed, but not astonish'd at poor Mr Whithed's[2] Insensibility. yet I had settled it with myself before, that he would give Mr Chute 500£ a Year, wch I thought at least by half too little. but this was just the Thing, in wch Mr Chute neither would, nor could, suggest to him what he ought to do; & so he has done accordingly. I hope, it was only negative Ingratitude; but (I own to you) I do suspect, there was a little Reflection in it, & that his Conversations with M^r L:, & perhaps with another Person, who knows the Value of Money, better than that of Friendship, might have had their Effect upon his Mind. I do not wonder, that Mr Chute is satisfied with every Thing: I even believe, that when Time shall convince him, that Whithed has fall'n extremely short in his Acknowledgements to him, it will rather add to his Concern, than diminish it. my best Wishes always accompany him; & I can only *wish*, that they were of more Consequence. what a Change this Lofs will make in his future Life! I can only guefs at the Extent of it. the Brothers are nasty People,[3] that don't deserve mentioning. I see *Alexander* sets himself up in his Brother's Room, w^ch (I hope in God) will considerably reduce his Share in the Inheritance.

You surprise me with the Account you give me of the Alteration in your own Family. what a Man must my L^d O:[4]

---

[16] See Letter 142, n. 1. The attack on Lyttelton was withdrawn by Smollett from the second edition.

LETTER 160.—First printed by Toynbee (1915), No. 174.

[1] The date of the year, which has been inserted in the original by Mason, is determined by the references to the deaths of Mr. Whithed and Lord Orford (see nn. 2, 4).

[2] Francis Whithed, the cousin and friend of John Chute, whose name was originally Thistlethwayte (see Letter 109, n. 36), had died at the Vyne, the residence of Chute's brother, on 30 March of this year (1751). Walpole had evidently informed Gray of the terms of Whithed's will. Chute had been left a legacy of £1,000, and appointed one of the trustees.

[3] 'Whithed's youngest brother, the clergyman, is the greatest brute in the world, except the elder brother, the layman' (Walpole to Mann, 1 April 1751). Alexander Thistlethwayte, the elder brother, succeeded to Whithead's estates.

[4] Robert Walpole, second Earl of Orford, Horace Walpole's eldest

have been, who might so easily have prevented it? I am heartily concerned for the Share you must bear in it. sure Your Uncle,[5] & M[rs] H:,[6] have it in their Power, if not to retrieve, at least much to alleviate, this Misfortune; for from the Mother[7] no body would expect anything. perhaps the good Qualities you mention in your Nephew[8] may go farther in repairing his Lofs, than any of his Relations could have done. from the little I had seen & heard of him, it did not seem probable, that he could continue long in the thoughtlefs Ways of Folly. You were very good, when you found Time to let me know, what I am interested in, not barely from Curiosity, but because it touches you so nearly. I can return that kindnefs no otherwise, than by not taking up your Attention longer, when it is so fully employed on your own Affairs. Adieu, my dear S[r], I am ever

Yours
T G:

Addressed: To The Hon[ble] Horace Walpole Esq in Arlington Street London
Postmark: CAMBRIDGE 17 AP

161. GRAY TO WALPOLE

HYMN TO ADVERSITY.[1]

DAUGHTER of Jove, relentlefs Power,
Thou Tamer of the human Breast!
Whose iron Scourge, & torturing Hour,
The bad affright, afflict the best,

brother, had died on 20 March. 'He ordered to be drawn and executed his will with the greatest tranquillity and satisfaction on Saturday morning. His spoils are prodigious—not to his own family! indeed I think his son the most ruined young man in England. My loss, I fear, may be considerable ... It is no small addition to my concern, to fear or foresee that Houghton and all the remains of my father's glory will be pulled to pieces!' (Walpole to Mann, 1 April 1751.)

[5] Horatio Walpole, Sir Robert's younger brother (see Letter 152, n. 2).

[6] Mary Magdalen, daughter and coheir of Peter Lombard; she married Horatio Walpole in 1720.

[7] The Countess of Orford (see Letter 92, n. 10).

[8] George Walpole (1730–91), third Earl of Orford. In later life he was frequently insane. On his death Horace Walpole succeeded to the title as fourth Earl of Orford.

LETTER 161.—First printed in part in *Works of Lord Orford*, vol. v, pp. 390–2; first printed in full by Toynbee (1915), No. 175.

[1] Gray's copy in his Commonplace-book has at the foot: 'at Stoke Aug: 1742'. Except for small differences of spelling and punctuation, the text is the same in both versions.

Bound in thy adamantine Chain
The Proud are taught to tast of Pain
And purple Tyrants vainly groan
With Pangs unfelt before, unpitied & alone.

When first thy Sire to send on Earth
Virtue, his darling Child, design'd,
To Thee he gave the heav'nly Birth
And bad to form her infant Mind.
Stern rugged Nurse! thy rigid Lore
With Patience many a Year she bore:
What Sorrow was thou bad'st her know,
And from her own she learn'd to melt at other's Woe.

Scared at thy Frown terrific, fly
Self-pleasing Folly's idle Brood,
Wild Laughter, Noise, & thoughtleſs Joy,
And leave us Leisure to be good:
Light they disperse, & with them go
The Summer-Friend, the flatt'ring Foe;
By vain Prosperity received,
To her they vow their Truth, & are again believed.

Wisdom in sable Garb array'd,
Immers'd in rapturous Thought profound,
And Melancholy, silent Maid,
With leaden Eye, that loves the Ground
Still on thy solemn Steps attend:
Warm Charity, the general Friend,
With Justice, to herself severe,
And Pity, dropping soft the sadly-pleasing Tear.

Oh! gently on thy Suppliant's Head
Dread Goddeſs lay thy chast'ning Hand,
Not in thy Gorgon-Terrors clad,
Nor circled with the vengeful Band,
As by the Impious thou art seen,
With thund'ring Voice, & threat'ning Mien,
With screaming Horrour's funeral Cry,
Despair, & fell Disease, & ghastly Poverty.

Thy Form benign, oh Goddeſs, wear,
Thy milder Influence impart;

Thy philosophic Train be there
To soften, not to wound, my Heart.
The generous Spark extinct revive,
Teach me to love, & to forgive,
Exact my own Defects to scan,
What others are, to feel, & know myself a Man.

I send you this (as you desire) merely to make up half a dozen;[2]
tho' it will hardly answer your End in furnishing out either a
Head or Tail-piece.[2a] but your own Fable[3] may much better
supply the Place. you have alter'd it to its Advantage; but
there is still something a little embarrafs'd here & there in the
Exprefsion. I rejoice to find you apply (pardon the Use of so
odious a Word) to the History of your own Times.[4] speak, &
spare not. be as impartial as you can; & after all, the World
will not believe, you are so, tho' you should make as many
Protestations as Bishop Burnet.[5] they will feel in their own
Breast, & find it very pofsible to hate fourscore Persons, yea,
ninety & nine: so you must rest satisfied with the Testimony
of your own Conscience. somebody has laughed at Mr Dodsley
or at me, when they talk'd of the *Bat*: I have nothing more,
either nocturnal or diurnal, to deck his Miscellany[6] with. we

[2] This with the other five—the *Ode on the Spring*, the *Eton Ode*, the *Ode on
the Cat*, the *Elegy* and *A Long Story*—made up the *Six Poems*, which Walpole
had arranged were to be printed with illustrations by Richard Bentley (see
Letter 162, n. 3). On June 13 Walpole had written to George Montagu:
'Our charming Mr Bentley . . . is drawing vignettes for his [Gray's] Odes.'
For the first time Gray had consented to a collection of his poems being published under his name.

[2a] As affording subjects for illustration.

[3] Miss Berry states that this was *The Entail*; but that fable was not written
until 1754. The reference is to *The Funeral of the Lioness* (printed in *Works
of Lord Orford*, vol. iv, pp. 377–80), which, as Walpole records in his *Short
Notes*, was written in this year (1751). A copy of this fable in Walpole's
handwriting, and with jottings on the back by Gray (evidently the copy
sent to him by Walpole), was among the Walpole MSS. in the Waller
Collection.

[4] His *Memoirs* (see Letter 128, n. 4), published after his death under
the title of *Memoires of the Last Ten Years of the Reign of George the Second*
(1822).

[5] In the preface to the *History of his own Time* Burnet writes: 'I do solemnly
say this to the world, and make my humble appeal upon it to the great God
of truth, that I tell the truth on all occasions, as fully and freely as upon my
best inquiry I have been able to find it out.'

[6] Dodsley was perhaps already projecting the fourth volume of his *Collection*

have a Man here that writes a good Hand; but he has two little Failings, that hinder my recommending him to you.[7] he is lousy, & he is mad: he sets out this Week for Bedlam; but if you insist upon it, I don't doubt he will pay his Respects to you. I have seen two of D^r M:^idns [8] unpublish'd Works. one is about 44 Pages in 4to against Dr Waterland,[9] who wrote a very orthodox Book on the Importance of the Doctrine of ye Trinity, & insisted, that Christians ought to have no Communion with such as differ from them in Fundamentals. M:^idn enters no farther into the Doctrine itself than to shew that a mere speculative Point can never be call'd a Fundamental; & that the earlier Fathers, on whose concurrent Tradition Wat:^d would build, are so far, when they speak of the three Persons, from agreeing with the present Notion of our Church, that they declare for the Inferiority of the Son, & seem to have no clear & distinct Idea of the H: Ghost at all. the rest is employed in exposing the Folly & Cruelty of Stiffneſs & Zealotism in Religion, & in shewing that the primitive Ages of the Church, in wch Tradition had its Rise, were (even by Confeſsion of the best Scholars & most orthodox Writers) the *Æra of Nonsense & Absurdity.* it is finish'd, & very well wrote; but has been mostly incorporated into his other Works, particularly the Enquiry: & for this Reason I suppose he has writ upon it, *This wholly laid aside.* the second is in Latin, on Miracles; to shew, that of the two Methods of defending Christianity, one from its intrinsic Evidence, the Holineſs and Purity of its Doctrines; the other from its external, the Miracles said to be wrought to confirm it. the first has been little attended to by reason of its Difficulty; the second much insisted upon, because it appear'd an easier Task, but that it can in reality prove nothing at all. 'Nobilis

of Poems, which did not appear until 1755. Gray talks of it as in prospect, when writing to Walpole in July 1752 (Letter 169).

7 As an amanuensis. *Berry.*—Gosse, in a letter to *The Athenæum* dated 1 June 1887, misquoted this passage as: 'Smart sets out for Bedlam'. The identification of the 'Man here that writes a good Hand' with Christopher Smart (see Letter 135, n. 8) is proved to be impossible by the fact that Smart at this date was not in Cambridge, but in London, actively engaged in editing and writing for *The Midwife, or Old Woman's Magazine.* The reference may be to Smart's copyist, Lawman, 'the mad Attorney' (see Letter 135, n. 13).

8 Conyers Middleton (see Letter 135, n. 18); he had died in July of the previous year, leaving behind him several works in manuscript.

9 See Letter 131, n. 3. His work, *The Importance of the Doctrine of the Holy Trinity Asserted,* was published in 1734.

illa quidem Defensio (the first) quam si obtinere potuifsent, rem simul omnem expediifse, causamᵩ penitús vicifse viderentur. at causæ hujus defendendæ labor cum tantâ argumentandi cavillandiᵩ molestiâ conjunctus ad alteram, quam dixi, defensionis viam, ut commodiorem longé & faciliorem, plerosque adegit——ego veró istiusmodi defensione Religionem nostram non modo non confirmari, sed dubiam potiús suspectamᵩ reddi existimo.' he then proceeds to consider Miracles in general, & afterwards those of the Pagans, compared with those of X^t. I only tell you the Plan, for I have not read it out (tho' it is short) but you will not doubt to what Conclusion it tends. there is another Thing, I know not what, I am to see. as to the Treatise on Prayer; they say, it is burnt indeed.[10] Adieu, I am ever

Yours
T G.

Sept: 8. [1751][11] Camb:

162. GRAY TO WALPOLE

I ASK your Pardon for not having immediately informed you, that I received the Parcel very safe; but I was in Huntingdonshire,[1] when it arrived, & did not return hither till Friday Evening. the Sionites,[2] I am sorry to say, are just where they were. so is Mr Bentley,[3] having had cold Water thrown upon him, wch stunted his Growth. the other I will send you in a few

---

[10] A treatise on the inefficacy of prayer is said to have been burnt by Dr. William Heberden (see Letter 135, n. 20), to whom Middleton's widow handed over his unpublished manuscripts. It was rumoured that several other works were destroyed at the same time. But see Letter 162, *ad fin.*

[11] The date of the year 1751 (which has been inserted in the original), is confirmed by the references to Walpole's *Fable* and *Memoirs* (see nn. 3, 4).

LETTER 162.—First printed by Toynbee (1915), No. 176.

[1] No doubt at Abbot's Ripton with the Bonfoys (see Letter 126, n. 11). His absence from Cambridge can only have been for a few days as it is not shown in the Peterhouse records.

[2] No explanation of what Gray meant by 'the Sionites' has been suggested.

[3] Richard Bentley (1708–82), son of the famous scholar of the same name, for many years a friend and correspondent of Horace Walpole, to whom his wit and artistic talents specially recommended him. Gray may have 'thrown cold water' on the illustrations, which he was designing for Gray's *Six Poems* (see Letter 161, n. 2).

Days, as you desire. I am going to see three of D^r M:^s little Works, that *were burnt.*⁴ Adieu! I am

Ever Yours

T G:

Camb: Sept: 29. Sunday [1751]⁵

Addressed: To The Honble Horace Walpole Esq in Arlington Street London
Postmark: SAFFRON WALDEN 30 SE

163. GRAY TO WHARTON

My dear Wharton

A LITTLE kind of Reproach, that I saw the other Day in a Letter of yours to Mr Brown, has made my Guilt fly in my Face, & given me Spirit to be a Beast no longer. I desired him to tell you in the beginning of the Summer, that I fear'd my Journey into the North would be prevented by the Arrival of my Cousin, Mrs Forster¹ (whom you remember by the Name of Pattinson) from India. she came in August; & I continued in Town with her a Month in order to do what little Services I could to a Person as strange, & as much to seek, as tho' she had been born in the Mud of the Ganges. after this the Year was too far advanced to undertake such an Expedition; & the Thought of seeing you here in the Spring² in some measure comforts me for the Disappointment; for I depend upon your coming then, when it will be far easier to confer together, & determine about a Thing, in w^ch (I fear) I am too much interes[ted to deserve having]³ any great share in the Deter-

⁴ See Letter 161, n. 10.
⁵ The date 1751, the year to which this letter obviously belongs, has been inserted in pencil in the original.
LETTER 163.—First printed (with omissions) by Mitford (1816), vol. ii, pp. 208–10; now reprinted from original.
¹ *Née* Alice Pattinson, daughter of Mary Gray (sister of Gray's father), who married a Pattinson; her husband was John Forster, Governor of Fort William, Bengal; she had an only daughter, John Anna, who married (8 Sept. 1767) Harry Goring (afterwards sixth Baronet of Highden), and is named as 'Anna Lady Goring, my second cousin by the father's side' in Gray's will (see Genealogical Table). As appears from Gray's letter to Wharton of 1 Aug. 1768 (Letter 480), Mrs. Forster and Gray had differences, which were made up at Wharton's instance, but Gray made no mention of her in his will (see Brown to Wharton, 31 July 1771, in Appendix W).
² Wharton went to Cambridge in April 1752 to take his M.D. degree (see Letter 166).
³ Piece cut out; text supplied by Mitford.

351

mination:[4] for * * * * * * * *
* * * * * * * * * * *
* * * * * * * * * * *[5]

People. you are aware undoubtedly, that a certain Deference, not to say Servility, to the Heads of Colleges is perhaps necefsary to a Physician, that means to establish himself here: you pofsibly may find a Method to do without it. another Inconvenience your Wife, rather than you, will feel, the Want of Company of her own Sex; as the Women are few here, squeezy & formal, and little skill'd in amusing themselves or other People. all I can say is, she must try to make up for it among the Men, who are not over-agreeable neither. I much approve of your settling seriously to your Profefsion; but as your Father is old, if you should lose him, what becomes of your Interest, & to whom is it then to be transfer'd? would you leave London & your Practise again to canvas an Election for yourself?[6] it seems to me, that, if you execute your present Scheme, you must (in case of M^r Wh:$^{n's}$[7] Death) entirely lay aside all Views of that Kind. the gradual Transition you propose to make thro' Bath or Cambridge to London is very well judged, & likely enough to succeed. for Bath, I am wholly unacquainted with it, & consequently can say little to the Purpose. the Way of Life there might be more amusing to Mrs Wharton, than this; but to You, I think, would be lefs satisfactory. I sincerely congratulate you on the good Effects of your new Medecine, wch is indeed a sufficient Recompence for any Pains you have taken in that Study. but to make a just Tryal of its Efficacy & of your own Constitution, you certainly ought to pafs a little Time at London (a Month or so) & that * * * * * *
* * * * * * * * * * *[8]

engaged himself to make it up 1000£, in case the Brothers will not do it, & they have (after some Hesitation) refused it.[9] our

---

[4] The matter in question was apparently that discussed below, whether Wharton should settle in Cambridge or Bath to practise as a doctor.

[5] About eight lines cut out.

[6] The allusions in this passage have not been explained.

[7] His father, who died early in 1752.   [8] About four lines cut out.

[9] The allusion is unexplained unless it is possible that Gray was writing to Wharton about the two Thistlethwaytes (see Letter 160: 'The Brothers are nasty People'). If so, the reference may be to a dispute about Whithed's will. Walpole, in his letter to Mann of 1 April 1751, says that Whithed 'left an annuity of one hundred and twenty pounds a year to his Florentine mistress, and six hundred pounds to their child'. From later letters of Walpole to Mann (7 July 1760, 26 Dec. 1764, and 26 March 1765) it appears that the brothers

good Mr Brown goes out of his Office¹⁰ today, of wch he is not a little glad. his College, wch had much declined for some time, is picking up again: they have had twelve Admiſsions this Year; & are just filling up two Fellowships with a Mr Cardell,¹¹ whom I do not know, but they say, he is a good Scholar; & a Mr Delaval,¹² a Fellow-Commoner (a younger Son to old Delaval¹³ of Northumberland) who has taken his Degree in an exemplary Manner, & is very sensible, & knowing. the Appeal,¹⁴ wch has been so long contended for, will, I believe, at last be yielded to with a good Grace, or rather bestowed, by the Advice of the D: of N:, & my Lord Ch:^r,¹⁵ & will be the best & most popular

refused to pay the legacies and disputed their validity. It is possible that a compromise had been proposed by which the brothers were to pay a certain sum, and Chute perhaps 'engaged himself to make it up to 1000£'. This offer was rejected.

¹⁰ As Proctor (see Letter 156, n. 24).

¹¹ William Cardale, from Eton, matriculated 1747; B.A. 1751; Fellow of Pembroke, 10 Oct. 1751; M.A. 1754; ordained Priest, 1752; died Nov. 1756.

¹² Edward Hussey Delaval (1729–1814), third son of Francis Blake Delaval (for his brother see Letter 127, n. 6); B.A. 1750; Fellow of Pembroke, 10 Oct. 1751; M.A. 1754; he was a distinguished classical scholar and linguist, and made a European reputation as a man of science, his attainments being chiefly in chemistry and experimental philosophy. He was elected F.R.S. in 1759, and was associated with Benjamin Franklin in a report to the Society on the means of securing St. Paul's Cathedral against danger from lightning. Among his achievements was the manufacture, under his direction, of the completest set of musical glasses in England [see Letter 309 *ad fin.*] (*D.N.B.*). An entry in the Pembroke register, dated 13 June 1757, records the granting of his request to be relieved from the obligation, as an M.A. of three years' standing, to study divinity. He was a candidate for the Professorship of Modern History in 1762, and again in 1768, when Gray was appointed (see Letters 363, 482). In some lines to Mason, Gray characterizes him as 'Delaval the loud', and elsewhere remarks on his loud voice (see Letters 461, 494).

¹³ Francis Blake Delaval, of Seaton Delaval, and Ford Castle, Northumberland (d. Dec. 1752); he married Rhoda, daughter of Robert Apreece, of Washingley, Hunts., and of Sarah, elder daughter, and eventually sole heiress of Sir Thomas Hussey, second Bart. of Honington, Lincs. (d. 1706), after whom his two younger sons assumed the name of Hussey.

¹⁴ This was the vexed question whether in cases of discipline there was any appeal from the Vice-Chancellor's Court (see Letter 156, n. 24). The matter was hotly disputed, but at length, after a proposal to refer the question to arbitration had been accepted by both sides, though no decision was given, it was allowed to drop, and the controversy came to an end (see Winstanley's *University of Cambridge in the Eighteenth Century*, pp. 215–22).

¹⁵ The Duke of Newcastle, Chancellor of the University, and the Earl of Hardwicke, Lord Chancellor.

Thing they can do, but you must not mention it, till it is actually done. I am sorry your friend Chapman will lose all the Merit of his Pamphlet,[16] w^ch (by the Way) has been answer'd exceedingly well, & with all due Contempt.[17] he seems much mortified, & was preparing a Reply; but this Event, I doubt, will cut him short.[18]

I know of nothing new in the literary Way, but the History of Lewis, 14th, by Voltaire;[19] not that I have yet seen it but my Expectations are much raised. Adieu, my dear Wharton, I am ever

Most truly Yours

T G.

P:S: I am ready to pay my Debts, if you will tell me to whom. my Compliments & good Wishes to Mrs Wharton, & the little Gentry.

[Oct. 10, 1751][20]

[16] *An Inquiry into the Right of Appeal from the Chancellor or Vice-Chancellor of the University of Cambridge in matters of Discipline: Addressed to a Fellow of a College . . .*, Lond., 1751, 8vo. Chapman, who was Master of Magdalene (see Letter 135, n. 17), maintained that Ansell had no right of appeal.

[17] Gray, no doubt, is referring to *The Opinion of an Eminent Lawyer concerning the Right of Appeal from the Vice-Chancellor of* Cambridge *to the Senate; supported by a short historical account of the Jurisdiction of the University. In answer to a late Pamphlet entitled* an Inquiry into the Right of Appeal. . . . *By a Fellow of a College*, Lond., 1751, 8vo. This was by Richard Hurd, afterwards Bishop of Worcester (see Letter 231*, n. 1). It was printed in the collected edition of his *Works*, vol. viii, pp. 185 ff.

According to Nichols (*Literary Anecdotes*, vol. ii, p. 230), who describes this answer as 'rather discourteous at the commencement', the eminent lawyer was Lord Hardwicke.

[18] Chapman published his reply, *A further Inquiry into the Right of Appeal from the Chancellor or Vice-Chancellor of the University of Cambridge in matters of Discipline, in which the objections of the author of a late pamphlet intitled* The Opinion of an Eminent Lawyer . . . *are fully obviated . . .*, Lond. and Camb., 1752, 8vo.

Chapman here maintained that the appeal lay only in *civil* cases. His *Further Inquiry* was answered by John Smith, Fellow of King's. Copies of all these pamphlets are in the Gough Collection in the Bodleian (see Wordsworth's *Social Life at the English Universities in the Eighteenth Century*, pp. 630–1).

[19] *Le Siècle de Louis XIV. Publié Par M.* de Francheville *conseiller antique de sa Majesté, & membre de l'académie roiale des sciences & des belles lettres de prusse.* A Berlin, Chez C. F. Henning, Imprimeur du Roi. M.DCC.LI. Tomes i, ii.

[20] Wharton's endorsement is 'Mr. Gray 10 Oct. 1750 or 1751'; but he has cancelled the latter, which is obviously the correct date.

164. GRAY TO WALPOLE
Tuesday [Nov. 26, 1751][1] Camb:ge

IF Etoughe[2] had any such Paper trusted to his Hands, I don't at all doubt, but it has been shew'd to some one here. it is about three Weeks ago, that he was here with his Budget of Libels (for it is his constant Practise twice in a year to import a Cargo of Lyes, & scandalous Truths mix'd) but his Confidents are caution'd against me, who have had more Squabbles than one either with him, or about him, so that *directly* it would be impofsible for me to come at it, or even to hear of any of the Contents: but I have a round-about Way, or two in my head: if I succeed, you shall be sure to know immediately; but this will take up a Week, or a Fortnight, for I must not seem too eager about it. I am amazed at the Impudence of the Fiend, (as much a Fiend as I knew him.)[3] you say you took him to task;[4] I am impatient to know in what Manner. for I imagine you sent to him, & that this has given him an Opportunity of writing those impudent Letters you mention to you. there are three Methods of taking him properly to task, the Cudgel, the Blanket, & the Horse-pond. if you are present at the Operation, you may venture to break a Leg or an Arm *en attendant*, & when I see you, I may pofsibly give you some Reasons, why you ought to have broke t'other Leg & t'other Arm also: for it is too long to stay, till he is a Bishop.

I do not wonder at their Rage venting itself on Mr Chute.[5] they think him easier to come at, & more open to Injury: I am glad he hears so little of the Matter. what my insipid Ld H:[..·]on[6] could poke out of his Memory against him, I don't conceive. would to God anything I could do, might make all the World

LETTER 164.—First printed by Toynbee (1915), No. 177.

[1] The date of the month is supplied by the postmark; that of the year has been inserted in the original by Mason. This letter evidently refers to the affair of Miss Nichol, to which Gray reverts in the next letter.

[2] See Letter 144, n. 50.

[3] So in the postscript of Letter 144 he refers to Etough as 'a Fiend of a Parson', and in his Epigram (quoted in Letter 144, n. 50) described him as 'the grinning Fiend'.

[4] Walpole had written to Etough (see Letter 165).

[5] See Letter 165, n. 1.

[6] This name was written by Gray partly above the line; the first part has been blotted out and is now illegible. The name may have been Haddington, Hamilton, Harrington, Hartington, or Huntingdon.

think of him as I do. but the way you propose, would signify very little. Adieu, S^r, I am

Yours ever

T G.

Addressed: To the Honble Horace Walpole Esq in Arlington Street London
Postmark: SAFFRON WALDEN 27 NO

165. GRAY TO WALPOLE

C[ambridge] Dec: 31 [1751][1]

YOU have probably before now met with the Paper[2] I enclose, itself; tho' when you wrote last, you had only heard of it from others. it must not be known on any account, that it came from me, for by that means it might easily be discover'd, whom I had it from, wch might be the Ruin of a Gentleman. I do not see any one End it can answer, but that of putting M^r C: in a silly Light to such, as do not know him. the Exactnefs of Dates, Hours, & Minutes with the Observation of his different Tones of Voice, betray it to be the Work of a Listener, placed on purpose. I am told, that old H:[3] does not deny his Design of getting her for D: W:,[4] after my L^d O: had refused her. he insists he was not once at C:^{rs}[5] Chambers, while she was in his

LETTER 165.—First printed by Toynbee (1915), No. 178.

[1] The date of the year is determined by the reference to the affair of Miss Nichol. Walpole, in his letter to Mann of 1 April 1751, informing him of the death of Francis Whithed (see Letter 160, n. 2), says that Chute 'had brought about a match for him, that was soon to be concluded with a Miss Nicoll, an immense fortune'. The lady was Margaret, daughter and heiress of John Nichol, of Minchendon House, Southgate. After Whithed's death in March of this year (1751), Chute, who according to Walpole's 'Narrative' (see n. 5) was 'as near a relation to the young lady as any that she has', endeavoured to arrange a marriage between Miss Nichol, who was said to have a fortune of above £150,000 (see Walpole to Mann, 30 May 1751; and *Short Notes* for that year), and Horace Walpole's nephew, the Earl of Orford, who had just succeeded to the title. But the match fell through, owing, as Walpole believed, to the intrigues of his uncle, Horatio Walpole (see n. 5), who tried to secure the lady for one of his own sons. In the event Miss Nichol married (in 1753) James Brydges, Marquess of Carnarvon, subsequently (1771) third Duke of Chandos.

[2] No doubt that mentioned at the beginning of the previous letter.

[3] Old Horace, Walpole's uncle, Horatio Walpole (see Letter 152, n. 2).

[4] Probably Dick Walpole, that is, his third son, Richard, who eventually (1758) married a daughter of Sir Joshua Vanneck, Bart.

[5] Walpole wrote a 'Narrative of the Proceedings in the intended Marriage between Lord Orford & Miss Nicholl. In a Letter addressed to Mrs Harris, My Lord's Grandmother'. A copy of this narrative, presumably sent to John Chute, is now at the Vyne. From the narrative it is clear that 'C:^{r}' was Capper, a solicitor and conveyancer recommended by Walpole's uncle: 'a

Hands, & that the Story of the 10,000£ is a manifest Lye. he affects to treat it as a Fact afserted by M^r C:, tho' no such thing appears, even in the Paper itself. I can't find for certain, that Et:[6] (tho he has been here a second time with his Budget) has given any Copies of this Paper about, yet I do not doubt but He has. this I know; he has shew'd your Letter to him, & his own Answers to a few People here, tho' I have not seen them. I am in hast, but shall write again soon. pray tell me, as soon as you receive this.

165.* Gray to Mason

*   *   *   *   *   *   *   *   *   *   *

[c. Dec. 1751][1]

Dear Sir—   **LETTER I**

Very bad!
I am Yours—equally bad![2] it is impossible to conciliate these passages to nature and Aristotle.

'*Allowed to modern caprice.*'[3]—It is *not* caprice, but good sense

fat headed Fellow, exceedingly mean & cringing in his Appearance and dull in his Intellects'.—Walpole suspected his uncle of underhand dealings (see letter to Mann, 31 Aug. 1751: 'The affair of Miss Nicoll is blown up by the treachery of my uncle Horace and some lawyers, that I had employed at his recommendation').   [6] Etough (see Letter 164).

Letter 165*.—First printed by Mitford (1835–43), vol. iv, pp. 1–5, with the heading: 'Mr. Gray's Remarks on the Letters prefixed to Mason's Elfrida'. The 'Remarks' were no doubt part of a letter sent to Mason. Mitford gives no information as to the source of his copy.

[1] Mason's *Elfrida* was published in March, 1752. Five 'Letters concerning the following Drama', addressed to a real or imaginary correspondent, were prefixed. These were dated 'Pemb. Hall. 1751'. Mason and Gray were both in residence until the second week of December, when Mason left Cambridge, and it is probable that towards the end of this month Mason submitted the letters to Gray's criticism. Warburton, in a letter of 16 January 1752, wrote that he 'had just received our amiable friend's letters, which are to be prefixed to his Elfrida' (*Letters from a late eminent Prelate to one of his Friends* (1808), pp. 73–4), and this was presumably after Mason had received Gray's criticisms.

[2] In his printed text Mason omitted the conventional beginnings and endings of the letters.

[3] In the first letter Mason, after explaining his design, proceeds: 'According to this notion, every thing was to be allowed to the present taste, which nature and Aristotle could possibly dispense with'. He must have originally written 'caprice' and substituted 'taste' to meet Gray's objection. Tovey, vol. ii, pp. 293 ff., points out in his notes other passages in Mason's *Letters*, which were the subject of Gray's criticism. Mason revised the *Letters* and increased the number to five, when he printed them.

that made these alterations in the modern Drama. A greater liberty in the choice of the fable, and the conduct of it, was the necessary consequence of retrenching the Chorus.[4] Love, and tenderness delight in privacy. The soft effusions of the soul, Mr. Mason, will not bear the presence of a gaping, singing, dancing, moralizing, uninteresting crowd. And not love alone, but every passion is checked and cooled by this fiddling crew. How could Macbeth and his wife have laid the design for Duncan's murder? What could they have said to each other in the Hall at midnight, not only if a chorus, but if a single mouse had been stirring there? Could Hamlet have met the Ghost, or taken his mother to task in *their* company? If Othello had said a harsh word to his wife before *them*, would they not have danced to the window, and called the watch?

The ancients were perpetually confined and hampered by the necessity of using the Chorus, and, if they have done wonders notwithstanding this clog, sure I am they would have performed still greater wonders without it. For the same reason we may be allowed to admit of more intrigue in our drama, to bring about a great action; it is often an essential requisite: and it is not fair to argue against this liberty, from that misuse of it, which is common to us, and was formerly so with the French, namely, the giving into a silly intricacy of plot, in imitation of the Spanish Dramas. We have also since Charles the Second's time, imitated the French (though but awkwardly) in framing scenes of mere insipid gallantry. But these were the faults of the writers, and not of the art, which enables us with the help of a little contrivance, to have as much love as we please, without playing the petits maîtres, or building labyrinths.

I forgot to mention that Comedy contrived[5] to be an odd sort of Farce, very like those of the Italian theatre, till the Chorus was dismissed. When Nature and Menander brought it into that beautiful form which we find in Terence. Tragedy was not so happy till modern times.

---

[4] Mason described *Elfrida* as '*A* Dramatic Poem Written on the Model of The Antient GREEK TRAGEDY', and the *Letters* profess to answer objections to the form of the drama and especially to the introduction of the Chorus. This subject he had discussed with Gray at an early stage, see Gray's letter to Walpole, of 20 Feb. 1751 (Letter 158).

[5] Tovey substituted 'continued' for 'contrived', which is in Mitford's text: but the emendation is not necessary.

II

I do not admit that the excellencies of the French writers are measured by the verisimilitude, or the regularities of their Dramas *only*. Nothing in them, or in our own, even Shakespeare himself, ever touches us, unless rendered *verisimile*, which by good management may be accomplished even in such absurd stories as the Tempest, the Witches in Macbeth, or the Fairies in the Midsummer Night's Dream: and I know not of any writer that has pleased chiefly in proportion to his *regularity*. Other beauties may indeed be heightened and set off by its means, but of itself it hardly pleases at all. Venice Preserved,[6] or Jane Shore,[7] are not so regular as the Orphan,[8] or Tamerlane,[9] or Lady Jane Grey.[10]

III

Modern Melpomene.—Here are we got into our tantarums! It is certain that pure poetry may be introduced without any Chorus. I refer you to a thousand passages of *mere* description in the Iambic parts of Greek tragedies, and to ten thousand in Shakespeare, who is moreover particularly admirable in his introduction of pure poetry, so as to join it with pure passion, and yet keep close to nature. This he could accomplish with passions the most violent, and transporting, and this any good writer may do with passions less impetuous, for it is nonsense to imagine that Tragedy must *throughout* be agitated with the furious passions, or attached by the tender ones. The greater part of it must often be spent in a preparation of these passions, in a gradual working them up to their height, and must thus pass through a great many cooler scenes and a variety of *nuances*, each of which will admit of a proper degree of poetry, and some the purest poetry. Nay, the boldest metaphors, and even description in its strongest colouring, are the natural expression of some passions, even in their greatest agitation. As to moral reflections, there is sufficient room for them in those cooler scenes that I have mentioned, and they make the greatest ornaments of such parts, that is to say, if they are well joined with the character. If not, they had better be left to the audience, than put into the mouths of a set of professed moralists,

---

[6] By Thomas Otway (1652–85), first produced in 1682.
[7] By Nicholas Rowe (1674–1718), first produced in 1714.
[8] By Otway (1680).   [9] By Rowe (1702).   [10] By Rowe (1715).

who keep a shop of sentences, and reflections, (I mean the chorus) whether they be sages, as you call them, or young girls that learnt them by heart, out of their samples and primers.

There is nothing ungracious or improper in Jane Shore's reflections on the fate of women,[11] but just the contrary, only that they are in rhyme, and in like manner it is far from a beautiful variety when the Chorus makes a transition in the ——[12] from plain Iambics to high flown lyric thoughts, expressions and numbers, and when their vagaries are over, relapse again into common sense and conversation. A confidante in skilful hands, might be a character, and have both sense and dignity. That in Maffei's[13] Merope has as much as any Chorus.

The Greeks might sing better than the French, but I'll be burnt if they *danced* with more grace, expression, or even pathos, yet who ever thought of shedding tears at a French Opera?

IV

If modern music cannot, as you say, express poetry, it is not a perfection, but a deterioration; you might as well say that the *perfectionment* of poetry would be the rendering it incapable of expressing the passions.

166. GRAY TO WHARTON

[Thursday, April 9, 1752][1]

My dear Wharton

I SHOULD not have made this little Journey to Town, if I had not imagined the Situation of your Affairs (after the Lofs[2] you have lately had) would have prevented your Design of coming to Cambridge.[3] the Pleasure I have here, is not sufficient, I am sure, to ballance a much slighter, than I shall

---

[11] At the end of Act I of Rowe's play—
'Such is the fate unhappy women find,' etc.

[12] Unless Gray had Mason's *Elfrida* in mind, he perhaps left a blank for the title of a Greek play which might suit his purpose.

[13] Scipione Maffei (1675–1755); his tragedy *Merope* was first performed in 1713.

LETTER 166.—First printed by Mitford (1816), vol. ii, p. 230; now reprinted from original.   [1] See n. 10.

[2] The death of his father, which had occurred a few weeks before.

[3] To take his degree. He signed the Registrary's book as M.D. on 14 April.

have in seeing you again: my Stay therefore, will at farthest not be longer than Wednesday next,[4] when [your][5] Businefs will be over, & we shall have time, I hope, to ma[ke up] in some Degree for so many Year's[6] Separation.[7]

My Thanks to M[r] Brown for his Letter, and I wi[ll trou]ble you to tell him, I see no Reason why the Person[8] he mentions should refuse the Proposal made him. he must necesfarily & I think, in Prudence sooner or later enter into the Profefsion, that qualifies him for it. & this is perhaps as creditable a Way of doing it, as ever will offer, besides that it need not oblige him to any thing he dislikes, & may perhaps lead to great Advantages . . .[9] if he be return'd. I need not tell you that [I am]

Ever Yours,

T GRAY.

Postmark: [1]o[10] AP

---

[4] 15 April (see n. 10).

[5] Here and elsewhere in the letter there are tears in the paper of the original, and the words missing have been supplied conjecturally.

[6] *Sic.*

[7] They seem to have met just five years before, in April 1747, at Stilton, when Wharton was on his way south with his bride (see Letter 137, n. 3).

[8] This most probably refers to Mason, who, as may be gathered from a letter of Warburton to Hurd, dated 9 May 1752, had had an offer made to him on behalf of Lord Rockingham. The proposal may have been that Mason should take Holy Orders and become domestic chaplain to his Lordship. Warburton wrote: 'Convey a word or two to M[r] Mason. You know how the thing stands with his Northern Lord, and you know my sentiment on it. A little after M[r] Mason had left us, M[r] C. Yorke . . . chanced to mention that affair. He said he had met the Earl of Rockingham at some public place, and complimented him on his disposition to M[r] Mason, saying what he thought most advantageous to him. . . . He thinks M[r] Mason is likely to attach the Lord's liking to him, as he is a young nobleman of elegance, and loves music and painting. . . . In a word [he] thinks M[r] Mason should not refuse the offer' (*Letters from a late eminent Prelate to one of his Friends* (1808), pp. 78–9). Mason, however, did not accept the offer, and was not ordained till 1754.

[9] Two or three words are missing owing to a tear in the paper (see n. 5). It may be conjectured that there should be a full-stop after 'Advantages' and that the missing words conveyed a greeting to Tuthill, who had recently been out of Cambridge.

[10] The first figure of the date is illegible, but the postmark must have been 10, as the College books show that Gray, who left Cambridge c. 1 April, returned on 15 April ('Wednesday next'); 9 April therefore would be the date of the letter. It is endorsed by Wharton: 'Mr Gray Apr. 1752 to me at Cambridge'.

167. GRAY TO WALPOLE

May 28. Camb:ᵍᵉ. 1752.

I AM sorry I am forced to tell you, that I can not have the Satisfaction of seeing you now at Strawberry.¹ here is a Dʳ Wharton (whose Name you remember) a particular Friend of mine, that I have not seen in several Years: his Errand hither has been chiefly to see me, & till he leaves the Place, it will be impofsible for me to stir.

I wish your Invitation had been some Weeks later,² but as it is, I must be content to lose that Pleasure, as I do most others, & only send my Love to Mʳ Chute, & Compliments to Mʳ Bentley.

I am
Yours ever,
T. GRAY

Addressed: To The Honᵇˡᵉ. Horace Walpole Esq in Arlington Street London.

168. GRAY TO WALPOLE

Wednesday—[July 8, 1752]¹ Stoke.

I AM at present at Stoke, to wᶜʰ I came at half an Hour's Warning upon the News I received of my Mother's Illnefs, & did not expect to have found her alive: but as I found her much better, & she continues so, I shall be very glad to make you a Visit at Strawberry, whenever you give me Notice of a convenient time. I am surprized at the Print,² wᶜʰ far surpafses my Idea of London Graving. the Drawing itself was so finished, that I suppose, it did not require all the Art I had imagined to

LETTER 167.—First printed in *The Times* of 15 May 1922, from copy of the original then owned by Messrs. Knight, Frank, and Rutley.
¹ Gray's presence at Strawberry Hill was probably desired by Walpole in connexion with Bentley's drawings (see Letter 161, n. 2). On 6 June Walpole wrote to George Montagu: 'Mʳ Bentley is with me finishing the drawings, for Gray's Odes'.
² The postponed visit came off in the summer, as appears from Gray's letter to Walpole of 8 July, and Walpole's to Montagu of 28 Aug. of this year.
LETTER 168.—First printed in part (in a garbled text, and in combination with a portion of another letter—see n. 4) by Mason in *Memoirs*, pp. 224–6; first printed in full by Toynbee (1915), No. 179.
¹ The date of the month is supplied by the postmark; that of the year is determined by the reference to the illustrations which Bentley was preparing for Gray's *Six Poems* (n. 2).
² A proof print of the Cul de Lampe, which Mr. Bentley designed for the Elegy in a country church-yard, and which represents a village-funeral; this occasioned the pleasant mistake of his two aunts. *Mason.*—This design,

Pencil drawing of Stoke Manor House
by Thomas Gray in the possession of W. S. Lewis, Esq.

copy it tolerably. my Aunts³ just now, seeing me open your Letter, take it to be a Burying-Ticket enclosed, & ask, whether any body has left me a Ring? and so they still conceive it to be, even with all their Spectacles on. heaven forbid they should suspect it to belong to any Verses of mine; they would burn me for a Poet. Mʳ Bentley (I believe) will catch a better Idea of Stoke-House from any old Barn he sees, than from my Sketch: but I will try my Skill. I forbid no Banes; but am satisfied, if your Design succeed so well as you intend it. and yet I know, it will be accompanied with something not at all agreeable to me.⁴ Adieu! I am

Yours ever

T G:

Addressed: To The Honᵇˡᵉ Horace Walpole Esq in Arlington Street London
   Postmark: 9 ɪʏ

169. GRAY TO WALPOLE

[Stoke, July, 1752]¹

YOUR pen was too rapid to mind the common form of a direction, and so, by omitting the words *near Windsor*, your letter has been diverting itself at another Stoke,² near Ailesbury, and came not to my hands till to-day. The true original chairs were all sold, when the Huntingdons broke;³ there are nothing now but Halsey-chairs,⁴ not adapted to the squarenefs of a

which is placed at the end of the *Elegy*, and is the last in the book, was engraved by Charles Grignion the elder (1717–1810). Gray's admiration for Bentley's work prompted him to write the 'Stanzas to Mr. Bentley' printed by Mason (*Memoirs*, p. 227).

³ Mrs. Rogers (Ann Antrobus) and Mrs. Olliffe (Jane Antrobus), Mrs. Gray's two surviving sisters, the unmarried sister, Mary Antrobus, having died in November 1749.

⁴ Mason here inserts: '—While I write this, I receive your second letter—' and then prints as part of this letter a garbled text of Gray's letter of 13 Feb. 1753 (Letter 173).

LETTER 169.—First printed in *Works of Lord Orford*, vol. v, pp. 392–3.

¹ This letter must have been written soon after Letter 168, at a time when Bentley was making his drawing to illustrate the *Long Story*.

² Stoke Mandeville.

³ Gray is referring to the Manor House at Stoke Poges, the 'ancient pile of building' of the *Long Story*, which, according to Lysons (*Magna Britannia*, vol. i, p. 635), had been built by Henry Hastings, Earl of Huntingdon, in the reign of Queen Elizabeth, and had soon afterwards been seized by the Crown for a debt.

⁴ Lady Cobham, the owner of the Manor House at this time, was the

Gothic dowager's rump. And by the way I do not see how the uneasinefs and uncomfortablenefs of a coronation-chair can be any objection with you: every chair that is easy is modern, and unknown to our ancestors. As I remember, there were certain low chairs, that looked like ebony, at Esher,[5] and were old and pretty. Why should not Mr. Bentley improve upon them?— I do not wonder at Dodsley.[6] You have talked to him of six *odes*, for so you are pleased to call every thing I write, though it be but a receipt to make apple-dumplings. He has reason to gulp when he finds one of them only a long story.[7] I don't know but I may send him very soon (by your hands) an ode to his own tooth, a high Pindarick upon stilts,[8] which one must be a better scholar than he is to understand a line of, and the very best scholars will understand but a little matter here and there. It wants but seventeen lines of having an end, I don't say of being finished. As it is so unfortunate to come too late for Mr. Bentley, it may appear in the fourth volume of the Miscellanies,[9] provided you don't think it execrable, and supprefs it. Pray, when the fine book is to be printed, let me revise the prefs, for you know you can't;[10] and there are a few trifles I could wish altered.

I know not what you mean by hours of love,[11] and cherries, and pine-apples. I neither see nor hear anything here, and am

daughter of Edmund Halsey (see Letter 155, n. 3). Walpole had evidently been asking for details of the furniture at the Manor House for the purposes of Bentley's drawing.

[5] Esher Place, in Surrey, the seat of Henry Pelham. Gray visited it probably in Walpole's company in 1747 or 1748 (see Letter 191, n. 22).

[6] Robert Dodsley (1703–64), the publisher of the *Six Poems*.

[7] Gray was having qualms about the book (see Letter 168 *ad fin.*) and especially about the *Long Story*. Mason, *Memoirs*, p. 227, states that: 'it was for the sake of the Design which Mr Bentley made for the Long Story, that Mr Gray permitted it to be printed: yet not without clearly foreseeing that he risked somewhat by the publication of it.'

[8] The *Progress of Poesy*, first printed at Strawberry Hill in 1757. Although Gray describes it as wanting but seventeen lines of having an end, he did not finish it for two years or more (see Letter 194). It may be assumed that its final form was very different from the first draft mentioned here.

[9] Dodsley's *Collection of Poems by Several Hands* (see Letter 161, n. 6).

[10] Walpole, when writing to Mason on 15 May, 1773, may have had this passage in mind: 'I have not the patience necessary for correcting the press. Gray was for ever reproaching me with it, and in one of the letters I have just turned over, he says, "pray send me the proof sheets to correct, for you know you are not capable of it".'

[11] Doubtless Walpole had made some allusion to Gray's relations with Miss Speed (see Letter 155, n. 1).

of opinion that is the best way. My compliments to Mr. Bentley, if he be with you.

I am yours ever,

T. GRAY.

I desire you would not show that epigram I repeated to you, as mine. I have heard of it twice already as coming from you.[12]

169*. GRAY TO WHARTON

Sept: 29 [1752].[1] Stoke.

My dear Wharton

I SHALL certainly be in Town on Monday next,[2] for Mr Brown informed me you would arrive there on the 30th, & I order'd my Matters here accordingly. you will see me the Instant I come, having (I need not tell you) not only nothing I like better to do there, but literally nothing else, than to see you. I have not time to enlarge, as I send this by a Person who is just going from our House to Uxbridge, tho' to my Shame I stand indebted to you for a very kind Letter I received long ago. Adieu, I am always

Very truly Yours,

T GRAY.

Addressed: To Dr. Wharton, M:D: at Mr. Espalin's, Barber, in Southampton Building's Holborn   *Postmark:* LONDON 30 SE

169**. Dodsley to Gray

[*Nov. 1752*]

[In his letter to Walpole of 17 Dec. 1752 (Letter 170) Gray speaks of having received a letter from Dodsley, written by Walpole's

---

[12] Miss Berry states that she was unable to discover the epigram alluded to. It is possible that this was the epigram on Etough (Letter 144, n. 50), which Cole, in his letter of 11 December 1769, states was written 'twenty years ago'. Cole's round number might be approximate.

LETTER 169*.—First printed by Mitford (1816), vol. ii, p. 243; now reprinted from original.

[1] This letter has hitherto been placed among letters of 1753, owing to Wharton's having so dated it; but as Gray was at Durham during the whole of September 1753 (see Letters 180, 182), and in Sept. 1754 Wharton was at another address (see Letter 192), the letter obviously belongs to 1752. It should be noted here that since the date (July 1752) of the last letter, the Calendar had been altered from Old to New Style, by the omission of eleven days from Sept. 3 to 13, N.S. beginning on 14 Sept. 1752.

[2] 2 Oct.

directions, with regard to the volume of Gray's *Six Poems*, with Bentley's designs, which Dodsley was preparing for publication.]

169***. Gray to Dodsley

[*Nov. 1752*]

[In his letter of 17 Dec. Gray tells Walpole that he had sent to Dodsley 'some time since' a reply to the above.]

169****. Dodsley to Gray

[*c. Dec. 15, 1752*]

[In his letter to Walpole of 17 Dec. Gray refers to a letter he had just received from Dodsley to say that he could have the volume of *Six Poems* finished in a fortnight, if Gray were to be in town.]

170. GRAY TO WALPOLE

Camb:ge Dec: 17. Sunday. [1752][1]

I SENT to Dodsley some time since, who wrote to me by your order, what little alterations[1a] I had to make, & should be glad to know, whether you thought them for the better or the worse. he tells me now, he could finish in a fortnight, if I were in town, but this would be very inconvenient to me at present, so I must

LETTER 170.—First printed by Toynbee (1915), No. 181.

[1] The date of the year (which has been inserted in the original by Mason) is determined by the reference to the volume of *Six Poems* in preparation by Dodsley (see Letter 169).

[1a] See Letter 169: 'there are a few trifles I could wish altered'.

Four of the poems had been published before; a comparison of the earlier texts with the texts in the Bentley edition shows that three of the poems were now revised, and given the final form, which was kept in later editions. The *Eton Ode* was unchanged, the *Ode to the Spring* had one amendment (see Letter 125, n. 6), there are small changes in the *Ode on the Death of a Favourite Cat*, but the *Elegy* was submitted to a careful revision. Corruptions which had appeared in some of the earlier editions were corrected, and it is worthy of note that Gray introduced new readings. The three manuscripts of the poem all have 'wind' in line 2; this was printed for the first time in place of 'winds', which had been the reading of all the published texts. Some variations that were now introduced were written on the margin of the manuscript in Gray's Commonplace-book, and it may be suggested that they were probably inserted after Gray had made his improvements for the Bentley edition. The Eighth Edition of the *Elegy*, which was published in December of this year, follows (with one error) the text now adopted, and the title-page describes it as 'Corrected by the AUTHOR'.

have the Sheets sent me to correct hither, & I suppose, it may come out in lefs than a Month². . . .

*   *   *   *   *   *   *   *   *   *   *

*   *   *   *   *   *   *   *   *   *   *³

. . . you may imagine, I do not expect any thing very particular on either of these subjects, but some sort of satisfaction you will easily know how to give me in a letter; as it will be a good while, before I can see you. Adieu, I am ever

Yours
T G.

Have you read Mad: Maintenon's Letters?⁴ or the Micromegas,⁵ or the dull Life of Dʳ Tillotson.⁶ I have gone thro' the 3ᵈ Vol: of the Biographia,⁷ wᶜʰ will be a great Relief to you after Bayle's⁸ pedantic bawdy: all the Lives, mark'd with an E or a C, have something curious in them, those with a G are abominable foolish.

I have just received the first Proofs from Dodsly. I thought it was to be a Qᵗᵒ, but it is a little Folio.⁹ the Stanzas are number'd, wᶜʰ I do not like.¹⁰

Addressed: To The Honᵇˡᵉ Horace Walpole Esq in Arlington Street London
   Postmark: SAFFRON WALDEN 18 DE

² Walpole, writing to Montagu on 28 Aug. 1752, had expressed the hope that the book would appear 'this winter'.
³ A piece, containing about five lines of text, has here been cut out and Gray's allusion cannot be explained.
⁴ *Les Lettres de Madame de Maintenon* (see Letter 171, n. 13) had been published in two volumes by L. A. de la Beaumelle in this year (1752).
⁵ A satirical romance by Voltaire published in this year. An English translation was published in 1753. Chesterfield wrote to his son on 1 Jan. 1753: 'A most poor performance, called *Micromegas . . .* is said to be Voltaire's; but I cannot believe it, it is so very unworthy of him; it consists only of thoughts stolen from Swift, but miserably mangled and disfigured.'
⁶ By Thomas Birch (see Letter 149, n. 20), published in this year.
⁷ *Biographia Britannica or, the Lives of the most Eminent Persons who have flourished in Great Britain and Ireland . . . in the manner of Mr. Bayle's Historical and Critical Dictionary* (see Letter 147, n. 2). The third volume was published in 1750. The articles are signed C, T, E, G, X, &c.
⁸ An English edition of Pierre Bayle's *Dictionnaire Historique et Critique* (first published in 1696–7) was published in 1710.
⁹ As published the volume was a small folio, measuring 15 × 10½ inches. of 45 leaves, the plates and poems printed on one side only.
¹⁰ The numbering of the stanzas was omitted.

171. GRAY TO WHARTON

[Dec. 19, 1752]¹

*   *   *   *   *   *   *   *   *   *   *

*   * oming.² I am sorry to tell you a sad story of our friend over the way.³ young V:⁴ who is now Chaplain to your new Bishop,⁵ & has had the promise of it for some time, applied to his little red L^dship,⁶ as a friend to him & to his family, to put him into orders. he begun by a direct Lie, & told him, he knew the B:ᵖ was absolutely engaged to two People of Oxford, whom he named. then he drill'd⁷ him on with various trifling pretences, & at last went to town without ordaining him, or appointing any time, when he would. in the mean time V: being prefs'd by Letters from home, went to town & was immediately ordain'd by the A:ᵖ of York,⁸ & soon after appointed Chaplain. he was inform'd from a very sure hand, that all this time his friend of Ch:ʳ⁹ had been making interest for R—fs¹⁰ against

LETTER 171.—First printed in part (in a garbled text) in Mason's *Memoirs*, pp. 223–4; first printed in full (as far as preserved) by Mitford (1816), vol. ii, pp. 231–3; now reprinted from original.

¹ The date was supplied by Wharton.

² MS. mutilated; about half a folio missing.

³ Keene, Master of Peterhouse, and since March of this year Bishop of Chester (see Letter 143, n. 3). Gray, himself a member of the College 'over the way', writes as if he belonged to Pembroke, Wharton's College, on the other side of the street.

⁴ This was Henry Vane (b. c. 1725) (not to be confounded with his relative of the same name, afterwards first Earl of Darlington—see Letter 143, n. 6), second son of George Vane, of Long Newton, co. Durham; admitted at Inner Temple, 1744; matriculated Trinity College, Cambridge, 1746; B.A. 1750; Fellow, 1752; M.A. 1753; LL.D. 1761; Deacon, Nov. 1752; Chaplain to Bishop of Durham, 1752; Priest, 1754; Rector of Great Stainton, co. Durham, 1754–60; Prebendary of Durham, 1758; cr. Baronet, 1782; d. 1794.

⁵ Richard Trevor (1707–71), who had been translated from St. David's to Durham in October of this year, in succession to Butler, of the *Analogy*, who died in June.   ⁶ Keene.

⁷ That is, put him off; perhaps a reminiscence of Addison's paper in the *Spectator* on the sect of women he calls 'demurrers': 'Strephon appears . . . irrevocably smitten with one that demurs out of self interest. He tells me . . . she has bubbled him out of his youth; that she has drilled him on to five and fifty; and that he verily believes she will drop him in his old age' (No. 89).

⁸ Matthew Hutton (1693–1758), formerly Fellow of Christ's College, Cambridge; Bishop of Bangor, 1743–7; Archbishop of York, 1747–57; of Canterbury, 1757–8.   ⁹ Keene, Bishop of Chester.

¹⁰ John Ross, Fellow of St. John's (see Letter 149, n. 13).

him, & particularly had said, that V: could not have it, for
he was a young man, *not in Orders* yet: I afsure you, they are
very angry (& with reason), at R:[11] Castle;   *   *   *
*   *   *   *   *   *   *   *   *   *
Birch, *   *   *   *   *   *   *   *   *   *·
between great Fact*   *   *   *   *   *   *   *
of none: however it is to be read. [I am reading Mad:][12] de
Maintenon's Letters; they are undoubtedly genuine. they
begin very early in her Life, before she married Scarron;[13]
& continue after the King's Death to within a little while of her
own. they bear all the Marks of a noble Spirit, (in her adversity
particularly) of Virtue, & unaffected Devotion, insomuch that
I am almost persuaded she indulged Lewis the 14th in no
Liberties, till he actually married her, & this not out of Policy
& Ambition, but Conscience; for she was what we should call
a Bigot, yet with great good-sense. in short she was too good
for a Court; Misfortunes in the beginning of her Life had
form'd her Mind (naturally lively & impatient) to reflexion, &
a habit of piety; she was always miserable, while she had the
care of Mad: de Montespan's[14] children; timid & very cautious
of making Use of that unlimited Power she rose to afterwards
for fear of trespafsing on the King's Friendship for her; & after
his death, not at all afraid of meeting her own. I don't know
what to say to you with regard to Racine: it sounds to me as if
any body should fall upon Shakespear, who indeed lies infinitely
more open to Criticism of all kinds, but I should not care to be
the person that undertook it. if you don't like Athaliah, or
Britannicus, there is no more to be said. I have done.

[11] Raby Castle was the seat of Henry Vane, afterwards Earl of Darlington
(see n. 4).
[12] MS. mutilated; about half a folio missing. The last four words are
supplied conjecturally, the lower part of 'I am' being visible. The reference
to Birch is doubtless in connexion with his *Life of Tillotson*, which is mentioned
with Mme de Maintenon's Letters, in PS. to Letter 170.
[13] Françoise d'Aubigné, Marquise de Maintenon (1635–1719); under
stress of poverty in 1651, at the age of sixteen, she married the poet Scarron,
who had just published his masterpiece *Le Roman Comique* (see Letter 140).
In 1669 she was given secret charge of the King's children by Mme de
Montespan, and in 1674 the King bestowed upon her the marquisate of
Maintenon. By her influence over Louis she succeeded in detaching him
from Mme de Montespan, and a year or two after the death of the Queen
(1683) she was secretly married to him.
[14] Françoise Athénaïse de Rochechouart, Marquise de Montespan (1641–
1707); she had eight children by Louis XIV, two of whom died in infancy.

Rofs bears, or difsembles his disappointment better, than I expected of him: perhaps indeed it may not turn out to his disadvantage at the end. he is in London about something. have you seen Bishop Hall's Satires, call'd Virgidemiæ, republish'd lately.[15] they are full of spirit & poetry; as much of the first, as Dr Donne,[16] & far more of the latter. they were wrote at this University, when he was about 23 years old, in Q: Elizabeth's time.[17] Adieu [Brown & Tuthill][18] send their best Compliments, with mine, to you & Mrs Wharton. I am ever

Very sincerely yours,

T G:

Addressed: To Dr Wharton M:D: at Durham   *Postmark:* CAMBRIDGE

171*. Walpole to Gray

[c. Feb. 11, 1753]

[From Gray's letter to Walpole of 13 Feb. 1753 (Letter 173) it is evident that Gray had received a letter from Walpole telling him of the proposal to prefix his portrait to the *Six Poems*. This letter, which Gray no doubt answered at once, has not been preserved.]

15 Joseph Hall (1574–1656), Fellow of Emmanuel College, Cambridge (1595); successively Bishop of Exeter, 1627–41, and of Norwich, 1641 until his ejection in 1647. His satires were first published in two volumes in 1597–8 *Virgidemiarum, Sixe Bookes. First three bookes of Toothlesse Satyrs,* and *Three last bookes of byting Satyres* (Lond. 12mo). The edition referred to by Gray was that edited by the Westmorland poet, William Thompson, Fellow of Queen's College, Oxford, which was published at Oxford with the date 1753.
16 John Donne (1573–1631), the famous Dean of St. Paul's, 1621–31.
17 Mason, who omits the conclusion of the letter, inserts here the following paragraph, which he doubtless transferred, *more suo*, either from the lost beginning of this letter, or from some other letter of Gray to Wharton: 'You do not say whether you have read the Crito. I only recommend the dramatic part of the Phædo to you, not the argumentative. The subject of the Erastæ is good; it treats of that peculiar character and turn of mind which belongs to a true philosopher, but it is shorter than one would wish. The Euthyphro I would not read at all.'
These four dialogues are among those annotated by Gray in the notes on Plato printed from his Commonplace-book by Mathias in vol. ii of his edition of the *Works of Gray* (Lond. 1814).
18 See Letter 120, n. 2. Mitford's restoration is not sufficient to fill the gap.

172. GRAY TO DODSLEY

Sr   Feb: 12. Camb:^{ge} [1753]

I AM not at all satisfied with the Title. to have it conceived, that I publish a Collection of *Poems* (half a dozen little Matters, four of wch too have already been printed again & again) thus pompously adorned would make me appear very justly ridiculous. I desire it may be understood (wch is the truth) that the Verses are only subordinate, & explanatory to the Drawings, & suffer'd by me to come out thus only for that reason. therefore if you yourself prefix'd this Title, I desire it may be alter'd; or if M^r W: order'd it so, that you would tell him, why I wish it were changed in the manner I mention'd to you at first, or to that purpose: for the more I consider it, the lefs I can bear it, as it now stands. I even think, there is an uncommon sort of Simplicity, that looks like affectation, in putting our plain Christian & Surnames without a M^r before them;[1] but this (if it signifies any thing) I easily give up; the other I can not. you need not apprehend, that this Change in the Title will be any prejudice to the Sale of the book. a showy title-page may serve to sell a Pamphlet of a shilling or two; but this is not of a price for chance-customers, whose eye is caught in pafsing by a window; & could never sell but from the notion the Town may entertain of the Merit of the Drawings, wch they will be instructed in by some, that understand such things.

I thank you for the Offer you make me, but I shall be contented with three Copies, two of wch you will send me, & keep the third, till I acquaint you where to send it. if you will let me know the exact day they will come out a little time beforehand, I will give you a direction. you will remember to send two copies to Dr Thomas Wharton, M:D: at Durham. perhaps you may have burnt my Letter, so I will again put down the Title

Designs by M^r R: Bentley
for six Poems of
M^r T: Gray.[2]

I am, S^r,   Your humble Servt
                                                  T G:

Addressed: To Mr Dodsley.

LETTER 172.—First printed by Mitford (1835–43), vol. iv, pp. 103–4; now reprinted from original.

[1] See Walpole's remarks on this in Letter 174.

[2] This was the title of the book when published (with the alteration of 'by Mr. T. Gray' for 'of Mr. T. Gray'.

173. GRAY TO WALPOLE

Camb:ᵍᵉ Feb: 13. 1753.

SURE You are not out of your Wits! this I know, if you suffer my Head to be printed,¹ you infallibly will put me out of mine. I conjure you immediately to put a stop to any such design. who is at the Expence of engraving it, I know not; but if it be Dodsley, I will make up the Lofs to him. the thing, as it was, I know will make me ridiculous enough; but to appear in proper Person at the head of my works, consisting of half a dozen Ballads in 30 Pages, would be worse than the Pillory. I do afsure you, if I had received such a Book with such a frontispice without any warning, I believe, it would have given me a Palsy. therefore I rejoice to have received this Notice; & shall not be easy, till you tell me all thoughts of it are laid aside. I am extremely in earnest, & can't bear even the Idea!

I had wrote to Dodsley to tell him, how little I liked the Title he had prefix'd, but your letter has put all that out of my Head. if you think it necefsary to print these Explanations² for the use of People that have no eyes, I could be glad, they were a little alter'd. I am to my shame in your debt for a long letter, but I can not think of anything else, till you have set me at ease. Adieu, I am

Yours ever,
T: G:³

LETTER 173.—First printed in part (in a garbled text, and in combination with part of Letter 168) by Mason in *Memoirs*, pp. 225-6; first printed in full by Toynbee (1915), No. 182.

¹ Dodsley had proposed to prefix Gray's portrait, engraved from the painting by Eckhardt in Walpole's possession, to the book. Mason (*Memoirs*, p. 225) states that the plate was actually more than half engraved, but was suppressed in consequence of Gray's protest. After Gray's death Mason, as he wrote to Walpole on 5 Nov. 1772 (*Walpole–Mason Correspondence*, vol. i, p. 42), found 'a proof of the unfinished head from your picture of Eckarts'. This proof he sent to Walpole and it is now in the possession of Dr. Rosenbach. It is inscribed in Walpole's hand: 'Mʳ Gray, from the picture at Strawberry Hill, the plate of which Mʳ Gray destroyed v. p. 225' (the reference being to Mason's *Memoirs*). It seems probable that the plate was not destroyed, and at some later date J. S. Müller, who had engraved it originally, finished the plate (or engraved another plate) and many copies of his engraving are known to be in existence.

² Four pages, containing *Explanation of the Prints* (written by Walpole), are printed at the end of the volume as published.

³ There was apparently a postscript in the original which has been torn off.

173*. Walpole to Gray

[*c. Feb. 15, 1753*]

[In his letter to Gray of 20 Feb. 1753 (Letter 174) Walpole refers to a note he had written to Gray to allay his uneasiness in reply to his protest (Letter 173) against the proposal to prefix his portrait. This note was written in haste, as Walpole explains.]

173**. Gray to Walpole

[*c. Feb. 17, 1753*]

[Walpole's note (Letter 173*) in reply to Gray's protest (Letter 173), instead of appeasing Gray, had, as appears from Letter 174, had 'quite the contrary effect' from what he intended, and had evidently elicited a further letter of complaint from Gray.]

174. WALPOLE TO GRAY

Arlington Street Feb. 20. 1753

I AM very sorry that the haste I made to deliver you from your uneasiness the first moment after I received your Letter, shoud have made me express myself in a manner to have the quite contrary effect from what I intended. You well know how rapidly and carelessly I always write my Letters; the note[1] you mention was written in a still greater hurry than ordinary, & merely to put you out of pain. I had not seen Dodsley, consequently coud only tell you that I did not doubt but he woud have no Objection to satisfy you, as you was willing to prevent his being a Loser by the plate.[2] Now, from this declaration how is it possible for you to have for one moment put such a construction upon my words, as woud have been a downright stupid brutality, unprovoked? It is impossible for me to recollect my very expression, but I am confident that I have repeated the whole substance.

How the bookseller woud be less a Loser by being at more expense, I can easily explain to you: He feared the price of half a guinea woud seem too high to most purchasers; if by the expence of ten guineas more he coud make the book appear so much more rich & showy (as I beleive I said) as to induce people to think it cheap, the profits from selling many more

LETTER 174.—First printed in part in *Works of Lord Orford* (vol. v, pp. 353–5); first printed in full by Toynbee (1915), No. 183.

[1] See non-extant Letter 173*.　　　　[2] See Letter 173, n. 1.

copies woud amply recompense him for his additional disbursement.

The thought of having the head engraved was entirely Dodsley's own, & against my opinion, as I concluded it woud be against yours, which made me determine to acquaint you with it before it's appearance.

When you reflect on what I have said now, you will see very clearly, that I had & coud have no other possible meaning in what I wrote last. you might justly have accused me of neglect, if I had deferr'd giving you all the satisfaction in my power, as soon as ever I knew your uneasiness.

The Head I give up. The Title I think will be wrong, & not answer your purpose, for, as the Drawings are evidently calculated for the poems, why will the improper disposition of the Word *Designs* before *Poems*, make the Edition less yours? I am as little convinced that there is any affectation in leaving out the M^r before your Names; it is a barbarous addition; the other is simple & classic, a rank I cannot help thinking due to both the Poet and Painter. Without ranging myself among Classics, I assure you, were I to print any thing with my name, it shoud be plain Horace Walpole: M^r is one of the Gothicisms I abominate.[3] The Explanation[4] was certainly added for people who have not Eyes—such are almost all who have seen Mr Bentley's drawings, & think to compliment him by mistaking them for prints. Alas! the generality want as much to have the words *a Man, a Cock*, written under his drawings, as under the most execrable hieroglyphics of Egypt or of sign post painters!

I will say no more now, but that you must not wonder if I am partial to you & yours, when you can write as you do & yet feel so little Vanity. I have used freedoms enough with your writings to convince you I speak truth: I praise & scold Mr Bentley immoderately as I think he draws well or ill; I never think it worth my while to do either, especially to blame, where there are not generally vast Excellencies. goodnight—dont suspect me when I have no fault but impatience to make you easy.

Yrs ever,

HW.

[3] It is a strange commentary on Walpole's 'abomination' that his own works were published as 'By Mr. Horace Walpole'.
[4] See Letter 173, n. 2.

1753

March. 15 – Stoke.

My dear Wharton

I judge by this time you are in town. the reason that I thought would have deprived me of the pleasure of seeing you is now at an end: my poor Mother, after a long & painful struggle for life, expired on Sunday morning. when I have seen her buried, I shall come to London, & it will be a particular satisfaction to me to find you there. if you can procure me a tolerable lodging near you, be so good (if you can conveniently) to let me know the night you receive this; if not, I shall go to my old Landlord in Jermyn Street. I believe, I shall come on Tuesday, & stay a few days, for I must return hither to pay my Aunt her Arrears, w:ch she will demand with great Exactness. Adieu, dear S:r, I am

Ever yours
TGray.

To me, at M:rs Rogers's of Stoke
near Windsor Bucks.

Facsimile of Letter 176

175. GRAY TO WALPOLE

Stoke. Feb: 27 [1753]¹

I AM obliged on the sudden to come hither to see my poor mother who is in a condition between Life & Death, tho' (I think) much nearer the latter. yet I could not help telling you, I had received your Letter, & am pleased to find, I was in the wrong. you may be sure, I was not willing to think you so. do what you please about the title, if it is time; but it seems to me the lefs of Puff or Ostentation it has, the better it will be, even for Dodsley.² excuse my brevity, Adieu, I am ever

Yours

T G:

Addressed: To The Honᵇˡᵉ Horace Walpole Esq in Arlington Street London
Postmark: 1 MR

176. GRAY TO WHARTON

March 15 [1753]¹—Stoke.

My dear Wharton

I JUDGE by this time you are in town. the reason that I thought would have deprived me of the pleasure of seeing you is now at an end. my poor Mother, after a long & painful Struggle for life, expired on Sunday morning.² when I have seen her buried, I shall come to London, & it will be a particular satisfaction to me to find you there. if you can procure me a tolerable lodging near you, be so good (if you can conveniently) to let me know the night you receive this; if not, I shall go to my old Landlord in Jermyn Street.³ I believe, I shall come on

LETTER 175.—First printed by Toynbee (1915), No. 184.
¹ The Letter is obviously an answer to Letter 174.
² The book was published on 29 March, price half a guinea.
LETTER 176.—First printed by Mitford (1816), vol. ii, pp. 235–6; now reprinted from original.
¹ Date of year added by Wharton.
² Mrs. Gray died on 11 March 1753, aged 68 (not 67, as Gray inscribed on her tomb). She was buried in the churchyard at Stoke Poges in the same tomb in which her sister Mary Antrobus had been laid in 1749, and in which Gray himself was laid eighteen years later. In the inscription on her tomb Gray described her as 'the careful tender mother of many children, one of whom alone had the misfortune to survive her'.
³ Mitford (*Works of Gray* (1836–43) vol. i, p. cx) quotes the following note

375

Tuesday,[4] & stay a few days, for I must return hither to pay my Aunt[5] her Arrears, wch she will demand with great Exactnefs. Adieu, dear S^r, I am

Ever yours,

T GRAY.

To me, at Mrs Rogers's of Stoke, near Windsor Bucks.

177. GRAY TO WHARTON

Camb: June 28 . . 1753.
Thursday.

My dear Doctor[1]

YOU may well suppose me no longer here, as I have neglected thus long to answer two very kind letters, & (wch is more) to congratulate you on what most of your friends regard as a very happy event: but to me, I own, it has another face, as I have a much greater regard for you than for the young Gentleman, whom I never saw; & foresee, that from this time you will never part with your bottle, wch is properly the father of this boy.[2] all my rhetorick will be thrown away, the Gout may groan at you, & brandish its crutches, the Stone rattle, & the Palsy shake its head unheeded. we shall be no match for Claret, if it can get an heir, as well as carry an election. now I talk of elections, we

by Norton Nicholls: 'Mr. Gray, when he came to town, lodged in Jermyn Street, St. James's, at Roberts's, the hosier, or at Frisby's, the oilman. They are toward the East end, on different sides of the street.' As appears from the address of Letter 509*, Roberts was a hosier and hatter, and his shop was called 'The Three Squirrels'. While Wharton was living in London Gray often stayed with him or took lodgings near him (see Letters 271, 285, 293). After Wharton left London in 1759 Gray for more than two years had rooms in the house in Southampton Row where Wharton had been living (see Letter 296).

[4] 20 March.

[5] Presumably Mrs. Olliffe, the aunt from whom probably the £100 was borrowed to meet the cost of rebuilding his house in Cornhill after the fire of March 1748 (see Letter 145, n. 7).

LETTER 177.—First printed by Mitford (1816), vol. ii, pp. 236–7; now reprinted from original.

[1] From this time onwards Gray not infrequently addresses Wharton by this title.

[2] This was Robert, familiarly known as 'Robin', his first son ('the ejected statesman' of PS. to Letter 209), who only survived until the spring of 1758 (see Letter 270). Wharton's second son, also Robert and 'Robin', was born in 1760 (see Genealogical Table).

have a report here that your friend M^r V: (I mean Ld Barnard)[3] means to bring in his Son-in-law[4] at Durham. is this true? H: Vane[5] sets out for the North on Saturday, so I suppose the Bishop's[6] entry will be over next week. and next Monday fort-night I hope to set out myself with Stonhewer, who is going down to his fathers,[7] in a Post-chaise. we shall not come very fast, as I propose to see Burleigh,[8] Bevoir-Castle,[9] &c: by the way. but I shall write again before I come, to tell you exactly what day we shall be at York. if the time does not suit you, you will inform me as soon as pofsible. I did not run away from his Grace,[10] but follow'd your advice, had a very affectionate squeeze by the hand, & a fine Complement in a corner. many people here have been curious to know what it was; but I have kept my own secret, for indeed I do not know myself: only I remember it felt warm, & sweated a little.[11] Adieu! you will not fail to present my Complements to Mrs Wharton. if she drank as much Claret, as you have done, we shall have the Boy *stand* for the County, as soon as he can walk alone. Mr Brown

---

[3] Henry Vane, the elder, had succeeded his father as third Baron Barnard on 27 April in this year; he was created Viscount Barnard and Earl of Darling-ton in 1754 (see Letter 143, n. 6).

[4] This was probably Ralph Carr, of Cocken, co. Durham, who in 1752 married Vane's daughter Mary. Vane, however, was followed in the repre-sentation of Durham, by his son Henry Vane, the younger, who held the seat from 1753 to 1758, when he succeeded his father as second Earl of Darlington.

[5] Rev. Henry Vane, chaplain to the Bishop of Durham (see Letter 171, n. 4).

[6] See Letter 171, n. 5.

[7] That is, to Houghton-le-Spring, Durham, of which his father was Rector (see Letter 120, n. 38).

[8] Burleigh House, Northants., near Stamford, seat of the Earl of Exeter.

[9] Belvoir Castle, Leicester, near Grantham, seat of the Duke of Rutland.

[10] Cooper in his *Annals of Cambridge* under the year 1753 records (pp. 290–1): 'The Duke of Newcastle the Chancellor of the University arrived at Clare Hall on the 14th of June. . . . On the 16th, he held a levee at Clare Hall. . . . On the 18th, his Grace left Cambridge.' Gray no doubt attended the levee.

[11] Tovey quotes Macaulay's description of Newcastle (at the end of his Edinburgh essay on Walpole's Letters to Mann): 'Whatever was absurd about him stood out with grotesque prominence from the rest of the charac-ter. He was a living, moving, talking caricature. His gait was a shuffling trot; his utterance a rapid stutter; he was always in a hurry; he was never in time; he abounded in fulsome caresses and in hysterical tears. . . . All the able men of his time ridiculed him as a dunce, a driveller, a child who never knew his own mind for an hour together; and he overreached them all round.'

377

(I believe) will be engaged here with Plummer¹² greatest part
of the Summer: [he and Tuthill]¹³ desire to be remember'd to
you both. I am ever

Truly Yours

T G.

Addressed: To D͏ʳ Thomas Wharton, MD, at Durham By Caxton *Postmark:*
CAMBRIDGE

178. GRAY TO WHARTON

Cambridge

My dear Doct͏ʳ   Saturday, July 14. 1753.

THIS is only to tell you, that we set out on Monday-Morning,
& shall travel leisurely, not by the direct road, for we intend
to see several houses & places, as we go; on Thursday we shall
see York, & next morning as early as we can (certainly before
ten o'clock) shall hope to meet you at Studley.¹ you will understand all this with Arch-Bishop Potter's² Proviso, God willing,
& provided nothing hinder, for if we are overturn'd, & *tous
fracafsés*, or if the Mob at Leeds cut us off, as friends to Turnpikes;³ or if the Waters be out, & drown us; or (as Herodotus

¹² William Plumer was entered at Pembroke in October 1752 as a Fellow-
commoner 'sub Tutore M͏ʳᵒ Brown Praeside'.

¹³ See Letter 120, n. 2.

LETTER 178.—First printed by Mitford (1816), vol. ii, p. 238; now reprinted from original.

¹ Studley Roger and Studley Royal (with Studley Park and the ruins of
Fountains Abbey) are both a few miles SW. of Ripon, where Gray slept on
the Friday (20 July) (see Letter 179). He visited Studley again, and
Fountains Abbey, in Nov. 1762 (see Letter 363).

² John Potter (c. 1674–1747), D.D., Fellow of Lincoln College, Oxford;
Regius Professor of Divinity, 1708–37; Bishop of Oxford, 1715–37; Archbishop of Canterbury, 1737–47.

³ Tovey notes: 'Those who travelled in post-chaises would be friends to
turnpikes; for only roads maintained by turnpikes were practicable for these
vehicles.' He refers to the *Gentleman's Magazine* for this year, which gives
accounts of serious riots in Yorkshire three weeks before the date of this
letter:

'*York, June 24.* A great number of persons having assembled in a riotous
manner, in the west riding of this county, and cut down and destroy'd
several turnpike gates, and burnt the toll houses, a party of *Hawley's* regiment
of dragoons quarter'd here are march'd to suppress them' (vol. xxiii, p. 294).

'*Leeds, June 25.* This morning a message was sent to *Edwin Lascelles* E͏ˢᑫ
that the rioters concern'd in cutting down the turnpikes, intended to
demolish the turnpike bar at *Harwood-Bridge*, and pull down his house.
Accordingly, in the afternoon, about 300, armed with swords and clubs,
appeared. M͏ʳ *Lascelles* armed about 80 of his tenants and workmen,

says) if we can go no farther *for feathers*,[4] in all these cases, & many more, we may chance to fail you. my respects to Mrs Wharton, I am ever

Yours
T GRAY

Addressed: To Dr Thomas Wharton M:D: at Durham By Caxton Bag *Post-mark:* CAMBRIDGE

179. GRAY TO BROWN[1]

Durham. July 24. Tuesday [1753]

Dear S^r

WE[2] perform'd our journey, a very agreeable one, within the time appointed,[3] & left out scarce any thing worth seeing in or near our way. the Doctor & Mrs Wharton had expected us about two hours when we arrived at Studley[4] on Friday; we pafsed that night at Rippon, & the next at Richmond, and on Sunday Evening[5] got to Durham. I can not now enter into the particulars of my travels, because I have not yet gather'd up my Quotations from the Clafsicks to intersperse, like Mr Addison:[6] but I hope to be able soon to entertain you with a dish of very choice erudition. I have another reason too, wch is, that the Post is just setting out. suffice it to tell you, that I have one of the most beautiful Vales here in England to walk in with prospects that change every ten steps, & open something new wherever I turn me, all rude & romantic, in short the sweetest

resolved to defend the bar, and march'd himself on foot at the head of them, to meet the rioters. After some skirmishing, in which several were wounded on both sides, he took about 30 prisoners, of whom ten were committed to York Castle the next day.' (p. 343.)

⁴ The reference is to Herodotus, iv. 7: 'Above, to the northward of the farthest dwellers in Scythia, the country is said to be concealed from sight and made impassable by reason of the feathers which are shed abroad abundantly' (tr. Rawlinson). 'Feathers', as Herodotus explains later (iv. 31), must be interpreted as 'snow flakes'. Mitford quotes Swift's humorous application of this passage in his *Tale of a Tub* (57) to the number of authors in England.

LETTER 179.—First printed by Mitford in *Gray–Mason* (1853), pp. 13–16; now reprinted from original.

¹ See Letter 115, n. 1. Mitford gave Mason as the addressee, and corrected the error in the Appendix (p. 491) to his second edition (1855).

² He was accompanied by Stonhewer (see Letter 177).

³ See Letter 178.

⁴ See Letter 178, n. 1.   ⁵ 22 July.

⁶ In his *Remarks on Several Parts of Italy, in the Years 1701, 1702, 1703*, Lond., 1705. See Walpole's burlesque of Addison's style in Letter 17.

Spot to break your neck or drown yourself in that ever was beheld. I have done neither yet, but I have been twice at the Races,[7] once at the Aſsembly, have had a visit from Dʳ Chapman[8] & dined with the Bishop.[9] I am very shabby, for Stonhewer's Box with my Coat in it, wᶜʰ went by Sea[10] is not yet arrived. you are desired therefore to send Lee the Bedmaker at Pet: house to the Master of the Lynn-boats[11] to enquire, what Veſsel it was sent by, & why it does not come. it was directed to Dʳ Stonhewer of Houghton[12] to be left with the Rector of Sunderland. another trouble I have to give you, wᶜʰ is to order Barnes to bring any Letters Stonhewer or I may have to you, & direct 'em hither. the Doctor & Mʳˢ Wh: desire their particular Compliments to you, & are sorry you could not be with us. Adieu, I am ever Sincerely

Yours

T G:

P:S: I have left my Watch hanging (I believe) in my bed-room. will you be so good to ask after it.

Addressed: To The Revᵈ Mʳ Brown, M:A: President of Pembroke Hall Cambridge By Caxton *Postmark:* DURHAM

180. GRAY TO MASON

Dear Mason, Durham. Sept: 21. [1753][1]

IT is but a few days, since I was inform'd by Avison,[2] that the alarm you had on your sister's[3] account served but to prepare

---

[7] The race-course was near Old Elvet (see Letter 143, n. 1).

[8] The Master of Magdalene, who was a Prebendary of Durham (see Letter 135, n. 17).

[9] Dr. Richard Trevor, the 'new Bishop' (see Letter 171, n. 5).

[10] It would go by the Cam and Ouse to King's Lynn (see n. 11), and thence by sea to Sunderland.

[11] In *Cantabrigia Depicta*, under the heading of '*Stage-Waggons* and other *Carriers*' is the following notice: 'Lynn Passage-Boats, go down from hence every *Tuesday* Morning, and return on *Sundays*.'

[12] Houghton-le-Spring is about five miles SW. of Sunderland (see n. 10).

LETTER 180.—First printed in part (in a garbled text) in Mason's *Memoirs*, p. 229; first printed in full by Mitford in *Gray–Mason* (1853), pp. 16–17; now reprinted from original.

[1] The date of the year was inserted by Mason.

[2] Charles Avison (c. 1710–70), musician, of Newcastle, where in 1736 he was appointed organist of St. Nicholas's Church, a post which he held till his death. For many years he was the chief of a small circle of musical amateurs in the north of England, among whom was Mason, and he seems

you for a greater Lofs,[4] wch was soon to follow. I know, what it is to lose a Person,[5] that one's eyes & heart have long been used to, & I never desire to part with the remembrance of that lofs, nor would wish you should. it is something, that you had a little time to acquaint yourself with the Idea beforehand (if I am inform'd right) & that He probably suffer'd but little pain, the only thing that makes death terrible.

It will now no longer be proper for me to see you at Hull[6] as I should otherwise have tried to do. I shall go therefore to York with intention to make use of the Stage-Coach either on Friday or Monday.[7] I shall be a week at Cambridge,[8] & then pafs thro' London into Buckinghamshire. if I can be of any use to you in any thing it will give me great pleasure. let me have a line from you soon, for I am very affectionately

Yours
T. GRAY

181. MASON TO GRAY

Dear Mr. Gray,

YOU have been rightly informd that I have lost a most affectionate Father. I have felt for him, all that a heart not naturally hard, & at the time already softend by preceeding anxiety could feel. But my Greifs rest not on him alone, only last tuesday my most intimate friend Dr Pricket[1] followd him, a Man who

to have been a friend of Wharton's (see Letter 184). In 1752 he published his *Essay on Musical Expression*, to which Mason contributed a note on the difference between ancient and modern music. (Mason, *Works*, 1811, vol. iii, p. 396.) For Avison's collaboration with Garth in the English version of Marcello's *Psalms*, see Letter 195, n. 10.

  [3] His half-sister Anne, then a child.
  [4] His father, Rev. William Mason, Vicar of Holy Trinity, Kingston-upon-Hull, 1722–53, had died, as Mason records, a few weeks before, on 26 Aug. (See 'Dates of the principal events relative to myself', printed from Mason's MS., in *Hurd–Mason Correspondence*, p. xxx.)
  [5] His own mother.   [6] Mason's home (see n. 4).
  [7] That is, Friday, 28 Sept., or Monday, 1 Oct. (see PS. to Letter 182).
  [8] In the event he only stayed a single day at Cambridge, being called to Stoke by the news of the illness of his aunt, Mrs. Rogers (see Letter 183).
  LETTER 181.—First printed by Mitford in *Gray–Mason* (1853), pp. 18–21; now reprinted from original.
  [1] Dr. Marmaduke Pricket, a young Physician of my own age, with whom I was brought up from infancy, who died of the same infectious fever [as my Father]. *Mason.*—Marmaduke Prickett, who was born at Hull in 1724, where he subsequently practised as a physician, was admitted as a pensioner at Trinity College, Cambridge, 1742; Scholar, 1743; M.B. 1748; admitted at Leyden, 1749; died 18 Sept. 1753.

I assure you had more good Qualities of the Heart, than the brightest of the Head could outballance either in mine or your estimation, we were brought up together from infancy & ever livd in the sincerest affection; in my long illness at London he attended me with a Care and assiduity almost unparralelld. I endeavord to repay that Care in my turn but alas his Fate did not give me time to discharge half the debt, yet what I could, I did.

O Mr Gray how dreadful is it to sit besides a Dying Friend! to see as I did, reason withdraw herself gradually, often return by starts, to a Memory evry Minute less capable of furnishing her with Ideas, and a tongue less able to give them utterance. I talk nonsence I beleive, but let me do it, it gives me some relief, what makes his Loss to me more deplorable is, that I am afraid either the Physician who constantly attended him mistook his Case, or that the other who was calld in afterwards hastend his End, for a sudden change ensued the alteration of his medicines. But I will check myself till I see you and then you must bear with me, if I am even a Child or a Woman in my complainings. I must add however that in a Will he made five year ago his Friendship bequeathd to me two hundred pounds wch when my Debt is dischargd to his executor will be reducd to one, yet the sum will come at present as oportunly as any thing of the kind possibly could, as My Father by the Strangest disposition of his affairs that can be conceivd has left all my paternal estate to my Mother in Law[2] for her life and entaild it so on my little sister, that I can take up no Money upon it, so that without this Legacy I should not have had a Shilling at present. I beleive I shall be obligd to take a journey to Mr. Huttons[3] near Richmond and may perhaps be at York next

---

[2] Here, as often in the eighteenth century and earlier, in the sense of stepmother. Sarah Mason, Mason's own mother, died within a year of his birth.

[3] In his 'Dates of the principal events relative to myself' (see Letter 180, n. 4), Mason records: 'John Hutton Esq. of Marske, near Richmond Yorkshire, died Jan^ry 12th 1768 by whose death an estate in the East Riding came to me in reversion.†' This John Hutton married as his second wife in 1726 Elizabeth, daughter of James D'Arcy, first Baron D'Arcy, of Navan, co. Meath, of the same family as Lord Holdernesse, through which marriage Mason was a distant connexion of the latter.

Mason also records (*loc. cit.*): 'Arch Bishop Hutton gave me the Prebend of Holme in the Church of York Dec. 6th 1756.' Matthew Hutton (1693–

---

† Probably from the family of Hutton's first wife, Barbara Barker, who was a distant cousin of Mason's.

sunday,[4] but this is so exceedingly uncertain that I only just name it but would not have you alter your schemes upon it for the sake of a meeting. Because my Mother is at present in a fever with three blisters but I hope on the recovery, yet I cannot leave her till there appears a greater certainty. Tom[5] has been also in a feavor and got out only to day, therefore I dont know whether he'll be in a condition to travel, and I cant easily relinquish the pomp of travelling with a Servt all on a sudden; and my Father's Servt, a Lad of the same age, died the week after his Master of a Fever also. from all this you may guess what a time I have gone thro lately. yet I am well myself at present except that my hands tremble, and my spiritts often, very often sink. yet have they supported me hitherto suppprizingly. Pray tell Mr Brown when you see him that I fear I cannot be up at College by the tenth of October,[6] yet I shall get there as soon as ever I can make any end of my perplext [affairs][7] here. I wish you had told me how long you would stay in Buckinghamshire I hope it will be short, and that we may meet again at Cambridge soon. adieu. My best complm^{ts} to Dr Wharton. I am Dr Sir

yours with sincerity and affection

W. Mason.

Hull Sept. 23^d—53

Do write to me again very soon.

Addressed: To Thomas Gray Esquire at Dr Whartons in Durham

182. Gray to Mason

My dear Mason,

I HAVE just received your Letter, & am both surprized, & angry (if you will suffer me to say so) at the weaknefs of your father. perhaps I ought not to use such words to a person, whose

---

1758), successively Bishop of Bangor, 1743–7; Archbishop of York, 1747–57; and of Canterbury, 1757–8, was the younger brother of the above John Hutton.   [4] 30 Sept.

[5] His servant, possibly the 'Tom' mentioned eight years later (see Letter 351).

[6] '*October-Term* begins *October* the 10th, divides *November* the 13th, and ends *December* the 16th' (Carter, *Hist. Univ. Camb.*, p. 10).

[7] MS. torn; text supplied by Mitford.

Letter 182.—First printed in part (in a garbled text) in Mason's *Memoirs*, pp. 229–30; first printed in full by Mitford in *Gray–Mason* (1853), pp. 21–3; now reprinted from original.

affliction for him is perhaps heighthen'd by that very weaknefs, for I know, it is pofsible to feel an additional sorrow for the faults of those we have loved, even where that fault has been greatly injurious to ourselves. this is certain, he has been (whether from his illnefs, or some other cause) at least guilty of a great weaknefs; & it is as sure, that there must have been a great fault somewhere, probably in the Person[1] who took advantage of his weaknefs, upon whom your care & kindnefs is very ill-bestow'd. tho' you do not at present shew any resentment, nor perhaps ever will; at least let me desire you not to expose yourself to any farther danger in the midst of that scene of sicknefs & death, but withdraw as soon as pofsible to some place at a little distance in the country, for I do not at all like the place you are in. I do not attempt to console you on the situation your fortune is left in. if it were far worse; the good opinion I have of you tells me, you will never the sooner do anything mean or unworthy of yourself, & consequently I can not pity you on this account. but I sincerely do so on the new lofs you have had of a good & friendly Man, whose Memory I honour. may I remind you, how, like a Simpleton, I used to talk about him? it is foolish to mention it; but it feels I don't know how like a sort of guilt in me: tho' I believe you knew, I could not mean any thing by it. I have seen, what you describe, & know how dreadful it is; I know too, I am the better for it. we are all idle & thoughtlefs things, & have no sense, no use in the world any longer than that sad imprefsion lasts, the deeper it is engraved, the better. I am forced to break off by the Post. Adieu, my dear S^r, I am ever yours,

T G:

P:S: I shall be at York on Sunday[2] at the Place the Stage-Coach goes from, having a place taken for Monday. pray remember James's Powder;[3] I have great faith in its efficacy,

---

[1] Presumably Gray meant Mason's step-mother.
[2] 30 Sept.
[3] This powder, which had a great vogue at this time, had been patented in 1746 by Robert James, M.D., the author of a *Medicinal Dictionary* published in 1743, the dedication of which to Dr. Mead was written by his friend, Dr. Johnson, who also contributed to the work. The powder, which was recommended by the patentee for use 'in acute continual *Fevers*, the *Small-Pox, Measles, Acute Rheumatisms, Colds, Headach*, and all *Inflammatory Diseases*', was made up in packets, each containing six powders, three for use in the morning, and three for night. The price was 2*s*. 6*d*. a packet, the

& should take it myself. here is a malignant Fever in the town.

Sept: 26. Durham [1753]

183. GRAY TO WHARTON

Oct: 18. Stoke. [1753]

My dear Doctor

YOU will wonder not to have heard sooner of me. the reason has been the instability of my own situation. as soon as I arrived at Cambridge,¹ I found a letter informing me my Aunt Rogers had had a stroke of the Palsy, so that I stay'd only a single day,² & set out for this place. I found her recover'd surprisingly from the greatest danger. her speech only is not yet quite restored; but it is easily intelligible to such as are used to her. is not this something extraordinary at seventy seven?³

I met Mason at York, & pafs'd that evening⁴ with him.* * * ⁵ he has absolutely no support at present but his fellowship; yet he looks more like a Hero, than ever I knew him, like one that can stare poverty in the face without being frighted, & instead of growing little & humble before her, has fortified his Spirit & elevated his brow to meet her like a Man. in short if he can hold it, I shall admire him, for I always maintain'd, that no body has occasion for Pride but the Poor, & that every where else it is a sign of folly. my journey was not so bad as usual in a Stage-Coach. there was a Lady Swinburne,⁶

sole authorized agents for its sale, being the owners of the patents, John and Francis Newbery (father and son), the publishers in St. Paul's Churchyard. (See *The Times*, 24, 28, 30 Dec. 1929.)

LETTER 183.—First printed by Mitford (1816), vol. ii, pp. 239–42; now reprinted from original.

¹ On 3 Oct. He left York on Monday 1 Oct. (see PS. to Letter 182), and, as he says below, left Stilton on the third day, and got to Cambridge that night.

² He had intended to stay a week (see Letter 180).

³ She survived until September 1758.

⁴ 30 Sept. (see PS. to Letter 182).

⁵ A piece, containing two words in one line and the two lines following, has been cut out, carrying with it the text on the other side (see n. 11). 'has' and 'great' begin the two lines that are missing.

⁶ This was the widow of Sir John Swinburne, third Baronet (1716), of Capheaton, co. Northumberland, to whom she was married in 1721, and who died in 1745. She was Mary, only daughter of Edward Bedingfield, of Gray's Inn, Barrister-at-law, youngest son of Sir Henry Bedingfield, first Baronet,

a Roman-Catholick, not young, that had been much abroad, seen a great deal, knew a great many people, very chatty & communicative, so that I pafs'd my time very well; & on the third day left them at Stilton, & got to Cambridge that night. as I know, & have heard mighty little to entertain you with, I can only tell you my observations on the face of the Country & the Season in my way hither, that you may compare them with what you see at Durham. till I came to York I thought the face of every thing rather alter'd for the worse, certainly not better than that corner of the Bishoprick about Darlington. at Topcliff[7] I saw a large Vine full of black Grapes, that seemd ripe. at Helperby[8] met a flock of Geese *in full song.* if their person had not betray'd them, one might have taken them for Nightingales. at York Walnuts ripe, 20 for a penny. from thence, especially South of Tadcaster, I thought the Country extremely beautiful, broke into fine hills cover'd with noble woods, (particularly toward the East) & every thing as verdant almost, as at Midsummer. this continued to Doncaster; the Hazle & White-thorn were turning yellow in the hedges, the Sycamore, Lime, & Ash (where it was young, or much exposed) were growing rusty, but far greener than in your County. The old Ash, the Oak, & other Timber shew'd no signs of winter. some few of the Lands were in stubble, but for the most part they were plough'd up, or cover'd with Turneps. I find Mr Evelyn in his book of Forest-trees[9] publish'd in Q: Anne's time takes notice 'That Shropshire & several other Counties, and rarely any beyond Stamford to Durham, have the Vernacula, (or French Elm) or the Mountain-Elm, (wch is what you call the English Elm,) growing for many miles together.' I cannot say I saw any, but about Scrubey[10] in Nottinghamshire,

of Oxburgh, co. Norfolk, and brother of the second Baronet (also Sir Henry), by Mary, youngest sister of Sir Clement Fisher, third Baronet, of Great Parkington, co. Warwick. She had four sons, and seven daughters, of whom the third, Mary, became the wife in 1754 of Gray's friend and correspondent, Edward Bedingfield (see Letter 210, n. 1). See Genealogical Table.

[7] Gray (who may have travelled by post-chaise from Durham to York) followed the main road as far as Topcliffe (twelve miles from Northallerton.)

[8] From Topcliffe he went about four miles to Helperby, and from there must have taken some by-road to join the road from Easingwold to York.

[9] John Evelyn (1620–1706) published his *Sylva; or a Discourse of Forest Trees and the Propagation of Timber* in 1664, it being the first book printed by order of the Royal Society. Gray quotes from the edition published in 1706 (p. 48).

[10] Scrooby, about two miles S. of Bawtry on the Yorkshire border.

& they were young ones newly planted near a hedge-row. he also mentions 'the Elm of a more scabrous Leaf, harsh, & very large, w^{ch}   *   *   *   *   *   *
*   *   *   *   for my part,   *
*   o sort   *¹¹   at least of any size, or growing in a wild way, till I came into Northamptonshire. I thought the winter more advanced in Lincolnshire, & so on, till I had pafs'd Huntingdon, than it was in the W: Riding of Yorkshire. in Northamptonshire I first observed the appearances of a long drougth, wch continued quite hither. the Turf is every where brown & burnt up, as in Italy, even the low Meadows want their usual verdure. at Cambridge the finest Grapes I ever saw there; the Lime-trees were only changing colour, but had drop'd few of their leaves. in the smoke of London they had almost lost their old leaves, but made fresh shoots, as green as in April. & here before my window are two young Sycamores, wch have done the same, but still retain all their old leaves too without any change of colour. at Trompington the new Rye was green in the fields, & three inches high. it is the same in this County. we are here upon a Loam with a bed of Gravel below, & Rag-stone beneath that. the Hay is usually all in by old Midsummer this year it was all cut by new Mids:^r,¹² but a great deal of it lost for want of rain, wch likewise spoil'd the Tares & Peas. in the beginning of August was rain for near three weeks, wch saved the Corn. Oats were in some places cut before the wheat, wch was all got in by the 20th of August. Barley, Beans, &c; by the 7th of Septr. I came hither the 6th of October, & they had then within a mile of the Thames (where the soil is better, than here) begun to sow wheat. for six weeks before my arrival it had been continued fine weather, & the air till Sunset was like July. never almost was such a year known for fruit. the Nectarines & best Peaches had been all gather'd three weeks before. the Grapes were then perfectly ripe, & still continue the best I ever eat in England. Oct: 9th it began to rain, & we have had showers every day since, with brisk winds in the S: & S:W:; today it is in the North, clear sunshine, but cold & a little wintry: & so ends

¹¹ Piece cut out (see n. 5). The passage from Evelyn's *Sylva*, p. 46 (see n. 9) which Gray presumably transcribed continues: 'becomes a huge tree mentioned in the Statute-Books under the name of the Wych-Hasel.' After this Mitford restored: 'for my part [I could find n]o sort [but the last].'

¹² That is, eleven days later, that being the difference between O.S. and N.S. in the eighteenth century.

my Georgick in prose. excuse me, if I had nothing better to send you. it is partly from my own eyesight, & partly from the report of such as have no prejudices in favour of their county, because they hardly know, there is any other.

I write chiefly to draw on a letter from you, for I am impatient to know many things; but remember, this election time[13] letters are apt to be open'd at the offices. pray, make my sincere acknowledgements to my *kind Hostefs:* I trust, she was not the worse for her journey. I hope, you know, that I am ever

Yours
T G:

P:S: Every thing resounds with the Wood-Lark, & Robin; & the voice of the Sparrow is heard in our land. remember me to all, that remember there is such a person. Adieu!
At Mrs Rogers's of Stoke near Windsor, Bucks

Addressed: To Dr Thomas Wharton, M:D: at Durham *Postmark:* 19 oc

184. GRAY TO MASON

Stoke—Nov: 5 [1753.][1]

My dear Mason,

I AM not in a way of leaving this place yet this fortnight, & consequently shall hardly see you in town. I rejoice in the mean time to think, that you are there, & have left (I hope) a part of your disagreable reflections in the place, where they grew. Stoke has revived in me the memory of many a melancholy hour, that I have pafs'd in it,[2] & tho' I have no longer the same cause for anxiety, I do not find myself at all the happier for thinking, that I have lost it. as my thoughts now signify nothing to any one, but myself, I shall wish to change the scene, as soon as ever I can.

I am heartily glad to hear Mr Hutton[3] is so reasonable, but

---

[13] 'All England is gone over all England electioneering', writes Walpole to Mann on 21 July 1753. The Parliament of 1747 was drawing near its term, and the constituencies were busy preparing for the dissolution, which took place at the beginning of April.

LETTER 184.—First printed by Mitford in *Gray–Mason* (1853), pp. 23–5; now reprinted from original.

[1] Date of year inserted by Mason.

[2] At the time of his mother's illness and death (see Letters 168 and 176).

[3] See Letter 181, n. 3.

am rather sorry to find that design⁴ is known to so many. Dʳ Wharton, who (I suppose) heard it from Avison,⁵ mentions it in a letter to me. were I you, I should have taken some pleasure in observing people's faces, & perhaps in putting their kindnefs a little to the tryal. it is a very useful experiment; & very pofsibly you will never have it in your power to put it in practise again. pray, make your bargain with all the circumspection, & selfishnefs of an old Hunks; when you are grown as rich as Crœsus, do not grow too good-for-nothing. a little good-for-nothing to be sure you will grow: every body does in proportion to their circumstances, else indeed what should one do with one's money? my third *Sentence* is, don't anticipate your revenues, & live upon air, till you know what you are worth. you bid me write no more than a scrall to you, therefore I will trouble you, as you are so busy, with nothing more. Adieu!
I am very sincerely & affectionately

Yours

turn over T G:

I should be obliged to you, if you had time to ask at Roberts's,⁶ or some place in Jermyn-street, whether I could be there about a fortnight hence. I won't give more than ½ a guinea a week, nor put up with a second floor, unlefs it has a tolerable room to the street. will you acquaint me of this?

Addressed: To William Mason Esqʳᵉ, at Mʳ Rowland Hosier's in Panton Square near the Haymarket London *Postmark:* 6 NO

⁴ This may refer to a proposal, due to Hutton (see Letter 181, n. 3), who was a connexion of both parties, that Mason should become private secretary to Lord Holdernesse, at this time Secretary of State for the Southern Department. Mason appears to have held this post for a time at the beginning of 1754; he was absent from Cambridge from about the middle of January till towards the end of March; and Walpole writes to Bentley on 6 March 1754 (the day of the Prime Minister, Henry Pelham's death): 'Lord Holdernesse . . . had but just taken Mʳ Mason the poet into his house to write his deserts'. Further confirmation is supplied by a remark of Mason printed in the *Harcourt Papers* (vol. vii, p. 191): 'I remember when first I went from Cambridge into Lord Holdernesse's family, Gray who went up to town in the same stage coach, told people in London "that he was come to put Mason apprentice to a Secretary of State"'.

⁵ See Letter 180, n. 2.
⁶ See Letter 176, n. 3.

184*. GRAY TO BROCKETT[1]

[c. 1754][2]

MR GRAY sends his Compliments to Mr Brocket. shall be extremely obliged to him, if he would make inquiry (when he has occasion to go into: Trin: Library) after the following old English Books

Paradise of dainty Devices. 1578. 4to & 1585
England's Helicon . . . . 4to
W: Webbe's Discourse of Eng. Poetrie. 1585. 4to
Fr: Meres[3] Wit's Commonwealth 1598 Lond: & 1634
Sam: Daniel's Musa or Defence of Rhyme 16[11.] [8]^vo3
Steph: Hawes Pastime of Pleasure 1555. 4[^to]3
Gawen Douglas' Palace of Honour 1553 Lond: [15]79 Ed[in:][3]
Earl of Surrey's Ecclesiastes 1567 4to
——————————— 2^d & 4th Books of the Æneid. 1557. 12mo
Gascoign's Works. 2 V: 4to. 1577. & 1587

If they should not be in the Library, Mr Gray believes that Professor Torriano[4] could favour him with a sight of some of them for a few days. he will take all imaginable care of them.

185. GRAY TO WALPOLE

Dear S^r   Friday [Feb. 15. 1754][1] . . . Cambridge

I SEND you my Story,[2] that you may not wait longer for it, tho' it does not at all satisfy me, but I do not know how to make it intelligible in fewer words.

LETTER 184*.—First printed in Tovey's *Gray and his Friends*, pp. 190–1; now reprinted from original. It was folded as a note and presumably sent by hand.   [1] See Letter 149, n. 7.

[2] Date conjectural; the reference to Professor Torriano (see n. 4), who was elected Regius Professor of Hebrew in 1753, in succession to Thomas Harrison (d. 3 July 1753), and resigned his Professorship 20 Oct. 1757, gives the limits within which the letter can be dated. As Gray's *Progress of Poesy* (in the notes to ll. 69 ff. of which he mentions Surrey) was in course of composition during 1754, and was completed by the end of this year (see Letter 194), this request for the loan of Surrey's works and of other contemporary poets may well have been made sometime in 1754.

[3] MS. damaged by damp; text restored conjecturally.

[4] Charles Torriano, of Trinity; Scholar, 1746; B.A. 1749; M.A. 1752; Fellow, 1751; Regius Professor of Hebrew, 1753–7; Rector of Chingford, Essex, 1757; d. c. 1778.

LETTER 185.—First printed by Toynbee (1915), No. 185.

[1] The date has been inserted in the original by Walpole; that of the month is supplied by the postmark, that of the year by reference to the next letter (see n. 6), which is dated in full.

Bianca Capello,[3]

Veneta, adolescenti nupsit nobili Florentino, quem ideó a patre domo expulsum uxor suâ operâ[4] diú sustentabat, donec Franciscus Mediceus M: Hetruriæ Dux, mulieris formâ captus eam in aulam perduxit, maritum ad summos honores extulit, qui potestate insolentér usus cum sæpe in crimina incurrifset, sæpé conjugis gratiâ (quam tamén asperiús tractaverat) supplicium effugifset, novifsimé suâ manu hominem confodit. Biancâ Ducis clementiam implorante, juravit Franc:[cus] se de marito pœnas non sumpturum, sed nec de illis, qui eum ipsum occidifsent. quo audito, vir ab inimicis interfectus est. viduam Franciscus justum in matrimonium duxit. hos ambos uno in convivio Ferdinandus Cardinalis, Fr:[ci] frater, veneno sustulit, ipse deinceps Hetruriæ Dux, cognomento Maximus.

I am collecting what I can about the two Marriages[5] & will send it you next week,[6] tho' I find the Chronicles of latter times do little more than copy Fabian.[7] they are excellent writers, & I thank you for bringing us acquainted. I am ever

Yours
T G:

Addressed: To The Honble Horace Walpole Esq in Arlington Street London
Postmark: ROYSTON 16 FE

186. GRAY TO WALPOLE

[Cambridge] March 3^d 1754.

YOU are to dispatch forthwith an Exprefs to Angers to fetch the windows of St Bonaventure's Chappel in the Church of

---

² Walpole had asked Gray to supply him with a brief account in Latin of Bianca Capello, for his picture of her by Vasari (see his letter to Mann of 28 Jan. 1754), which in the *Description of Strawberry Hill* is said to have been 'bought out of the Vitelli palace at Florence by sir Horace Mann, and sent to Mr Walpole' (*Works of Lord Orford*, vol. ii, p. 469). Bianca's story, 'written in a cartouche on the frame', is there given in English, which, however, is obviously based on the Latin version supplied by Gray in this letter.

³ A Venetian (d. 1587), who was first the mistress, and subsequently the wife, of the Grand-Duke Francis I of Tuscany.

⁴ Gray wrote first, 'suis laboribus'.

⁵ Of Henry VI and Henry VII (see next letter).

⁶ Actually, in the letter of 3 March.

⁷ Robert Fabyan (d. 1513), author of a Chronicle from the time of the arrival of Brutus in England down to the death of Henry VII. It was first printed by Pynson in 1516.

LETTER 186.—First printed by Toynbee (1915), No. 186. On the

the Cordeliers there; in them are painted Margaret of Anjou herself kneeling; her Mother Isabella, Dutchefs of Lorraine, first Wife of René, K: of Sicily; Joan de la Val, his second wife; Yolande, his eldest daughter, also D:ᶠˢ of Lorraine; & John, Duke of Calabria, his eldest Son. these are not mobbled Queens¹ upon a tomb, but fair & flourishing figures with entire faces: the hair of the four Women is dishevel'd below their girdle, wᶜʰ one would think was a fashion peculiar to them, for no other cotemporary Lady have I ever seen, that did not wear hers trufsed up & plaited, or quite hid. to stay your stomach till the return of the Courier, you may see them all in Montfaucon's Antiquities, (Tom: 3. Plates 47, & 63.) I think you have the Book, & pray observe, if the Mother does not resemble that figure in the Picture² with the large sleeves & hair at length on the foreground. now for the time, place, & circumstances of the marriage, here begins Wyllyam Wyrcester³ (p. 462.) 'A:D: 1444, & anno Regis Hen: 6ᵗⁱ 23°, Rex accepit in uxorem dominam juvenem, filiam Regis Neapolis, Ceciliæ, & Jerusalem, quæ desponsata erat in abbaciâ de Tycchefield in Comitatu Suthampton . . A:D: 1445. Coronacio uxoris Henr: 6ᵗⁱ apud Westmonast:ᵐ 30ᵐᵒ Maii.' next comes Mʳ Alderman Fabian.⁴ 'A:D: 1444. the Marquefs of Suffolke soon after with his wyfe & other honourable Personages as well of men as of women with great Apparayll of chayris and other costious ordenaunce for to convey the forenamed Lady Margerete into Englande sayled into Fraunce, & so tarryed there all this Mayres year . . A:D: 1445. This 23ᵈ Year (of Henry 6ᵗʰ) & monthe of . . . the

original has been written in pencil, 'Containing large quotations relative to the subject of the historic doubts'; but this is an error, for Walpole did not begin his *Historic Doubts on Richard the Third* until the winter of 1767 (see *Short Notes*, under 1 Feb. 1768). The extracts in fact relate to the marriages of Henry VI and Henry VII, about which Walpole was anxious for information in order to identify the personages in two pictures of these subjects which he had recently acquired (see nn. 2, 23).

¹ *Hamlet*, ii. 2.

² This was 'an ancient and valuable piece, representing the marriage of Henry VI', which afterwards hung 'over the chimney' in the Library at Strawberry Hill. This picture, which is in possession of the Duke of Sutherland, is figured and described in the second chapter of Walpole's *Anecdotes of Painting in England* (see *Works of Lord Orford*, vol. iii, pp. 37–9).

³ William of Wyrcester or Worcester (c. 1415–82), author of *Annales Rerum Anglicarum*. It was first printed by Hearne in 1728.

⁴ See Letter 185, n. 7. He was Alderman of the Ward of Farringdon Without.

foresayd Lady Margerete came over into Englande, & in the monthe of . . . following she was maryed at a towne called Southwyke in the countre of Hamshyre, and from thence she was convey'd by the Lordes & Estates of this Lande, wch mette with her in sundry places with great retynewe of men in sundry Lyveryes with their slevys browderyd & some betyn with goldsmythe's werkes in most costly maner, & specyally (of) the D: of Glouceter mette with her with 500 Men in one lyverye, & so was convey'd unto Blackhethe, where upon the 18th of Maye she was mette with the Mayer, Ald:^{n} & Sheryffes of the Citie & the Craftes of the same in *Browne* blew with brawderyd slevys, that is to meane, every maister or crafte with the conysaunce of his *maister* (read, *mystery*) & red hoodes upon eyther of their heddes, and so the same day brought her unto London, where for her were ordeyned sumptuous & costly Pagentes & resemblaunce of dyverse old hystorics to the great comfort of her & such as came with her—& so with great triumphe she was brought unto Westminstre, where upon the 30th of May, the day after Trinitie Sonday she was solemply crowned.' (fol: 199.) As to Grafton,[5] Hall,[6] Speed,[7] Hollingshed,[8] & other Chroniclers[8a] of Q: Eliz:^{s} time I transcribe nothing from them, because they add nothing new to Fabian's account, indeed only copy him, or one another: Stow[9] only, as he is more particular, I shall make use of. 'This noble Company (Ld Suffolk, & others not named) came to the City of Towers in Touraine, where they were honourably received & entertain'd both of the 'French King & Duke Reiner, where the Marquefs of Suffolke, as Procurator to K: Henry, espoused the said Lady in the Church of St Martin. at wch marriage were present the Father & Mother of the Bride, the French King who was[10] Uncle to

---

[5] Richard Grafton (d. c. 1572), author of an *Abridgement of the Chronicles of England* (1562), and of a *Chronicle at Large* (1568).

[6] Edward Hall (d. 1547), author of the *Union of the Noble and Illustre Famelies of Lancastre and York* (1542).

[7] John Speed (c. 1552–1629), author of the *History of Great Britaine* (1611).

[8] Raphael Holinshed (d. c. 1580), author of *Chronicles of England, Scotland and Ireland* (1578).

[8a] In the Pembroke College Library Register Gray's name is entered as borrowing in Jan. and Feb. 1754, Strype's *Annals*, Wood's *Institutes*, and Rymer's *Fœdera*.

[9] John Stow (c. 1525–1605), author of a *Summarie of Englyshe Chronicles* (1565), and of the *Chronicles of England* (1580).

[10] This is a mistake: he was indeed Uncle to K: Henry 6th, but Cousin only to René, K: of Sicily, &c. *Gray*.

Duke Reiner, & the French Queen[11] Aunt to the Dutchefs his Wife. also the Dukes of Orleans,[12] of Calabre,[13] of Alanson[14] & of Brytaine,[15] 7 Earls, 12 Barons, 20 Bishops, besides Knights & Gentlemen, when the feast, triumphs, banquets, & justs were ended, the Lady was deliver'd to ye Marquefs of Suffolk, wch in great estate conveied her thorow Normandy unto Diepe, where awhile they remained. the Lady, being transported from Diepe, landed at Portchester, from whence she was conveyed by water to Hampton, & rested there in a place call'd Gods-House;[16] from thence she went to Southwicke,[17] & was married to the King in the Abbey of Tichfield[18] on the 22^d of April &c:'

Now you are to determine whether the Picture represent the marriage at Tours, (wch may be; & yet Henry 6th may be introduced, tho' not there in person). this must be the case, if one of those women be the Queen of Sicily, for neither she, nor any of the family accompanied Margaret to England. they took leave of her at Bar-le-Duc with abundance of tears, & at Rouen she was consign'd to her English attendants, who made their entry with great pomp into that city. I can tell you exactly, who they were, & what they did there. shall I? if it is nothing to your purpose, you may pafs it over.

'Le Roy Henry envoya plusieurs Seigneurs & Dames de son pays au dit lieu de Rouën fort hautement & richement habilléz, c'est a scavoir le Duc d'Jorcq, le Comte de Suffort, le Seigneur de Tallebot, le Marquis de Susalby, (Salisbury) le Seigneur de Clif (Ld Clifford) le Baron de Gruisot, Mefsires Jamet d'Ormont,

[11] Another mistake. she was René's own Sister, & Aunt to the Bride. *Gray.*
[12] Charles, who had been prisoner 25 years in England, & return'd home about four years before this marriage. *Gray.*
[13] Brother to the Bride. *Gray.*
[14] John, the 2^d of the name. *Gray.*
[15] Francis, first of the name. he had married Margaret's Aunt. *Gray.*
[16] An Hospital for poor folkes at Southampton. (Leland. V: 3. p. 92.) *Gray.* —Gray's references are to Hearne's edition of Leland's *Itinerary.* John Leland in 1533 was appointed 'King's antiquary', an office created for him. In the same year a commission was granted to him to search for English antiquities in the libraries of all cathedrals, abbeys, colleges, &c.
[17] It is a good big thoroughfare, but no celebrate market. the fame of it stood by the Priory of the black Chanons there, & a pilgrimage to our Lady. (Leland. ib: p. 98.) *Gray.*
[18] It was a monastery of Premontrés, founded by Henry 3^d, given at the reformation to Mr Wriothesley, who pull'd it down, & built a right stately house there. (Leland, p. 95.) *Gray.*

Jean Bolledit, Guil: Bonnechille, Rich: Rios, Jean Secalay, Ed: Hoult, Rob: de Willeby, Rob: de Harcourt, & plusieurs autres Chevaliers & Ecuyers de grand etat. au regard des Dames y estoient la Comtefse de Suffort, la Dame de Talbot, la Dame de Salsebery, la Dame Marguerite Hoult, & autres en grand nombre. il y avoit aufsi des chariots couverts & plusieurs haquenées houfsées de si riches habillemens, que peu avoient eté veus de pareils, venans du susdit royaume d'Angleterre; sur tout a leur entrée de Rouën, ou ils pouvoient bien etre 1500 chevaux. or faut il declarer la maniere comment les Seign:^{rs} & Dames devant dits & leurs gens entrerent en bel ordre en ladite ville. premierement pour l'Estat de la Reyne y estoient les premiers entrans les defsus nommez (here he names all the Men again, but the 3 first) & avec eux Mefsire Huy Coquesin, lesquels tous en leur compagnie avoient quelque 400 Archers pour l'estat de la maison d'icelle Reyne, tous vestus d'une meme parure de gris. aprés lesquels suivoient les Ecuyers & Officiers d'icelui Estat; & outre ce il y avoit avec les defsusdits 200 Archers de la grande Garde du Roi d'Angleterre, portans ses couleurs & livrées, c'est a scavoir, sur chacune de leurs manches une couronne d'or, lesquels estoient trés richement habillez: aprés les Chevaliers defsusdits venoient 6 Pages montéz sur six haquenées, richement vestus de robes & de chaperons noirs, chargez d'orfevrerie d'argent doré, qui estoient tous fils de Chevaliers; & menoit le premier Page par la main une haquenée de son costé dextre, que ledit Roy d'Anglet:^{e} envoyoit a la Reyne sa femme, ornée d'une selle & de paremens, tels que le tout en estoit de fin or, & les paremens des autres haquenées estoient tous d'argent doré. aprés suivoit le chariot, que le dit Roy lui envoyoit, lequel estoit le plus richement orné & paré que depuis trés long tems il n'en estoit party du Royaume d'Ang:^{re} un pareil; car il estoit couvert d'un trés riche drap d'or, & armoyé des armes de France & d'Angleterre: lequel chariot estoit tiré par 6 chevaux blancs de grand prix, & estoit icelui chariot figuré par dedans & dehors de plusieurs & diverses couleurs, dans lequel estoient la Comtefse de Suffort, les Dames de Talbot, & de Salsebery, & estoit ladite Comtefse en l'estat de la Reyne pareil au jour qu'elle espousa. les autres dames ensuivans de degré en degré venoient aprés ce chariot montées sur haquenées. au plus prés d'icelui chariot estoit le Duc d'Jorcq d'un costé, & le S^{gr} de Talbot de l'autre, tenant maniere et contenance, comme si la Reyne eust eté dedans. le Comte de Suffort alloit chevauchant devant le chariot representant la personne du Roy d'Ang:ʳʳᵉ, & aprés luy il y avoit 36 tant chevaux qu'haquenées de grand parage tous houfséz de vermeil armoyé de ses armes. aprés icelui chariot il y avoit encore 5 chevaux richement ornéz, dont 2 estoient couverts de velours vermeil battu à or, seméz de roses d'or dedans, & les autres estoient couverts de drap de damas cramoisy. aprés tout ce que dit est, venoit encore un chariot richement orné, dedans lequel estoient la Dame de Talbot la jeune, la Dame Marg:ᵉ Hoult, & autres, lesquelles estoient toutes ordonnées & destinées pour recevoir icelle nouvelle Reyne d'Angleterre.' (Matth:ᵘ de Coucy;[19] a Cotemp:ʳʸ p. 553).

Out of these, if the Scene of the Picture lies in England, you may pick & chuse; for it is likely they all waited upon her to Southwick. I am sorry Duke Humphrey could not be there, but you see he did not meet her till after the marriage in her way to London. much lefs could his Wife Jaqueline appear, as that marriage was set aside 18 years before: indeed his Dutchefs Eleanor Cobham was now in prison, & had been so (in spite of Shakespear[20]) 3 or 4 years, before Margaret came over. the Cardinal Beaufort, then at least 70 years old, one would think should have the honour of joining their hands, especially in his own Diocese; but I recollect no marks of a Cardinal, & what I take for the Pallium, wᶜʰ he holds over their hands, is (I believe) peculiar to Archbishops: so it may be John Stafford, Archb:ᵖ of Canterbury, who certainly crown'd her the next month. I could tell you many small particulars, as the name of the Ship she came over in, wᶜʰ was *Coq Johan de Charburgh*; Thomas Adams, Master. the Ring she was married with, wᶜʰ was a *fair Ruby, sometime yeven unto us* (says the King) *by our bel Oncle the Cardinal of Englande, with the wᶜʰ we were sacred in the day of our Coronacion at Parys, & wᶜʰ was broke, thereof to make another ring for the Quene's wedding.* the Jewels he gave for New-year's gifts before the marriage to the D: of Gloucester, the Cardinal, the D: of Exeter, the Archbishop, Dutchefs of Buckingham, Earl of Warwick, &c: the George he wore himself, wᶜʰ cost 2000 Marks; *the Puson of Golde, call'd Iklyngton Coler, garnish'd with 4 Rubees, 4 greet Saphurs, 32 greet Perles & 53 other Perles; & the*

---

[19] Otherwise Matthieu d'Escouchy; he continued Monstrelet's *Chroniques* (see n. 21) down to the accession of Louis XI (1461).

[20] 2 *Henry VI*, ii. 3.

Pectoral of Golde garnished with rubees, perles & diamondes; & also the greet Owche garnished with diamondes, rubees & perles, that cost 2000 Marcs, wch the Quene wore at the solempnitee of hir Coronation. if these suit your palate, you may see them all, & many other curious Papers, in Rymer's Fœdera, V: 11. some dated from the Priory of Southwyk, & witnefs'd by the Marquefs of Suffolk, the Tresorer of Englande (wch was Sr Ralph Boteler, Ld Sudeley,) & the Privy-Seal (Adam Moleyns, Dean of Salisbury, afterwards Bishop of Chichester, & murther'd by the Mob at Southampton).

Now I shall set down the ages of the parties concern'd. the King was barely 23 years old. (what shall we do with this stubborn date?) the Queen was in her 15th Year. her mother Isabella was probably about 35. René, her father, was 36. (see his picture, when old; done by himself, in Montfaucon). Mary, Q: of France, her aunt, was 40 (see her, ibid: with a very odd face, an odder Coif, & high, but not pointed bonnet, from an original) Charles the 7th of France was 41. (see him in the same plate). John, her brother, D: of Calabria, was about 19. Yolande, her Sister, was not a year older than herself.

There is so particular a description of the drefses in use about the middle of the 15th Century extant, that (long as it is) I must send it you. 'En ceste année delaifserent les dames & damoiselles les queues a porter a leurs robes: & en ce lieu meirent bordures a leurs robbes de gris de lestices, de martres, de veloux & d'autres choses si larges, comme d'un veloux de haut ou plus. & si meirent sur leurs tetes bourrelets a maniere de bonnet rond, qui s'amenuisoient par defsus de la hauteur de demie aulne, ou de trois quartiers de long tels y avoit: & aucunes les portoient moindres, & deliez couvrechefs par defsus pendans par derriere jusques a terre, les aucuns & les autres: & prindrent aufsi a porter leurs ceintures de soye plus larges beaucoup qu'elles n'avoient accoutumé & de diverses façons; & les ferrures plus somptueuses afsez, & coliers d'or a leurs cols autrement & plus cointement beaucoup qu'elles n'avoient accoutumé. et en ce temps aufsi les hommes se prindrent a vestir plus court, qu'ils n'eurent onques fait; tellement que l'on veoit la façon de leurs culs & de leurs genitoires, ainsi comme l'en souloit vestir les singes, qui estoit chose tres malhonnête & impudique. & si faisoient les manches fendre de leurs robbes & de leurs pourpoints pour monstrer leurs chemises deliées, larges, & blanches. portoient aufsi leurs cheveux si longs, qu'ils leur empêchoient leurs visages, mesmement leurs yeux. & sur leurs testes portoient bonnets de drap hauts & longs d'un quartier ou plus. portoient aufsi, comme tous indifferemment, chaines d'or moult somptueuses chevaliers & escuyers: les varlets mêmes, pourpoints de soye, de satin & de veloux. et presque tous, especiallement és cours des Princes, portoient poulaines a leurs soulliers d'un quartier de long; et á leurs pourpoints gros mahoitres á leurs espaules pour monstrer, qu'ils fufsent larges par les espaules; qui sont choses moult vaines, & par adventure fort haineuses a Dieu. & qui estoit huy court vestu, il estoit le lendemain long vestu jusques a terre.'

(Monstrelet.[21] V: 3. aprés P: 130).

The Date he afsigns to these new fashions is 1467. yet it is sure the sugar-loaf caps, the long close Hose, & long-pointed shoes, are seen in paintings a good while before. as in Montfaucon, (V: 3. Plate 46.) where one of the Lords has a Hawk on his fist, *marque d'une grande qualité dans ces tems lá.* Charles the 6th used to go to Council, *l'epervier sur le poing.* (ibid: p. 189.) Mary, the Heirefs of Burgundy, is the last Lady with a high Cap that I meet with. she died 1481, & from what I recollect of the drefses in your picture, they are all older than that date, for about this time very different fashions came in. I even believe it was painted soon after 1445, & the Glory about the King's head might be added afterwards; tho' Jo: Blackman,[22] a Carthusian, who has wrote a short account, as an eye-witnefs, of Henry 6th's private Life, treats him already as a sort of Saint. the Pomegranates are only a fashionable Pattern for Embroidery & Brocades about that time. Philip, D: of Burgundy made his entry into Ghent in such a robe, & Charles the 7th into Paris (V: 3. Pl: 39, & 45.) &c:

This is what I have yet met with to your purpose at all, tho' perhaps little to your satisfaction, with regard to that picture. now for the other,[23] I must tell you my disappointment, w[ch] has

[21] Enguerrand de Monstrelet (c. 1390–1453), author of *Les Chroniques de France, d'Angleterre et de Bourgogne. . . .* The edition used by Gray was that published at Paris in 3 vols., fol., in 1572, with continuations down to 1516 (see Letter 543, n. 10). Monstrelet's own work covers the period from 1400 to 1444.

[22] Otherwise Blakman or Blakeman (fl. 1436–48); his memoir of Henry VI, which was written in Latin, was printed in 1732 by Hearne in his *Duo Rerum Anglicarum Scriptores.*

[23] The 'Marriage of Henry VII and Elizabeth of York; by Mabeuse',

been the reason why I have made you & *the world* wait so long for this first volume of my Antiquities. a Senior-Fellow of Trinity, I was told, had got a Mſs, in wch were painted Henry 7th, & many of his court: he was absent, & I have stayed with impatience for a sight of it: I have now met with him, but the painting is at his living in Cheshire. it is not a Mſs, but a Roll of Vellom, as long as the Room (he says) in wch are represented that King and all his Lords going to Parliament. this must be a great curiosity, but we are not like to be the better for it. another disappointment! in reading Thomas of Otterbourne's[24] Chronicle I found mention of a Sainte-Ampoule kept in Westm:^r Abbey. he speaks of Henry 4th's being inunctus sancto oleo, quod S: *Thomæ* martyri dedit beatiſs:^a Virgo Maria in exilio ejus. this seem'd to account for S: Thomas' attending Elizabeth of York as the future anointed Queen of England. but alas! on second thoughts these words must mean S: Thomas Becket.

Immediately after the Battle of Bosworth, Aug: 22, 1485, the King sent Sr Rob: Willoughby to the Castle of Sheriff-Hutton in Yorkshire with orders to conduct the Princeſs Eliz:^th to her Mother at London. he himself enter'd the City 5 days after; was crown'd, Oct: 30, by Card^l Tho: Bourchier, Archb^p of Canterbury, & married Jan: 18, 1486, at Westminster, being then in his 31st year, & Elizabeth turn'd of 20. he (you see) is in his kingly ornaments; but he would not suffer her to be crown'd till almost two years after, when she had brought him a Son. if you are sure the Person who accompanies the King is a Cardinal, it must be Bourchier, who died very soon after this marriage, for the Writ, de custodiâ commiſsâ to Jo: Morton, B^p of Ely, who succeeded him, is dated July 13. 1486. Bourchier was not Legate de latere, but perhaps may bear the Legatine double-Croſs as Archb: of Canterbury; for both our Archbishops were styled *Apostolicæ Sedis Legati* (see Rymer. V: 12. p. 208 & 245.) but I take the Person there represented to be James, Bishop of Imola, who granted the Dispensation for this marriage (they being in the 4th degree of Consanguinity to one

which afterwards hung at the east end of the Gallery at Strawberry Hill. The picture, which is now at Sudeley Castle, is figured and described in the third chapter of Walpole's *Anecdotes of Painting in England* (see *Works of Lord Orford*, vol. iii, pp. 50–1).

[24] Thomas Otterbourne (fl. 1400), author of a Chronicle extending to 1420, which was printed by Hearne in 1732.

another) & was then *Orator & Commifsarius cum potestate Legati de latere in regnis Angliæ et Scotiæ.* (see the Bull, in Rymer, V: 12. p. 213.) and somewhere, tho' I can not turn to the place, I found the King returning the Pope thanks for honouring the solemnity with the presence of his *Ambafsador.* 'tis true, this Legate was no Cardinal, but (I believe) as Legate he might wear the Purple: tho' I am not sure, his drefs is any thing more, than a D^r in Divinity's scarlet robe, & the hood, as usual, lined with Meniver. it is certain, there is no hat, tho' this was the distinction of a Cardinal long before these times.

This is all at present compyled by the paynful hand & symple engyne of your honour's pour bedesman

T: G:

My Love to M^{r}C:, pray tell me about him, & about the Vine.[25] I have not found his Dugdale[26] yet; it is not in Emanuel, nor the Publick Library.

187. GRAY TO WALPOLE

[Cambridge, March 17, 1754][1]

Dear S^r

I DO not at all wonder at you for being more curious about an interesting point of modern history,[2] than a matter that happen'd 300 years ago.[3] but why should you look upon me as so buried in the dust of an old Chronicle, that I do not care what happens in George, 2$^{d's}$, reign? I am still alive (I'd have you to know) & tho' these events are indeed only subjects of speculation to me, feel some difference still between the present & the past. you are desired therefore to look in the annals of Strawberry, March ... 1754. & when you can find time, please to transcribe me a little paragraph or two; that when I come,

---

[25] Gray, no doubt, had heard of the serious illness of John Chute's elder brother, Antony, owner of the Vyne, with whom he was on bad terms, and was anxious to know whether John Chute was likely to succeed to the family estates. Antony Chute died on 20 May of this year (see Letter 189, n. 1).

[26] See Letter 188, nn. 2, 3.

LETTER 187.—First printed by Toynbee (1915), No. 187.

[1] The date of the month is supplied by the postmark; that of the year by the reference in the letter to the current year.

[2] Henry Pelham, the Prime Minister, died on 6 March, and a new administration was in course of formation under his brother, the Duke of Newcastle. At the ensuing General Election Walpole was elected (20 April) M.P. for Castle Rising.

[3] The marriage of Henry VI (1445), discussed in the previous letter.

like the rest of my brethren here, to ask for some little thing, I may know at least, what door to knock at. Adieu, I am ever
Yours
T G:

Addressed: To The Honble Horace Walpole Esq in Arlington Street London
Postmark: SAFFRON WALDEN 18 MR

188. GRAY TO WALPOLE

Dear S^r   Camb:^{ge} April 11. 1754.

I AM very glad my objections serve only to strengthen your first opinion about the subject of your picture:¹ if I casually meet with any thing more, I shall send it you. the reason I trouble you at present is to tell you, that I have got into my hands the Dugdale Mr Chute enquired after.² a great number of the arms are blazon'd in the margin, not very neatly, but (I suppose) they are authentic; tho' in it I find written in an old hand

> This volume no Errata's has;
> The Whole may for Errata's pafs.
> If to correct them you intend,
> You'll find it labour without end.
> 'Tis therefore better let them goe.
> God only 'tis knows, who gets who.

Whether this is wit only, or a censure upon Dugdale's work, or upon the Heraldry added to it, I leave you to judge. the arms were done by a Sergeant-Surgeon to K: Charles 2^d, who made this art his particular Study, & the book belongs to Caius-College.³ you are desired to send your queries forthwith, for I can not keep it a great while.

I return you thanks for the civilities you have shew'd Mason, who is here, & speaks much of your politenefs to him. Adieu, I am
Ever Yours
T G:

Addressed: To The Honble Horace Walpole Esq in Arlington Street London
Postmark: CAMBRIDGE 12 AP

LETTER 188.—First printed by Toynbee (1915), No. 188.
¹ See Letter 186, n. 2.
² See Letter 186 (postscript). The work in question was Dugdale's *Baronage of England*, London, 1676, 2 vols., fol.
³ This copy of Dugdale is still preserved in the Library of Caius College. The arms are painted by hand on the margins, in some cases 'not very neatly'. The verses quoted by Gray (who has not transcribed them quite accurately) are written on the reverse of the leaf, in the second volume, bearing the dedication to Charles II.

189. GRAY TO WALPOLE

My dear S^r

I HAVE scarce time to thank you for your kindnefs in immediately telling me the unexpected good news.¹ I must trouble
you to send this² to the Vine, as I do not rightly know the
direction. Adieu, I am

Ever Yours

T G:

May 23. [1754]³ Cambridge

189*. Gray to Chute

[23 May 1754]

[Gray wrote to congratulate Chute on succeeding to the Vyne. See
Letter 189.]

190. Gray to Wharton

[20 July 1754]

[In MS. Brit. Mus. *Egerton*, 2400, between Gray's letter to Wharton
of 18 Oct. 1753 (Letter 183) and that of 13 Aug. 1754 (Letter 191)
there is a blank sheet of paper, similar to that used by Gray, which
has Wharton's endorsement: 'Mr Gray 20 July 1754'. This evidently belonged to a letter which cannot now be traced.]

191. GRAY TO WHARTON

Stoke. Aug: 13. [1754]¹

My dear S^r

HAVING been some little time absent from hence² I mifsed of
your letter, or I had answer'd it as soon as you desire me.
the opportunity of a good House³ I hope you will not suffer to
escape you. whether the rent be too high, you alone can pro-

LETTER 189.—First printed by Toynbee (1915), No. 189.
  ¹ Anthony Chute died on 20 May 1754, intestate. His estate of the Vyne
passed to John Chute, his only surviving brother.
  ² Evidently an enclosure for John Chute (see Letter 189*).
  ³ The date of the year is determined by the reference to Chute (see n. 1).
  LETTER 191.—First printed in part in Mason's *Memoirs*, p. 232; first
printed in full by Mitford (1816), pp. 245–7; now reprinted from original.
  ¹ Date of year added by Wharton.
  ² There is nothing to show where Gray had been.
  ³ Wharton was looking for a house in London, where he proposed to
practise as a physician.

perly judge. there is great comfort to be sure in a good house. some appearance of Œconomy I should think would give you credit in that part of the town you are to be well with: they pride themselves in living much within their income. upon the whole I seem to have a partiality for Mr Crumpe, but be sure never to repent. if you think, you shall, by all means settle yourself in the great house. besides I do not know but some great old Doctor may come & squat himself down there at your elbow (for I suppose there may be some convenience in succeeding to a house of the same Profefsion) & then you would be horridly out of humour. in short you see with your own eyes, you know the Quarter, & must necefsarily be best qualified to decide. Dr Fothergill's[4] invitation is very civil. as to the depth of Science, wch you seem to dread, it always grows shallower, as one comes nearer, tho' it makes a great noise at a distance. the design of the Society[5] at least is a good one. but if they are warm & profefs'd Enemies of the College,[6] I should think the same reason, that makes Heb:^{n}[7] withdraw himself, should prevent your admifsion into it: it will be easy to delay it however on various pretences without disobliging any one.

I am glad you agree with me in admiring Mr Southcote's Paradise,[8] wch whenever you see it again, will improve upon

[4] John Fothergill (1712–80), quaker physician; M.D. Edin. 1736; he began practice in London in 1740, was admitted licentiate of the College of Physicians in 1744, and was elected F.R.S. in 1763. He was in attendance on Lord Clive at the time of his death (see Walpole to Lady Ossory, 23 Nov. 1774).

[5] 'The Medical Society to which Dr Wharton was invited by Dr Fothergill, was the Medical Society of Physicians, founded in 1752 by Fothergill. This Society met at the Mitre Tavern, and was composed mainly of Licentiates of the College of Physicians who were violently opposed to the Fellows of the College on account of their action in refusing to elect as Fellows those Licentiates who were not Doctors of Medicine of either Oxford or Cambridge. Later this dispute came into the Courts, where Fothergill, who was a Licentiate, figured prominently' (extract from letter of Dr. Arnold Chaplin, Harveian Librarian of the Royal College of Physicians).

The Society, at whose meetings medical communications were read, was formed for the purpose of 'collecting and publishing all such observations and inquiries in medicine, that seemed to deserve public notice' (see Lettsom's *Memoirs of John Fothergill*, Lond., 1786, p. 254 n.).

[6] The Royal College of Physicians in Warwick Lane (see Letter 114, n. 7).

[7] Dr. William Heberden, one of the most distinguished Fellows of the College of Physicians (see Letter 135, n. 20).

[8] Woburn Farm, near Weybridge, in Surrey. Of this, which Lord Bath in his *Ballad of Strawberry Hill* terms 'but a dainty whim', Walpole writes: 'Philip Southcote Esq. a Roman Catholic gentleman, . . . was the first

you. do you know, you may have it for 20,000£. but I am afraid, the Lands are not very improveable. you do not say enough of Esher.[9] it is my other favourite place. it was a Villa of Cardinal Wolsey's,[10] of wch nothing but a part of the Gateway[11] remain'd. Mr Kent[12] supplied the rest, but I think with you, that he had not read the Gothic Clafsicks with taste or attention.[12a] he introduced a mix'd Style, wch now goes by the name of the *Battey Langley* Manner.[13] he is an Architect, that

Designer of the Ferme Ornée; but tho That appellation is more humble than That of garden, the composition is rather less natural, at least as Mr Southcote exhibited It. . . . Wooburn farm near Weybridge in Surry where Mr. Southcote displayed his peculiar Style with happiness & Taste, is the habitation of such Nymphs & Sheperds as are represented in landscapes & novels, but do not exist in real life'. (*Notes on Mason's Satirical Poems*, ed. Toynbee, pp. 39–40.)

[9] Esher Place, Surrey, the seat of the recently deceased (6 March) Henry Pelham, which he bought in 1729, and, with the aid of Kent, greatly improved. Pope in *Epilogue to the Satires* writes of

> Esher's peaceful Grove
> (Where *Kent* and Nature vie for Pelham's Love)
>   (*Dialogue*, ii. 66–7.)

Walpole writes to Montague (11 Aug. 1748): 'Esher I have seen again twice, and prefer it to all villas, even to Southcote's; Kent is Kentissime there'.

[10] It was a house belonging to his Bishopric of Winchester; hither he retired by the King's order in Oct. 1529, after he had been deprived of the great seal.

[11] The gatehouse, known as Wolsey's Tower, but apparently part of the mansion founded by William of Waynflete, *c*. 1450, is still standing.

[12] 'William Kent, Painter & Architect in the reign of George the 2^d was Author of the modern taste in English gardening; or in other words, the First who discovered that the Imitation of Nature was the true Style in gardening, as in all other Arts'. (Walpole, *Notes on Mason's Satirical Poems*, ed. cit., p. 39; he gives a full account of Kent and his science in his essay *On Modern Gardening*, published in the fourth volume of his *Anecdotes of Painting*.) Kent (1684–1748) was employed by Sir Robert Walpole on the decoration of Houghton, and was the architect, among other buildings, of Lord Leicester's house at Holkham, of Devonshire House, Piccadilly, and of the Horse Guards and Treasury Buildings.

[12a] Gray means that Kent had not studied the classical examples of Gothic Architecture.

[13] Batty Langley (1696–1751), writer on architecture, 'who endeavoured to adapt Gothic architecture to Roman measures; . . . and (for he never copied Gothic) *invented* five orders for that style. All that his books achieved, has been to teach carpenters to massacre that venerable species, and to give occasion to those who know nothing of the matter, and who mistake his clumsy efforts for real imitations, to censure the productions of our ancestors' (Walpole, *Anecdotes of Painting*, chap. 22, in *Works of Lord*

has publish'd a book of bad Designs. if you have seen M^r W:^{s14} pray let me hear your opinion, wch I will not anticipate by saying any-thing about it. to be sure its extreme littlenefs will be the first thing, that strikes you. by all means see Ld Radnor's^{15} again. he is a simple old Phobus,^{16} but nothing can spoil so glorious a situation, wch surpafses every thing round it. I take it ill, you should say any thing against ye Mole.^{17} it is a reflection, I see, cast at the Thames. do you think, that Rivers, wch have lived in London & its neighbourhood all their days, will run roaring & tumbling about, like your Tramontane Torrents in the North. no, they only glide & whisper. in your next expedition you will see Claremont,^{18} & Ld Portmore's,^{19} wch joins my Ld Lincoln's,^{20} & above all Mr Hamilton's, at Cobham^{21} in Surrey, wch all the world talks of & I have seen

Orford, vol. iii, p. 485). 'Batty Langley Gothic' came to be a by-word. The work referred to by Gray was probably his *Gothic Architecture, improved by Rules and Proportions in many grand Designs.*

14 Walpole's house at Strawberry Hill. The allusion in the next letter suggests that Wharton had then visited 'Strawberry Castle'. When Wharton went to reside at Old Park, the family mansion, and was busy renovating it, Gray sent him details of the decorations at Strawberry Hill (see Letters 302, 373).

15 John Robartes (c. 1686–1757), fourth and last Earl of Radnor of that name. His fantastic residence, Radnor House, known to Walpole and Bentley as 'Mabland', at Twickenham, adjoined Strawberry Hill (see Walpole to Conway, 8 Nov. 1752; to Mann, 12 June 1753; and to Bentley, 18 May 1754).

16 'Fobus', a vulgar term of abuse, frequently applied by Gray and Mason to the former's pet aversion, the Duke of Newcastle (see Letters 212, 261, 262, 263, 275, 313, 314, 334, 335, 547), occurs in Wycherley's *Plain Dealer*, a play with which Gray was familiar (see Letter 3, n. 5), whence no doubt he borrowed it: ii. 1: '*Widow Blackacre*. Wouldst thou make a candle-maker, a nurse of me . . . *Oldfox*. O heavens! *Jerry Blackacre*. Ay, you old fobus, and you would have been my guardian, would you?'

17 The tributary of the Thames which drains the district in which the various country-seats mentioned in this letter are situated.

18 Claremont Park, near Esher, seat of the Duke of Newcastle, after whose death in 1768 the place was bought and the house rebuilt (to the plans of Lancelot Brown) by Lord Clive.

19 Ham Haw Park, Weybridge, belonging to Charles Colyear (1700–85), second Earl of Portmore.

20 Oatlands Park, near Weybridge, belonging to the Duke of Newcastle, at this time the residence of his nephew, and successor in the dukedom, Henry Fiennes Pelham-Clinton (1720–94), ninth Earl of Lincoln (1730). The estate was bought in 1788 by the Duke of York.

21 This was Painshill, the seat of the Hon. Charles Hamilton, fifth son (d. 1787) of the sixth Earl of Abercorn. In his letter to Montagu of 11 Aug.

seven years ago.[22] the Year indeed does not behave itself well. but think, what it must be in the North. I suppose the roads are impafsable with the deep snow still.

I could write abundance more, but am afraid of losing this Post. pray, let me hear from you as soon as you can, & make my Compliments to M[rs] Wharton. Mason is by this time in Town again. [Tuthill * * *][23] Brown, I believe, at Cambridge. Adieu, I am ever

Yours

T G:

I am obliged to you for sending the Tea, w[ch] is excellent.

Addressed: To D[r] Thomas Wharton M:D: in Pancras-Lane[24] near Cheapside London *Postmark:* 14 AV

192. GRAY TO WHARTON

Stoke, Sept: 18. 1754.

Dear S[r]

I REJOICE to find you at last settled[1] to your heart's content, & delight to hear you talk of *giving your house some Gothic ornaments* already. if you project any thing, I hope it will be entirely within doors; & don't let me (when I come gaping into Coleman-street[2]) be directed to the Gentleman's at the ten Pinnacles, or with the Church-porch at his door. I am glad you enter into

1748 Walpole writes: 'I have been to see Mr. Hamilton's near Cobham, where he has really made a fine place out of a most cursed hill'. See also Walpole's *Essay on Modern Gardening* (*Works of Lord Orford*, vol. ii, p. 541). Mitford says that Hamilton 'formed many of the beautiful scenes in the grounds at Paineshill from the Pictures of Poussin and the Italian Masters'.

[22] If Gray had visited Painshill (and the other places mentioned in this letter) 'seven years ago', his visit would have been in 1747: but it seems probable that he was a year out in his reckoning, and that it was in the summer of 1748 that he made his tour of the Surrey houses, in the company of Walpole. Walpole, in a letter to Montagu of 11 Aug. 1748, in which he mentions that Gray had been at Strawberry Hill, speaks of having recently visited Painshill, Esher, and Claremont.

[23] See Letter 120, n. 2.

[24] Pancras Lane runs on the south, and parallel to Cheapside, from Queen Street to Bucklersbury.

LETTER 192.—First printed in part (in a garbled text) in Mason's *Memoirs*, pp. 230–1; first printed in full by Mitford (1816), vol. ii, pp. 247–51; now reprinted from original.

[1] See Letter 191, n. 3.

[2] As appears from the address of the next letter, Wharton's new abode was in King's Arms Yard, Coleman Street (see Letter 193, n. 6).

Horace Walpole in the Library at Strawberry Hill

from a watercolour drawing by J. H. Müntz

the Spirit of Strawberry-Castle. it has a purity & propriety of Gothicism in it (with very few exceptions,) that I have not seen elsewhere. the eating-room & library³ were not compleated, when I was there, & I want to know, what effect they have. my Lᵈ Radnor's Vagaries⁴ (I see) did not keep you from doing justice to his situation, wᶜʰ far surpaſses every thing near it, & I do not know a more *laughing* Scene, than that about Twickenham & Richmond. Dʳ Akenside⁵ (I perceive) is no Conjurer⁵ᵃ in Architecture, especially when he talks of the Ruins of Persepolis, wᶜʰ are no more Gothic, than they are Chinese. the Egyptian Style (see Dʳ Pococke,⁶ not his discourses, but his prints) was apparently the Mother of yᵉ Greek; & there is such a similitude between the Egyptian, & those Persian Ruins, as gave room to Diodorus⁷ to affirm, that the old buildings of Persia were certainly perform'd by Egyptian Artists. as to the other part of his opinion, that the Gothic manner is the Saracen or Moorish, he has a great Authority to support him, that of Sʳ Christ:ʳ Wren,⁸ & yet (I can not help thinking) is undoubtedly wrong. the Palaces in Spain I never saw but in description,

---

³ In his *Description of Strawberry Hill* Walpole says: 'the library, and refectory or great parlour, were entirely new built in 1753'.

⁴ See Letter 191, n. 15.

⁵ See Letter 115, n. 2. Akenside's remarks on the ruins of Persepolis have not been traced.

⁵ᵃ 'No conjurer' was used as an ironical description of one who was far from clever. Congreve, *Love for Love*, II, ix has 'By the account I have heard of his education, [he] can be no conjurer' (*O.E.D.*). Gray uses the phrase again in Letters 296, 353.

⁶ Richard Pococke (1704–65), the well-known traveller. He visited Egypt and Palestine in 1737–8, and in 1743–5 published *A Description of the East* (Lond., 2 vols., fol., with 178 Plates), the first volume containing his 'Observations on Egypt'. Gray's notes (dated 25 April 1745) on Part I of vol. ii, are in the possession of Hon. Geoffrey Howard, at Castle Howard.

⁷ Mitford refers to Lib. i, c. 46, where Diodorus says, that the Royal Palaces in Persepolis, in Susa, and those in Media, were built by Egyptian architects, when Cambyses burnt the temples of Egypt, carried their riches into Asia, and transported their artificers there.

⁸ Wren's opinion is recorded in a 'Memorial, by Sir Christopher Wren, to the Bishop of Rochester, in 1713, in connexion with the restoration of Westminster Abbey', printed in *Parentalia: or Memoirs of the Family of the Wrens . . . but chiefly of Sir Christopher Wren . . . compiled by his son* Christopher Wren (Lond., 1750, p. 297): 'This we now call the Gothick manner of Architecture (so the Italians call'd what was not after the Roman style) tho' the Goths were rather destroyers than builders; I think it should with more reason be call'd the *Saracen* style; for those people wanted neither Arts nor Learning, and after we in the West had lost both, we borrowed again from them.'

wch gives us little or no Idea of things; but the Doge's Palace at Venice I have seen[9] (wch is in the Arabesque manner) & the houses of Barbary you may see in Dr Shaw's book,[10] not to mention abundance of other eastern Buildings in Turky, Persia, &c: that we have views of, & they seem plainly to be corruptions of the Greek Architecture, broke into little parts indeed, & cover'd with little ornaments, but in a taste very distinguishable from that we call Gothic. there is one thing, that runs thro' the Moorish Buildings, that an Imitator would certainly have been first struck with, & would have tried to copy, & that is the Cupola's, wch cover everything, Baths, Apar[t]ments, & even Kitchens. yet who ever saw a Gothic Cupola? it is a thing plainly of Greek original. I do not see any thing but the slender Spires, that serve for steeples, wch may perhaps be borrowed from the Saracen Minarets on their Mosques.

I was in Northamptonshire,[11] when I received your Letter, but am now returned hither. I have been at Warwick, wch is a place worth seeing. the Town is on an eminence surrounded every way with a fine cultivated Valley, thro' wch the Avon winds, & at the distance of 5 or 6 miles, a circle of hills well wooded, & with various objects crowning them, that close the Prospect. out of the town on one side of it rises a rock, that might remind one of your rocks at Durham, but that it is not so savage, or so lofty, & that the river, wch washes its foot, is perfectly clear, & so gentle, that its current is hardly visible. upon it stands the Castle, the noble old residence of the Beauchamps & Neville's, & now of Earl Brooke.[12] he has sash'd the

[9] He was in Venice from May to July, 1741.

[10] Thomas Shaw (1694–1751), the African traveller. From 1720 to 1733 he was chaplain to the English factory at Algiers, during which time he travelled in Egypt, Palestine, and N. Africa. In 1738 he published at Oxford his *Travels, or Observations relating to several Parts of Barbary and the Levant* (fol., with maps and Plates). Gray's abstract (dated 6 Dec. 1744) of this work, consisting of more than fourteen closely written 4to pages, is in the possession of Hon. Geoffrey Howard, at Castle Howard.

[11] Perhaps with Frederick Montagu (see Letter 216, n. 8), whose father, Charles Montagu was M.P. for Northampton, in the representation of which borough Frederick succeeded him in 1759. George Montagu had a house at Greatworth, near Brackley, in this county at this time (see Walpole to Montagu, 22 May 1753, and 7 Oct. 1755).

[12] Francis Greville (1719–73), eighth Baron Brooke (1727); created Earl Brooke of Warwick Castle, 1746; and Earl of Warwick, 1759.

There had been six Earls of Warwick of the Beauchamp family, from 1268 to 1446; the only Earl of the Nevill family was Sir Richard, 'the King-

great Appartment, that's to be sure, (I can't help these things) & being since told, that square sash-windows were not Gothic, he has put certain whim-wams withinside the glaſs, wch appearing through are to look like fretwork. then he has scooped out a little Burrough in the maſsy walls of the place for his little self & his children,[13] wch is hung with Paper & printed Linnen, & carved chimney-pieces, in the exact manner of Berkley-square or Argyle-Buildings. what in short can a Lord do now a days, that is lost in a great old solitary Castle, but sculk about, & get into the first hole he finds, as a Rat would do in like case. a pretty long old stone-bridge leads you into the town with a Mill at the end of it, over wch the rock rises with the Castle upon it with all its battlements & queer ruin'd towers, & on your left hand the Avon strays thro' the Park, whose ancient Elms seem to remember Sr Philip Sidney,[14] (who often walk'd under them) and talk of him to this day. the Beauchamp Earls of Warwick[15] lie under stately Monuments in the Choir of the great Church, & in our Lady's Chappel adjoining to it. there also lie Ambrose Dudley, E: of Warwick;[16] & his Brother, the famous Ld Leicester, with Lettice, his Counteſs.[17] this Chappel is preserved entire, tho' the Body of the Church was burnt down 60 years ago, & rebuilt by S^r C: Wren. I had heard often of Guy-Cliff two miles from the town, so I walked to see it; & of all improvers commend me to Mr Greathead,[18] its present Owner. he shew'd it me himself, & is literally a fat young Man with a head & face much bigger than they are usually worn. it was

Maker', who was created Earl of Warwick in 1450, and was killed at the battle of Barnet, 1471, leaving no son.

[13] He had at this time six children, of whom the eldest was eleven.

[14] The famous soldier, statesman, and poet (1554–86); he was nephew of Ambrose Dudley, Earl of Warwick, 1561–89, and of Robert Dudley, Earl of Leicester, 1564–88, whose guest he was at Kenilworth when Leicester entertained Queen Elizabeth there in 1576.

[15] See n. 12.   [16] See n. 14.

[17] Leicester (see n. 14) married in 1578, Lettice, daughter of Sir Francis Knollys, K.G., and widow (1576) of Walter Devereux, first Earl of Essex (1572); she died at the age of 95 in 1634.

[18] This was Samuel Greathed (d. 1765), who married in 1748 Lady Mary Bertie (d. 1774), eldest daughter of second Duke of Ancaster. Walpole, writing to Chute on 4 Aug. 1753, speaks of him as 'that foolish Greathead, who quarelled with me (because his father was a gardener) for asking him if Lord Brook had planted much'. When Lady Ossory visited Warwick Castle in 1777 Walpole asked her, 'Did you go to Guy's Cliffe, and see how Lady Mary Greathead had painted it straw-colour, and stuck cockle-shells in its hair?'

naturally a very agreeable rock, whose Cliffs cover'd with large trees hung beetleing over the Avon, wch twists twenty ways in sight of it. there was the Cell of Guy, Earl of Warwick, cut in the living stone, where he died a Hermit[19] (as you may see in a penny History, that hangs upon the rails in Moorfields)[20] there were his fountains bubbling out of the Cliff; there was a Chantry founded to his memory in Henry the 6th's time.[21] but behold the Trees are cut down to make room for flowering shrubs, the rock is cut up, till it is as smooth & as sleek as sattin; the river has a gravel-walk by its side; the Cell is a Grotta with cockle-shells[22] and looking-glafs; the fountains have an iron-gate before them, and the Chantry is a Barn, or a little House.[23] even the poorest bits of nature, that remain, are daily threatned, for he says (& I am sure, when the Greatheads are once set upon a thing, they will do it) he is determined, it shall be *all new*. These were his words, & they are Fate. I have also been at Stow,[24] at Woburn[25] (the Du[ke] of Bedford's), and at Wroxton[26] (Ld Guilford's) but I defer these Chapt[ers] till we meet. I shall only tell you for your Comfort, that th[e] part of Northampt:^{re}, where I have been, is in fruits, in flowers [& in] corn very near a fort-

---

[19] The story of Guy of Warwick, which is mentioned by Chaucer in his *Rime of Sir Thopas* (c. 1380), and was adopted as authentic history by the fourteenth-century chroniclers, was versified by Lydgate about 1450, and became popular as a prose romance and in ballads, one of which was included by Bishop Percy in his *Reliques of Ancient English Poetry* (1765). (*D.N.B.*)

[20] The hanging of their wares by catchpenny ballad-mongers on the railings in Moorfields, where was the asylum known as Bethlehem (or Bedlam) Hospital, and elsewhere, is alluded to by Pope in his *Imitations of Horace* ('Epistle to Augustus', Bk. ii, Epist. 1):

> And when I flatter, let my dirty leaves
> (Like Journals, Odes, and such forgotten things
> As Eusden, Philips, Settle, writ of Kings)
> Clothe spice, line trunks, or, flutt'ring in a row,
> Befringe the rails of Bedlam and Soho. (ll. 415–19).

[21] The Beauchamp Earls of Warwick, the second of whom was named Guy, claimed descent from Guy of Warwick, and in 1422–3 Earl Richard, the fifth Earl, erected a chantry or chapel for the repose of the souls of the legendary Guy and others of his ancestors, and provided endowment for the maintenance of two priests.

[22] See Walpole's description quoted in n. 18.   [23] A privy.

[24] Stowe, the seat of Richard Grenville-Temple, second Earl Temple, in Buckinghamshire.

[25] Woburn Abbey, in Bedfordshire, the seat of John Russell, fourth Duke of Bedford.

[26] Wroxton Abbey, near Banbury, in Oxfordshire, the seat of Francis North, first Earl of Guilford.

night behind this part of Buckinghamshire, that they have no nightingales, & that the other birds are almost as silent, as at Durham. it is rich land, but upon a Clay, & in a very bleak, high, exposed situation. I hope, you have had some warm weather, since you last complained of the South. I have thoughts of seeing you about Michaelmas, tho' I shall not stay long in town. I should have been at Camb:ᵍᵉ before now, if the D: of Newc:ˡᵉ & his foundation-stone²⁷ would have let me, but I want them to have done before I go.²⁸ I am sorry Mʳ Brown should be the only one, that has stood upon Punctilio's with me, & would not write first. pray tell him so. Mason is (I believe) in town, or at Chiswick.²⁹ [no news of Tuthill]:³⁰ I wrote a long letter to him in answer to one he wrote me, but no reply. Adieu, I am ever Yrs,

T G:

Brown call'd here this morning, before I was up, & breakfasted with me.

Addressed: To Dʳ Thomas Wharton M:D: in Pancras-Lane, near Cheapside London *Postmark:* 20 SE

193. GRAY TO WHARTON

Dear Doctor   Oct: [Nov.] 10¹. Camb: 1754

I AM clear, that you are in the right way & that you ought to make your excuses at the Queen's Arms² with all poſsible

---

²⁷ Plans for erecting a new front to the University Library were approved on 11 June 1754 and on 16 Sept. the Duke of Newcastle, as Chancellor of the University, visited the site and inspected the trenches dug for the foundations. The foundation stone was not laid until 30 April 1755 (see Willis and Clark, *Architectural History of the University of Cambridge*, vol. iii, pp. 63–6.

²⁸ At this time, and on many other occasions, when the Duke paid his ceremonial visits to the University, Gray made plans to be out of Cambridge, so as to avoid meeting him.

²⁹ With Lord Holdernesse, who, as appears from the note to Mason's 'Elegy addressed to Miss Pelham on the Death of her Father' (*Works*, ed. 1811, vol. i, p. 97), written in March 1754, at that time 'rented a small villa at Chiswick'. Mason's letter to Gray of 25 Dec. 1755 (Letter 212) is dated from there.

³⁰ See Letter 120, n. 2. Mitford's restoration, which is printed above, is not enough to fill the space.

LETTER 193.—First printed by Gosse in *Works of Gray*, vol. ii, pp. 259–60; omitted by Mitford; now reprinted from original.

¹ As the postmark is 11 Nov., Gray must have written 10 Oct. by mistake for 10 Nov.

² Gray evidently intended 'the Queen's Arms' (which in the next letter

civility to Foth:[11];[3] and perhaps the civilest excuse is to tell the truth, to him at least, that it would be neither grateful, nor prudent, to hazard disobliging the Gentlemen at the Mitre,[4] among whom you have several Friends, & besides it will be always more in your power to recommend moderate measures, while you continue connected with one Party, than if you should lose yourself with both by seeming to divide yourself between them. but how far this is to be said, & to whom, you are best able to determine.

*   *   *   *   *   *   *   *   *   *   *

*   *   *   *   *   *   *   *   *   *   *

*   *   *   *   *   *   *   *   *   *   *[5]

Addressed: To Dr Thomas Wharton, M:D: in Kings-Arms Yard, Coleman Street[6] London   *Postmark:* SAFFRON WALDEN 11 NO

194. GRAY TO WHARTON

ODE, IN THE GREEK MANNER[1]

Strophe 1.

Awake, Æolian lyre, awake,
And give to transport all thy trembling strings!
From Helicon's harmonious springs
A thousand rills their mazy progrefs take:

becomes 'the King's Arms') to represent Fothergill's Society, while by the 'gentlemen at the Mitre' he meant the Royal College of Physicians with which it was at variance. But this is a mistake or misunderstanding (which is repeated in the next letter), for it was Fothergill's Society which met at the Mitre Tavern (see Letter 191, n. 5); so that he has said the opposite of what he intended, for it was clear that he was of opinion that Wharton should avoid being drawn into joining the Society lest he should embroil himself with the College. The representatives of the College would naturally meet in their own building in Warwick Lane.

3 Fothergill (see Letter 191, n. 4).

4 This was presumably the well-known tavern of that name in Mitre Court, Fleet Street, frequented by Dr. Johnson; but it may have been the Mitre in Fenchurch Street.

5 The rest of the letter has been cut away.

6 Coleman Street runs from Lothbury to Fore Street, Cripplegate. King's Arms Yard extends from Coleman Street to Tokenhouse Yard.

LETTER 194.—First printed in part (in a garbled text) in Mason's *Memoirs*, p. 232; first printed in full (but without the *Ode*) by Mitford (1816), vol. ii, pp. 251–3; now reprinted from original.

1 This is the 'high Pindarick upon stilts' about which he wrote to Walpole in July 1752 (Letter 169). It had taken a long time to complete: he described it later to Bedingfield (Letter 215) as 'being wrote by fits & starts at very

The laughing Flowers, that round them blow,
Drink life & fragrance, as they flow.
Now the rich stream of musick winds along
Deep, majestic, smooth, and strong,
Thro' verdant vales, & Ceres' golden reign:
Now rolling down the steep amain
With torrent-rapture see it pour;
The Rocks & nodding Groves rebellow to the roar.

(Antistrophe 1.)

Oh Sovereign of the willing Soul,
Parent of sweet & solemn-breathing airs,
Enchanting Shell! the sullen Cares;
And frantic Pafsions hear thy soft controul.
On Thracia's hills the Lord of war
Has curb'd the fury of his car,
And drop'd his thirsty lance at thy command.
Perching on the sceptred hand
Of Jove thy magick lulls the feather'd King
With ruffled plumes, & flagging wing:
Quench'd in black clouds of slumber lie
The terrour of his beak, & light'nings of his eye.

Epode 1.

Thee the Voice, the Dance, obey
Temper'd to thy warbled lay.
O'er Idalia's velvet-green
The rosy-crowned Loves are seen
On Cytherea's day
With antick Sports, & blew-eyed Pleasures,
Frisking light in frolick measures:
Now pursuing, now retreating,
Now in circling troops they meet;
To brisk notes the cadence beating
Glance their many-twinkling feet.
Slow melting strains the Queen's approach declare;

different intervals'. Gray's copy in his Commonplace-book is dated 'Finish'd
in 1754'; the poem may have been finished some months before he sent it
to Wharton, for the corrections made in the margin of the Commonplace-
book are all shown in the copy printed here. The title 'Ode in the Greek
Manner' is that given to the poem in the Commonplace-book: in his agreement with Dodsley Gray called it The Powers of Poetry (see Letter 243,
n. 1). When it was first published (Letter 240) it was called 'Ode': in the
Poems of 1768 it had the title 'The Progress of Poesy. A Pindaric Ode'.

Wher'e'er she turns, the Graces homage pay,
With arms sublime, that float upon the air,
In gliding state she wins her easy way.
O'er her warm cheek & rising bosom move
The bloom of young Desire, & purple light of Love.

(Strophe 2ᵈᵃ.)

Man's feeble race what Ills await,
Labour & Penury, the racks of Pain,
Disease, and Sorrow's weeping Train,
And Death, sad refuge from the storms of Fate?
The fond complaint, my Song, disprove,
And justify the laws of Jove.
Say, has he given in vain the heavenly Muse?
Night, & all her sickly Dews,
Her Spectres wan, and Birds of boding cry,
He gives to range the dreary sky:
Till fierce Hyperion from afar
Pours on their scatter'd rear his glitt'ring shafts of war.

(Antistrophe 2ᵈᵃ.)

In climes beyond the solar road,
Where shaggy Forms o'er ice-built mountains roam,
The Muse has broke the twilight-gloom
To chear the shivering Native's dull abode;
And oft beneath the od'rous shade
Of Chili's boundlefs forests laid
She deigns to hear the savage Youth repeat
In loose numbers wildly sweet
Their feather-cinctured Chiefs & dusky Loves.
Her track wher'e'r the Goddefs roves,
Glory pursue, and generous Shame,
Th' unconquerable Mind, & Freedom's holy flame.

(Epode 2ᵈᵃ.)

Woods, that wave o'er Delphi's steep,
Isles, that crown th' Egæan deep,
Fields, that cool Ilifsus laves,
Or where Mæander's amber-waves
In ling'ring labyrinths creep,

How do your tuneful Ecchoes languish
Mute, but to the voice of Anguish?
Where each old poetic Mountain
Inspiration breath'd around;
Every Shade & hallow'd Fountain
Murmur'd deep a solemn sound:
Till the sad Nine in Greece's evil hour
Left their Parnaſsus for the Latian plains.
(Alike they scorn the pomp of tyrant Power,
And coward Vice, that revels in her chains.)
When Latium had her lofty spirit lost,
They sought, oh Albion, next thy sea-encircled coast.

(Strophe 3ª.)

Far from the Sun and summer-gale
In thy green lap was Nature's Darling laid,
What time, where lucid Avon stray'd,
To him the mighty Mother did unveil
Her aweful face: the dauntleſs Child
Stretch'd forth his little arms, & smiled.
'This pencil take, (she said) whose colours clear
'Richly paint the vernal Year.
'Thine too these golden keys, immortal Boy,
'This can unlock the gates of Joy:
'Of Terror that, & thrilling Fears;
'Or ope the sacred Source of sympathetic tears.

(Antistrophe 3ª.)

Nor second He, that rode sublime
Upon the seraph-wings of Extasy
The secrets of th' Abyſs to spy.
He paſs'd the flaming bounds of Place & Time.
The living Throne, the sapphire-Blaze,
Where Angels tremble while they gaze,
He saw: but blasted with exceſs of light,
Closed his eyes in endleſs night.
Behold, where Dryden's leſs presumptuous car
Wide o'er the fields of Glory bear
Two Coursers of ethereal race
With necks in thunder cloth'd, & long-resounding pace.

(Epode 3ᵃ.)

Hark! his hands the Lyre explore.
Full-plume'd Fancy, hov'ring o'er
Scatters from her pictured Urn
Thoughts, that breath, & Words, that burn:
But ah! 'tis heard no more——
Oh Lyre divine, what daring Spirit
Wakes thee now? tho' he inherit
Nor the pride, nor ample pinion,
That the Theban Eagle bear
Sailing with supreme dominion
Thro' the azure deep of air:
Yet oft before his infant-eyes would run
Such Forms, as glitter in the Muse's ray
With orient hues, unborrow'd of the Sun.
Yet shall he mount, & keep his distant way
Beyond the limits of a vulgar fate,
Beneath the Good how far!—but far above the Great.

If this be as tedious to You, as it is grown to me, I shall be sorry that I sent it you. I do not pretend to *debellate*² any one's Pride: I love my own too well to attempt it. as to mortifying their Vanity it is too easy & too mean a task for me to delight in. you are very good in shewing so much sensibility on my account. but be afsured, my Taste for Praise is not like that of Children for fruit. if there were nothing but Medlars & Blackberries in the world, I could be very well content to go without any at all. I dare say that M——n (tho' some years younger than I,) was as little elevated with the approbation of Lᵈ D: and Lᵈ M:³, as I am mortified by their silence. I desire you would by no means suffer this to be copied; nor even shew it, unlefs to very few, & especially not to mere Scholars⁴, that can scan all the measures in Pindar, & say the Scholia by heart. the oftener, &

---

² A reminiscence of *Aen.* vi. 853: 'Parcere subjectis, et debellare superbos').
³ These two Lords have not been identified; 'Lᵈ D:' may be Lord De La Warr, who was a friend of Mason. See Letters 359, 383.
⁴ Nichols, *Literary Anecdotes*, vol. v, p. 615 n., quotes from a life of Dr. Taylor (see Letter 212, n. 18) in *Some Account of the antient and present State of Shrewsbury School*, 1810 (pp. 388 ff.):
'The learned world at Cambridge at that time was divided into two parties; the polite scholars and the philologists. The former, at the head of

(in spite of poor Trollope[5]) the *more* you write to me, the happier I shall be. I envy your Opera. your Politicks I don't understand; but I think, matters can never continue long in the situation they now are. Barbarofsa[6] I have read, but I did not cry: at a modern Tragedy it is sufficient not to laugh. I had rather the King's Arms[7] look'd askew upon me, than the Mitre; it is enough to be well-bred to both of them. You do not mention L[d] Strathmore,[8] so that I doubt, if you received my little Letter about him. Mas[n] is still here: we are all mighty glad he is in Orders,[9] & no better than any of us. pray inform me, if Dr. Clerke[10] is come to Town, & where he is fix'd, that I may

which were Gray, Mason etc, superciliously confined all merit to their own circle, and looked down fastidiously on the rest of the world'.

[5] See Letter 114, n. 1.

[6] This tragedy, which was produced anonymously at Drury Lane on 17 Dec. 1754, was by Rev. John Brown (see Letter 144, n. 27). Garrick acted in *Barbarossa*, which had considerable success, and wrote the prologue and epilogue to it; but a line in the latter: 'Let the poor devil eat, allow him that', gave Brown great offence.   [7] See Letter 193, n. 2.

[8] John Lyon (1737–76), eldest son of Thomas Lyon, eighth Earl of Strathmore and Kinghorn, who married in 1736 at Houghton-le-Spring, co. Durham, the daughter and heiress of James Nicolson, of West Rainton, in that county. Lord Glamis, as he was styled, succeeded as ninth Earl on the death of his father, 18 Jan. 1753. In Feb. 1767 he married Mary Eleanor Bowes (see Chesterfield's letter to his son, dated 13 Feb. 1767: 'the greatest heiress, perhaps, in Europe, and ugly in proportion'), daughter of George Bowes, of Streatlam Castle and Gibside, co. Durham.

Tovey quotes the following passage from a letter of Lord Chesterfield, written 10 Feb. 1753, on hearing of the death of the eighth Earl: 'The present Lord is seventeen, a good classical scholar, and with a turn to learning. At this age Lady Strathmore will probably think it proper to send him either to an university or to travel; and if to an university, I should much prefer an university in Scotland to either of ours here'. That he was sent to Cambridge, and to Pembroke College (see Letter 196, n. 6) was perhaps due to Stonhewer (whose father was Rector of Houghton-le-Spring, where Lady Strathmore was married) and to Wharton, both of them natives of Durham, large estates in which county (lying between Houghton-le-Spring and Durham) had come to the Strathmore family through Lady Strathmore, with whom probably both Stonhewer and Wharton were acquainted. Lady Strathmore's two younger sons, James Philip Lyon, and Thomas Lyon, followed their brother to Pembroke, the former in 1756, the latter in 1758 (see Letters 233, n. 3; and 332, n. 14).

[9] He had been ordained Deacon on 17 Nov., and Priest on 24 Nov. of this year, and on 27 Nov. he had been instituted Rector of Aston, Yorks., on the presentation of the Earl of Holdernesse, who appointed him domestic chaplain. This was the occasion of Garrick's verses (published in the *Gentleman's Magazine* for April 1755, xxiv, p. 179): '*An Address to the R— H— the Earl of H—ld—ss, on the Preferment of the celebrated Mr M—son.*'   [10] See Letter 79, n. 11.

write to him, angry as he is. my Compliments to my Friend Mrs. Wharton, to your Mother, & all the little Gentry. I am ever, dear D^r, most sincerely

Yours.

Camb: Dec: 26. 1754.

195. MASON TO GRAY

Dear S^r

I AM gathering together my disjecta Membra[1] & as a specimen I send you the enclosd Ode,[2] of wch perhaps you may remember one Stanza. It is not what *I can* make it at present,[3] but I wont give myself any more trouble with it, till it has had your desp'rate Hooks.[4] but spare it as much as you can, for I dont mean to draw you into any scrape by the conclusion of it but shall leave you quite at your liberty to write my Epitaph[5] or no, as you please. As soon as you have interlind it send it me back again & dont let any body see it except the President[6] & Tuthill[7] and *Old Cardale*[8] *& the Master.*[9]

Marcello[10] has set out from Newcastle & is travelling hither

LETTER 195.—First printed by Mitford in *Gray–Mason* (1853), pp. 26–9; now reprinted from original.

   [1] A reminiscence of Horace, 1 *Sat.* iv. 62: disjecti membra poetae.

   [2] This was the *Ode On Melancholy. To a Friend*, one of the Odes which Mason published in the following year (see Letter 214, n. 10); after a mention of 'pensive Gray', and a reference to the *Elegy*, it concludes:

     He, too, perchance, when these poor limbs are laid,

     Will heave one tuneful sigh, and sooth my hov'ring shade—

lines which explain what Mason says as to Gray's writing his epitaph.

   [3] 'At present', in contrast to the time when he wrote the poem—Mason means he could do better now.

   [4]   Not that I'd lop the Beauties from his book,

      Like slashing Bentley with his desp'rate hook

          (Pope, *Imitations of Horace*, ii. 1, ll. 103–4),

where the word 'hook' is used in the double sense of 'pruning-hook' and 'bracket', in allusion to Bentley's statement in the preface to his edition of *Paradise Lost* that his emendations of the text were 'printed in the Italic letter', and 'inclosed between two hooks'.   [5] See n. 2.

   [6] James Brown (see Letter 115, n. 1), who had been appointed President (or Vice-Master) by the Master in 1749 after the death of Trollope.

   [7] This word, which has been heavily scored through in MS., is still legible. See Letter 120, n. 2.

   [8] See Letter 163, n. 11.   [9] Dr. Long (see Letter 39, n. 2).

   [10] Mitford ineptly conjectured that Marcello was a nickname for Edward Delaval. There is no doubt that Mason was referring to a book. Benedetto Marcello in 1724–7 published his musical setting of the first fifty Psalms (see Letter 374, n. 5). An English version: *The First Fifty Psalms, set to Music by Benedetto Marcello and adapted to the English Version*, by J. Garth, 8 vols., was

as fast as a Northumberland Waggon[11] can bring him you must not expect him at Cambridge this fourthnight. Pray is the Thane of Glamis[12] come.

I wish I could put that good creature Fraser[13] up in his own frank, to transcribe your Ode for me for I want it vastly.

I have no *Lueurs* yet about Hanover.[14] My Lord[15] did speak to Lord Hertford[16] to make me Chaplain to his Embassy. but he was preengaged; tell this to no Body but Old Cardale and the Master.

I send you also an Epistle wch Folks say Voltaire[17] writ lately to himself, but you must Judge whether they are right in their Assertion * * * *[18]. . . . you must return it in a Post or two. I am (as you must say if youve any gratitude in you)

Your very obliging friend

W MASON.

Arlington Street[19] March 1st—55

I am dissapointed of Voltaires Verses. but you shall have them very soon.[20]

published in 1757. To this work Charles Avison contributed 'Remarks' and a life of Marcello. Avison was a Newcastle musician and a friend of Mason (see Letter 180, n. 2). The book may have been in the press in 1754 (it was announced as forthcoming in Avison's *Essay on Musical Expression* in 1753). It may be concluded as probable that Avison, at Mason's request, was sending proof-sheets to Gray.

[11] Stage-wagons were used for the conveyance of goods and parcels.

[12] Lord Strathmore (see Letter 194, n. 8).

[13] William Fraser, an official under Lord Holdernesse, at this time Secretary of State (see Letter 60, n. 3); Fraser was subsequently for many years (from 1760) Under-Secretary of State and eventually (1782) Under-Secretary for Foreign Affairs. He often franked letters for Gray and Mason.

[14] As to whether he should accompany Lord Holdernesse to Hanover; the King went over at the end of April, and Mason was there in June and wrote thence to Gray (see Letter 197).

[15] Holdernesse, whose chaplain Mason now was.

[16] See Letter 60, n. 2. On 8 Feb. 1755 Walpole wrote to Bentley that an ambassador was to be sent immediately to Paris, and 'to my great satisfaction, my cousin and friend Lord Hertford is to be the man'; but on 6 March he had to write, 'The state of affairs is much altered since my last epistle. . . . that my Lord Hertford does not go.' He went as Ambassador to Paris in 1763.

[17] No doubt *Épitre de M^r de V***. en arrivant dans sa Terre près du Lac de Genève, en Mars*, 1755.

[18] Several words are here heavily scored through in MS. and are illegible.

[19] Lord Holdernesse's town-house was in this street.

[20] Stonhewer some months later sent Gray a copy in manuscript (see Letter 204, n. 3).

196. GRAY TO WHARTON

March, 9. 1755. Camb^ge:

My dear Doctor

ACCORDING to my reckoning M^rs Wh: should have been brought to bed before this time; yet you say not a syllable of it. if you are so loth to publish *your productions*, you can not wonder at the repugnance I feel to spreading abroad mine. but in truth I am not so much against publishing, as against publishing *this*[1] alone. I have two or three Ideas[1a] more in my head. what is to come of them? must they too come out in the shape of little six-penny flams,[2] dropping one after another, till Mr Dodsley thinks fit to collect them with M^r this's Song, and M^r t'other's epigram, into a pretty Volume? I am sure Mason must be sensible of this, & therefore can never mean what he says. to be sure, Doctor, it must be own'd, that Physick, & indeed all Profeſsions, have a bad effect upon the Mind. this it is my Duty, & Interest to maintain; but I shall still be very ready to write a Satyr upon the Clergy, & an Epode against Historiographers,[3] whenever you are hard prefs'd; & (if you flatter me) may throw in a few lines with somewhat handsome upon Magnesia alba, & Alicant-Soap. as to Humanity you know my aversion to it; wch is barbarous & inhuman, but I can not help it. God forgive me.

I am not quite of your opinion with regard to Strophe &

LETTER 196.—First printed in part (in a garbled text) in Mason's *Memoirs*, pp. 232–3; first printed in full by Mitford (1816), vol. ii, pp. 253–5; now reprinted from original.

[1] His Ode on the progress of Poetry. *Mason.*—See Letter 194, n. 1.

[1a] Mason states that one of these 'lyrical ideas' was the *Bard*, 'the exordium of which was at this time finished' (see Letter 199, n. 9): and another was the Ode, of which Gray left a fragment, which Mason entitled *Ode on the Pleasure arising from Vicissitude*: the plan of this Ode Mason found sketched in Gray's pocket-diary for 1754.

[2] The *Oxford English Dictionary* defines 'flam' as a fanciful composition, a conceit, and quotes Swift to Pope (1725): 'Philips writes little flams (as Lord Leicester called those sort of verses) on Miss Carteret', but Gray uses the word, here and in Letter 230, in the sense of a pamphlet.

[3] The reference is undoubtedly to Richard Stonhewer (Letter 120, n. 38). In January 1755 Thomas Philips Jenkins, Historiographer to his Majesty, died (*Gentleman's Magazine*, vol. xxiv, p. 92), and he was succeeded by Richard Stonhewer (*Rider's British Merlin*, 1756, p. 79). The office carried a stipend of £200 a year.

Antistrophe.[4] setting aside the difficulties, methinks it has little or no effect upon the ear, wch scarce perceives the regular return of Metres at so great a distance from one another. to make it succeed, I am persuaded the Stanza's must not consist of above 9 lines each at the most. Pindar has several such Odes.

L^d S:[5] is come, & makes a tall genteel figure in our eyes. his Tutors[6] & He appear to like one another mighty well. when we know more of him than his outside, You & the Historian[7] shall hear of it. I am going to ask a favour of you, wch I have no better pretence for doing, than that I have long been used to give you trouble. it is, that you would go to the London Insurance Office in Birchin-Lane[8] for me, & pay two Insurances, one of my House at Wansted[9] (Policy, N° 9675.) the other of

[4] He often made the same remark to me in conversation, which led me to form the last Ode of Caractacus in shorter stanzas: But we must not imagine that he thought the regular Pindaric method without its use; though, as he justly says, when formed in long stanzas, it does not fully succeed in point of effect on the ear: For there was nothing which he more disliked than that chain of irregular stanzas which Cowley introduced, and falsely called Pindaric; and which from the extreme facility of execution produced a number of miserable imitators. . . . Mr. Congreve, who (though without any lyrical powers) first introduced the regular Pindaric form into the English language, made use of the short stanzas which Mr. Gray here recommends. See his Ode to the Queen. *Mason.*

[5] See Letter 194, n. 8.

[6] In the Pembroke College Admission Book is the following entry: '1755 March 3. Honoratissimus Joannes Comes de Strathmore et Kinghorn admissus est ad mensam Sociorum [corrected in margin to 'in ordinem nobilium'] sub Tut^{bus} M^{ris} Brown et Tuthill'. Tuthill, who was not a College tutor, was doubtless Strathmore's private tutor.

[7] This must be Stonhewer, see n. 3.

[8] Birchin Lane runs from Cornhill, opposite the east end of the Exchange, to Lombard Street. The premises of The London Assurance (the correct title of the office in which Gray's houses were insured) were situated at the time of the Cornhill fire in Castle Court. (See Letter 145, n. 6.)

[9] See Letter 156, n. 7. Mason, in *Memoirs*, pp. 119–20, says of Gray's father that 'his indolence had led him to neglect the business of his profession; his obstinacy, to build a country-house at Wanstead, without acquainting either his wife or son with the design (to which he knew they would be very averse) till it was executed. This building, which he undertook late in life, was attended with very considerable expence; which might almost be called so much money thrown away: Since, after his death, the house was obliged to be sold for two thousand pounds less than its original cost.' Mason's statement that the house was sold after Philip Gray's death needs explanation. The house was owned by Gray as late as 1760 (as is known from Gray's pocket-diary for that year). It had been rented by Frederick Bull,

that in Cornhill[10] (N° 23470.) from Lady-Day next to Lady-Day, 1756. the first is 20 Shillings; the 2^d, 12 Shill^{gs} & be pleased to inclose the two Receipts (stamp'd) in a Cover, and send them to me; the sooner the better, for I am always in a little apprehension during this season of Conflagrations.[11] I know you will excuse me, & therefore will make no excuses. I can not think of coming to town, till sometime in April myself.[12]

I know, you have wrote a very obliging Letter [to Tuthill][13] but as I have not seen it, & he is not in my way at present, I leave him to answer for himself. Adieu, Dear S^r, & make my Compliments to your Family, I am ever

Yours

T GRAY.

197. MASON TO GRAY

Dear Sir

AMONGST the variety of rational entertainments that Travel affords to a thinking mind, I have always rankd with the principal that fund wch it presents of new Ideas, peculiarly proper to be thrown upon paper in order to form that wch we call a free Epistolary correspondence.[1] An easy Communication of Sentiments neither obscurd by a cloud of reserve, wch is always dissagreable to an amicable reader nor embarrassd by a Burthen of terms recherchés wch is always full as unpleasing to a negligent writer, is the very thing wch I should always labor to attain in my productions of this kind, tho perhaps my aim

Alderman of the City of London (see Letter 556, n. 7) since 1751, and was bought by him between 1760 and 1763. According to Mr. C. H. Crouch ('Ancestry of Thomas Gray', in *Genealogists' Magazine*, vol. iii, no. 4, p. 78) the house was built about 1736, and was known as Oak Hall. After his father's death (Nov. 1741) the house seems to have come into Gray's possession, as did the house in Cornhill.

[10] See Letter 145, n. 2.

[11] It was in March 1748 that the Cornhill fire took place in which Gray's house was destroyed.

[12] In Gray's pocket-diary for 1755 (now at Pembroke College) under date April 24 is the entry: 'Go to Town'.

[13] Words heavily scored through in MS. (see Letter 120, n. 2).

LETTER 197.—First printed by Mitford in *Gray–Mason* (1853), pp. 29–34; now reprinted from original.

[1] The greater part of the letter is written in a burlesque vein. In the last paragraph Mason says: 'how strangly is my stile changed since the beginning!'

is totally chimerical as the stile I speak of may be calld with the Poet

　　　A faultless Monster wch the world neer saw.[1a]

Therefore without further apology I shall trust to the sincerity of your friendship for a plenary Absolution in this case And proceed in all the simplicity of Narration.

　　Germany[2] is a country—But why should I tell my Friend who has seen France who has seen Italy what kind of a country is Germany. And yet perhaps he will not dispise me for it. For tho France is remarkable for its savoir-vivre and Italy for its Virtù. Yet Germany is the reservoir of solid Litterature & therefore not unworthy of the attention of a Person who unites all these qualifications in his own particular and may be calld without flattery a Microcosm of the talents both of his own Island & the continent. But Hard very hard is my fate that I cannot give him any satisfactory account of the state of Germanic Learning Having only as yet had a single Interview with Myn-Herr Shite the Royal Librarian of this place. MynnHerr Shite is of a roundish squab figure and of a face corresponding, that is as his Body is cylindrical, his face is rather circular than Oval, He apparells himself generally in a decent grass-green Suit. With a fair full Peruke not too full to break upon the spherical form of his cheeks & yet full enough to add a graceful squarness on each side of them. The Altitude of his square-toed-shoe heels the breadth of his Milk and waterd Rollups[3] and the size of his amber-headed Cane are all truly symbolical not only of his own Genius but of that of all his Compatriots. When I say that Mynheer Shite is the only erudite person whom I have yet seen, I must be understood to mean in this place, for when I lately made a tour to Hamburg, I met with another tho of a different Sex, her name Madam Belcht. Her person I will not attempt to describe But will endeavor to give you a morceau of Her Conversation, for I was honord with it, She askd me who was the famous Poet that writ the Nitt toats. I replyd Doct^r

---

[1a] From *Essay on Poetry* by John Sheffield, Duke of Buckingham:
　　'Reject that vulgar Error which appears
　　So fair, of making *perfect Characters*,
　　There's no such thing in Nature, and you'l draw
　　A faultless Monster which the world ne'er saw.'
[2] Mason was now in Hanover (see Letter 195, n. 14).
[3] See Letter 61, n. 2.

Yonge.[4] She begd leave to drink his Health in a Glass of sweet wine adding that he was her favrite English Author. We toasted the Doctor. Upon wch having a mind to give my Parnassian Toast, I askd Madame Belch if she had ever read La Petite Elegie dans La Cœmeterie Rustique, C'est Beaucoup Jolie je vous Assure! (for I had said fort jolie very often before). Oui Monsr (replyd Madame Belch) Je lu, & elle est bien Jolie & Melancholique mais elle ne touche point La Cœur comme mes tres cheres Nitt toats.

The Prudence you recommended to me at parting & wch you yourself are so remarkable for I shall strictly observe & therefore will say nothing of the Place I am in. Indeed I have nothing to say if I was not prudent, only that it is the noisiest Place I ever was in, & that I want to get out of it, wch I hope is no treason. I have sent Lord John Cavendish[5] a list of the Noises & their times of beginning wch will give you some Idea if he shews you the Letter.

Oh Mr Gray! I bought at Hamburg such a piano Forte,[6] and so cheap, it is a Harpsichord too of 2 Unisons & the Jacks serve as mutes (when the Piano Forte stop is playd) by the cleverest mechanism imaginable.[7] Wont you buy my Kirkman?[8]

Pray Mr Gray write soon (how strangly is my stile changd since the beginning!) and tell me about Rousseau or any thing. It's great Charity, I do assure you; I would have writ to you before but Hamburg & Reviews prevented me. White-

---

⁴ Edward Young (1683–1745), Fellow of All Souls College, Oxford, 1708; D.C.L. 1719; author (1742–5) of *The Complaint; or Night Thoughts on Life, Death, and Immortality.*

⁵ Fourth son (1732–96) of William Cavendish, third Duke of Devonshire; he was at Peterhouse, Cambridge (M.A. 1753), (where Mason was his private tutor); M.P. 1754–96; an adherent of Rockingham, he was a Lord of the Treasury in his first Ministry, 1765, and Chancellor of the Exchequer in his second Ministry, March–July 1782. Mason's *Elegy to a Young Nobleman leaving the University* ('Ere yet, ingenuous Youth, thy steps retire From Cam's smooth margin') was addressed to him. Mitford quotes George Selwyn's description of him as 'the learned canary bird', on account of his fair little person, and the quaintness with which he untreasured, as by rote, the stores of his memory. He was a friend of Gray, who in a letter to Mason (Letter 237) called him 'the best of all Johns'.

⁶ The earliest instance of this word in *O.E.D.* is dated 1767.

⁷ For explanation of this mechanism see Tovey's note, vol. i, p. 265.

⁸ Jacob Kirchmann, a German, who anglicized his name as Kirkman, came to London, early in the eighteenth century, and set up as a maker of harpsichords at the sign of the King's Arms in Broad Street, London.

head is here with his two lordlings.[9] You would delight in Lord Newnam,[10] he's so peevish & hates things so much & has so much sense. Lord Villiers[11] is Plumer[12] exceedingly polishd. Whitehead talks rather too much of Princesses of the Blood in a way between jest & earnest that most people must mistake & take for Admiration. The rest of the English are Earl[13] of Peterhouse, Sutton,[14] & just now Bagnal[15] of Trinity, With Grooms, Dogs, Tutors & all. Whitworth[16] is also soon expected so that I think we shall soon have a pretty Partie enough. O the Duce take that confounded Drum & fife it plagues me past endurance. I cannot write a word more adieu & beleive me Yours

with the greatest Sincerity
W. MASON.

Hanover June 27th 55

[9] William Whitehead (see Letter 44, n. 8); he was travelling as tutor to Lord Villiers and Lord Nuneham; they left England in June 1754, and after a stay at Leipzig made a tour in Germany and Italy, returning home towards the end of 1756.

[10] George Simon Harcourt (1736–1809); from 1749, when his father, second Viscount Harcourt, was created Viscount Nuneham and Earl Harcourt, till he succeeded to the Earldom in 1777, he was styled Viscount Nuneham. He became the intimate friend of Mason, whose correspondence with him has been preserved (see the *Harcourt Papers*, vol. vii, pp. 7 ff.). He paid Gray a visit at Cambridge at the beginning of April 1757 (see Letter 236).

[11] George Bussy Villiers (1735–1805); from 1742, when his elder brother died, until 1769, when he succeeded his father as fourth Earl of Jersey, he was styled Viscount Villiers. He accompanied Lord Nuneham on his visit to Gray at Cambridge in April 1757 (see n. 10).

[12] Presumably the Plummer of Gray's letter to Wharton of 28 June 1753 (see Letter 177, n. 12).

[13] Erasmus Earle, of Pembroke, B.A. 1748; Fellow of Peterhouse, 1748–51; d. 1768.

[14] Richard Sutton (son of Sir Robert Sutton, K.B., Ambassador at The Hague, Constantinople, and Paris) admitted to Trinity College, Cambridge, from Westminster in 1750, M.A. 1753. He was created a baronet on retiring from the office of Under-Secretary of State in 1772, and died in 1802.

[15] Beauchamp Bagenal, son of Walter Bagenal of Dunleckney, co. Carlow, admitted as a Fellow-commoner to Trinity in 1753. He had succeeded to the Carlow estate in 1745. He was subsequently member for co. Carlow and a friend of Grattan. He died in 1802.

[16] Perhaps Henry Whitworth, of St. John's, where he was a contemporary of Mason; B.A. 1745; priest, 1747; d. 1768.

198. GRAY TO WALPOLE

The Vine. Tuesday. July 22. [1755]¹

Dear Sʳ

I SHALL be very sorry, if I have been the occasiō² of interrupting any party or design of yours. when Mʳ C:³ thought to carry me to the Vine, I was hardly recover'd from a fit of the Gout, & was obliged to delay my journey thither till the week afterwards; and the uncertainty of my own motions has made me defer answering your meſsage without reflecting, that it might be troublesome to you. my intention is to wait upon you tomorrow se'nnight at Strawberry: if you go to Col. Conway's,⁴ or have any other design, that makes mine inconvenient to you at present, be so good to let me know, at this place, where I shall stay till the end of this week. we return'd yesterday night from Portsmouth, Southampton, & Winchester. I leave to Mʳ Ch: (who will write next post) to display to you all the beauties of Netley-Abbey.⁵ the two Views⁶ of this House go on apace, & grow every day under our eyes. Adieu, I am ever

Yours

T G:

Addressed: To The Honᵇˡᵉ Horace Walpole Esq in Arlington Street London
  Postmark: BASINGSTOKE⁷ 23 IY

LETTER 198.—First printed by Toynbee (1915), No. 190.
    ¹ The date of the year is determined by Gray's letter to Wharton from Stoke of 6 Aug. 1755 (Letter 199), in which he speaks of being 'just returned from my Hampshire expedition'. Gray's pocket-diary for 1755 (see Letter 196, n. 12) has the following entries: 'July 15 went into Hampshire to the Vine: 19 Go to Portsmouth: 21 Return to the Vine'.
    ² So in MS.; Gray not having left himself room for the *n* at the end of the line, made use of this sign of abbreviation to indicate the missing letter.
    ³ Mr. Chute.
    ⁴ At Park Place, in Berkshire, opposite Henley, which Conway had purchased three years before.
    ⁵ See Letter 199, n. 7. Walpole visited Netley Abbey with Chute a few weeks later (see his letter to Bentley of 18 Sept. 1755).
    ⁶ Painted by Müntz (a Swiss artist employed by Walpole) (see Letter 203, n. 3), who was now at the Vyne (see Walpole to Bentley, 4 Aug. 1755). A view of the Vyne by Müntz hung 'over the chimney' in Walpole's bedchamber at Strawberry Hill (see *Description of Strawberry Hill*, in *Works of Lord Orford*, vol. ii, 452).
    ⁷ The stamp was not inked, but the impress is legible.

John Chute

from a painting by Pompeo Battoni at the Vyne

199. GRAY TO WHARTON

Aug: 6. 1755. Stoke.

Dear Doctor

I WAS just returned from my Hampshire expedition,[1] & going to enquire after your little family, & how they had got over the measles, when I found a Letter from Stonhewer, in wch he says nothing on that head; whence I conclude they are out of danger, & you free from anxiety about them.[2] but he tells me, you expect me in town, for wch I am at a lofs to account, having said nothing to that purpose, at least I am sure, nothing with that meaning. I said, I was to go to Twickenham,[3] & am now expecting a letter from Mr. W: to inform me, when he shall be there. my stay will be at farthest a week with him, & at my return I shall let you know, & if the season be better than it now is, enquire, if you continue inclined to visit Windsor & its Environs. I wished for you often on the Southern Coast, where I have been,[4] & made much the same Tour, that Stonhewer did before me. take notice, that the Oaks grow quite down to the Beach, & that the Sea forms a number of Bays little & great, that appear glittering in the midst of thick Groves of them. add to this the Fleet (for I was at Portsmouth two days before it sail'd)[5] & the number of Vefsels always pafsing along, or sailing up Southampton-River (wch is the largest of these Bays I mention) and enters about 10 mile into the Land, & you will have a faint Idea of the *South*. from Fareham to Southampton, where you are upon a level with the coast, you have a thousand such Peeps & delightful Openings, but would you see the whole at once, you must get upon Ports-Down 5 Mile on this side Portsmouth. it is the top of a ridge, that forms a natural Terrafs

LETTER 199.—First printed by Mitford (1816), vol. ii, pp. 256–8; now reprinted from original.   [1] See Letter 198, n. 1.

[2] For 'about them' Gray wrote originally 'on that head', a phrase he had used just before.

[3] Strawberry Hill,where he went on Sept. 3 as he records in his pocket-diary.

[4] He visited Southampton and Portsmouth with Chute (see Letter 198).

[5] Sir Edward Hawke, K.B., who, after having been in command of the home fleet for four years, struck his flag in November 1752, 'in February 1755 was again ordered to hoist it on board the St. George at Portsmouth. On 16 July he was appointed to the command of the western squadron, with orders from the lords justices (22 July) to go to sea with sixteen sail of the line, and cruise between Ushant and Cape Finisterre in order to intercept a French squadron which . . . had been cruising in the neighbourhood of Gibraltar and had put into Cadiz' (*D.N.B.*).

3 Mile long, literally not three times broader than Windsor-
Terraſs with a gradual fall on both sides & cover'd with a turf
like New-Market. to the North opens Hampshire & Berkshire
cover'd with woods, & interspersed with numerous Gentlemen's
Houses & Villages. to the South, Portsmouth, Gosport, &c:
just at your foot in appearance, the Fleet, the Sea winding, &
breaking in bays into the land, the deep shade of tall Oaks in
the enclosures, wch become blue, as they go off to distance,
Portchester-Castle, Carshot-Castle,[6] & all the Isle of Wight,
in wch you plainly distinguish the fields, hedge-rows, & woods
next the shore, & a back-ground of hills behind them. I have
not seen a more magnificent or more varied Prospect. I have
been also at Tichfield, at Netly-Abbey,[7] (a most beautiful
Ruin in as beautiful a situation) at Southampton, at Bevis-
Mount,[8] at Winchester, &c: my Gout is gone, but I am not
absolutely well yet. I hear Mason was expected on Monday
last, but was not to speak of it, therefore you will say nothing
till you see him. I do not understand this, nor what he means
by coming. It seems wrong to me. what did you think of the
Morceau[9] I sent you, pray, speak your mind.
My best Compliments to Mrs. Wharton. Adieu, I am
Ever Yours
T G.

Addressed: To Dr Thomas Wharton, M:D: in Kings-Arms Yard, Coleman
Street London   *Postmark:* 7 AV

[6] 'Calshot-castle'; the Tudor fortress of that name on a spit at the mouth
of Southampton Water.
[7] Netley was a Cistercian abbey, founded in 1237 by Henry III; the ruins
include a great part of the cruciform church, abbot's house, chapter-house,
and domestic buildings. Gray visited Netley Abbey again in 1764 (see his
description of it in Letters 392, 397).
[8] The name formerly of a house and grounds about a mile north of Southampton, outside the city walls. The name is now applied to a small suburb
on the site of the former estate. In Gray's catalogue of sites, buildings, etc.,
which he wrote in the pages of a pocket Atlas (printed by Mason in 1773
with the title *Catalogue of the Antiquities, Houses, Parks, Plantations, Scenes, and
Situations in England and Wales*, see Letter 267, n. 4), among the places in
Hampshire noted as particularly worth seeing is 'Bevis Mount, (Sir J. Mordaunt's) near Southampton'—the owner at that time being General Sir John
Mordaunt, K.B.
[9] A copy of the *first* part of the Bard, but which, I am sorry to say, is not
preserved among Dr Wharton's MSS. *Mitford.*—This consisted of the first
56 lines; a second portion, consisting of lines 57 to 100, Gray sent to Stonhewer (to be communicated to Wharton) on 21 Aug. (see Letter 204, n. 4); a
draft of lines 63–144 he sent subsequently direct to Wharton (see Letter 205A).

200. GRAY TO WALPOLE
Aug: 8. Stoke 1755.

I INTEND to be at Strawberry on Monday[1] before dinner. but as Saints have the Diabetes,[2] you will not wonder if a miserable Sinner can not answer a day beforehand for his own constitution. seriously it has not been fair weather within me, eversince I came into this country. at Mr Chute's I was not quite right; & since my return, particularly this morning, I am sensible of a feverish disposition, & little wandering pains, that may fix into the Gout, & confine me again. if so, you will excuse the caprices of my distemper, & conclude, that it came upon me too suddenly for me to give you notice in time. I am

Yours ever
T G:

Addressed: To The Honble Horace Walpole Esq in Arlington Street London
Postmark: 9 AV

201. GRAY TO WALPOLE
Aug: 10. 1755. Stoke.

A s they have order'd me to bleed presently, I write to you, while I can make use of my arm, to desire you would excuse me. I have had advice, as they call it, & am still as uncertain as ever, whether I am to expect the Gout or Rheumatism. one thing is certain, that I am to expect medecines enough; & as I do not think it civil to bring an Apothecary's shop[1] to Strawberry, & am told besides, that it is not very safe, I hope you will forgive

Yours ever
T G:

Addressed: To The Honble Horace Walpole Esq in Arlington Street London
Postmark: 11 AV

LETTER 200.—First printed by Toynbee (1915), No. 191.
[1] August 11.
[2] Walpole had evidently repeated to Gray a *mot* which appears in his letter to Bentley from Strawberry Hill of 4 Aug.: 'We have been exceedingly troubled for some time with St. Swithin's diabetes, and have not a dry thread in any walk about us.'
LETTER 201. First printed by Toynbee (1915), No. 192.
[1] See his letters to Chute of 14 Aug. (Letter 203), and to Wharton of 21 Aug. (Letter 205).

202. GRAY TO WALPOLE

Stoke. Aug. 14. 1755.

WHEN you name a Fever & Rash in the middle of August,[1] I can not but enquire (as soon as I am able[2]) what you are doing to get rid of them, & how you are, since I heard from you. I do not at all expect an answer from yourself; but should be much obliged to you, if you would order Harry[3] or Louis[4] to write me a line of information. I myself am a little better & a little worse for my *advice*. the heats I felt in a morning are abated, if not gone; and in their room I have got the head-ach, wch with me is a very unusual thing. Adieu! I hope to hear a better account of you. I am ever

Yours

T G:

If you easily get rid of your fever; pray, do not think of going so soon near the coast of Efsex.[5]

Addressed: To The Honble Horace Walpole Esq in Arlington Street London
Postmark: 15 AV

203. GRAY TO CHUTE

Stoke. Aug: 14. 1755.

Dear S^r

I WRITE to the Vine imagining you may be still there to tell you, that I was to have gone to Strawberry on Monday last, but being ill was obliged to write the day before, & excuse myself. M^r W: could not receive my letter till Monday afternoon, & had therefore sent a Mefsenger from London early that morning to

LETTER 202.—First printed by Toynbee (1915), No. 193.
[1] See his letter to Chute of 14 Aug. (Letter 203).
[2] He had been 'bloodied' recently (see Letter 201), when '10 or 11 oz of blood' had been taken from his arm (see Letter 205).
[3] Walpole's valet (Henry Jones).
[4] A Swiss servant of Walpole's; he died of drink in 1767 (see Walpole to Montagu, 14 Oct. 1760; 8 April 1763; 13 Jan. 1767).
[5] Walpole writes to Bentley on 15 Aug.: 'I am going to Mr Rigby's for a week or ten days'; that is, to Mistley Hall, near Manningtree, in Essex. 'The house stands on a high hill, on an arm of the sea, which winds itself before two sides of the house' (Walpole to Montagu, 25 June 1745).
LETTER 203.—First printed by Mitford in *Works of Gray* (1835–43), vol. iii, pp. 133–4; now reprinted from original.

say, that he was very ill of a Fever & Rash, & unable to go himself to Twickenham. I know this is a dangerous season, & that malignant Fevers are now very common, & am therefore something alarmed at his situation. if you have heard anything, you will let me know; & particularly, if any thing should carry you soon to Town. I myself have been ill, eversince I came out of Hampshire. I have had *advice*, & have been bloodied, & taken draughts of salt of Wormwood, Lemons, Tincture of Guiacum,[1] Magnesia, & the Devil. you will immediately conclude, they thought me rheumatic & feverish. no such thing! they thought me gouty, & that I had no fever. all I can say is, that my heats in the morning are abated, that my foot begins to ach again, & that my head achs, & feels light & giddy. so much for me. my Comp:[ts] to the Gentleman with the Moco[2]-smelling-bottle, the Muntz's,[3] the Betties, & the Babies. Adieu, I am ever

[
                                                                ][4]

Addressed: To John Chute Esq, of the Vine near Basingstoke Hampshire
     Postmark: 15 AV

   [1] A drug made from the resin obtained from the Lignum vitae (*Guaiacum officinale*).
   [2] Moco (otherwise mocho or mocha) is a kind of chalcedony of the nature of moss-agate.
   [3] John Henry Müntz (d. 1775); in his letter to Mann of 9 Sept. 1758, from Strawberry Hill, Walpole says of him: 'I have a painter in the house, who is an engraver too, a mechanic and everything. He was a Swiss engineer in the French service; but his regiment being broken at the peace, Mr. Bentley found him in the isle of Jersey, and fixed him with me. He has an astonishing genius for landscape, and added to that, all the industry and patience of a German.' Müntz was employed at the Vyne for some weeks in the summer of 1755, and was there when Gray visited Chute in July (see Letter 198, n. 6). It was probably at this time that he painted the oval portrait of Chute and the view of the Vyne which were formerly at Strawberry Hill, and are now at the Vyne. Walpole, who had allowed him '100*l.* a year, my house, table, and utmost countenance', dismissed him in 1759. (See his letter to Montagu of 17 Nov. of that year.)
   [4] Signature cut off.

204. GRAY TO STONHEWER

August 21, 1755.

I THANK you for your intelligence about Herculaneum,[1] which was the first news I received of it. I have since turned over Monsignor Baiardi's book,[2] where I have learned how many grains of modern wheat the Roman Congius, in the Capitol, holds, and how many thousandth parts of an inch the Greek foot consisted of more (or lefs, for I forget which) than our own. He proves also by many affecting examples, that an Antiquary may be mistaken: That, for any thing any body knows, this place under ground might be some other place, and not Herculaneum; but neverthelefs, that he can shew for certain, that it was this place and no other place; that it is hard to say which of the several Hercules's was the founder; therefore (in the third volume) he promises to give us the memoirs of them all; and after that, if we do not know what to think of the matter, he will tell us. There is a great deal of wit too, and satire and verses, in the book, which is intended chiefly for the information of the French King, who will be greatly edified without doubt.

I am much obliged to you also for Voltaire's performance;[3] it is very unequal, as he is apt to be in all but his dramas, and looks like the work of a man that will admire his retreat and his Leman-Lake no longer than till he finds an opportunity to leave it: However, though there be many parts which I do not like, yet it is in several places excellent, and every where above mediocrity. As you have the politenefs to pretend impatience, and desire I would communicate, and all that, I annex a piece

LETTER 204.—First printed in Mason's *Memoirs*, pp. 240–1.

[1] See Gray's account of his visit to the site in Letter 88.

[2] Ottavio Antonio Baiardi (c. 1690–c. 1765), of Parma, Apostolic Notary—was in 1747 invited from Rome by the King of Naples (see Letter 76, n. 2) to describe the antiquities which were being collected from Herculaneum in the museum at Portici under the care of Camillo Paderni. By way of preliminary he published at Naples in 5 vols. 4to (1752–6) his *Prodromo delle Antichità d'Ercolano*, but the King, impatient of the delay, this work being no more than an introduction to the desired description, founded the Accademia Ercolanese, to whom he entrusted the task. This body published in 9 vols. fol. *Le Antichità di Ercolano* (Naples, 1757–92).

[3] See Letter 195, n. 17. In the Catalogue of the Sale of Gray's MSS. and books in 1751 there was included in lot 53 *Epitre de M. de Voltaire en arrivant dans sa terre près du Lac Leman*, described as in Stonhewer's Autograph.

of the Prophecy;[4] which must be true at least, as it was wrote so many hundred years after the events.

205. GRAY TO WHARTON

Aug: 21. 1755. Stoke.

Dear Doctor

INSTEAD of going to Twickenham I was obliged to send my excuses,[1] & the same day Mr. W: sent a mefsenger to say he was confined in Town with a Fever & a Rash.[2] he has since wrote me word, that he is well again; but for me I continue much as I was, & have been but once out of the house to walk, since I return'd from Hampshire. being much inclined to bleeding myself, I yet was fearful to venture, least it should bring on a regular fit of the Gout, so I sent for advice at last, & expected Dr Hayes[3] should tell me presently, whether it were Gout or Rheumatism. in his talk he treated it rather as the former, but his prescription appears to me to be meant for the latter. you will judge. he took away 10 or 11 *Oz* of blood, & order'd these draughts night & morning:—*Sal: Absinth. Succ: Limon. finitâ effervescentiâ add: Aqu: Alexit. Simpl:, Menth: Piperit, Magnes. alb., Tinct: G. Guiac. Spirituos.* the quantities I can't read; only I think there is a Dram of the Tincture, & ½ a Dram of Magnesia in each draught. the Blood had no sign of inflammation, but of a bright red: the Serum of a dark yellow with little transparency, not viscid to the touch. the draughts (wch I took over night only) made me sweat almost immediately, & open'd a little in the morning. the consequence is, that I have still many slight complaints. broken & unrefreshing sleeps, as before. lefs feverish than I was, in a morning: instead of it a sensation of wearinefs and sorenefs in both feet, wch goes off in the day. a frequent dizzinefs & lightnefs of head.

---

[4] The second Antistrophe and Epode, with a few lines of the third Strophe of his Ode, entitled the Bard, were here inserted. *Mason.*—This fragment consisted of lines 63 ('Mighty Victor, mighty Lord') to 100 ('The web is wove. The work is done'). This is not with the letter.

LETTER 205.—First printed in part in Mason's *Memoirs*, p. 244; first printed in full by Mitford (1816), vol. ii, pp. 258–63; now reprinted from original.

[1] See Letter 201.   [2] See Letters 202, 203.

[3] This was Cherry Hayes, Scholar of Eton 1711; Scholar of King's College, Cambridge, 1716; B.A. 1720; M.A. 1723; M.D. 1728; Fellow of King's 1719–63; d. 25 Oct. 1763. He practised at Windsor. He was in attendance on Gray's aunt, Mrs. Rogers, at Stoke at the time of her death in Sept 1758 (see Letter 280).

easily fatigued with motion. sometimes a little pain in my breast, as I had in the winter. these symptoms are all too slight to make an illneſs; but they do not make perfect health. that is sure.

Tho' I allow abundance for your kindneſs & partiality to me, I am yet much pleased with the good opinion you seem to have of the *Bard*. you may alter that *Robed in the Sable*, &c,[4] almost in your own words, thus

> With fury pale, & pale with woe,
> Secure of fate, the Poet stood &c:

Tho' *haggard*, wch conveys to you the Idea of a *Witch*, is indeed only a metaphor taken from an unreclaim'd Hawk, wch is call'd a *Haggard*, & looks wild & *farouche* & jealous of its liberty. I have sent now Stonhe^r a bit more of the *prophecy*,[5] & desire him to shew it you immediately: it is very rough & un-polish'd at present. Adieu, dear S^r, I am ever

Truly Yours
T G.

Addressed: To Dr Thomas Wharton M:D: in Kings-Arms Yard Coleman Street London   *Postmark:* 22 AV

205A. TEXT OF 'THE BARD', LL. 57–144.

[Letter 205 is followed in the Wharton manuscripts by a copy, in Gray's handwriting, of part of *The Bard*. Sometime before 6 August 1755 Gray had sent Wharton a *Morceau*, which, it is assumed, was the first part of the Ode (see Letter 199, n. 9). On 21 August, the same day that he wrote to Wharton, he sent to Stonhewer another piece of the *Prophecy* (ll. 63–100), which was to be shown to Wharton (see Letter 204, n. 4). The passage printed here contains from l. 57 to the end of the poem. It obviously cannot have been written until nearly two years after the date of Letter 205, as it contains the conclusion of the Ode in a later recension than that which Gray sent to Mason in his letter of [31] May 1757 (Letter 238). It was probably earlier than the letter to Mason of [11] June (Letter 239). Gray went to London about the middle of June 1757, and may have given Wharton his rough copy, when he saw him.

Note.—Words and passages enclosed in square brackets represent cancellations made by Gray in the manuscript. The substituted readings, which in the manuscript are inserted for the most part overline, but occasionally in the margin or on the opposite leaf, are here printed, in smaller type, immediately above the cancellations which they replace.]

*   *   *

⁴ Lines 17–18; the alteration was not ultimately adopted.
⁵ See Letter 204, n. 4.

She-Wolf of France with unrelenting fangs
That tear'st the bowels of thy mangled Mate
From thee be born, who o'er thy country hangs
The Scourge of Heaven. what Terrors round him wait!
Amazement in his Van with Flight combined,
And Sorrow's faded form & Solitude behind.

                    ANT: 2
          Victor
Mighty [Conqu'ror], mighty Lord,
    his
Low on [the] funeral couch he lies.
   No   no
[What] pitying heart, [what] eye afford
A tear to grace his obsequies?
Is the sable Warrior fled?
Thy Son is gone. he rests among the Dead.
              in thy noontide beam were born
The swarm, that [hover'd in thy noontide ray?]
                  morn
Gone to salute the rising [day].
Fair laughs the Moon, & soft the Zephyr blows
While proudly riding o'er the azure realm
In gallant trim the gilded Vefsel goes,
Youth in the prow, & Pleasure at the helm,
Regardlefs of the sweeping Whirlwind's sway
That hush'd in grim repose expects his evening-prey.
[Mirrors of Saxon truth & loyalty,
Your helplefs old expiring Master view
They hear not. scarce Religion dares supply
Her mutter'd Requiems, & her holy Dew.
Yet thou, proud Boy, from Pomfret's walls shalt send
A sigh, & envy oft thy happy Grandsire's end.]

                    EPODE 3[6]
Fill high the sparkling bowl,
The rich repast prepare,
Reft of a crown he yet may share the feast.
Close by the regal chair
Fell Thirst & Famine scowl
A smile of horror on their baffled guest.

          [6] *Sic* in MS. It should be 2.

                    435

Heard ye the din of battle bray,
Lance to lance & horse to horse!
Long Years of havock urge their destin'd course,
And thro' the kindred squadrons mow their way.
<u>Ye</u>
[Grim] Towers of Julius, London's lasting shame,
With many a foul & midnight-murther fed,
Revere his Consort's faith, his Father's fame,
And spare the meek Usurper's hallow'd head
Above, below, the Rose of snow
Twined with her blushing Foe we spread:
The bristled Boar in infant gore
Wallows beneath the thorny shade.
Now, Brothers, bending o'er th' accursed loom
Stamp we our vengeance deep, & ratify his doom.

STROPHE 3

Edward, lo, to sudden fate
(Weave we the woof. the thread is spun)
Half of thy Heart we consecrate
(The Web is wove. the Work is done.)
<u>thus</u>
Stay, oh stay, nor [here] forlorn
<u>me unblefs'd, unpitied here</u>
Leave [your despairing Caradoc] to mourn!
<u>track</u>
In yon bright [clouds], that fires the western skies,
<u>melt</u>
They [sink], they vanish from my eyes.
<u>solemn scenes</u>
But ah! what [scenes of heav'n] on Snowdon's height
<u>glitt'ring</u>
Descending slow their [golden] skirts unroll!
Visions of glory, spare my aching sight,
Ye unborn ages, crowd not on my soul.
No more our long-lost Arthur we bewail.
All hail, ye genuine Kings, Britannia's Issue, hail!
[From Cambria's thousand hills a thousand strains
Triumphant tell aloud, another Arthur reigns]

ANTIST: 3

<u>Girt with many a Baron</u>
[Youthful Knights & Barons] bold
<u>Sublime their starry fronts they rear</u>
[With dazzling helm & horrent spear]

436

And gorgeous Dames, & Statesmen old
In bearded majesty appear:
In the midst a Form divine.
Her eye proclaims her of the Briton-line;
Her   her
[A] lyon-port, [an] awe-commanding face,
Attemper'd sweet to virgin-grace.
What strings symphonious tremble in the air!
What strains of vocal transport round her play!
Hear from the grave, great Taliefsin, hear;
They breath a soul to animate thy clay.
Bright Rapture calls, & soaring, as she sings,
Waves in the eye of Heav'n her many-colour'd wings.

EPODE 3

The verse adorn again
Fierce War, & faithful Love,
And Truth severe by fairy-Fiction drest.
In buskin'd measures move
Pale Grief & pleasing Pain
With Horrour, Tyrant of the throbbing breast.
A Voice as of the Cherub-Quire
Gales from blooming Eden bear;
And distant Warblings lefsen on my ear,
That lost in long futurity expire.
Fond impious Man, thinkst thou, yon sanguine cloud
Rais'd by thy breath has quench'd the Orb of day?
Tomorrow he repairs the golden flood
And warms the Nations with redoubled ray.
Enough for me. with joy I see
The different doom our Fates afsign.
Bc thinc Dcspair & sccptrcd Carc.
To triumph & to die are mine.
He spoke, & headlong from the Mountain's height
Deep in the roaring tide he sunk to endlefs night.[7]

[7] Eventually this line was altered to 'Deep in the roaring tide he plung'd
to endless night' (see Letter 38, n. 5). In his own copy of the Strawberry Hill
edition of *Odes by Mr. Gray*, Walpole wrote: 'In the original this word was
sunk but Mr Garrick suggested *plung'd* as a more emphatic word on such an
occasion' (see *Journal of the Printing-Office at Strawberry Hill*, p. 29, n. 6).

206. MASON TO GRAY

Tunbridge Sept 10ᵗʰ 55.
Dear Mʳ Gray

I PROMISD to write to you from Tunbridge And now I perform it. You can't imagine how much people lye with one another here. I had the narrowest escape in the world. The Countess of Schoonfeld¹ lay with evry body and she was but just gone when I came hither. However since I came We have sent Miss Ash² to Town with Child some people say twas Count Bryll³ that did it But I say nothing, I had been here two days before she went; thats all. Lady Caroline⁴ who corresponds with her evry post, tells it publickly on the pantiles, then Ladies are surprizd. & She crys out "Lord how can ye I wonder she is not with Child evry year." Heres a Monˢ de Sᵗ Simon⁵ here, much laid with also. but The property of one Lady only who as Sʳ John Falstaffe says makes him "her Philosophers two stones".⁶ You cant conceive how she pillages him. Sometimes they take their pastime in the midst of a Curricle sometimes in a feild sometimes at his Lodgings & where not? Lady Rotchfort⁷ has

LETTER 206.—First printed in part by Mitford in *Gray–Mason* (1853), pp. 35–7; now first printed in full from original.

¹ Schoenfeld. Miss Speed (see Letter 155, n. 1) was at Tunbridge in July and August of this year, and in a letter to Lord Nuneham of 26 Oct., she gives a lively description of a German Countess 'about seventy years old, . . . who dresses as if she was sixteen'.

² Miss Elizabeth Ashe was an intimate friend of Lady Caroline Petersham (see n. 4). There are allusions to both the ladies in Walpole's letters to Mann of 2 April and 2 August 1750, and to George Montagu of 23 June in the same year.

³ Nothing seems to be known of this individual.

⁴ Lady Caroline Fitzroy (1722–84) was eldest daughter of Charles Fitzroy, second Duke of Grafton; she married, in 1746, William Stanhope, Viscount Petersham, eldest son of the first Earl of Harrington, to whose title he succeeded in 1756.

⁵ This was Maximilien Henri (1720–99), Marquis de St. Simon, of the Sandricourt branch of the family to which the famous Duc de St. Simon belonged. He had been aide-de-camp to the Prince de Conti, and was the author of numerous works, which included translations of Swift's *Tale of a Tub*, Pope's *Essay on Man*, and Macpherson's *Temora*. Walpole met him in the summer of this year while on a visit to Lord Tilney at Wanstead; see his letter to Bentley of 17 July. In his letter to Conway of 24 Jan. 1756 Walpole describes a fracas at the theatre where the Marquis was in company with Miss Ashe and Lady Caroline Petersham in the latter's box.

⁶ *2 Henry IV*, iii. 2 (*ad fin.*).

⁷ Countess of Rochford—Lucy Young (d. 1773), daughter of Edward Young, of Durnford, Wilts.; she married (1742) William Henry Nassau de

been here three Days with Lady H[8] A delightful Character! so full of the Rheumatics and Achs & Pains all over and then so Genède you know & so detesting of Public places, because People dont dress so strangely as they did four year ago, and are not frightful enough to make one Laugh.—I was told yesterday by Lady H that it was her Birthday and she wondered I had not writ her some Verses. so I did, & here they are.[8a]

> Had R—d[9] bad my muse essay
> To hail her, on her natal day
> I soon had Ransackd Natures bowers
> For Blushing fruit & fragrant flowrs
> And sworn till Fops believd it true
> That all their sweetness all their hue
> Were nought to what her cheekes advance
> Adornd tout alamode de France
>   Or had gay Lady C***[10]
> Been bent on such an odd design,
> And deignd my verses to receive,
> (For Verse is all I have to give)
> It soon had been my tuneful prayr
> To beg propitious Fate to spare
> The Bliss she has, & alway lend
> An easy Lord and genrous friend.
>   But how to suit my song to you
> Is mighty hard, for entre nous
> You're most unfashionably fair,
> Content with your own face & air,

Zulestein (1717–81), fourth Earl of Rochford. She was among the first of Walpole's visitors to the Strawberry Hill printing-office in August 1757, when the following lines were addressed to her from the press:

> 'In vain from your properest name you have flown,
> And exchang'd lovely Cupid's for Hymen's dull throne:
> By my art shall your beauties be constantly sung,
> And in spite of yourself you shall ever be YOUNG.'

[8] Countess of Holdernesse—Mary Doublet (1720–1801), daughter of Francis Doublet, member of the States of Holland; she married (1743), at The Hague, Robert Darcy (1718–78), fourth Earl of Holdernesse (see Letter 60, n. 3).

[8a] In Mason's Commonplace-book (now in the Cathedral Library at York) there is a copy of these verses 'written at Tunbridge Wells, Aug. 1755'. There are variations from the text sent to Gray, which no doubt represent Mason's final improvements.

[9] Rochford (see n. 7).   [10] Caroline (see n. 4).

And more unfashionably true,
A Husband bounds your utmost view.
This then the Case, my Rhymes I'll close,
And wish in verse as plain as prose,
That Tunbridge from her springs may grant
The little added health you want;
And that for many a happy year
You need not to her fount repair,
Unless to see as now you see   •
Each varied form of vanity,
And candid laugh, as now you do,
At all the fools her walks can shew.
　　Yet one wish more—May Fortune kind
Soon briskly blow a North-east wind;[11]
And then some few days past & gone
Youll scarce pull Coifs for St Simon.[12]

You must observe this is not the St Simon mentioned in a Book
you have formerly read calld the Testament, But another quite
of a different family and whose name is pronounced Sĕnsĭm-
mong like a Dactyle.[13] Well, how do you like my Verses?
Whether shall I call them, To Lady H on her Birthday; or a
Lampoon on Lady R & Lady C? one talks of nothing but
Lampoons here, pray unde derivatur Lampoon?[14] You have
a pretty knack at an oldfashioned Welch Ode,[15] but you are
nothing like me at an Impromptu. If you write to me Direct
to The young Man that my Aunt Dent had like to have
ravishd. Axton[16] writ to me yesterday about his fellowship. twas
rather a sesquipedalian Letter; however I answerd it today, &
hopd he would behave gratefully to Mr Brown who I sayd was
much his friend, & would secure him his fellowship. and so
having concluded my Paper I am yours

[11] To bring Lord Holdernesse back from Hanover, where as Secretary of
State he was in attendance on the King.
[12] See n. 5.
[13] Mason apparently could not distinguish an anapaest from a dactyl.
[14] *O.E.D.* accepts the etymology given by Littré of Fr. *lampon*, from
lamper, a nasalized form of *laper* (Eng. *lap*), to gulp down, *lampons*, that is,
buvons, being a common refrain of scurrilous drinking-songs.
[15] Gray's unfinished *Bard*.
[16] Thomas Axton, of Pembroke, admitted Sizar, 1750; matriculated,
1751; B.A. 1755; Fellow, March 1757; M.A. 1758; Vicar of Frindsbury,
Kent, 1762–4; d. 1764. He is mentioned in Mason's letter to Gray of 28 Nov.
1760 (Letter 326).

207. GRAY TO WALPOLE

Oct: 14. 1755.

I DO not think of leaving this place[1] till about a fortnight hence, & as I doubt if you will continue at Twickenham so late in the year, shall then call upon you at your house in Town. I heartily pity poor G: Montagu,[2] who never was made for solitude, & who begins to feel it at a time of life, when every body grows unfit for it. pray tell Mr Chute, I have been tolerably well,[3] eversince I saw him. I am ever

Yours

T G:

Addressed: To The Honble Horace Walpole[4] in Arlington Street London
Postmark: 15 OC

208. GRAY TO WHARTON

[18 Oct., 1755][1]

My dear Doctor

I OUGHT before now to have thanked you for your kind offer, wch I mean soon to accept for a reason, wch to be sure can be no reason to you or Mrs Wharton, & therefore I think it my duty to give you notice of it. it is a very poſsible thing I may be ill again in Town, wch I would not chuse to be in a dirty inconvenient lodgeing, where perhaps my nurse might stifle me with a pillow, and therefore it is no wonder, if I prefer your house. but I tell you of this in time, that if either of you are frighted at the thought of a sick body, you may make a handsome excuse, & save yourselves this trouble. you are not to imagine my illneſs is in *Eſse;* no, it is only in *Poſse,* otherwise I should myself

LETTER 207.—First printed by Toynbee (1915), No. 194.
[1] 1 Stoke (see n. 3).
[2] Montagu had just lost his sister, Miss Harriet Montagu, who lived with him at Greatworth, in Northamptonshire (see Walpole to Montagu, 7 Oct. 1755).
[3] Writing to Chute from Arlington Street on 20 Oct., Walpole says: 'I had a note from Gray, who is still at Stoke; and he desires I would tell you that he has continued pretty well.'
[4] It will be noted that from now on Gray adopts the modern usage, and addresses Walpole as 'Honble' without 'Esq.'
LETTER 208.—First printed in part (in a garbled text) in Mason's *Memoirs,* pp. 244–5; first printed in full by Mitford (1816), vol. ii, pp. 265–6; now reprinted from original.
[1] Date added by Wharton; Gray was still at Stoke (see Letter 207, n. 3).

be scrupulous of bringing it home to you. I shall be in town in about a fortnight.[2] you will be sorry (as I am) at the destruction of poor   [3] views, wch promised so fair: but both he & I have known it this long time, so, I believe, he was prepared, & his old Patron is no bad refsource.[4] I am told, it is the fashion to be totally silent with regard to the ministry.[5] nothing is to be talked of, or even suspected, till the Parliament meets.[6] in the mean time the new *Manager* has taken what appears to me a very odd step.[7] if you do not hear of a thing, wch is in it's nature no secret, I can not well inform you by the Post. to me it is utterly unaccountable.

Pray what is the reason I do not read your name among the Censors of the College?[8] did they not offer it you, or have you refused it? I have not done a word more of *Bard*, having been in a very listlefs, unpleasant, & inutile state of Mind for this

[2] In his pocket-diary (see Letter 196, n. 12) Gray noted: 'Oct. 30. came to Town. Nov. 26. go to Cambridge.'

[3] The name is obliterated. Mitford printed 'Stonehewer's' without note or explanation. It is possible that at the time, when Mitford had the manuscript before him, some letters could be traced beneath the obliteration, but the restoration must be regarded as uncertain.

[4] If the reference is to Stonhewer, nothing is known as to the destruction of his views. It might be conjectured that 'his old Patron' was the Duke of Grafton, to whose son, the Earl of Euston, Stonhewer had been private tutor. It was perhaps to the Duke that Stonhewer owed his appointment, in this year, to the post of Historiographer to his Majesty (see Letter 196, n. 3).

[5] There was a crisis in the Newcastle administration. Walpole in letters written at the end of September to Mann, Chute, and Bentley gives an account of what was intended. Legge, the Chancellor of the Exchequer, and Pitt, the Paymaster of the Forces, who had opposed the subsidies to Hesse-Cassel and Russia, were to be dismissed from their posts, and Henry Fox was 'to be Secretary of State and to have the conduct of the House of Commons'. But the changes were not to be made 'till after the Parliament is met'. So far as Newcastle's intentions were not matters of common knowledge, Gray had probably been informed of them by Walpole.

[6] Parliament met on 13 Nov.

[7] 'The new *Manager*' can scarcely be Newcastle, as Tovey suggested, as he had been Prime Minister since March 1754. Probably Henry Fox is meant. Walpole, in his letter to Chute, says that Fox is 'to have the management of the House of Commons'. It is possible that the 'very odd step', that he had taken, may be explained by Walpole's statement that he was 'endeavouring to bring the Bedfords to court'.

[8] The officers in the College of Physicians who grant licences. Wharton's great-grandfather, Thomas Wharton, was six times Censor, and his uncle, George Wharton, four times. Wharton himself, who became a Fellow in 1754, was Censor in 1757.

long while, for wch I shall beg you to prescribe me somewhat strengthning & agglutinant, lest it turn to a confirm'd Pthisis.[9] to shew you how epidemical Self-Murther is this year,[10] Lady M. Capel (Ld Efsex's Sister)[11] a young Person, has just cut the veins of both arms acrofs, but (they say) will not die of it. she was well & in her senses, tho' of a family that are apt to be otherwise.[12] Adieu, dear Doct^r, I should be glad of a line from you, before I come. believe me ever

Most sincerely Yours,
T G:

209. MASON TO GRAY

Wadworth[1] Nov: 26th 55.

Dear Mr Gray

IT is not true that I again make interest to be transported into Ireland;[2] and yet I beleive too it will be my fate. I am totally passive in the whole affair, and shall remain so, the only step I ever took, wch could be calld active, was to write a Letter to Mr Bonfoy,[3] simply to enquire whether it was true that the Marquiss[4] intended to take me next; wch he has now answerd

---

[9] *Sic* for phthisis.

[10] In his letter to Bentley of 9 Jan. 1755 Walpole mentions no less than four recent suicides, those of Lord Drumlanrig, Lord Montford, Sir John Bland, and another, unnamed; he mentions yet another in his letter to the same of 17 July; and on 19 Oct. he writes: 'The invasion . . . begins, like Moses's rod, to swallow other news, both political and *suicidical*.'

[11] Lady Mary Capel, fourth daughter (b. 1722) of William, third Earl of Essex, and sister of William Ann Holles, fourth Earl (1743); she survived, and married in 1758 Admiral Hon. John Forbes, (1714–96), second son of George, third Earl of Granard.

[12] Gray alludes to the fact that her father, the third Lord Essex, was insane and died in confinement in 1743 (see Walpole's letters to Mann of 23 Oct. 1742, and 13 June 1743).

LETTER 209.—First printed by Mitford in *Gray–Mason* (1853), pp. 37–41; now reprinted from original.

[1] Four miles south of Doncaster. Mason's first cousin, Ann Robinson, daughter of Arthur Robinson, of Hull, and of Mary Mason, his father's sister, married Josiah Wordsworth, of Wadworth (see Letter 438, n. 1).

[2] See n. 4.

[3] See Letter 126, n. 11. Bonfoy seems to have been intimate with the Marquis of Hartington of that day; after the Marquis had succeeded to the dukedom Walpole met him at Chatsworth as the guest of the Duke (see Walpole to Montagu, 1 Sept. 1760).

[4] William Cavendish (1720–64), eldest son of the third Duke of Devonshire; styled Marquis of Hartington from 1729 (when his father became

in the affirmative; but as Louth[5] is still to continue first Chaplain, the time when is uncertain, & cannot be these two years, in wch space you know a Man may die or do a hundred pretty things.—But I hear, since I came into these parts, that Seward the Critic[6] is very anxious about taking my Place, & has made offers of making over to me a great living in the Peak,[7] if he may go in my stead. Here too I preserve my Passivity. It being totally indifferent to me whether they thrust me into the Devil's A—e,[8] or an Irish Bog.

Yet, tho I say I am indifferent to both these, I will in my present circumstances embrace either. The world has nothing to give me that I really care for, therefore Whatever she gives me, or however she gives it, does not matter a rush. And yet I own I would have some thing more of her too, merely because I have not Philosophy, or a better thing Œconomy, to make what I have a Competency.[9] *   *   *   *   *   *   *
*   *   *   *   *   *   *   *   *   *   *
*   *   *   *   *   *   *   *   *   *   *

Whitehead has sent me some Verses from Vienna,[10] treating of my Indolence, & other weighty matters, & exhorting me not to detach myself too much from the World. The Verses are

Duke) till 5 Dec. 1755, when he succeeded to the dukedom. In February of this year (1755) he had been appointed Lord Treasurer of Ireland, and on 27 March Lord-Lieutenant, which office he held until November 1756, when he was summoned to England, and became Prime Minister in the short-lived Devonshire–Pitt administration. Mason's expectation of being appointed chaplain to the Lord-Lieutenant was not realized.

[5] Robert Lowth (1710–87), scholar and afterwards Fellow of New College; Professor of Poetry at Oxford, 1741–51; D.D. 1754. While first chaplain to Lord Hartington in Ireland he was offered the Bishopric of Limerick, which he declined. In 1766 he was appointed Bishop of St. Davids, and in the same year was translated to Oxford (see Letter 415, n. 9).

[6] Rev. Thomas Seward (see Letter 144, n. 28); he published an edition of the works of Beaumont and Fletcher in 10 vols., 8vo., in 1750.

[7] Seward, who at this time was resident in Lichfield, was Rector of Eyam, in the Peak district of Derbyshire, about five miles north of Bakewell. It was at Eyam that his daughter Anna, 'the Swan of Lichfield', was born in 1747.

[8] The Great Cavern of the Peak, as is recorded by the German traveller, Carl Philipp Moritz, who visited it in 1782, 'goes commonly by a name that is shockingly vulgar: in English it is called *The Devil's Arse o' Peak*'.

[9] The next thirteen lines in MS. have been heavily scored through, and are undecipherable.

[10] Whitehead was travelling with 'two lordlings' (see Letter 197, n. 9). The verses here mentioned do not seem to have been published.

really very easy, & natural, & I would transcribe them for you if it was not too much trouble. & yet you would not like them, if I did; because of some Words, wch I know would not digest upon your Stomach; neither do they on mine; for I dont know how it is, but the slops you have given me have made my Digestive facultys so weak, that several things of that sort, wch were once as easy to me as hasty pudding, never get thro the first concoction, & lay as heavy in the prima Via as toasted Cheese. All wch I impute to your Nursery, where you would never let one eat any thing that was solid, as I did at St Johns.[11]

"Write (you say) something stately at Aston."[12] I writ nothing there but Sermons, & those I only transcribd. Write yourself if you please, at least finish your Welch Ode[13] & send it me to Hull, for there is an Alderman there, that I want to give his opinion about it.

But pray Why Mr Gray! must I write & you Not? Upon my word S^r! I really dont mean it as a flattery or any thing of that sort, no S^r I detest the insinuation. but, Blast my Laurells S^r if I dont think you write vastly better than I do. I swear by Apollo (my dear S^r) That I would give all my Elfrida[14] (Odes included) to be the Author of that pretty Elegy, that Miss Plumbtree can say off book. And I protest to you, that my Ode on Memory[15] after it has gone through all the Limæ Labor that our friend Horace prescribes, Nay Si prematur Nonum in Annum[16] (above half of wch time it has already I assure you been conceald Malgre my Partiality to it), I say that that very Ode is not, nor ever will be, half so terse, & complete as the fragment of your Welch Ode; wch is as one may say now just warm from your Brain, & one would expect as callow as a new-hatchd Chicken (pardon the barndoor Simile) but all your productions are of a different sort, they come from you Armd Capapee at all points, as Minerva is said to have issued from the Head of Jupiter. I have thus said enough to shew you that however I may have laid aside the practical part of poetry I retain all that internal force, that Ignea vis, wch inspires evry true Son of parnassus with all wch I am fervently yours

W Mason.

---

[11] Mason's College before he was elected Fellow of Pembroke.
[12] See Letter 194, n. 9.   [13] The *Bard*.
[14] See Letter 158.
[15] Ode i, *To Memory* (see Letter 214, n. 10).
[16] 'Nonumque prematur in annum', Horace, *Ars Poet.* 388.

Pray give my best Compliments to Dr Wharton & his Lady & the ejected Statesman,[17] and if youll write to me immediatly to Hull, Ill tell you when Ill meet you at Cambridge. Do you know what Whiteheads place[18] is worth?—[19]

210. GRAY TO BEDINGFIELD[1]

S^r

Dec: 25. Cambridge. 1755

IT is not oweing to insensibility (as by this time you may possibly imagine) but to the misfortune I had of staying longer than usual this winter in Town,[2] that I have not sooner return'd you my thanks for the particular honour you did me,

---

[17] This was Robin, Wharton's two-year old son (see Letter 177, n. 2), whose nose had been put out of joint by the birth of another child, Deborah, this year. (See Genealogical Table.)

[18] While still abroad he had been appointed by the Duke of Newcastle, through the influence of Lady Jersey, the mother of one of his 'lordlings' (see n. 10), to the patent places of Secretary and Registrar of the Order of the Bath.

[19] Mitford printed this postscript at the end of Letter 206.

LETTER 210.—Now first printed from original. On the first page of the letter, which is endorsed by Bedingfield: 'Dec: 28. 1755', Mason has noted: 'Printed', but it was not published in his *Memoirs*.

[1] Edward Bedingfield (or Bedingfeld, as the name is now spelt) was the youngest son of Sir Henry Arundell Bedingfield, third Baronet of Oxburgh, Norfolk, and of Lady Elizabeth Boyle, eldest daughter of Charles Boyle, second Earl of Burlington; he was born at Oxburgh 2 Feb. 1730, and married, 21 March 1754, Mary Swinburne (born at Capheaton 13 May 1729), third daughter of Sir John Swinburne, third Baronet of Capheaton, Northumberland, and of Mary Bedingfield, only daughter of Edward Bedingfield, youngest son of the first Baronet (see Letter 183, n. 6); he had ten children, of whom the second son, Thomas (1760–89), a conveyancer, was the author of poems, which were published after his death. (See Genealogical Table.) Edward Bedingfield himself had a poetical gift, one of his poems, written in March 1753, being 'On receiving from the Countess of Burlington Mr Gray's Poems with Designs by Mr Bentley'. (From information kindly supplied by Mrs. Paston-Bedingfeld, and from Edward Bedingfield's *Journal*, kindly lent by Sir Henry Paston-Bedingfeld.)

From a series of 18 letters written by Mason to Edward Bedingfield between 29 Sept. 1769 and 19 July 1775, now in the Henry E. Huntington Library, it appears that Mason was largely indebted to Bedingfield not only for correcting the proofs of his own poems and of his *Memoirs of the Life and Writings of Mr. Gray*, but also for the revision of the latter, and for not a few of the notes.

[2] See Letter 208, n. 2.

when you were at Cambridge.[3] You tell me with so much
warmth & franknefs, that I have given you pleasure, that it would
be mere hypocrisy in me, if I did not confefs to you with the
same opennefs of mind, that I am pleased. my wish & the only
reward I ask in writing is to give some little satisfaction to a
few Men of sense & character. I say *a few*, because there are
but few such: were they more numerous, I would wish (I own)
to please them all; & yet not fear being censured for too eager
a desire of fame. but as much as your proceeding may have
raised my vanity, I shall by no means promise that you will like
your new acquaintance, when you see him *out of print*. however
with all his imperfections on his head[4] he will, be afsured, make
the experiment the very first opportunity, & claim in person the
honour you offer him, whenever he is so happy to find himself
in the same place with you.[5]

I am much obliged to you for the Iris & Aurora[6] they are
more elegant & have more of the relish of antiquity than any
thing I have met with in modern Italy. permit me to present
my Compliments to Lady Swinburn.[7] I am not known to her
at all, and yet have had the honour of pafsing three days in her
company. when & where it was, I leave to her Ladyship's
recollection.[8] I am S^r

Your obliged & obedient Servant
T GRAY

[3] This is explained by the following passage in Gray's letter to Wharton of
9 Jan. 1756 (Letter 213): 'Mr Bedingfield, who . . . desired to be acquainted
with me, call'd here (before I came down), & would pay a visit to my rooms.
he made Dr Long conduct him thither, left me a present of a Book (not of
his own writing) & a Note with a very Civil Compliment.'

[4] *Hamlet*, i. 5.

[5] They had not met when Gray wrote to him a year later (Letter 231); but
in his letter of 12 Feb. 1757 (Letter 232) Gray refers to their having met
recently before Bedingfield paid a visit to Bath for his health; no doubt
Bedingfield visited Cambridge in January of that year, for Gray was in residence during the whole of that month.

[6] The book left by Bedingfield (see n. 3) was the Italian version of two
Latin poems by Carlo Noceti: *L'Iride e l'Aurora Boreale descritte in verso latino
dal P. Carlo Noceti d. C. d. G. e tradotto in verso toscano dal P. Antonio Ambrogi
della med. Comp.* Firenze, Stamperia Imperiale, 1755. The book is described
as 'magnificently printed'.

[7] See Letter 183, n. 6.

[8] It was in the stage-coach between York and Stilton, 1–3 Oct. 1753 (see
Letter 183, n. 1).

211. WALPOLE TO GRAY[1]

ADVICE OF D[r] OLIVER[2] TO S[r] JOHN COPE[3] ON HIS
GETTING ST ANTONY'S FIRE[4] BY DRINKING THE
BATH WATERS OUT OF MISS MOLLY'S HAND.

BY LORD BATH.[5]

SEE gentle Cope with gout and love opprest,
 Alternate torments raging in his breast,
Tries at his cure, but tampers still in vain;
What lessens one, augments the other pain.
 The charming Nymph, who strives to give relief,
Instead of comfort, heightens all his grief:
For health he drinks, then sighs for love, & cries,
Health's in her hand, destruction in her eyes.
She gives us water, but each touch alas!
The wanton Girl electrifies the glass.
To cure the gout, we drink large draughts of Love,
And then, like Ætna, burst in flames above.

The ⎱ Sip not, dear Knight, the Daughter's liquid fire,
Advice ⎰ But take the healing bev'rage from the Sire:
Twill ease thy gout—for Love no cure is known;
The God of physic coud, not cure his own.

ON LD DARL——'S[6] BEING MADE JOINT PAYMASTER.

Wonders, Newcastle,[7] mark thy ev'ry hour;
But this last Act's a plenitude of pow'r:

LETTER 211.—First printed by Toynbee (1915), No. 195.
 [1] This letter and three others from Walpole to Gray (Letters 319, 474, and 546) were preserved among the Walpole MSS. in the Waller Collection, in a packet endorsed by Horace Walpole: 'Letters from M[r] Walpole to M[r] Gray. returned by M[r] Mason to M[r] W. after M[r] Gray's death.'
 [2] William Oliver (1695–1764), M.D. of Pembroke College, Cambridge, the famous Bath physician, inventor of the well-known 'Bath Oliver' biscuit.
 [3] 'Johnnie Cope', the General (d. 1760) who in command of the Royal forces was routed by the Young Pretender at Prestonpans on 21 Sept. 1745.
 [4] A name for erysipelas.
 [5] See n. 11. In the article on Dr. Oliver in the *Dictionary of National Biography* these lines are said to be by him, their attribution to Lord Bath by Horace Walpole having apparently not been known.
 [6] Henry Vane, first Earl of Darlington (see Letter 143, n. 6), was appointed Joint Paymaster of the Forces, with Viscount Dupplin (see Letter 262, n. 13), in this year (1755).
 [7] Thomas Pelham-Holles (1693–1768), Duke of Newcastle (1715), who became Prime Minister on the death of his brother, Henry Pelham (6 March 1754).

448

Nought but the force of an almighty reign
Coud make a *Paymaster* of Harry V——.[8]

On splitting the Pay office.

Holles,[9] not past his childhood yet, retains
The maxims of his Nurse or Tutor's pains:
Thence did the mighty Babe this truth derive,
Two negatives make one affirmative:
But ah! Two Dunces never made a Wit,
Nor can two Darlingtons compose a Pitt.[10]

To draw poetry from you, I send you these mediocre verses, the only ones in fashion. the first lines indeed are pretty, when one considers they were writ by a Man of seventy, Lord Bath.[11] the first Epigram was a thought of George Selwyn,[12] rhimed; the last is scarce a thought at all.

Ministers, Patriots, Wits, poets, paymasters, all are dispersed & gone out of town. The Changes are made, & all preferments given away:[13] you will be glad to hear that our Colonel Montagu[14] has got a regiment. Lord Waldgrave[15] last night hearing them talk over these histories, said with a melancholy tone, alas! they talk so much of giving places for life, I wish they dont give me mine[16] for life!

Adieu! I expect prodigious interest for my pômes.

Yrs ever

Arlington street   HW.
Christmas day 1755.

[8] See n. 6.   [9] See n. 7.

[10] William Pitt (1708–78), afterwards (1766) first Earl of Chatham, had been Paymaster-General of the Forces from 1746 till November of this year.

[11] See n. 5. William Pulteney, Earl of Bath (1742), at this time 71, died in 1764, aged 80 (see Letter 390, n. 12).

[12] 'Lord Duplin and Lord Darlington are made joint Paymasters: George Selwyn says, that no act ever showed so much the Duke of Newcastle's absolute power as his being able to make Lord Darlington *a paymaster*' (Walpole to Bentley, 17 Dec. 1755). Both epigrams were no doubt written by Walpole (see *Horace Walpole's Fugitive Verses*, edited by W. S. Lewis, pp. 121–2).

[13] For a list of the changes in the Government see Walpole's letters to Montagu of 20 Dec., and to Mason of 21 Dec. 1755.

[14] Colonel Charles Montagu, George Montagu's brother, was appointed Lieutenant-Colonel of General Bockland's Regiment in this month (*Gent. Mag.*, 1755, p. 572).

[15] James Waldegrave (1715–63), second Earl Waldegrave (1741), who afterwards (1759) married Walpole's niece, Maria Walpole.

[16] Of Governor to the Prince of Wales. *Walpole.*—He was Governor of the Prince (afterwards George III) from 1752 to 1756.

212. MASON TO GRAY

Chiswick[1] Dec. 25th –55

Dear S[r]

Y OU desird me to write you news, but tho there are a great many promotions[2] they seem to me as far as I can judge all such dirty ones, that you may spare me the trouble of naming them & pick them out of a news paper if you think it worth While. There is a Bon mot of M[r] Pitts handed about out of the late debate about the treaties. some Body had compard the Russians to a Star rising out of the north &c. Pit replyd he was glad the place of the Star was thus fixd for he was certain it was not that Star w[ch] once appeard in the East & *w[ch] the wise Men worshipt*, tho it was like it in one particular for it made its Worshipers *bring Gifts.*[3] Charles Townshend[4] in the same debate calld Lord H[5] an unthinking unparliamentary Minister, for w[ch] he was severely mumbled by M[r] Fox[6] w[ch] I am glad of because he is certainly a most unprincipled Patriot.[7] But perhaps all this is old to you, Im tird of the subject and will drop it——

LETTER 212. First printed in part by Mitford in *Gray–Mason* (1853), pp. 42–5; now first printed in full from original.

[1] At Lord Holdernesse's villa (see Letter 192, n. 29).

[2] See Letter 211, n. 13.

[3] This was on 15 Dec.; see Walpole, *Memoirs of George II* (ed. 1847, vol. ii, pp. 134 ff.).

[4] Charles Townshend (1725–67), second son of Charles, third Viscount Townshend, best known as Chancellor of the Exchequer (1766–7) in Pitt's second ministry, was at this time M.P. for Yarmouth. In the reconstructed ministry after Pelham's death in 1754 he was a Lord of the Admiralty, but was dismissed in the present year (1755) by Newcastle, whose 'little petulant mechanic activity' he vigorously denounced in the speech here referred to.

[5] Mitford printed 'Lord Holland'; but, as Tovey recognized, there was no Lord Holland at this date. The reference is to Lord Holdernesse and is explained by Walpole in his *Memoirs of George II*. Charles Townshend, he records, who 'spoke for three-quarters of an hour against the treaties with infinite rapidity, vehemence, and parts', remarked that 'the King went abroad with only an unthinking and unparliamentary Minister at his ear'— to which Walpole adds in a note, 'Lord Holderness' (*op. cit.*, pp. 121, 124).

[6] Now Secretary of State in place of Sir Thomas Robinson, and leader of the House of Commons (see Letter 208, n. 5).

[7] Johnson defined *patriot* in the fourth edition of his *Dictionary* (1773): 'It is sometimes used for a factious disturber of the government.'

There is a sweet Song in Demofoonte[8] called Ogni Amante sung by Riccarelli.[9] Pray look at it. Tis almost $\frac{\text{Notatim}}{\text{verbatim}}$ the Air in Ariadne,[10] but I think better. I am told tis a very old one of Scarlattis[11] wch if true Handel is almost a musical Lauder.[12]

Voltaires Mock Poem calld La Pucelle[13] is to be met with, tho not sold publickly, in town, I had a short sight of it the other day. If you have any curiosity to see it I can send it you with Frasers[14] assistance in a couple of Covers.

I have been here ever since I left Cambridge except one Opera night.[15] My Absence from my Piano forte almost makes me peevish enough to write a Bolinbrokian Essay upon exile.[16]

[8] The libretto of this opera was written c. 1732 by Metastasio and was set to music by many composers. 'The opera of *Demofoonte* came out December the 9th [1755], and in the course of the winter was performed more than twenty times' (Burney, *Hist. of Music*, vol. iv, p. 466) in a version that was a *pasticcio*. *The Favourite Songs in the Opera called Il Demofoonte*, printed for I. Walsh [in 1755], contains the song mentioned by Mason.

[9] Ricciarelli had been singing in England during the summer season o this year (see Burney, *op. cit.*, vol. iv, p. 464).

[10] Handel's *Ariadne in Crete* was first produced in 1734.

[11] There were two famous Scarlattis, father and son. Alessandro (1659–1725) and his son Domenico (1683–1757). Both composed operas, and the younger was an intimate friend of Handel.

[12] William Lauder (d. 1771), a literary forger, in 1750 published *An Essay on Milton's Use and Imitation of the Moderns in 'Paradise Lost'*. He foisted into his quotations from modern Latin poets lines which he himself translated from *Paradise Lost* in order to accuse Milton of plagiarism. He had been exposed in 1756.

[13] Voltaire's scandalous burlesque epic, *La Pucelle*, was written at intervals between 1734 and 1739 during his residence with Madame du Châtelet at the château of Cirey, and was first published in this year.

[14] See Letter 195, n. 13.

[15] It was no doubt on this occasion that he attended the performance of *Demofoonte* (see n. 8). He left Cambridge about a week before the date of this letter, having vacated his Fellowship 'a year after his presentation' to Aston. He was elected Smart Fellow (a bye-Fellowship) on 23 March 1757 (see Letter 284, n. 4).

[16] Henry St. John (1678–1751), Viscount Bolingbroke (1713); after the death of Queen Anne (1714) he fled to France, was attainted of high treason, and entered the service of the Pretender; he remained in exile until 1725, when his attainder was reversed, and he returned to England. His *Reflections upon Exile*, written, in the manner of Seneca, in 1716, were first published by David Mallet, to whom he left all his works, in 1752; they were reprinted in his *Collected Works* in 1754.

Why will you not send me my inscription?[17] and with it be sure add a dissertation upon Sigmas, and tell me with all Dʳ Taylors[18] accuracy whether a Σ or a C or a Є[18a] is the most classical. You can write dissertations upon the Pelasgi, & why not upon this when it is for the use of *a learned friend?* Allways twitting you (you say) with the Pelasgi.[19] why, tis all I can twit you with. I wish you good success at Brag as well as sweet Temper.

May the Latter be ΠΟΛΥ ΠΑΚΤΙΔΟϹ ΑΔΥΜΕΛΕϹΤΕΡΑ and the former make your purse ΧΡΥΣΩ ΧΡΥΣΟΤΕΡΑ.[20]

I see in the papers Dodsley has publishd An Ode on the Earthquake at Lisbon with some Thoughts on a Church yard.[21] I suppose You are the Author and that you have taggd your Elegy to the tail of it. However if I dont suppose so I hope the world will, in order that people may lay out their sixpences on that, rather than on Duncombs[22] flattery to Fobus,[23] & the Old Horse.[24]

[17] Mason apparently had asked Gray for a verse translation of a Greek inscription on a tripod (see Letter 216).

[18] John Taylor (1704–66), of St. John's College, Cambridge; B.A. 1724; M.A. 1728; Fellow, 1729; University Librarian, 1732; Registrary, 1734; LL.D. 1741. Besides editions of the Greek orators, he wrote *Marmor Sandvicense* (Cambridge 1744), a dissertation on an inscription brought from Athens by Lord Sandwich in 1739.

[18a] Mason seems to have been confused in assuming that Є could stand for Sigma.

[19] The point of this reference, which recurs in Gray's letter to Mason of 23 July 1756 (Letter 218), is obscure. It may have had some connexion with Gray's Chronological Table (see Letter 129, n. 4).

[20] Πόλυ πάκτιδος ἀδυμελεστέρα, χρύσω χρυσοτέρα (Sappho, *Fr.* 122), 'far sweeter-sounding than the harp, more golden than gold.'

[21] *A Poem on the Late Earthquake at Lisbon.* To which is added, *Thoughts in a Churchyard*, was published by Dodsley (price sixpence) on 5 Jan. 1756. Mason, no doubt, saw an advertisement of it. There is no clue to the authorship.

[22] John Duncombe (1729–86), Fellow of Corpus Christi College, Cambridge; B.A. 1748; M.A. 1752. In 1753 he published a parody on Gray's *Elegy*, entitled *An Evening Contemplation in a College*. On 19 Dec. of this year, but with the date 1756, Dodsley published a volume of his *Poems* (1s.). The third of these is an *Ode presented to the Duke of Newcastle, Chancellor of the University, on his Arrival there, June 14, 1753.*

[23] See Letter 191, n. 16.

[24] In the *Ode to the Duke of Newcastle* (see n. 22) Duncombe refers, in a footnote, to his having set on foot a subscription for the University Library, 'towards which his Majesty with his usual Magnificence, contributed 2000 l.' The king's praises are celebrated in the sixth stanza. Mitford was no doubt right in saying that by the 'Old Horse' Mason meant George the Second.

What a scribbling Humor am I in! Ill releive you however
by adding only my Love to Mr Brown Tuthill[25] & all friends &
assuring you that I am yours with the greatest sincerity

SCRODDLES.[26]

Shall I trouble you Dear S^r to wish Dr Long & Old Cardale[27] a merry Xt.mas in my Name. Lady Rotchford[28] assures
me that Lady Coventry[29] "has a mole on *one* of her Ladyship's
Necks" Pray tell Dr Gascarth,[30] that the Neck has descended
some inches in the Human frame & deviding itself into two
Hemispherical excrescences forms those parts wch Sally
erroneously calls her Bubbies, & wch he feels for such.

[25] This name is scored through in MS., but is still legible (see Letter 120,
n. 2).
[26] The nickname by which Gray occasionally addresses Mason (see
Letters 216, 489).
[27] See Letter 163, n. 11.   [28] See Letter 206, n. 7.
[29] The celebrated beauty, Maria Gunning, elder daughter of John
Gunning, of Castle Coole, co. Roscommon, married in 1752 George William
Coventry, sixth Earl of Coventry, Lord of the Bedchamber to George II, and
died of consumption at the age of twenty-seven, 30 Sept. 1760. Mason wrote
an *Elegy* on her death (see Letters 322, 326, 364).
[30] Gaskarth may have been studying medicine (he ultimately practised
it in the West Indies, see Letter 148, n. 17): hence Mason calls him jocosely
'D^r'

PRINTED IN
GREAT BRITAIN
AT THE
UNIVERSITY PRESS
OXFORD
BY
JOHN JOHNSON
PRINTER
TO THE
UNIVERSITY